Strategic Management and Organisational Dynamics

The Challenge of Complexity

Fourth Edition

Strategic Management and Organisational Dynamics

The Challenge of Complexity

Ralph D Stacey

Prentice Hall
FINANCIAL TIMES

An imprint of **Pearson Education**
Harlow, England • London • New York • Boston • San Francisco • Toronto
Sydney • Tokyo • Singapore • Hong Kong • Seoul • Taipei • New Delhi
Cape Town • Madrid • Mexico City • Amsterdam • Munich • Paris • Milan

Pearson Education Limited
Edinburgh Gate
Harlow
Essex CM20 2JE
United Kingdom

and Associated Companies throughout the world.

Visit us on the World Wide Web at:
www.pearsoneduc.com

First published under the Pitman Publishing imprint 1993
Second edition published 1996
Third edition 2000
Fourth edition 2003

© Pearson Education Limited 1993, 1996, 2000, 2003

The right of Ralph D Stacey to be identified as author of this work has been asserted by him in accordance with the Copyright, Designs and Patents Act 1988.

ISBN 0 273 65898 0

British Library Cataloguing-in-Publication Data
A catalogue record for this book is available from the British Library

Library of Congress Cataloging-in-Publication Data
Stacey, Ralph D.
    Strategic management and organizational dynamics: the challenge of complexity /
  Ralph D. Stacey.—4th ed.
      p.   cm.
    Includes bibliographical references and index.
    ISBN 0-273-65898-0 (pbk.)
      1. Strategic planning.   2. Organizational behavior.   I. Title.
  HD30.28 .S663 2002
  658.4′012—dc21

                                                                    2002075980

10 9 8 7 6 5 4
09 08 07 06 05

Typeset in 10/12.5 pt Sabon by 35
Printed and bound by Ashford Colour Press, Gosport
The publisher's policy is to use paper manufactured from sustainable forests.

To the memory of my mother Auriel

Contents

List of figures

List of tables

Preface

Most books on organisational strategy seek to account for superior performance in organisations and they prescribe methods by which to secure competitive advantage as the basis of improved performance. The tendency is to reify the organisation and regard it as a system. There is also a tendency to reify an organisation's strategy, defining that strategy as the direction of the whole organisation's movement into the future. The concern is then with identifying the forces operating on that direction so that the forces may be manipulated by managers to secure their desired outcome for their organisation's future.

This book differs from those just mentioned. Instead of being concerned with superior performance, it focuses on a prior concern, which is the matter of how we are thinking about organisations and strategy. For example, why do we think that an organisation is a system and what are the consequences of doing so? What view of human psychology is implicit in prescribing measures that managers should take to select the direction of an organisation's movement into the future? This book differs from many others in seeking to locate current thinking about strategy in the history of Western thought and thereby identify taken-for-granted assumptions about human psychology and human interaction. It seeks to challenge thinking rather than describe the current state of thinking about strategy and organisational dynamics.

The challenge to current ways of thinking is presented in the contrasts that this book draws between systemic and process ways of thinking about strategy and organisational dynamics. While the systemic perspective is concerned with improvement and movement to a future destination, process thinking is concerned with complex responsive processes of human relating in which strategies emerge. From this perspective, strategy is defined as the emergence of organisational and individual identities so that the concern is with how organisations come to be what they are and how those identities will continue to evolve. From a process perspective, the question of performance improvement has to do with more authentic participation in processes of communicative interaction, power relating and the creation of knowledge and meaning.

The challenge to ways of thinking presented in this book also comes in the form of insights from the complexity sciences. The book will explore the differences for organisational thinking between a way of interpreting these insights in systemic terms and a way of interpreting them in process terms.

In this fourth edition I have made a number of changes. The number of chapters on the theory of strategic choice has been reduced because that theory is extensively covered in a number of other books. The intention here is not to provide a detailed coverage of the theory but to tease out the way of thinking it reflects. This edition makes a sharper distinction between systemic and process thinking than the third edition did, particularly by including new chapters on the philosophical origins of systems and process thinking and by adding new chapters on second-order and critical system thinking. New material has also been included on the theory of complex responsive processes, particularly to do with control, leadership and ethics.

The purpose of this book is to assist people to make sense of their own experience of life in organisations. For this reason the case studies included in the third edition have been removed because they tend to be carefully structured accounts of someone else's organisational experience, usually written with some point in mind, which the reader is supposed to see. This is not consistent with the purpose of assisting readers to make sense of their own experience. So, instead of case studies, there are seven management narratives, that is, personal accounts of the experience of life in organisations. Readers are invited to think about the sense they make of this experience. The main point, however, remains for readers to use the material in this book to make sense of their own experience.

I am grateful to users of previous editions who have made helpful comments and to my colleagues and other participants in the MA/Doctor of Management programme on organisational change at the University of Hertfordshire (in association with the Institute of Group Analysis).

Ralph Stacey
London
May 2002

Supplements

Online support materials for students and lecturers including additional references and useful weblinks, and a commentary on the text for lecturers are available at www.booksites.net/stacey.

Acknowledgements

We are grateful to the following for permission to reproduce copyright material:

Figure 3.3 from *Introduction to Cybernetics* published by John Wiley (Ashby, W. R. 1956) by permission of A. P. Watt Ltd on behalf of Mrs J. Ashby; Figure 5.2 from *Behaviour in a Business Context* published by Chapman and Hall (Turton, R. 1991) by permission of Thompson Learning; Figure 5.3 from *The Social Psychology of Organizing* published by McGraw-Hill (Weick, K. 1979), reproduced with permission; Figures 5.5, 5.6, 5.7 and 5.8 from *The Fifth Discipline* by Peter M. Senge, copyright © 1990 by Peter M. Senge. Used by permission of Doubleday, a division of Random House, Inc. Figure 5.9 from M. Porter, *The Competitive Advantage of Nations*, 1990, Macmillan, reproduced with permission of Palgrave Macmillan; Figure 6.4 from *Power and Organization Development: Mobilizing Power to Implement Change* by Greiner/Schein, © Reprinted by permission of Pearson Education, Inc., Upper Saddle River, N. J.; Figure 7.2 from *Improving Skills in Working with People: The T Group*, published by HMSO (Smith, P. B. 1969). Crown copyright material is reproduced with the permission of the Controller of HMSO and the Queen's Printer for Scotland. Figure 7.3 adapted from *Work and Creativity* published by Tavistock (Miller, E. H. 1983); Figure 7.4 from *The Psychoanalysis of Organizations* published by Tavistock (de Board, R. 1978); Figures 10.1, 10.2, 10.3 and 10.4 from *The Chaos Frontier* by R. Stacey. Reprinted by permission of Elsevier Science. Figures 17.1 and 17.2 adapted from *The Paradox of Control in Organizations* published by Routledge (Streatfield, P. 2001).

Jane Blacketer: "Global competences", Jose Fonseca: "Innovation in a water industry", David Scanlon: "The diversity project", Patricia Shaw: "Consulting and culture change" and "Culture change at a factory", and Philip Streatfield: "The budget meeting" and Performance measurement".

In some instances we have been unable to trace the owners of copyright material, and we would appreciate any information that would enable us to do so.

Chapter 1 ● ● ● ●

The nature of strategy and organisational change

1.1 Introduction

This book is concerned with ways of thinking about how organisations change over time. It explores explanations of how organisations have become what they are, and how they will become whatever they will be in five, ten or however many years' time.

There are many different theories that seek to explain how organisations change, or fail to change, but none of them is universally accepted. Even those that dominate academic and management discourses provide only partial explanations of life in organisations. The purpose of this book is to examine what is similar in these competing theories, and how they differ. To put it another way, the purpose of this book is to explore different ways of making sense of one's experience of life in organisations. It is from my own experience that I describe, compare and comment on the various theories I will be presenting in the chapters that follow. My own experience inevitably colours how I describe those theories and what I have to say about them. In writing this book, therefore, I am revealing how I currently make sense of my experience of life in organisations and I am inviting you to consider whether this resonates in any way with your own experience.

This book differs in its focus of attention from many other books on strategy and organisational dynamics. Most strategy books focus attention, either explicitly or implicitly, on what managers do, or should do, to improve the performance of an organisation. The immediate concern is then with the scope of an organisation's activities, its future direction and how it secures competitive advantage. This book explicitly focuses attention on how managers, researchers and writers are thinking about organisations, strategy and change, as well as on the kinds of questions they pose about these matters.

The chapters that follow will summarise various organisational theories, including their descriptions of, and prescriptions for, managing change. The aim will be to point to the assumptions made, and reasoning processes used, in these theories, matters that are often not made explicit by those presenting them. A distinction will be drawn between systemic and process ways of thinking about organisations and their strategies.

Two basic questions

What I am setting out to do in this book, then, is to review and compare different ways of explaining what strategy is and how organisations change. It is very tempting to jump straight into defining what a strategy is and how it should be formulated and implemented, or to explain immediately how organisations change and how this change should be managed. I want to avoid this temptation because, as I hope to show, the result of such haste is the obscuring of what lies behind the definitions and prescriptions. There is no universally true explanation of how organisations evolve, only a number of increasingly contested accounts. If one is to avoid blindly following one of these accounts, mistakenly taking it to be the truth, then I think that it is necessary to stand back and ask two fundamental questions:

1 What are the phenomena that are being talked about when the terms 'strategy' and 'organisational change' are used?
2 How do human beings make sense of phenomena, including those that this book is concerned with?

The second question is important because there are different explanations of how humans make sense of anything. The particular explanation one adopts directly affects the particular account one gives of any phenomena, including those to which the concepts of strategy and organisational change apply.

1.2   The phenomena of interest

Before attempting any definition of what a strategy is, or what is meant by organisational change, consider the general phenomena that strategy and organisational change are both concerned with.

To some extent, you can see what the phenomena are simply by turning to the business section of any daily newspaper. For example, if you had turned to the business section of the *Sunday Times* newspaper on 13 January 2002 you would have read that a new UK airline was ready for take-off. In a travel industry still experiencing the aftermath of the attack on the World Trade Center in New York on 11 September, a new organisation was being created, while older organisations such as British Airways were worrying about declining activity and others, like Swissair, had gone out of business altogether. In the same newspaper, it was reported that the UK based cruise-line group, P&O, was seeking a non-returnable deposit from its American rival. Carnival, the largest cruise company in the world, was in the process of making a takeover bid for P&O in an attempt to break up a proposed merger between P&O and Royal Caribbean Cruises. P&O wanted Carnival to make a voluntary payment, just to show whether they were serious about acquiring P&O or simply trying to destroy the merger with Royal Caribbean. In the *Independent* newspaper, the UK water regulator called for government legislation to speed up competition in the water industry and in the *Financial Times* on 4 January it was reported that the US congress was probing into the collapse of the energy company Enron. It was also reported that improved jobless data had lifted US treasuries. All of this was happening as the United States forces continued to search for Osama bin Laden in Afghanistan.

Populations of organisations

These newspaper reports are examples of populations of interacting organisations. Over any time period, say one, five, ten years, in any geographic region, say Europe, thousands upon thousands of new organisations are set up and within the same time frame many thousands are dissolved. In each period, there are large numbers of small organisational dissolutions and small numbers of large ones. Some organisations, however, go on for a very long time: the Roman Catholic Church is more than 1,500 years old and a few commercial organisations have survived for more than a century. On average, however, the life span of commercial organisations in Western countries is about 40 years. In any time period, some organisations merge into others, while yet others split into separate organisations. Many acquire others and some sell parts of their organisation to others as those reported above were doing. Organisations supply each other with goods and services. Some exert regulatory power over others.

Over the years, surviving organisations change their structures and their direction and as they do so they threaten, or create opportunities for, others. Whole new industries appear as new technologies are developed, creating niches of new activities for both new and old organisations, while other industries disappear. Many organisations reduce their workforces in downsizing, delayering activities. Many relocate their activities from one country to another. Some focus on one locality while others operate globally. There are private and public, commercial and charitable, governmental and industrial organisations all interacting with each other in many different ways.

Dynamic phenomena

What is striking, I think, as one reads such reports day after day, is just how much change is going on. In other words, the phenomena of interest, namely populations of organisations, are highly dynamic ones. *Dynamics* means movement and concern with the dynamics is concern with how phenomena move, unfold or evolve over time. Dynamic phenomena are ones that display patterns of change over time and a study of dynamics is concerned with what generates these patterns and what properties of stability and instability, predictability and unpredictability they display. One of the key features distinguishing one theory of strategy and organisational change from another is how they deal with the matter of dynamics. I will be pointing to this in reviews of a number of theories in the chapters that follow.

It is striking how unstable the dynamics of populations of organisations are, on the one hand, but how stable they are, on the other. Or, to put it another way, what is striking is just how unpredictable are the moves made by organisations and yet how predictable they are. What I mean by this is that it is virtually certain that mergers and takeovers will take place and it is often clear in which industries this will happen. At the same time, however, it is often very surprising that one particular organisation should buy, or merge with, another. Members of an organisation, including its most senior managers, often experience such unpredictability and instability as anxiety provoking and stressful. Another striking point is how some organisations are merging with others, while yet others are splitting themselves into two or more parts. In other words, some are integrating while others are dividing.

Paradoxical phenomena

Populations of organisations change over time in ways that display both stability and instability at the same time, both predictability and unpredictability at the same time, both creation and destruction at the same time. What is one to make of it when the phenomena one is trying to understand, change in populations of organisations, display such contradictory tendencies? Is this an apparent contradiction, which arises for me simply because I do not understand the phenomena fully? Or is it a paradox, the genuine, simultaneous coexistence of two contradictory movements? How one answers these questions has important implications for the kind of theory of organisational change one develops. Some theories see only contradictions to be solved by further work, while others see paradox that can never be resolved. This position on paradox will be one of the features I will use to distinguish one theory of organisational change from another. I will return to this point later in this chapter and take it up again in subsequent chapters as I review a number of theories of organisational change.

Degrees of detail

Now, however, I think it is important to notice how the newspaper reports describe and so define the phenomena of interest. The descriptions and definitions are given in terms of named organisations interacting with each other in national and global societies. The descriptions are of 'whole' organisations interacting 'within' a whole population as if they were individual entities. In other words, the descriptions are at the macro level, that is the level of the large, or the whole, rather than the small, or the entities that make up the whole, that is the micro level. This too will be an important feature in the comparison between different theories of organisational change in the chapters that follow. Some theories focus on the macro level, some on the micro level and yet others on both.

More fundamentally, however, is the matter of how one thinks about these 'levels'. In some theories, the micro and the macro are thought of as distinct levels of reality, each of which has its own distinctive properties as wholes. So, one level is the human being understood from some psychological perspective. The next level is the group having its own properties. The level above that may be the oganisation consisting of groups of individuals to be understood in terms of organisational principles. In these theories, then, organisational phenomena are wholes classified at different ontological levels. In other theories, however, the micro and the macro are not thought of as separate levels with distinctive properties. Instead, they are thought of as simply different degrees of examination. In these theories, individuals, groups and organistions are not wholes at different ontological levels but are simply aspects of the same processes of human interaction.

Moving now to the micro degree of examination, each organisation is itself a population of interacting groupings of individual people. The newspaper reports sometimes provide glimpses of what might be going on within some particular organisation. The companies and markets section of the *Financial Times* on 2 January 2002 reported that the new chief executive of ARC International, the semi-conductor chip manufacturer, had been granted 10 million share options. This was a controversial award because it was not tied to any performance criteria.

Emotion

It is necessary to call on one's own experience of life in organisations to imagine what interactions lay behind this announcements. I would suspect that it was preceded by intense political activity as people sought to push for, or stop, the award of so many options not tied to any performance measure. I would imagine that people might have become angry with each other or felt betrayed. It is not hard to imagine what kinds of conversations the directors involved had with their partners when they returned home. If you think of your experience of being promoted, having others promoted above you, having the threat of downsizing hanging over you, you can see how emotions of some kind are inseparable from interactions within and between organisations. Another feature I will be pointing to, as I review a number of theories in the chapters that follow, is just how much account they take of the emotion involved in organisational evolution.

The objective observer and the participant enquirer

The phenomena of interest in this book have to do with life in organisations and this is not some interaction between abstract entities, but interactions between people that directly affect the meaning of their lives and their health. Furthermore, these interactions between people in an organisation are not richly documented either in the newspapers or in management books. To gain some understanding of these interactions one has to participate in them and one's understanding will arise in one's own experience. From a macro perspective, it may well be possible to take the position of the objective observer who stands outside the phenomena of interest and offers explanations of their behaviour. However, explanation and understanding from the micro perspective relies much more on one's own personal experience. Here the explanation is offered from the position of a participant in organisational life. This is another distinguishing feature of the theories I will review, namely the extent to which the theory is offered from the position of the objective observer as opposed to the enquiring participant.

Interaction

Another important point to note about the phenomena that strategy and organisational change are concerned with is this: the newspaper reports I have referred to are all describing interactions. For example, one kind of interaction takes place when one company buys another and another kind of interaction takes place when one company supplies another. From the perspective of an individual organisation, one kind of interaction takes place when a director resigns and another kind takes place when a director is handsomely rewarded.

Furthermore, although the newspapers report one interaction, it requires only a moment's thought to see that this interaction will inevitably touch off many more. When one pharmaceutical company merges with another, it changes the competitive balance for all of the others, making it highly likely that many of them will look for merger partners. This is because they are interconnected. Another very important feature distinguishing one theory of strategy and organisational change from another is the manner in which interaction and interconnection are understood.

Most theories think of interaction as constituting a network or a system. Individual minds might be thought of as a system consisting of, say, interacting concepts. A group may be thought of as a system consisting of, say, interacting individuals, while an organisation might then be thought of as a system consisting of interacting groups. An industry would then be thought of as a suprasystem consisting of interacting organisations. When thought of in this way, interaction is always interaction between systems producing yet another system, all of them nesting hierarchically in each other at different levels. Different theories of strategy and organisational change are built on different theories of the nature of a system. One of the main focuses of this book will be on different theories of systems and how these underpin different theories of organisational evolution. However, although most theories of strategy and organisational change are couched in systemic terms, there is an alternative. This is to think of interaction as processes of direct communicating and relating between human bodies. Such a perspective yields process theories of strategy and organisational change. This distinction between systemic and process theories provides the principal way of distinguishing between different theories of strategy and organisational change. Parts One and Two will review systemic theories and Part Three will explore process theories.

In summary, then, the phenomena that this book is concerned with are continuously evolving populations of organisations where each organisation is itself an evolving population of groupings of individual people, each of whom is also evolving. In other words, we are concerned with dynamic patterns of interaction and interconnection. We can think about these patterns of interaction in terms of *systems* or in terms of *processes*. We can take a macro or micro perspective and we can think of these as different ontological *levels* or simply as different *degrees of detail being examined*. We can notice the contradictions and we can adopt a *dualistic* way of thinking that resolves them or we can adopt a way of thinking that sees the contradictions as essential *paradoxes* that cannot be resolved. Finally, we can try to think from the position of the *objective observer* or from that of the *participative enquirer*. Which of all of these choices is made determines the kind of theory of strategy and organisational change one comes up with.

Having obtained some idea of the nature of the phenomena that strategy and organisational change are concerned with, consider now the second question posed at the end of section 1.1, namely how to make sense of the phenomena.

1.3 Making sense of the phenomena

The question of how we make sense of ourselves in our world is, of course, a very old one. One answer to that question is realism. From this perspective, it is the nature of reality itself that determines the patterns we perceive and the meaning we make of our experience. The notion here is that there is a reality external to humans that exists before they try to interpret or explain it; that is, reality is pre-given. This means that the categories into which people classify specific instances are already there in the phenomenon they are trying to explain. A rose falls into the category 'roses' because there is a real difference between roses and other categories of flowers. An organisation falls into the category 'coal industry' because there is a real difference between organisations in this industry and those in the gas industry. If the categories exist in reality then any other classification people might make would not produce an adequate explanation, a fact that they would discover when they tried to act in accordance with that explanation. Most natural scientists would probably adopt this position in relation to the natural phenomena that they try to explain. If one adopts this position then it is quite natural to suppose that a human being can stand outside the phenomena to be explained, taking the role of the objective observer who builds increasingly accurate explanations, or models, through experimentation. Mostly, realists do not see any inherent limitation on human ability to comprehend reality in its entirety. For them, it is only a matter of time before research progressively uncovers more and more of reality.

The opposite position to realism is relativism or scepticism, nowadays know as postmodernism. Here the categories into which people classify their experiences are held to exist only in their minds, not out there in reality. Any explanations they come up with are, therefore, simply projections of their own minds. Those who hold this position maintain that there is no pre-given reality outside of humans. There is no reality, only the stories we tell each other and one story is as good as another.

Another position avoids the extremes of both realism and scepticism and this is idealism. Here too, it is held that it is way we think which determines the patterning of our experience. However, idealists do not believe that this means that our entire sense making is purely relative. Chapters 2 and 13 will explore idealist ways of making sense in more detail. Chapter 2 will describe Kant's transcendental idealism, in which it is argued that humans inherit mental categories and understand their world in terms of them. Understanding is then not relative at all but determined by pre-given categories in individual minds. Chapter 13 will briefly review Hegel's absolute idealism according to which human understanding is a social process that avoids relativism.

There are also more recent views that might be understood as idealist. Constructivists (*see* Chapter 2) hold that, because of biological evolution, humans are capable of perceiving the world in one way but not others (Maturana and Varela, 1987). For example, the human visual apparatus receives light waves on three channels; it is trichromate. Some other animals have dichromate (two channels) or quatrochromate (four channels) vision. Each type of creature, therefore, sees the world of colour in a different way, in effect, through biological evolution, selecting aspects of reality for attention. It is impossible for one type of creature to see the world of colour that another type sees. Similarly, constructivists would point to limitations on human capacity to perceive reality imposed by the evolved nature of the human brain. By its very nature, the human brain selects aspects of reality to pay attention to. This position has something in common with realism in that it supposes a reality that exists outside of the human organism and is not simply the result of the mind's projection. However, unlike realism, this is not an unproblematically pre-given reality but, rather, a constructed, enacted or selected reality.

Another position taken on the nature of the human capacity to explain experience is that of social constructionism (Gergen, 1985). Some social constructionists adopt the sceptical position, holding that there is no reality out there, but others tend towards an idealist position in which social reality is socially constructed in language. Here, reality is not a pre-given world determining our explanation but, rather, our explanation is being socially constructed in our encounter with each other in the world. This form of social constructionism is similar to constructivism but with a very important difference. While constructivists focus upon the selecting nature of the individual human being, social constructionists point to social interaction, particularly in conversation, as the selecting process. The constructionist position is this: every explanation people put forward of any phenomenon is a socially constructed account, not a straightforward description of reality. If this view is held then it is impossible to adopt the role of the independent, objective observer when trying to explain any phenomenon. Instead, one could only come up with an explanation through participation in what one is trying to explain.

Social constructionists hold that it is impossible to take the position of objective observer and that those who claim to do so are simply ignoring the impact of their own participation or lack of it. This leads to the closely related notion of reflexivity (Steier, 1991). Reflexive entities are entities that bend back upon themselves. Humans are reflexive in the sense that any explanations they produce are the products of who they are, as determined by their histories. For example, I am trying, on these pages, to explain different ways in which humans explain their experience. If I hold the reflexive position then I cannot claim any objectively given truth for my way of doing this. Instead, I have to recognise that the approach I am adopting is the product of who I am and how I think. This, in turn, is the distillation of my personal history of relating to other people over many years. If I accept the argument about reflexivity, I can never claim to stand outside my own experience, outside the web of relationships that I am a part of, and take the role of objective observer. Instead, I have to take the role of enquiring participant (Reason, 1988).

The individual and the group

The move to a reflexive, social constructionist position is very significant in terms of what is being assumed about the relationship between the individual and the group. Realist, transcendental idealist and constructivist positions are all presented in terms of the capacities and limitations of the human individual. The individual is taken to be prior and primary to the group and groups can then only be seen as consisting of individuals. Some social constructionists see the group as prior and primary. Individuals are then the products of the group in some way. Other perspectives, mostly derived from absolute idealism, are more paradoxical in that neither the individual nor the group is primary. One forms and is formed by the other. This question of how to think about the individual and the group is central to the reviews of theories of strategy and organisational change in this book.

So, there are a number of different, contradictory ways of explaining how human beings come to know anything. Furthermore, there is no widespread agreement as to which of these explanations is 'true' or even most useful. The realist position probably commands most support amongst natural scientists and those social scientists, probably the majority, who seek the same status for their field as is accorded to the natural sciences. Social constructionists point to a significant difference between natural and social phenomena. Humans interpret natural phenomena, those phenomena do not interpret themselves. However, when it comes to human phenomena, we are dealing with ourselves, phenomena that are already interpreting themselves. Many constructionists hold, therefore, that while the scientific approach might be applicable in the natural sciences it is not in the human sciences.

At this point, you might be wondering why I have apparently moved so far away from the central concern of this book, namely strategy and organisational dynamics. The reason is this: any view you take of the nature of strategy and change in organisations immediately implies a view on the nature of human knowing. If you think that an organisation's strategy is the choice made by its chief executive, following a rational process of formulation, then you are assuming a realist, transcendental idealist or perhaps constructivist position. You are implicitly assuming that the individual is primary. Since this tends to be the dominant approach to explaining what strategy is, it is quite easy to take it for the truth. However, what I have been trying to show in the above paragraphs is that this would be a completely unwarranted assumption. Just how human beings know anything, whether the individual or the group is primary, are hotly contested issues with no clear truth. Simply going along with today's dominant views on strategy, without any questioning of the foundations upon which they are built, amounts to shutting one's eyes to other possibilities, which might make more sense of one's experience. For example, if one shifts perspective and considers that an organisation's strategy might emerge from conversational processes in which many participate, then one would be moving towards a social constructionist position and assuming that the group is primary or to some kind of absolute idealism where neither the individual nor the group is primary. Perhaps this might assist in making more sense of experience of life in organisations.

Different theories of strategy and organisational change imply different ways of explaining how human beings know or do anything. If one wants to understand just what the differences are between one explanation of strategy and organisational change and another, then one needs, I believe, to understand what assumptions are implicitly being made about how humans know anything. The key aspect distinguishing explanations of human knowing is the way they treat the relationship between the individual and the group. In the rest of this book, I will be reviewing how various ways of understanding strategy and organisational change differ. I will be pointing to how some of the most important differences relate to the implicit assumptions made about human knowing and the relationship between the individual and the group.

I now want to move on to another extremely important aspect of how we make sense of the world and this has to do with the nature of causality.

The nature of causality

One way of thinking about the relationship between cause and effect in Western culture is linear and unidirectional. There is some variable Y whose behaviour is to be explained. It is regarded as dependent and other 'independent' variables, X_1, X_2, . . . , are sought that are causing it. Linear relationships mean that *if* there is more of a cause *then* there will be proportionally more of the effect.

For example, in organisations, a frequent explanation for success is that it is caused by a particular culture, a particular management style, a particular control system. The more that culture, style or control system is applied the more successful the organisation will be. Opposition parties always say that the government of the day has caused recession and inflation. More of the government's policies will, they say, lead to more recession and more inflation. All of this is what is meant by straightforward unidirectional, linear connections between cause and effect.

Many scientists, both social and natural, are increasingly realising that this view of the relationship between cause and effect is far too simple and leads to inadequate understanding of behaviour. They hold that greater insight comes from thinking in terms of the mutual or circular causality. The demand for a product does not depend simply on customer behaviour; it also depends upon what the producing firm does in terms of price and quality: the firm affects the customer who then affects the firm. Management style may cause success but success affects the style managers adopt. The government's policies may cause recession and inflation, but recession and inflation may also cause the policies they adopt.

When organisms and organisations are thought of as systems then complex forms of causality become evident to do with interconnection and interdependence, where everything affects everything else. In addition to the circular causality and interdependence of systems, there is also *nonlinearity*. This means that one variable can have a more than proportional effect upon another. Nonlinear systems then involve very complex connections between cause and effect. It may become unclear what cause and effect mean. The links between them may become distant in time and space and those links may even disappear for all practical purposes. If in these circumstances one proceeds as if simple linear links exist even if one does not know what they are, then one is likely to undertake actions that yield unintended and surprising results.

How one thinks about causality, then, will have an important impact on how one thinks about strategy and organisational change. This is a matter to which subsequent chapters will pay a great deal of attention.

Closely linked to the matter of causality is that of paradox. I have already said that how different theories deal with paradox is an important feature distinguishing them, so it will be important to be clear what paradox means.

The nature of paradox

There are a number of different ways in which we deal with the contradictions we encounter in our thinking. The first is to regard them as a *dichotomy*, which is a polarised opposition requiring an 'either . . . or' choice. For example, managers faced with the need to improve quality, requiring an increase in costs, may also be faced with the need to cut costs. If they think in terms of a dichotomy then they choose one or the other of these opposing alternatives. Or they could think of the choice facing them as a *dilemma*, which is a choice between two equally unattractive alternatives. Improving quality is unattractive because it increases costs and cutting costs means destroying jobs, which is unattractive for humanitarian reasons. Dilemmas also present 'either . . . or' choices. Thirdly, a contradiction may be thought of in terms of a *dualism or a duality*. For example, managers may be faced with the need to customise their products to meet localised customer requirements but they may also be faced with the need to standardise their products to meet global competition. If those managers think about this in dualistic terms then they might come up with the resolution or elimination of the contradiction through '*both* thinking globally *and* acting locally'. The mode of thinking in dualistic terms has a 'both . . . and' structure. Instead of choosing between one or the other, one keeps both but locates them in different spaces or times. So in the above example, one pole of the contradiction is located in thinking and the other in acting. The 'either . . . or' thinking of dichotomies and dilemmas and the 'both . . . and' thinking of dualisms/dualities all satisfy a precept of Aristotelian logic, which requires the elimination of contradictions because they are a sign of faulty thinking.

Finally, one might think of a contradiction as a *paradox*. There are a number of different definitions of a paradox. First, it may mean an apparent contradiction, a state in which two apparently conflicting elements appear to be operating at the same time. Paradox in this sense can be removed or resolved by choosing one element above the other all the time or by reframing the problem to remove the apparent contradiction. There is little difference between paradox in this sense and dualism/dualities and this is the meaning of paradox that is usually taken up in the literature on systemic views of organisations.

However, paradox may mean a state in which two diametrically opposing forces/ ideas are simultaneously present, neither of which can ever be resolved or eliminated. There is, therefore, no possibility of a choice between the opposing poles or of locating them in different spheres. Instead, what is required is a different kind of logic, such as the dialectical logic of Hegel (*see* Chapter 13). As it is used in this book, the word paradox means the presence together at the same time of self-contradictory, essentially conflicting ideas, none of which can be eliminated or resolved.

There are many examples of paradoxes in organisations. Each individual in an organisation has a paradoxical desire for freedom and the excitement that goes with chance and uncertainty, while at the same time fearing the unknown and wanting order and discipline. Businesses have to produce at the lowest cost, but they have to increase costs to provide quality. Organisations have to control what their employees do, but they have to give them freedom if they want to retain them and if they want them to deal with rapidly changing circumstances.

Many theories of organisation emphasise either/or choices. They prescribe either stability and success, or instability and failure. They usually do not recognise paradox as fundamental and, when they do, they prescribe some kind of harmonious, equilibrium balance between the choices. In this way the paradox is in effect eliminated; its existence is a nuisance that is not fundamental to success.

The way one perceives paradox says much about the way one understands organisational dynamics. The idea that, for success, paradoxes must be resolved, and that the tension they cause must be released, is part of the paradigm that equates success with the dynamics of stability, regularity and predictability. The notion that paradoxes can never be resolved, only lived with, leads to a view of organisational dynamics couched in terms of continuing tension-generating behaviour patterns that are irregular, unstable and unpredictable, but lead to creative novelty.

1.4   Key features in comparing theories of organisational evolution

In the previous sections of this chapter, I have been describing what I think the phenomena are that I am trying to explain when I talk about strategy and organisational change. Those phenomena are populations of organisations of various kinds and populations of people and groupings of people that make up each of those organisations. These populations of organisations and people are continuously interacting with each other in ever-changing but also repetitive ways. I have also been talking about how human beings come to know the phenomena of their worlds, including those of populations of organisations and people dynamically interacting with each other. In the course of describing the phenomena and how one might come to know them, I have listed a number of factors that I want to use to distinguish between various theories of strategy and organisational dynamics. These factors are:

- How the dynamics are understood.
- How paradox is handled.
- What degree of descriptive detail is focused upon.
- What part emotion is seen to play.
- How the interactive/relational nature of the phenomena are conceptualised.
- How causality is understood.
- Whether the theory assumes a pre-given or a constructed reality.
- Whether it takes the methodological stance of the objective observer or the reflexive, participative enquirer.
- What theory of human knowing and behaving it assumes, particularly how it deals with the relationship between individuals and groups.

I now want to pull these factors together into four questions that I will put to each of the theories to be considered in the chapters that follow. The questions are:

1 How does the theory understand the nature of human interacting and relating? I will be considering whether the theory takes a systemic or a process perspective, and how it deals with the dynamics and the nature of causality.

2 What theory of human psychology, that is ways of knowing and behaving, does each theory of strategy and organisational change assume? I will be focusing particularly on how each psychological theory deals with the relationship between individual and group and the questions of emotion and power.

3 What methodology underlies each theory of strategy and organisational change? I will be asking whether the theory takes the position of objective observer of a pre-given reality or whether it takes the position of the reflexive, participative enquirer seeking to understand a constructed reality.

4 How does each theory of strategy and organisational change deal with the possible paradoxical nature of the population of organisations and groupings of people? I will be asking whether the theory sees opposing ideas as dichotomies, dualisms/dualities or paradoxes.

In the chapters that follow I am going to classify different explanations according to the answers they give to the above four questions. What I am trying to do is to tease out strands of theory in order to expose assumptions and reasoning processes for comparison.

1.5   Outline of the book

Part One reviews theories of strategy and organisational change that are based on some form of systems thinking.

Chapter 2 explores the origins and development of system thinking, the main pillar of the theories of strategic choice, organisational learning and knowledge management. Chapter 3 describes the two pillars upon which the first of these theories, strategic choice, is built. The first pillar is cybernetic systems theory and the second is cognitivist psychology. Strategic choice theory prescribes a procedure involving the formulation of long-term strategies and then their implementation. Chapter 4 reviews the theory of strategic choice.

Chapter 5 turns to the foundations of the second theory to be reviewed. The theory is that of the learning organisation and the foundations are systems dynamics, cognitive and humanistic psychology. Chapter 6 reviews the theory of the learning organisation. It concludes with an examination of how it answers the four key questions set out in the previous section.

Chapter 7 reviews a combination of open systems theory and psychoanalytic perspectives on human nature. Chapter 8 explores the development of second order systems thinking and the theory of autopoiesis. It relates these to strategy thought of as knowledge management. Chapter 9 reviews the move system thinkers have been making to more social perspectives. It covers critical systems thinking and the notion of communities of practice.

Part Two of the book moves from the systems theories developed in the late 1940s and early 1950s to those developed more recently. Chapter 10 describes the theories of chaos and dissipative structures, also making a brief reference to synergetics. Chapter 11 describes the agent-based models of complex adaptive systems.

Chapter 12 reviews some recent publications that explore the application of chaos and complexity theory to organisations. I argue that they do this from the systemic and cognitivist psychological perspective and in doing so collapse the potentially radical insights of chaos and complexity theory into management orthodoxy.

Part Three moves from systemic to process thinking.

Chapter 13 reviews the origins and development of process thinking. Chapters 14 and 15 review the theory of complex responsive processes as a perspective from which to understand strategy and organisational change. They develop an alternative psychological perspective in which the individual is decentred and relationship is key to understanding human nature. Chapter 16 explores the nature of complex responsive processes in organisations. This theory focuses on the self-organising and constructive nature of conversation and power relations in organisations. Chapter 17 looks at the implications of the complex responsive processes theory for control, leadership and ethics. Chapter 18 examines how such a theory might answer the four key questions.

The final section of the book consists of Management narratives in which managers and consultants write about some aspect of their work in organisations.

PART ONE ● ● ● ●

Systemic perspectives on strategy and organisational dynamics

The first chapter in this part, Chapter 2, explores the origins of systems thinking, which underlies today's dominant theories of strategy and organisational change. Subsequent chapters in this part review a number of theories of organisational strategy and change and examine how each directs attention in a particular way to the four key questions posed at the end of Chapter 1:

1 What is the nature of interaction?
2 What is the nature of human beings?
3 What method is used to understand human interaction?
4 How does this method deal with paradox?

The different theories described are as follows.

The first is the theory of strategic choice. In simple terms, this theory holds that organisations change primarily in ways that are chosen by their most powerful members. It prescribes the making of such choices on the basis of predicted future outcomes and rational selection criteria. Although subjected to increasing criticism over recent years, this theory, in various forms, is probably the one that continues to dominate discussions of strategy and organisational change amongst both practitioners and researchers. Although some of its analytical methods are derived from economic theories of the market and the firm, the theory of strategic choice is mainly built on the foundations of cybernetic systems theory and takes a largely cognitivist view of human nature. Chapter 3 will explain what cybernetics and cognitivism mean and then Chapter 4 will describe how they are used in strategic choice theory.

The second theory to be reviewed is that of the learning organisation. In very simple terms, this theory holds that an organisation evolves through the learning processes that take place within it. It prescribes ways of thinking and behaving that are supposed to enhance this learning process. Here the systems theory is provided by systems dynamics and the psychological theory is also cognitivist with some elements of humanistic psychology. Chapter 5 explains what systems dynamics is and how it differs from cybernetics and Chapter 6 indicates how these ideas are used in the theory of the learning organisation.

The third theory, which is explored in Chapter 7, combines open systems theory with a psychoanalytic understanding of human nature. This theory is primarily concerned with unconscious processes and neurotic forms of leadership, demonstrating how these might impede rational choice and learning. It takes account of the impact on organisations of anxiety and the ways it is contained or defended against.

Finally, in Chapters 8 and 9, more recent developments in systems thinking are reviewed, namely second order and critical systems thinking, and their implication for thinking about strategy and organisational change in terms of knowledge creation and management.

Chapter 2 ● ● ● ●

The origins of systems thinking

2.1 Introduction

I recently joined a task force of senior executives in a large international corporation. This task force had been appointed by the chief executive who was concerned about the strategic direction of the corporation. He felt that the corporation had become increasingly unable to cope with the rapid changes confronting it. It seemed to carry on operating as it always had done in a world that was now completely different. The chief executive believed that the organisation needed to change substantially from an inflexible bureaucracy into a nimble entrepreneurial organisation capable of developing new forms of competitive advantage. He also believed that this change would only take place if the people throughout the *whole* organisation changed the way they behaved and he was convinced that such behavioural change would only happen if the values driving behaviour were transformed. This was the task he set for the task force I joined. This task force had been meeting for some time and when I joined them their frustration was evident. Despite sharing the chief executive's beliefs and despite their undoubtedly intelligent efforts, they had been unable to identify the required values, let alone how such values might be installed in the *whole* corporation. Furthermore, they had no satisfactory way of explaining why they had not been able to carry out their task.

What struck me when I joined them was how they had not been questioning the way of thinking that led them to believe that they could change their whole corporation in the manner proposed. They were not exploring the assumptions they were making. Instead, they were simply taking it for granted that it was possible to do what they had been asked to do. It seemed to me that they were thinking of their organisation as a whole, as a system, operating according to particular values. They thought that if they could identify these values and then change them, they could then change the direction, the strategy, of the organisation. They seemed to be thinking about themselves as autonomous individuals who could objectively observe the organisational system and determine the values according to which it should operate and then ensure that it did in fact operate according to these values.

For me, the big question was whether it was possible to do what they were proposing to do and it was clear that they were not even asking themselves this question. Unless they could begin to reflect upon their way of thinking and its taken-for-granted assumptions, they would probably continue with their frustrating attempts to formulate and change values. To take the reflective stance I am suggesting, it seems to me to be essential to understand how particular ways of thinking originated. Ways of thinking evolve – they have a history and understanding this history enables us to understand the nature of the assumptions we are making now as we approach important practical issues. It is for this very practical reason that this chapter introduces the subjects of strategy and change by turning to philosophy and the history of Western thought.

In order to understand the taken-for-granted assumptions made in theories of strategic management, therefore, it is helpful in a very practical way to understand something of the history of those theories within the wider history of Western thought. The chapters in this part of the book will be drawing attention to the manner in which all of the major theories of strategic management today depend upon systems thinking and take for granted the assumptions upon which that thinking is built. This chapter will explore the origins of systems thinking in Western philosophy and to do this it is necessary to go back some four hundred years and consider how people in the West thought about themselves and the world they lived in, and how they thought about the way in which they came to know anything about themselves in the world they lived in.

In the Middle Ages, people in the West thought that the world was created by God and they thought about themselves as creatures in nature and therefore also made by God. The purpose of nature was to express the glory of God in following His eternal, timeless laws. These laws applied to human beings too but with one major difference: unlike other creatures, humans were believed to have souls enabling them to choose whether to obey the laws of God or not. Obedience led to rewards in the afterlife and disobedience led to eternal punishment. Knowledge of God's creation was through divine revelation so that humans knew what they knew because God had revealed it to them in the Scriptures. Knowing was a process of interpreting the eternal truth to be found in the Holy Scriptures.

People thought in this way for hundreds of years and then about four hundred years ago changes in social and political structures began a long process of weakening the Church and absolute monarchies, and this process was intertwined with changes in the way people thought. This gradual process of change in the way people thought has come to be known as the Scientific Revolution, leading to the Age of Enlightenment.

●●●● 2.2   The Scientific Revolution

The Scientific Revolution was a movement of thought in which people came to hold that the eternal, timeless laws of nature could be understood not through revelation but through human reason. For example, Copernicus and others worked in the early sixteenth century, observing and measuring the movement of the planets and putting forward theories on the laws governing their movement. Galileo took this work up in the early seventeenth century, as did Newton and Leibniz later on in the seventeenth century. Also during this period, the philosophers Bacon and Descartes

powerfully articulated the way in which people were coming to experience themselves as individuals with minds inside them. As Descartes put it, human minds are
'thinking things' and all we can be sure of is our own individual capacity to doubt.
Everything is to be subjected to doubt and it is in this rational process of doubting
that humans can come to know themselves and their world. By the end of the seventeenth century, then, the scientific method had been established, as had a highly
individualistic way of thinking about ourselves.

Central to the scientific method is the individual scientist who objectively
observes nature, formulates hypotheses about the laws governing it and then tests
these laws against quantified data, so progressively moving towards a fuller and
more accurate understanding of the laws. These laws were understood to take the
form of universal, timeless, deterministic, linear 'if–then' causal links. For example,
if twice as much force is applied to an object in a vacuum *then* it will move twice
as far. The consequence of this Scientific Revolution, extending over more than a
century, was that people in the West had come to experience themselves as autonomous individuals with a non-corporeal mind inside them, taking the form of
internal worlds consisting of representations of the external world. This view of
how people experienced themselves was concisely formulated in the philosophy
of Leibniz. He saw individuals as windowless monads who internally represented external worlds, perceived both consciously and unconsciously, and related
to each other across an existential gulf.

However, this way of thinking posed fundamental questions. First, the question
arose as to how reasoning individuals were able to formulate hypotheses, involving
the categorisation of phenomena in nature and the identification of relationships
between them. For the realists, the answer lay in the nature of reality. There was no
problem about knowing because our bodies simply perceived reality as it was
through the senses. For others, however, there was a problem about knowing that
needed explanation. Descartes and Leibniz dealt with the problem by arguing that
the mind contained innate ideas through which it recognised clear, distinct truths
about the real external world. In other words, there is nothing problematic about
knowing: external reality exists and we directly know it because we are born with
minds having the capacity for knowing reality. However, Locke took a more sceptical position and argued that the mind had no innate ideas of reality but was initially
a blank tablet waiting for experience to write upon it in the form of sensory impressions that represent external, material objects. The question then became how we
could know that mental representations correspond to reality.

Writing around the middle of the eighteenth century, Hume took a radically
sceptical position and said that the mind imposes an order of its own on the sensations coming from the external real world but this order is simply an association of
ideas, a habit of human imagination through which it assumes causal connections.
There is nothing innate about knowing and the causal connections we postulate are
simply the accidents of repeated connections in the mind. Ideas result from connections in experience, not from an independent reality, and intelligibility reflects
habits of mind, not the nature of reality. Hume claimed that there was no necessary
order to our ideas other than the ways they were combined in our minds according
to habit and the laws of association.

With this radically sceptical argument, Hume threw into doubt the Enlightenment idea that reason could unaided discover the order of the real world. As a result the philosophy of Descartes, Leibniz and Locke no longer seemed to provide a firm foundation for science. Scepticism, with its conclusion about the relativity and unreliability of knowledge, threatened the very basis of science. This debate between the dogmatic rationalists, or realist scientists, and the radical sceptics about the nature of human knowledge is much the same as the much more recent debate between modernist science and postmodernism. In both cases science posits the existence of a unitary reality that can be reliably observed as truth, while radical scepticism/postmodernism points to the constructed, relative and plural nature of accounts of the world in which there is no truth, only many different 'stories' with none necessarily better than any other.

Another fundamental question posed by the Scientific Revolution had to do with human freedom and choice. Since humans were part of nature they had to be subject to its deterministic laws but if they were, then it followed that they could not be free.

These two questions, one to do with the nature of human knowing and the other to do with the possibility of human choice, were taken up by the philosopher Kant. Systems thinking can be said to have originated in Kant's answers to these questions.

2.3 Kant: natural systems and autonomous individuals

Kant was greatly impressed by the advances in human knowledge brought about by the scientific method but he also recognised that it was not sufficient to simply dogmatically postulate that we know reality directly. He accepted that we know what we know through sensations coming from the real world and that the mind imposes some kind of order on this sense data so that we cannot know reality in a direct manner. He therefore postulated a dualism. On the one hand there was reality, which he called noumenal, and on the other hand, there was the appearance of reality to us in the form of sensations, which he called phenomenal. He argued that we could never know reality in itself, the noumenal, but only the appearance of reality as sensation, the phenomenal. This bears some similarity to the position of the radical sceptics but Kant departed from them when he held that our inability to know reality itself does not mean that all our knowledge is purely relative, simply the result of habits of association. Instead, the mind consists of innate categories which impose order on the phenomenal.

In this way he agreed with the radical sceptics in holding that we could not know reality directly but also agreed with the scientific realists in holding that there were innate ideas that imposed order on experience so that knowledge and truth were not simply relative. Examples of the innate categories of mind are time, space, causal links and what Kant called 'regulative ideas'. Regulative ideas are to be distinguished from constitutive ideas. A constitutive idea, or hypothesis, is a statement of what actually happens in reality. For example if we say that an organisation actually is a system operating to fulfil some real purpose, then we are putting forward a constitutive idea. We are saying that the organisation really exists and it is really fulfilling some real purpose. However, if we put forward an hypothesis in which we are thinking about an organisation 'as if' it were a system operating 'as if' it had a purpose, then we are thinking in terms of regulative ideas. Obviously Kant would not talk about constitutive ideas because he held that we could never know reality in itself. The activity of the scientist then becomes clear in Kant's scheme of things. The scientist has a mind consisting of categories of time, space, causal links and the capacity for forming 'as if' hypotheses, which enable him or her to formulate hypotheses about the appearances of reality and then test them.

Scientists, such as Newton and Leibniz, had understood nature in mechanistic terms and Kant was able to explain why this understanding was neither purely relative nor directly revealing of the reality of nature. He resolved the contradiction between realist and relative knowledge by taking aspects from each argument and holding them together in the 'both . . . and' way of a dualism. Knowledge of appearances was real and reliable while knowledge of reality itself was indeed impossible. In a sense both the scientific realists and the radical sceptics had a point and the contradictions between them could be eliminated by locating their conflicting explanations in different realms. This is typical of Kant's dualistic thinking in which paradoxes are eliminated so satisfying the rule of Aristotelian logic according to which paradox, the simultaneous existence of two contradictory ideas, is a sign of faulty thinking. I want to stress this key aspect of Kantian thinking because it has become very widespread in the West. The ideas of figure and ground, of different lenses through which to understand the world, and different levels of existence, are examples of this.

Kant, then, developed transcendental idealism as an alternative to realism, on the one hand, and scepticism, on the other. His thinking can be labelled as idealism because he held that we know reality through the capacities of the mind and it is transcendental because the categories through which we know are given outside our direct experience. In this way, Kant provided a sophisticated justification for the scientific method.

Self-organising systems

However, Kant went further than providing a philosophical justification of the mechanistic understanding of nature provided by scientists. He held that while it was useful to understand inanimate nature in this way, it was not adequate for an understanding of living organisms. He suggested that organisms could be more usefully understood as self-organising systems, which are very different to mechanisms.

A mechanism consists of parts that form a functional unity. The parts derive their function as parts from the functioning of the whole. For example, a clock consists of a number of parts, such as cogs, dials and hands, and these are assembled into a clock, which has the function of recording the passing of time. The parts are only parts of the clock insofar as they are required for the functioning of the whole, the clock. Therefore, a finished notion of *the whole is required before the parts* can have any function and the parts must be *designed* and assembled to play their particular role, without which there cannot be the whole clock. Before the clock functions, the parts must be designed and before they can be designed, the notion of the clock must be formulated.

However, the parts of a living organism are not first designed and then assembled into the unity of the organism. Rather, they arise as the result of interactions within the developing organism. For example, a plant has roots, stems, leaves and flowers which interact with each other to form the plant. The parts emerge, as parts, not by prior design but as a result of internal interactions within the plant itself in a self-generating, self-organising dynamic in a particular environmental context. The parts do not come before the whole but emerge in the interaction of spontaneously generated differences that give rise to the parts within a unity (Goodwin, 1994; Webster and Goodwin, 1996). The parts, however, have to be necessary for the production of the whole, otherwise they have no relevance as parts. The parts have to serve the whole; it is just that the whole is not designed first but comes into being with the parts. Organisms develop from a simple initial form, such as a fertilised egg, into a mature adult form, all as part of an inner coherence expressed in the dynamic unity of the parts. An organism thus expresses a nature with no purpose other than the unfolding of its own form. The organism's development unfolds what was already enfolded in it from the beginning.

Kant described this unfolding as 'purposive' because although an organism is not goal oriented in the sense of having a movement towards an external result, it is thought of as moving to a mature form of itself. The development to the mature form, and the mature form itself, will have some unique features due to the particular context in which it develops but the organism can only ever unfold the general form already enfolded in it. In talking about development being purposive, Kant introduced his notion of organism developing according to a 'regulative idea'. Since he held that we could not know reality, it followed that we could not say that an organism actually was following a particular idea. In other words, we cannot make the claim of a constitutive idea in relation to the organism. Instead, as observing scientists, we can claim that it is helpful to understand an organism 'as if' it were moving according to a particular purpose, namely, the regulative idea of realising a mature form of itself, that is, its true nature or true self.

For Kant, the parts of an organism exist because of, and in order to sustain, the whole as an emergent property (Kauffman, 1995). Organisms are self-producing and therefore self-organising wholes, where the whole is maintained by the parts and the whole orders the parts in such a way that it is maintained. In suggesting that we think in terms of systems, Kant was introducing a causality that was teleological and formative rather than the simple, linear, efficient (if–then) causality assumed in the mechanistic scientific way of understanding nature. In systems terms, causality is formative in that it is in the self-organising interaction of the parts that those parts and the whole emerge. It is 'as if' the system, the whole, has a purpose, namely, to move towards a final state that is already given as a mature form of itself. In other words, nature is unfolding already enfolded forms and causality might be referred to as formative (Stacey, Griffin and Shaw, 2001) in which the dominant form of causality is the formative process of development.

Note how this understanding of nature as system is quite consistent with the scientific method in that it is the human objective observer who identifies and isolates causality in natural systems and then tests hypotheses ('as if' or regulative ideas) about the purposive movement of those systems. It is not that organisms actually are systems or that they actually are unfolding a particular pattern in movement to a mature form. It is the scientist who finds it useful to think 'as if' they are. It is not that the laws are actually in nature but that the scientist is giving the laws to nature.

A very important point follows from this way of thinking about organisms, namely that it is *a way of thinking that cannot explain novelty*, that is, how any new form could come into existence. In thinking of an organism as unfolding an already enfolded form, Kant's systems thinking can explain the developmental cycle from birth to death but cannot explain how any new form emerges, that is, how evolution takes place. This is obviously a serious problem if what one wants to understand is creativity, innovation or novelty. The key point is that in Kant's systems thinking, causality is formative rather than transformative.

Also, Kant argued that the systemic explanation of how nature functioned could never be applied to humans because humans are autonomous and have a soul. Humans have some freedom to choose and so the deterministic laws of nature cannot be applied to rational human action.

The autonomous individual

For Kant, the human body could be thought of as a system because it is an organism. As such, it is subject to the laws of nature and when human action is driven by the passions of the body then it too is subject to the laws of nature and so not free. However, when acting rationally, humans could not be thought of as parts of a system because then they would exist because of, and in order to maintain the whole. A part of a system is only a part because it is interacting with other parts to realise themselves in the purposive movement of the emergent whole and the emergence of that whole is the unfolding of what is already enfolded, so excluding any fundamental spontaneity or novelty. If a part is not doing this then it is irrelevant to the system and so not a part. However, a part in this sense cannot be free, that is, it cannot follow its own autonomously chosen goals because then it would be acting for itself and not as a part. Furthermore, as parts of a whole that is unfolding an already enfolded final state, neither whole nor parts can display spontaneity or novelty. There can be nothing creative or transformative about such a system.

It follows that rational human action has to be understood in a different way. Kant held that human individuals are autonomous and so can choose the goals of their actions and they can choose the actions required to realise them. The predominant form of causality here is teleological, namely, that of autonomously chosen ends made possible because of the human capacity for reason. The principal concern then becomes how autonomously chosen goals and actions mesh together in a coherent way that makes it possible for humans to live together. This is a question of ethics and Kant understood ethical choice in terms of universals, namely, those choices that could be followed by all people. We may call this rationalist causality.

So, Kant developed a systems theory with a theory of formative causality to explain how nature developed, arguing that this could not be applied to human action, and another kind of explanation for human action, involving rationalist causality. It is particularly important to note these points because when later forms of systems thinking were developed in the middle of the twentieth century, they were directly applied to human action, and individuals came to be thought of as parts in a system called a group, organisation or society. It immediately follows that any such explanation cannot encompass individual human freedom, or individual agency. Nor can a systemic explanation encompass the origins of spontaneity or novelty. To explain these phenomena within systems thinking, we have to rely on the autonomous individual standing outside the system. In other words change of a transformative kind cannot be explained in systemic terms, that is, in terms of interactions between parts of the system, with one important exception that I will come to in Chapter 11. Any transformative change can then only be explained in terms of the mental functioning of the individual.

There are two other points to be borne in mind about Kant's systems thinking. It is essentially dualistic, that is, it takes a 'both . . . and' form that eliminates paradox (Griffin, 2001) by locating contradictions in different spaces or time periods. So, with regard to knowing there is *both* the known relating to phenomena *and* the unknown relating to noumena. With regard to the paradox of determinism and freedom there is *both* the determinism of mechanism and organism in nature *and* the freedom of rational human action. Linked to this there is the essentially spatial metaphor underlying all systems thinking. A system is a whole separated by a boundary from other systems, or wholes, In other words, there is an 'inside' and an 'outside'. For example, one thinks of what is happening inside an organisation or outside in the environment. Or one thinks of the mind inside a person and reality outside it.

2.4   Systems thinking in the twentieth century

Kant's thinking provoked many controversies and has continued to have a major impact on the evolution of Western thought up to the present time. This impact is evident in the major development of systems thinking in the twentieth century. Scholars in many different areas were working from the 1920s to the 1940s to develop systemic ways of thinking about physiology, biology, psychology, engineering and communication. This work culminated in the publication of a number of very important papers around 1950. These papers covered systems of control, the development of computer language, and the development of a new science of mind in reaction to behaviourism, namely, cognitivism (Gardner, 1985; McCulloch and Pitts, 1943). These ways of thinking amounted to a new paradigm, namely, a shift from mechanistic, reductionist science in which the whole phenomenon of interest was understood to be the sum of its parts, requiring attention to be focused on the nature of the part rather than the interactions between them. In the new paradigm of systems thinking, the whole phenomenon was thought of as a system and the parts as subsystems within it. A system in turn was thought to be part of a larger suprasystem. The parts were now not simply additive in that they affected each other. The whole came to be understood as more than the sum of the parts. The focus of attention shifted from understanding the parts, or entities, of which the whole was composed, to the interaction of subsystems to form a system and of systems to form a suprasystem. An essential aspect of this way of thinking is the different levels of existence it ascribes to phenomena. For example, individual minds are thought of as subsystems forming groups, which are thought of as systems forming an organisation, which is thought of as a suprasystem. Here each level is a different kind of phenomenon to be understood in a different way.

The new systems theories developed along three pathways over much the same period of time:

- General systems theory (Boulding, 1956; von Bertalanffy, 1968). The central concept here is that of homeostasis, which means that systems have a strong, self-regulating tendency to move towards a state of order and stability, or adapted equilibrium. They can only do this if they have permeable boundaries that are open to interactions with other systems. This strand in systems thinking will be explored in Chapter 7.
- Cybernetics (Ashby, 1945, 1952, 1956; Beer, 1979, 1981; Wiener, 1948). Cybernetic systems are self-regulating, goal-directed systems adapting to their environment, a simple example being the central heating system in a building. Here, the resident of a room sets a target temperature and a regulator at the boundary of the heating system detects a gap between that target and the actual temperature. This gap triggers the heating system to switch on or off, so maintaining the chosen target through a process of negative feedback operation. The impact of this strand of thinking on strategic management will be explored in Chapters 3 and 4.
- Systems dynamics (Forrester, 1958, 1961, 1969; Goodwin, 1951; Philips, 1950; Tustin, 1953). This was also developed largely by engineers who turned their attention to economics and industrial management problems. In systems dynamics, mathematical models are constructed of how the system changes states over time. One important difference from the other two systems theories is the recognition that the system may not move to equilibrium. The system is then no longer self-regulating but it is self-influencing: it may be self-sustaining or self-destructive. The impact of this strand of systems thinking will be explored in Chapters 5 and 6.

These three strands of systems thinking began to attract a great deal of attention in many disciplines from around 1950, as did the new cognitivist psychology, and of course, computers. Engineers, bringing with them their notion of control, took the lead in developing the theories of cybernetic systems and systems dynamics, while biologists, concerned with biological control mechanisms, developed general systems theory. This systems movement, particularly in the form of cybernetics, has come to form the foundation of today's dominant management discourse, so importing the engineer's notion of control into understanding human activity. The development of systems thinking amounted to the rediscovery of formative causality. The move from mechanistic thinking about parts and wholes to systems thinking, therefore, amounted to a move from a theory of causality couched entirely in efficient terms (if–the) to one of both efficient causal links and formative causal process as found in Kant's philosophy.

It is important to note that in applying systems thinking to human action, all of the strands of systems thinking indicated above did exactly what Kant had argued against. They postulated that human action could be understood in terms of systems.

2.5   Thinking about organisations and their management

So far in this chapter, I have been describing the movement from revelation as a way of knowing to the Scientific Revolution with its rational way of knowing. I have talked about some of the reactions to the scientific method and to some key aspects of its development, namely, the move from mechanistic and reductionist ways of thinking to holistic and systemic ways of thinking. These developments have, of course, been reflected in thinking about organisations and their management during the course of the twentieth century.

Scientific management

The mechanistic and reductionist approach of the early Scientific Revolution is quite evident in what has come to be known as scientific management. Frederick Taylor (1911) in the United States and Henri Fayol (1916) in Europe were the founding figures of scientific management and both were engineers. Taylor's central concern was with the efficient performance of the physical activities required to achieve an organisation's purpose. His method was that of meticulously observing the processes required to produce anything, splitting them into the smallest possible parts, identifying the skills required and measuring how long each part took to perform and what quantities were produced. His prescription was to provide standardised descriptions of every activity, specify the skills required, define the boundaries around each activity and fit the person to the job requirement. Individual performance was to be measured against the defined standards and rewarded through financial incentive schemes. He maintained that management was an objective science that could be defined by laws, rules and principles: if a task was clearly defined, and if those performing it were properly motivated, then that task would be efficiently performed. Fayol's approach to management was much the same. He split an organisation into a number of distinct activities (for example, technical, commercial, accounting and management) and he defined management as the activity of forecasting, planning, organising, co-ordinating and controlling through setting rules that others were to follow.

Management science equated the manager with the scientist and the organisation with the phenomenon that the scientist is concerned with. The particular approach that the manager is then supposed to take towards the organisation is that of the scientist, the objective observer, who regards the phenomenon as a mechanism. The whole mechanism is thought to be the sum of its parts and the behaviour of each part is thought to be governed by timeless laws. An organisation is, thus, thought to be governed by efficient (if–then) causality and the manager's main concern is with these causal rules. There is a quite explicit assumption that there is some set of rules that are optimal, that is, that produce the most efficient global outcome of the actions of the parts, or members, of the organisation.

There is, however, an important difference between the scientist concerned with nature and the analogous manager concerned with an organisation, which is rarely acknowledged in scientific management. The scientist discovers the laws of nature while the manager, in the theory of management science, chooses the rules driving the behaviour of the organisation's members. In this way, something like Kant's autonomous individual and the accompanying rationalist causality is imported into theories of scientific management, but with some important differences. First, it is only the manager to whom rationalist causality applies. It is he who exercises the freedom of autonomous choice in the act of choosing the goals and designing the rules that the members of the organisation are to follow in order to achieve the goals. Those members are not understood as human beings with autonomous choice of their own but as rule-following parts making up the whole organisation. Closely linked to this point about freedom is that of acting into the unknown. Kant argued that the choices humans make are unknown. In its use in scientific management, rationalist causality is stripped of the quality of the unknown, and also of the ethical limits within which action should take place, to provide a reduced rationalist causality. In fact scientific management does what Kant argued against. It applies the scientific method in its most mechanistic form to human action. Secondly, Kant's coupling of autonomous human action with universal ethical principles is absent in the rationalist causality of management science, which regards human action as a reflex-like response to stimuli in accordance with the behaviourist psychology of its time.

The ethical aspect appears to some extent in the reaction of the Human Relations school to scientific management. By the 1930s, the view that Taylor and Fayol took of human behaviour was being actively contested by, for example, Elton Mayo (1945), a social psychologist. He conducted experiments to identify what it was that motivated workers and what effect motivational factors had on their work. He pointed to how they always formed themselves into groups that soon developed customs, duties, routines and rituals and argued that managers would only succeed if these groups accepted their authority and leadership. He concluded that it was a major role of the manager to organise teamwork and so sustain co-operation. Mayo did not abandon a scientific approach but, rather, sought to apply the scientific method to the study of motivation in groups.

From the 1940s to the 1960s, behavioural scientists (for example, Likert, 1961) continued this work and concluded that effective groups were those in which the values and goals of the group coincided with those of the individual members and where those individuals were loyal to the group and its leader. Efficiency was seen to depend upon individuals abiding by group values and goals, having high levels of trust and confidence in each other in a supportive and harmonious atmosphere. In extending freedom to all members of an organisation and paying attention to motivational factors, the Human Relations school took up a fuller notion of rationalist causality.

Taking scientific management and Human Relations together, we have a theory in which stability is preserved by rules, including motivational rules, which govern the behaviour of members of an organisation. Change is brought about by managers when they choose to change the rules, which they should do in a way that respects and motivates others so that the designed set of rules will produce optimal outcomes. Organisations are thought to function like machines achieving given purposes deliberately chosen by their managers. Within the terms of this framework, change of a fundamental, radical kind cannot be explained. Such change is simply the result of rational choices made by managers, and just how such choices emerge is not part of what this theory seeks to explain. The result is a powerful way of thinking and managing when the goals and the tasks are clear, there is not much uncertainty and people are reasonably docile, but inadequate in other conditions. Truly novel change and coping with conditions of great uncertainty were simply not part of what scientific management and Human Relations theories set out to explain or accomplish.

The principles discussed above were developed a long time ago, and they have been subjected to heavy criticism over the years, but they still quite clearly form the basis of much management thinking.

The shift to systems thinking

The wider paradigm shift from mechanistic to systemic thinking described in previous sections is also evident in theories of organisations and their management. For example, general systems theory was combined with psychoanalysis to develop a systemic understanding of organisation (*see* Chapter 7) which emphasises clarity of roles and task definition and equates management with a controlling role at the boundary (Miller and Rice, 1967). The influence of the cybernetic strand of systems thinking is even more in evidence (*see* Chapters 3 and 4). All planning and budgeting systems in organisations are cybernetic in that quantified targets are set for performance at some point in the future, the time path towards the target is forecast and then actual outcomes are measured and compared with forecasts, with the variance fed back to determine what adjustments are required to bring performance back to target. All quality management systems take the same form as do all incentive schemes, performance appraisal and reward systems, management and culture change programmes, Total Quality Management and Business Process Re-engineering projects. The thinking and talking of both managers and organisational researchers, therefore, tends to be dominated by cybernetic notions. The third strand of systems thinking, namely systems dynamics, originally had little impact on management thinking but more recently it has attracted much interest as a central concept in the notion of the learning organisation (*see* Chapters 5 and 6). Here, instead of thinking of a system moving towards an equilibrium state, it is thought of as following a small number of typical patterns or archetypes. Effective management requires the recognition of these archetypes and the identification of leverage points at which action can be taken to change them and so enable management to stay in control of an organisation, in effect controlling its dynamics.

The shift from reductionist management science to holistic, systemic perspectives on organisations does not, however, entail any substantial challenge to the scientific method. The manager continues to be equated with the natural scientist, the objective observer, and just as the scientist is concerned with a natural phenomenon, so the manager is concerned with an organisation. Now, however, the organisation is understood, not as parts adding to a whole, but as a system in which the interactions between its parts are of primary importance. The manager understands the organisation to be a self-regulating or a self-influencing system and it is the formative process of self-regulation or self-influence (formative cause) that is organising the pattern of behaviour that can be observed. In the case of general systems and cybernetics, that pattern is movement towards a chosen goal, an optimally efficient state, and the pattern of behaviour is held close to this goal/state when the system is operating effectively. In the case of systems dynamics, the form towards which the system moves is a typical pattern or archetype enfolded in the system, which the manager can alter by operating at leverage points. In all of these systems theories, therefore, the final form of the system's behaviour, that towards which it tends, is a state already enfolded, as it were, in the rules governing the way the parts interact.

In the decades after 1950, the first wave of modern systems thinking about organisation, described above, paid as little attention as management science did to ethics, ordinary human freedom and the unknown nature of the final state towards which human action tends. As soon as one thinks of a human organisation as a system that can be identified or designed one immediately encounters the problem that the identifier or the designer is also part of the system. This problem was recognised by the systems thinkers of the mid-twentieth century and later led to the development of second order systems thinking (*see* Chapter 8). Also, some more recent developments of systems thinking (soft systems and critical systems) in the 1980s and 1990s actively took up the issues of participation and ethics, but they did so in a way that did nothing to alter the underlying theory of causality (*see* Chapter 9). The systems movement continues to build on a theory of rationalist causality applied to the understanding and design of organisations as systems that are governed by formative causality (*see* Chapters 8 and 9).

Back to the values task force

I started this chapter by referring to the task force appointed by the chief executive of a major international company. I suggest that the way he and the members of the task force were thinking about change in their organisation clearly reflects the history of systems thinking outlined in this chapter. They were taking it for granted that they, as autonomous individuals, could objectively observe their organisation, understood as a system, and change the values that drive its operation. In other words, they were assuming that they could enfold into the organisational system the purposes that it would then unfold. In doing this, they had lost sight of Kant's notion of a regulative idea. Instead of thinking that they could understand the system 'as if' it were unfolding a purpose they were hypothesising, they were thinking that their organisation was a system that really could/would unfold the purpose they determined for it. More than that, however, they were doing what Kant strongly advised against. They were applying the notion of system to the human actions that are the organisation and thereby thinking of the organisation's members, including themselves, as parts of the system. In this way of thinking, ordinary human freedom to make a choice is lost sight of. However, all individuals in an organisation have some choice regarding the part they play in together forming the values that guide their behaviour. Attempts to determine these values for them are then bound to fail, if indeed individuals are at all autonomous. Furthermore, the systemic way of thinking cannot explain in its own terms the very matter that these managers were concerned with, namely the transformation of their organisation. This is simply because systems thinking cannot explain, in its own terms, novelty or creativity. What may seem, in this chapter, to be a rather abstract philosophical discussion is in fact a highly practical matter.

2.6 How systems thinking deals with four questions

Systems thinking essentially seeks to understand phenomena as a whole formed by the interaction of parts. Whole systems are separated from others by boundaries and they interact with each other to form a suprawhole. There are thus different levels at which phenomena either exist or need to be thought about. These notions of wholes, boundaries and levels are central distinguishing features of systems thinking. How does this kind of thinking deal with the four questions posed at the end of Chapter 1?

The first questions has to do with how interaction is understood. In systems thinking, interaction between parts produces the whole and the parts are relevant as parts only because they produce and sustain the whole. The form of causality is the formative process of interaction between parts. Process here means the process of producing a whole and participation means participating in the production of a whole.

The second question has to do with the nature of human beings. In systems thinking, the answer to this question is a dualism. On the one hand, humans are thought of as rational, autonomous individuals who objectively observe systems and ascribe purposive behaviour to them. Causality here is rationalist and rational humans are free to choose. On the other hand, humans are also thought of as parts or members of the system being observed and so subject to formative causality. As such they cannot be free to choose but are subject to the purpose and formative process of the system. This problem has not gone unnoticed by systems thinkers but in Chapters 8 and 9 I will argue that the problem has not been resolved.

Taken together, the systems thinkers' answers to these two question imply a particular way of thinking about human experience, that is, the patterning of interaction between people. The implication is that the cause of experience, the cause of the patterning of interaction between people, lies in some system, created by people, that lies above or below that experience. So, in the task force I referred to, the particular patterning of the interactions between people in the organisation was assumed to be a system of values existing somehow outside the direct experience of people interacting.

Turning to the third question to do with the method used to understand human action, it is clear that the method of the systems thinking so far discussed is that of objective observation. Generally, when applied to organisations, this is done in a realist way. People then think that systems actually exist in reality and organisations really are systems that have their own purposes. Organisations and systems are thereby reified, that is, understood to have an existence as things. Kant's idealist position on systems is thereby lost. However, in later critical systems thinking (*see* Chapter 9) Kant's 'as if' position has been recovered. Critical systems thinkers argue against the notion that systems actually exist and regard them as mental structures. Second-order systems thinking (*see* Chapter 8) also moves away from simple object-ive observation and seeks to understand humans as participants in systems.

The fourth question has to do with paradox. Systems thinking originated as a dualistic way of thinking that eliminated paradox, for example by postulating one causality for nature and another for human action. Since Kant, systems thinkers have retained, often implicitly, a dual theory of causality, formative and rationalist, and applied them both to human action. They eliminate the paradox, not by differ-ent spatial locations, but in different temporal sequencing. First, managers are thought of as autonomous individuals subject to rationalist causality when they are determining the organisational system's purpose and then as subject to formative causality in their role as members of the system. In this way they preserve the 'both . . . and' structure of Kantian thinking.

●●●● 2.7 Summary

This chapter has described some key aspects in the development of Western thought over the last four centuries. Its particular concern has been with the origins of systems thinking in Kantian philosophy and its later development and application to human action around the middle of the twentieth century. The purpose has been to highlight the key aspects of systems thinking and the particular problems it poses when applied to human action. The main problem has to do with how, in system terms, we are to understand human participation, freedom and transformation. The chapters that follow will explore systemic theories of organisational strategy and change.

Further reading

The origins and philosophical nature of systems thinking are reviewed in more depth in Stacey *et al.* (2001) and in Griffin (2001).

Chapter 3 ● ● ● ●

The foundations of strategic choice theory
Cybernetic systems and cognitivist psychology

3.1 Introduction

The purpose of this chapter is to review the theoretical foundations of the theory of strategic choice. Although there has recently been a shift to notions of the learning organisation (*see* Chapters 5 and 6), strategic choice is still probably the dominant theory of strategy and organisational change. You can hear it in the way that most management practitioners talk about strategy and change in their organisations, and you can read it in most of the books and articles written about strategy and organisational design and development.

The next chapter provides a summary of some of the key elements of this theory but here it will suffice to give a very brief definition of what the theory of strategic choice has to say before going on to its theoretical foundations in the theories of cybernetic systems and cognitivist psychology.

The theory of strategic choice holds that the strategy of an organisation is the general direction in which it changes over time. The general direction encompasses the range of activities it will undertake, the broad markets it will serve, how its resource base and competences will change and how it will secure competitive advantage. This general direction is chosen by the most powerful individual in the organisation or by a small group of managers at the top of the management hierarchy, that is, the dominant coalition.

This notion places the individual, and the choices made by the individual, at the very centre of the theory. It therefore immediately implies a particular theory of human psychology, that is, a theory of how humans know and behave. The theory implied is that of cognitivism, a term I will explain later in this chapter.

Having chosen the general direction, or strategy, the managers at the top of the hierarchy are supposed to design an organisational structure to implement it. The structure they design is supposed to be a largely self-regulating one in which people are assigned roles and given objectives to achieve that will realise the chosen strategy.

This requirement assumes that these is a particular way in which people are thought to interact with each other. They are thought to interact within a particular kind of system, namely a cybernetic system, the nature of which I will explain in the next section of this chapter. Furthermore, the need to motivate people to achieve objectives also implies a psychological theory of motivation and this is usually based on humanistic psychology. I will also explain what this is later in the chapter.

Having set out what cybernetic systems and cognitivist psychology are, I will then pursue the four questions posed at the end of Chapter 1. I will ask how cybernetic systems theory and cognitivist psychology deal with those four questions. This enables one to see how the theory of strategic choice, to be described in Chapter 4, displays its theoretical origins in cybernetic systems theory and in cognitivist psychology.

3.2   Cybernetic systems

Cybernetics is an application of the engineer's idea of control to human activity. During the Second World War, the superiority of the German air force led British scientists to consider how they might improve the accuracy of anti-aircraft defences. One of these scientists, Norbert Wiener, saw a way of treating the evasive action of enemy aircraft as a time series that could be manipulated mathematically to improve the gunner's predictions of the enemy plane's future position:

> *When we desire a motion to follow a given pattern, the difference between the pattern and the actually performed motion is used as a new input to cause the part regulated to move in such a way as to bring the motion closer to that given pattern. (Wiener, 1948, p. 6)*

It is important to note how cybernetics immediately focuses attention on performing a given pattern. This is the realist position described in Chapters 1 and 2. There is an already existing, or pre-given, reality outside the individual who is trying to understand it. What Wiener is describing here is the process of negative feedback.

Negative feedback and equilibrium

Negative feedback simply means that the outcome of a previous action is compared to some desired outcome and the discrepancy between the two is fed back as information that guides the next action in such a way that the discrepancy is reduced until it disappears. Thus when anything at all disturbs a system from its state of stable equilibrium it will return to that equilibrium if it is governed by some form of negative feedback control. Negative feedback is the process required to produce the dynamics of stability. Consider two commonly quoted examples: a domestic central heating system and the Watt steam engine governor.

A domestic heating system consists of an appliance and a regulator. The regulator contains a device that senses room temperature connected to a device that turns the heating appliance on and off. A desired temperature is set in the regulator. When the room temperature falls below this desired level, the control sensor detects the discrepancy between actual and desired states. The regulator responds to a negative discrepancy with a positive action – it turns the heat on. When the temperature rises above the desired level the opposite happens. By responding to the

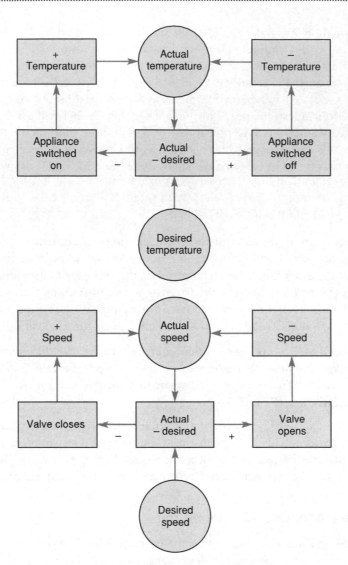

Figure 3.1   Negative feedback

deviation of actual from desired levels in an opposite or negative way, the control system dampens any movement away from desired levels. The controls keep the room temperature close to a stable level over time utilising negative feedback. Figure 3.1 illustrates this negative feedback loop.

The same principle applies to the steam engine governor. As the boiler of the engine is stoked, steam pressure rises causing the engine to speed up. If this speed exceeds a preset desired level, the governor responds by opening a valve to release the steam and so pull the engine speed back to the desired level. As soon as the speed falls below the desired level the valve closes, steam pressure rises and the engine speed increases to the desired level. Here too the operation of the control system is such that fluctuations around the desired level are damped and predictable. Stable equilibrium behaviour is thus preserved through the use of negative feedback. Figure 3.1 also illustrates this example.

Equilibrium is a possible state of behaviour for a system. It takes a stable form when the behaviour of a system regularly repeats its past and when it is very difficult to change that behaviour to some other state. It requires significant change to shift a system from a state of stable equilibrium. For example, in economic theory markets are assumed always to tend to a state of stable equilibrium. If there is an increase in demand, then prices will rise to encourage an increase in supply to match the demand. If demand then stays constant, so will price and supply. Any chance movement of the price away from its equilibrium level will set in train changes in demand and supply that will rapidly pull price back to its equilibrium level. It will take a noticeable change in demand or supply to alter this behaviour.

Equilibrium can take an *unstable* form. Here the system's state is easily perturbed from, and does not easily return to, its original state.

Dynamic equilibrium is a state in which a system continuously adapts to alterations in a continually changing environment.

The key point about all forms of equilibrium behaviour is that they are regular, orderly and predictable. Most theories of management and organisation have been developed within an equilibrium framework. Of course, to be regular, orderly and predictable, the links between cause and effect have to be clear-cut. In equilibrium there are clear-cut links between cause and effect and consequently behaviour is predictable.

Negative feedback and human action

Wiener and his colleagues held that negative feedback loops were important in most human actions – a loop in which the gap between desired and actual performance of an act just past is fed back as a determinant of the next action (*see* Figure 3.2).

If you are trying to hit an object by throwing a ball at it and you miss because you aimed too far to the right, you then use the information from this miss to alter the point at which you aim the next shot: you aim further to the left, trying to offset the last error. In this sense the feedback is negative – it prompts you to move in the opposite direction. You keep doing this until you hit the object. Wiener and his colleagues thought that this negative feedback was essential to controlled behaviour and that breaking the feedback link led to pathological behaviour.

Cyberneticists also realised that when such negative feedback becomes too fast, or too sensitive, the result could be uncontrolled cycles of over- and under-achievement of the desired state. So, for example, you may be taking a shower and find the water too hot. This leads you to raise the flow of cold water. If you do not take sufficient account of the lag between your action and the subsequent drop in temperature you may increase the cold water flow again. This may make the water too cold so you raise the flow of hot water which then makes it too hot again. Unless you get the time lag between your action and its consequence right, you may increase the hot water flow until it becomes too hot again. So, if your negative feedback control system is operating too rapidly, the temperature of the water will fluctuate in an unstable manner instead of settling down to a desired level. Negative feedback systems can be highly unstable.

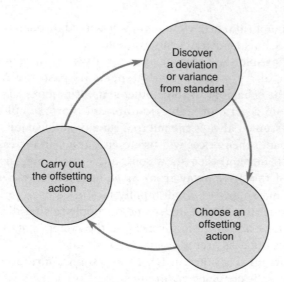

Figure 3.2   Negative feedback in cybernetics

Those studying such systems therefore became very concerned to establish the conditions for stability and instability in negative feedback control systems. As a result of this kind of work governments came to accept that their attempts to remove cycles in the level of activity in the economy were usually counterproductive. Just as the economy was recovering from a slump, impatient governments tended to cut taxes and increase expenditure, so fuelling an excessive boom accompanied by rapid inflation. Just as that boom was collapsing on its own, fearful governments increased taxes and cut expenditure, so pushing the economy into a deeper slump than it would otherwise have experienced. To secure stability through negative feedback you must be able to predict not only the outcome of an action but also the time lag between an action and its outcome. The design of a control system that works at the right speed and the right level of sensitivity relies upon such predictions. Given the ability to predict, it is then possible to specify in a precise mathematical way exactly what conditions will produce stability for any negative feedback system.

Having outlined what cybernetics is all about I now turn to how it has been applied to the control of organisations. Two writers have been of major importance in developing cybernetic theory, particularly in its early applications to organisations: W. Roy Ashby (1945, 1952, 1956) and Stafford Beer (1959/67, 1966). Ashby and Stafford Beer made the key points set out in the paragraphs below.

Goal-seeking adaptation to the environment

Cybernetics postulate that two main forces drive an organisation over time. The first force is the drive to achieve some purpose: from this perspective organisations are goal-seeking systems and the goal drives their actions. The second force arises because organisations are connected through feedback links to their environments:

they are subsystems of an even larger environmental suprasystem. Reaching the goal requires being adapted to those environments.

Thus, in the cybernetics tradition, organisations are driven by attraction to a predetermined desired state which is equilibrium adaptation to the environment. The state a given organisation comes to occupy is determined by the nature of its environment.

For example, on this view, a company operating in, say, the electronics industry may be driven by the goal of achieving a 20 per cent return on its capital. In order to achieve this it must deliver what its customers want. If customers have stable requirements for standardised low-cost silicon chips to be used as components in their own products, then the company has to adapt to this environment by employing mass production methods to produce standardised products at lower costs than its rivals. It will have to support these production methods with particular forms of organisational structure, control systems and cultures: functional structures, bureaucratic control systems and conservative, strongly shared cultures. The company will look much the same as its rivals in the same market because the overall shape of each is determined by the same environment.

If, however, the electronics market is a turbulent one with rapidly changing technology and many niche markets where customers look for customised chips, then there will be very different kinds of organisation, according to cybernetics theory. A company will have to adapt by emphasising R&D and continually developing new products to differentiate itself from its rivals. It will support these production methods with particular forms of structure, control systems and culture: decentralised structures of separate profit centres, greater emphasis on informal controls, and change-loving cultures.

But how do organisations come to be adapted to their environments and achieve their goals?

Regulators

According to cybernetics, organisations deploy regulators that utilise negative feedback in order to reach their goals and the desired states of adaptation to their environments. The central problem is how to keep an organisation at, or near to, some desired state and the answer to the problem lies in the design of the regulator, that is, the design of the control system. Cybernetics is the science of control and management is the profession of control. At the heart of that science and that profession lies the design of regulators. You can see how this kind of thinking accords with a major management concern – that to do with being in control.

There are two types of regulator: the error-controlled regulator and the anticipatory regulator. In Ashby's scheme, disturbances from its environment (D in Figure 3.3) impact on the organisation (T in the figure) leading to an outcome (E in the figure). The problem is where to put the regulator (R in Figure 3.3).

Anticipatory regulation

If the regulator is placed so that it senses the disturbance before that disturbance hits the organisation, then it can take anticipatory action and offset the undesirable impact of the disturbance on the outcome (part A of Figure 3.3).

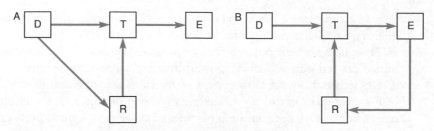

Figure 3.3   Regulation in control systems
Source: W. R. Ashby (1956), *Introduction to Cybernetics*, New York: John Wiley.

An immediately recognisable example of this kind of regulator is of course a planning system. Such a regulator takes the form of a sensing device using market research questionnaires or analyses of market statistics. On the basis of these, realistically achievable desired states are established. These desired states are forecasts of sales volumes, prices and costs at some future point; that is, the positions and postures required to achieve the performance target or goal. Action plans to realise these forecasts are also prepared; that is, patterns in future actions are identified. As the company moves through time it continually senses the environment, picks up disturbances before they occur and prepares planned actions to deal with them before they hit the organisation. This is ideal control without making mistakes: preventing deviations from plan occurring in the first place.

Error-controlled regulation

If it is not possible to establish such an anticipatory regulator, or if such a regulator cannot work perfectly, then a regulator must be placed so that it can sense the outcome once that outcome has occurred. This is the classic error-controlled regulator (part B of Figure 3.3).

An immediately recognisable example of this type of regulator is the monitoring, reviewing and corrective action system of an organisation. It is what a company's board of directors does each month when it meets to review what has happened to the business over the past month, monitors how the performance measures are moving and decides what to do to correct deviations from plan that have already occurred.

It is clearly preferable to anticipate disturbances as far as possible because there are time lags: first in detecting what is happening; then in deciding what should be done; then in doing it; and then in the outcome materialising from the action. These time lags mean that relying entirely on the error-control system will not produce the intended performance. Since it takes time to correct a deviation, and since time lags can cause instability in performance, managers should aim to prevent deviation in the first place. But anticipating disturbances relies on the ability to forecast them and this can never be perfect. Therefore an organisation will have to rely on both anticipatory and error-control regulators. This is exactly what the managers of a business do when they prepare budgets and plans and then monitor and review the environment and the company's performance each month. Note, however, that even error-controlled regulators depend on some form of predictability. When a deviation between a desired and an actual outcome appears, you take action in one period. When the next period comes around and the deviation has still not been removed, do you take further action? You would only do so if the last period's action has already had its effect and that effect was insufficient. You would not do so if the effects were still working their way through. This means that when you take a corrective action you have to be able to predict the timing of its effects if error-controlled regulation is to be reliable.

Reliance on statistics

An essential requirement for the most effective application of this whole approach to control is the availability of quantitative forecasts of future changes in the organisation and its environment, as well as forecasts of the consequences of proposed actions to deal with these changes. For self-regulating control to work adequately the forecasts need to be at a rather detailed level of description and can only function, therefore, over a time span where this is possible. The tools available for such quantitative forecasts are those derived from statistical theory. Statistical forecasting methods are based on the assumption that the disturbances hitting the organisation from its environment take the form of groupings of large numbers of closely similar events that can be described by a probability distribution. It is implicitly assumed that uniquely uncertain events will be relatively unimportant.

This distinction can be clarified by two examples. An example of a unique event is the terrorist attack on New York's World Trade Center in September 2001. It is of course unique because it only occurs once. It cannot be described in terms of an observed probability distribution – either it occurs or it does not. Because of its uniqueness standard statistical techniques cannot be used to forecast its occurrence. An example of a grouping of events that can be described by a probability distribution is the number of television sets a company sells each month. By looking at the records for a number of months it will be possible to say what the most likely level of demand will be. These different possibilities are illustrated in Figure 3.4.

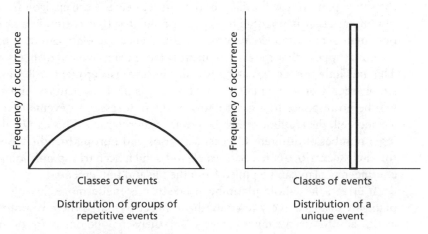

Figure 3.4   Distribution of events

If the business is primarily affected by events that can be described by probability distributions it will be possible to use tried-and-tested statistical techniques to forecast them. Statistical techniques require data generated by many repetitions. If most of the events hitting a business are unique it will not be possible to rely on these techniques. If they cannot be used, then practising anticipatory and error-controlled control in the way proposed by cybernetics will not be possible.

The law of requisite variety

However, cybernetics sees the main cause of the difficulty in designing regulators not in terms of the uniqueness of events, but in terms of their variety, or complexity. Variety is the number of discernibly different states the environment can present to the organisation and the number of discernibly different responses the organisation can make to the environment. It is the function of the regulator to reduce variety so retaining stability within a system, despite high variety outside it. In other words, the huge variety of disturbances presented by the environment must be neutralised by a huge number of responses such that the outcome can match the one desirable state selected in advance that will fit the environment. In order to be able to do this, the regulator must be designed to have as much variety as the environment; the number of potential responses must match the number of potential disturbances so that they can cancel each other out and produce a single desired outcome. This is Ashby's law of requisite variety: the complexity and speed of the firm's response must match the complexity and speed of change of the environment.

Suppose an organisation faces a stable environment in which changes follow regular predictable patterns. Then it will succeed when it uses an anticipatory regulator of the comprehensive planning kind. Here it forecasts the changes that will occur and prepares a single comprehensive plan to deal with all the future changes it faces over a given time period: it decides in advance on the sequence of actions it is to follow for a particular time period and then it implements that sequence of actions.

In this case there is a simple rather than a complex environment. There is also an environment in which there is little variety: it is regular and it is possible to predict the single pattern it will follow in the future. Because the environment is simple and low in variety it is possible to design a regulator that is simple and low in variety; one single set of intended actions, the comprehensive plan, can then be followed.

Now suppose that the environment is more complex and displays greater variety. This inevitably means greater difficulty in forecasting what will happen. Using the simple regulator – one plan for the future – is likely to lead to failure because there will be no response to a great many of the unforeseeable events that are occurring. To succeed, the regulator must be given greater variety. This can be done by preparing a number of different forecast scenarios and putting together contingency plans for each scenario. As it becomes clearer which scenario is unfolding, the requisite contingency plan can be pulled from the file and implemented.

In effect, the whole planning procedure is made more flexible and long-term plans are changed every few months in order to match them to unforeseen changes as those unforeseen changes emerge. So, there may be one plan for an environment in which oil prices are low, exchange rates favourable, rates of growth in demand high, own product prices high and competitor moves sluggish. A different plan can be developed for the reverse of all of these environmental conditions, or for only some of them.

Notice how a higher level of complexity and variety is responded to by increasing the complexity and variety of the regulator, in this case the planning system, the range of plans available and the frequency with which they are changed.

At some point the changes in the environment may become so rapid and unpredictable that even contingency planning will not work; too many contingencies may arise to make it practicable to have a plan ready for all of them. The regulator will therefore no longer take the form of a planning system. Instead it may take the form of a loose, changing set of project teams or what Peters and Waterman called skunkworks (Peters and Waterman, 1982). Here each team is working on some project to deal with some possible change in the environment. Each team conducts trials to test out possible market responses. One team will be experimenting with one kind of product that might suit, say, a rapid-growth, low-oil-price environment and another may be experimenting with a product that suits a slow-growth, high-oil-price environment. The regulator takes the form of trial-and-error testing of responses that the changing environment might require. The organisation is thus developing a large number of potential responses to a large number of potential environmental changes. Those experiments that succeed are continued with and those that fail are abandoned. The more experiments conducted, the greater and faster the action, the more likely the organisation is to deal with what the environment throws at it.

Here then there is a regulator that has even more variety and complexity built into it so as to match the much higher level of complexity and variety in the environment. Systemic views of strategic management depend crucially upon the validity of this idea.

You can see how this notion of requisite variety underlies popular approaches to success prescribed by writers such as Tom Peters (1985). He presses managers to form a vision, a picture of a future state, and then reach that vision by undertaking hectic trial-and-error actions that satisfy criteria set by shared values and logical connection to the existing business.

Note how Ashby's law depends upon the proposition that it is enough to have the same number of responses as environmental shocks, not that each response to each shock has to be the right one. In other words, the mechanism is trial and error and all that is necessary is to get the speed of the trial and error right. What is the justification for this?

The justification is the law of large numbers, or probability. If large numbers of random shocks, or unforeseeable changes, keep hitting a system and if that system undertakes large numbers of basically random small trial actions in response, then obviously only some random actions will match some of the random shocks in the sense of being appropriate responses. Most will not but, because of the large numbers involved, the inappropriate responses will tend to cancel each other out – the law of large numbers. Provided that a system acts fast enough it will maintain stability and move towards its goal but only if shocks and responses are closely similar, or repetitive events of the kind obtained, for example, when a coin is tossed, where the result is always either heads or tails. It is only with large numbers of repetitive events that one can rely on the cancelling out of mismatches between random shocks and random actions because it is only then that the law of large numbers works.

It will be shown in Chapter 10 that a nonlinear feedback system may operate in conditions where no specific event is ever repeated in exactly the same way. The probability of any specific event occurring is therefore infinitely small. Each specific event is unique, falling only into general qualitative categories in which items bear a family resemblance to each other. An organisation does not typically get a large number of chances to repeat events that bear a family resemblance close enough to apply probability in even an approximate way.

Under these circumstances there is no guarantee that trial-and-error mismatches with random environmental shocks will cancel out. Large numbers of random actions, even within boundaries set by logical connection with the existing business and core values, cannot be relied on as a search technique that will take the business to its intended vision. Right at the outset, then, there is a problem in building a theory of organisational change based on cybernetics.

Cybernetics and causality

The law of requisite variety makes it unnecessary, according to the cybernetics tradition, to understand the internal feedback structures of the organisation and the environment. Let me explain.

Cyberneticists recognised that feedback means circular causality – event A causes event B which then causes event A. They argued that one can determine the direction this circular causality takes for any pair of events simply by observing which precedes which in a large number of cases. But when dealing with large numbers of interconnected pairs it all becomes too difficult. These internal structures are so complex that one cannot hope to understand them – they constitute a 'black box'. Note how an unquestioned assumption is being made here. Those arguing this position are assuming that there is always a specific cause for each specific outcome, the problem being that it is all too complex for us to understand. Chapter 10 will suggest that there is another way to tackle this difficulty: it may be impossible to reduce our understanding to specific cause-and-effect links because the links themselves are lost in the detail of what happens; the alternative is then to think in terms of patterns in behaviour.

The cyberneticists, however, argued that causal connections exist but one does not need to understand them because one can observe a particular type of disturbance impacting on a system and also can observe the outcome of that disturbance; that is, how the system responds. If the regulator has requisite variety, that is a large enough variety of responses to counteract the variety of disturbances, then it will normally respond to a particular type of disturbance in the same way. From large numbers of observations of such regularities statistical connections can be established between particular types of disturbance and particular organisational responses.

The importance of this notion of causal connection is that it allows the use of statistical techniques for control in a negative feedback way, despite system complexity so great that one cannot hope to understand it, at least according to the cyberneticists. What matters to them are pragmatic factors such as what is observed and what is done. It is not necessary to devote much energy to understanding and explaining, they claim, because observing and doing is what matters in a complex world. These writers were not concerned with the dynamic patterns of behaviour that organisations generated or with the complexities of the internal workings of the organisation. No importance was attached to perceptions of the patterns of behaviour.

Note how the law of requisite variety and the view taken of complex causality amount to an assumption that the laws of large numbers, or probability, apply. Large numbers of random disturbances from the environment are to be offset by equally large numbers of responses from the organisation. But since one cannot know the complex causal relationship between these, according to cybernetic theory, it is necessary to rely on a process of cancelling out. Because causality is so complex one cannot determine exactly the right response for each disturbance, so some responses will be too weak and others too strong, but taken together the deviations from what is required should cancel out over large numbers.

Now, this is only possible if the disturbances and responses are not unique; that is, they do not take the form of a disturbance requiring one and only one response at a particular time if it is to be handled effectively in goal-seeking terms. If amplifying feedback could cause a tiny disturbance to escalate, then it would require an immediate response of exactly the right offsetting nature to stop this happening. If such escalation was not immediately stopped it could swamp the behaviour of the whole system – the cancelling out of inappropriate responses to disturbances would not occur. Without this cancelling out, the law of requisite variety would not be enough to secure control.

This assumption about uniqueness and large numbers is therefore of great significance to the view of control, a matter to which I will be returning in Chapter 6. There, it is shown that amplifying feedback raises problems for cybernetic ways of thinking about control.

Cybernetics, then, is an approach that seeks to control an organisation by using feedback without understanding the feedback structure of the organisation itself. It sees effective regulators as those that cause the system to be largely self-regulating, automatically handling the disturbances with which the environment bombards it. It sees effective regulators as those that maintain continual equilibrium with the environment. The result is stable behaviour, predictable in terms of probabilities of specific events and times.

The key points on organisational dynamics made by the cybernetics tradition are summarised in Figure 3.5. Whenever managers use planning, monitoring, reviewing and corrective action forms of control, they are making the same assumptions about the world as those made by cyberneticists. Whenever management consultants install such systems they too make the same assumptions. Whenever managers engage in trial-and-error actions in the belief that this will take them to an envisioned end-point in a turbulent environment, that is, whenever they implement the advice of writers such as Peters and Waterman (1982), then they are assuming that the law of requisite variety is valid. The problem is that managers and consultants

---

Figure 3.5

Cybernetics: main points on organisational dynamics

- Organisations are *goal-seeking*, *self-regulating* systems adapting to pre-given environments through negative feedback.
- Cybernetics thus takes a realist position on human knowing.
- The system is *recursive*. This means that it feeds back on itself to repeat its behaviour.
- It follows that causality is circular. However, although the causality is circular it is *linear*. Cybernetics does not take account of the effects of nonlinearity. Causal structures cannot be understood because they are too complex. However, regularities in the relationships between external disturbances and the system's response can be statistically identified. Circular causality is thus recognised but then sidestepped by saying that it is too complicated to understand.
- Predictability of specific events and their timings is possible in a probabilistic sense. Disturbances coming from the environment are not primarily unique.
- Effective control requires forecasts and a control system that contains as much variety as the environment. Change must be probabilistic so that large numbers of random changes and random responses cancel out, otherwise unique small changes might amplify and swamp the system.
- No account is taken of positive, or amplifying, feedback. There is thus no possibility of small changes amplifying into major alterations.
- Behavioural patterns themselves, especially of the system as a whole, are not thought to be interesting enough to warrant special comment.
- The self-regulation process requires the system's actual behavioural outcomes to be compared with some representation of, or expectation about, its environment. There is an external point of reference according to which it is controlled. The system internally *represents* its environment and then responds to that representation.
- There is a clear boundary between system and environment, between inner and outer. Although the system is adapting to its environment, it is itself a closed system. It operates/changes with *reference to a fixed point at the boundary* with its environment.
- Its state is determined by flux in the environment expressed through the fixed point of reference. Instability comes from the environment.
- It is a homeostatic, or *equilibrium-seeking*, system.
- *History is not important* in that the current state of the system is not dependent upon the sequence of previous states, only on the 'error' registered at the regulator. The system does not evolve of its own accord. Any change must be designed outside the system and then installed.
- Effective organisations are self-regulating, an automatic mechanical feature flowing from the way the control system is structured.
- Success is a state of stability, consistency and harmony.

---

are normally not fully aware of what they are assuming. It is extremely important to be aware of these assumptions because if life in organisations diverges significantly from them, cybernetic systems will not work. For example, if unique tiny changes can escalate through amplifying feedback, a cybernetic system will no longer be able to self-regulate.

●●●● 3.3 Cognitivist psychology

The review of cybernetic theory in section 3.2 has already brought out how cybernetics is a theory about human behaviour. It assumes that human beings are cybernetic entities and that they learn through an essentially negative feedback process. In fact, the development of cybernetic systems theory was closely associated with the development of cognitive science, or a cognitivist approach to human psychology. Furthermore, both cybernetics and cognitivism were closely associated with the development of computers. The central aim was to develop a science of mind.

In 1943, McCulloch and Pitts (1943) published an important paper in which they claimed that brain functioning and mental activity could be understood as logical operations. They held that the brain was a system of neurones that functioned according to logical processing principles. The brain was thought to be a deductive machine and this notion was applied to develop machines that could operate in the same way, namely computers. In essence, the claim was that human beings are cybernetic systems. So, a theory about the operation of the brain was fundamental to the development of computers and those computers then came to be taken as an analogy for brain functioning. Computers were developed to mimic what brains were thought to be and this having been done, the brain was then thought to be like a computer, an essentially circular argument.

The next significant development in cognitive science occurred in 1956 at two meetings in Cambridge, Massachusetts, when Simon, Chomsky, Minsky and McCarthy set major guidelines for the development of cognitive science (Gardner, 1985). Their central idea was that human intelligence resembles computation so much that cognition, that is, human knowing, could be understood as a process of computing representations of reality, those representations being made in the form of symbols. So, just as computers process digital symbols so the human brain processes symbols taking the form of electrochemical activity in the brain. This is the central idea, just as it is with cybernetic systems. Humans are assumed to act on the basis of representations of their environment that are processed in their brains. Learning is a process of developing more and more accurate representations of external, pre-given reality utilising negative feedback processes.

Bateson (1972), an important figure in the development of both cybernetics and cognitivism, distinguished between different levels of learning. He used the example of the central heating system already given in section 3.2. The central heating system itself is capable only of Learning Level 0; that is, no learning. The central heating system simply repeats its behaviour without change. It cannot change its own setting and so it cannot learn. He then used this example to demonstrate how a cybernetic system can be considered at a higher logical level. He introduced the resident into the room and the resident can, of course, change the temperature setting. Now the system consists of the resident and the central heating system and the environment is still, of course, the temperature in the room. The skin of the resident becomes part of the boundary of this larger system. When the skin of the resident registers an uncomfortably low temperature for a while, the resident turns the regulator setting up and the boiler is turned on. Later the resident may feel too warm and turn the setting down.

In a cognitivist approach to psychology the brain of the resident is seen to be a cybernetic device in much the same way as the heating system. Temperature variations are registered by sensing nerve cells in the skin and this perception is then represented in a specific part of the brain. The representation triggers the motor action of turning the setting on the thermometer up or down.

The structure of this larger system has changed in that the number of states it can move through is now much larger. The change in the total system is not due to one specific error, as it was before, but to a range of errors, that is, a number of fluctuations that do not fit the resident's requirements. With one exception, stated below, the properties of this larger system are the same as for the logically lower system. Note particularly how there is still a fixed point of reference. The external environment is still internally represented, and the behaviour of the system is still determined by the flux of the environment as expressed through the fixed point of reference. From the perspective of the logically lower system, the heating system, the addition of the resident amounts to the appearance of an observer who can control it. The implicit assumption is that the move to a system of a higher logical level creates the observer position with regard to the system of the lower level. The one difference brought about by adding the resident to the system has to do with learning:

- The resident/heating system displays Learning Level 1 in that the resident changes the system by changing the setting, so increasing the number of alternatives open to the whole system. Note how this learning is error activated in that it is triggered by a gap between the resident's comfort level and the resident's current experience.
- Furthermore, if the resident were to change long-held habits of altering the setting then the system would display Learning Level 2 because there is once more a widening of the range of alternatives open to the system. This level of learning is of a higher logical category in that it expands the range of Level 1 alternatives. Again, it is error activated in that the resident will change habits because the old ones do not meet some required standard.
- The system could potentially display Learning Level 3, which expands the range of Level 2 alternatives. Bateson thought that humans very rarely achieved this level of learning and the examples he gave of it were religious conversion and personal change through psychotherapy.

What should be noted here is the importance of internal representations of the external environment and the error-activated nature of the learning process that cybernetics specifies. These are central assumptions in a cognitivist approach to psychology and they have enormous implications for how human agency, groups and organisations are understood.

Human beings are regarded, in this theory, as living cybernetic systems that can understand and control inanimate cybernetic systems. The implication is that an individual human can stand alone as a system. Implicit in a cybernetic approach to human affairs, then, is the assumption that humans are monads, that is, autonomous individuals who can exist outside relationships with others. The individual is prior and primary to the group. Again, there is the assumption, dominant in Western thinking, of the primacy of the masterful, autonomous individual. This is the same point as that made in the previous chapter, namely that of formative causality applied to the system and rationalist causality applied to the autonomous individual.

The cognitivist perspective

From a cognitivist perspective, the brain is a network of neurones, each of which is connected to a number of other neurones. When any neurone receives a powerful enough electrochemical pulse from another, it is triggered into firing a pulse to yet other neurones to which it is connected, and they in turn transmit further charges which trigger yet other neurones. Each neurone functions according to rules stipulating when to respond to an incoming impulse and when to transmit charges to particular other neurones. Neurones, therefore, transmit symbolic information, that is, code in the form of pulses of electrochemical activity. The brain is thus a rule-driven mechanism that processes symbols that represent stimuli, more or less as a computer does. The notions of symbol and representation lie at the heart of the cognitivist perspective and in this perspective they have substantial implications. The main points are set out in Figure 3.6.

Figure 3.6

Cognitivism: main points on human knowing and behaving

- The brain processes symbols (electrochemical pulses) in a sequential manner to form representations or internal templates that are more or less accurate pictures of the world. This means that the brain is assumed to act as a passive mirror of reality. Furthermore, these mirror images are, according to cognitivists, stored in specific parts of the brain in the sense that a stimulus, say a particular light wave, would always trigger the same sequence of firing neurones. In other words, the same electrochemical pattern would be produced in a specific part of the brain when the body was presented with the same external stimulus.
- The world so pictured by the brain can be specified prior to any cognitive activity. This means that the world being perceived would have particular properties, such as light waves, and it would be these already existing real properties that would be directly registered by the brain. The world into which humans act is found, not created.
- The templates formed are the basis upon which a human being knows and acts. Repeated exposure to the same light wave would strengthen connections along a specific neuronal pathway, so making a perception a more and more accurate representation of reality. This would form the template, stored in a particular part of the brain, against which other light wave perceptions could be compared and categorised, forming the basis of the body's response. Representing and storing are, thus, essentially cybernetic processes. There is a fixed point of reference, external reality, and negative feedback of the gap between the internal picture and this external reality forms a self-regulating process that closes this gap. Knowing, knowledge creation and learning are essentially adaptive feedback processes.

Figure 3.6 continued

● There is a separate entity that does this representing and storing. This is a 'centred' theory in the sense that the biological individual is at the centre of the whole process of knowing and acting and also in the internal sense of processes centred in particular parts of the brain.

● Since all normal individuals have much the same biologically determined brain structures and all their brains are processing symbolic representations of the same pre-given reality, there is no fundamental problem in individuals sharing the same perceptions. The transmission of messages from one brain to another and the sharing of information between them simply do not pose significant questions.

3.4   Brief review: how cybernetics and cognitivism deal with four key questions

In this section, I want to take a brief look at how cybernetics and cognitivism deal with the four questions posed at the end of Chapter 1.

What kind of system does cybernetics posit?

First, the level of description of the system is at a macro level. The entities of which the system is composed are all the same. In other words, differences amongst the system entities are averaged out. Interactions between the entities are assumed to be average, or at least normally distributed around the average. This allows the cyberneticist to disregard the dynamics of interaction between entities of which the system is composed and concentrate on the system as a whole. What is then focused on is the regularities in the system's responses to changes in its environment. The system responds to differences between externally imposed goals and its actual behaviour. Or, it responds to differences between an expectation, or prediction, of some state it should achieve and what it actually does. In organisational terms, the focus of attention is on how the whole organisation responds to the actions of other whole organisations that constitute its environment. Little attention is paid to the differences in the people that belong to the organisation or the nature of their interactions with each other.

Secondly, the time-span of concern is that over which the level of detail required for control is predictable. A cybernetic system's operation depends crucially on the ability to predict outcomes and time lags, or on the cancelling out of random changes.

Thirdly, the dynamics, that is, the kinds of movement over time displayed by the system, are that of an automatic move to stable equilibrium.

Fourthly, the cause of the system's movement is the formative process of negative feedback. From this perspective, organisations are thought of as wholes formed by interacting parts. These parts exist in order to sustain the purpose of the whole and so cannot be free. The cybernetic system unfolds the purpose already enfolded in it, namely the target set from outside of it. Cybernetics cannot explain novelty or transformation.

What kind of understanding of human nature does cognitivism present?

Cognitivism is built on the assumption that the individual is primary and prior to the group. First, there are individuals who process symbolic representations of a pre-given world, building ever more accurate representations through the process of learning. They arrive in the world with the inherited capacity to do this. Then there are groups composed of these autonomous individuals. The representations are of regularities extracted from behaving in an environment. They take the form of rules that govern behaviour. In later chapters I will refer to them as schemas, scripts, mental models, cognitive maps. When people use terms like these to describe how humans behave, they are making assumptions of a cognitivist kind.

From this perspective, human beings are essentially rational, logical animals. Emotion plays a rather unimportant part in how humans are held to behave. Also conspicuously absent is any notion that power and ideology structure relationships between people. There is no notion that unconscious processes might influence how people perceive and know anything.

Although the strategic choice theory to be reviewed in the next few chapters primarily assumes a cognitivist theory of human behaviour, it does take account of motivational factors in a particular way. The appeal then is to humanistic psychology, represented by writers such as Hertzberg, Mausuer and Snyderman (1959) and Maslow (1954), who stress the emotional and inspirational factors required to motivate human beings. Maslow talks about the individual's need for self-actualisation. Humanistic psychology, however, retains the emphasis on the autonomous individual.

While the organisation as a system is understood to be driven by formative causality, a different theory of causality applies to the humans who design it. This is the rationalist causality of the autonomous individual choosing goals and actions.

What methodology underlies cybernetics and cognitivism?

Both cybernetics and cognitivism take a realist position on human knowing. In other words, they assume that there is a reality to be dealt with that exists before people perceive it. They take the traditional scientific perspective of looking for laws, or regularities, to explain behaviour. They seek to apply the principles of logic. In doing this they take the position of the objective observer who stands outside the system of interest and makes hypotheses about it. They build models of the system to guide behaviour. The emphasis is on the ability to control. No importance is attached to the notion that people may construct reality in their social interaction with each other. There is no notion of reflexivity and the position of understanding through participating.

How do cybernetics and cognitivism deal with the possibly paradoxical nature of existence?

Little attention is paid in either of these theories to the possibility of paradox, that is, the simultaneous presence of contradictory ideas. The primary example of this is the way in which people are implicitly regarded as parts of an organisational cybernetic system, and so not free, on the one hand, and yet also as autonomous individuals and so free, on the other hand. This is not sensed as paradoxical at all. In fact any paradox has been eliminated in a temporal sequencing in which the human is first thought of as a part and then thought of as autonomous.

3.5 Summary

This chapter has reviewed the theory of cybernetic systems and the closely associated cognitivist theory of human behaviour. These theories are the foundations upon which the strategic choice theory of organisational change is built. Cybernetic systems depend upon the possibility of prediction over a long enough time period at a fine enough level of detail, if they are to achieve the control that is their central concern. Cognitivist psychology assumes that individuals are autonomous and that they learn in an essentially negative feedback manner. It heavily emphasises the logical capacities of the human being and it is these that enable choices to be made. These are central themes that run through strategic choice theory, to which the next chapter turns.

Further reading

Richardson (1991) provides an excellent account of cybernetics and the use of feedback thinking about human systems. Baddeley (1990) provides a very good exposition of the cognitivist position and Varela, Thompson and Rosch (1995) provide a cogent critique of cognitivism.

Chapter 4 ● ● ● ●

Strategic choice

4.1 Introduction

Strategic choice theory makes a distinction between the formulation of a strategy and its implementation. The formulation of the strategy is the analytical procedure of preparing a plan, that is a set of goals, the intended actions required to achieve the goals, and forecasts of the consequences of those actions over a long period of time. The plan, therefore, plays the role of the externally set point of reference required for the operation of a cybernetic system. The plan is to the organisation what the setting of a target temperature is to the domestic heating system discussed in Chapter 3. Implementation is the procedure of designing systems to ensure that the plans are carried out in the intended manner and periodically adjusted to keep the organisation on track to achieve its goals.

The plan is chosen by the most powerful individual in the organisation or by a small group of top executives – the dominant coalition. The choice is said to be made by individuals, displaying the cognitivist assumptions upon which this theory is based. The prescription is for this choice to be made following a rational sequence of logical steps, using rational evaluative criteria.

This chapter reviews how a plan is supposed to be formulated and implemented and it points to the theoretical foundations of these prescriptions. The subject matter of this chapter often takes up most of a textbook on strategic management and I will point to literature that goes into this matter in greater depth. However, my purpose here is to set out the key elements of the theory of strategic choice in the interest of understanding the way of thinking that it reflects. For most of the chapter, I will summarise what the theory has to say, providing little critique, although of course the way I summarise it already expresses something of my opinion. In the final section, I will express that opinion more explicitly.

The essence of strategic choice theory, I think, is that it assumes that it is possible for powerful individuals to stand outside their organisations and model them in the interest of controlling them. The theory assumes that organisations change success-fully when top executives form the right intention for the overall future shape of the whole organisation and specify in enough detail how this is to be achieved. It prescribes the prior design of change and then the installation of that change. Again, the cognitivist basis of this theory is clear. Autonomous individuals are assumed to be able to model their organisations from the position of the objective observer. Just as with any cybernetic system, the ability to predict is crucial to the ability to control an organisation understood as a cybernetic system.

●●●● 4.2   Formulating long-term strategic plans

The words 'plans' and 'planning' are often used loosely by managers. For example, managers may say that they have a long-term plan simply because they have set out some long-term financial targets or because they have identified one or two specific actions that they intend to undertake, for example make an acquisition. Students of strategic management need to be more precise than this.

Managers can only be said to be planning the future of their organisation when, as a group, they share a common intention to achieve a particular future composition and level of performance; that is, when they select aims and objectives well in advance of acting. In addition to choosing a future state, managers must also share a common intention to pursue a sequence of actions to achieve that chosen future state, if their behaviour is to qualify as planned. Before managers can intentionally choose an intended state and an intended sequence of future actions, however, they have to identify the future environment in which they are to achieve their aims – their intentions must be anchored to a specific future reality. In other words, managers cannot possibly plan unless they can also make reasonably reliable forecasts of the future time period they are planning for. The future must not only be knowable, it must be sufficiently well known in advance of required performance. The time span and the level of detail must be that which produces the required performance.

In addition, to qualify as controlling and developing an organisation's long-term future in the planning mode, managers must set milestones along the path to the intended future state, couched in terms of results. This will enable the outcomes of actions to be checked and deviations from plan to be corrected. Action is both implementation of the planned sequence of actions and corrections to keep results on course. Only then is control being exercised in a planned manner. The ability to control by plan depends upon the possibility of establishing intention relating to the organisation as a whole and making predictions at the appropriate level of detail over the relevant time span.

In order to formulate a long-term plan, managers must first identify and agree upon the performance levels, both financial and operational, that they are going to achieve by some point in the long-term future. In other words, they must set the quantitative and qualitative objectives that they are going to strive for. Those objectives must satisfy the rational criteria of acceptability, feasibility and suitability to be discussed below.

The second step in formulating a long-term plan is the specification of the future actions that will produce the performance objectives. However, before much can be said about appropriate actions for an organisation, it is necessary to find out something about the future environment in which they are to be taken; some actions are possible and successful in some environments but not in others. The requirement for success is that an organisation must be adapted to its environment. It follows that managers cannot plan future actions until they know something about what that environment will be.

Finding out about a future environment is a process of analysing the past and the present and then using that analysis as the basis for forecasting. Once managers know something about the nature of their future environment they can then deduce what alternative action options might deliver their performance objectives. The rational criteria of acceptability, feasibility and suitability, to be discussed below, must then be applied to evaluate each option and select that option which best satisfies the criteria. This then becomes an organisation's strategy.

Different kinds of plans

Now consider the different kinds of planning that are prescribed for organisations. Since most organisations of any size consist of a collection of different activities organised into units, a distinction is drawn between corporate plans and business unit plans (Hofer and Schendel, 1978; Porter, 1987). The corporate plan is concerned with what activities or businesses the organisation should be involved in and how the corporate level should manage that set of businesses. In other words, corporate strategy is about a portfolio of businesses and what should be done with them.

Business unit plans set out how a business unit is going to build a market position that is superior to that of its rivals, so enabling it to achieve the performance objectives set by the corporate level. In other words, business unit strategy is about the means of securing and sustaining competitive advantage. Since business units are generally organised on a functional basis –[finance, sales, production and research]departments, for example – the business unit strategy will have to be translated into functional or operational strategies.

Functional and operational plans set out the actions that a function is to take to contribute to the whole strategy of the business unit, just as the business unit strategy contributes to the corporate one. The key question for functional plans is: what actions must be taken to contribute an appropriate share to the business unit plan?

The result is a hierarchy of long-term objectives and plans, the corporate creating the framework for the business unit, and the business unit creating the framework for the functional. Furthermore, this collection of long-term plans provides the framework for formulating shorter-term plans and budgets against which an organisation can be controlled in the short term.

The question to address now is how managers at whatever level are supposed to select the plans that will lead them to success. The prescribed way of selecting successful plans is to use analytical criteria to evaluate the options.

Evaluation criteria are intended to enable managers to conclude whether or not a particular sequence of actions will lead to a particular future state that will produce some target measure of performance. The criteria are there to enable managers to form judgements about the outcomes of their proposed actions before they take those actions; that is, judgements as to whether a choice of strategy is likely to turn out to be a good one before they do anything at all to implement it. The purpose is to prevent surprises and ensure that an organisation behaves over long time periods in a manner intended by its members and leaders. There are three very widely proposed sets of criteria for doing this:

1 acceptibility or desirability
2 feasibility
3 suitability, or fit.

Each of these will be briefly reviewed in the following sections.

4.3   Evaluating long-term strategic plans: acceptability

There are at least three senses, it is argued, in which strategies have to be acceptable if they are to produce success. First, performance in financial terms must be acceptable to owners and creditors. Secondly, the consequences of the strategies for the most powerful groupings within an organisation must be acceptable in terms of their expectations and the impact on their power positions and cultural beliefs. Thirdly, the consequences of the strategies for powerful groups external to an organisation must be acceptable to those groupings. Consider what each of these senses entails.

Acceptable financial performance

If they are to be successful, managers must determine in advance of acting whether their long-term plans are likely to turn out to be financially acceptable. They are supposed to determine this by forecasting the financial consequences of each strategic option open to them: cash flows, capital expenditures and other costs, sales volumes, price levels, profit levels, assets and liabilities including borrowing and other funding requirements. Next, managers are supposed to use the forecasts to calculate prospective rates of return on sales and capital. A rate of return is calculated by expressing some measure of profit as a percentage of some measure of the sales that yield that profit or the assets used in generating it.

However, complexities arise because it is possible to define profits and assets in many different ways. Managers may be interested in profits before tax or after tax, before allowing for the depreciation of assets or after depreciation, before interest paid on loans or after interest. They may be interested in total assets employed or in net assets employed, that is, after deducting amounts owed by the organisation. They may be interested in fixed assets (land, buildings, plant and machinery) or variable assets such as inventories and debtors. There are therefore many different rates of return on sales and capital and the one used depends upon the purpose of use and also on accounting conventions.

No matter what particular rate of return is selected, there will be many difficulties of measurement to be overcome. For example, it may be difficult to measure just how much of an asset has been used up in a particular period of use – the problem of measuring depreciation. Or it is often difficult to know how to allocate the costs of the corporate level of management to the business units.

Acceptable financial performance is a relative concept and is defined in terms of the next best opportunity open to the owners of an organisation for using or investing their funds. In the case of state and not-for-profit organisations those alternatives are established through political choices and those choices depend upon the relative power of people interested in the choice.

In 1991, the UK government decided to permit British Rail to build a Channel Tunnel rail link to pass through east London rather than south London. The reason for choosing an eastern rather than a southern route was most probably because the pressure groups of people living in the east are far less powerful than the pressure groups of the much more affluent inhabitants of the southern parts of the city. Furthermore, the decision to invest government funds in this project constituted a choice not to use those funds to build, say, a refuge for the homeless. Again that choice reflected the relative power positions of industry that wanted the rail link and the homeless who needed somewhere to live.

Although the alternative uses of funds in state and not-for-profit bodies are inevitably the result of political decisions, those who wish to apply a more scientific approach prescribe the use of analytical techniques to identify and compare the costs and benefits of alternative political choices. The argument is that, even if at the end of the day the choice is made on the basis of relative power, those making the choice should at least be aware of what the costs will be of the benefits provided by each option open to them.

The method for doing this is cost–benefit analysis (Mirsham, 1980; Rowe, Mason, Dickel and Snyder, 1989), which attempts to place money values on all the costs and benefits of a particular strategic action option. The difficulty lies in the fact that state bodies and not-for-profit organisations are particularly concerned with intangible, non-traded costs and benefits. The analysis therefore involves many subjective judgements upon which there is likely to be disagreement that cannot be resolved by rational argument. In the end the decision has to be made by political processes of persuasion and conversion, or even force. The analysis is there to aid this process by making the factors that need to be taken into account explicit and by creating the appearance of rationality. This appearance of rationality can be instrumental in persuading people to accept a particular choice and it legitimises the decision, in effect giving it a seal of 'scientific' approval even though such rationality was not actually used to make the choice.

In the business sector, the ability to measure and value costs and benefits is far greater although even here, the growing importance of the knowledge economy (*see* Chapter 8) renders such measurement increasingly problematic. The following are some important ways of measuring the acceptability of financial performance: performance benchmarks, where performance in the most successful companies is taken as a standard of comparison; gap analysis, where profit forecasts are compared with benchmarks and the gap between them calculated in order to identify the magnitude of the steps required to close the gap; financial models and scenarios (Beck, 1982; Cooke and Slack, 1984; Rowe, Mason, Dickel and Snyder, 1989; Shim and McGlade, 1984); financial appraisal techniques such as payback period, average rate of return and discounted cash flow analysis.

The use of scenarios and simulations at both total corporate and specific invest-ment project levels allows sensitivity analyses to be performed. The purpose of these analyses is to identify those variables to which performance is particularly sensitive. So a particular company, or a particular investment project, may not be particularly sensitive to changes in the exchange rate, but it may be highly sensitive to changes in regulations on pollution control. Sensitivity analysis allows managers to gain some idea of how serious a change in some variable, such as the interest rate, will be for the future performance of an investment or for the corporation as a whole. There are a number of indicators of the level of financial risk that are used to make judgements about the acceptability or otherwise of performance in financial terms. These indicators take the form of financial ratios such as gearing ratios, which measure how heavily an organisation depends on borrowed funds; liquidity ratios, which provide a measure of how quickly an organisation can realise its assets; inventory turnover, which measures how many times a year the inventories of a business are realised.

Even if plans pass the test to produce financial performance acceptable to share-holders and creditors in terms of both risk and reward levels, however, they must still pass other tests – they must meet the expectations of those with power in an organisation.

Acceptable consequences for internal power groups

If carried out, strategic plans may well change the way people work, who they work with, what relative power they have, how they are judged by others and so on. Long-term plans could produce consequences that people believe to be morally repugnant or against their customs and beliefs in some other way. If this is the case, those plans are unlikely to succeed because people will do their best to prevent the plan being implemented. Managers must therefore submit their long-term plans to another acceptability test: they must analyse the impact of their plans on the expectations, relative power positions and cultural beliefs of key individuals and groups within the organisation. Consider now what must be analysed

- *Organisational culture.* The culture of any group of people is understood to be that set of beliefs, customs, practices and ways of thinking that they have come to share with each other through being and working together. It is a set of assumptions people simply accept without question as they interact with each other. In order to determine whether a plan is likely to be acceptable in cultural terms it is necessary to analyse people's shared beliefs. Analysis of the culture is thought to reveal whether options being considered fall within that culture or whether they require major cultural change. One would not necessarily reject options that require major cultural change, but then plans to bring this about would have to be formulated. The nature of an organisation's culture can be analysed by studying the stories told by people in that organisation. For example, there may be well-known stories about the organisation's founder or other memorable leaders that are always told to new joiners. The story is a way of emphasising one of the rules that all accept.

- *Power structure*. It will also be necessary to analyse the power structure of an organisation to determine whether plans are likely to be acceptable. Power flows from relationships, built up over time, between individuals and groups that determine how one affects or responds to another in making organisational choices. Power enables one person or group to force or persuade another to do something that the other does not want to do, or could not otherwise do, or would not otherwise have thought of doing. The sources of power lie in sanctions, interdependence and contribution. The source of power has much to do with the form it takes. Power can take the form of authority when it is exercised and consented to because of hierarchical position and because of the rules and regulations of the organisation. Or power can take the form of influence where it is based on interdependence between people and the contributions they make to common endeavours. Or, power can take the form of force. Having analysed the source and form of power, the strategist has to identify its location and that means identifying the dominant coalitions in the organisation. This may be difficult because the power structure does not necessarily accord with the formal hierarchy – it will be necessary to identify which individuals and groups exercise influence even though they have less authority. It will be necessary to look for potential alliances between coalitions.

Acceptable consequences for external power groups

Power groups outside an organisation also determine the acceptability of that organisation's strategies. A community pressure group may find the noise level of a proposed factory expansion unacceptable. Even if the factory itself turns out to be a financially acceptable investment, the total consequences for the image of the corporation could render the strategy unsuccessful. Another example is provided by the electricity and gas industries in the UK. To succeed, strategies of companies in these sectors have to be acceptable to the industry regulators and consumer pressure groups. A further example is where the strategies of one organisation could have damaging consequences for the distributors of that organisation's products or for the suppliers to that organisation. Such damage could provoke those distributors and suppliers to retaliate in highly detrimental ways.

The reactions of competitors to strategies are also of major importance. Some strategies pursued by one company could provoke more than normal competitive responses from competitors. Those competitors may regard the strategies of the first company as unfair competition and this could lead to price wars, hostile mergers, lobbying of the national political institutions, all of which could cause a strategy to fail.

4.4   Evaluating long-term strategic plans: feasibility

Analysis may show that strategies are likely to be acceptable in terms of financial performance, and to major power groupings both within and outside an organisation, but yet fail because they are not feasible. To be feasible there must be no insurmountable obstacle to implementing a strategy. Such obstacles could be presented by:

- *Financial resources*. One of the immediately obvious resources that must be available if a strategy is to be carried out is the money to finance the strategy over its whole life. If a company gets half-way through a strategy, which is on target to yield acceptable performance, but nevertheless runs out of the funds to continue, then clearly the strategy will fail. The prescription is therefore to carry out a flow-of-funds analysis of the strategy options, before embarking on any of them, to ascertain the probability of running into cash flow problems. A flow-of-funds analysis identifies the timing and size of the capital expenditures and other costs required for each project that makes up the strategy, and the timing and size of the revenues that those projects will generate. A flow-of-funds analysis makes it possible to calculate the break-even point, where a project, a set of projects constituting a strategy or a corporation as a whole makes neither a loss nor a profit. What managers should do, therefore, to establish the feasibility of their strategy is to calculate the flows of funds and the break-even points for different strategic options in different scenarios. This will help them to identify the financing requirements for their strategy, the timing of those requirements and the key conditions required for the move out of any initially negative cash flow situation.
- *Product life cycle*. To be feasible in market terms a strategy must take account of the stages in the product life cycle. Most products are thought to follow a typical evolutionary pattern:
  - An *embryonic* stage in which the product is developed. Here market growth potential may be great but it will be very uncertain.
  - A *growth* stage in which rapid market growth materialises, attracting other competitors.
  - A *shake-out* stage in which some of the competitors who entered find that they cannot compete and therefore leave.
  - A *mature* stage in which growth in the demand for the product slows and a small number of competitors come to dominate the market.
  - A *saturation* stage in which demand for the product stabilises and competitors have difficulty in filling their capacity.
  - A *decline* stage in which demand begins to switch to substitute products.

  These stages in the evolution of a product indicate different general types of strategies – different generic strategies. Which of these generic strategies is appropriate is said to be dependent upon the stage of evolution of the product's market and the competitive strength of the company producing it. So a company with a strong capability should invest heavily in the embryonic stage and establish a position before others arrive. During the growth phase it should continue investing, push for rapid growth, and so defend its strong position against new arrivals. By the time the mature phase is reached, this company should have established market leadership and, as the product gets to saturation level, the ageing stage, the dominant company should defend its position but withdraw cash from the business. In a declining market it will be able to continue harvesting cash, while weaker competitors withdraw.

● *Experience curves*. The idea of the experience curve is based on the observation that the higher the volume of a particular product that a company produces, the more efficient it becomes at producing it. The cost per unit therefore declines as volume increases, at first rapidly and then more slowly as the learning opportunities for that particular product are exhausted. As a company moves down the learning curve it is in a position to reduce the price it charges customers for the product because its costs are falling. These price and cost curves can be linked to the idea of a product life cycle and the different strategies that strong and weak competitors should pursue. In the early stages of product evolution, a strong competitor will achieve higher volumes than a weak one and so move further down the learning curve. This will enable the strong competitor to reduce prices faster, stimulating demand and so increasing volumes even more to move even faster down the learning curve. Soon, the weaker competitor, or the latecomer, will have no chance of catching up.

● *Product portfolio*. The earliest and simplest form of product portfolio analysis is the growth share matrix of the Boston Consulting Group (BCG) (Henderson, 1970). To analyse their organisation in this way, managers review their whole business, dividing it up into all its different products, or market segments, or business units. They then calculate the relative market share they hold for each product, or market segment or business unit. The relative market share provides a measure of the firm's competitive capability with regard to that product, segment or business unit, because a high market share indicates that the firm is well down the experience curve compared with rivals. Next managers must calculate the rate of growth of the product demand or market segment. The rate of growth is held to be a good measure of the attractiveness of the market – the stage in its evolution that it has reached. Rapid rates of growth indicate the entrepreneurial and growth stages of evolution. Different combinations of market share and growth rates yield the following possibilities:

– *Question marks* are products, market segments or business units that are growing rapidly, and the company has a relatively low share. The product life cycle and the experience curve analysis indicate that question marks will require heavy investment, are unlikely to yield profit for some time and may face strong competitors.

– *Stars* are products, markets or businesses that are growing rapidly, and the firm has a high relative share. Product life cycle and experience curve analysis indicate that these products will require heavy investment (negative cash flow) but may produce high levels of profit. The strategy indicated is one of concentrating effort and money on the stars.

– *Cash cows* are products in mature slow-growth markets in which the firm has a relatively high market share. The prescription is to cut down on investment in these products and harvest the cash.

– *Dogs* are products in slowly growing markets in which the firm has a low share. Both cash flow and profit could be negative. It is in a weak position and the firm should therefore withdraw.

The feasible options will be those that have some balance between the different possibilities. If a firm has enough cash cows, it will be able to use the money milked from those businesses to support the stars and perhaps try to develop some of the question marks. It can sell dogs and use the money so raised for the same purposes. An unbalanced portfolio – too many stars and not enough cows, for example – will mean that the company has to borrow heavily. The opposite will generate big cash surpluses without knowing what to invest them in.

- *Human resources.* In addition to financial resources, the availability of the right quality of skilled people will also be a major determinant of the feasibility of strategic options. This makes it necessary for managers to audit the human resources inside their organisation, those available outside and the availability of training resources to improve the skills of people.

Consider now the third criterion for the evaluation and selection of successful strategies.

4.5   Evaluating long-term strategic plans: suitability or fit

Having established that their strategies are acceptable and feasible, the next hurdle managers must cross to achieve success is that of demonstrating that those strategies have a *strategic logic*. Strategic logic means that a proposed sequence of actions is consistently related to the objectives of the organisation on the one hand and matches the organisation's capability (including its structure, control systems and culture) in relation to its environment on the other. The idea is that all the pieces of the strategic puzzle should fit together in a predetermined manner – the pieces should be *congruent*. When this happens we can say that the strategies fit, that they are suitable. The prescription is to use analytical techniques to determine the strategic logic of a sequence of actions, how all the pieces do or do not fit together (Hofer and Schendel, 1978). The analytic techniques available to do this are:

- *SWOT analysis.* This is a list of an organisation's strengths and weaknesses indicated by an analysis of its resources and capabilities, plus a list of the opportunities and threats that an analysis of its environment identifies. Strategic logic obviously requires that the future pattern of actions to be taken should match strengths with opportunities, ward off threats and seek to overcome weaknesses.
- *Industry structure and value chain analysis.* Michael Porter (1980, 1985) has put the classical economic theories of market form into a framework for analysing the nature of competitive advantage in a market and the power of a company in that market, as well as the value chain of the company. These analytical techniques identify key aspects determining the relative market power of an organisation and its ability to sustain excess profits. Strategic logic entails taking actions that are consistent with and match the nature of the organisation's market power. Industry structure is held to determine what the predominant form of competitive advantage, and thus the level of profit, is. Some market structures mean that sustainable competitive advantage can be secured only through cost-leadership strategies. Other structures mean that competitive advantage flows from differentiation. Strategic logic means matching actions to those required to secure

competitive advantage. Value chain analysis identifies the points in the chain of activity from raw material to consumer that are crucial to competitive advantage.

Contingency theory

Contingency theory states that success will be secured when an organisation secures a good match between its situation and its strategies and structures. For example, mechanistic bureaucracies are said to be appropriate for stable environments, but flexible, organic structures are required for turbulent environments.

Contingency is thus a theory about the nature of cause and effect. It makes statements like these: if an organisation is operating in an environment that is very complex and changing rapidly, then it requires organic forms of organisation to succeed. If, however, it operates in a simple, slow-moving environment, then it requires mechanistic structures to succeed. If an organisation is small, then it requires a simple structure. If an organisation is large, then it requires a division-alised structure.

Contingency theory postulates a complex web of interconnections between the features of organisations and their environments in which the causal connections are linear in the sense that they run in one direction. It is a particular environment that causes a particular kind of successful strategy and that causes a particular kind of successful structure. The theory does not contemplate circular causation in which the structures of organisations cause them to follow certain strategies which then create certain kinds of environment to which they respond.

Contingency theory is based on the assumption that approximately the same cause will have approximately the same effect. It does not envisage escalation in which a tiny difference between two causes leads to two completely different outcomes. It does not, for example, allow for the possibility that two organisations operating in the same environment may develop in totally different directions simply because one gained a slightly bigger market share than the other in a particular product line at a particular point in time.

By making particular assumptions about the nature of cause and effect, contingency theory is making particular assumptions about the dynamics of organisations. Success is assumed to be a state of equilibrium and, because they are close to equilibrium, the future time paths of successful organisations are predictable. These are all assumptions that are open to question, as we shall see in Chapters 10 and 11.

The contingency concept, and its consequent prescription of consistency and congruence, runs in terms of a large number of different combinations of strategies, structures, cultures and so on, each suited to a particular environment and a particular set of objectives at a particular time. Organisations then adopt whichever of these satisfies the consistency criteria.

●●●● 4.6 Implementing long-term strategic plans

Once long-term plans have been formulated and evaluated, they need to be implemented. The prescriptions for doing this are set out in this section.

Designing organisational structures

The structure of an organisation is the formal way of identifying who is to take responsibility for what; who is to exercise authority over whom; and who is to be answerable to whom. The structure is a hierarchy of managers and is the source of authority, as well as the legitimacy of decisions and actions. It is normally held that the appropriate structure follows from the strategy that an organisation is pursuing and that organisational structures display typical patterns of development or life cycles (Chandler, 1962). Chandler identified four stages in the structure life cycle. Embryonic organisations have very simple structures in which people report rather informally to someone that they accept as their leader. They tend to do whatever needs to be done with relatively little separation of functions. When they embark on a growth strategy, however, they will find it necessary to change the structure to one based on more formal specialisation of functions and identification of authority and responsibility. If this is not done, managers will find it impossible to implement their strategy of growth and the organisation will probably fail. As they pursue their growth strategy, managers will find that they have to carry out strategies of cost reduction to stay ahead and they will be more and more confronted with the problem of integrating specialised functions. The structure will therefore have to be made even more formal with clearer definition of lines of authority and communication. It will also be necessary to systematise and improve the techniques of marketing, manufacturing and materials procurement. Then, as managers pursue strategies of diversification into new products and markets, they find it necessary to set up marketing and manufacturing organisations in different geographic areas: they install additional structures. As they continue their strategy of diversification, the number of additional structures multiplies and they have to restructure to ensure a better 'fit' with the diversification strategies they are pursuing. They might secure this fit by forming a larger functionally departmentalised structure, with departments at the centre shared by many geographic areas; or by setting up largely independent subsidiaries as divisionalised or holding company structures.

Designing systems of information and control

The information and control systems of an organisation are basically procedures, rules and regulations governing what information about the performance of an organisation should flow to whom and when. It also covers who is required to respond to that information and how they are authorised to respond, in particular what authority they have to deploy the resources of their organisation. To implement the strategies they have formulated, managers will have to ensure that their information and control systems are adequate for the flows of information that implementation requires and provide appropriate control mechanisms to enable managers to monitor the outcomes of the strategy implementation and do something if those outcomes are not in accordance with the strategy.

Management control is defined as the process of ensuring that all resources – physical, human and technological – are allocated so as to realise the strategy. It is a process in which a person or a group of people intentionally affects what others do.

Control ensures proper behaviour in an organisation and the need for it arises because individuals within the organisation are not always willing to act in the best interests of the organisation (Wilson, 1991). The process of control involves setting standards or targets for performance, or expected outcomes of a sequence of actions, then comparing actual performance or outcomes against standards, targets or expectations, and finally taking corrective action to remove any deviations from standard, target or expectation.

The principal form taken by the control system in most organisations is that of the annual plan or budget. Strategy implementation is held to depend upon an effective budgeting system. The budget converts strategy into a set of short-term action plans and sets out the financial consequences of those action plans for the year ahead. Control is then a process of regularly comparing what happens with what the budget said would happen. Budgets allocate the resources of an organisation with which different business units and functions are charged to carry out the strategy. Budgets establish the legitimate authority for using the resources of the organisation. The budget will normally be prepared in great detail, showing what people in each business unit and function are required to bring in as revenue, what they are permitted to spend and on what, and therefore what surplus they are required to earn, or deficit they will be allowed to incur.

The budget, however, is a short-term instrument, only the first step in the implementation of the strategy. Some have therefore sought to identify the differences between short-term control and strategic control. For example, Hurst (1982) points out that strategic control requires more data from more sources, particularly external sources, and the data must be oriented to a longer-term future. Strategic control is therefore inevitably less precise and less formal than budgetary control. It is concerned more with the accuracy of the premises on which decisions are based and much less with quantitative deviations from standard. Strategic control has to be more flexible and to use variable rather than rigidly regular time periods for reporting. The relationships between corrective action and outcome are therefore weaker in strategic control. The conclusion drawn is that although planning and control in a strategic sense is very difficult, a system to compare expectations and outcomes is even more necessary than it is for the short term.

Goold and Quinn's (1990) research shows that very few companies have a strategic control process that is anything like as formal and comprehensive as their budgetary control system. Even where managers do set strategic milestones that would allow them to check on their progress as the strategy was implemented, those milestones take the form of events rather than results. So the milestone might be the completion of a new factory; managers might set this for a period two years hence and then after two years check if the factory is indeed complete. If it is, they may conclude that they are keeping to their strategy. However, since this is an event rather than a result, they will not know if the financial results their strategy was supposed to achieve are in fact being achieved. The reasons for the lack of a proper results-based monitoring and control system were identified as the length of time lags between action and outcome and the risks and uncertainties that long-term plans were subject to. Despite the difficulties, however, Goold and Quinn recommend trying harder to use formal strategic control systems based on milestones for comparison.

Installing and operating human resource systems

Effective strategy implementation should occur when the people required to take action to this end are motivated to do so. One of the most powerful motivators is the organisation's reward system (Galbraith and Kazanian, 1986). Appropriate rewards stimulate people to make the effort to take actions directly relevant to an organisation's strategy. The way in which people's jobs are graded and the pay scales attached to these grades will affect how people feel about their jobs and the effort they will make. Differentials need to be perceived to be fair if they are not to affect performance adversely. Bonuses, profit-related pay, piecework and productivity schemes are all ways of tying monetary rewards to the actions that strategy implementation requires.

Non-monetary rewards are also of great importance in motivating people. These rewards include promotion, career development, job enrichment, job rotation, training and development. They all help individuals to be more useful to an organisation while developing greater self-fulfilment. Simpler forms of reward are also of great importance, for example praise, recognition and thanks.

Training and development is an important implementation tool, not only because it motivates people, but also because it provides the skills required for strategy implementation (Hussey, 1991). The objectives of training and development programmes should be aligned with those of an organisation's strategy and those objectives should consist of measurable changes in corporate performance.

Culture change programmes

Just as the reporting structure of an organisation should fit the particular strategy it wishes to pursue, so should its culture, the attitudes and beliefs that people within an organisation share. Handy (1981) classifies organisational cultures into four categories:

1 The *power* culture is typically found in small entrepreneurial companies controlled by powerful figures. People in this culture share a belief in individuality and in taking risks. They believe that management should be an informal process with few rules and procedures.
2 The *role* culture is associated with bureaucracies where people's functions are defined in a formal way and they specialise. People here share a belief in the importance of security and predictability. They equate successful management with rules and regulations.
3 The *task* culture is found where people focus on their job, or on a project. People share a belief in the importance of teamwork and expertise and in being adaptable.
4 The *person* culture occurs where people believe that the organisation exists so that they can serve their own personal interest, for example barristers and architects, and many other professionals.

Just as structures need to fit a particular strategy and just as they tend to follow a life cycle from the simple to the functional to the divisional, so too do cultures. The power culture is appropriate to the early stages of a firm's life when its structure is simple. Later it will have to change to the role culture as it grows and installs a functional structure. Then it will have to develop a task culture to fit in with a divisionalised structure.

Implementation may well therefore require that an organisation change its culture and the conventional wisdom prescribes that such change should be planned. The reasons why people might resist a change in culture need to be identified and plans formulated to overcome the resistance. Participation, communication and training are all seen as ways of overcoming resistance. The process of overcoming resistance involves a stage called unfreezing when the existing culture is questioned, and is followed by a period of reformulation where people consider what new beliefs they need to develop and share with each other. Finally there is the re-freezing stage where the new culture is fixed in place. We will be returning in Chapter 6 to these matters of planned change in belief systems – the discipline of organisation development.

Developing appropriate political behaviour

It is inevitable that people in an organisation will conflict and, when they do, they engage in political behaviour (Pfeffer, 1981). As an organisation differentiates into functions and units, those functions and units develop their own objectives, some of which will differ from those of the organisation as a whole. But differentiation brings with it interdependence so that no single function or unit can achieve its objectives on its own. They will have to compete with each other for scarce resources and to co-operate with each other to reach their objective. Interdependence, heterogeneous goals and scarce resources taken together produce conflict. If the conflict is important and power is distributed widely enough, then people will use political behaviour, that is persuasion and negotiation, to resolve their conflict. If power is highly centralised then most will simply do as they are told – they will not have enough power to engage in political behaviour.

The kinds of political strategies people employ to come out best from conflict are the selective use of objective criteria, the use of outside experts to support their case, forming alliances and coalitions, sponsoring those with similar ideas, empire building, intentionally doing nothing, suppressing information, making decisions first and using analysis afterwards to justify them, and many more.

The above view of politics as a manipulative process of dubious ethical validity leads to the belief that steps should be taken to reduce the incidence of political behaviour. Such steps are those that reduce the level of conflict and the most powerful of these is to preach and convert people to a common ideology.

I now turn to a matter closely connected with strategy implementation and strategic control, namely, motivation.

4.7 Motivation

So far, this chapter has reviewed the stages of formulation, evaluation and implementation of long-term strategic plans, which is the centrepiece of the theory of strategic choice. However, those writing in this tradition also recognise that the factors of human motivation and leadership affect how an organisation's strategy unfolds. For example, Peters and Waterman (1982) questioned the rational techniques of decision making and control reviewed in this chapter, pointing to their limitations in conditions of turbulence. Instead, they emphasised human motivation, values, beliefs and the importance of leadership. They stressed the importance of working harmoniously together, and strongly sharing the same culture, values, beliefs and vision of the future. Their prescriptions were to establish a vision of the whole organisation's future, convert people to believing in it, promote internal harmony by encouraging the strong sharing of a few cultural values, and empowering people.

However, although critical of rational techniques, Peters and Waterman did not depart in any way from cognitivist assumptions about human nature, nor in any essential way from the assumption that an organisation is a cybernetic system. This is evident when they talk about charismatic leaders who choose a vision of the future and certain core values that they then inspire others with, converting them into believing the vision and the values. If anything, the autonomous individual becomes even more heroic in their view of organisational change. The system is still cybernetic because it is controlled by referring to the vision and the values and damping out any deviations from them.

A number of similar theories of motivation have been put forward in the management literature on how to secure consensus, co-operation and commitment. For example, Hertzberg (1966) pointed out that people are motivated to work in co-operation with others by both extrinsic motivators such as monetary rewards and intrinsic motivators such as recognition for achievement, achievement itself, responsibility, growth and advancement. Intrinsic motivation is the more powerful of the motivators and is increased when jobs are enriched, that is when jobs are brought up to the skill levels of those performing them.

Maslow (1954) distinguished between: basic physiological needs, such as food and shelter; intermediate social needs, such as safety and esteem; and higher self-actualisation needs, such as self-fulfilment. Maslow held that when the conditions are created in which people can satisfy their self-actualisation needs, those people are then powerfully motivated to strive for the good of their organisation.

Schein (1988) and Etzioni (1961) distinguished three categories of relationship between the individual and the organisation. The relationship may be coercive, in which case the individual will do only the bare minimum required to escape punishment. The relationship may be a utilitarian one where the individual does only enough to earn the required level of reward. Thirdly, the relationship may take a normative form where individuals value what they are doing for its own sake, because they believe in it and identify with it. In other words, the individual's ideology coincides with an organisation's ideology. This provides the strongest motivator of all for the individual to work for the good of an organisation.

Pascale and Athos (1981) stressed organisational culture as a result of their study of Japanese management. They recognised that people yearn for meaning in their lives and transcendence over mundane things. Cultures that provide this meaning create powerfully motivated employees and managers.

What all these studies point to is this. An organisation succeeds when its people, as individuals, are emotionally engaged in some way, when they believe in what their group and their organisation are doing, and when the contribution they make to this organisational activity brings psychological satisfaction of some kind, something more than simple basic rewards.

A sense of mission

People believe and are emotionally engaged when their organisation has a mission or set of values and when their own personal values match those of the organisation. Organisational missions develop because people search for meaning and purpose and this search includes their work lives (Campbell and Tawady, 1990). To win commitment and loyalty and to secure consensus around performing tasks it becomes necessary to promote a sense of mission.

The development of a sense of mission is seen as a central leadership task and a vitally important way of gaining commitment to, loyalty for and consensus around, the nature and purpose of the existing business. An organisation with a sense of mission captures the emotional support of its people, even if only temporarily.

A sense of mission is more than a definition of the business, that is, the area in which an organisation is to operate. A sense of mission is also to be distinguished from the ideas behind the word 'vision' or 'strategic intent'. The word 'vision' is usually taken to mean a picture of a future state for an organisation, a mental image of a possible and desirable future that is realistic, credible and attractive. The term mission differs in that it refers not to the future but to the present. A mission is a way of behaving. Mission is concerned with the way an organisation is managed today, with its purpose or reason for being. Strategic intent is a desired leadership position. It too, therefore, is a desired future state, a goal to do with winning. Mission is to do with here-and-now purpose, the culture, the business philosophy. A sense of mission is an emotional response to questions to do with what people are doing, why they are doing it, what they are proud of, what they are enthusiastic about, what they believe in.

Campbell and Tawady also sound warnings about developing a sense of mission. The strategies and values embodied in the mission could become inappropriate as the world changes and continued reinforcement of them would then lead to failure. Strong belief in a mission leads people in an organisation to resist change and to keep outsiders from occupying positions of any importance.

The underlying assumption is that organisations succeed when individuals are motivated to perform, as individuals. The humanistic psychology on which the above writers draw accords the same primacy to the individual as cognitivism does. The difference is that the former places much more emphasis on emotional factors, predominantly of a positive inspirational kind. Note how leaders are supposed to choose appropriate motivators.

●●●● 4.8   Leadership and the role of groups

The primary focus is on the leader as one who:

- translates the directives of those higher up in the hierarchy into the goals and tasks of the group;
- monitors the performance of the task in terms of goal achievement;

- ensures that a cohesive team is built and motivated to perform the task;
- supplies any skills or efforts that are missing in the team;
- articulates purpose and culture, so reducing the uncertainty that team members face.

When leadership is defined in these terms, the concern is with the qualities leaders must possess and the styles they must employ in order to fulfil these functions effectively and efficiently. Those who have put forward explanations of this kind on the nature of leadership have differed from each other over whether the effective leader is one who focuses on the task, or one who focuses on relationships with and between people. A related area of concern is whether the effective leader is one who is autocratic, or one who delegates, consults and invites full participation. The question is which style of leadership motivates people more and thus gets the task done better. Consider three prominent theories (Fiedler, 1967; Hersey and Blanchard 1988; Vroom and Yetton, 1973). According to these theories leadership styles are to be chosen by the individual manager and to be successful a style that matches certain pre-given situations must be chosen. The leader should arrive at the group with particular skills developed beforehand. The required personality, skills and styles (or, as they are sometimes called, competences) are supposed to be identified in advance since they depend upon the situation. Here leadership is about motivating people and the concern is with the appropriate role of the leader in securing efficient performance of known tasks.

The relevance of the group

A group is understood to be any number of people who interact with each other, are psychologically aware of each other and perceive themselves to be a group. Formal groups in an organisation may be permanent, for example the sales department; or they may be temporary, as is the case when special task forces or multi-disciplinary teams are appointed to deal with a particular task. Whether they are temporary or permanent, formal groups have clear goals and tasks; it is the purpose of formal groups to find solutions to structured problems. They usually have appointed leaders – leaders and managers have power given to them. However, they may also be autonomous, self-managing or democratic work groups that elect their own leader and design their own approach to a given structured task. Note that procedures are laid down in advance on how leaders are to be appointed and roles determined. This has sometimes been done to improve motivation and thus efficiency (Lindblom and Norstedt, 1971). However, even self-managing groups still have clear structures, tasks, objectives and procedures and so are formal groups, parts of an organisation's legitimate system.

Within, alongside and across the formal groups, there is a strong tendency for informal groups to develop. These may be horizontal cliques amongst colleagues on the same hierarchical level, vertical cliques that include people from different hierarchical levels, or random cliques. Informal groups develop primarily because of proximity (Festinger, Schachter and Back, 1950): through the contacts people make with each other given their physical location in relation to each other, the nature of their work and the time pressures they are under. The immediate concern about these informal groups is whether they will support or counter the operation of formal groups. The concern is with motivating people to cohere into functional teams that will focus on clearly defined tasks, not dissipate energies in destructive informal groups.

The concern is primarily with the authority, responsibility and performance of individual managers in carrying out their pre-assigned tasks. From this perspective, the interest in groups relates to the circumstances in which groups may be more effective than individuals. Groups can:

- accomplish complex interdependent tasks beyond the ability of individuals working alone;
- solve complex problems that require many inputs;
- provide a means of co-ordinating activities;
- facilitate implementation through generating participation and commitment;
- generate new ideas and creative solutions within the paradigm;
- provide the opportunity of social interaction that improves morale and motivation.

Groups, both formal and informal, meet human needs for affiliation and self-esteem. They provide individuals with a sense of security, they reduce anxiety and the sense of powerlessness and they provide opportunities for individuals to test reality through discussion with others. But they also create a vehicle for individuals to pursue their own self-interested tasks and problem-solving activities. The central concern in relation to groups is that of motivating people to perform known tasks efficiently. This requires that people should behave in a cohesive manner and develop supportive informal groups.

It has been recognised for a long time that bureaucratic control is neither rational nor efficient outside certain limited conditions and that it produces a number of negative behavioural consequences that undermine its effectiveness. The need for an informal organisation arises, then, simply because the formal bureaucracy often cannot work. There are two major reasons why a bureaucracy fails so frequently to produce what it is supposed to. The first is the adverse human reaction to bureaucracy. Bureaucracies have an alienating impact on people because they are allocated to narrowly defined roles and repetitive tasks and are thus treated as the means to some end. This leads to feelings of powerlessness, isolation, frustration, dissatisfaction and aggression (Blauner, 1964). Bureaucracies also tend to make people subordinate, passive, dependent and lacking in self-awareness (Argyris, 1957). Bureaucracies may lead to work that has lost its moral character and cultural significance. People then perform according to rules they do not believe in. Without shared values to govern their work, their behaviour and the sharing of rewards, people feel that their work has no meaning – a state of anomie. Bureaucracies can deskill people, leading to trained incapacity (Merton, 1957). The operation of bureaucracies can contravene or provoke certain kinds of social behaviour and so touch off vicious circles (Gouldner, 1964).

Secondly, bureaucracies are unable to handle ambiguity and uncertainty. They cannot cope with complex, unstable, unpredictable environmental and working conditions because they are inevitably too inflexible and slow to respond to change

(Burns and Stalker, 1961). Rules and regulations cannot be established in advance to deal with the unforeseen.

People deal with these shortcomings of the bureaucratic system by colluding to operate a 'mock' bureaucracy (Gouldner, 1964) and acting instead within an informal organisation that they set up themselves (Blauner, 1964). The 'mock' bureaucracy is one in which all pay lip-service to the rules but tacitly agree not to enforce them. The appearance of rationality and order is thus maintained, and any conflict that might have been generated by the application of inappropriate rules is avoided.

The underlying assumption about the relationship between individuals and groups in the notions reviewed in this section is that of the objective observer standing outside the system of groups and teams. The explicit or implicit prescription is that leaders and managers should take this position too, identify the nature of the situation and select leadership styles and motivational factors that are appropriate in the sense that they fit the situation. In essence, this amounts to installing appropriate feedback loops in the organisation so that it operates like a cybernetic system.

As far as the relationship between individuals and groups is concerned, again it is clear how the primacy of the individual is assumed. Groups are made up of individuals and these groups then affect those individuals, meeting some of their needs but deskilling them in other ways. In order to prevent adverse effects of groups on individuals, leaders need to pay attention to factors to do with the environment of the group, its composition in terms of members and their sensitivity to group dynamics. Formal groups are to be preferred over informal ones. It is recognised that informal groups are inevitable but the mainstream view seems to be that they threaten control. This attitude towards groups reflects cognitivist and humanistic assumptions.

4.9 Taking account of uncertainty

So far this chapter has reviewed the theory of strategic choice, that is, the view that organisations change in ways that are chosen by their most powerful executives. The strategy of an organisation, on this view, is the intention formed by an individual, or a small group of individuals. This intention is formed well in advance of change and it relates to the shape and direction of the organisation as a whole. Organisational change is the realisation of this individually formed, overall, prior intention. Such realisation is accomplished through the design, installation and operation of an essentially cybernetic system that is supposed to ensure change in products and/or services, financial flows and member behaviour according to the intended goals. Both the organisation and the individuals who form it are understood to be cybernetic systems. The focus is very much on control.

As Chapter 3 pointed out, cybernetic control depends on the possibility of making reasonably reliable forecasts of outcomes and timings at the required level of detail and over the required time span. When this is not possible, cybernetic control may still be effective if small and essentially random actions by the organisation can be relied upon to cancel out small and essentially random changes in the environment – the law of requisite variety. In other words, cybernetic systems require a fairly high degree of certainty about environmental change, either in the sense that a specific cause can be related to a specific effect or in the probabilistic sense of small changes cancelling out. This is the same thing as saying that cybernetic systems function effectively when they operate in rather repetitive environments.

Many writers on strategic management have, of course, been well aware of the uncertainty, ambiguity and conflicting goals that managers have to deal with and have developed different ways of understanding the nature of strategic choice. One influential example is the notion of logical incrementalism.

Trial and error – logical incrementalism

Based on his study of ten large corporations, Quinn (1980) identified a pattern of strategic change which he called logical incrementalism. Here managers have an intended destination for their organisation, but they discover how to reach it by taking logically connected decisions step by step. They do not make major changes but build incrementally in a consistent manner on what they already have. They sense the changes in their environment and gradually adapt to those changes so maintaining a continuing dynamic equilibrium with their environment.

Quinn's (1980) research into the decision-making process of a number of companies revealed that most strategic decisions are made outside formal planning systems. He found that managers purposely blend behavioural, political and formal analytical processes together to improve the quality of decisions and implementation. Effective managers accept the high level of uncertainty and ambiguity they have to face and do not plan everything. They preserve the flexibility of an organisation to deal with the unforeseen as it happens. The key points that Quinn made about the strategic decision-making mode are as follows:

- Effective managers do not manage strategically in a piecemeal manner. They have a clear view on what they are trying to achieve, where they are trying to take the business. The destination is thus intended.
- But the route to that destination, the strategy itself, is not intended from the start in any comprehensive way. Effective managers know that the environment they have to operate in is uncertain and ambiguous. They therefore sustain flexibility by holding open the method of reaching the goal.
- The strategy itself then emerges from the interaction between different groupings of people in the organisation, different groupings with different amounts of power, different requirements for and access to information, different time spans and parochial interest. These different pressures are orchestrated by senior managers. The top is always reassessing, integrating and organising.
- The strategy emerges or evolves in small incremental, opportunistic steps. But such evolution is not piecemeal or haphazard because of the agreed purpose and the role of top management in reassessing what is happening. It is this that provides the logic in the incremental action.
- The result is an organisation that is feeling its way to a known goal, opportunistically learning as it goes.

In Quinn's model of the strategy process, the organisation is driven by central intention with respect to the goal, but there is no prior central intention as to how that goal is to be achieved; the route to the goal is discovered through a logical process of taking one small step at a time. In logical incrementalism, overall strategy emerges from step-by-step, trial-and-error actions occurring in a number of different places in an organisation; for example, some may be making an acquisition while others are restructuring the reporting structure. These separate initiatives are pushed by champions, each attacking a class of strategic issue. The top executives manage the process, orchestrating it and sustaining some logic in it. It is this that makes it a purposeful, proactive technique. Urgent, interim, piecemeal decisions shape the organisation's future, but they do so in an orderly logical way. No one fully understands all the implications of what they are all doing together, but they are consciously preparing to move opportunistically.

Logical incrementalism represents a move from the more mechanistic view of classical strategic choice theory towards an understanding of strategy as a continual process of an organisation learning its way into the future. Others, for example Mintzberg (1994), make a more direct call for a move from strategic choice and long-term planning to an understanding of strategic management as a process of learning. This kind of move will be discussed in Chapters 5 and 6.

●●●● 4.10   Competitive advantage

Previous sections have described strategic choice as a comprehensive choice of the overall direction and shape of an organisation for some long time period into the future. Alternatively, the choice can be understood as a series of shorter-term, logically connected choices in which the longer-term strategy emerges. In both cases, the central purpose of the choices is to secure competitive advantage for the organisation. The key concern of strategic choice theory is to identify, secure and sustain an advantage over competitors such that superior performance will be achieved.

During the 1980s, the most influential view of competitive advantage was based upon neo-classical economic theory, particularly theories to do with industry structure. The idea was that managers needed to analyse and understand the structure of their industry or market and select strategies that were appropriate to that structure. This was supposed to enable them to sustain competitive advantage for their organisation over long periods of time. The most prominent writer in this tradition was Porter, whose work on industry structure has already been referred to in section 4.5.

The view that competitive advantage could be sustained for long time periods was criticised by some who pointed to the rapid change in competitive conditions. They held that hypercompetition made it impossible to sustain competitive advantage for any length of time.

Hypercompetition

Those taking this view argue that hypercompetition requires a new view of strategy (D'Aveni, 1995). From this perspective, one firm outperforms another if it is adept at rapidly and repeatedly disrupting the current situation to create a novel basis for competing. Hypercompetition requires a discontinuously redefined competitive advantage and radical changes in market relationships. Success is not built on existing strengths as in the resource-based view, to be discussed below, but on repeated disruptions. This enables a firm to continuously establish new but temporary competitive advantages. Tactical actions keep competitors off-balance. Competitive advantage is temporary and firms destroy their own and others' competitive advantage. Organisation units and actions are loosely coupled and competition requires aggressive action unconstrained by loyalty and compassion. Successful strategies rely on surveillance, interpretation, initiative, opportunism and improvisation.

Others were critical of the view that industry or market structure was the determinant of competitive advantage. Instead of focusing on neo-classical theories of market or industry structure, they turned to more recent economic theories of the firm to develop a resource-based view of strategic management. The source of competitive advantage was then understood to be the resources or competences of the firm rather than the structure of the industry.

Resource-based view

Here a firm is viewed as a blend of resources that enable certain capabilities, options and accomplishments (Wernerfelt, 1984). One firm outperforms another if it has superior ability to develop, use and protect core competences and resources, which are the foundations for creating the future (Hamel and Prahalad, 1990, 1994). Internal capabilities are what enable a firm to exploit external opportunities and competitiveness is a function of the exploitation and leveraging of these internal resources. Strategies are designed to capitalise on core competences and distinctive assets form the basis of creating a sustainable competitive advantage. Complementary interdependence makes a firm's capabilities difficult to imitate. Resource and competence is built up historically, evolving in a continuous way with cumulative effects. Capabilities are building blocks that can be combined in mutually reinforcing ways into unique capacities and the different unique combinations lead to different unique futures. To prevent imitation, attention is focused on intellectual capital, firm-specific practices, relationships with customers and other intangible ways of working together. Strategic intent relates to choices about competences to secure a desired future and success comes from focusing attention on a few primary success factors.

A core competence is one that defines a firm's fundamental business; for example Kodak's core competence is imaging and IBM's is integrated data processing and service (Teece, Pisano and Shuen, 1992). Distinctive competences reflect the organisation's capabilities to organise, manage, co-ordinate, control and govern sets of activities. It is a set of skills, complementary assets and routines that enable a firm to co-ordinate its activities, so providing the basis for competitive advantage. The routine is the basic unit of analysis (Nelson and Winter, 1982).

Hamel and Prahalad (1989) also stress the role of organisations in creating their own environments instead of simply adapting to them. They have studied a number of global companies in North America, Europe and Japan and they suggest that what distinguishes the noticeably successful (Honda, Komatsu and Canon, for example) from the noticeably less so (General Motors, Caterpillar and Xerox, for example) are the different mental models of strategy guiding their respective actions.

This research questions one of the basic tenets of strategic choice, namely the notion that successful organisations are those that fit, or adapt to, their environments.

Hamel and Prahalad found that the less successful companies follow strategic choice prescriptions and so seek to maintain strategic fit. This leads them to trim their ambitions to those that can be met with available resources. Such companies are concerned mainly with product market units rather than core competences. They preserve consistency through requiring conformity in behaviour, and they focus on achieving financial objectives. These companies attempt to achieve their financial objectives by using generic strategies, selected according to criteria of strategic fit, in order to secure sustainable competitive advantage. Hamel and Prahalad report that this approach leads to repetition and imitation.

On the other hand, Hamel and Prahalad found that successful companies focus on leveraging resources, that is, using what they have in new and innovative ways to reach seemingly unattainable goals. The main concern of these companies is to use their resources in challenging and stretching ways to build up a number of core competences. Consistency is maintained by all sharing a central strategic intent and the route to this successful state is accelerated organisational learning, recognising that no competitive advantages are inherently sustainable. Here, managers are not simply matching their resources to the requirements of the environment, leaving to others those requirements their resources are incapable of delivering. Instead, managers creatively use the resources they have, they create requirements of the environment which they can then meet, they push to achieve stretching goals and so they continually renew and transform their organisation.

While these authors question some assumptions of strategic choice theory, they preserve others. In particular, they continue to see organisational success as flowing from clear, prior, organisation-wide intention. They stress what they call strategic intent, a challenging, shared vision of a future leadership position for the company. This strategic intent is stable over time. It is clear as to outcome but flexible as to the means of achieving the outcome. It is an obsession with winning and winning on a global scale cannot be secured either through long-term plans or through some undirected process of intrapreneurship or autonomous small task forces. Instead success is secured by discovering how to achieve a broad, stretching, challenging intention to build core competences.

This study questions the idea of adapting to the environment, proposing instead creative interaction and stresses the importance of local learning, providing a further example of the shift from classical strategic choice theory towards the perspective of strategy as a learning process, which will be taken up in Chapters 5 and 6. However, in other respects – intention, harmony and consistency – it falls within strategic choice theory.

●●●● 4.11 How strategic choice theory deals with four key questions

The purpose of this section is to reflect upon the underlying assumptions and reasoning processes of strategic choice theory in order to identify what it focuses attention on and the extent to which it helps to make sense of one's experience of life in organisations.

In Chapter 1, I suggested that the phenomena of interest when one talks about strategy are populations of organisations of various kinds that interact with each other. Each organisation is itself a population of groupings of individuals that interact with each other. These populations are continually changing in that new organisations and groups within them come into being, while already existing ones disappear altogether, merge with others, split apart, develop new activities, alter structurally, grow or decline. As they relate to each other in their groups, people experience enthusiasm and boredom, excitement and anxiety, anger and fear, jealousy and envy, fulfilment and disappointment, pleasure and frustration.

Making sense of the phenomena

Strategic choice theory makes sense of these phenomena from a realist position. In other words, the theory assumes a pre-given reality. Sections 4.2 and 4.3 on the formulation and evaluation of a strategy show how each step in the formulation process makes this assumption. For example, a suitable strategy is one that fits, or is adapted to a particular market. In order to determine whether or not this is so, the market must be analysed in terms of customer requirements, competitor positions, entry barriers and so on. These factors are treated as realities that already exist, not stories about a reality that is being socially constructed by those who are participating in that market.

In addition, to establish the suitability of a strategy, managers must forecast, envision or imagine the state of these market factors some years into the future. That future is talked about as a pre-given reality too. You can hear this when people talk about getting to the future first, or use the analogy of Columbus setting sail for America, or President Kennedy announcing the dream of putting a man on the moon. These are all metaphors of a future reality that already exists, waiting to be discovered rather than created. Another example of this realist position is the discussion of leadership in section 4.8. Different leadership styles are related to different situations and the recommendation is that individuals should choose a leadership style that fits the situation. Again, the situations and the styles already exist before any individual comes to take them up. They are not created in the act of leading but discovered and adopted in advance.

Furthermore, strategic choice theory makes a particular assumption about the nature of causality. It assumes that linear causal links can be identified and that, therefore, predictions can be made. For example, it states that success is caused by choosing a strategy that is feasible, acceptable and suitable. Another example is provided by the understanding of groups (*see* section 4.8). It is postulated that groups of people will function effectively as teams if certain environmental factors and certain kinds of members are chosen to form the group. Such linear causality is not the only possible view. Chapters 10 and 11 will review notions of nonlinear causal connections and look at theories indicating that it could be impossible to identify causal links at all in certain circumstances.

The point I am making, then, is that strategic choice theory takes a particular position in relation to the way that humans know anything. As with any other position, this immediately moves the reasoning process down one avenue and excludes others. The result is to deal with the four questions posed in Chapter 1 in a particular way. Consider how strategic choice theory deals with these four questions.

The nature of interaction

In strategic choice theory, interaction is understood in systemic terms, where the entities comprising the system are organisations that interact with each other in industry groupings, or markets. An organisation is also thought of as a system that consists of people grouped into divisions, subsidiary companies, departments, project teams and so on. The immediate consequence is a tendency to reify, that is to think of an organisation and a system as a thing.

The concept of a system in strategic choice theory is a very specific one. It is a cybernetic system, that is, a goal-driven, self-regulating system. The self-regulation takes the form of a negative feedback process through which an organisation adapts to its environment, that is, its markets. Negative feedback is a process of referring back to a fixed point of reference established outside the organisation. The market demand to which the organisation must adapt provides the fixed point of reference. The negative feedback works through the system taking account of the difference between its offering and that market demand, so as to remove the difference. The organisation is itself also a cybernetic system consisting of groups of people. The fixed point of reference for these groups is the set of goals and targets set for them by their manager. Negative feedback operates by taking account of the difference between performance and targets, so as to remove the difference. Uncertainty, ambiguity and conflict are supposed to be dealt with largely by more elaborate negative feedback loops. Thinking about motivation, political activity and culture change is all in terms of negative feedback loops. Note how strategic choice theory takes no account of the effect of positive or amplifying feedback loops in human affairs.

The result is a theory that focuses primarily on the macro level. A single, whole organisation is the primary unit of analysis. Intention, or choice, is related to this whole. By focusing attention on a single organisation, 'the organisation', strategic choice theory ignores the fact that other organisations are making choices too. What happens to one depends not only on what it chooses but on what all the others do too.

You can see the importance attached to a single organisation making choices for the whole, in isolation, in the emphasis placed on: strategic intent, choosing a vision, choosing financial targets, choosing a culture, choosing strategic management styles and so on. The possibility of making such choices successfully depends heavily on the ability to predict at rather fine levels of detail and over rather long time spans. That in turn depends upon the possibility of identifying causal links between action and outcome at a rather fine level of detail over rather long time spans.

For example, to achieve financial targets, investments must be chosen to deliver those targets. The discounted cash flow method prescribed for choosing between alternative investments requires the forecasting of detailed cash flows over periods as long as 25 years. Whether an investment is a success or not depends on the fine detail of what it costs and what revenues it generates over many years, once it is in operation. Forecasts at a coarse level of detail, or for short time periods, will then not capture the factors upon which success depends. The choice cannot then be made as prescribed, which is to make the choice in a rational way that takes account of the actual factors that lead to success. Success will not be the result of rational choice but will depend on the chance capturing of the most important factors in the coarse detailed forecasts. Much the same point applies to choices of values and cultures. If a group of people is to be reliably moved from behaving according to one set of values to another then it is necessary to make a prediction of how they will respond to some measure to persuade them to do so.

There is an alternative to prediction at fine levels of detail over long time periods required by rational choice. This is the kind of very general prediction called for in setting a direction, or articulating a vision, and trusting trial-and-error activities to carry it out. Chapter 3 made the point that this can work only if small random changes in the environment and small trial-and-error actions cancel each other out. In other words, it can only work if the law of requisite variety is valid. Chapter 10 will question this.

Strategic choice theory takes a particular view of organisational dynamics. Since it is a cybernetic theory, the dynamics are those of a move to stable equilibrium. Success is equated with stability, consistency and harmony. Instabilities arise largely in the organisation's environment.

Strategic choice theory is usually formulated in a way that focuses on the interaction between components and so ignores the richness of human relationships. In viewing people as parts of a system it fails to take account of ordinary human spontaneity, which will always be affecting what happens. Cybernetic systems are incapable of any kind of novelty, innovation, creativity or transformation. They can only unfold what their designers, the observing humans outside them, put into them.

Nature of human beings

This chapter has indicated how strategic choice theory is built on a particular view of human nature. It is assumed that individuals are essentially cybernetic entities. They make representations of a pre-given reality taking the form of regularities built up from previous experience and mentally stored in the form of sets of rules, or schemas, cognitive maps or mental models. Through experience they make more and more accurate representations, more and more reliable cognitive maps. This process is essentially one of negative feedback in which discrepancies between the cognitive map and external reality are fed back into the map to change it, closing the gap between it and reality. Strategic choice theory pays very little attention to emotion and the impact that this might have on how an organisation functions. To the extent that this theory does pay attention to emotion it does so from a humanistic psychology perspective.

Humanistic psychology was developed mainly in the United States as a reaction to what was felt to be the pessimism and conservatism of psychoanalysis. Humanistic psychology takes a basically optimistic view of human nature and its perfectibility. One of its roots was in inspirational religious revivalism and it saw the main problem of human existence as the alienation of an individual from his or her true self. From this perspective people can be motivated by providing experiences for them in which they can experience more of their true selves. You see the influence of these ideas in the theories of motivation of Maslow and Hertzberg, mentioned in section 4.7. The prescriptions for establishing visions and missions that inspire people also arise from this kind of thinking about human nature.

So, when it comes to the micro level, strategic choice theory alternates between two views of human nature, the cognitivist and the humanistic. The former tends to be predominant when the theory focuses on control systems and the latter when it focuses on motivation, leadership and culture. The way both are used, however, has an element in common. It is implicitly assumed that the individual members of an organisation are all the same and that interactions between them are all the same. It is assumed that everyone responds in the same way to the same motivational factor, for example. Another example is the implicit assumption, when talking about leadership styles, that everyone will respond in the same way to a given leadership style. Differences between individuals, and deviant and eccentric behaviour have no role to play in how an organisation evolves. Indeed, they are seen as dangerous disruptions to be removed by more controls or additional motivators. The emphasis is on everyone sharing the same values to produce uniformity and conformity. The very way members of an organisation are referred to as the staff, or the management, indicates how differences within the categories are obliterated while differences between them are highlighted.

There is an important consequence of this ignoring of individual differences and deviant behaviour that will be taken up in Part Three. Systems in which the entities and their interactions are all the same cannot spontaneously generate anything new. For strategic choice theory this means that the only possible explanation of creativity is located in the individual's intention to do something creative. How individuals do this is not explained in strategic choice theory. It is simply assumed.

Individuals feature in strategic choice theory primarily in terms of how they affect the organisation as a whole. Individuals make the choices and do the controlling. Individuals appoint people to roles and they put them into teams. They set targets for those teams and motivate, reward or punish people according to performance. An individual forms a vision and individuals articulate missions for others. Power is possessed by individuals who exert it over other individuals. In this way the individual is consistently held to be prior and primary to the group. A group consists of individuals and may then affect how they behave.

The point I am making here is that strategic choice theory implicitly makes a number of important assumptions about human nature that should not be mistaken for the 'truth'. They are all assumptions that can quite properly be contested and when they are, the whole of strategic choice theory is questioned too.

Methodology and strategic choice

I have pointed a number of times in this chapter to how researchers writing in the strategic choice tradition and how managers talking in this way explicitly or implicitly take the position of the objective observer. They stand outside the system they are talking about and construct models of it as the basis for prescription and action. This has methodological implications for research and it has even more important consequences for how managers understand their role.

When a manager takes this position, that manager immediately assumes that it is his or her task to design and install some system, set of actions, motivators and so on. For example, the top executive is supposed to analyse the cultural values of an organisation. This requires the executive to step outside the value system of which he or she is a part and look at it from the outside, as it were. The next step is to design and install a new value system. Another example is provided by the discussion of leadership styles. Again, the manager is required to step outside the situation and determine whether it is one in which a particular leadership style is required. If this differs from the one the manager currently practises, then the appropriate one must be installed.

Paradox

Strategic choice theory does not understand an organisation in paradoxical terms at all. Contradictions are to be solved, tensions and conflicts smoothed away and dilemmas resolved. In terms of what might be major paradoxes of organisational life, strategic choice consistently occupies one pole of the contradiction. Individuals and groups are not paradoxical since groups simply consist of autonomous individuals. They are not seen to constitute a paradox. Predictability is emphasised and the possible implications of simultaneously present unpredictability are not seriously explored. Control is emphasised and freedom to act is made consistent with it through motivational factors. Order is the requisite for success and disorder or any form of deviance or eccentricity is to be curbed and removed. Success is equated with determinism and chance with the potential for failure.

Again, the point I am making is that strategic choice theory implicitly makes assumptions about opposing forces in organisational life that cannot simply be taken for granted. It is quite possible to take a different view and so construct a different theory.

Making sense of experience

The question now is how this theory assists one to make sense of one's experience of life in organisations. My experience is that, despite the rational analysis, the forecasts, the visions, strategic intents, team building and so on, organisational outcomes are very frequently surprising and unexpected. I find it very difficult to make sense of this experience by taking a strategic choice perspective. The theory leads one to believe that it is possible to make choices that lead to organisational success if one follows the prescribed procedures. So when managers follow the prescriptions and the surprising, the unexpected and the downright unpleasant occur, they are left with little option but to conclude that they have been incompetent in some way. Or, more likely, that other people have been incompetent in some way. A variation on this is to blame the surprise on ignorance of enough facts. Alternatively, the blame might be placed on people who do not implement the strategic choice as required. When one makes sense of experience from the strategic choice perspective the most widespread response to the unexpected takes the form of some kind of blame.

The response is then to put more effort into gathering and analysing information to overcome ignorance. Or more intensive efforts are made to acquire the necessary competences to manage strategically and so avoid accusations and feelings of incompetence. Or new motivating and controlling systems are installed to prevent poor implementation and bad behaviour. When the surprise is a large one, these responses are usually accompanied by the removal from the organisation of individuals who are conspicuously associated with the surprise. However, none of these responses puts a stop to the whole sequence of events happening again. Instead, in my view, these responses raise levels of fear and place people under increasing stress. Is this inevitable or is there a problem with trying to make sense of experience from the strategic choice standpoint?

If you take the psychoanalytic perspective to be reviewed in Chapter 7, you might reach a different conclusion. It could be that many of the prescriptions of strategic choice theory are little more than defences against the anxiety of not being able to forecast and stay in control. If this is so, then they are not very good defences because, as I have just suggested, they may actually increase levels of anxiety. If you take the perspective that I will suggest in Part Three, you might conclude that it is the nature of organising itself that generates the unexpected and the surprising. Then it may be that no one is to blame but, rather, uncertainty needs to be accepted as an inescapable fact of life that need not provoke despair or paralyse action.

●●●● 4.12 Summary

This chapter has reviewed the rational, analytic sequence of steps prescribed by strategic choice theory for the formulation and evaluation of long-term strategic plans. The steps involve analysing and forecasting market development, as well as the financial, other resource or competence and power implications of alternative action options. The result should be a blueprint to guide the development of the organisation for some reasonably long period into the future. It is the template against which the actions of individual managers are to be measured. The assumption is that if the plan has been put together skilfully enough it will go a long way to ensuring the organisation's success. However, the formulated plan only provides the blueprint against which action is to be evaluated. Success requires effective implementation.

Implementation is in effect the construction of cybernetic systems. Detailed targets and objectives are derived from the strategic plan and hierarchical structures and detailed sets of procedures for measuring and comparing outcomes with expectations are designed to monitor movement towards the detailed objectives. Even 'softer' elements such as belief systems, power and management style are prescribed in much the same way.

The chapter then reviewed behavioural factors in organisations from a strategic choice perspective. These were the motivation of people working in the organisation, the nature of leadership, the application of power in political processes and the impact of values, belief systems and culture. There were common assumptions underlying the approach in all of these areas. They were all understood in terms of what amounts to negative feedback loops, displaying the way in which organisations are treated as if they are, or should be, cybernetic systems. In all of these areas the individual is treated as primary, displaying the underlying assumption of cognitivism and humanistic psychology. Another common assumption is that managers can and should take the position of independent observer and choose appropriate feedback loops in relation to motivation, leadership, politics and culture. Throughout, the assumption is that human beings behave like cybernetic systems themselves, the underlying tenet of cognitivism. Throughout, the individual is unquestioningly held to be prior and primary in relation to the group.

The conclusion I reach is that this theory provides a partial and limited explanation of how organisational life unfolds. It provides powerful explanations of, and prescriptions for, the predictable, repetitive aspects of organisational life over short time frames into the future. These are indeed very prominent and important aspects of organisational life. However, if you believe, as I do, that life in organisations is woven from inextricable strands of the predictable and the unpredictable, the stable and the unstable, the orderly and the disorderly, then it provides a very partial explanation. On its own, it leaves one feeling puzzled by constant surprise and worried about the inability to stay in control that it prescribes. Creativity and innovation remain largely mysterious if strategic choice theory is the only way to understand organisations. The richness and importance of relationships between people is absent. It prescribes predominantly top-down processes, even when empowerment and self-managing teams are suggested. They are always the result of decisions made by those at the top of the hierarchy.

Further reading

To obtain further information on analytical techniques and models for evaluating strategies *turn to* Hofer and Schendel (1978) as well as Rowe, Mason, Dickel and Snyder (1989) and Johnson and Scholes (2001). *Also see* Ansoff (1990) for a very different perspective to the one presented in this book. Hussey (1991) provides further material on management control and Goold and Campbell (1987) provide a thorough analysis of strategic management styles. Campbell and Tawady (1990) should be referred to for a greater understanding of the mission concept. For further detail on particular decision-making modes *turn to* Quinn (1978), Mintzberg, Théorêt and Raisinghani (1976) and Cohen, March and Ohlsen (1972). Good summaries of counter views are to be found in Hurst (1982), Hurst (1986), Argyris (1990) and Schein (1988). Morgan (1997) and Mintzberg (1994) are well worth reading. For the resource-based view *see* Hamel and Prahalad (1989).

Chapter 5 ●●●●

The foundations of learning organisation theory
Systems dynamics and cognitivism

5.1   Introduction

Chapters 3 and 4 reviewed strategic choice theory, showing how its theoretical foundations are to be found in the theory of cybernetic systems and a primarily cognitivist view of human nature. This chapter turns to another way of understanding organisational change, namely the notion of the learning organisation, which has attracted increasing attention since the early 1990s. This approach has much in common with strategic choice theory but there are significant differences. Most important, perhaps, is how it points to the limits of predictability. The purpose of this chapter is to explore the theoretical foundations of learning organisation theory and the next chapter will then review that theory and compare it with strategic choice perspectives. The main theoretical difference is that learning organisation theorists employ a somewhat different theory of interaction. They still see interaction in systemic terms but the systems theory is systems dynamics rather than cybernetics. The difference and the significance of the shift will be explored in the next section and how it connects with life in organisations is dealt with in subsequent sections. An important point to note at the outset is this: while the underlying systems theory changes from cybernetics to systems dynamics, the same cognitivist view of human nature is retained. Furthermore, the way systems dynamics is interpreted as feedback structures retains an essentially cybernetic perspective on control.

5.2   Systems dynamics: nonlinearity and positive feedback

As Chapter 3 explained, cybernetics and cognitivism both developed from common origins. Essentially, cognitivism assumes that the human individual is a cybernetic entity. Cybernetic entities are driven by negative feedback towards states of equilibrium. The negative feedback process is one in which the behaviour of the entity or system is compared with some feature external to it, such as a goal, an expected sequence of behaviours, or a pre-given reality in the environment. Information on the difference between system/entity behaviour and this fixed, external point of reference is then fed back to modify the behaviour of the system/entity so that the difference is damped and removed.

Cybernetic explanations of behaviour focus on the operation of negative feedback loops and no attention is paid to the possibility of positive feedback loops. While the former dampen down differences, the latter amplify them. If amplifying feedback were applied to a steam engine it would blow up. Cybernetics also assumes linear connections between cause and effect and pays no attention to possible nonlinearities in the behaviour of a system. Consequently, it avoids the consideration of complex dynamics, seeing patterns of change purely in terms of an orderly and predictable movement towards stable equilibrium. A cybernetic system has no internal capacity for changing its state. It moves in a steady, orderly trajectory to equilibrium until some change in the environment occurs. Departures from this steady trajectory are due to errors in forecasts, particularly of time lags, not the structure of the system itself.

Systems dynamics has its intellectual roots in the same tradition as cybernetics. It is also built on the engineer's notion of control. However, from this common root and around the same time, it developed in a somewhat different way to cybernetics. While cyberneticists focused on the structure of negative feedback loops those who developed systems dynamics sought to model the system as a whole in mathematical terms. The most important figures in this development were economists seeking to model economic cycles for whole economies or some aspect of them such as inventory (stock) cycles. Some of the most important figures here were Goodwin (1951), Philips (1950) and Tustin (1953). Systems dynamics thinking was also extended to industrial management problems (Simon, 1952; Forrester, 1958). It is important to note, right from the start, that when these writers referred to human beings they saw them as decision rules in a system. The understanding of human nature was essentially cognitivist, as it was with cybernetics.

In their modelling work systems dynamicists used nonlinear equations that incorporated positive feedback effects and generated rather complex dynamics. These models also display some cyclical behaviour that is due to the structure of the system itself, not just changes in the environment. However, just as with cybernetics, the system cannot spontaneously change its state, a matter I will return to in Chapter 11. The point is that systems dynamics makes a number of assumptions that lead it to differ in some respects from cybernetics. These are nonlinear causality, the possibility of positive, as well as negative, feedback and the possibility of internally generated cyclical behaviour and non-equilibrium. However, the interpretation of systems in terms of feedback loops retains some links with cybernetics.

This section will give a brief review of some of the key concepts in systems dynamics, starting with the nature of nonlinearity.

Nonlinearity

Nonlinearity occurs when some condition or some action has a varying effect on an outcome, depending on the level of the condition or the intensity of the action. For example, the availability of a stock of goods in an inventory affects shipment rates of those goods, but the effect varies. When the stock is close to a desired level, there will be virtually no impact of stock levels on shipment rates. The firm ships according to its order inflow rate. However, when inventory is very low, stock availability has a powerful constraining effect on shipments.

Another example is where extra labour is hired. At first, extra labour may lead to proportionally extra output but, given fixed equipment, a point will be reached where extra labour adds proportionally less and less output. Eventually, adding extra labour causes output to decline as large numbers interfere with efficient operation. These effects cannot be captured in simple linear relationships where a cause always exerts the same degree of effect on an outcome.

Nonlinear interaction can be modelled as a system of nonlinear equations, as you can see in the following simple example. The size of a population of, say, insects is determined by the difference between birth rates and death rates so that today's population size (P_t) is some multiple or some fraction (c), of yesterday's population (P_{t-1}). This can be written as:

$$P_t = cP_{t-1} \tag{1}$$

When birth rates exceed death rates, then c is greater than 1 and the population grows. However, this is not the only set of forces governing the population level. As the population rises, food becomes scarcer and conflict and stress rise as overcrowding increases. This dampening impact of population increases can be represented mathematically as follows:

$$P_t = 1 - P_{t-1} \tag{2}$$

Since both of these forces are acting upon the population at the same time, the relationship can be expressed by combining them as follows:

$$P_t = cP_{t-1}(1 - P_{t-1}) \tag{3}$$

This is the famous logistic difference equation that has been widely used in analyses of populations of all kinds and many other phenomena besides. I will be returning to this in Chapter 10.

This equation models nonlinear behaviour in that, for the same birth and death rates, a level of population today exerts a different effect on tomorrow, depending on just how high or low it is today. It is important to note how this equation is iterative and self-referential and how it generates a history. It is iterative because it is repeatedly applied from one period to another and it is self-referential because what P is today depends upon what it was yesterday. In other words, it refers back to itself in order to determine what it is and in doing so traces a path over time. I will be returning to this point in Chapters 10 and 11. I am making this point now to draw attention to the fact that this kind of structure is not spoken about in self-referential terms in the literature on the learning organisation. Instead, it is interpreted from a feedback point of view. This takes the reasoning process down a very different route to that which a self-referential interpretation takes. I will be returning to this point in Part Three.

Although interpreted in feedback terms, the equation itself is not a feedback structure in the cybernetic sense in that it does not feed back a difference between its behaviour and some fixed, external point of reference. You may say that it feeds

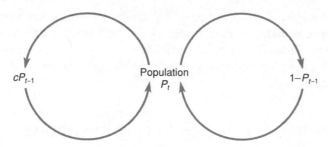

Figure 5.1   Positive and negative feedback in population growth

back on itself but this would be a very different notion of feedback from the cybernetic one. I will use the term self-referential when referring to the kind of process that the logistic equation represents. I think that this is important because organisation theorists describe such processes in the terminology of feedback and so, I think, import a cybernetic mode of thinking into systems dynamics. The radical potential of systems dynamics is then, I believe, lost. I will explain what I mean by this in Chapter 10. In the meantime, let me explain how I see self-referential relationships of the kind depicted in equation (3) above being used as feedback loops. Consider how you might interpret that equation as a feedback model of the insect population.

Equation (1) might be interpreted as a positive, or amplifying, feedback loop. When birth rates exceed death rates, the population grows for ever more, according to equation (1). This is amplifying growth. When c is less than 1, the population declines until none is left. Again, this is amplifying feedback. Equation (2) might then be interpreted as a negative feedback loop of the kind familiar from cybernetics. High levels of population dampen the growth effects of equation (1). So instead of a system that operates only according to negative feedback, as in cybernetics, there is now a system that operates according to both positive and negative feedback as shown in equation (3). These feedback loops can be represented in the diagrammatic form shown in Figure 5.1.

Systems dynamics therefore introduces the possibility that a system may display non-equilibrium behaviour as it flips between positive and negative feedback. The result is much more complex patterns of movement over time, that is, much more complex dynamics. Behaviour can now be cyclical and those cycles might be very irregular if the system is perturbed by environmental fluctuations. Systems dynamics was very important in understanding the nature of economic cycles, such as cycles in inventory and other forms of investment. Systems dynamics also points to the limits of predictability by introducing nonlinear circular causality which makes it difficult to say what causes what, or what precedes what.

Before exploring further how systems dynamics ideas are used in understanding organisations I want to reiterate a point I have already made. One way of interpreting systems dynamics is to see the system as a self-referential one. The line of reasoning pursued is then to try to understand how the system determines what it is by reference to itself. Another route to take is to interpret systems dynamics in terms of feedback loops, that is, to see it as a feedback system. The latter is the route that most have taken. I will be taking up the self-referential route and looking at the difference it makes in Part Three. The point I want to emphasise here, however, is that the feedback system route implicitly retains a conception of the system as cybernetics plus positive feedback and in doing so remains a systemic theory of organisational change.

●●●● 5.3   Positive feedback in organisations

Consider some important examples of positive feedback in organisations.

Vicious circles

The vicious (or virtuous) circle is a widely used concept and this is a positive feedback loop. An early model of vicious circles in organisations is provided by Gouldner (1964). He studied a gypsum plant in the United States and developed a model to explain what he observed. This is illustrated in Figure 5.2.

Senior managers at the gypsum plant were concerned to manage efficiently and believed that this required reduced tension between managers and workers. Such tension could be reduced, they thought, if power relations became less visible and

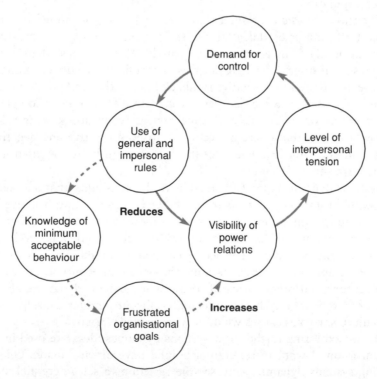

Figure 5.2   Gouldner's model of intended and unintended consequences
Source: R. Turton (1991), *Behaviour in a Business Context*, London: Chapman and Hall.

all behaved according to impersonal rules. The intention was to emphasise the 'rationality' of the rules and conceal the fact that power was being exercised. No reasonable person could object to rules designed to improve efficiency and those who had to enforce them could deny the personal exercise of power and simply say they were doing their job. Conflicts around the distribution of power would then be removed.

Thus, the demand by senior managers for greater control led to the use of general and impersonal rules intended to decrease the visibility of the power of senior management and hence interpersonal tension. In this way managers hoped to establish a damping, negative feedback loop producing the intended consequences of reduced tension.

These actions, however, set up another loop that produced unintended consequences. The rules created norms about minimum performance in terms of time of attendance and output levels. People stuck to the minimum norms, frustrating senior management expectations of increased performance. That led to a call for closer supervision and closer control, which had the effect of increasing the visibility of power and thus increasing the level of tension. More impersonal rules were then required. An unintended positive loop was generating unintended consequences. And that loop came to dominate what was going on, causing a vicious spiralling circle of tighter controls and more tension.

Self-fulfilling prophecies

Merton (1957) developed a model of organisations in terms of self-fulfilling prophecies, another example of positive feedback at work. Many managers argue that most people are not very competent and cannot be left to make decisions for themselves in relation to their work. They argue that efficiency requires rules. But constant compliance with rules causes individuals eventually to lose the capacity to make decisions for themselves. The constant reliance on rules leads to the rules becoming ends in themselves instead of means to ends. As a consequence of being compelled to obey rules they did not originate, employees lose the capacity for independent thought. The result is trained incapacity. Rule-bound organisations encourage unimaginative people to join them and the imaginative leave. The prophecy that people are incompetent is fulfilled by the means taken to deal with its originally supposed existence.

For example, managers may demand greater control in order to secure reliability in service terms. Employees fulfil the stipulated reliability criteria by sticking to the rules. The result is employees who stick to the rules and supply customers strictly in accordance with them. If this leads to trouble with customers, employees can show how they have kept to the rules. This is the intended feedback loop – negative and damping. But such rigid behaviour and the organisational defences it involves lead to more and more difficulties with clients. Growing customer dissatisfaction leads to top managers calling for greater reliability and more rules. So another positive loop is set up, a vicious circle with unintended consequences.

Bandwagon effects and chain reactions

A bandwagon effect is the tendency of a movement to gain supporters simply because of its growing popularity; or it is the well-observed economic phenomenon of 'keeping up with the Joneses' – the demand for a product increases simply because more and more people see that other people have it. This phenomenon of products spreading through consuming populations is another example of a positive feedback loop, this time creating a virtuous circle for the producer of the product. A small gain in market share by one product can, through this spreading and copying effect, be escalated into market domination. So although Sony's Betamax was the technically superior video recorder, Matsushita's VHS recorder obtained a small market lead in the early days of market development. This led to more stores stocking titles in the VHS format. That led to a further increase in VHS recorder market share and therefore more stockists turned to VHS films, and so on.

A similar phenomenon is the chain reaction. Here a positive feedback process escalates a small change into major consequences. Police firing a shot into a demonstrating crowd may touch off a chain reaction which leads to a massive riot or even the overthrow of a government. If relationships between people in a group take complicated, changing feedback forms, then decision making cannot be as coherent a process as rational models of any kind would lead one to believe.

Tight and loose coupling

The complexity in interrelationships and decision making grows as a move is made from single groups to the collections of groups that constitute an organisation. Organisations are typically not tightly coupled sets of groups alone. Organisations are more typically sets of groups that are tightly coupled for some purposes, but constitute a loosely coupled system for other purposes (Weick, 1979).

Groups or systems are *tightly coupled* when there are clear-cut direct connections between them and when they are so closely co-ordinated that a decision or action in one has immediately apparent implications for decisions or actions in another. Tight coupling is present in an efficient assembly production process, where one group assembling the components on a television set work in a highly co-ordinated way with another group putting the components into a plastic casing. Any failure in the first assembly operation has an immediate impact on the later operation and vice versa. Tight coupling is highly efficient while all moves according to plan. But unforeseen changes in one area have rapid and major implications for what happens in other areas. A small failure in one small part could bring the whole system down. Tight coupling is characterised by (Perrow, 1984):

- no delays in processing;
- no variation in sequences of events;
- only one method of achieving the goal;
- no slack in the flow of activity from one part of the system to another;
- any buffers built in at the design stage;
- possible substitution of supplies or equipment built in at the design stage.

Loose coupling, on the other hand, means that there is a buffer between one group and another. There is the possibility of delays and changes in the sequences of events. Parts of the system can continue to function while failures in other parts of the system are attended to. Alternative methods can be employed and additional resources called upon. Buffers and redundancies are available to deal with the unforeseeable.

Clearly, loosely coupled systems are less efficient, but they are also far safer. The more unpredictable the situation, the more helpful it will be to have a loosely coupled system. So in the assembly operation above the system could be turned into a loosely coupled one by introducing the possibility of building up unplanned inventories at each stage. If the group putting the assemblies into plastic cases fails to maintain its speed, the supervisor of the group assembling the components could decide to continue production and add to inventories, even though there is no plan to do so. Decisions or actions in one group would then not have immediate implications for another.

Because of this possibility of loose coupling, a change in one part of the system need not immediately affect the other parts. Loosely coupled systems are characterised by the possibility of delays and changes in the sequences of events. And because of this it is difficult to predict what one group will do when another takes some action. The system becomes safer in the face of uncertainty, but the safety factor itself adds a level of complexity that makes it more difficult to determine how the system will behave or why it is behaving as it does.

Loose coupling means that the connections between decisions and actions in one part of the organisation and decisions and actions in other parts are often obscure. The connections between means and ends, and between problems and solutions, also become less clear. People, problems and choice opportunities are combined in confusing ways that make it difficult to predict agendas of matters to be attended to, and the outcomes of those matters.

When they deal with the day-to-day management of their existing businesses, successful organisations set up tightly coupled systems. Modern methods of operations management and inventory control, such as just-in-time delivery and materials resource programming, are examples of this. But successful organisations always also have to face unpredictable changes to their activities. To deal with this they also evolve loosely coupled systems. Because they face both the predictable and the unpredictable, most organisations are systems that combine tight and loose coupling. The element of loose coupling often makes it very difficult to identify the events in one part of the system that are causing changes in other parts.

Links with the environment

Weick (1979) also explains the organisation's links with the environment in terms of feedback loops. The nature of these loops is illustrated in Figure 5.3.

First consider what the terms used in Figure 5.3 mean and then what the loop connections between them signify.

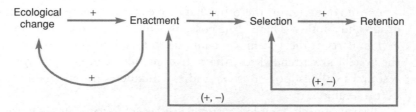

Figure 5.3 Weick's model: links with the environment
Source: K. Weick (1979), *The Social Psychology of Organizing*, New York: McGraw-Hill. Reproduced with permission.

1 *Ecological change* means the changes occurring in the market and wider environments that an organisation operates in. Such changes are primarily the actions undertaken by actors in the environment. These external actions may lead people in an organisation to undertake actions too – hence the arrow and the + sign running from ecological change to enactment.

2 *Enactment* describes what the actors within the organisation itself do; it is the actions they undertake. The term enactment is used rather than the term action, to indicate that people within an organisation do not simply anticipate, react or adapt to what actors in the environment can be objectively observed to do. Instead, people within an organisation are prompted by their subjective perceptions of what actors in the environment are doing or might do. It is those perceptions that drive their actions. Here Weick has moved from a cognitivist to a constructivist notion of human psychology. In the cognitivist perspective, an individual perceives an objective reality and then acts on that. In a constructivist perspective, an individual acts on the basis of perceptions built up through past experience and in so doing selects, or enacts, an environment. Here, the individual calls forth responses from other individuals and this constitutes his or her reality. This introduces an important notion of constraint. An individual cannot perceive objective reality but only what his or her experience makes it possible to perceive. Constructivism and cognitivism, however, both accord primacy to the individual.

  Furthermore, actions of the above kind may lead environmental actors to do what they do. Those within an organisation then perceive this and undertake further action. So they all keep going around a positive feedback loop, represented by the + signs in the loop shown in Figure 5.3 between ecological change and enactment. By taking a particular action, people within an organisation may cause people outside it to do what they do – the former are therefore in a real sense creating, or enacting, their own environment. Because they are driven by subjective perceptions it is also quite possible for people within an organisation to invent an environment and then cause it to occur. The question now is this: what causes actors within the organisation to perceive and act in the way they do? The answer lies in what they remember about what they have done before.

3 *Retention* is the process of storing what has been perceived and learned from previous actions. It is the shared memory of the collection of people constituting the

organisation, built up from what they have done together over the past, reflecting their perceptions of what has worked and what has not worked. If particular actions worked in particular circumstances before, this will prompt a similar enactment now. So the link running back from retention to enactment can be positive or negative; that is, the organisational memory could prompt an action or stop it. The terms retention and organisational memory as they are used here mean the same thing as the culture of the organisation, its recipe, the paradigm its managers subscribe to, their received wisdom. These terms all have to do with the shared mental models of organisational actors, that is, it is a cognitivist notion. The next question is this: how does retention come about? The answer lies in a process of selection.

4 *Selection* is the process through which organisational actors focus on some meanings of what they are doing and some perceptions of what others are doing, while ignoring yet others. What is selected for retention depends upon what has been done or enacted and what has been perceived (the positive arrow running from enactment to selection). And the selection itself is affected by what has been previously retained about how things should be perceived and done (the loop running back from retention to selection). What is selected to focus on now depends on the mental models already built up. These may cause people to accept or reject a perception hence the positive and negative signs in the retention–selection loop.

By looking at the interactions between an organisation and its environment in this way, Weick clarifies the concept of managers creating the reality they respond to.

Self-designing systems

The feedback system view of how an organisation works led Weick (1977) to the concept of an organisation as a self-designing system. Rigid rule-bound organisations that spell out exactly how people should behave are incapable of generating new forms of behaviour to meet new situations. To be able to meet the unexpected new situation, organisations need to be loosely coupled, self-designing systems. That requires establishing the following patterns:

- valuing improvisation more than forecasts;
- dwelling on opportunities rather than constraints;
- inventing solutions rather than borrowing them;
- cultivating impermanence instead of permanence;
- valuing argument more highly than serenity;
- relying on diverse measures of performance rather than on accounting systems alone;
- encouraging doubt rather than removing it;
- continuously experimenting rather than searching for final solutions;
- seeking contradictions rather than discouraging them.

Such patterns of behaviour will make organisations less efficient but more adaptable. Weick has made a number of key points that are summarised in Figure 5.4.

Figure 5.4

Weick's model: key points on organisational dynamics

- Organisations are feedback systems, starting right at the fundamental level of inter-action between two or more people within the organisation.
- The systematic feedback structure of the organisation itself determines the pattern of behaviour over time. The standard assumption in strategic choice theory is that the dynamics, the pattern of change, is due mainly to environmental forces outside the organisation. The proposition being made in Weick's models is that patterns of change are determined by the inherent nature of the system structure itself.
- A group of people does not necessarily have to have a shared, common purpose in order to be a group. People form groups before they have a common purpose because they have interdependent needs that require the resources of others. People group because they need each other's support, because of the means not the ends. Purpose comes later. So an organisation is not necessarily driven by goal-seeking behaviour, that is, achieving a given goal. It may well be driven by searching for a goal in the first place. This is a very different perspective from strategic choice theory.
- Meaning for an organisation is retrospective not prospective. People can only under-stand what they are doing by interpreting what they have done. They impose meaning on what they have done. So a vision would not be a picture of a future state but an interpretation of where they have now got to. Meaning, purpose, vision and mission emerge from what people have done and are doing – they are not prior organisation-wide intentions.
- Organisations create and invent their own environment in the sense that the environ-ment is their perception of what is happening and in the sense that their actions impact on the environment which then impacts back on the organisation. This is different to the simple adaptive view that is common in strategic choice theory.
- Predicting what feedback systems will do is very difficult. It is difficult to guess what people's preferences will be in the future and it is these preferences that will drive what they do.
- But despite the unpredictability and the complexity, people can operate as part of a sys-tem that is too complex for any one person alone to understand. Each plays a part in the complex unfolding of events, understanding only a part, and relies on others to play their parts.
- Loose coupling is important in the ability of such complex systems to remain flexible, but that loose coupling adds to system complexity and makes it even harder to under-stand and predict its behaviour.
- Such systems are essentially self-designing.
- Positive feedback and self-reinforcing processes play a very important part in what hap-pens. Instability is an essential part of what goes on and one cannot simply ignore it or write it off as something to be banished by negative feedback controls. There is too much evidence that this focus on negative feedback alone leads to unintended positive loops and unintended consequences.

●●●● 5.4   Systems thinking

Perhaps the most important development of systems dynamics models for application to organisational and social policy issues has been by Jay Forrester (1958, 1961). His background was that of a servomechanisms engineer, digital computer pioneer and manager of a large R&D effort. He developed an approach to understanding human systems that is based on concepts of positive and negative feedback, nonlinearity and the use of computers to simulate the behaviour patterns of such complex systems. Feedback is the basic characteristic of his view of the world:

> Systems of information feedback control are fundamental to all life and human endeavour, from the slow pace of biological evolution to the launching of the latest satellite. A feedback control system exists whenever the environment causes a decision which in turn affects the original environment. (Forrester, 1958, p. 4)

Here human decision making is firmly linked to the feedback concept.

Production and distribution chains

Forrester has illustrated his approach by modelling the behaviour of production and distribution chains. A factory supplies a product, say beer, to a number of distributors who then ship it to an even larger number of retailers. Orders for the product flow back upstream from retailers to distributors and from them to the factory. The factory, the distributors and the retailers form a system and the links between them are flows of orders in one direction and flows of product in the other. Each part of the system tries to do the best it can to maintain inventories at minimum levels without running out of product to sell. Each attempts to ship product as fast as possible. They all do these things because that is the way to maximise their individual profits.

But because of its very structure – the feedback and lags in information flows – this system shows a marked tendency to amplify minor ordering disturbances at the retail level. An initial 10 per cent increase in orders at the retail level can eventually cause production at the factory to peak 40 per cent above the initial level before collapsing.

Peter Senge (1990) reports how he has used this example as a game with thousands of groups of managers in many countries. Even when people know about the likely consequences of this system, he has always found that the consequences of a small increase at the retail level are, first of all, growing demand that cannot be met. Inventories are depleted and backlogs grow. Then beer arrives in great quantities while incoming orders suddenly decline as backlogs are reduced. Eventually almost all players end up with large inventories they cannot unload. It is exactly this kind of cyclical behaviour that we observe in real-life businesses.

Only by being aware of how the system as a whole functions, rather than simply concentrating on one's own part of it, can we try to ensure that the extreme instabilities of the cycles are avoided. It seems, however, that these cycles can never be removed altogether.

The lessons of systems thinking

The lessons of the game are the following.

- The structure of the system influences behaviour. The cycles in ordering, inventory levels and production in the game are really the consequence of the structure of the system. But, when people play the game in a classroom, or in real life, they blame others in the system for what is going on. For example, the retailers blame the distributors for running out of stock and not delivering fast enough.
- Structure in human systems is subtle. Structure is the set of interrelationships between people and, because of negative and positive feedback loops, that structure can generate unintended results.
- Coping effectively often comes from a new way of thinking. If one simply focuses on one's own part in the system, thinks for example always as a retailer, then one's behaviour of over- and under-ordering will simply contribute to the system's instability. If, instead, players think in terms of the whole system, they will behave differently. For example, they will realise that widespread over-ordering is likely to occur. They will realise that doing so themselves in this situation will not help them much in the short run, but will eventually lead to stock levels that are too high. They will avoid doing what everyone else is doing, even if this reduces profitability in the short run.

Principles of systems dynamics

By running computer simulations of a great many different human systems, researchers in the systems dynamics tradition have identified a number of principles about complex human systems. These are set out below.

1 Complex systems often produce unexpected and counterintuitive results. In the beer game, retailers increase orders above their real need expecting this to lead to bigger deliveries, but because all retailers are doing this, and because of lags in information flows, the unexpected result is lower deliveries. Simulation of other situations suggests that increased low-cost housing in an inner city will exacerbate rather than arrest the decline of inner cities, because it creates ghettoes where social mobility is impossible. Policies of demolishing slum housing and discouraging the construction of cheap housing make the centre more desirable for the better-off, but also create a more balanced social system in which there is the opportunity for upward mobility.

2 In complex systems – nonlinear relationships with positive and negative feedback – the links between cause and effect are distant in time and space. In the beer game, the causes of increased demand appeared at the retail end, distant in space from the factory and distant in time because of the lags in order flows. Such distance between cause and effect makes it very difficult to say what is causing what. Those playing the beer game always think that the fluctuations in deliveries are being caused by fluctuations in retail demand when in fact they are due to the manner in which the system operates. The problem is made worse by many coincident symptoms that look like causes but are merely relational. This means

that it is extremely difficult to make specific predictions of what will happen in a specific place over a specific time period. Instead, quantitative simulations on computers can be used to identify general qualitative patterns of behaviour that will be similar to those one is likely to experience, although never the same. Simulation here is being used not to capture the future specific outcome within a range of likely outcomes, but to establish broad qualitative features in patterns of behaviour. Senge (1990, p. 73) puts it like this:

> *The art of systems thinking lies in being able to recognise increasingly (dynamically) complex and subtle structures . . . amid the wealth of details, pressures and cross-currents that attend all real management settings. In fact, the essence of mastering systems thinking as a management discipline lies in seeing patterns where others see only events and forces to react to.*

3 Complex systems are highly sensitive to some changes but remarkably insensitive to many others. Complex systems contain some influential pressure, or leverage, points. If we can influence those points we can have a major impact on the behaviour of the system. The trouble is that these are difficult to identify. Note how this concern with leverage points relates to the ideas introduced at the beginning of this chapter on chain reactions, bandwagon effects and virtuous circles of behaviour. In the beer game, the leverage points lie in the ordering practices of retailers and distributors. Unfortunately these pressure points, from which favourable chain reactions can be initiated, are extremely difficult to find. More usually, it seems, complex systems are insensitive to changes and indeed counteract and compensate for externally applied correctives. So when retailers find that deliveries from the distributors are curtailed, they respond by ordering even more and so make the situation worse. When aid programmes provide more dams and water pumps to halt the expansion of the Sahara, tribesmen simply enlarge their herd sizes, leading to overgrazing and the even more rapid encroachment of the desert.

 Because of this natural tendency to counteract and compensate, that is to move to stability, it is necessary to change the system itself rather than simply apply externally generated remedies. By their very nature, complex systems often react to policy changes in ways that are the opposite to those which policy-makers intend; and complex systems tend to a condition of poor performance because they resist change.

The above points lead inevitably to the conclusion that, because an organisation is a complex system, attempts to plan its long-term future and plan changes in its culture and behaviour patterns are all likely to prompt counter-forces and lead to little change at all or to unexpected and unintended changes.

Archetypes of feedback processes

Once the strong possibility that complex systems will counteract correctives and produce unintended consequences is recognised, it becomes essential to analyse and understand the feedback connections in the system, to understand the system as a

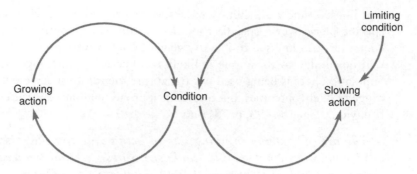

Figure 5.5   Limits to growth
Source: P. Senge (1990), *The Fifth Discipline*, New York: Doubleday.

whole. It becomes vital for effective intervention in the behaviour of the system to understand the dynamics of the system.

Through their simulations, systems dynamicists have built up a set of templates, or archetype feedback processes, that are very commonly found in organisations of all kinds. The purpose of these archetypes is not to make specific predictions of what will happen, but to recondition perceptions so that people are able to perceive the structures at play, to see the dynamic patterns of behaviour and to see the potential leverage in those structures. The templates are meant to be used in a flexible way to help understand patterns in events. The template is used as an analogy with which to build an explanation of each specific situation that people in organisations are confronted with. Some examples of these templates are as follows.

1 Limits to growth

Limits to growth occur when a reinforcing positive feedback process is installed to produce a desired result (a positive growth loop) but it inadvertently creates secondary effects (a negative limiting loop) that put a stop to the growth. The 'limits to growth' structure is found wherever growth bumps up against limits. (*See* Figure 5.5.)

The most immediate response to this structure is that of pushing harder on the factors that cause growth. In fact this is counterproductive because it causes the system to bump even more firmly against the limits. The solution is to work on the negative loop, on relaxing the limits.

For example, a company may grow through introducing new products flowing from its R&D efforts. As it grows it increases the size of the R&D department which becomes harder to manage. Senior engineers then become managers and the flow of new product ideas slows. Pressing for more new product ideas will simply lead to a bigger R&D department and that will exacerbate the management problems, so reducing the flow of new ideas. Instead, there is a need to rethink the whole process of developing new products and running R&D activities. The leverage point is the way in which the actual R&D effort is organised and to see how this should be done one needs to understand the whole system of which R&D is a part.

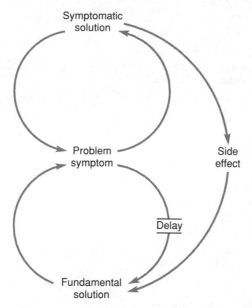

Figure 5.6   Shifting the burden
Source: P. Senge (1990), *The Fifth Discipline*, New York: Doubleday.

2 Shifting the burden

Shifting the burden (*see* Figure 5.6) happens where some underlying problem generates a number of symptoms. Because the underlying problem is difficult to identify, people focus on the symptoms. They look for the quick, easy fix. While this may temporarily relieve the symptoms, the underlying problem gets worse. People do not notice at first how the underlying problems are getting worse and as they avoid dealing with these problems the system loses its ability to solve them.

An example is bringing an expert into an organisation to solve a problem. This may leave a manager's ability unaltered and when related problems arise again the manager will be unable to cope without the expert.

3 Eroding goals

Another template is that of eroding goals (*see* Figure 5.7), where a short-term solution is effected by allowing fundamental goals to decline. This happens when managers accept a decline in performance standards as a temporary measure to deal with a crisis.

So, for example, a company producing a good product attracting high levels of demand increases its delivery time to accommodate a backlog crisis. It then does little to increase production capacity. The next time it goes around the circle, it experiences even bigger backlogs and so it extends delivery time even further. This goes on until customer dissatisfaction suddenly reaches a critical point and demand falls away rapidly.

Simulations show that when firms allow their goals for quality and delivery time gradually to slip it has dramatic effects on their profitability. The message is

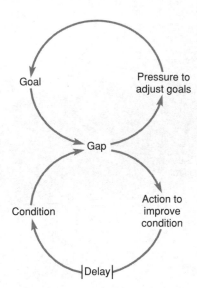

Figure 5.7   Eroding goals
Source: P. Senge (1990), *The Fifth Discipline*, New York: Doubleday.

to beware the symptomatic solution and seek to understand how the system is working.

4 Growth and underinvestment

Growth and underinvestment occur when new investments in capacity are not made early enough or on a large enough scale to accommodate continuing growth (*see* Figure 5.8). As growth approaches limits set by existing capacity, the attempts made to meet demand result in lower quality and service levels. The consequence is customer dissatisfaction and declining demand.

Another example of systems thinking: Porter's analysis of the competitive advantage of nations

Porter (1990) puts forward an explanation of how nations develop competitive advantage. This approach sees a particular company as part of a complex system consisting of other competing, supplying, supporting, customer and governmental organisations. The pattern of change any one company in this system displays depends upon a self-reinforcing interplay between what all of them are doing. Clusters of supporting and competing companies emerge in particular areas as a result of spreading benefits between them – a form of feedback between them that amplifies advantages and disadvantages and sets off virtuous and vicious circles of development. In this process, partly affected by chance, the cause and effect of individual determinants becomes blurred.

Porter's industry structure and value chain analysis, mentioned briefly in Chapter 4, paints a picture of managers in an organisation who analyse a given environment and then choose a particular strategy that they then implement. If they choose the

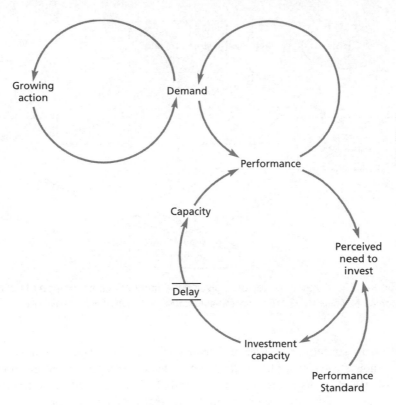

Figure 5.8   Growth and underinvestment

Source: P. Senge (1990), *The Fifth Discipline*, New York: Doubleday.

right strategy, that is, if they formulate the right organisational intention and then actually carry it out, they will succeed. This is a picture of orderly, intentional adaptation to the environment. In the later analysis being discussed here, however, each firm is part of a system and therefore what happens to any individual firm will be a consequence, not of the shared intention of its top managers, but of the evolution of the whole system of which that firm and its top managers are a part.

The analysis is conducted in terms of what Porter calls the 'national diamond' reproduced as Figure 5.9. A nation, and therefore any individual firm within it, achieves success in a particular industry when it develops a favourable configuration between the following:

- *Factor conditions* such as skilled labour, the transport and education infrastructure, knowledge resources.
- *Demand conditions* such as the size of markets and the sophistication of buyers.
- *Related and supporting industries*. The point here is that one firm has competitive advantage when it is part of a whole value chain that is competitive. So Italian shoe manufacturers have advantages because they are part of a cluster of industries containing support in the form of leather suppliers and designers. This support industry is made possible by the existence of related firms such as handbag manufacturers.

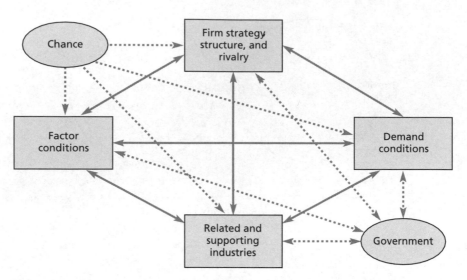

Figure 5.9 Porter's model for analysing the competitive advantage of nations
Source: M. Porter (1990), *The Competitive Advantage of Nations*, London: Macmillan.

- *Firm strategy*, structure and rivalry. The way firms are managed and formulate their strategies affects their competitive advantage. The more intense the rivalry between firms the more effective and efficient they will have to be to survive and therefore the more internationally competitive they will be.

In addition to these four determinants, the development of firms in a cluster depends on chance and on the government. Chance inventions or other events outside the control of companies or their governments create discontinuities that can reshape an industry. Government policies are part of the system too because they can add to or detract from competitive advantage.

These determinants create a system within which the nation's firms are born and develop. They gain advantage when the cluster of which they are part is more favourable than competing clusters. This is a self-reinforcing system because the effect of one determinant depends upon the state of the others. Favourable demand conditions only lead to success if the state of rivalry is such that firms respond.

5.5 How systems dynamics differs from cybernetics

Figure 3.5 in Chapter 3 summarised the key features of cybernetic systems and Figure 5.10 presents a similar summary for systems dynamics. By comparing them, one can see that the key differences are as follows. While cybernetics assumes linear causality, systems dynamics takes account of nonlinearity. Cybernetics deals only with negative feedback processes through which self-regulating control is maintained while systems dynamics also incorporates the effects of positive feedback as well. Consequently, non-equilibrium is a highly likely state according to systems

Figure 5.10

Systems dynamics: main points on organisational dynamics

- Organisations are goal seeking but amplifying feedback loops and nonlinearity mean that they are not self-regulating in the cybernetic sense. Instead, they are self-influencing and this may take a self-sustaining or a self-destructive form. They may be adapting to pre-given environments through negative feedback or diverging from them through positive feedback.
- Systems dynamics takes a realist position on human knowing.
- The system is recursive. This means that it feeds back on itself to repeat its behaviour.
- It follows that causality is circular. However, in systems dynamics causality is nonlinear. Causal links are distant and often difficult to identify.
- Predictability of specific events and their timings is very difficult and this makes it important to recognise qualitative patterns.
- Control becomes difficult but if the structure of the system is understood, leverage points can be identified. These are points where efforts to change behaviour have the most effect. These points are difficult to find. Changes there might simply provoke compensating and offsetting behaviour.
- Positive, or amplifying, feedback is seen to be of great importance.
- Behavioural patterns of the system as a whole are of great importance. Behavioural patterns can emerge without being intended; in fact they often emerge contrary to intention. The result is unexpected and counterintuitive outcomes.
- Because the analysis is conducted in feedback terms there is still the notion of an external point of reference. The system still operates on the basis of representations of its environment.
- There is a clear boundary between system and environment, between inner and outer. Although the system is adapting to its environment, it is itself a closed system. It operates/changes with reference to a fixed point at the boundary with its environment, either amplifying or damping in relation to that fixed point.
- Its state is determined by its own structure as well as flux in the environment expressed through the fixed point of reference. Instability comes from within the system as well as the environment.
- The system is no longer homeostatic, or equilibrium seeking, but far more likely to be in non-equilibrium. However, left to its own devices, the system has a tendency to stabilise and so deteriorate in the face of change.
- History is important in that the current state of the system does depend upon the sequence of previous states. However, the system does not evolve of its own accord. Any change must be designed outside the system and then installed.
- Effective organisations are self-regulating, an automatic mechanical feature flowing from the way the control system is structured.
- The goal is still to achieve as much stability, consistency and harmony as is compatible with changing to adapt to the environment.

dynamics while systems move to equilibrium according to cybernetics. The possibility of prediction is not seen as problematic from the cybernetic perspective but it is from a systems dynamics one. Discussions about organisations from a systems dynamics perspective, therefore, present much more complex dynamics and much more problematic possibilities for control than do discussions from a cybernetic perspective.

5.6 Summary

This chapter introduced systems dynamics theory and clarified how it differs from cybernetics. The most significant difference relates to the introduction of nonlinearity and positive feedback. The way in which positive feedback processes have been used to understand life in organisations was reviewed. From this it can be seen that a systems dynamics perspective presents a richer, more complex insight into the dynamics of life in organisations. The next chapter carries this review further to see how systems dynamics underlies the theory of the learning organisation.

Further reading

Richardson (1991) provides an account of the use of feedback thinking in human systems and Senge's (1990) book gives a summary of systems thinking.

Chapter 6 ● ● ● ●

The learning organisation

6.1 Introduction

This chapter explores how those who provide theories of the learning organisation employ systems dynamics. Strategic choice theory held that organisations change when their managers make choices about a wide range of issues. According to the theory of the learning organisation change flows from a process of organisational learning. It is when people in an organisation learn effectively together that it changes.

The chapter first summarises the key points of learning organisation theory made by Senge (1990) and then explores them in later sections. The key notions focused on are to do with mental models and their connection with learning, how learning in an organisation may be blocked and the role that leaders and groups play in this learning.

6.2 Senge's conception of the learning organisation

One of the most influential expositions of the concept of the learning organisation is that given by Senge (1990). Senge believes that an organisation excels when it is able to tap the commitment and capacity of its members to learn. He sees this capacity as intrinsic to human nature and he locates it in the individual, although he does see such learning as occurring when individuals experience profound teamwork. He identifies five disciplines required for an organisation that can truly learn.

Systems thinking

Senge understands organisations from the perspective of systems dynamics and holds that a learning organisation requires its people to think in systems terms. The last chapter reviewed at some length what he means by that. People should not think about their work purely in terms of their own roles. Instead, they should develop an understanding of the negative and positive feedback structure of the system of which they are a part. This should enable them to obtain some insight into the unexpected consequences of what they are doing. The purpose of thinking in systemic terms is to identify leverage points, that is, those points in the web of negative and positive feedback loops where change can have the largest beneficial effects. As in strategic choice theory, the purpose is to stay in control as much as is possible in a very complex system. This chapter will say no more about systems thinking because it was covered in the last chapter.

Personal mastery

The second discipline required in a learning organisation is personal mastery. Senge does not mean by this some form of domination but, rather, a high level of proficiency such as that possessed by a master craft worker. Those who have personal mastery consistently obtain the results that they want and it requires commitment to lifelong learning. It is a process of continually deepening one's personal vision, focusing energy, developing patience and seeing reality objectively. He links it with spiritual foundations. The strongly humanistic flavour of his view of human nature is evident and takes the same line of inspirational motivation as that described in Chapter 4 in relation to strategic choice theory.

Mental models

The third discipline required for the learning organisation is an understanding of the notion of mental models. These are deeply ingrained assumptions, or generalisations, often taking the form of pictures or images. Individuals are mostly not aware of their mental models. They are hidden, or unconscious, mental constructions. Senge emphasises how mental models restrict perceptions and points to Royal Dutch Shell, claiming that it developed the skill of surfacing and challenging the mental models of managers. Mental models are internal pictures of the world and he claims that individuals can learn to surface them and subject them to rigorous scrutiny. Institutional learning is a process in which management teams work together to change their shared mental models of their company and its markets.

This is, of course, pure cognitivism of exactly the same kind as that assumed in strategic choice theory. The whole topic of mental models and learning to change them will be the subject of the next section.

Building a shared vision

The fourth discipline of the learning organisation is that of building a shared discipline. A shared vision inspires people to learn. It is a lofty goal and requires the skill of identifying inspiring pictures of the future. It is important that this vision should not be dictated but developed by people working together. Again, the humanistic foundations of this idea are evident.

Team learning

The final discipline of the learning organisation is that of team learning. Senge maintains that teams can learn and when they do the intelligence of the team exceeds that of the individual members and produces extraordinary results. When this happens the individuals learn more rapidly too. The basis of team learning is dialogue and Senge's discussion of dialogue is based on the views of Bohm (1965, 1983; Bohm and Peat, 1989). According to Bohm, dialogue means the free flow of meaning through a group of people, allowing them to discover insights not attainable individually. This is a collective phenomenon that occurs when a group of people becomes open to the flow of a larger intelligence. Bohm talks about a new kind of mind that comes into existence. People are said to participate in this pool of common meaning, which is not accessible individually. He talks about the whole organising the parts. The whole here is this common pool of meaning, a kind of transcendent mind analogous to the idea in quantum physics that the universe is an indistinguishable whole. This is Bohm's idea of an implicate order that is unfolded by experience. The parts in this way of thinking are individual mental maps that guide and shape individual perceptions. Here, Bohm is clearly thinking in terms of formative causality, in which the future is the unfolding of what is already enfolded as implicate order, rendering any true novelty impossible. This idea of an already enfolded implicate order is expressed in the notion of a common pool of meaning, a kind of transcendent whole or group mind which people access when they interact with each other in dialogue. Bohm takes a perspective in which there is *both* a collective pool of meaning *and* an individual mind that is shaped by the common pool, quite outside individuals, in dialogue.

For Bohm and Senge, then, dialogue is a special kind of collaborative conversation, quite distinct from discussion, which is primarily competitive. Dialogue, as special conversation with a life of its own, is said to be rare nowadays and the call is for a return to ancient wisdom, to ways characteristic of so-called 'more primitive' people who used to practise it. North American Indians are often given as an example of the few people who still practise it today. Senge says that when we do (rarely) experience dialogue nowadays, it is a chance product of circumstance. So he calls for systematic effort and disciplined practice of the art of dialogue, which we need to rediscover to satisfy a deep longing. If we do it right we will all win. In order to do it right, people have to participate in a particular way: they must suspend, that is, be aware of, their assumptions; they must regard each other as colleagues and friends; and there should be a facilitator present who holds the context. Resistance and defensive routines are then diminished and dialogue can take place. Bohm claims that in these circumstances people can become observers of their own thinking and that once they see the participative nature of their thought they separate themselves from it. Conflict then becomes conflict between thoughts and not conflict between people. Dialogue, therefore, offers a safe environment in which it can be balanced with discussion. Dialogue becomes a new tool and a prescription for management behaviour (Isaacs, 1999), although Bohm himself thought dialogue was virtually impossible in hierarchical organisations.

Team learning also requires skill in identifying factors that block true dialogue. These blockages must be recognised and surfaced. Senge claims that it is teams rather than individuals that learn. The points about blockages to learning and about the role of groups in that learning will be taken up in later sections of this chapter. It is important to signal here, though, how Senge handles this question of the individual and the team. It sounds as though he is making the group primary to the individual. However, this is not so. Although he says that it is the team that learns, when he develops what he means by team learning it is clear that he is saying that an effective team provides the context within which a number of individuals together learn more than they could on their own. It is still the individuals who learn. They arrive to form a team and the atmosphere of that team then affects their capacity for learning together. Part Three will take a very different view of the relationship between the individual and the group, arguing that individual minds are formed by the group while they form it at the same time. This perspective also takes a very different view of the nature of conversation, avoiding the positing of a special form called dialogue in the way that Bohm and Senge do.

The key points that Senge makes will now be explored more fully in the sections that follow, starting with mental models and the notion of single- and double-loop learning.

6.3   Mental models: single- and double-loop learning

One of the foundations upon which the notion of single- and double-loop learning is built is research on human cognitive ability. According to this research, humans are capable of retaining only up to seven bits of information in the short-term memory at any one time. A bit is a digit, or a letter of the alphabet, or some chunk of them such as a word. The new information-processing capacity of the human brain is thus limited. The capacity of the long-term memory is apparently infinite, but it takes seconds to store new information in that long-term memory. Human ability to absorb and process new information is therefore painfully slow, much slower than computers. However, human ability to recognise patterns in information and to extract new meaning from them is considerably greater than that of computers. Note how it is assumed that brains store information in much the same way as computers – the cognitivist position.

Humans are therefore compelled by their limited brain capacity for processing new information to simplify everything they observe; they are unable to know reality itself; all they can do is construct simplifications, that is, mental models of reality. What they discover and therefore what they choose and how they act, all depend upon the mental model they bring to the task. When they look at a particular situation, they see it through the lens provided by the mental models built up through past experience and education. Humans approach each situation every day with a mindset, a recipe they have acquired from the past, that they use to understand the present in order to design actions to cope with it. When they take actions that fail to have the desired result, the reason often lies in the way the problem is perceived in the first place. The remedy is to amend the mental model, the perspective, the mindset, the paradigm with which the task is being approached.

The methods used to store mental models and to use what has been stored for subsequent discovery and choice have important implications. Research on cognitive ability claims that people do not normally store what they have previously observed and processed in any detailed form. They only store items and recall them in exact detail in exceptional circumstances, for example when they learn the lines of a play or prepare for certain kinds of examination. Normally people store and recall only some important category features of the items observed. It is as if people label items according to the category they belong to, according to the strength of association they have with other similar items. People are said to store schemas, frames or scenes, particularly noting exceptions. Mental models are sketchy, incomplete constructs used in a feedback way to affect what is discovered next (Baddeley, 1990). When confronted by some situation people do not observe its complete detail. They select certain items and fill in others using previously stored frames or scenes. Experiments have shown that people can be quite convinced that they have witnessed an event, even though it has not occurred, simply because that event normally occurred in a particular situation the experimenter now presents (Baddeley, 1990).

These points about how people build partial, loose, flexible mental models based on similarities and irregularities in the patterns of events observed, and then use them later partially to reconstruct what they then observe, are said to be of great importance to an understanding of management. These points mean that managers will not simply observe a given environment and a given organisational capability – the facts. They, like all other humans, will sometimes inevitably invent what they observe. The whole process of simplifying and selecting means that the environment is in a real sense the invention and the creation of the managers observing it. It will then only be possible for managers to make sense of what they are doing after they have done it (Weick, 1969/1979). In highly complex and uncertain situations, then, explanations of strategic management need to take account of the possibility that environments may be invented or created in managers' minds and that they can often only make sense of what they are doing with hindsight.

Mental models

So far, a number of ways in which humans compensate for their limited brain-processing capacity have been referred to. According to learning organisation theory, they simplify complex reality by constructing mental models of that reality in which data are classified in loose categories. They store those models and use them later to understand the next situation and indeed to fill in some of the detail of the next situation. They do not always use algorithmic step-by-step reasoning, but sometimes make intuitive jumps. In this way they can handle far greater levels of complexity and uncertainty, as well as far faster rates of change, than a straightforward use of processing capacity would allow. But the consequence of this way of operating is that people may invent the reality around them.

In addition to all this there are two further means of great importance that are said to be used to compensate for the limited capacity of the brain to process new information in a complex world. First, mental models are automated, so speeding up the process of recall and application to a new situation. Secondly, those automated models are shared with others to cut down on the need to communicate before acting together.

Experts and unconscious mental models

A person would function very slowly if for every action that person had consciously to retrieve and examine large numbers of previously acquired mental models and then choose an appropriate one. Experts therefore push previously acquired models below the level of awareness into the unconscious mind. One aspect of learning is through repetition of an action in order to make the design of later similar actions an automatic process. The expert seems to use some form of recognisable pattern in a new situation automatically to trigger the use of past models developed in relation to analogous previous situations. Experts do not examine the whole body of their expertise when they confront a new situation. Instead they detect recognisable similarity in the qualitative patterns of what they observe and automatically produce models which they modify to meet the new circumstances.

For example, an expert chess player differs from a novice in terms of the richness of their mental store of patterns and relationships between the pieces on a chess board. On being confronted with some new juxtaposition of pieces, the expert perceives patterns missed by the novice. It is from these perceptions that the expert derives superiority. This conclusion is supported by the fact that the expert is no better than the novice in deciding what to do when the pieces have been set out randomly. It is not therefore that the expert has a better short-term memory or can process information faster. The expert's superiority arises because models of the moves appropriate to different patterns are stored in the expert's memory and drawn on as required through some form of analogous reasoning.

Analogy has been found to pervade thought. People use analogies to make the novel seem familiar by relating it to prior knowledge. They use analogies to make the familiar seem strange by viewing it from a new perspective. These are fundamental aspects of human intelligence used to construct new scientific theories, design experiments and solve new problems in terms of old ones (Gick and Holyoak, 1983).

One form of learning, then, is that which uses some form of repetition to push mental models into the unconscious where they can be recalled and used very rapidly. The richer the store of unconscious models the more expert the person. This is single-loop learning. Each time people act they learn from the consequences of the action to improve the next action, without having consciously to retrieve and examine the unconscious models being used to design the action.

But expert behaviour based on single-loop learning and unconscious mental models brings not only benefits; it carries with it significant dangers. The fact that the mental models being used to design actions are unconscious means that they are not being questioned. The more expert one is, the more rapidly one acts on the basis of unconscious models. This means that one more easily takes for granted the assumptions and simplifications upon which the mental models are inevitably built. This is highly efficient in stable circumstances but when those circumstances change rapidly it becomes highly dangerous – in other words, it is an appropriate way to learn in conditions close to certainty and agreement, but more and more dangerous the further one moves away from certainty and agreement. Mental models used without question can rapidly become inappropriate in rapidly changing conditions. The possibility of skilled incompetence (Argyris, 1990) then arises. The more expert people are, that is, the more skilled they are in designing certain actions, the greater the risk that they will not question what they are doing. It follows that they are more likely to become skilled incompetents. This gives rise to the need for double-loop learning. Here people learn not only in the sense of adjusting actions in the light of their consequences, but in the sense also of questioning and adjusting the unconscious mental models being used to design those actions in the first place.

To summarise, mental models are the simplifications that humans construct and store in their brains of the world they encounter. These models are the lenses through which they perceive the world they have to operate in, the constructions they make to explain how it and they are behaving, the structures they use to design their actions. These models are based on loose, flexible categories of information, where categories appear to be defined in terms of similarity and irregularity. In totally new situations, people use processes of analogous reasoning to construct new mental models using those already stored. Coping with the world can be seen as a continuing feedback from one set of models to another.

People automate mental models by pushing them into the unconscious – this is the process of becoming an expert. Some models, the expert ones, are therefore implicit and hardly ever questioned while others are explicit and are more likely to be questioned. The latter are the explanations of what people are doing that they articulate. People share the expert unconscious models when they work together in a group. Automation and sharing lead to the strong possibility of expert incompetence and groupthink when conditions are changing rapidly. In the literature a number of words are used to mean much the same thing as mental models – paradigms, mindsets, frames of reference, company and industry recipes, schemas, scripts. Note that the culture of a group is its shared mental model according to this perspective.

Teams and shared models

Managers do not choose and act as isolated individuals. They interact with each other, choosing and acting in teams or groups. Simply by being part of a group, individuals learn to share the mental models they use to discover, choose and act. In this way they cut down on the communication and information flows that are required before they can act together. In particular, the more they share those implicit, expert models that have been pushed into the unconscious, the less they need to communicate in order to secure cohesive action. This sharing of implicit models is what is meant by the culture of the group or the organisation. Groups and organisations develop cultures, company and industry recipes or retained memories, as they perform together, in order to speed up their actions.

Individuals who are part of any group are put under strong pressure by group processes to conform, that is, to share the mental models of the other members. While this may have great benefits in terms of efficient action in stable conditions, it becomes a serious liability when conditions are changing rapidly. It then becomes necessary to question the implicit, unconscious group models that are being used to design actions. As conditions change the unquestioned models may well become inappropriate. The powerful pressures that grow up within groups of experts to accept rather than question very fundamental values open up the strong possibility of skilled incompetence in group behaviour, of groupthink.

Espoused models and models in use

People overcome limited brain-working capacity to produce unlimited mental capacity by simplifying and selecting, building models, automating those models by pushing them below the level of awareness, and learning to share them with others in their group. They use qualitative similarities and dissimilarities between one situation and another to develop more appropriate models in new situations. Managers design their expert actions in this way, just as physicians and physicists do. The more expert an individual or a group, the more actions are designed in ways determined by unconscious, implicit models. Because the assumptions under-lying those models are not surfaced and questioned it is quite possible that experts will articulate one model while designing their actions according to another. There may well be a difference between espoused models and models in use (Argyris and Schon, 1978). Experts are quite likely to say one thing and do another. The more expert people become in working together as a group the more prone they are to do this too. Ask managers what they do and most will say that they organise and plan. Observe what managers actually do and you may see that they dash from one task to another in a manner which is not very planned or organised.

When it is recognised that there are frequent differences between what expert managers say they are doing and what they are actually doing, differences of which they themselves are not usually aware, it can be seen how easy it is for managers to play games and build organisational defences against facing up to what is really happening (Argyris, 1990). For example, most managers espouse a rational model of action and believe that they should uncover the facts and consider a sensible range of options before they take action. Most espouse free and open discussions because that is a rational position to take. But at the same time there is a widespread norm in organisations requiring subordinates to withhold the truth from their superiors, especially if they believe that the superior will find the truth unwelcome and accuse them of being negative. Games of deception and cover-up are therefore played. All know they are being played but none openly discusses what is happening, despite espousal of rational behaviour. Managers sometimes say one thing, do the direct opposite, and rarely find this strange. Add to this the exis-tence of skilled incompetence and you can see how very difficult it will be to change these games and break down these defences. Attempts to explain how strategic management is actually carried out and attempts to prescribe how to do it better will be misleading and perhaps dangerous unless they explicitly recognise the existence of skilled incompetence, the difference between espoused models and models in use, and the behavioural dynamics these lead to. These are matters that I will deal with in more detail later in this chapter. I turn now, however, to a further examination of how mental models are used and changed; that is, the process of learning and the single- and double-loop forms that it takes.

Single- and double-loop learning

The single-loop form of learning can be illustrated by the activity of reviewing a budget and taking corrective action. There is a monitoring, or discovery, step in which an actual profit outcome is compared with the desired outcome set in the budget. If actual is below budget, the reason is discovered, a choice of corrective action is made, and action is taken. That action affects profit in the next period as do external changes, leading to the need for the next round of discovery, choice and action. Managers involved in this single loop are controlling and they are also learning. They are discovering the consequences of their actions and amending their behaviour according to what they discover. This kind of learning is single loop because managers are not questioning what they are doing in any fundamental sense. The budget, for example, is not questioned. Taking another example, General Motors thought that high fuel costs and therefore smaller cars were the key issues and Japanese competence in offering small cars the key reason for their success in the 1970s. General Motors' managers focused on this explanation, never questioning their assumptions, and so missed the importance of quality as the source of competitive advantage. This kind of single-loop learning is depicted in Figure 6.1.

Now consider what these managers would do if they were to learn in a double-loop way. When they analyse why profit is coming in below budget, they do so using their expertise, that is, the implicit unconscious mental models they have built up through past experience and have come to share through working together. They

Figure 6.1   Single-loop learning

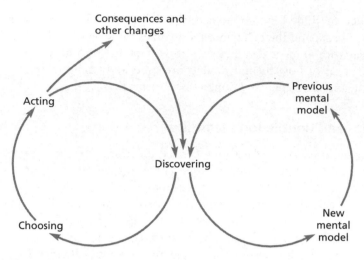

Figure 6.2   Double-loop learning

have a recipe on how their organisation and its industry or environment work. The reasons they produce to account for poor profit performance will be determined by these unconscious shared mental models. Consequently their choice and their action will also depend on these mental models. In the single-loop case they do not surface what the model is or question it; they simply use it. In double-loop learning they would, as part of the discovery stage, surface and question that model. They would be discovering not only what is changing outside and what the consequences of their actions are, but also what this all means for the unconscious models they are using, for their recipes and received wisdom. This simultaneous journey around two loops is depicted in Figure 6.2.

Double-loop learning, then, involves changing a mental model, a recipe, a mindset, a frame of reference or a paradigm. It is a very difficult process to perform simply because one is trying to examine assumptions one is not normally even aware one is making. People will therefore keep slipping into single-loop learning because that is easier. But it is important to encourage double-loop learning since it is this that produces innovation. Managers who would innovate need constantly to be shifting, breaking and creating paradigms – they must engage in double-loop learning.

To summarise, single-loop learning is when one learns from the consequences of previous actions to amend the next action. It is a feedback process from action to consequence to subsequent action, without questioning the mental model driving the action.

Double-loop learning involves another feedback loop. It occurs when the consequences of actions lead to a questioning of the mental model, the underlying assumptions, that have been driving the actions. That questioning may lead to the amendment of the mental model, the reframing of the problem or opportunity, before action is amended. There is a double loop in which not only are actions amended, but the model driving the actions is too. Double-loop learning requires destruction – old ways of viewing the world have to be destroyed. Double-loop learning also involves creation – new ways of viewing the world have to be developed. Double-loop learning is the shifting, breaking and creating of paradigms.

- Single-loop forms of organisational learning take the form of negative feedback loops in which groups of people review and learn from the actions they have just undertaken.
- Single-loop forms of learning are conducted within a given paradigm and sustain the group learning in a state of stability, moving towards the realisation of a vision or the achievement of a goal.
- Double-loop learning is partly the negative feedback learning about the consequences of actions, but also partly an amplifying, positive feedback loop of questioning the underlying assumptions.
- Double-loop learning is therefore potentially destabilising and revolutionary, but it is vitally necessary for innovation.

6.4   Covert political processes and their impact on organisational learning

Double-loop learning begins when people question their own unique mental models and when together they start questioning the mental models they share with each other. As soon as they do this they arouse fears to do with failing to produce anything that functions in place of what they are destroying, as well as the fear of embarrassing themselves and others with questioning and discussion that may appear incompetent, or threatening or even crazy. As soon as such fears are aroused people automatically defend themselves by activating defence routines of one kind or another. The raising of such defensive routines in an organisational setting is what I mean by covert politics. It is a form of game playing that all are aware is going on but which all agree, tacitly, not to discuss (Argyris, 1990).

Organisational defence routines

One of the main reasons for the failure of groups of people to engage in double-loop learning is that the questioning of deeply held individual and shared assumptions about the world in which they are operating may well provoke and reinforce powerful organisational defence routines that are very difficult to identify and even more difficult to deal with effectively (Argyris, 1990). The activation of such defence routines is a specific example of a general point: namely, that complex systems tend to counteract planned changes to the system because they also unintentionally provoke positive feedback loops called organisational defence routines.

For example, top managers may try to abandon a command and control model of managing in the belief that this will make their organisation more flexible and entrepreneurial. This may be an example of double-loop learning if they are genuinely trying to question the assumptions underlying their currently shared mental model of management – the command and control one. Consider first what is meant by a command and control model of managing. It is one in which:

- the manager's power is derived from position in the hierarchy;
- people are motivated by the task; and
- people respond most to short-term rewards in relation to task achievement.

These beliefs about the source of power and the way to motivate people are closely associated with the suppression of negative feelings and judgements about people's performance. Such judgements are usually not publicly exposed and tested in case they upset and demotivate others, so reducing levels of task performance. Instead evaluations are made privately and covered up in public – covert politics. All understand that this is what is happening but they accept it as a necessary defence against hurting people's feelings and against the consequent organisational inefficiency.

When a manager is fired, this is frequently presented as a resignation due to health reasons or some other factor. Memoranda are distributed thanking the fired person for years of valued contributions. All know that this is a tissue of lies but none publicly say so. This is an example of a defence routine, a game people play to protect each other from having to face unpleasant organisational truths in public. As a result, the real reason for firing the person, a judgement that the person is incompetent, is never properly examined; it could well have been unjustified and turn out to be harmful to the performance of the organisation.

These kinds of beliefs about control lead to win/lose dynamics in which people adopt tactics of persuasion and selling, only superficially listening to others. People driven by win/lose behaviour also tend to use face-saving devices for themselves and each other. They save face by avoiding the public testing of the assumptions they are making about each other's motives or statements. This behaviour produces skilled incompetence: skilled in that the behaviour is automatic; incompetent in that it produces obstacles to work, real learning and effective decision making. These obstacles take the form of organisational defence routines that become embedded in behaviour and are extremely difficult to change.

Defence routines become so entrenched in organisations that they come to be viewed as inevitable parts of human nature. Managers make self-fulfilling prophecies about what will happen at meetings, because they claim it is human nature; they indulge in the game playing, so confirming their belief in human nature. The defence routines, game playing and cover-ups can become so disruptive that managers actually avoid discussing contentious issues altogether. Even if this extreme is not reached, the dysfunctional learning behaviour blocks the detection of gradually accumulating small changes, the surfacing of different perspectives, the thorough testing of proposals through dialogue. When they use the control management model with the organisational defence routines it provokes, managers struggle to deal with strategic issues. They end up preparing long lists of strengths and weaknesses, opportunities and threats that simply get them nowhere. They produce mission statements that are so bland as to be meaningless, visions not connected to reality, and long-term plans that are simply filed. Or they may decide on an action and then not implement it.

Managers collude in this behaviour and refrain from discussing it. They then distance themselves from what is going on and blame others, the chief executive or the organisational structure when things go wrong. They look for solutions in general models, techniques, visions and plans. All the while the real causes of poor strategic management – the learning process itself, the political interaction and the group dynamic – remain stubbornly undiscussable.

People within an organisation collude in keeping matters undiscussable because they fear the consequences if they do not. Consultants too find themselves sucked into defence routines because they are nervous of the consequences of exposing them – they may be fired. The result of the defence routines I have been talking about is passive employees and managers, highly dependent upon authority, who are not well equipped to handle rapid change. In these conditions, managers produce vague, impractical prescriptions as a defence against having to do anything in difficult situations, such as 'we need more training' or 'we need a vision'. The organisation loses out on the creativity of people because of the management model it uses.

The way out of this impasse, proposed by Argyris, is for managers and managed to reflect jointly, as a group, on the processes they are engaged in. If this can be perceived as a challenge rather than a potential source of embarrassment and fear, then managers are able to engage in double-loop learning. For example, joint reflection might lead them to consider the extent to which:

- power flows from expertise and contribution, not simply position in the hierarchy;
- people are motivated primarily by their own internal commitment; and
- people respond to long-term rewards.

These beliefs about power and motivation are said to encourage the public exposure and testing of relevant feelings and judgements, even if they are negative, in order to ensure that decisions are being taken on the basis of valid data. Behaviour according to such a 'commitments' model should lead to co-operative dynamics and mutual control, allowing people to put their own creativity to use for the organisation.

The problem is that the attempt to move to such a 'commitment' model is itself likely to provoke the damping feedback loops of organisational defences. When people behave according to the control model, they set off damping loops of organisational defence which have the effect of blocking the double-loop learning process, so trapping an organisation in a state of stable equilibrium – that is, within the same mental model. One of the main fears touching off such damping loops is the fear that managers have of losing control. This can quite easily completely immobilise learning, decision making and action.

The fear of losing control

If people are to engage in double-loop learning then they must expose relevant negative feelings, the basis of the judgements they make on the performance of others, the cover-ups and games they are playing.

Such learning is therefore bound to upset people and to arouse management fears of losing control. Such fears will reduce commitment to double-loop learning, and consistent with the control model they are still using, even though they are trying to get away from it, people will also tend to conceal the diminishing commitment. The effect is to reduce the effectiveness of any attempt to engage in double-loop learning and the possibility of switching to some other model of control. The harder they try, the more it provokes the fears that impede it.

The result is a positive feedback loop running from the control mental model to anomalies and contradictions that weaken the control model and build up an alternative model. But movement around this loop itself touches off movement around another loop. This is a negative, damping loop that undermines the complex learning process and therefore strengthens the control model.

The problems pointed to in this section are primarily due to the fact that people try to hang on to their existing model of how to learn as they learn. How can they overcome this? Well, one popular prescription for promoting the learning organisation is that of empowering people throughout the organisation, where empowerment is equated with democracy, dispersed power and widespread participation. However, simply dispersing power, inviting widespread participation, is no guarantee whatsoever that the organisation will function more effectively or make better decisions. First, widespread participation means that, although more people are being invited to take part in decision making, they are all still using the control model. There are simply more people behaving incompetently. There is no guarantee that lower-level managers or employees behave better than top executives. While the larger numbers involved in decision making continue to use the control model they simply spread the win/lose dynamics more widely. The negative damping loops of organisational defences will be reinforced. Widespread participation is no

---

Figure 6.3

Defence routines and covert politics: main points on organisational dynamics

- The behaviour of people in organisations is dominated by what Argyris has called the control model of management. This is usually operated within a pluralistic political system, in which a number of groupings have countervailing power.
- Use of the control model, the existence of different power groups, leads to win/lose behavioural dynamics. Here people employ a number of organisational defence mechanisms to protect themselves and others from the consequences of the win/lose pressures. They play games and make matters undiscussable. Consequently, decisions are often not made on the basis of valid data, implementation of decisions is often obstructed, small changes go undetected for lengthy periods. In short the ability of the organisation to develop strategically is severely impaired.
- But movement from the control model/pluralistic political system is fraught with difficulty. The most widespread idea of what to move to is a commitment model of control operating within a collegiate political system. This is the OD programme. Movement away from the control model, and particularly movement to the collegial model, touches off many positive amplifying feedback loops which undermine that movement.
- These positive feedback loops are activated because any attempt to change an organisation in a fundamental way upsets the balance and nature of power and raises the levels of uncertainty and ambiguity. All of these changes increase anxieties of one kind or another. And it is the anxiety that provokes positive feedback loops.

guarantee of more effective learning or better decision making at all. People first have to learn how to operate on the basis of continuing complex learning and that is very difficult to achieve. Simply inviting people to do so will not have the required result. Widespread participation is no guarantee of better learning.

Emotion plays a major role in this double-loop learning process. As soon as people embark upon double-loop learning they must confront their own fear of failing. This triggers avoidance of the fear, and hence the learning, altogether by engaging in organisational defence routines – summarised in Figure 6.3. If people can hold the fear, see it as a challenge, then they can proceed with the double-loop learning.

6.5   The impact of vested interests on organisational learning

The previous section looked at how attempts to learn in a double-loop way can give rise to a number of fears, such as the fear of failing, of being embarrassed and of embarrassing others. These fears tend to trigger defensive routines, game playing and covert politics that block the learning. The whole point of double-loop learning is to bring about organisational change and it is highly likely that change of an important kind will alter power relations between people. Change threatens vested interests and the prospect of losing power is likely to trigger action to prevent this from happening. That action is also likely to block the process of double-loop learning. In other words, the nature of an organisation's political system, the way in which power is used, is likely to have an important impact on its capacity to learn.

Authoritarian use of power

The authoritarian use of power may be relatively benign when it is based on legitimate positions in the hierarchy and exercised according to the accepted procedures of the organisation. This is likely to be accompanied by a group dynamic of compliance, especially when followers strongly share the same ideology. Compliance amounts to the suspension of intellectual and moral judgement about the appropriateness of superiors' choices and actions. People then willingly do what the powerful want (Bacharach and Lawler, 1980). Clearly this is incompatible with double-loop learning. Where power is exercised as force over unwilling followers the dynamics tends to be much more volatile. It is characterised by sullen acceptance, covert resistance and at times outright rebellion. Again, this is inimical to double-loop learning.

Collegial use of power

Highly authoritarian political systems based on mechanistic rules are, however, rather rare in practice. There is far more likely to be a complex pluralistic political system in which power is already spread around an organisation in groups with vested interests (Greiner and Schein, 1988). Thus, the typical modern corporation does not have a political system in which one or two powerful executives at the top control what goes on throughout the company. Instead there are powerful subsidiary companies and powerful departments in many different parts of the organisation and those at the top have to sustain enough support to govern. Any change of any significance is going to affect the balance of power, making one department, subsidiary company or management grouping weaker or stronger than it was before. Any sign of change will touch off fears that such power shifts might occur even before it is clear what they might be. People and groups will therefore start taking protective action as soon as they get wind of any possible change.

Any attempt to engage in double-loop learning, to change mental models, is likely to be just such a change, one that is directly concerned with changing power positions. It is therefore highly likely to touch off damping feedback loops of a political nature that will undermine and perhaps eventually destroy it. The more people are persuaded to move to a consensus collegiate way of making choices, the more powerful groups with vested interests are threatened and the more likely they are to put a stop to the programme. The more managers try to head off this threat, the more they have to play by the rules of the political system they are trying to replace. If they do this they simply reinforce what they are trying to remove.

Once again, initiatives will fail if they do not recognise and deal with the damping feedback loops that are always present in organisations. And how to deal with these loops is far from clear.

Power vacuums and organised anarchies

If managers do succeed in installing a collegiate political system and the commitment management model, yet other damping feedback loops may be activated by the shift in the distribution of power.

As authority and other forms of power are dispersed, as organisational structures are flattened, as job descriptions become looser and as the establishment of widespread consensus comes to be required before decisions are possible, so the likelihood of a power vacuum at the centre increases. It becomes more and more difficult for anyone to exercise much authority; more and more people have to be able to handle their own independence. In situations in which most people seek the comfort of dependency this could create serious difficulties. One way of understanding the consequences of changes in power distribution is provided by Greiner and Schein (1988).

Greiner and Schein use the device given in Figure 6.4 to relate changes in willingness to assert and to accept power to the consequent group dynamic. When both leaders and followers consent freely to the exercise of power, there is a high probability of active consensus. When the leader exerts power but the followers do not consent, then we get the behaviour of covert resistance. It can be seen from Figure 6.4 that as the leader becomes less able or willing to exert power, while followers still look for a lead, then the behaviour is that of passive loyalty. If, in the same circumstances, the followers too become less willing to accept the exercise of power, the group's behaviour is characterised by peer rivalry.

So the dispersal of power and the spread of participation could set off feedback loops in which declining central power leads to greater rivalry throughout the organisation, or to passive loyalty, both of which will block double-loop learning.

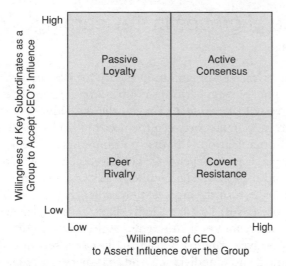

Figure 6.4   Power and group dynamics

Source: L. E. Greiner and V. E. Schein (1988), *Power and Organization Development: Mobilizing Power to Implement Change*, Reading, MA: Addison-Wesley.

Figure 6.5

Vested interests: main points on organisational dynamics

- Positive feedback loops are activated by any attempt to change an organisation in a fundamental way. This is because change upsets the balance and nature of power and raises the levels of uncertainty and ambiguity. Consequent anxiety provokes offsetting negative feedback loops.
- One feedback loop has to do with the fears of existing power groups that they will lose control. As change programmes are pushed, so these fears are increased, leading usually to covert undermining of the programme. Organisational defence routines are then strengthened rather than weakened.
- Dispersing power and weakening central authority can set off loops leading to peer rivalry or passive loyalty. Both determine creativity and decision-making ability.

Indeed events could be much more complex than this if at the same time levels of uncertainty and ambiguity are raised by loosely defining people's jobs.

The point to be made here is this. When decision-making procedures are highly unstructured, as they tend to be when power is dispersed and widespread participation invited, then the particular decision taken on a particular occasion will depend almost entirely on the detailed context at the time. Here context means details such as: who attended the meeting at which the decision was taken; how important those attending were; what other matters they had on their minds. In this sense the particular decision made comes to depend upon chance. And in these circumstances there is a high level of probability that decisions will be postponed and, even if made, not implemented.

The main points are summarised in Figure 6.5.

● ● ● ● 6.6 The role of groups in the learning organisation

The kind of group that learning organisation theory focuses on is the team and the key question is what kind of team performs double-loop learning effectively.

Argyris (1957) stressed the conflict between the individual and the group. He maintained that there is a conflict between the needs of healthy individuals and the demands of formal organisation. Chains of command and task specialisation require people to be passive and dependent, but psychologically mature individuals seek to be unique and different. The conflict leads to frustration, hostility and rivalry and a focus on a part of the organisation rather than the whole, as well as a focus on short-term objectives. To adapt, individuals develop defence routines that then feed back into the organisation and reinforce the adverse effects. The learning theory developed by Argyris, summarised in the last two sections, is built on this view that a group is made up of individuals and that there is a fundamental conflict between being an individual and being in a group.

From this perspective, the key concern is that of understanding how a group can evolve into a functioning team in which individuals can learn. The basic premise is that this will happen when people can engage in true dialogue rather than in the kind of defensive conversational cover-ups discussed in the previous section. This requires that members of a group trust each other enough to expose their shared assumptions to public scrutiny. It is held that this is possible only when the team is cohesive, that is, when there is good team spirit. Today, organisations spend considerable sums of money to provide social and training events where teams can be together in the belief that this fosters the required team spirit. In addition, attention is paid to the composition of the team in terms of different personality types. It is believed that a balance of different personality types will enable a team to function and learn effectively. This section looks at what has been written about phases in group development and about the effect of different compositions of membership in terms of personality type.

Patterns in small-group development

Gibbard, Hartman and Mann (1974) distinguish between models of group development, for example, linear progressive and life-cycle models. They describe these models in the following terms.

Linear progressive model

In the linear progressive model the explanations of group behaviour run in terms of progressive stages that the members of a group pass through and the resolutions they achieve in each stage before they can work effectively together. One of the best known descriptions of group development (Tuckman, 1965) identifies the four sequential steps that, it is claimed, all groups follow during the course of their development:

1 *Forming*. When people first come together to form a group, they go through a hesitant testing stage in which they begin to identify their task, form relationships and develop roles. It is a stage in which people are typically dependent and look for guidance.

2 *Storming*. Having acquired some sense of security, the members of a group then conflict over what it is they should be doing, how they should do it and what roles each should occupy. This is a stage of emotional expression.

3 *Norming*. The next stage is that of working through the conflict and developing shared values or norms to govern how they are to operate together. The outcome is conformity and cohesion.

4 *Performing*. This is the stage in which the group produces what it has gathered together to produce; it performs its primary task.

Lewin described the stages of change in an organisation and a group in terms of a period of 'unfreezing' (similar to forming and storming), followed by a period of 'reformulation' (similar to norming), followed in turn by 'refreezing' (similar to performing). Another model identifies two phases in group development, each of which consists of a number of subphases (Bennis and Shepard, 1956):

1 *The authority phase*. When people first come together to form a group they are preoccupied with the question of authority; that is, who is to be in charge, who is to be looked to for guidance, who is to be depended upon in performing the primary task? This phase is typically divided into subphases. First, people in the group behave in a submissive way, looking for and being willing to take guidance on what to do and how to do it. The hope is that some leader will provide the solutions that will allow the group to work. This is followed by the next subphase in which people rebel against those they have at first depended upon, hoping that conflict will provide a solution to the problems of group life. The third subphase is one in which members find a compromise solution and partial resolution of the dependency–authority/submission–rebellion issue, one that accepts their simultaneous presence.

2 *The interpersonal phase*. Once the group has at least partially worked through the questions of authority and dependence, submission and rebellion, the concern then becomes that of interdependence between the members of the group. The first subphase here is one in which members of the group identify with each other, the subphase of 'enchantment'. The psychological force here is a desire on the part of individuals to find the security that comes from fusing themselves into the group. This is a primitive defence in which members seek the route to performing their primary task through group cohesion. This gives way to the second subphase in which members of the group experience 'disenchantment' with their interdependence and seek to establish their own individuality and independence of the group. The third subphase here is one in which there is some resolution of the fusion–individuation tension, one in which fusion and individuation are both present.

It is easy to see how these models assume that groups move to stable equilibrium when they are effective. These models appear to assume that a group reaches a peak of efficient work and then ends or continues at that level.

Life-cycle models

Life-cycle models are an elaboration of the linear progressive models, the principal addition being the emphasis on the terminal phase for small groups. Thus Mills (1964) adds a stage of 'separation' in which the group begins to face and cope with its own death and members assess the success or failure of their efforts.

Having discussed how small groups develop, we now turn to the roles people take up in those small groups.

Roles and leadership in groups

In the formal system, leaders are appointed to an office in a bureaucracy, or perhaps elected to a position in some representative body, where they take charge of a group of people who have also been appointed or elected in some formal way. People come to their roles in a formal fashion in groups that already have structures, procedures, norms, cultures, systems, goals and relatively clear primary tasks. In these circumstances the important question quite clearly is one of identifying how groups can most effectively and efficiently perform the task and reach the goal. When it is observed that people, as they work together, have a natural tendency to develop informal social groupings in addition to the formal, the concern becomes one of harnessing that informal group to support and not obstruct the performance of the main task. The concern is with motivation and the prime role of the leader is to motivate, form the vision and clarify the cultural values. One then looks to personality traits, styles and skills as the determinants of good leaders. One reaches the conclusion that techniques and programmes can be installed to develop good leaders and cohesive groups, ones that are aware of the social and psychological self-realisation needs of individuals.

Jung stressed the differences between people that flow from the many archetypes that drive them. He identified a number of common psychological types, preferred ways of behaving and temperaments. From this perspective, patterns in the behaviour of small groups would be explainable from the manner in which different temperaments typically interact.

The impact of personality

Jung distinguished between preferences that go to make up different temperaments (Kiersey and Bates, 1978). First, people express preferred modes of behaviour somewhere between extroversion (E) and introversion (I). The E person derives energy from contact and interaction with others, while the I person is exhausted by such contact and seeks energy from internal, reflective sources.

Secondly, people have a preference along a spectrum that stretches from sensation (S) at one end to intuition (N) at the other. The S person prefers facts and knows through experience; such a person is firmly anchored to reality. The N person lives in anticipation and looks for change, skipping from one activity to another; such a person values hunches and prefers speculation.

The third pair of preferences is thinking (T) and feeling (F). The T person prefers the logical, impersonal basis for choice, while the F person prefers the personal, emotional basis.

Finally, there is the spectrum running from perceiving (P) to judging (J). The P person prefers to keep options open and fluid, seeing things from different points of view, while the J person prefers closure, that is, narrowing choices down and reaching solutions.

The 4 pairs of preferences lead to 16 possible temperament types and the possibility of having evenly balanced preferences adds a further 32 combinations to these. All these temperaments, however, can be sorted into four broad categories:

1 *The Dionysian or SP person.* As a manager this type of person prefers not to be tied down by routine, but focuses on the present, seeks action and tends to be impulsive.
2 *The Epimethean or ST person.* As a manager this type of person is dutiful and desires to belong to the organisation. Such a manager is careful, thorough and accurate, a giver rather than a taker.
3 *The Promethean or NT person.* As a manager this personality type is interested in power, control and predictability. They avoid the personal and emotional and want to be competent and in charge.
4 *The Apollonian or NF person.* As a manager this type makes intuitive decisions, seeks to be unique and finds it difficult to take negative criticism.

When people come together, their temperamental differences lead to misunderstandings and the widest gulf is that between the sensing and the intuitive types – the one insisting on logic and the facts, the other pushing proposals based on intuition and experience. People with the same personality type can also clearly have difficulties – a whole group of NT types all trying to control the group, for example, is a recipe for destructive conflict and inactivity. But differences bring contributions to relationships that would otherwise be lacking and some similarity provides the basis of understanding each other.

The behaviour patterns of groups of people would on this view be driven by the understanding and misunderstanding generated by the range of temperaments of the people constituting the group. The implication is that effective groups can be designed if one finds out enough about the personality composition of sets of people, or group functioning can be improved if one becomes more aware of the difficulties and contributions flowing from temperamental preferences.

Belbin's classification

Belbin has used teams of managers playing business games to identify the effects on group performance of different personality types (Belbin, 1981). He showed how some types work effectively together while others do not and that this has a greater impact on performance than the individual abilities of the people involved. Teams made up of people simply on the basis of their ability – how clever they are – do not make winning teams. Teams designed to include a balance of different personality types are much more likely to win even if they do not contain the most able individuals; it is actual contribution and interdependence that determine performance.

In Belbin's terms the basis of a good team is the Company Worker types – the conservative, dutiful and predictable, even if inflexible, people (much the same as the Epimethean manager above). These Company Workers are the basis of a good team because of the stability they provide and the steady work contributions they make.

This is not enough for superior performance, however. In addition a team needs members paired into the 'Chairman' (Promethean) and the 'Shaper' (Apollonian) types. The 'Chairman' is calm, self-confident and controlled, arouses the contributions of many types, has a strong sense of objectives, but is average in creative ability. The 'Chairman' therefore needs to be balanced with a 'Shaper' who is highly strung and dynamic, challenges complacency and self-deception, and is impatient and irritable. The team is strengthened by the addition of the 'Plant' (Apollonian) and the 'Resource Investigator' (Dionysian). The 'Plant' is an unorthodox individualist who contributes new ideas but is apt to be 'up in the clouds'. The 'Resource Investigator' is an enthusiastic extrovert, eager for challenge but apt to lose interest quickly. These two types need to be balanced with sober and prudent 'Monitor Evaluators' and the orderly, conscientious 'Completer Finishers' (both Epimethean). Finally, superior teams contain 'Team Workers' who are socially oriented but tend to be indecisive in times of crisis (Apollonian, perhaps).

6.7 How learning organisation theory deals with four key questions

At the end of Chapter 1, I posed four questions that I would ask of each of the theories of organisational change that this book is concerned with. They were:

1 How does the theory view the nature of interaction?
2 What view does it take of human nature?
3 What methodology does it employ?
4 How does it deal with paradox?

Then in Chapter 3, I examined the answers to these questions suggested by cybernetics and cognitivism. They are summarised in Figures 3.5 and 3.6. In Chapter 4, I looked at them again in relation to strategic choice theory as a whole. Figure 5.10 in Chapter 5 sets out the key points made in systems dynamics theories and by comparing it with Figures 3.5 and 3.6 one can see how the theories differ. In this section I will briefly review the questions again in relation to learning organisation theory. First, how does learning organisation theory deal with the nature of interaction?

The nature of interaction

Learning organisation theory sees interaction in systemic terms just as cybernetics does. It is concerned with how components, entities or individuals interact to produce patterns of behaviour. It understands the system in the terms of systems dynamics and this, like cybernetics, is a theory that focuses on the macro level. It identifies the feedback structure of the system. It does not attempt to model the micro detail of the entities constituting a dynamic system. Two assumptions are implicitly made about these entities, events or individuals in systems dynamics (Allen, 1998a):

- First, it is assumed that micro events occur at their average rate and that it is sufficient to take account of averages only. Interactions between entities are then homogeneous.
- Secondly, it is implicitly assumed that individual entities of a given type are identical, or, at least, that they have a normal distribution around the average type. The entities, or events, are thus implicitly assumed to be homogeneous. Within a category, distinctive identities and differences are not taken into account.

These assumptions make it possible to ignore the probabilistic dynamics governing the micro entities, events or individuals and model the system at the macro level. This is done by specifying the structure of negative and positive feedback loops that drive the system. For example, the beer distribution system, described in the last chapter, is specified in terms of damping and amplifying loops between orders, inventories and shipments between the different components of the system, namely customers, retailers, wholesalers and producers. Nothing is said about how customers, retailers, wholesalers and producers are organised or how they make decisions. This kind of model yields insight into the dynamics of the system as a whole and the possibility of unexpected outcomes. The way systems dynamics is used in learning organisation theory amounts to adding positive feedback loops to a cybernetic system. Systems dynamics is not used in a self-referential sense. I will explore in Chapter 11 how developments of systems dynamics point to how this might be done.

However, there are also major differences compared to cybernetics. Because of the presence of positive feedback loops the dynamics is no longer an automatic movement towards an equilibrium state. Instead, the system is a non-equilibrium one with the dynamics of fluctuating patterns that create considerable difficulties for prediction over longer time periods. However, it is claimed that if the feedback structure of the system is understood, then leverage points can be located. Action at these leverage points makes it possible to control the system. In the end, however, the theory of causality underlying systems dynamics is formative cause just as it is with cybernetics. In systems dynamics, the system unfolds archetypes already enfolded in it. People are still thought to be parts of a system and so not free. Because of its theory of causality, systems dynamics cannot explain novelty or creativity.

The nature of human beings

Learning organisation theory draws on cognitivist, constructivist and humanistic psychology to understand the nature of human beings. The cognitivist assumptions are particularly clear in that individuals are understood to act upon the basis of mental models built from previous experience and stored in the individual. They are representations of the individual's world. Part of each individual's model is shared with others and this forms the basis of their joint action together. The focus on the individual nature of these models, their representation function, the claim that they are stored and shared, the belief that they can be surfaced and subjected to rational scrutiny, are all hallmarks of a cognitivist psychology. However, the way in which mental models select some aspects of reality for attention and exclude others is a feature of a constructivist approach to psychology. The emphasis placed on individual vision and fulfilment, as part of the learning process, is evidence of the humanistic leaning in the theory of the learning organisation.

In all of these psychological theories the individual is held to be prior and primary to the group. Mental models are individual constructs that are shared with others. Effective teams are composed of a balance of different types of individual. Note, however, how differences between individuals do not feature in a fundamental way in the learning organisation theory. A small number of different categories may be identified but the difference is located between categories, while within those categories everyone is implicitly assumed to be the same. This is consistent with a systems dynamics approach in which micro entities are all assumed to be average and their interactions are assumed to be homogeneous. What I am trying to emphasise is this: cohesion and sharing are seen as the foundations of effective learning. There is no notion that deviant and eccentric behaviour might be essential to any creative and innovative thinking and behaving. In Part Three, I will be arguing that organisations change in novel ways through deviant behaviour.

The group is treated in a particular way. It consists of individuals and develops in phases, only some of which are conducive to members learning together as individuals.

So, learning organisation theory uses the same psychological theories as strategic choice theory but does place more emphasis on emotion and relationships between people. It also identifies more clearly what may block people from changing and learning. Perhaps the importance of power receives more attention but power is still located in the individual. However, there is no fundamental change in the view of human nature as one moves from the one theory to the other.

Methodology and organisational learning

The methodological stance in learning organisation theory is similar to that in strategic choice theory in some respects. A realist position is sometimes implied in which managers are assumed to be able to stand outside the system of which they are a part and think systemically about it. They are also supposed to be able to stand outside their own mental models, rigorously scrutinise them and then rationally change them. However, at other times an idealist position is suggested in that managers are assumed to respond not to the real world but to their idea of the real world as represented in their mental models.

Dealing with paradox

The notion of paradox does not play a fundamental part in learning organisation theory. Tensions, contradictions and dilemmas are certainly recognised but they are thought to be resolvable. As with strategic choice theory, learning organisation theory takes a position at one of the poles of what seem to me to be fundamental paradoxes of organisational life. This is very clear in the case of the individual and the group. I argue above that this is not seen as a paradox at all. The individual is given primacy and understood to be in fundamental conflict with the group. This conflict must be resolved through building relationships of trust in teams if learning is to take place. Sameness and difference are not held in mind at the same time. For example, individuals within a personality category are treated as if they were all the same and all different from individuals in another category. Although unpredictability is pointed to, it is predictability and the possibility of control that is emphasised. As with strategic choice theory, order, stability, consistency and harmony are all seen as prerequisites for success and the role that the opposites of these might play in creativity is largely ignored.

Making sense of experience

At this point, I invite you to reflect on how this theory assists you to make sense of your experience of life in organisations.

For me, the focus on learning, and what blocks it, provides a rich addition to strategic choice theory when it comes to making sense of my experience. I certainly recognise my own involvement in defence routines and political struggles. I also recognise the difficulty of learning in a fundamental way. However, I think the theory holds out a rather idealised picture of what it is possible for people in an organisation to do.

For example, Argyris reports that he has worked with large numbers of managers in many countries, coaching them to engage in double-loop learning. He reports that they find it difficult and rarely engage in it when they return to their workplace. Instead, they carry on with their win/lose dynamics and their defence routines. I think this immediately raises a question mark over his theory on learning as a change in mental models. Many organisations clearly do change, often in quite creative ways. How does this happen if double-loop learning is such a rarity? Furthermore, I wonder whether it really is possible for people to surface their mental models and change them. Where are they located? It is far from clear that brains store anything that could be correlated with a map or a model. If it is possible for people to identify assumptions of which they are unaware and change them, then why is mental illness so prevalent and difficult to deal with? I greatly doubt my own ability to identify whatever it is that makes me think the way I do, and then simply change it.

In the hurly-burly of organisational life, with its political intrigues and the possibility of losing one's job, is it at all wise to expose the defence routines that one is taking part in? If it is so important to do so, why is it so rare to find people doing it?

When I ask myself questions such as these I have serious doubts about the practicality of the prescriptions this theory presents for successful organisational learning. For example, the kind of conversation that the theory of organisational learning presents is a special kind called dialogue which has the rather mystical tones of people participating in a common pool of meaning as if it were an already existing whole outside of their experience. There seems to be no constructive place here for ordinary conversation. Also participation has a special meaning – participation in some whole system outside of our direct experience of interacting with each other (Griffin, 2001).

●●●● 6.8   Summary

This chapter has reviewed learning organisation theory. According to this theory, organisations are systems driven by both positive and negative feedback loops. The interactions between such loops tend to produce unexpected and often counterintuitive outcomes. Perfect control is not possible but it is possible to identify leverage points where control may be exerted. Perhaps the most important loops relate to learning. Organisations learn when people in cohesive teams trust each other enough to expose the assumptions they are making to the scrutiny of others and then together change shared assumptions which block change. The theory identifies some important behaviours that block this learning process. Although learning organisation theory uses a different systems theory to strategic choice theory, its conceptualisation of that systems theory in terms of feedback loops keeps it close to cybernetics. Learning organisation theory is built on the same psychological theories as strategic choice theory. Control and the primacy of the individual are central to both.

Further reading

Rush, White and Hurst (1989) explain how personality types affect decision making, as does Belbin (1981). Kiersey and Bates (1978) give a questionnaire that you can use to identify your own personality type. Senge (1990) and Argyris (1990) are important reading. Critiques of learning organisation theory from a system perspective are to be found in Flood (1999) and from a process perspective in Griffin (2001).

Chapter 7 ●●● ●

Obstacles to strategic choice and organisational learning
Open systems and psychoanalytic perspectives

7.1 Introduction

Chapters 3 and 4 explored the foundations upon which the theory of strategic choice rests. These are a theory of interaction to be found in cybernetic systems theory and a theory of human nature to be found primarily in cognitivism, but also in humanistic psychology. Then Chapters 5 and 6 examined the theoretical foundations of learning organisation theory. Here there is some shift from a theory of interaction based on cybernetics to one based on systems dynamics. However, the way systems theory is used retains a link with cybernetics through the conceptualisation of systems dynamics in feedback terms. There is much less of a shift in the basic theory of human nature. This remains heavily cognitivist, although with the addition of a constructivist slant in that mental models are seen to select features for attention, so constructing rather than purely representing experience. The reliance on humanistic psychology is even stronger than it is in strategic choice theory. A link is developed with Eastern spirituality so that participation comes to be understood as participation in a whole that is greater than the individuals comprising it and this greater whole has a mystical aspect.

This chapter reviews a theory of organisational change that is built on both a different theory of interaction and a different theory of human nature. Interaction continues to be seen in systemic terms but this time from the perspective of open systems theory. The theory of human nature is provided by psychoanalytic perspectives. The chapter first reviews open systems theory and then turns to relevant psychoanalytic notions, before showing how they can be combined to shed light on life in organisations.

7.2 Open systems theory

Around the same time as the development of cybernetics and systems dynamics, there also appeared the closely related ideas of general systems theory. In a number of papers and books between 1945 and 1968, the German biologist von Bertalanffy put forward the idea that organisms, as well as human organisations and societies, are open systems. They are systems because they consist of a number of component subsystems that are interrelated and interdependent on each other. They are open because they are connected to their environments, or suprasystems, of which they are a part.

Each subsystem within a system and each system within its environment has a boundary separating it from other subsystems and other systems. For example, the sales department in an organisation is a subsystem separated by a boundary from the production and accounting departments. One organisation such as IBM is a system separated by a boundary from the other organisations and individuals that form its environment.

Within each system or subsystem, people occupy roles, they conduct sets of activities, and they engage in interrelationships with others. They do this both within their part of the system and in other parts or other systems.

Each subsystem within a system and each system within an environment is open. It imports materials, labour, money and information from other subsystems or systems. It also exports outputs, money and information to other subsystems and systems.

Open systems explanations of managing and organising therefore focus attention on:

- organisations, industries and societies as systemic wholes;
- the behaviour of people within a subsystem or system;
- the nature of the boundary around a subsystem or system;
- the nature of the relationships across the boundaries between subsystems and systems;
- the requirements of managing the boundary.

The open systems concept provides a tool for understanding the relationship between:

- the technical and the social aspects of an organisation;
- the parts and the whole organisation (e.g. the individual and the group, the individual and the organisation);
- the whole organisation and the environment.

Negative feedback

Changing one component in an open system will clearly have knock-on effects in many other components because of the prevalence of interconnection. Changes in the environment will have an impact on changes in the subsystems of an organisation. What happens in one system will affect what happens in another system and that in turn will affect the first.

One can see the importance of the insight provided by open systems theory if one considers how the technical subsystem of an organisation is interconnected with its social subsystem (Trist and Bamforth, 1951).

Scientific rational management tends to concentrate on the technical subsystem. This system consists of the primary tasks that the organisation is there to carry out: for example, the techniques, technology and sets of tasks required to produce coal in the case of a coal mining business. The prescription for success put forward by scientific management is to make the task subsystem as efficient as possible. So, if you introduce the latest technology for mining coal, together with rules and regulations about quality and efficiency to govern the work of coal miners, then you should succeed according to scientific management. Success here depends primarily on the technical subsystem.

The behavioural school of management, on the other hand, focuses primarily on the psychosocial subsystem. Its prescriptions for success stress the establishment of a social system in which people are motivated and participate in making decisions about the nature of the tasks and the technology. To succeed you must consult those who perform the organisation's primary tasks, involve them in decision making, and introduce reward structures that will motivate them to operate efficiently. Success here depends primarily on the social subsystem.

The insight that comes from open systems theory is that the technical and social systems are so interconnected that it makes no sense to regard one as dominant and the other as subordinate. Both subsystems have to be handled together in a manner that takes account of their interdependence.

The importance of this interconnection was demonstrated many years ago in a study of the coal-mining industry in the UK by Trist and Bamforth (1951). In the late 1940s, the British coal industry introduced the long-wall method of mining coal, which was more efficient than previous method. The new technology, however, required changes in the set of tasks performed by coal miners. These changes broke up the co-operative teams in which miners were accustomed to working, teams that reflected their social arrangements in the coal-mining villages in which they lived. Because of the consequent resistance to working in the new way, the technology failed to yield its technical potential.

The message is that, if changes are to succeed, then they have to be based on a realistic understanding of the interconnection, or feedback, between the social and the technical subsystems. And that interconnection is not simply taken account of by introducing participation or reward schemes for individuals. Instead, general systems theory prescribes a match between the two subsystems, one that establishes stable equilibrium

Like cybernetics and systems dynamics therefore, the general systems strand of thinking sees an organisation as a feedback system. It also sees that feedback system as one that maintains equilibrium with its environment, and between its parts, by utilising the mechanisms of negative feedback.

Conflicting subsystems

In general systems theory, open systems are thought of as having maintenance subsystems to sustain orderly relationships between the parts of the system (Lawrence and Lorsch, 1967). In an organisation this would be the management information and control systems and the cultures that keep people working harmoniously together. However, it is recognised that these maintenance systems are conservative by nature. They are intended to hold the system together; to prevent it from changing too rapidly; to keep it efficiently carrying out its main tasks. The inevitable consequence of this maintenance form of control is that the overall system and its subsystems become out of balance as time goes by and things change. They become out of balance with each other and with the environment.

But organisations also have adaptive mechanisms that promote change so as to keep them in dynamic equilibrium with the environment. These two subsystems, the maintenance and the adaptive, inevitably conflict, but successful organisations sustain a stable balance between them, according to general systems theory. Note that general systems theory recognises a fundamental conflict inherent in the structure of the system, but assumes that successful systems deal with this by sustaining equilibrium.

Differentiation and integration

Lawrence and Lorsch (1967) used the conceptual approach of open systems to research the functioning of a number of large organisations. They concluded that as organisations increase in size they differentiate into parts, and the more they differentiate, the more difficult becomes the consequent task of integration.

So as the environment becomes more complex and as they grow in size, companies differentiate into functions – finance, operations, sales and so on. But each part or function then faces the problem of relating to the other parts, if the firm is to operate effectively. Integrating what people in the production department do with what those in the sales or finance departments do then becomes more and more of a problem.

As organisations deal with their external environment they become differentiated into separate units, each dealing with a part of the environment. Think of large multinational companies, such as GE or IBM, with perhaps hundreds of different subsidiary companies across the world. They have reached advanced stages of differentiation and face well-known and very difficult-to-solve problems of integrating all their activities.

The authors found a relationship between variables external to the organisation and the states of differentiation and integration within that organisation. They found that organisations become more differentiated as their environments become more diverse.

Citibank operates in a large number of countries, a complex environment, through a great many national subsidiaries. This is a differentiated organisation. Since the environment demands more interdependence and co-operation, the organisation responds with greater integration. So, Citibank superimposes upon its national subsidiaries a central activity to serve its multinational clients wishing to deal with one central point, not hundreds of subsidiaries (Buzzell, 1984).

As environments become more diverse and organisations more differentiated, the tasks of integration become greater, leading to a proliferation of complex integrating devices. Citibank finds that conflicts grow up between the national subsidiaries and the central body dealing with multinational clients. It has to set up rules and systems to try to resolve the conflicts.

Lawrence and Lorsch also found that the more unpredictable the environment becomes the more decentralised the organisation becomes, pushing the locus of decision making down the hierarchy.

Note how general systems theorists recognise fundamental conflicts in organising: the need to divide tasks up and to integrate them; the need for maintenance control systems for stability but the inevitable drift from the demands of the environment as such maintenance control is applied. Note how they interpret organisations dealing with these conflicts. In effect, they see the organisations as solving the conflicts, the solutions being dictated by the need to adapt to the environment.

General systems theory has made an important contribution to an understanding of the nature of managing and organising in a number of ways. It focuses attention on:

- interdependence, interaction and interconnection between parts of an organisation and between organisations;
- the importance of the boundaries between parts of an organisation and between one organisation and others;
- the roles of people within and across the boundaries and the nature of leadership as management of the boundary.

These ideas are summarised in Figure 7.1.

I now want to move on from open systems theory to some relevant psychoanalytic concepts. I will return to open systems theory in section 7.4.

Figure 7.1

General systems theory: the main points on organisational dynamics

- An organisation is an open system: a set of interconnected parts (individuals, informal groups, formal groups such as departments and business units) in turn interacting with other organisations and individuals outside it.
- Interconnection means that a system imports energy and information from outside itself, transforms that energy and information in some way and then exports the transformed result back to other systems outside of itself.
- An organisation imports across a boundary separating it from other systems, transforms the imports within its boundary and exports back across the boundary. The boundary separates a system from its environment but also links it to its environment.
- Relationships across the boundary are always changing, the environment is always changing. The boundary therefore exercises a regulatory function: on the one hand it protects the system from fluctuations in the environment and on the other it relays messages and prompts changes within the boundary so that the system adapts to its environment.
- It is the role of leadership to manage the boundary, to regulate so that the system is protected and changes adaptively.
- Successful management keeps an organisation adapted to its changing environment through a process of negative feedback producing stable equilibrium.
- Adaptation to the environment determines the stable equilibrium balance between differentiation and integration, between maintenance control systems and change, required for success. Organisational paradoxes are thus solved in a unique way determined by the environment.
- Success is therefore a state of stability, consistency and harmony.

●●●● 7.3   Psychoanalysis and unconscious processes

In developing psychoanalysis, Freud focused attention on the unconscious. He believed that people repress dangerous desires and painful memories but that this repression does not get rid of them and they remain in the unconscious as determinants of behaviour. Repression is one of the major defences against anxiety, that is, a painful state of unease for which no clear reason can be found. It is also held that people's behaviour can be driven by unconscious group processes.

Unconscious processes in organisations

An unconscious group process is one in which a group of people engage without consciously agreeing to it or even realising that they are doing it. When groups of people are in this state they find what is happening to them both puzzling and upsetting and it makes it impossible for them to engage in double-loop learning. Covert politics is a defence against anxiety that people are more or less conscious of practising but unconscious processes are defences they indulge in quite automatically without being aware of what they are doing.

So, anxiety triggers an automatic negative feedback loop, a damping process that inhibits movement away from a currently shared mental model so trapping a group of people in stability. A group of people can only learn in a double-loop way when they are able to contain the anxiety such learning provokes, as opposed to avoiding it through covert politics, on the one hand, or becoming overwhelmed by it in the form of unconscious processes, on the other hand.

When people's ways of thinking are challenged, they become anxious. That anxiety may rise to such high levels that people swing into automatic basic assumption behaviour – an unconscious process. This is a notion developed by Wilfred Bion that I will review in some detail in this section. When groups are dominated by basic assumption behaviour they cannot learn and therefore their organisation cannot develop new strategic direction. On the other hand, if there is a good enough holding environment so that people can contain rather than submit to or avoid the anxiety, then insight and creativity may be generated by and accompany the anxiety of learning.

I now go on to consider the work of Bion, and others, on the nature of unconscious group processes.

Bion's models: unconscious group processes

The nature of interaction between people depends upon the extent to which those people are aware of the nature of their own and each other's behaviour. This point is made in Figure 7.2, a diagram known as JOHARI's window.

When people are aware of their own behaviour and those with whom they are interacting are also aware of that behaviour, then interaction between them takes on a Public form – they all know what they are doing together and why. But one group of people may be doing something of which they are completely aware, to

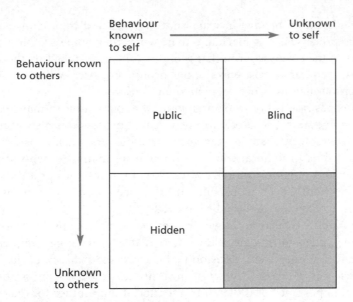

Figure 7.2   JOHARI window
Source: P. B. Smith (1969), *Improving Skills in Working with People: The T Group*, London: HMSO.

others who are unaware of what is going on. Such behaviour is labelled Hidden in Figure 7.2; some are manipulating others. Again, one group may be performing in a particular way, for reasons of which they are unaware, but their behaviour is transparent to others. Such behaviour may be called Blind: some pretend they are doing one thing while they do another, but other people can see through this. The figure also shows a quadrant that is shaded, depicting behaviour where those behaving and those responding are unaware of the true nature of their interaction. This is unconscious behaviour.

When individuals behave in such a way that they are not explicitly aware of the nature, or the quality or the causes of that behaviour, then one can say that they are behaving unconsciously. For example, when I react in a hostile manner to a total stranger I have never heard about or met before, then I am behaving unconsciously – there is no obvious reason, no clear connection with external reality, to explain my reaction. The reason for such a reaction is held by psychoanalysis to lie in the unconscious mind; the particular person has activated a response from some other experience in the past that has been pushed into the unconscious and this process of activation is know as transference. Whenever people react to some stimulus in a manner which others, and later they themselves, perceive to be out of all proportion to the stimulus, then in all probability the cause of that behaviour lies in their unconscious.

When you lose your temper at a typist for making a small spelling error, the true source of the anger is most probably not the typist at all; you are simply projecting anger felt for someone else, who might well be yourself, on to the unfortunate typist. This kind of projection is an unconscious process in which all humans regularly indulge, according to psychoanalysis.

Since all people behave in ways that are directed by unconscious as well as conscious processes, it is inevitable that, when they come together as a group, at least part of their behaviour in that group will be determined by those unconscious processes. In other words, unconscious group processes will inevitably be part of most decision-making processes in an organisation.

This proposition is not recognised in most explanations of managing, organising and decision making. The role of unconscious processes is also firmly denied any explicit attention by many management practitioners. Such considerations tend to be dismissed as peripheral concerns for mature managers who are supposed to make decisions in largely rational ways. When unconscious processes are discussed they are normally seen as peripheral influences on a decision, usually adverse influences, which must and can be removed.

More careful reflection, however, suggests that unconscious processes are so deeply embedded in human behaviour that it is only some completely inhuman, and therefore non-existent, decision-making process that can occur in the absence of unconscious processes, or with those processes occupying a position of only peripheral importance. It is therefore a matter of importance for the effectiveness of strategic management to explore what impact these processes may have and how they come about. First consider one way of becoming aware of what the processes I am talking about are.

Group relations conferences

A very powerful way of experiencing what unconscious group processes actually feel like is provided by what are known as group relations conferences (Miller, 1989). This approach to training in group awareness was popular in the 1960s but fell from favour largely because it did not produce predictable, long-lasting changes in people's skills in building cohesive teams. From a psychoanalytic perspective, this is not the only aim, so the criticism need not deter one from learning from this approach. I would therefore like to describe some of the kinds of behaviour that always emerge in such events and then outline the explanations that have been put forward to account for the behaviour.

What I am going to describe is based on three separate conferences, each lasting two days over a weekend. The participants on each occasion were about thirty part-time MBA students, with an average age of around 35. Some points on the composition of these groups are as follows: about 15 per cent were female; perhaps 10 per cent of the total were from minority groups; about 70 per cent of the total were from the commercial and industrial sector and the remainder from public sector and charitable bodies; over 90 per cent had degrees or professional qualifications. All of these intelligent people held responsible managerial positions in their organisations.

Participants arrived at the residential weekend with some feelings of apprehension because they had heard rumours from others about the strange happenings likely to occur. At the start of the weekend, all of the participants met in a plenary session with the staff who were to act as consultants to groups of participants. The staff consisted of three visiting consultants with considerable experience in running such conferences and two teachers from my own institution who played a relatively minor consulting role. The task of the weekend was briefly outlined: it was to study group processes, particularly unconscious processes, so enabling each individual to examine the part he or she plays in those processes, including the exercise of authority.

Participants were then divided into study groups of 10–12 members each and the task of the study group was stated to be that of studying intra-group processes in the here and now, when they happen and as they happen. It was clearly explained to the participants that each study group would be attended by a consultant, who would be there not to teach, but to provide working hypotheses about the processes occurring in groups. It was quite clearly stated that participants must take responsibility for their own learning.

The study groups were therefore set up in such a way that there was nothing that the managers involved recognised as the kind of objective and task to which they were accustomed. Managers do not normally simply examine their own behaviour in a group – the behaviour normally lies in the background of dealing with an objective and a task. Here the behaviour itself is brought out of the background actually to provide the, rather unfamiliar, objective and task. The role that the consultants steadfastly occupy is also not one to which the participants are accustomed. The consultant clearly occupies some position of authority as far as the participants are concerned, but that consultant abandons the participants in the sense that the consultant refuses to occupy the expected role of teacher, expert or leader. Then, however, having abandoned them in this sense, the consultant nevertheless keeps intruding in the role of consultant to offer interpretations of what the participants are doing (Gustafson and Cooper, 1978).

These two changes, the removal of what is normally regarded as a task and the removal of what is normally regarded as a teacher or leader, always provoke high levels of anxiety in the participants, anxieties which they are reluctant to recognise. Those anxieties find expression in all manner of strange behaviours. Group discussions may take on a manic form with asinine comments and hysterical laughter. In a remarkably short space of time the participants attack the visiting consultant for not playing a more usual and active role and openly question whether they are earning their consulting fees. Participants become incredibly rude to the consultants, behaviour they would not normally display to a visitor, no matter how poor the visitor's performance might be. Significantly, however, participants rarely attack the two teachers, perhaps because they represent the ongoing authority figures for the MBA course.

Members of study groups might try to find a leader to replace the non-functioning consultant but they rarely seem to be successful in this endeavour for very long. They begin to pick on an individual, usually some highly individualistic or minority member of the group, and then treat this person as some kind of scapegoat. They all become very concerned with remaining part of the group, greatly fearing exclusion. They show strong tendencies to conform to rapidly established group norms and suppress their individual differences, perhaps because they are afraid of becoming the scapegoat.

The study group events are followed by the inter-group event. Here the participants are invited to organise themselves into groups and then study inter-group behaviour in the here and now as it happens. The sight of these mature people organising themselves into groups is quite astonishing. They do so without any fore-thought, all seemingly in a panic at the thought of being left out of a group. Within seconds the room is cleared of people who have all rushed off, away from the con-sultants, in one group or another. Then they begin to interact and within minutes the win/lose dynamic takes powerful hold. Even though there is no specific objective, other than studying behaviour, even though the groups have formed without any common purpose whatsoever, some groups at least start to talk about dominating the others. They then proceed to try to do so, brushing aside any quiet, puzzled voice that might ask why they are doing this. In their pursuit of domination, group mem-bers lie to each other, spy on each other and play one deceitful game after another.

The one thing they hardly do at all is examine the behaviour they are indulging in, the task they have actually been given. Individuals and whole groups become scapegoats, set up by others and collaborating in that set-up. Very real emotions of anger and fear are evoked by what goes on, despite the fact that all know that this is 'only a training weekend'. Rumours spread about what other groups are doing, fantasies that participants afterwards realise are completely false. But at the time little effort is made to check on the data: all is wild assertions, building up fantasies of attacking and being attacked, rejecting and being rejected. People talk all the time about the group as some real thing separate from themselves as individuals. They place enormous store on being part of the group and on the group being cohesive. They talk about belonging to the strongest, most cohesive group, the best group, in a fantasy-like manner.

I personally found it most surprising that undoubtedly competent, mature people in responsible managerial positions react so strongly to two rather small changes from the normal. After all, there is a task: it is to study group processes as they happen and there is certainly much happening. There is assistance in performing the task in the form of comments and guidance from the experienced consultants, even though they refuse the role of teacher. But it seems that the original stimulus of two rather unusual changes sets off some kind of amplifying feedback loop in the behaviour of the groups of participants from which they seem incapable of escaping during the whole weekend. They, and even I as a rather peripheral consultant, become totally caught up in very strong and difficult-to-understand amplifying processes. The fact that the magnitude of the response is out of all proportion to the stimulus is a sign of unconscious processes. Throughout the experience it becomes apparent to many participants that processes of this kind occur every day within their own real-life organisation, although usually at a much lower level of intensity. I personally found it even more surprising that I too behaved in this way when I joined a group relations conference as a member.

How is one to explain the nature and cause of these unconscious processes that make it virtually impossible for a group of intelligent and competent managers to work on a task for a whole weekend? A psychoanalytical explanation is that, when humans are confronted by high levels of anxiety provoked by unfamiliar tasks and lack of leadership, they revert very easily to infantile mechanisms. They begin to behave according to patterns they learned as infants. So first look briefly at an explanation of how infants cope with their world provided by the object relations school of psychoanalysis (Klein, 1975).

Infantile mechanisms

According to Melanie Klein's explanation (1975), infants are born with two power-ful drives: the libido, or life force, which is the drive to love; and the morbido, or death wish, which is the fear of death and destruction, the feeling of persecution. The inner life of the infant is very simple – it is dominated by these two extremes of love on the one hand and persecutory fear on the other.

The infant's perception of its external world is also very simple, consisting of two part-objects: a good part of the mother that feeds and comforts it and a bad part that denies it food and comfort.

The infant copes with this simple and also powerfully distressing world by split-ting its inner life into a loving part that is projected on to the good part of the mother. The infant then identifies itself with that good part and introjects it back into itself. The same thing is done with the persecutory feelings and the aggression and hatred they arouse. These are all projected on to the bad part of the mother, and the infant identifies its own violent impulses with that bad part – it then intro-jects that bad part of the mother back into itself.

The infant projects its feelings and then perceives those feelings as coming from the outside object. It therefore reacts to the object in a manner provoked by the feel-ings which originally come from itself. So it projects its own fears of persecution and then reacts to the object projected upon as if that object is actually persecuting it. This leads to a reaction of hate and aggression, strengthening the feeling of perse-cution. If the projection affects the behaviour of the object, then the whole feedback process becomes even stronger. It is through this feedback that the character of the infant is formed. If it experiences loving responses to its loving projections then the loving side of its character is strengthened. If the persecutory projections are reinforced by lack of love and actual persecution then this side of the character is reinforced. Right at the earliest stages of behaviour, then, positive and negative feedback loops play major parts in the development of an infant.

This first stage of infantile development is known as the paranoid-schizoid posi-tion. It is schizoid because the infant splits the external world and it splits its own internal world too. It is paranoid because of the persecutory fears of the infant. The infant deals with these fears by using the mechanisms of splitting and projective identification, putting what is inside its own mind out into some external object or person and then identifying with and reacting to what it has projected. It copes with harsh reality by creating a fantasy world of separate objects, some of which are persecuting it. It is idealising the good parts and denying its own bad parts by projecting them, so building the external bad into a demon.

The infant who develops normally works through this position and comes to realise that the bad and good objects in its external world are really one and the same whole person. But for the infant having learned how to defend against the earliest anxieties, these defences remain in the unconscious. In later life when people con-front anxiety again, they are highly likely to regress to the infantile mechanisms of splitting the world and themselves into extreme and artificial categories of the good and the bad, projecting the parts of themselves they do not like on to others, so creating fantasies that have little to do with reality.

Once the infant realises that it loves and hates the same person it is filled with anxiety because of the feelings of anger and hatred previously projected on to the mother. This causes the depressive position. The normal infant works its way through this position too, developing strong feelings of love and dependence on the mother, while seeking to make amends for previous bad feelings. It experiences hope from the more mature relationship with the mother. Once the infant can hold the depressive position, that is, hold in the mind the paradox of simultaneously loving and hating, then that child can go on to make reparative acts and have reparative feelings. If these are responded to with love then a lifelong cycle of experiencing guilt, making reparation and receiving forgiveness is put in place. Melanie Klein saw this as the basis of all later creative behaviour. So, it is when people are in the depressive position, when they can hold in their minds the paradoxes and ambiguities of organisational life, that they are able to engage in double-loop learning. When they regress from that depressive position to the paranoid-schizoid position they become trapped in primitive ways of thinking and behaving. And this, it is held, happens to all of us when we cannot contain the anxiety of learning and when our environment provides us with no anxiety containment either.

Transitional objects, learning and play

Winnicott's (1971) work gives further insight into the development of the ability to learn and be creative. He identified child development with a process of separation from the carer and he stressed the vital importance of 'good enough holding' by the carer in this process. He defined the good enough carer as one with a fine judgement of just how much to gratify the child to sustain a sufficient degree of security, and just how much to frustrate that child to provoke exploration of and relation to the environment: that fine balance constitutes 'good enough holding' and comes from the instinctive empathy the carer has with the child. Good enough holding enables children to cross the boundary of their own minds and begin to explore, relate to and manipulate the real world outside their minds.

However, eventually the child has to develop its own holding mechanisms as it were, since reliance cannot be placed on the carer to do this all the child's life. Winnicott proposed that such holding mechanisms take the form of what he called transitional objects. As they mature children develop the ability to compensate for short absences of their carer by developing a very powerful relationship with some special object such as a blanket or a teddy bear. Winnicott suggested that this object stands for the carer: it is treated for short periods as if it were the carer and so it provides enough security for the child to continue exploring the environment. In this sense the object is a transitional one: it is a transition from a present carer to an absent carer; it stands for the carer although it is not the carer. This is how the child begins to use symbols, the beginning of all language and reasoning powers.

In fact the teddy bear soon comes to stand for anything the child wants it to be, providing experiences of play which develop the imagination and the ability to manipulate symbols. It is through this experience of play that the child learns and develops imaginative, creative powers. The child discovers how to control and manipulate objects outside the mind, first by manipulating the transitional object

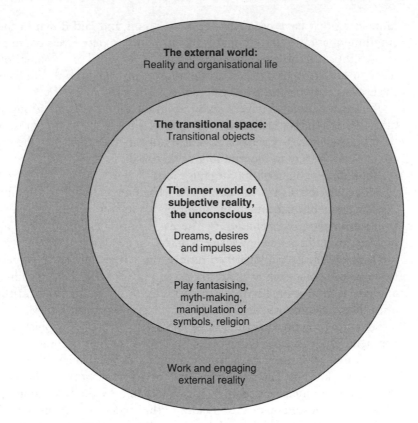

Figure 7.3   The creative space
Source: Adapted from E. H. Miller (1983), *Work and Creativity*, Occasional Papers. London: Tavistock.

and then by controlling real objects. The play takes place in a transitional space between the inner fantasies of the mind and the outer reality of a concrete world, as depicted in Figure 7.3. Here the child holds ambiguity and paradox: the transitional object is one thing but stands for something else. In this sense the transitional space is close in meaning to the depressive position (Miller, 1983; Gordon, 1993).

Play continues to be a major source of learning and it continues throughout life to be closely associated with creativity. It is when individuals are able to play, when they are able to manipulate symbols, when they are able to occupy the illusionistic world, that they are able to be creative. Winnicott argued that the transitional space continues throughout life to be the area in which people develop cultures, myths, art and religion. So, double-loop learning in organisations would have to do with creating the space for play and with creating the conditions that will hold the anxiety such creative play arouses.

Groups and infantile mechanisms

When mature, competent managers come together as a group, each brings along the infantile mechanisms of dependence, idealisation, denial, splitting, projection and fantasising that have been learned as an infant and laid down in the unconscious. Anything that raises uncertainty levels and thus anxiety levels could provoke regression to those infantile mechanisms. Bion has provided an explanation of how these mechanisms are manifested in group behaviour, leading to the kinds of behaviour at the group relations conferences described earlier (Bion, 1961).

Bion distinguishes between two important aspects of any group of people. The first aspect is the sophisticated work group. This is the primary task that the group has come together to perform. So a team of top executives has the primary tasks of controlling the day-to-day running of the business of the organisation and also the strategic development of that organisation.

All groups are also at the same time what Bion called 'basic assumption groups'. A basic assumption group is one that behaves as if it is making a particular assumption about required behaviour. The assumption becomes most apparent when uncertainty and anxiety levels rise. What Bion is talking about here is the emotional atmosphere, the psychological culture, of the group. All groups of people have these two aspects: some task they are trying to perform together, accompanied by some emotional atmosphere within which they are trying to perform their task. That atmosphere can be described in terms of a basic assumption they are all making.

So, at any one time, a group of people may constitute a sophisticated work group characterised by a basic assumption on behaviour that occupies a kind of low-level background position, influencing the conduct of the primary task but not dominating or blocking it. Then when uncertainty and anxiety levels rise markedly the group can become suffused with and dominated by the basic assumption; a strong emotional atmosphere, or group culture, that blocks the group's ability to function as a sophisticated work group. The primary task will not be carried out, or it will be carried out in an ineffective manner.

Bion distinguished between three basic assumptions:

1 *Dependence*. Here the group behaves as if it has come together to depend on some leader. The members of the group seek a leader on whom they can depend. They abandon their individuality and critical faculties in favour of some kind of adoration of a charismatic leader. They actively seek a charismatic person who will tell them what to do. Charisma lies not in the person of the leader but in the interrelationship between the followers and the leader.

   In this state, members of a group will idealise the leader, expecting completely unrealistic performance from the leader. Groups working on this assumption are destined to be disappointed and will quickly abandon the leader. This dependence is an infantile mechanism because the members of the group are projecting their requirements for something to depend upon on to someone else. This projection will in effect select the leader. Note how this raises a possibility not normally thought of. When a group is behaving in this mode it is creating its own leader through projecting demands on to a person – it is not the leader who is creating the group. If the person selected for this projection does not co-operate or disappoints, then members of the group project their frustration and fear on to that person and begin to attack. This brings us to the second basic assumption.

2 *Fight/flight*. Here it is as if the group has come together for the purpose of fighting some enemy or for the purpose of fleeing from some enemy. Members project their desire for fight or flight on to someone to lead them in fight or flight. Once again they may rapidly become disappointed with and attack the leader. Groups in this state invent fantasy enemies in some other department or some other organisation. The energy goes into competition and win/lose dynamics.

3 *Pairing*. Pairing is another mode in which a group might operate. Here it is as if the group has come together to witness the intercourse between two of their number which will produce the solution to their anxieties. The atmosphere here is one of unrealistic hope that some experts will produce all the answers.

Turquet (1974) has added a fourth basic assumption:

4 *Oneness*. Here it is as if the group has come together to join in a powerful union with some omnipotent force which will enable members to surrender themselves in some kind of safe passivity. Members seem lost in an oceanic feeling of unity.

The dynamics

The explanation presented so far is summarised in Figure 7.4.

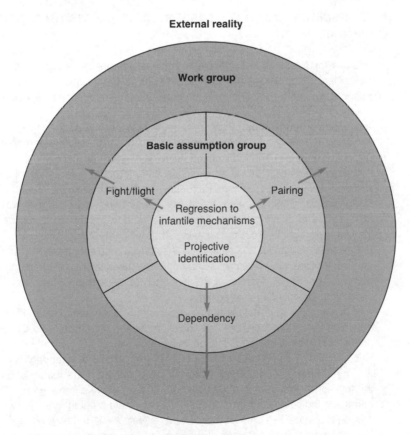

Figure 7.4   Unconscious group processes
Source: R. de Board (1978), *The Psychoanalysis of Organizations*, London: Tavistock.

Once a group of people come to be dominated by one of the basic assumptions, they enter into volatile dynamics in which they switch, for apparently no reason, from one basic assumption to another. While people in a group are behaving like this they are incapable of performing the primary task or acting as a work group. They cannot remember what they have just discussed; they go around and around in incompetent circles; they suck unsuitable people into leadership positions; they create scapegoats; they act on untested myths and rumours; they build fantasies and lose touch with reality. Individuals sink their individuality in group uniformity and become deskilled.

What provokes the switch from a work group with some background basic assumption, being used in a sophisticated way to support their task, to a group dominated by a basic assumption? The provocation seems to have a great deal to do with levels of ambiguity and uncertainty on the one hand, and with certain styles of exercising power on the other. If leaders abandon groups in times of great

---

Figure 7.5

Unconscious group processes: main points on organisational dynamics

- Positive feedback loops are activated by any attempt to change an organisation in a fundamental way. This is because change upsets the balance and nature of power and raises the levels of uncertainty and ambiguity. Consequent anxiety provokes positive feedback loops.
- Increased anxiety unleashes unconscious processes of regression to infantile behaviour. Work groups become swamped with basic assumption behaviour in which they are incapable of undertaking strategic developments.
- A group of managers facing strategic issues is turning up the levels of uncertainty and ambiguity since these are characteristics of strategic issues. Such issues threaten power positions. It is therefore inevitable that strategic issues themselves will touch off the positive amplifying loops of basic assumption behaviour. Such behaviour is an inevitable part of the process of making strategic decisions.
- In these circumstances it is quite likely that long-term plans, mission statements, visions and the like are simply being used as defence mechanisms. Perhaps people cling to a dominant paradigm despite all the evidence to the contrary because it is their main defence mechanism against anxiety.
- The dynamics of any real-life organisation is inevitably unstable, unless it is completely dominated by rules, fears or force, in which case it will atrophy and die. Strategic management proceeds as part of this unstable dynamic.
- Success has to do with the management of the context or boundary conditions around a group. The main factors that establish the context are the nature and use of power, the level of mutual trust and the time pressures on people in the group. The purpose of managing the context, or the boundaries, is to create an emotional atmosphere in which it is possible to overcome defences and to test reality rather than indulge in fantasy. In other words, the context must be managed to create an atmosphere that enables double-loop learning.

uncertainty and ambiguity then they will develop into basic assumption groups and become incapable of handling the uncertainty and ambiguity.

But note that this is not clear-cut causality between a specific action, say the withdrawal of power, and specific outcomes in behavioural terms. All one can say is that, when the nature of power in a group is changed so that people's requirement for dependency is frustrated, they will display general patterns of behaviour that can be labelled as fight/flight or some other label. It will not be possible to say what form such fighting or such flight may take, or when it will occur. The key points about the dynamics and unconscious processes are summarised in Figure 7.5.

7.4   Open systems and unconscious processes

The combination of open systems theory and psychoanalysis originated in the Tavistock Institute of Human Relations. This was set up London in 1946 by a group of psychoanalysts from the Tavistock Clinic and social scientists from other institutions. During the 1950s and 1960s a distinctive approach to understanding life in organisations was developed by members of this Institute, for example Trist, to whom I have already referred, Rice and Miller (Miller and Rice, 1967).

As I have already said, an open system exists by importing energy/materials from its environment across a boundary, transforming them and then exporting them back across the boundary (Miller and Rice, 1967). This boundary is seen as a region in which mediating, or regulating, activities occur to protect the system from disruption due to external fluctuations but also allow it to adapt to external changes (Miller, 1977). The boundary region must therefore exhibit an appropriate degree of both insulation and permeability if the system is to survive. This makes regulatory functions at the permeable boundary region of central importance. In organisational terms, these regulatory functions are performed by leaders/managers at the organisation's boundary with other organisations. It is the activities of leaders and managers at the boundary that are key to the process of change. It then becomes quite logical to think about change in terms of rational design and to look for what might inhibit such rational designing activity. Disorder is seen as an inhibitor that must be removed. The disorder is due to the unconscious processes described in the last section.

Miller and Rice (1967) used Bion's (1961) insights to see a group of people as an open system in which individuals, also seen as open systems, interact with each other at two levels. At one level they contribute to its purpose, so constituting a sophisticated (work) group, and at the other level they develop feelings and attitudes about each other, the group and its environment, so constituting a more primitive (basic assumption) group. Both of these modes of relating are operative at the same time. When the basic assumption mode takes the form of a background emotional atmosphere it may well support the work of the group, but when it predominates it is destructive of the group's work. So, individuals are thought of as open systems relating to each other across their individual boundary regions. In this way they constitute a group, which is also thought of as an open system with a permeable boundary region. Furthermore, Miller and Rice argue that it is confusing to think of organisations, or enterprises, as open systems consisting of individuals and groupings of individuals. So, an intersystemic perspective is adopted in which an enterprise is thought of as one open system interacting with individuals and groupings of them as other open systems.

Enterprises are seen as task systems – they have primary tasks that they must perform if they are to survive. There are various definitions of the primary task. It may be the task that ought to be performed. It may be the task people believe that they are carrying out. It may be a task that they are engaged in without even being aware of it and this probably means that it is a defensive mechanism. The primary task requires people to take up roles in order for it to be carried out and the enterprise, or task system, imports these roles across its boundary with the system consisting of individuals and groupings of them. Roles, and relationships between roles, fall within the boundary of the task system. However, groups and individuals, with their personal relationships, personal power plays and human needs not derived from the task system's primary task, fall outside it: they constitute part of the task system's environment. So, there is one system, a task system, interacting with other systems, individuals and groups, and the groups are always operating in two modes at the same time: work mode and basic assumption mode.

When the individual/group system has the characteristics of a sophisticated group with basic assumption behaviour as a supportive background atmosphere, then it is exporting functional roles to the task system and the latter can perform its primary task. The enterprise, or task system, is thus displaying the dynamics of stability – that is, equilibrium or quasi-equilibrium. When, however, the individual/group system is flooded with basic assumption behaviour it exports that behaviour into the task system so disrupting the performance of the primary task. The dynamics is then that of instability or disintegration. Miller (1993, p. 19) argues that this intersystemic view encourages one to focus on interdependence: people supplying roles to enterprises and those enterprises requiring performance in role from people in order to survive. He argues that when individuals and groups are seen as parts of the whole enterprise the focus shifts to a subordinate–superior relationship.

Part of the task system, a subsystem of it, might be set up to contain imported basic assumption behaviour such as fight. Its primary task is then to operate as an organisational defence that allows the rest of the task system to carry out its primary task. Without such organisational defences, the task system as a whole would import fantasies and behaviours that are destructive of the primary task – the dynamics of instability. These undesirable imports are to be diminished by:

- clarity of task;
- clearly defined roles, and authority relationships between them, all related to task;
- appropriate leadership regulation at the boundary of the task system;
- procedures and structures that form social defences against anxiety (Jacques, 1955; Menzies Lyth, 1975);
- high levels of individual maturity and autonomy.

Most of these factors seem to me to emphasise design and some joint intention relating to the system as a whole. Furthermore, there is, it seems to me, a strong implication that the dynamics of stability is a prerequisite for a functioning task system, while the dynamics of instability is inimical to that functioning. There is little sense in this formulation of the creative potential of disorder. I am making this point here because the theory to be presented in Part Three takes a different view on these matters.

Shapiro and Carr (1991) employ the above model in their interpretation of the role of the consultant. The consultant uses counter-transference feelings to formulate hypotheses about the transferential and projective processes at work in an organisation, and about the impact of basic assumption behaviour on the work of that organisation. They see the function of the consultant as one of feeding back those hypotheses into the life of the organisation and so fostering a collaborative, negotiated understanding and verbalisation of the unconscious, irrational processes at play. It is believed that this process enables the reclaiming of projections and distorted impressions of reality, so restoring to the group its work function. The consultants engage with and understand the complexity of organisational life by adopting an interpretive stance. This stance is seen as the most important element in creating a holding environment and they draw an analogy with a therapeutic setting: 'containment and holding ordinarily refer to symbolic interpretive ways in which the therapist manages the patient's (and his own) feelings' (Shapiro and Carr, 1991, p. 112).

Another feature of the holding environment, one that interpretation aims to secure, is the clarity of task, boundary and role. This is seen as containing, for example, sexual and aggressive feelings. Empathic interpretation affirms individuals in their roles and the resulting containment establishes a holding environment. This provides for safe regression, a shift from rationally organised words to the primitive distortions of fantasy images and simple metaphors which can then be articulated and so disarmed. The aim of interpretation is to move people from states of irrational anxiety and fantasy that distort work to the more reality-based taking of roles that support it.

According to Shapiro and Carr, the aim of the consultant's work is to identify whether an organisation is functioning according to its design. This will happen when members of the organisation understand their tasks so that roles within and across parts of the organisation can be legitimately authorised and fully integrated. This, in turn, requires clarification of authorisation from one level to another in the hierarchy and a structure of meetings to promote effective communication. Shapiro and Carr stress the need to develop a culture in which people bring their work-related feelings to legitimate forums where they can be made available for examination in relation to the work rather than discharged in informal subgroups. What they mean by an interpretative stance, then, is a collaborative verbalisation of unconscious processes leading to withdrawal of projections that might be adversely affecting task performance. The objection to informal subgroups seems to be based on the belief that, since they are based purely on personal relationships rather than task, they are fertile ground for projections and basic assumption behaviour. Note how this model of organisational functioning leads to a focus on the legitimate relationships in an organisation.

●●●● 7.5 Leaders and groups

In both strategic choice and mainstream learning organisation theory, leaders are assumed to be perfectly healthy, balanced people, who set the direction of the organisation for others to follow. However, as soon as it is recognised that basic assumption groups can very quickly emerge from work groups, the possibility arises that leaders can also be the creations of the group. It is quite possible that leaders are vainly trying to act out the fantasies that those in the management team are projecting. Leaders affect what groups do, but groups also affect what leaders do through processes of unconscious projection.

Leadership

Bales (1970) identified the emergence of two kinds of leaders in small task-oriented groups: the task leader who gives suggestions, shows disagreement and presses the group to focus on task completion; and the social-emotional leader who asks for suggestions, shows solidarity and soothes tempers by encouraging tension release. These leadership roles are mutually supportive in that each helps the group solve different problems, provided that the role occupants can work together. Sometimes one person can combine both roles – the 'great man' leader (Borgatta, Couch and Bales, 1954). When specialist leaders of this kind do not emerge or cannot work together, then members begin to deal with their frustration in unconscious ways that lead to the emergence of scapegoat roles, enemy roles, messiah roles and so on. Bion (1961) distinguishes between different types of leader in the basic assumption group: the fight leader, the flight leader, the dependency leader and the leader who symbolises some unrealistic utopian, messianic or oceanic hope. Bion points to the precarious position these leaders occupy. The important point here is that the leader is sucked into that position by the group and is controlled by the group, not the other way around as we usually believe.

An important distinction is that between the leader of a work group and a basic assumption leader. An effective leader is one who maintains a clear focus on and definition of the primary task. That task determines the requirements of the leader, who must continually struggle to synthesise, participate and observe. The effective leader operates on the boundary of the group, avoiding both emotional immersion and extreme detachment. Leaders are there to regulate transactions between their groups and other groups. Both immersion and distance make this impossible. When a group is dominated by basic assumption behaviour it sucks into the leadership position one who is completely immersed in the emotional atmosphere, the basic assumption behaviour of the group. This leader is subjected to conflicting and fundamentally impossible roles – to provide unlimited nurturance, to fight and subdue imaginary enemies, to rescue the group from death and dissolution, to fulfil utopian or messianic hopes.

One of the most intriguing aspects of relatively unstructured and ego-involving small groups is the evolution of a constellation of informal roles that serve important social and psychological functions for the group. Most small-group research has addressed itself to groups that do not have formal statuses and ascribed social positions. The roles that emerge are usually described as 'behaviour patterns,' 'individual roles,' or 'interpersonal styles.' Under relatively unstructured conditions, psychological factors, conscious and unconscious, become increasingly important as determinants of role structure . . . Explicit and formal social prescriptions are replaced by fantasy conceptions of norms and sanctions. At the same time, it is assumed that such roles are not simply expressive of idiosyncratic needs but perform necessary and recurrent functions for the social system – such functions as impulse expression, group maintenance, tension release. (Gibbard, Hartman and Mann, 1974, p. 179)

The kinds of roles that have been distinguished are those of the aggressor, the seducer who tries to seduce people into exposing their feelings and positions, the scapegoat, the hero, the resistors, the anxious participators, the distressed females, the respected enactors, the sexual idols, the outsiders, the prophets (Dunphy, 1968). These informal roles develop in order to contain and deal with internal conflict, the tension of fusion and individuation. One of the key roles is that of leader. Managers' choices and actions may have more to do with unconscious processes than any rational consideration.

Neurotic forms of leadership

Strategic choice and mainstream learning organisation theory focus on what leadership means when it is functioning well. However, leaders often do not function very well and quite often they are definitely dysfunctional. Such dysfunctional leadership has not attracted very much attention in most of the management literature, but it occurs frequently and it is therefore a matter of importance to understand something about it. Functional leaders assist in the containment of anxiety and thus help to create the possibility of double-loop learning, but dysfunctional, neurotic leaders may well become caught up, and drive others to become caught up, in neurotic defences that will block such learning.

Kets de Vries (1989) explains the nature of neurotic leadership in the following way. Everyone behaves in a manner that is affected by what one might think of as an inner theatre. That theatre consists of a number of representations of people and situations, often formed early in childhood, and those that have come to play the most important roles are core conflictual relationships. It is as if people spend much of their lives re-enacting conflicts that they could not understand in childhood, partly because they are familiar to them, and partly, perhaps, because they are always seeking to understand them. What they do, then, is project this inner play with conflictual situations out on to the real world they have to deal with. Leaders do this just as others do, the difference being that they project their inner conflicts on to a much larger real-world stage that includes their followers. A leader projects internal private dialogues into external public ones and these dialogues are about core conflictual themes from childhood. The particular neurotic style a leader practises will be determined by the nature of these core conflicts.

Followers also project their inner plays on to the leader and these leader/follower projections keep leaders and followers engaged with each other in a particular manner. Followers project their dependency needs into leaders and displace their own ideals, wishes and desires on to them too.

The inner theatre in which leaders and followers join each other contains scenarios which are the basis of imagined, desired and feared relationships between them. There are typical scenarios that are found over and over again and they constitute typical dispositions, typical ways of defending against, repressing, denying and idealising particular leader/follower relationships. Everyone uses such devices and everyone has a number of prominent dispositions that constitute that person's neurotic style. This is quite normal and it becomes a problem only when people massively, compulsively and habitually use a rather small number of defences. This blocks their ability to relate to reality effectively and it is then that they might be labelled 'neurotic'.

Kets de Vries (1989) distinguishes between a number of such dispositions or neurotic styles as follows. Every leader will display a combination of some of these styles and it becomes a problem only when a rather small number of these come to dominate the behaviour of the leader and the followers.

1 The *aggressive* disposition tends to characterise many who become leaders and rather fewer who are followers – aggression is often acceptable in leaders but creates problems for followers. Tough chief executives who are socially forceful and intimidating, energetic, competitive and power oriented fall into this category. People are not important to them and they want to dominate. They tend to be impulsive and to believe that the world is a jungle. They expect people to be hostile to them and they become aggressive in advance to counteract such expected hostility. Of course their behaviour may well provoke the hostility they expect. Such leaders probably experienced parental rejection or hostility.

2 The *paranoid* disposition is found frequently amongst leaders and less amongst followers. Such people are always looking for hidden motives and are suspicious of others. They are hypervigilant, keep scanning the environment and take unnecessary precautions. They deny personal weakness and do not readily accept blame. They tend to be restricted and cold in relationships with little humour. They are fond of mechanistic devices to measure performance and keep track of people. Such people may have had intrusive parents and may feel uncertain of themselves.

3 The *histrionic* disposition is characterised by a need to attract the attention of others at all costs. Such people are alert to the desires of others, they are sociable and seductive with their sense of self-worth heavily dependent on the opinion of others. They love activity and excitement and tend to overreact to minor incidents, often throwing tantrums. Such people may have had difficulty attracting the attention of parents.

4 The *detached* disposition is displayed when people find it difficult to form close relationships. They tend to be cold and aloof and this may be a response to parental devaluation.

5 The *controlling* disposition is high in leaders and low in followers and it is displayed by people who want to control everything in their lives. They have an excessive desire for order and control. This is a way of managing hostile feelings

that may have arisen from the behaviour of controlling parents. The resultant hostility may emerge as tyrannical ways of behaving or its opposite of submission.

6 The *passive-aggressive* disposition tends to be found more in followers than in leaders. Such people are highly dependent but tend to attack those they depend upon. They resist demands for performance, they are defiant, provocative and negative, complaining all the time and demanding much from their leaders. They tend to blame others all the time, they are ambivalent and pessimistic. This difficulty might arise because such people find it difficult to assess what is expected of them. They are likely to have parents who presented them with conflicting messages.

7 Other dispositions are the *narcissistic* one when people see themselves as exceptional and special; the *dependent* disposition in which people are excessively dependent upon others; and the *masochistic* disposition.

It is not just the style of the leader or the style of the followers on their own that determines how their joint behaviour unfolds. It is how the styles engage each other that will create the environment within which they have to work. So, an aggressive, controlling leader interacting with dependent, masochistic followers will produce a rather different context and pattern of behaviour compared with such a leader interacting with, say, passive-aggressive followers. These patterns of interaction will have a powerful impact on how effectively an organisation learns. Such neurotically based interactions, therefore, have to be understood as central to processes of management.

● ● ● ● 7.6   How open systems/psychoanalytic perspectives deal with four key questions

This chapter now turns to how open systems/psychoanalytic perspectives answer the four questions posed at the end of Chapter 1. These were:

1 How does the theory view the nature of interaction?
2 What view does it take of human nature?
3 What methodology does it employ?
4 How does it deal with paradox?

You can compare how the theories surveyed in this chapter answer the questions with the kind of answers found in strategic choice theory (section 4.10). You can also make comparisons with learning organisation theory (section 6.7). Consider now how open systems/psychoanalytic perspectives deal with the questions.

The nature of interaction

Interaction within and between organisations is understood in systems terms as with strategic choice and learning organisation theory. While cybernetics analyses a system in terms of self-regulating negative feedback loops and systems dynamics takes account of amplifying positive feedback loops, open systems theory focuses attention on regulatory functions at the system's boundary. Essentially, these functions regulate the flows of imports into, and exports out of, the system so that the system adapts to its environment. The dynamics, the way the system moves, is therefore the same as for cybernetics, that is a tendency to move towards stable equilibrium when it is succeeding.

Open systems theory pays more attention to the micro level than cybernetics and systems dynamics do. In other words, it pays attention to the subsystems of which the whole is composed. This is especially so when it is combined with psychoanalytic perspectives because they are very much concerned with the individuals and the groups that make up an organisation. The disorderly dynamics generated by individuals relating to each other in groups then becomes very important as an obstacle to the successful movement towards adaptive equilibrium. Those writing in the Tavistock tradition distinguish between the task/role system and the system of individuals/groups. The task/role system is a subsystem of the organisation that is open to the other subsystem consisting of individuals and groups, and also open to the environment consisting of other organisations. When the imports from the individuals/groups subsystem are adequately regulated then the task/role subsystem can make rational choices about adapting to the environment of other organisations.

So, this is a theory that pays considerable attention to both macro and micro levels and it envisages both orderly and disorderly dynamics. The former is equated with successful adaptation to the environment and the latter as an obstacle to this process. The orderly operation of the task/role system is understood in much the same way as strategic choice or learning organisation theory. However, the attention to micro detail brings in very important processes that can disrupt the rational processes.

The theory of causality, however, is the same as that for cybernetics/strategic choice and systems dynamics/learning organisation, namely formative cause. The emphasis is on already enfolded archetypes that are unfolded as the system develops. The same problems to do with ordinary human freedom and novelty follow. This opens systems/psychoanalytic approach cannot explain how novel, transformative changes come about. These are matters that rely on some kind of explanation in terms of the individual.

The nature of human beings

The theory reviewed in this chapter takes a very different view of human nature to the mainly cognitivist and humanistic perspectives on which strategic choice and learning organisation theories are built. The main difference is the emphasis it places on unconscious processes, the effects of anxiety and the ever-present possibility of defensive and aggressive behaviour. Human ability to behave rationally and altruistically is seen as highly problematic and the capacity for learning as very fragile. Attention is focused on power and dysfunctional behaviour in a way that the use of cognitivist and humanistic assumptions in the other theories largely ignores.

However, there are also significant similarities. First, the notion of representation is as central in psychoanalysis as in cognitivism. In other words, in both of these theories it is assumed that individuals somehow form inner mental representations of outer reality and then act on the basis of those representations. However, the nature of the representations and the processes through which they are formed are very different. Consider what representation means in most psychoanalytic theories:

- In classic, Freudian drive theory, a representation is a conscious or unconscious idea that represents an instinct and as such it is the expression of some basic, inherited body function. So, here there is no notion of a more or less accurate picture of a pre-given external world. Instead, there is a unique expression of general bodily functions internal to the individual body, developed from the interaction of inherited instincts and actual experience. In early object relations theory (Klein, 1975) the notion of representation is developed in a different way. Representations are of part-objects and objects encountered in relationships. Object here is mainly a person or some part of a person and the nature of the representation is highly complex. It is not at all a more or less accurate picture of an external reality but rather an internal construct developed through experience on the basis of inherent, inherited fantasies common to all humans. The earliest object is that of the mother's breast and what is being represented is not so much the object itself as the experience and fantasied relationship with the object. Later object relations theorists (Bion, Winnicott, Fairbairn) placed much more emphasis on the relationships as did attachment theorists (Bowlby, Balint), self psychologists (Kohut) and relational psychologists (Sullivan, Stern), for all of whom representations are primarily of relationships with other human beings.
- As with cognitivism, representations are made up of symbols that form 'internal' templates (drive derivatives, forbidden wishes, objects, relationships) which are the basis upon which a human being knows and acts. 'Internal' here refers not to the brain but to a mental apparatus or process. This is described in terms of mental components or agents – the ego, the id and the superego, various object and self-object representations, relational interactions that have been generalised. The question of where such an apparatus might be located, or where the fantasies and other psychological processes might actually be, is never addressed
- As with cognitivism, representations are built up through a process of symbol processing but there is no suggestion that this is like a computer. Indeed, the process through which the representations are constructed becomes highly complex. Freudian drive theory emphasises processes of defence and suppression. Object relations theory presents highly complex mental processes of splitting, projecting, introjecting, identifying, idealising, denigrating, making reparation and so on. Attachment theorists, self and relational psychologists talk about processes of evocation, resonance, mirroring, attunement and empathy. All of these processes build up representations of objects and relationships.
- As with cognitivism, representing is a process of recovering or reconstructing templates from a memory bank but these now take different forms. They could be drive-driven wishes that are permissible in terms of external reality or suppressed wishes expressive of the pleasure principle. Or, they could be recoveries of past object relationships. Representing, as a process of comparing new stimuli with past representations of external, environmental features, receives little

emphasis. Instead the representations are used to interpret reality and may well distort it in various transferential and projective processes.

The above usage of 'representation' clearly carries with it substantial implications. It postulates that the individual human mind is formed by the clash of inherited drives and social constraints, out of which there emerges a mental apparatus that mediates the clash. Later developments in psychoanalytic theory increasingly see humans occupying a world formed by relationships with other human beings, with representations of these relationships emerging from them and coming in turn to govern them. There is a separate entity that does this representing, namely a mind or psyche of the individual. These separate individual entities cannot easily share the same representations because each individual uniquely constructs his or her own psyche. However, psychic processes are postulated that allow some degree of sharing of mental contents or states. These processes include projective identification, resonance, mirroring, empathy, attunement and, of course, talking. The world into which the human acts is primarily created rather than found. This, of course, is the reverse of the cognitivist implication.

There is a decentring of the individual in an inner sense in that the individual is not clearly in control of his or her mind, but, rather, is buffeted about by the id. However, in any external sense there is no significant decentring of the individual. It is true that the social prohibition is part of the process of structuring the psyche, particularly in the form of the superego, but groups arise when members identify with the same leader. There is no sense of individuals and groups co-creating each other. The social plays a part only in terms of the reality principle. This curbs the limitless drive for pleasure on the part of the individual, a drive which has to be mediated first by an ego and then by a superego. The process of mental structuring is essentially the feat of the individual infant as it copes with unconscious fantasy, proceeding from primitive dependency to autonomy. This is very much within the dominant Western paradigm of the autonomous individual.

To summarise, in both cognitivism and psychoanalysis, the individual is prior and primary to the group. In both theories individuals build representations of reality. However, they do so in very different ways and build very different kinds of representations. In doing so, they present very different views on human nature and the ability of an individual to control his or her own mental processes. The impact of unconscious group processes on the individual's ability to think and act rationally receives a great deal of attention in this theory. The individual is primary in the sense that he or she is born with inherited drives and fantasies that are constrained by social forces. The individual is not primary if one takes the view that an individual mind is socially constructed within the constraints provided by biological inheritance. If one takes the latter view then a different theory of organisations is arrived at. I will be discussing this possibility in Part Three.

Methodology

In strategic choice and learning organisation theory the researcher, consultant and manager are assumed to be able to stand outside the organisational system and take the position of the objective observer. The perspectives in this chapter take a similar methodological stance but with an important difference. The consultant, researcher and manager are assumed to stand at the boundary of the organisational system. In this position one is not so immersed in the organisational culture that one loses a rational, objective perspective. However, one is immersed enough to experience how being in that culture feels. These feelings are part of the information that can be used to understand the organisation.

Paradox

While strategic choice and learning organisation theory do not recognise paradox, it is central to a psychoanalytic perspective. The struggle between ego, id and superego is never resolved. The capacity to think and learn requires an individual to take the depressive position where it is possible to hold ambiguity and paradox in the mind. Creativity requires the individual mind to occupy the transitional space. This is essentially paradoxical since it is both fantasy and reality at the same time.

Making sense of experience

The perspectives in this chapter are particularly useful when it comes to making sense of experiences that feel stressful or bizarre. It might be possible to understand them by paying attention to the effects of anxiety on people's behaviour and how they defend against it. It also offers ways of understanding the nature and impact of dysfunctional leadership and inappropriate applications of power. It is important to bear in mind that the processes I have been describing affect how an organisation evolves. They are as important as rational choice in determining what happens to an organisation.

7.7 Summary

This chapter has reviewed open systems theory and psychoanalytic perspectives, pointing to how they focus attention on aspects of life that do not feature in strategic choice and learning organisation theory.

The open systems/psychoanalytic approach opens up insights like these:

- Charismatic leaders and the strong cultures of dependence they provoke in followers may well be extremely unhealthy for organisations. Researchers (e.g. Peters and Waterman, 1982) may therefore note the presence of charismatic leaders and superficially conclude that this is the reason for success, when it might well be a neurotic phenomenon that is about to undermine the company.
- A cohesive team of managers may not be a healthy phenomenon at all. It may be an unhealthy and unproductive reflection of the fantasy of basic assumption groups acting out dependence or oneness assumptions. Again researchers not considering an organisation from a psychoanalytic point of view may well conclude that such neurotic cohesion is a reason for success.

- The idea of the group or the management team may itself be a defence mechanism. So, faced by high levels of strategic uncertainty and ambiguity, managers may retreat into the 'mother figure' of the team for comfort and in so doing fail to deal with the strategic issues.
- Groups clearly do not have to have a purpose or even a task to function very tightly as a group, even if it is a misguided one. Again, signs of close teams should provoke suspicion, not praise.
- Groups or teams are a two-edged sword. People need them to establish their identity. They need them to operate effectively. But they can also deskill people.
- The desire for cohesion may well be a neurotic phenomenon.
- Plans and rigid structures and rules may all be defences against anxiety instead of the rational way of proceeding usually considered.
- One aspect of culture is the emotional atmosphere, the basic assumption, that a group of people create as they interact.

Further reading

Hirschorn (1990) provides an important exposition of the role of the informal organisation as a defence against anxiety. I would also recommend Shapiro and Carr (1991) and Kets de Vries (1989), as well as Miller (1993), Oberholzer and Roberts (1995) and Gould, Stapely and Stein (2001). They all give deeper insight into the psychodynamics of organisations. Winnicott (1971) is also well worth reading.

Chapter 8

Knowledge creation in organisations
Second-order systems, autopoiesis and constructivist psychology

8.1   Introduction

Previous chapters in this part of the book have described the origins of modern systems thinking in the philosophy of Kant and how the idea of systems was significantly developed around the 1950s in what might be called the first wave of twentieth-century systems thinking. That first wave had three strands, namely, cybernetics, systems dynamics and general system theory and it also reflected a shift in psychological theories from behaviourism to cognitivism and later constructivism to some extent. So far, the chapters have reviewed how these theories of systems and psychology have formed the basis of three important theories of organisation and management. First, there is the theory of strategic choice and it was pointed out how it is built on theoretical foundations provided by cybernetics and cognitivist psychology. Here, an organisation becomes what it becomes through the strategies chosen by its dominant coalition in a rational manner. The second theory is that of the learning organisation built on the theoretical foundations of systems dynamics, humanistic and cognitivist psychology, and to some extent constructivist psychology. Here, an organisation becomes what it becomes through the processes of learning in which its managers and other members engage. Leadership, motivation, inspiration and widespread participation in a greater whole become important concepts. Discussion of this theory was followed by a chapter discussing the behavioural obstacles to strategic choice and organisational learning to be found in a theory combining general systems theory with psychoanalytic perspectives on human psychology. Here, an organisation becomes what it becomes through strategic choice and learning intertwined with complex unconscious processes. The manner in which anxiety is contained becomes very important.

This chapter explores the more recent interest shown in the importance of knowledge in organisational life. This is a development of the resource-based view of strategy mentioned in Chapter 3 and of the learning organisation discussed in Chapters 5 and 6. Here, the central question for strategy becomes how people in an organisation create knowledge and what needs to be done to manage an organisation's knowledge assets. When one focuses on knowledge in organisations, one cannot escape the fact that knowing is a human activity and a self-referential one at that. The psychological theory underlying the theorising about organisational knowledge therefore acquires a much stronger constructivist angle. Furthermore, the self-referential nature of knowledge management demands a self-referential perspective on systems and this is provided by what has come to be known as second-order systems thinking. Those writing on knowledge in organisations also frequently appeal to the notion of autopoiesis. This chapter will, therefore, explore second-order systems thinking, the theory of autopoiesis and constructivist psychology in the context of knowledge management.

Many argue that the global change toward the knowledge economy has major implications for the strategic management of organisations. First, professional knowledge workers need to be managed in different ways to those of the industrial age. Unleashing the creativity of knowledge workers requires them to be empowered so that they can participate more fully in the development of the organisation and special measures need to be taken to ensure that individual knowledge becomes organisational knowledge. Many argue that this is to be done by codifying the knowledge held by key knowledge workers and by taking steps to retain their services. The new knowledge economy also has major implications for the nature of an organisation's assets. In the industrial age, accounting measures of asset values were close to the capital market valuation of the organisation because market pricing of the main assets, namely physical resources such as plant and equipment, enabled them to be measured. Managing the value of a corporation meant managing measurable physical assets and the 'human resources' who used them. In the new knowledge economy, however, knowledge is said to be the major asset and since it is not directly traded in markets, it is not measured and recorded in corporate balance sheets. As a result, enormous gaps have opened up between the asset values recorded by a corporation and the value capital markets place on the corporation itself. This creates problems for managing assets to produce shareholder value. The response to this has been a call to measure the intellectual capital of a corporation and manage its knowledge assets.

Some strands of thinking about knowledge creation in organisations represent a continuation of the thinking about learning organisations reviewed in Chapters 5 and 6. The theory of interaction is largely provided by systems dynamics and the theory of psychology is that of cognitivism. This will be reviewed in section 8.2. Another strand draws on a different systems theory, namely, autopoiesis, and a different psychological theory, namely constructivism. This will be explored in section 8.3.

8.2 Knowledge management in the tradition of the learning organisation

Nonaka's writings (Nonaka, 1991; Nonaka and Takeuchi, 1995) have exerted a major impact on the development of theories of knowledge creation in organisations (for example, Brown, 1991; Burton-Jones, 1999; Davenport and Prusak,

1998; Garven, 1993; Kleiner and Roth, 1997; Leonard and Strauss, 1997; Quinn, Anderson and Finkelstein, 1996; Sveiby, 1997). Like Senge (*see* Chapters 5 and 6), Nonaka draws on the systems dynamics strand of systems thinking, including some concepts from chaos and complexity theories, which he treats as extensions of that thinking (*see* Chapter 12), and Argyris and Schon whose learning theories he traces back to Bateson (1972). In addition, he relies heavily on Polanyi's (1958; 1960) distinction between tacit and explicit knowledge.

Creating new knowledge

According to Nonaka (1991) new knowledge is created when tacit knowledge is made explicit and crystallised into an innovation, that is, a re-creation of some aspect of the world according to some new insight or ideal. New knowledge, according to Nonaka, comes from tapping the tacit, subjective insights, intuitions and hunches of individuals and making them available for testing and use by the organisation as a whole. For him tacit knowledge is personal and hard to formalise. It is rooted in action and shows itself as skill, or know-how. In addition to being in technical skills, tacit knowledge lies in the mental models, beliefs and perspectives ingrained in the way people understand their world and act in it. Tacit knowledge is below the level of awareness and is therefore very difficult to communicate. The nature of explicit knowledge, however, is easy to understand: it is the formal and systematic knowledge that is easily communicated, for example in the form of product specifications or computer programs.

Tapping tacit knowledge

Nonaka gives an example of how tacit knowledge is to be tapped. In 1985, product developers at Matsushita could not perfect the kneading action of the home bread-baking machine they were developing. After much unhelpful analysis, including comparisons of x-rays of dough kneaded by the machine and dough kneaded by professionals, one member of the team proposed a creative approach. She proposed using a top professional baker as a model, so she trained with a top baker to acquire his kneading technique and after a year of trial and error she was able to help her colleagues reproduce a mechanical kneading action that mimicked that of the professional. This example describes a movement between different kinds of knowledge, the tacit and the explicit:

- tacit to tacit as the product developer acquires the skill of the professional baker through observation, copying and practising, so internalising it and learning;
- tacit to explicit as the product developer articulates the foundations of her newly acquired tacit knowledge to her colleagues;
- explicit to tacit as the colleagues internalise the knowledge made explicit by the product developer and use it to alter their own tacit knowledge or mental models – in other words, they learn;
- explicit to explicit as the newly formulated product specifications are communicated to the production department and embodied in working models and final production processes.

Innovation then flows from a form of learning, that is, new knowledge creation, that in turn flows from moving knowledge between one type and another.

New knowledge starts with an individual, according to Nonaka. Tacit knowledge has to travel from one person to another, in a way that cannot be centrally intended because no one knows what is to travel, or to whom, until it has travelled. New knowledge can therefore only be created when individuals operate in empowered teams.

A key difficulty in the creation of new knowledge is that of bringing tacit knowledge to the surface of individual awareness, conveying tacit knowledge from one person to another, and finally making it explicit. This is so difficult because it requires expressing the inexpressible and this needs figurative rather than literal language.

- *Metaphors*. Metaphors have to be used to link contradictions to each other. It is when people juxtapose seemingly illogical and contradictory things that they are stimulated to look for multiple meanings, to call upon tacit knowledge and so develop new insights. The ambiguity of metaphors provokes and challenges people to define them more clearly. Metaphors are formulated through intuition, a form of tacit reasoning that links images that may seem remote from each other. Nonaka describes how, in 1978, top management at Honda inaugurated the development of a new car concept with the slogan 'Let's gamble', indicating the need for a completely new approach. The development team expressed what they should do to deal with this metaphor in the form of another slogan: 'Theory of Automobile Evolution' (a contradictory idea of a car as both a machine and an organism). This posed the question: if a car was like an organism how would it evolve? The designers discussed what this might mean and produced another slogan: 'Man–maximum, Machine–minimum'. This conveyed the idea that the car should focus on comfort in an urban environment. The idea of evolution prompted the designers to think of the car as a sphere, a car that was 'short' and 'tall'. This gave birth to the idea of a 'Tall Boy' car, eventually called the Honda City.
- *Analogy*. Once metaphors have provoked new ideas, analogies between one thing and another can then be used to find some resolution of the contradictions that have provoked people into thinking new things. Analogy is a more structured process of reconciling opposites and making distinctions, clarifying how the opposing ideas are actually alike or not alike. To illustrate this, Nonaka recounts the story of Canon's development of the mini-copier. To ensure reliability, the developers proposed to make the copier drum disposable – the drum accounted for 90 per cent of maintenance problems. Team members were discussing, over a beer, the problem of how to make the drum easily and cheaply, when the team leader held up his beer can and asked how much it cost to make one. This led the team to examine the process of making cans to see if it could be applied to the manufacture of photocopier drums. The result was lightweight aluminium copier drums.
- *Models*. Finally, models are used actually to resolve the contradiction and crystallise the new knowledge: for example, a prototype kneading machine, or a prototype small photocopier.

As new knowledge is dispersed through a group and an organisation, it must be tested – that means that there must be discussion, dialogue and disagreement.

The distinction Nonaka makes between tacit and explicit knowledge (Griffin, Shaw and Stacey, 1999) is derived from Polanyi (Polanyi and Prosch, 1975). Nonaka and Takeuchi maintain that 'knowledge is created and expanded through social interaction between tacit and explicit knowledge' (1995, p. 61) in the four modes of knowledge conversion described above. However, as Tsoukas points out, Polanyi was actually arguing that tacit and explicit knowledge are not two separate forms of knowledge, but rather that:

> *Tacit knowledge is the necessary component of all knowledge; it is not made up of discrete beans which may be ground, lost or reconstituted . . . to split tacit from explicit knowledge is to miss the point – the two are inseparably related. (Tsoukas, 1997, p. 10)*

Another point to note is how Nonaka and Takeuchi (1995) talk about knowledge as embodied, rooted in experience and arising in interaction between individuals:

> *Our dynamic model of knowledge creation is anchored to a critical assumption that human knowledge is created and expanded through social interaction between tacit knowledge and explicit knowledge. We call this interaction 'knowledge conversion.' It should be noted that this conversion is a 'social' process between individuals and not confined within an individual. (p. 10)*

They emphasise the importance of dialogue and discussion in this conversion process (p. 13), pointing to the importance of intuition, hunches, metaphors and symbols (p. 12). They see knowledge as essentially related to action and arising from a process in which interacting individuals are committed to justifying their beliefs. They talk about knowledge as justified belief closely related to people's values. They talk about the context of ambiguity and redundancy in which knowledge is created (p. 12). However, they then take their argument in a direction that leaves the importance of relationships and the social undeveloped and unexplored. Having emphasised the social, they locate the initiation of new knowledge in the individual:

> *In a strict sense, knowledge is created only by individuals. The organization supports creative individuals or provides contexts for them to create knowledge. Organizational knowledge creation, therefore, should be understood as a process that 'organizationally' amplifies the knowledge created by individuals and crystallizes it as a part of the knowledge network of the organization. The process takes place within an expanding 'community of interaction,' which crosses intra- and interorganizational levels and boundaries . . . Tacit knowledge is personal, context-specific. (p. 59)*

In this way of seeing things, tacit knowledge is possessed by individuals and the knowledge creation at an organisational level is the extraction of this already existing tacit knowledge from individuals and spread across the organisation by socialising processes. This leads to a rather linear sequential view of individuals passing tacit knowledge to others, primarily through imitation, then formalising and codifying it so that it can be used.

The emphasis of Nonaka and Takeuchi on the individual as the origin of knowledge, on the other hand, leads them to emphasise the organisation-wide intentional character of knowledge creation:

The knowledge spiral is driven by organizational intention, which is defined as an organization's aspiration to its goals. Effort to achieve the intention usually takes the form of strategy within a business setting. From the viewpoint of organizational knowledge creation, the essence of strategy lies in developing the organizational capability to acquire, create, accumulate, and exploit knowledge. The most critical element of corporate strategy is to conceptualize a vision about what kind of knowledge should be developed and to operationalize it into a management system for implementation . . . Organizational intention provides the most important criterion for judging the truthfulness of a given piece of knowledge. If not for intention, it would be impossible to judge the value of information or knowledge perceived or created. (p. 74)

Having emphasised the ambiguity of the situation in which knowledge arises, Nonaka and Takeuchi leave this behind and move to the strategic choice view of strategy. Nonaka and Takeuchi do not pay much attention to the ever-present possibility of groups of people becoming stuck in some stable dynamic, or some fragmenting one that kills off the knowledge-creating process. What Nonaka and Takeuchi end up with, then, is a process for knowledge creation that can be managed and controlled.

The individual and the organisation

Many writers have written in the same vein as Nonaka. Like him they all posit a fundamental split between the individual and the organisation. The individual and the organisation are always treated as two distinct phenomenal levels requiring different explanations of how learning and knowledge creation takes place. The connection between the two levels is usually understood as follows. Individuals in interaction with each other together create the levels of organisation and society and those collective levels constitute the context within which individuals act. In other words, individuals construct organisational/social levels, which then act back to affect those individuals. It is usually explicitly stated that it is individuals who learn and create knowledge, although this is almost always coupled with an emphasis on the importance of the teams within which that individual learning takes place. A key question then becomes whether a team, group or organisation can be said to learn or whether it is just their individual members who do so. For these writers, in the end, it is usually individuals who learn and create knowledge and the principal concern from an organisational perspective is then how that individual learning and knowledge might be shared across an organisation and how it might be captured, stored and retained by the organisation. Sometimes, the group/social level is treated as a kind of transcendent group mind, common pool of meaning or flow of a larger intelligence, for example, in Senge's treatment of Bohm's notion of dialogue (*see* Chapter 6).

Since it is usually assumed that it is individuals who learn it follows that knowledge creation involves the transmission of knowledge from one individual to another. This notion derives from information theory (Shannon and Weaver, 1949) and it posits a sender–receiver model of knowledge transmission in which one individual sends some kind of signal to another, who receives it and then sends a responding signal back to the first. These signals are often categorised in the following way (for example, *see* Davenport and Prusak, 1998):

- Data are usually defined as a set of discrete objective facts about events.
- Information is then data that make a difference. It is a message passed from a sender to a receiver that shapes the perception of the receiver. Information has a meaning; it has a shape and it is organised for some purpose. Data become information when the creator of information adds meaning to the data.
- Knowledge is taken to be a framework for evaluating and incorporating new experiences and information. This framework originates in the mind of the knower and it is formed by past experience as well as by current values and beliefs. It is stored as memory in fluid and structured forms. It may be explicit or tacit, a distinction to be further examined later on in this section, and it is transmitted from one knower to another. Insight and wisdom are sometimes classified under knowledge and sometimes regarded as higher forms of more intuitive knowing. In other words, knowledge is equated with the notion of mental models described in Chapter 7.
- Action is a choice made on the basis of knowledge and that knowledge is evaluated in the light of the consequences of the decisions and actions it leads to. This is a systemic, error-activated notion of learning.

It is assumed that data, information and knowledge are transmitted from one individual to another and it is here that the distinction between explicit and tacit knowledge (Nonaka and Takeuchi, 1995) becomes particularly important. Explicit knowledge is formal, systematic knowledge, easily transmitted from one person to another in the form of language (verbal, mathematical and numerical). What is transmitted is thought of as a translation of already existing tacit knowledge into language, that is, into a codified form. Immediately, a particular assumption is being made about the nature of language, namely, that it is a formal, objective system of symbols located outside people and employed by them as a tool to translate already existing ideas and concepts into a form that can be readily transmitted to the others. Criticisms of this view will be taken up in Part Three. Tacit knowledge is subjective insights, intuitions and hunches, below the level of awareness and is, therefore, hard to formalise and communicate. It is rooted in action and shows itself as skill or know-how, lying in the beliefs and perspectives ingrained in the way people understand their world and act in it. In other words, tacit knowledge takes the form of mental models that are below the level of awareness.

New knowledge

New knowledge is said to come from tapping the tacit knowledge located in individual heads and this process of tapping is understood as one of translating the tacit knowledge in individual heads into explicit forms. Knowledge management writers focus attention on this process of translation but do not explain how completely new tacit knowledge comes to arise in individual heads. The explanation starts from the point where some individual already possesses important tacit knowledge. What is explained is how some novelty arising in an unexplained way is subsequently transmitted to others so that it can become organisational knowledge. This knowledge may be 'new' to the organisation but it is not 'new' per se.

New knowledge, arising in an unexplained way in some individual, is transferred as movement in tacit form from one individual to another. This movement takes place through a process of mimicry. The possessor of tacit knowledge expresses it in the form of skilled action, that is, as the professional, expert, mentor or teacher. The acquirer of this tacit knowledge observes, copies and practises the skilled action of the expert, so internalising and learning it. Having acquired the tacit knowledge through this process of mimicry, the now skilled novice may translate it into explicit form for communication to others. This step of translating tacit into explicit knowledge is recognised as being problematic because it requires expressing the inexpressible. The translation therefore requires the figurative language of metaphor and analogy to bring what is below the level of awareness into awareness.

This is where it becomes important to work and learn in teams. How members of those teams relate to each other, how they converse with each other and what kind of language they use, all become important matters. Once tacit knowledge has been made explicit then others must internalise it so that it becomes part of their tacit store. Or the explicit knowledge may be embodied in working models and prototypes of one form or another, in cultural artifacts, or in written and unwritten codes and procedures. As knowledge is dispersed through an organisation by this process of movement between tacit and explicit it must be tested and this requires discussion, dialogue and disagreement. Some distinguish between discussion and dialogue, where the former is a competitive form of conversation and the latter a co-operative one in which people suspend their assumptions and learn collectively far more than they can learn individually (Bohm, 1983; Senge, 1990).

Knowledge creation is basically a process of transmission between individuals in which data are converted into information through the medium of knowledge, which may be explicit but, far more importantly, may be tacit. The transmission of knowledge between people is a process of conversion between tacit and explicit forms based on mimicry in tacit–tacit transfers, group dialogue and discussion in metaphorical and analogical language in tacit–explicit transfers, formalisation and codification in explicit–explicit transfers, and internalisation in explicit–tacit transfers. Knowledge is understood to move about in this way through the interplay of individual and group/organisational/social levels.

This understanding of mind is drawn from cognitivist psychology (*see* Chapter 3). The brain, according to this approach, forms representations of external reality, structures them into patterns, or models, which are stored in memory, and then later retrieved in order to process new sense data encountered by the individual. Mental models, then, provide the means for an individual to process data about the world and the means for making a choice of actions to take. Much knowledge management thinking, therefore, is based on a very particular view of the nature of mind and of the functioning of the brain. It is a view in which the mind and the brain, of which it is a function, form representations, store them in memory, process information and data and then make a choice. It is a theory in which thought and choice precede action. All of these assumptions are taken for granted.

The theory of knowledge management leads to a number of prescriptions. The first is that of measuring the intellectual capital of an organisation (for example, Roos *et al.*, 1997; Sveiby, 1997). The aim of measuring intellectual capital is that of managing its contribution to shareholder value. Writers on knowledge management seem much concerned with people leaving an organisation and taking their implicit knowledge with them. This leads to prescriptions to do with the conversion of individual tacit knowledge into explicit form and the storing of that explicit knowledge in either centralised or distributed systems. Linked to this are the prescriptions to do with developing Information Technology so that knowledge held by individuals can be captured and so owned and controlled by organisations. Related to these prescriptions are others to do with hiring and retaining a professional elite. It is argued that professionals must be managed in a different manner to others to persuade them to stay in an organisation. The call is for greater flexibility and empowerment because professionals require more autonomy. However, prescriptions of this kind tend to be immediately coupled with further prescriptions to do with the setting of stretch targets, monitoring of performance and linked financial reward systems. The autonomy of the professional is thereby heavily subscribed. Linked to this, there are prescriptions for 'downsizing' and leaner organisations to be accomplished by the outsourcing of work, including non-core professional work. Closely linked to prescriptions for hiring and retaining of professionals are those for training and developing people. The aim of training and development is to increase the competence, skill and knowledge of the individual, including the capacity to work as a member of a team. The emphasis is placed on managing not just the activities of training and development but the quality of the learning process itself. Management is understood in systemic terms and the prescriptions relate to the design and operation of a system to ensure the quality of the learning process.

Next, there are prescriptions concerned with spreading knowledge around an organisation. If knowledge is created in individual heads, and if human nature is such that individuals selfishly seek to keep it to themselves, then it becomes a prime management task to design structures, systems and behaviours to overcome these selfish tendencies and spread knowledge around the organisation. The prescriptions relate to designing organisational structures that are more flexible. This means flattening the hierarchy and decentralising decision making and control in project-based, network or web-like structures such as self-managing teams. Other prescriptions relate to engineering new cultures and inspiring people through the visions of leaders so that they will share their knowledge and work toward achieving the inspiring vision.

The split between the individual and the social

In the strand of knowledge management thinking just reviewed, there is a circular, systemic interaction between individuals at one level and the group/organisation/ society at a higher level. Effective learning and knowledge creation require widespread sharing of values to do with openness, trust, affirmation, dialogue and empowerment. Effectiveness of these processes is also said to require particular forms of leadership that establish values of this kind and provide a central vision to guide the learning and knowledge-creation process. It is recognised that it is difficult to establish and sustain group, organisational and societal relationships of this kind and this leads to the consideration of some of the obstacles to the required leadership and value formations required.

Implicitly, the perspective so far described presents the dual causal structure of rationalist and formative causality. The knowledge-creating system is basically one in which tacit knowledge already stored in the heads of some individuals, already enfolded as it were, is unfolded by processes of conversion. Mental models are already there, as are the learning models according to which they are supposed to be changed, and so are the visions that are supposed to guide the learning and knowledge creation of the whole system. System archetypes (Senge, 1990) are already there. Bohm's (1983) 'common pool of meaning' is an implicate, hidden order that is already there.

As I have repeatedly pointed out, this systems perspective cannot succeed on its own as an explanation of how new knowledge is created. It can only explain how already enfolded knowledge is unfolded by the system. Within its own terms this systems view does not, indeed cannot, explain how completely novel knowledge arises. It simply assumes that it arises as tacit knowledge in the heads of some individuals, or exists in a common pool of meaning, and the explanation starts from there. The same point applies to the requirement for a vision to guide the functioning of the system. There too, there is no explanation within systems thinking itself of how such a guiding vision is formed. It follows that the origin of novel knowledge, and of the vision supposed to guide it, lies outside the system and it is here that rationalist causality is relied upon. It is special individuals, an elite, standing outside the system, who make autonomous choices. This becomes very clear when one considers the prescriptions since they mainly have to do with designing systems of one kind or another by individuals who stand outside the systems and choose their designs. The choices arise in dialogue that employs metaphor and analogy as well as rational reasoning but there is little explanation of the origins of creativity within that dialogue. In the end even the move from formative to rationalist causality fails to explain how truly new knowledge is created.

In other words, the writing on knowledge management so far reviewed answers the four questions posed at the end of Chapter 1 in essentially the same way as learning organisation theory does. In both theories, there is little attempt to deal with the paradox of managers being observers of an organisational system while being parts of it at the same time. However, this problem of the observer outside the system was identified early on in the development of twentieth-century systems thinking and it led to the development of second-order systems thinking.

●●●● 8.3 Second-order systems thinking

If I am trying to understand some natural phenomenon, say a colony of ants, it is reasonable to think of myself as an observer of that colony and I can identify it as if it were a system. Of course, by observing the colony I may be disturbing it but since I am not an ant, I am quite clearly outside it. However, if I am trying to understand a human group, it is highly problematic to think of myself as an observer outside that group simply because I am a human. In other words, as soon as a human group or organisation is identified as if it were a system, the problem arises that the identifier is also part of the system. When we try to understand human groupings, we are trying to understand ourselves and the process is then inevitably self-referential. The systems thinking that has so far been reviewed in this book does not address that issue – it is first-order systems thinking quite clearly built on the dual theories of formative and rationalist causality. However, systems thinkers have sought to deal with the self-referential nature of understanding groups and organisations in what is called second-order systems thinking. One might include in this category second-order cybernetics (Bateson, 1972; von Foerster, 1984), soft systems thinking (Checkland, 1981; Checkland and Scholes 1990), and critical systems thinking (Churchman, 1968, 1970; Flood, 1990, 1999; Jackson, 2000; Midgley, 2000). Chapter 9 will return to soft and critical systems thinking while the rest of this section will explore the distinction between first- and second-order systems thinking.

First-order systems thinking

The general systems, cybernetics and systems dynamics strands of systems thinking all departed from mechanistic and reductionist approaches in that they stressed dynamic interaction between parts of a system and between systems in an environment. However, they did not make a major move away from the radical separation of the observer (the subject and rationalist causality) from the observed (the object and formative causality). Like mechanistic and reductionist thinking, the first wave of twentieth-century systems thinking, often called hard systems thinking, assumes an objective reality that is observed by an observing individual. The assumption is that the world is made up of systems having a purpose, which can be objectively observed and modelled. The boundaries of a system are taken to be given by the structure of reality. In other words reality is held to consist of systems in a realist perspective. On the whole, most hard systems thinkers forgot the 'as if' of Kant's regulative idea in relation to systems (see Chapter 2) and reified the organisation as a real system. This approach allows managers to imagine that their organisation is a system that they can control in an optimal manner. First-order systems thinking is concerned with intervening in the system to define clear goals, identify problems and propose rational solutions. This involves characterising a situation in terms of identifiable objects with well-defined properties; finding general rules that apply to situations in terms of those objects and properties; applying the rules logically to the situation and drawing conclusions as to what is to be done. The approach is clearly scientific and it emphasises thought and its application as independent activities. It is concerned with transferable knowledge and it is based on the sender–receiver model of communication.

Second-order thinking

Second-order systems thinking is built on the understanding that human beings determine the world they experience (constructivist psychology) and this requires that we reflect upon how we operate as perceiving and knowing 'observers'. Second-order thinking is the continual attempt of managers and researchers to be aware of their own framework of understanding. One key name associated with the origins of second-order systems thinking is that of von Foerster (1984) who said that he was part of the universe and whenever he acted he was changing both himself and the universe. Another key name is that of Bateson who explored how the observer could be included in the system being observed.

Bateson (1972) starts with the classic example of the cybernetic system, namely, the central heating system (*see* section 3.3 in Chapter 3). You will recall that Bateson identified three levels of learning: Level 1, which is single loop learning where mental models stay the same; Level 2, which is double loop learning where mental models are changed; and Level 3, examples of which are religious conversion and deep personal change.

Consider what happens as we move from one level of learning to the next. The boundary of the system is redrawn. Before Level 1, the system contains only the central heating device. To reach Level 1, the boundary of the system has to be redrawn to include the human operator of the central heating system because it is the human who sets goals for the system. The human operator sets such goals according to some mental framework in his or her mind, that is, a mental model. The system now includes a person who can detect an error, a gap, between what he or she experiences and what he/she wants as determined by his/her habits, or mental model. The human operator can respond to this error and set a new goal for the system without in any way changing habits, mental models, or way of understanding the world. In other words the person's mental model, which remains the same, is now part of the higher-order system and this higher-order system can learn. This learning is itself a cybernetic process in that experience of an error triggers a change in the goal set for the lower-order system.

Mental models, then, are higher-order cybernetic devices that change the goals for the lower-order cybernetic system. Learning Level 1, or single loop learning, is therefore made possible by including the objective observer's fixed mental model in a widened system. Note that the process of changing mental models remains outside the definition of the Learning Level 1 system.

However, the system can now be widened to include this observer's observing of him/herself performing the single loop learning. The observer may find that as he/she changes the temperature setting according to his/her habit, or mental model, this does not yield the satisfaction he/she is seeking. This error could trigger him/her into changing his/her habits, that is, mental model. The process for changing the mental model is now part of an even higher order system and the mental model can also change as a result of the choice of the human. When it does so, Learning Level 2, or double loop learning, is achieved. The system is now widened to include the process of changing mental models and this too is thought of as a cybernetic system. However, the process that triggers the process of changing the mental model, something to do with satisfaction and dissatisfaction, or preference, is still outside the definition of the Learning Level 2 system.

This too is dealt with by redrawing the boundary of the system, widening it even further to include this observer observing him/herself changing his/her preferences that trigger the choice to change his/her mental model. The observer becomes aware of him/herself learning in a double loop way and this is presumably made possible by a mental model of the process of changing the mental model. This process of changing preferences is now included in an even wider system. However, once again, there is now the problem of defining the process by which the observer becomes aware of the need to change his/her preferences. Bateson found he could not identify what this would be and fell back on mysticism.

The problem with second-order system thinking, then, is that it rapidly runs into an infinite regress and some kind of mysticism. It seems to me that this problem of infinite regress, which second-order systems thinking immediately runs into, is a key conceptual concern. It is a sign that second-order systems thinking is not addressing the paradox of the observing participant but eliminating it through the device of redrawing boundaries and changing levels of description. I will argue in Chapter 9 that later systems thinkers in the second-order tradition of soft and critical systems thinking have not been able to overcome this problem. I think that failure to do so leaves us with the necessity of appealing to some kind of mystical whole in order to account for transformative learning and knowledge creation. Of course, an appeal to the mystical is not an explanation.

This problem is fundamental to all forms of systems thinking simply because systems thinking is built upon a spatial metaphor. It always involves postulating a whole separated by a boundary from other wholes. There is always an 'inside' and an 'outside'. Drawing a boundary creates an 'inside', which has to be different to what is outside. This cannot be other than a dualism in which one kind of causality applies to the inside and another kind to the outside. There always has to be something outside the system that is drawing the boundary around it and what that something is must eventually be a mystery. Systems thinking is fundamentally Kantian 'both . . . and' thinking. This matters in practical terms because it ends up with an appeal to mysticism. Part Three of the book will move from systems thinking with its spatial metaphor to temporal process thinking, which makes no use of concepts such as 'inside', 'outside', 'wholes' and 'boundaries'.

●●●● 8.4   The move to the mystical

Bateson's notion of Level 3 learning with its rather mystical implications is also reflected in writings on the learning organisation. Chapter 6 has already referred to Senge's notion of dialogue as an essential aspect of the learning organisation. Dialogue is understood as a form of communication between people in which they hold in abeyance their conflicting assumptions about the world, so enabling them to come into contact with a rather mysterious pool of 'common meaning'. This notion is greatly elaborated by one of Senge's collaborators, Scharmer, who outlines a theory of learning as the sensing and enacting of emerging futures.

Scharmer (2000) distinguishes between two different sources of learning and argues that both are required for organisations to succeed. He calls the first 'reflecting on the experiences of the past' and the second 'sensing and embodying emergent futures' *rather than* re-enacting the patterns of the past. One kind of learning is, therefore, relevant to the past and another to the future.

The first kind of learning involves uncovering the past and bringing it into awareness as a process of 'presencing'. This occurs at the surface level of concrete experience. It is the cognitive process of downloading mental models and simply re-enacting old habits of thought. It also occurs below the surface level of action, involving the uncovering of common will and the changing of consciousness and then embodying the changes in the form of behavioural routines and procedures. In other words, this is close to single loop learning.

The second kind of learning, to do with the future, is called generative learning, which is understood as cognitive processes involving the reframing of mental models, that is, double loop learning. This requires a special conversational process called dialogue where assumptions are suspended and one takes account of the views of others, enabling access to a common pool of meaning. It also requires imagination, which is described as becoming aware through the redirection of attention from an object to its source. Scharmer talks about generative learning as the deepest level and presents it as an essentially mystical experience, the manifestation, or coming into awareness, of a deeper, hidden reality. Here, individual intention is at one with the intention of the emerging whole. It is a process of bringing the emerging whole into reality 'as *it* desires' rather than as the ego desires and this is what he means by the coming into presence of the emerging future.

Presencing is a process of becoming aware which involves taking off one's self-created cognitive filters, turning inward to the source of oneself, redirecting attention from current reality to an emergent reality, and letting go, that is, emptying or surrendering to a deeper higher will. Scharmer then adds another stage which he calls 'letting come'. For him surrender means switching from 'looking for' to 'letting come', a phase of quickening or crystallisation in which one allows the arrival of the highest possible future, the highest presence, the highest Self. What is received is an emerging heightened quality of will and a more tangible vision of what the individual and the group want to create. The language is strikingly mystical.

Accessing the generative level of learning

The key question for generative learning is how to access this level for it is here that transformation occurs, where transformation is understood as the coming into presence of emerging futures. Scharmer emphasises that presencing is as much a collective phenomenon as it is an individual one and by this he seems to mean that individuals fuse together into the collective when they reach this stage. Scharmer describes presencing as a mystery and says that it is a mode of relating in which the individual relates to the collective whole of the community, team and organisation. In this state people become more 'selfless' and become aligned with their true selves and with the intention of the emerging whole. Scharmer's understanding of generative learning, therefore, is one of accessing, even immersing in, a transcendent whole. It is essentially a mystical process in which there is participation in a mystical whole. This amounts to postulating a transcendent system and ascribing to it an actual intention rather than the 'as if' intention to be found in Kantian thinking. Emergence means bringing into being what this transcendent system desires.

For Scharmer transformation is the enactment of a deep spiritual process in which individuals fuse into a common will. The origin of transformation, and thus novelty, lies in a transcendent whole that is brought into being, is presenced, by the basically meditative practices of a group of people. Individuals and groups are simultaneously transformed but this is in no way paradoxical because the individuals and the group are fused. The process is the same and there is nothing contradictory in terms of individual and group. There is no mention of difference, conflict or power, which implicitly play no part whatsoever in the transformative process. The social is not thought of as a responsive relating of a co-operative/competitive nature but as fusion in a transcendent whole. Participation means individuals participating in a transcendent whole.

So far, the theory of causality is clear. Individuals fuse together and submerge in the 'whole', the transcendent system. This system is the formative cause of action in that action is clearly understood as unfolding the enfolded will of the whole. Scharmer suggests that this is transformative causality but if it is then it is of a mystical kind.

The role of leaders

Scharmer says that it is the role of leaders to choose the learning level at which to operate. The key challenge for leaders is how to enable teams to uncover layers of reality that will move them from one level of learning to another. Scharmer defines leadership as the activity of shifting the place from which a system operates and he defines this as shifting the conversation from talking 'nice' and talking 'tough' to reflective and generative dialogues. Generative dialogues lead to an intentional quietness or sacred silence. The only sustainable tool for leading change is the leader's self as the capacity of the 'I' to transcend the boundaries of its current organisation and operate from the emerging, larger whole, both individually and collectively. The leader's role is to create the conditions that allow others to shift the place from which their system operates. The leader, then, is understood as an autonomous individual standing outside the system and choosing the level at which to operate. Causality here is of the rationalist kind.

This immediately exposes the dual causality typical of systems thinking. There is a transcendent system of which individuals become a part in order to transform and there is an autonomous leader standing outside this and deciding whether to operate at that level. This is clearly 'both . . . and' thinking that eliminates paradox. The 'both . . . and' nature of the thinking is evident in the postulation of *both* a system with an actual intention/desire *and* autonomous individuals who create conditions for shifting the system.

Note also how the systems thinking underlying Scharmer's theory is a distancing from experience in that the causes of the experience of interaction do not lie in the interaction itself but in systems above the interaction.

This section has given an example of how some systems thinkers have tried to deal with the problem of the paradox of the participant observer and with the nature of novelty and transformation by turning to mysticism. They halt the infinite regress involved in systems thinking by locating the potential for transformation in a transcendent whole. This kind of approach will be explored further in relation to the notion of organisations as living systems in Chapter 12.

Another approach to the problem of infinite regress is suggested by the theory of autopoiesis. In this theory, the ultimate cause of change in a system lies within itself, rather than some higher-level system. If the cause of change is within the system then it seems that there is no question of the infinite regress of appealing to higher systems but the question is whether there is an explanation of transformation. I will be suggesting that the theory of autopoiesis cannot explain transformation.

8.5   Autopoiesis and enactment

The biologists Maturana and Varela (1992) developed the notion of autopoiesis to account for what was distinctive about living systems, starting with a living cell. An autopoietic system is one whose components participate in production processes that produce those components and the boundary that separates the system from its environment. In doing this, Maturana and Varela are taking up a notion that is very similar to that of self-organising wholes. The autopoietic system consists of a circular organisation of production processes that continually replace the components necessary for the continuation of that system. In other words, the system creates itself. What this means can be seen most clearly in relation to living cells, which have: *identifiable components*, such as the nucleus and mitochondria in a cell, which produce a cell as a cell produces the nucleus and mitochondria; *mechanistic interactions* between components, such as the general physical laws that determine changes that occur within a cell; and an *identifiable boundary* produced by the system itself, such as a plasma membrane around a cell.

These properties have a number of distinctive consequences. The boundary is not imposed from outside but determined by internal relationships, and in producing its own boundaries, an autopoietic system establishes its own autonomy, that is, its identity. The focus of attention is, therefore, on single, self-defined individuals as parts of organisms, populations and species operating in an environment.

Maturana and Varela distinguish between the organisation and the structure of an autopoietic system. The organisation is the nature of the components and the relations between them required for an entity to belong to a particular category or type. It is thus an abstract generalisation that determines the identity of a system and this identity must remain constant and invariant if the system is not to disintegrate. The organisation of the system prescribes the properties of its components and the relationships between them that permit them to enter into a limited, but large, number of relations to each other while still preserving the fundamental form of the system. Organisation is, thus, the dynamics of interaction within the system, the context within which the components interact. Structure is the mode of operation that produces the potential range of structural arrangements that retain identity. The structure, then, is an actual example of the organisation. In other words, the structure embodies the abstract principles that define the organisation, or identity, of the system. It is the specific arrangement of the components at any particular moment. So, the organisation of a prokaryote cell, that which gives it its identity as this kind of cell, is the abstract features of cell membrane containing nucleoid material. The structure of a prokaryote cell is some living example that has the features just described. The organisation emerges from component interactions, while those interactions flow from the organisation so that the circular, self-referential process functions to sustain the organisation.

Identity determined from within

Autopoietic systems are organisationally closed. This means that the system's organisation, or identity, is not determined by anything outside of it. It may import energy or information and export waste but its identity is determined by its own operations. There are no instructive interactions with its environment so that it can receive no constructive instructions from outside of itself. This does not mean that it is isolated: it is structurally coupled to other systems in its environment. The structural coupling means that change in other systems can perturb the system in question and so trigger internal change, but the nature of the change itself will be determined entirely by the production processes within the system.

The structural coupling between systems leads to evolution as structural, or natural drift rather than adaptation to the environment. Evolution is the history of structural coupling and it is this history that is referred to as structural or natural drift. It is the system's own nature, identity and operational processes that determine the structural shape it takes on, not the particular environmental perturbation it experiences. In this sense the system does not adapt to a unique pre-given environment. However, because it is structurally coupled to other systems, they together determine the history of structural coupling. Evolution is thus codetermined or co-created. Evolution is a reciprocal adjustment between structurally coupled entities that continually trigger changes in each other but these changes are always internally driven. Those changes that facilitate the process of autopoiesis, that is, the maintenance of identity, are maintained and conserved. The loss of identity is the destruction of the system. This leads to natural drift, which is change in the total population of species due to the success of some groups which maintain their identity and the dying out of others through the loss of their identity.

Comparisons with other systems theories

General systems theory is concerned with open systems. It explains how living systems function through importing energy from a pre-given environment, across the system's boundary with that environment, transforming the imports into a form of functioning, and then exporting waste to the environment. The boundary is a given and its formation is not due to the functioning of the system. The theory explains how the system sustains homeostasis, or equilibrium, through adaptation to the environment. The history of the system is not important in that what matters is the process of adaptation to the current environment. The principle of equifinality means that the state of homeostasis can be achieved from a large number of starting points and it is this that renders history unimportant.

Autopoietic systems are substantially different in that they produce their own boundaries. They are organisationally or operationally closed, which means that the state of the system is determined by its own operations, triggered by changes in other systems constituting the environment. This means that the system cannot be said to be adapting to a current state of the environment but, rather, that its current state reflects the history of its structural couplings with other systems. There is a similarity with homeostasis in that all structural changes must be consistent with the conservation of system identity. The only alternative is system destruction. While general systems theory understands the dynamics as simple movement to stability, autopoiesis theory understands the dynamic as wide variations consistent with identity. Open systems are self-regulating but they are not self-organising or emergent in the Kantian sense, while autopoietic systems are.

The cybernetic branch of systems thinking explains system stability in terms of negative feedback applied to information about the external environment with the system structure playing little part in the nature of change. A cybernetic system functions with reference to some state in its environment, adapting to that environment. Again, history is not important as far as the current adapted state is concerned, although it plays a part in movement towards that state. The internal structure of the cybernetic system is not considered to be important, only the gap between current state and the environmental state to which the system must adapt. An autopoietic system is substantially different in that it is the internal structure that determines how it changes in a way consistent with the conservation of its identity. History is important in the form of a history of structural coupling with other systems. Again, while cybernetic systems are self-regulating, they are not self-organising or emergent, while autopoietic systems are.

The systems dynamics branch of systems thinking understands systems change in terms of damping and amplifying feedback loops. Here the internal dynamic of the system determines the pattern of change. This is similar to autopoiesis, the difference being the emphasis the latter places on the conservation of identity, a concept lacking in systems dynamics. In systems dynamics, the system is self-influencing but not self-organising and emergent in the way an autopoietic system is.

Despite the significant differences between autopoietic systems theory and these other three systems theories, there is one important matter that they all have in common. This is the underlying causal framework, namely, that of formative causality (*see* Chapter 2). They all assume that the future is the unfolding of what is already enfolded in the system or its environment. So, in general systems theory, an open system moves toward its homeostatic state of adaptation to the current environment. In cybernetics, the system moves toward the stable state specified in the external reference point. In systems dynamics, the system realises archetypal patterns of damping and amplifying feedback. Although autopoietic systems co-construct their environment rather than adapt to it, they also unfold an already enfolded identity. Autopoiesis quite explicitly excludes transformation of identity. As with other systems theories, autopoiesis cannot explain the emergence of novelty as the transformation of identity – the system either survives or it does not. Indeed, it quite explicitly excludes this possibility in its insistence on the conservation of identity.

This inability to explain the origins of novel identities is revealed in the concept of structural or natural drift. Natural drift is the history of structural coupling between systems, where either each system conserves its identity or that identity is destroyed. Natural drift discards systems that do not manage to conserve their identities. It explains the history of the destruction of species but does not explain new speciation. Evolution is understood as variations on a central theme, some of the variations being destroyed as they lose their identity. This is a view that understands evolution not as the transformation of identity, as the emergence of the truly novel, but as a continuing unfolding of an already enfolded central theme.

Autopoietic systems are cognitive systems

Maturana and Varela argue that all autopoietic systems are cognitive systems. By this they mean that in operating in an environment, an autopoietic system makes distinctions in that it does not simply respond to stimuli presented by the environment but selects aspects of its environment according to its own identity. In other words, it enacts, or brings forth, the environment that is relevant to it. This is a view of cognition, that is, of recognising and responding, that is active rather than simply passively registering what is already there. For an autopoietic system, the world is an active construction of its own world, not a passive representation of a pre-given world. Each autopoietic system in a sense creates its own world.

This notion of selecting, or calling forth, a world is illustrated by the perception of colour (Varela *et al.*, 1995). Primates have evolved a trichromate system for perceiving colour. That is, they possess one channel, or receptor, which responds to medium-wave light, another which responds to an excess of long-wave over short-wave light and a third to an excess of medium- over long-wave light. The colours perceived depend upon which receptors are dominant and which are dormant. Not all species, however, have trichromate systems. Squirrels and rabbits, for example, have dichromate systems, that is, two receptors, while pigeons and ducks have tetrachromate systems, that is, four receptors. These other creatures, therefore, cannot see the world of colour that humans see and similarly humans are at a loss to know what the world of colour looks like to a duck or a rabbit. Which is reality? The question is meaningless because specific evolutionary histories have produced one of a number of possible visual systems for each species. Evolutionary history has operated to select, to call forth or enact, one of a number of possible worlds for a particular species.

Maturana and Varela present evidence for their view that the human brain does not simply register stimuli but creates patterns associated with them. The brain does not process information or act as a passive mirror of reality to form more or less accurate representations of the world. Instead, it is perturbed, or triggered, by external stimuli into actively constructing global patterns of electrochemical activity. Furthermore, these patterns are not stored in specific parts of the brain because each time a stimulus is presented to the body, the brain constructs a pattern anew that involves whole ensembles of neurons in many different parts of the brain. This leads Maturana and Varela to conclude that the nervous system does not simply represent a world; rather, it creates, calls forth or enacts a world. The world people act into is the world they have created by acting into it.

This is the notion of enactment, namely, a process of selecting, or calling forth a world (*see* Chapter 5). Humans do not simply perceive a pre-given world in the only possible way, building up more and more accurate representations of it but, rather, they select those sense perceptions they are biologically and socially enabled to select. In other words, Maturana and Varela adopt a constructivist perspective rather than the cognitivist one underlying the theories of strategic choice and the learning organisation. Trying to understand organisations from an autopoietic systems perspective, therefore, involves a shift from the three strands of systems thinking so far discussed but also a shift in the underlying psychological theory from cognitivism to constructivism.

This change in the underlying theory of psychology is important because it presents a serious challenge to the cognitivist underpinnings of the theories of strategic choice and the learning organisation. It presents a view of mental process as one of perpetual construction, thereby moving away from the notion that brains faithfully represent an external reality and also any idea of the brain as storing and retrieving representations in any simple way. The Maturana and Varela perspective brings bodily action to the forefront and develops the notion of enactment, that is, of humans acting into what they have constructed.

However, the individual is still held to be primary and the theory is still a systems theory. Autopoiesis takes the individual, understood as a system, as its fundamental unit of analysis and presents the conservation of individual identity as the fundamental principle. Here, individuals are bounded, self-determining entities. The constructivist position is not inconsistent with the notion of mental models since it can be taken to be an alternative way of understanding how mental models are constructed. The individual mind is then functioning purely in terms of an identity, on one side of a boundary, constructing variations in itself, triggered by changes in other identities contained within their boundaries.

Those taking up the theory of autopoiesis to understand human action also apply the notion of autopoietic systems to groups and organisations. An organisation, for example, is thought of as a higher-level autopoietic system. An organisation then is a self-contained entity functioning according to the principles of its own identity. It is an organisationally closed system but it is perturbed by changes in other organisations, which are also autopoietic systems. These perturbations trigger change but the change itself proceeds according to its own internal dynamics, its identity. It can receive no constructive instructions from outside. Instead organisations co-evolve, reflecting the history of their structural coupling.

Industries and societies can then also be understood as autopoietic systems (Luhmann, 1984). In Luhmann's formulation, a social system is a system of communicative events in that one communicative event produces another. This satisfies the condition of an autopoietic system that it should produce the components that constitute it because communications always refer to previous communications and lead on to others. Communicative events are not thoughts, behaviours or actions. They are utterances of information by one individual that have meaning for another individual. This system of communications is at a different level to people and their thoughts. In fact, people are the environment of a social system. The communicative events are separate from the people, who come and go, while the self-referring communication goes on.

Mingers (1995) critiques the work of Luhmann, pointing out that he does not adequately solve the problem of boundaries because his system of communicative events cannot be said to produce a boundary between communicative events and people. Secondly, he does not demonstrate how communicative events could emerge from the interactions of humans and yet constitute a domain independent of them. Communications require people to make them but in Luhmann's theory people disappear into the environment of disembodied communicative events.

Novelty and infinite regress

Earlier on, this chapter pointed to the problem encountered in the first wave of systems thinking, often called hard systems thinking. The problem was twofold. First, as soon as a system of the general, cybernetic and systems dynamics kinds is specified by an observer that system can only unfold what the observer has specified or enfolded in it. In other words, the causality is of the formative kind. The source of any transformative change, therefore, has to be the functioning of the observer. The observer is understood in terms of cognitive psychology as an individual who can choose to change. This is rationalist causality. The second problem is that the observer of the human system is also always a part of that system. The observer, therefore, is subject to two quite different kinds of causality. Second-order systems thinking sought to deal with this problem by incorporating the observer into the system. However, this immediately means that there is then no explanation of how the system can transform, simply because the source of that transformation, the observer, is now subject to formative causality, which cannot explain transformation. This leads to the problem of infinite regress in which there is first the mental model outside the system, then the learning model that changes the mental model. This exposes the inability of the cognitivist position to explain transformational change and the only way to stop the infinite regress is to appeal to some transcendent whole. The source of transformation is then of a mystical kind. The question now is whether the shift to autopoietic systems and constructivist psychology escapes this problem. It does not for the following reasons.

An autopoietic system changes when triggered by perturbations in its environment but the change itself is entirely determined by the internal dynamics of the system. Nothing outside it causes the change so it looks as if the problem of infinite regress does not even arise. However, the change that takes place can be one of only two possibilities. Either the change is such as to conserve the identity of the system or the system ceases to exist. There is no possibility of transformation in identity. The infinite regress does not get going because there is no question of the transformation of identity. However, a collection of autopoietic systems, in which each is triggering others, is co-creating the environment. That collection could then be understood as a higher-level autopoietic system that evolves through natural drift. This means that some of the lower-level systems survive while others become extinct. The higher-level system, therefore, changes. However, because it too is autopoietic it can only either sustain its identity or become extinct. Again there is no possibility of the higher-level system transforming its identity. However it too could be one of many autopoietic systems co-creating an environment as a higher-level system. That higher-level system could change because some of the lower-level systems are surviving while others are becoming extinct. However, it too can only sustain its identity or become extinct. In the end there is the same problem of infinite regress in order to explain the transformation of identity. Perhaps this is why Varela *et al.* (1995) also appeal in the end to Eastern mysticism.

8.6 The application of autopoietic thinking to organisations

Many believe that the notion of autopoiesis is useful in understanding the nature of single cells, but there is considerable disagreement as to whether other living systems are autopoietic. Maturana and Varela have not given definite or consistent views on whether multicell organisms are autopoietic. Varela claims that the human nervous and immune systems are operationally closed. Both he and Maturana have said that they do not believe that social systems are autopoietic.

Some (Morgan, 1997) suggest that autopoiesis provides one of many possible metaphors for organisations, while others claim that social systems are autopoietic. Some have incorporated the work of Maturana and Varela into their thinking about knowledge creation and the management of intellectual capital (for example, Roos *et al.*, 1997). They draw on this work to conclude that knowledge is always located in the individual and created within autopoietic brains. For them, knowledge is always tacit and what is called explicit knowledge is data that help individuals to create their own knowledge.

Knowledge and autopoietic social systems

Von Krogh *et al.* (1994) suggest that the transformation of contemporary society requires rethinking the meaning of strategic management through taking the view that an organisation is a knowledge system. They think of an organisation as a stream of knowledge and appeal particularly to the work of Luhmann to propose autopoiesis as a new theory of the knowledge possessed by a social system. They hold that cognitive systems are created and re-created in a recursive, self-generating, closed and autonomous manner and propose to use this autopoietic view to understand the evolution of organisational knowledge, which they define as shared knowledge. For them, knowledge development at this social level resembles knowledge development at the individual level. They reject the cognitivist notion of representations of a pre-given world, storing, retrieval and processing, arguing that cognition is the active calling forth of a world. Knowledge is said to be intimately connected to observation and thus dependent upon the point of observation of the manager. Knowledge enables managers to make distinctions in their observations, based on their norms and this determines what they see. Von Krogh *et al.* claim that applying distinctions allows new knowledge to develop through making finer and finer distinctions in a self-referential way. As an autopoietic system the manager is closed to knowledge, including knowledge of the environment, but open to data. Books, memos and so on are data that become information through the interpretation or knowledge of the manager.

Organisational knowledge is shared knowledge allowing shared distinction making, which is created and maintained in conversations in which new knowledge develops in a self-referential manner. Organisations too are open with respect to data but closed with respect to knowledge. Von Krogh *et al.* regard individual cognition as relatively unproblematic but organisational cognition as dynamic, fragile and developed through a self-referential, simultaneously open and closed process of relating. They talk about an organisation observing itself as a self-description or identity. This provides the criteria for selecting what passes for knowledge as opposed to noise in that organisation, so preventing the organisation from drowning in knowledge complexity. Generally, organisational members do not question the knowledge structure or identity of the organisation – they filter out new data not consistent with it. However, eventual massive criticism leads to change. As members observe events, applying and inventing distinctions, they participate in developing organisational knowledge. New distinctions often vanish so the key question has to do with what leads to their being sustained. Von Krogh *et al.* talk about the external observer who can see the blind spots in the system.

Again the dualism of rationalist causality applying to the observer and formative causality applying to the system is evident, as is the primacy accorded to the autopoietic individual.

Breaking out of traditions of thinking

Another example of the application of autopoiesis to strategic matters is provided by Ison and Russell (2000). They are concerned with technology transfer in agriculture in Australia, arguing that it is less effective than it could be because interventions to secure it have been first-order systemic ones based on the idea that communication is the transfer of knowledge. However, they do not propose to replace first-order with second-order thinking because they regard second-order thinking as providing the context for first-order thinking. Second-order thinking builds on the insights gained from first-order thinking but instead of talking about transferring knowledge Ison and Russell see conversation as the vehicle for genuine commitment and enthusiasm for action and thus as the crucial element in corporate success.

They summarise the characteristics of the second-order approach as follows:

- It is doing by extending invitations to others who willingly accept joining together in making sense for mutually satisfying action.
- The reality that is brought forth in this process includes the researcher, constituting a duality of researcher and participant.
- All participants share responsibility.
- The study is of relationships.

- It is grounded in an explanation of what is experienced, not the replication of principles. It has no imperative character.
- The contextual grounding has to do with an increasing understanding of the social construction of the very concepts used.
- The essence is self reference.

In order to break out of the first-order tradition, they say that one must be aware of and explore one's context. This means that, as experts, they stand back and explore the wider context of the issue they are studying before inviting stakeholders to participate in a process of formulating issues and problems understood as systems of interest. In doing this, experts are trying to break out of the traditions of stakeholders and also out of the traditions of their own thinking. In order for stakeholders to break out of their traditions it is necessary for the experts to trigger the enthusiasm of stakeholders. They talk about a research design that triggers enthusiasm. They place a considerable emphasis on the prior design of their participation with stakeholders while realising that there is a disparity between design and its realisation. Their design aim is to enable stakeholders to see themselves as researchers and they do this by designing a context and a process. Their challenge is to design contexts that provide the capacity for effective response by stakeholders.

They do not see this as empowering people. Instead they describe what they are talking about as the emergent relationship between the enthusiasm of the individual and the consensus that is generated responsibly and accountably by the collective. For them, the individual and the collective are two different levels that they understand to be the unity of a duality, which resolves the apparent paradox of the one and the many, forming the unity of a whole. The paradox is only apparent and due to dependence on the observer. They hold that it is possible for intervening researchers to trigger the enthusiasm of the stakeholders as well as to trigger other processes that lead to consensus. They point out how enthusiasm (and individual emotion) can get in the way of consensus (a collective phenomenon) and vice versa as consensus leads to a loss of emotional energy.

They explain the process of breaking out of traditions of thinking in terms of the theory of autopoiesis. Biological systems cannot be thought of in terms of the sender–receiver model because humans are structure-specified systems and they cannot be instructed with knowledge by other living systems. Humans are closed, self-generating structures coupled to others but what they make of the coupling depends upon their own internal dynamic. Instead of instructing each other, humans trigger each other. The real world can only ever be the world of our experience, by which they mean the operation of the nervous system. This means that we all have different worlds so that shared meaning requires participation in conversation. Ison and Russell see such conversations as a dance in which we cannot determine the outcome.

They define a social system as a set of operations and relationships that have some specified outcome. When such systems are judged to be problematic, or are failing to achieve the desired outcome, then they become the focus of planned intervention. The naming of the problem and the attribution of problem ownership are often contentious. They claim that human 'organisation' differs from the purely biological ones because humans can choose to change the identity of their groupings.

They, therefore, develop what they call a second-order approach which they describe as action research and systemic learning based on the theory of autopoiesis.

Critique

In Chapter 2, I made the point that systems thinking reflects Kantian causal dualism, which eliminates paradox in 'both . . . and' thinking. The paradox is eliminated by ascribing different causalities to human action and to natural organisms. With regard to human action there is the rational autonomous individual subject to the causality of freedom and with regard to natural organisms there is the system subject to the formative causality of the 'regulative idea', that is, the 'as if' purpose hypothesised by an autonomous individual. Contrary to Kant, modern systems thinkers think of human collectives as systems. The result is a causality of human action in terms of the autonomous individual and a causality of human action in which humans are parts of a system. The system changes when the autonomous individual chooses a different system design. No paradox is sensed in having humans autonomous in some respects and subject to systems with a purpose of their own in other respects. The paradox is eliminated in the 'both . . . and' way of thinking. This is clearly what Ison and Russell do when they refer to the duality of individual and collective as resolving paradox. This duality locates the individual and the individual's enthusiasm at one level and the collective and its consensus at another level. You can see the result when they define the social as a system with a purpose and how autonomous individuals see when the system is not working, name it and design changes to it. Notice also their 'both . . . and' thinking when they retain the strengths of both first-order and second-order thinking. So they have a social 'reality' that is deterministic in the first-order sense within what they call a context, the social, which is socially constructed. Again they do not notice any contradiction or paradox. When they claim that human 'organisation' (that is, identity) can be voluntarily changed they escape the requirement of autopoiesis that autopoietic systems cannot be changed from the outside and that identity cannot be changed without destroying the system.

The second point I have repeatedly made is that this causal dualism cannot explain novelty in its own terms. The system cannot explain novelty because it unfolds its enfolded purpose. Any potential for novel change is thus located in the individual and there is no explanation of how such novel individual changes occur.

The third point is that 'both . . . and' thinking renders human freedom problematic. Sometimes we are free and autonomous as individuals and sometimes we are parts of a social system and so not free because we are subject to its consensual purpose. The dependence on autopoiesis is essentially a dependence on a theoretical construct of formative causality in which humans are considered to be closed and autonomous. The underlying psychology of constructivism is focused on the individual.

The fourth point about systems thinking raised in this chapter has to do with infinite regress. The first-order system cannot transform of its own accord and it is the autonomous individual observer who designs the change. The second-order system incorporates the observers, who can be understood as a social system. Now, however, there is the problem of just how they change in novel ways and the explanation of this requires something outside the system. In Ison and Russell's scheme this seems to be the team of researchers who first decide upon the context before they invite the participants to join them. However, they do not really explain how the team of researchers comes up with the design of the intervention. They say that we should be continually aware of our way of thinking and that in our action we are changing the universe and ourselves. I suggest that they do not provide a satisfactory account of this process – it remains outside the explanatory framework of systems thinking.

Emancipation from dependency

Of their research in the semi-arid rangelands of western New South Wales, Ison and Russell (2000) say:

> Our aim was to generate, through our research, new understandings which might guide the design of future R&D systems. We did this by 'braiding' theory with subsequent practice in an attempt to create a context in which second-order R&D was possible. From the start we did not set out to pursue a 'fact finding' mission but rather, via the medium of 'stories', to invite pastoralists (graziers) to tell of their experience. (p. 133)

They based their design on the need to emancipate the participants from dependency and empower them through collaboration based on the mutual acceptance of different realities. Families of pastoralists were invited to tell of their day-to-day experience and their interpretation of this experience. Ison and Russell used semi-structured interviews to trigger accounts of their stories and the interviews were designed to map out patterns of meaning across time: the historical context; current experience; anticipated context. They coupled this phenomenological data with hermeneutic data to constitute the contextual research focus on second-order data. First-order data were social, ecological and pastoral events as patterns of analysis and these were mapped as second-order data, that is, data about themselves and how they were making sense. They claim that they were holding first and second order in creative tension. They invited participants to specially designed workshops to identify their enthusiasms for taking action. They constituted user-initiated R&D groups along lines of shared enthusiasms to generate, manage and evaluate actions in particular domains (political, social, pastoral).

Ison and Russell claim that they triggered enthusiasm by valuing and appreciating people for who they were and what they were doing. For them enthusiasm has to do with individuals managing their own realities and accommodating change. They set up processes in which people were listened to with acceptance for what they had done because each individual possesses a reservoir of unexpended energy and excitement which is a resource for collective action if it can be effectively organised or elicited. They see enthusiasm as an individual drive, and the methodology for eliciting it is based on narrative. By listening to stories elicited by the right questions they listen for moments of enthusiasm. The enthusiasms could then be brought together and mapped out to be presented to graziers, who could then be invited to work together on their common enthusiasms. Meeting rituals were developed to facilitate intellectual and emotional appreciation, for example, a tea ceremony. They talk about the need to design each meeting carefully in terms of process, use of language and sharing of expectations.

At workshops, Ison and Russell invite participants to listen to their interpretations of main concerns and issues gathered in interviews and stories. Local people are then offered a space to consider these issues. They developed a 12-stage workshop design with introductions, small groups, plenary meetings and follow-up workshops. They talk about an experiential learning cycle of planning, action, observation and reflection, with stages of evaluation and implementation. The stages are: bringing the system into existence, that is naming it; evaluating the effectiveness of the system as a vehicle to elicit useful understanding and acceptance of social and cultural context; generation of a joint decision-making process involving all key stakeholders; evaluating the effectiveness of the decisions made, that is, how the action taken has been judged by the stakeholders.

From the above description, one can see that the central concern is with a problem, an issue or a system of interest. The practitioners first stand back and identify the wider context before they invite stakeholders to participate in the designed processes and contexts, which are supposed to enable effective responses from stakeholders by triggering their enthusiasm. Engagement with others then takes the form of conversation involving appreciation and enthusiasm. Strikingly absent is the anxiety and the destructive processes it calls forth, power, ideology and unconscious processes. This systemic way of reflecting upon what one is doing ignores the more informal, shadow, unconscious emergent nature of interaction, which I will be taking up in Part Three. As a consequence, attention is focused upon rational design.

8.7 Enactment and sense making in organisations

Constructivist psychology need not necessarily be combined with autopoietic systems theory. For example, one influential writer on organisations already referred to in Chapter 5 is Weick (1995), who adopts a constructivist approach without moving to an autopoietic notion of systems. He emphasises enactment and also a topic that will be taken up in the next chapter, namely, the role of storytelling and communities of practice. Together they constitute sense making, which has the following features (Weick, 1995):

- Active agents place stimuli in some kind of framework so that they can comprehend, explain, attribute, extrapolate and predict. Weick often uses the metaphor of a map and talks about individual mental models.
- Individuals form conscious and unconscious anticipations and assumptions as predictions of what they expect to encounter and sense making is triggered when

there is a discrepancy between such expectations and what they encounter. The need for explanation is triggered by surprise and takes the form of retrospective accounts to explain those surprises. Meaning is ascribed retrospectively as an output of a sense-making process and does not arise concurrently with the detection of difference.

- Sense making is the process people employ to cope with interruptions of ongoing activity.
- It is a process of reciprocal interaction of information seeking and meaning ascription, that is, it includes environmental scanning, interpretation and associated responses.
- A distinction may be drawn between generic (collective) and intersubjective (individual-relating) forms of sense making.

Weick regards sense making as both an individual and a social activity and argues that it attends to both how a 'text' is constructed and how it is interpreted, to both creation/invention and discovery. He argues that sense making is grounded in identity construction, where identities are constructed in the process of interaction between people. He emphasises its retrospective nature, where meaning is the kind of attention directed to experience. Sense making is a process of relating in which people co-create, or enact, their environment. This leads him to place particular emphasis on talk, discourse, conversation, storytelling and narrative. In this process, people notice, extract and embellish cues, which he regards as the simple, familiar structures from which people develop a larger sense of what may be occurring. For him, the metaphor of a 'seed' captures the open-ended quality of sense making because a seed is a form-producing process. He quotes Shotter (1983), who describes how an acorn limits the tree that grows from it to an oak tree but does not specify it exactly. Rather, it grows unpredictably. Notice here how this assumes a theory of formative causality.

Weick ascribes particular importance to novel moments in the process of sense making. He locates the origins of novelty in dissonance, surprise, gaps, differences, disruptions, unexpected failures and uncertainty. For him it is events of this kind that trigger sense making, which could produce novel explanations. He describes the process as one that involves emotion and is necessarily confusing. What he does not question is the split between individual and social and the dual causality that goes with it.

8.8   Summary

This chapter first described the development of organisational learning theory as theories of knowledge creation and management and the measurement of intellectual capital. It then turned to the development of constructivist psychology and autopoietic systems theories. These developments point to important challenges to the theories of strategic choice and organisational learning. There is the challenge to the view that the mind is a processor of information that stores accurate representations of external reality and the suggestion that the brain-mind perpetually constructs meaning and knowledge. Weick's linking of difference/discrepancy and the origin of novelty is a highly important one to be taken up in Part Three of this book. The writers surveyed in this chapter make significant moves to seeing the importance of social and conversational processes in the construction of strategies. These are all matters that will be taken up in Part Three.

However, all the writers surveyed continue to argue within the framework of systems thinking. They all conceptualise the individual as one level and the social as another level in a system in which one level impacts on the other sequentially. It is a 'both . . . and' approach implicitly retaining the underlying split causality of previous theories. The system is assumed to unfold that which is already enfolded, that is, formative causality, whether it be the system of the social or the system of the mind. However, the origin of change is then understood from a perspective outside the system, where causality is rationalist.

This chapter also provided a brief description of second-order systems thinking and pointed to the conceptual problem of dual causality and the infinite regress associated with it. This problem is either ignored or eliminated in an appeal to some kind of mysticism. However, the move to theories of organisational change viewed in terms of knowledge does represent a much fuller taking into account of social processes, conversation and narrative. It shows considerable concern with matters of participation and inclusion based on a view of the co-construction of the realities into which organisational members act.

Further reading

Nonaka and Takeuchi (1995) is a one of the major texts on knowledge management. Mingers (1995) provides an important review and critique of autopoiesis.

Chapter 9 ● ● ● ●

A social perspective
Critical systems thinking and communities of practice

9.1 Introduction

In the last decades of the twentieth century, many presented criticisms of hard systems thinking (cybernetics, systems dynamics and general systems theory) in addition to those raised by second-order thinking to do with the participant nature of the observer as discussed in the last chapter. One criticism was that early systems theories implied that organisations were physical entities like organisms with clear boundaries, structures and functions and this limited the domain of effective application. Allied to this was the criticism that hard systems theories presented individuals as deterministic, thinking machines and ignored the aspects of emotion, conflict, politics, culture and ethics. In other words, the critics of hard systems thinking were taking a much more social perspective. For example, Churchman (1968, 1970) focused on boundaries and ethics; Ackoff (1981, 1994) developed interactive planning; and Checkland (1981, 1983; Checkland and Scholes, 1990) developed soft systems thinking, arguing that very few real-world situations allowed one to think of them as systems with clearly defined goals and objectives. Later, critical systems thinking grew out of the critiques of Churchman, Ackoff and Checkland. Since the main approaches to strategic management are based on systems thinking, it is important to explain how systems thinking has been evolving and what the implications for strategic management are.

9.2 Interactive planning and soft systems thinking

As examples of the critical attitude towards the first wave of twentieth-century systems thinking, consider the work of Ackoff on interactive planning and then that of Churchman and Checkland on soft systems.

Interactive planning

Ackoff (1981, 1994) holds that obstructions to change lie in the minds of the members of an organisation, that is, in their mental models. He believes that it is not practically feasible to surface these mental models and change them as many learning organisation theorists believe. Instead, he argues that members of an organisation should participate in formulating an idealised design of the future they desire and create ways of achieving it. They should seek to close the gap between their present situation and this desired future. The central message is to plan or be planned for. Ackoff developed a method of interactive planning to do this, one that focuses on the participative development of scenarios for desired futures. The first step in the rather detailed process he proposes is systems analysis, that is, the formulation of a detailed picture of the organisation as it is today in terms of process, structure, culture and relationships with the environment. He is concerned with what can be done now to create the future.

Ackoff presents a version of strategic choice theory that emphasises not just the roles of leaders but the participation of members of an organisation in making the strategic choice. It seems to me, therefore, that his perspective represents a shift in ideology from 'command and control' to teamwork and democratic participation. Ackoff is not explaining how managers and others actually do behave. Instead, he is prescribing what they should do to act more effectively.

While Ackoff clearly continues within the theory of strategic choice, Churchman moves to a theory of the learning organisation.

Churchman's critique

Like Ackoff, Churchman (1968, 1970) argued that human systems are best understood as systems of meaning (ideas, concepts, values) and learning. Churchman set out the conditions required for a system to be purposeful. Purposeful systems are characterised by a decision maker who can produce change in performance measures, a designer whose design influences the decision maker, a design aimed at maximising value and a built-in guarantee that the purpose can be achieved. He stressed the importance of critical reflection on system design and operation.

Notice here the distinction between decision maker/designer and the system of ideas, concepts and values about which performance measurement decisions and design changes are made. The decision maker/designer is clearly understood to be rationally seeking to maximise value and achieve a purpose through the system of ideas, concepts and values. The action of this decision maker/designer is thus thought of in terms of Kantian autonomous individuals to be explained in terms of rationalist causality. However, the systems of ideas, concepts and values, which the autonomous individuals design and measure, must be subject to some other causality for they are clearly not autonomous individuals. What causes the system's movement has to be the formative process of interaction between the ideas, concepts and values that produce the whole conceptual or value system. In other words, the conceptual and value system unfolds what the designers and performance-measuring autonomous individuals have designed into them. Furthermore, the designer/decision maker is a participant in the ideas, concepts and values of the system. The designer/decision maker must think in terms of the ideas and concepts and act in accordance with the values in order to count as relevant to the system. If they deviate then they are no longer relevant to the construction of the social system of ideas, concepts and values.

Churchman's thinking, therefore, has the same structure as that of all the other system thinkers so far reviewed in this Part of the book, namely that human interaction is first understood in terms of the rationalist causality of the designer/decision maker and then in terms of the formative causality of the conceptual and value systems they have designed. In the former they are free to choose the design of the system and in the latter they are not because they are subject to the formative causality of the system they have designed. This is not sensed as a paradox and no explanation is offered of how people manage to live with alternating between being free and being not free.

Churchman also placed great importance on moral practice. For him, the first step in systems thinking was to draw a boundary around the system, which is essentially a choice that opens up ethical questions because drawing a boundary always includes some and excludes others, dominating some and liberating others. For Churchman, the aim of systems thinking was to emancipate people from domination so that they could participate on a free and equal basis in the process of system design, that is, in the design of their own thinking. The way in which particular views are privileged over others was to be identified (Flood, 1990) and exposed so that people could be liberated from dominant worldviews (Phelan, 1999). Churchman also stressed participation, debate and trans-discipline and trans-function team working. The response to the criticism that systems are designed by technocrats, who exclude people, is to focus on democracy and participation in the process of design. What this move does is substitute a group, be it a democratic or some other kind, for the individual designer of the system. The understanding of a system or the design of a system is now a task for a team in dialogue with each other. The method of their thinking and talking to each other is still supposed, however, to be systemic. So, the idea of human systems as systems of meaning is closely linked to an emphasis on participation as equality and an idealised, democratic freedom. The ideological basis of Churchman's thinking is thus quite transparent. It is based upon a belief in liberation and participation. It presents a prescription for better ways to manage human affairs. Churchman is not explaining what actually does happen but is calling for a better way of making decisions.

Notice, however, that although Churchman is deeply concerned with participative social interaction and human freedom, he employs a framework that has problems with freedom. The autonomous individuals who are designing and making decisions about the systems of ideas and values are clearly free because they are choosing the system design. However, what they are designing is their own systems of ideas and value. If these systems are to mean anything to them then they and others must adhere to the formative purpose and process of the system. The ideas, concepts and values of the system must also be their ideas, concepts and values. As such they cannot be free and this is why Kant warned against thinking of human action in terms of systems. The problem of freedom applies as much to the idealist position of Churchman as it does to the realist position of earlier hard systems thinkers. In the realist position people are actually taken to be parts of a real system while in the idealist position the system is thought of as the mental construct of the people involved. However, even though the system is their own mental construction, the very act of this construction means that they must be thinking of themselves as parts of the system they are constructing, otherwise they are not really thinking in systems terms at all. Notice, also, a point already made about hard systems. Since the system, whether it be a real system or a system of ideas, is subject to formative cause, it cannot produce anything new. The source of novelty, therefore, lies in the individual and systems thinking does not explain how such novelty arises.

This feature of dual causality and the problems it brings to do with freedom and novelty are also evident in Checkland's thinking.

Soft Systems Methodology

Checkland (1983) was critical of the positivist, engineering view of systems to be found in the three strands of systems thinking discussed in the previous chapters of this Part of the book. These views of systems took the realist perspective, regarding the world as actually consisting of systems having an objective existence. Instead, Checkland proposed that systems were the mental constructs of observers, in effect bringing back Kant's idealist view of the regulative, 'as if' nature of systems. For Checkland, the notion of systems related to the process of inquiry, meaning and intention and he developed Soft Systems Methodology (SSM) as a reflection of this view. Notice how this approach implies the notion of the autonomous individual, the inquiring scientific observer who hypothesises about reality 'as if' it were a system.

SSM approaches a problem situation on the basis that people possess free will rather than being subjected to forces beyond their control and because of this they must be involved in any changes to the systems they create. This is precisely the Kantian position of humans to be understood as autonomous individuals acting in an ethical manner in relation to each other. Checkland is thus implicitly assuming some kind of rationalist causality, this time including emotion, as applying to human action. The implicit assumptions around human psychology are those of cognitivism. The aim of the methodology is to integrate multiple viewpoints of free participants in order to assist them *to predict and control the changes to their systems* in vague situations in which there are no agreed goals. The assumption of rationalist causality and cognitivist psychology is again made clear.

The key phases of SSM are as follows:

- An initial phase of analysis that should *not* be pursued in systems terms but should build up what Checkland calls a 'rich picture' of the problem situation. This is to avoid jumping too rapidly to conclusions about representing the situation in systemic terms.
- In the next phase, a number of systems are drawn from the 'rich picture'. These are systems regarded as relevant to improving the problem situation and each system represents a particular viewpoint because it is not obvious which system design is appropriate to the particular problem situation. Notice here that Checkland is thinking in Kantian terms in that he posits a rich reality from which categories of the mind called systems are to be drawn to form understanding.

Here, the autonomous individual is hypothesising systems as mental constructs just like Kant's regulative ideas, which impart 'as if' purpose to the system.

- The third phase is the construction of a number of system models. These models are not blueprints for the design of an objective system but conceptual models contributing to a debate about change. This again is pure Kant in that the conceptual models are subject to formative causality. The interaction of their parts, the concepts of which the system consists, produces the whole conceptual system, which unfolds the purpose ascribed to it by its designers. As soon as a designer defines a system in terms of the interaction of its parts, that designer enfolds in it that which is to be unfolded by it.

The second and third steps in Checkland's approach are essential if it is to qualify as systems thinking. One has to posit wholes formed by interacting parts within a boundary to qualify as thinking in systems terms. However, this very act of thought entails exactly the same causal dualism as that found in Churchman's version of systems thinking and brings with it the same problems to do with freedom and novelty. There are thus autonomous individuals, the designers of the system, who are subject to a causality of freedom of choice and there is the system they have designed, which is subject to formative causality. Soft systems thinking is thus clearly a form of thinking in terms of causal dualities. One implicitly thinks about oneself as designer in terms of a causality of autonomy and then one thinks of oneself as part of the designed system in some sense and so subject to formative causality.

An early version of SSM set out stages to be followed: arising of a problem; expressing the problem situation; making root definitions of relevant purposeful activity systems; conceptual models of the relevant systems identified in the root definitions; comparison of models with the real world; changes to be made that are systemically viable and culturally feasible; action to improve the problem situation. *The root definitions and the conceptual models are systems thinking about the world. The real world is the problem situation and the changes to be made.* A clear distinction is made between the real world of problems and changes, including those relating to social relations, and the explanation of such problems and changes.

In a later version of SSM Checkland identified two strands. The first was a cultural strand consisting of a view of the interventions and rules of clients, problems solvers and other stakeholders. This involves taking a cultural view of the social systems, roles, norms and values, as well as the politics and sources of power. The second strand is the logical analysis. Both strands are modelled as systems and compared to the real situation to learn from differences.

Checkland, therefore, did not stop at the level of the cognising individual. In developing soft systems thinking, he (Checkland, 1981; Checkland and Scholes, 1990) advocated an interpretive approach to systems in which account is taken of the social rules and practices of participants in a problem situation. He defined a model, a learning cycle, with a number of steps that constitute the SSM, which is a methodology for systems designers to follow when facing soft, ill-structured problems *that include social practices, politics and culture*. Intertwined with this designed intervention is an investigation of the process of designing the intervention itself and the culture and politics this process involves. In other words, Checkland is taking account of the need for second-order systems thinking, or reflexivity, in which people seek to understand their own processes of interaction in systemic terms. In short people are being advised to think of their interaction with each other as creating a system of values, culture, ideas, power interests, social relations and so on.

In SSM, the subjective aspects of decision making are brought into consideration and a number of different systems models are developed to make explicit the implications of different viewpoints so that the consequences of alternative courses of possible action can be compared. The purpose is to provide a systemic learning process in which participants can come to appreciate more fully their differing viewpoints and how they might come to some kind of consensus or accommodation as the basis of change. Instead of replicating the method, that is models designed for repeated use, it is the methodology that is replicated as a means to designing specific models for specific situations. SSM does not seek to study objective facts or search for causal relations because it views systems as the creative mental constructs of the human beings involved in the problem situation. Researchers and practitioners, therefore, need to understand subjectively the viewpoints and the intentions of all involved in a problem situation. SSM is a way of probing alternative worldviews and it uses specific models of systems to explicate those worldviews in specific situations rather than trying to identify the 'truth' about the nature of systems.

Note how Checkland is not explaining how people actually do go about dealing with life in organisations. Instead he presents prescriptions for dealing more effectively with problem situations. This heavily prescriptive rather than descriptive stance points to the underlying ideology to do with participation and the validation of alternative viewpoints.

The learning paradigm

In putting forward SSM, Checkland moved from a paradigm of goal seeking and optimisation, as in hard systems thinking, to a paradigm of learning, understood as the maintaining and development of relationships. Unlike Ackoff, Checkland does not seek to define an ideal future and identify ways of achieving it. Checkland moves from a positivist, functionalist philosophy to a phenomenological and interpretivist one, in which social reality is constructed and re-constructed in a social process in which meanings are negotiated. For him, an organisation is not an entity but part of the sense making of a group of people engaged in a dialogue. *Action is the managing of change in a set of relationships rather than taking rational action to achieve goals* (Checkland and Holwell, 1998). SSM helps to *manage relationships by orchestrating a process* through which organisational actors can learn about accommodations to each other that are feasible and desirable. Checkland provides lists of constitutive rules prescribing what constitutes a genuine soft systems study (Checkland, 1981; Checkland and Scholes, 1990), which ensures that the soft systems philosophy is carried out in practice. Managers are supposed to step out of the hurly-burly of ongoing events to make sense of these events and apply structured, systemic thinking to them. The use of systems models is meant to facilitate social processes of enquiry in which social realities are constructed. Notice here how the underlying notion of autonomous individuals is subtly retained although Checkland distances himself from 'rational action to achieve goals'. There is still a straightforward causality of individual freedom as evidenced in the managing and orchestrating of relationships and the intentional use of systems models to facilitate social processes.

SSM is, therefore, a systemic process in that it combines a cyclical process of learning with the use of systems models. The aim is to structure the debate in which different assumptions can be held up for examination and systems models are said to be ways of understanding the world outside ourselves. Central to the SSM learning cycle is the requirement for systemic thinking about the world and the building of systems models of that world. So, in order to cope with the ill-structured problems created by 'soft' issues such as culture, the system boundary must be widened to include such matters and incorporated in models. The model is then taken to the real-world problem area and change proposals are thought through. This approach recognises that problems are not isolated or confined to a delineated technical system but are part of even wider cultural and political systems. However, that recognition takes the form of expanding the systems definition to take account of culture and politics as systems themselves, systems that intertwine with and impact on the problem that is the focus of attention. The goal here is to surface divergent models that individuals have of the system of concern to them. The purpose of surfacing these divergent models is to generate a shared understanding and consensus so that action can be taken to improve the system. The approach is one of facilitating a participative approach to learning about the world using mental constructs of systems as part of problem solving.

Comment

The thinkers reviewed in this section have made an important move from a realist to an idealist view of systems. Instead of being taken actually to exist, systems have come to be understood as mental constructs. To qualify as a system such mental constructs must constitute meaningful wholes produced by interacting ideas, beliefs, habits, values and so on. Such conceptual wholes can, of course, only be wholes if they are separated by boundaries from other conceptual wholes. Soft systems thinkers consider themselves to be engaging with others in the construction of social reality, which may not be systemic. However, it is of the essence that such reality be thought of conceptually 'as if' it were a system, otherwise one could not qualify as a systems thinker.

What is the social reality that people are constructing? It is defined above as problem situations and changes to be made in organisations and societies. Soft systems thinkers prescribe the construction of systems models to facilitate the process of constructing solutions to problems and changes to organisations and societies. As soon as one makes this distinction between a reality that we are together constructing and a systemic way of thinking about it, a systems model of it, which we are also constructing, then one is thinking in causally dualistic terms. First there is the 'real' causality and we can only know about it through the model we construct. If we construct a systems model then the causality is formative in that the whole is formed by the process of interaction stipulated in the model. This cannot be a causality of freedom because models cannot themselves choose but only follow their 'rules' of interaction. Next, there is the causality of the constructor of the model, that is, the cognitive, rational (or irrational) process of the person choosing the model or viewpoint. This is causality of autonomous choice as in the rationalist causality of Kant's autonomous individual. Both forms of causality are applied to humans but no paradox is noticed. Soft systems thinkers, therefore, think in terms of causal dualisms, just as hard systems thinkers do.

I want to point here to the notion of process involved in systems thinking. I will be coming back to the nature of process in Part Three, where a very different notion of process is explored. In hard systems thinking, *process means interaction between real parts to produce a system*. In human terms, process is straightforward interaction between people in which they together produce the real system of which they are parts. In soft systems thinking, *process means interaction between ideas, values, power positions and so on, to produce whole conceptual and value systems*, or paradigms. Mental and social interaction between people is thought of as producing conceptual wholes of some kind. In the kind of process thinking to be explored in Part Three, process means interaction between human bodies that simply produces further interaction. In this kind of thinking the word process does not mean the production of some whole outside of the direct interaction itself. This difference amounts to a difference in ways of thinking about experience. In soft systems thinking, there is a clear distinction between the socially constructed changes of social relations/ problems in the real world and the socially constructed systems models used to explain that real world. There is a distinction between experience, or practice, and explanation, or theory. There is no such distinction in the view of process taken in Part Three.

Another point to emphasise about soft system thinking is its ideological basis. It is a way of thinking that reflects a belief in improvement, liberation, participation and respect for diverse views. Clearly connected to this is the focus of this systems thinking on prescribing what should be done rather than describing and explaining what people actually do. Soft systems thinkers do not explore whether, in their ordinary lives, people do go about following soft systems kinds of methodology or whether they do something else. Indeed, the need to make the prescriptions arises because people in organisations do not normally think and interact in the way that soft systems thinkers recommend. They have to be assembled in special settings and facilitated in their use of soft systems methodology.

Finally, the psychological assumptions underlying both interactive planning and soft systems thinking remain those of cognitivism or sometimes constructivism.

● ● ● ● 9.3 Critical systems thinking

In their critiques of the approaches of Checkland, Ackoff and Churchman, Jackson, Mingers, Flood and Midgley took critical systems thinking further. This section takes the work of Midgley and Jackson as examples of this development.

Midgley on critical systems thinking

Midgley (2000) is concerned with problem situations faced by people and his question has to do with how they may be assisted by systems thinkers to deal with those problem situations, understood in terms of wholes. As with all systems thinkers, Midgley's approach is based upon the assumption that people are facing a systemic problem or issue to which they must find a solution or answer in order to act.

Midgley argues that systems thinkers seek to be as comprehensive as possible in their analyses but because everything is connected to everything else, it is impossible to be totally comprehensive. It therefore becomes essential to make boundary judgements. For him, the making of boundary judgements is the core of systems thinking; it is what he calls systems philosophy. Prior to the work of Churchman, most systems thinkers assumed that the boundaries of a system were given by the structure of reality but Churchman saw boundaries as social and personal constructs that define the limits of the knowledge to be taken as pertinent (first-order system) and the people who may legitimately be considered as decision makers or stakeholders (second-order system). It is the inclusion of stakeholders that yields the second-order system and this means that there are no experts and that far form being comprehensive, systems thinking highlights the bounded nature of understanding. However, systems thinkers need to widen boundaries so as to sweep in more information because, even though understanding will never be comprehensive, it can be greater than what we currently have.

Of boundaries, Midgley says:

> everything is distinguished from that which it is not, and that which it is not comes to be distinguished in turn with reference to another boundary. (2000, p. 37)

What he is pointing to here is the problem of infinite regress in systems thinking – having identified something in terms of what it is not, one can only understand what it is not by drawing yet another boundary. Midgley sees and admits this but regards it as a theoretical problem – in practice people would simply stop drawing boundaries at some point and take action.

Midgley argues that systems thinking departs from mechanistic and reductionist thinking, which assumes an objective reality that is observed by an observing individual so radically separating the observer from the observed in a subject/object dualism. Midgley says that the move to second-order systems overcomes this dualism because the second-order system includes the stakeholders. The key process is that of making boundary judgements in which subjects are defined, just as objects are.

A boundary judgement defines the object of attention, namely, what is to be taken as pertinent at any moment in an analysis. Where there are multiple objects in a relationship with one another, there are multiple boundaries. The set of objects is then delineated by a wider boundary that defines that set in relation to everything that is excluded from attention.

> I would hope that this can be accepted as uncontroversial so I will not dwell on it. Where controversy might surface, however, is when we ask, who or what is

drawing the boundary? What gives rise to the boundary's existence? What gives rise to the possibility that an object appears the way it does? (Midgley, 2000, p. 79)

Midgley says that who or what draws the boundaries depends upon where the boundaries are drawn. It is possible to look outward towards the world and draw a first-order boundary or to look back at the knowledge-generating system which produces the outward judgements, so drawing a second-order boundary, that is, denoting the identity of the knowledge-generating system. One could draw any number of second-order boundaries, for example, one that identifies the individual, a group and so on.

In any second order analysis . . . at least two boundary judgments need to be identified: one specifying the extent of the knowledge generating system; and one specifying the nature of the sentient being(s) who are part of it. The placing of the boundaries is always dependent upon the purposes being pursued, and the theoretical ideas employed, in a local situation – so, as purposes change (allowing a different point of view to be taken), so there is always the possibility of identifying a second order generating system and associated sentient being(s); and a third one beyond that, etc. Also, every time the question is asked, 'what gives rise to the purposes motivating this second-order boundary judgment?' another second order boundary judgment needs to be made – and, in theory, this can go on ad infinitum. (p. 82)

Here it is quite clear that Midgley is talking about an observer drawing boundaries around problems and people and he quite explicitly sees the infinite regress problem but it simply does not bother him. What is implicit here is that some independent person is drawing the boundary by making first- or second-order judgements. Midgley has, therefore, not moved away from the dualism of formative and rationalist causality at all.

The difficulty he has in escaping the dualism is linked to the way he deals with time and paradox. He takes a linear view of time and quite explicitly avoids any notion of paradox.

In my own version of process philosophy, when a knowledge generating system external to the self is identified, there is no problem: as I have suggested, knowledge generating systems containing sentient beings are delineated through boundary judgments in exactly the same way as non-sentient objects. However, introduction of the self as a special case of a knowledge generating system (even a self with a variety of possible boundaries) introduces the spectre of a similar kind of recursion that I have claimed is an issue for Fuenmajor's position. It is not quite the same recursion, because in this case it arises when a boundary judgment is made about the nature of the self and we then ask, what is the identity of the self making this boundary judgment? When this is answered, the question can be asked again ad infinitum. *In my view the means of resolving this problem is to introduce the concept of time. Instead of seeing oneself as simultaneously giving rise to boundary judgments about another self, we need to view this as an activity happening over time. Witness the following hypothetical scenario. At one moment the self feels the need to define its boundaries. Having done so, the very next moment the question is asked, what is the self that gave rise to this definition? Reflections may produce a second, different definition of the self (or possibly the same one). If we see this as a process happening over time, then there is no recursion; rather there is a spiral of reflection involving movement from questioning the nature of the self, to defining the self, to questioning the self, etc. Theoretically the spiral can go on indefinitely – but this never happens in practice because the need to make boundary judgments concerning matters other than the self inevitably intrudes. Indeed I suggest that relatively little time is spent in self reflection of this kind compared with the time spent on making first- and second-order boundary judgments. (pp. 87–8)*

This quotation is a striking example of 'both . . . and' dualistic thinking that eliminates paradox. First one takes one position, then one takes another position in a time sequence that is intended to avoid the paradox of simultaneously doing two things. It seems to me that Midgley simply evades the question of who is drawing boundaries and that of infinite regress. He addresses the subject/object dualism and says he moves away from it but all he does is posit a process of reflecting on the boundary, on the one hand, and the issue, problem or knowledge-generating system, on the other. The former is subject and the latter is object by another name.

However, the reader may be left wondering why I have only talked in broad terms about the process of making boundary judgments, and have not specified exactly how these are generated. The answer is that, as soon as we move from discussing boundaries in general to a generative mechanism, we have moved away from process to content! In this sense it would be contradictory to create a supposedly universal theory of what generates boundary judgments. (pp. 88–9)

When it comes to interventions, Midgley says that a variety of boundary judgements should be used. So in addition to theoretical pluralism he advocates methodological pluralism – the use of many different methodologies. He advocates a practice of systemic intervention. This is purposeful action by an agent to create change in relation to reflection on boundaries. The purpose is to take action for improvement. He says that the definitions of action and of improvement depend upon the local situation but he defines improvement to mean realising desired consequences that can be sustained into the indefinite future without the appearance of undesired consequences (p. 130). He sees this as a learning process and he equates boundary judgements with values and ethics. The boundary includes, excludes and marginalises and so it is an ethical matter. The boundary is a mental construct limiting the problem/issue to be analysed and limiting those who are to do the deciding.

Summary and comment

The perspective Midgley seems to be writing from is that of an agent (individual or group) confronted with some situation in which that agent must make a decision or choose an action. He advocates a particular approach to such a situation called systemic intervention. This is an approach to analysing the situation by making boundary judgements and the creative design of systemic methods of intervention to enable agents to look 'outwards' at the situation understood as a first-order system and to look 'back' to the knowledge-generating system (biological organisms, mind, social group, society, etc.) in which the agents/stakeholders are embedded. He understands the latter to be a second-order level or system. The first-order boundary judgement is one of including all those relationships judged to be pertinent to the situation to be analysed and in relation to which action must be taken. The second-order boundary judgement is one of including legitimate stakeholders, that is, those who have the legitimate right to be involved in or be affected by the situation or action. Boundary judgements are therefore matters of values and ethics and particular attention has to be paid to who or what is being excluded or marginalised. The excluded or marginalised can only be identified or understood in terms of a further boundary judgement. Although this involves infinite regress in theory, in practice people will not go on making boundary judgements but will act so that this is not a practical problem.

Since everything is connected to everything and since agents/stakeholders are embedded in or actually are autopoietic systems there are essentially many multiple realities. It is therefore necessary to make many different boundary judgements in any situation and this requires using many different theories and methodologies. This underlies the prescription of the creative design of methods, which means tailoring a mix of methods (critical systems heuristics, viable systems model, etc.) to the situation and varying them during the work of systemic intervention. Systemic intervention is always purposive and the purpose is improvement, that is, the realisation of a desired consequence that can be sustained indefinitely.

This approach, it seems to me, has a number of key features:

1 Thought in the form of reflection, analysis, determination of desired consequences, intervention design, all of which are either before or apart from action.
2 How agents come up with creative boundary judgements and subsequent actions is not explained.
3 Participation is systemic, that is, embedded in a knowledge-generating system. Despite moving to a second-order level – the knowledge-generating system – the whole implication is one of agents who step outside the first-order level when they look outwards at it and outside the second-order level when they look back at it. It is recognised that this involves infinite regress but this is not regarded as a problem. In my view it is a serious problem because in practical situations people are trying to understand how to act creatively. When they start asking questions about who draws the boundaries, for example, the explanation tends to end up in mystical terms. This shuts down thinking with very important practical consequences. The infinite regress of systems thinking thus avoids explaining how novelty and creativity come about and also does not deal with the contradiction of freedom when individuals become parts of knowledge-generating systems.
4 Midgley's argument reflects 'both . . . and' thinking. There is both the first-order and the second-order system. There are both systems and autonomous agents drawing boundaries.
5 He implicitly assumes cognitivist/constructivist psychology.

Jackson on critical systems thinking

Jackson (2000) says that systems thinking is a holistic way of thinking that respects profound interconnectedness and pays attention to emergent properties in reaction to the reductionism of positivist science. Systems thinking is said to be more appropriate than reductionism for real-world social issues. Jackson calls for systems thinking to put people, with their different beliefs, purposes, evaluations and conflicts, at the centre of its concerns. Systems thinking uses models to try to learn about behaviour and does not take for granted, or impose, boundaries on situations. Instead, it reflects upon and questions where the boundary has been drawn and how this impacts on the kind of improvement that can be made. It encourages different perspectives and values as contributing to holistic appreciation.

Jackson says that the core systems concepts are:

- Holism, which means either taking the whole into the models or continually reflecting on the inevitable lack of comprehensiveness in a system design.
- Knowledge as inevitably organised into cognitive systems, which are structured frameworks linking elements of knowledge into coherent wholes. System is the fundamental element in ordering human thinking. This indicates the basis of critical systems thinking in cognitivist psychological theories.
- Boundaries drawn in different ways according to different worldviews.

Jackson seeks to re-establish the hegemony of systems thinking by developing a coherent multi-perspective, multi-methodological framework encompassing all strands of systems thinking. He draws on Burrell and Morgan's (1979) categorisation of sociological paradigms to locate the various strands of systems thinking and to develop a System of System Methodologies (SOSM). Jackson identifies four ways of thinking about social systems according to the emphasis placed on change as opposed to regulation and on subjective versus objective factors. These four paradigms are:

- Objective + regulation = functionalist.
- Objective + change = radical structuralism.
- Subjective + regulation = interpretive.
- Subjective + change = radical humanism.

He wants to show that systems thinking is not confined to the functionalist thinking of the first wave of twentieth-century systems theories but can contribute to radical and interpretive discourses. He believes that systems thinking must offer theoretical and methodological coherence in a world of multiple paradigms and clear, non-contradictory advice on how systems thinking can be put to use.

Viewed from the *functionalist* paradigm, systems are seen as objective systems existing outside of observing humans. Human beings are component parts and not particularly problematic. This approach focuses on the status quo and builds models with the aim of prediction and control. Jackson locates the first wave of twentieth-century hard systems thinking in this paradigm.

Viewed from the perspective of *radical structuralism*, systems seem to have a hard existence that is external to human observers who look for causal regularities relating to the whole with the aim of understanding radical change. Contradictions and conflict between different groups are focused on in order to promote emancipation. This is in contrast to understanding radical change in terms of the intentions of individuals.

Viewed from the *interpretive* paradigm, systems are seen to be the elusive, precarious creations of human beings. Jackson claims that human beings with free will are present in the system but does not address the contradiction between individuals being part of a system, even if only in their minds, and being autonomous at the same time. Systems can only be understood by trying to subjectively understand the points of view and intentions of the humans who construct them. Instead of constructing a model, those trying to understand the system have to get involved by 'getting inside the system'. The purpose, however, is still prediction, control and preservation of the status quo. Jackson argues that the soft systems thinking of Checkland falls in this interpretive paradigm because his methodology aims to structure and enhance debate but does not address conflict.

Viewed from the radical *humanist* paradigm, systems are also the creative constructions of humans and once again to analyse and learn about them human observers have to get involved and understand the intentions of the human members of the system. However, now those trying to understand the system look for those current arrangements that are constraining people and intervene to assist emancipation, so releasing the ability of people to transform the system they have created. Jackson locates emancipatory systems thinking in this paradigm.

Jackson defines the essence of critical systems thinking as critical and social awareness. Critical awareness is the differentiation of different strands and paradigms of systems thinking and social awareness is the understanding of the social contexts which lead to the popularity and use of the different systems methodologies. Postmodern critical awareness questions the legitimacy of all systematising and totalising efforts. Jackson's classification of all strands of systems thinking has been criticised as providing a totalising framework that includes everything, while arguing for a pluralist approach in which no single paradigm is privileged overall. Jackson, however, argues that his various classifications of other systems theories does not amount to an overall paradigm that incorporates all of the others. The various strands of systems thinking are not to be critiqued from some overall standpoint but from within the paradigms of the others. The apparent strengths and weaknesses of any one systems approach will depend upon which of the other systems approaches it is viewed from. How is one to develop a system of all the strands of thinking without claiming that it is a totality? This is what Jackson sets out to do in his System of System Methodologies.

The System of Systems Methodologies

Critical systems thinking seeks to address the problem created by the strengths and weaknesses of any particular systems approach depending upon the paradigm from which it is observed. Jackson develops what he calls the System of System Methodologies (SOSM) to encompass all methodologies and indicate how they create particular problem contexts, that is, how they depend upon different sets of assumptions.

> *Once it became clear that different systems approaches had different strengths and weaknesses it also became apparent that they could be seen as a set with individual approaches, within the set, being more or less appropriate to particular problem situations and purposes . . . [Jackson's approach was] . . . aimed theoretically at explaining the relationship between different systems-based methodologies and practically at discovering the efficacy of particular approaches in various problem contexts. (Jackson, 2000, pp. 357–8)*

Jackson distinguishes between method, methodology and meta-methodology in an ascending hierarchy. The method is the specific systemic tool applied in a particular problem situation. Methodology is the principles underlying methods, encompassing a number of methods. Meta-methodology is the relationship between methodologies.

At the meta-methodological level, Jackson identifies four problem contexts created by the nature of a systems methodology. The context varies according to whether the methodology assumes that the relationships and perspectives of the participants are unitary, pluralist or coercive and according to whether the system is assumed to be simple or complex. Unitary means that the participants, or stakeholders, in a problem situation are assumed to be in a unitary relationship with each other in the sense of sharing values and interests. Plural means that although the participants have many different views, they are assumed to share enough to make some kind of accommodation possible. In conflictual and coercive situations, the difference in values is assumed to be so great that some form of power is brought to bear. Simple means that the interrelationships are assumed to be few while complex means an assumption of many and highly interconnected relationships, giving rise to turbulence and unpredictability. The six contexts are produced by methodologies assuming:

- Simple system with unitary values or intentions of participants, creating a simple, unitary context.
- Simple system and pluralist values or intentions of participants, creating a simple, pluralist context.
- Simple system and conflicting or coercive values or intentions of participants, giving the simple, coercive context.
- Complex systems with unitary, pluralist and coercive values or intentions of participants, creating complex unitary, complex pluralist and complex coercive contexts.

An immediate implication of this meta-methodology is that it includes all systems thinking in a pluralist framework that can be used to select a particular form of systems thinking, or some combination of them, or some combination of parts of them, as being appropriate to a particular problem context. For example if one identifies the context as a simple/unitary one, then it is appropriate to apply hard systems thinking, such as cybernetics. Simple/pluralistic contexts call for soft systems thinking and interactive planning. Emancipatory systems thinking (Ulrich, 1983) would be applied in either simple/coercive or complex/coercive contexts. According to Jackson, complex/unitary contexts are those that complexity theories deal with – this classification will be critiqued in Chapter 12. Jackson suggests that complex/conflictual contexts have not received much attention.

The SOSM, which is at the heart of Jackson's critical systems thinking, is thus a meta-methodological framework relating all systems methodologies to appropriate contexts, that is, according to the assumptions made about the nature of the problem. It brings pluralism to systems thinking. Jackson talks about the above six contexts as ideal problem contexts that differ from one another in a meaningful way. The existence of these ideal problem contexts implies, says Jackson, the need for a variety of problem-solving methodologies. Important differences in context should be reflected in differences of methodology. This view was criticised by some as implying that it enables us to identify real-world problem situations according to ideal problem contexts and choose appropriate systems methodologies. However, Jackson (2000, p. 360) says that this is a functionalist interpretation, which is not necessary because the SOSM is simply a classification enabling one to critique one strand of systems thinking from the perspective of another in a pluralist perspective that denies any objective observer or meta-paradigm or grand narrative. So, despite calling SOSM a meta-methodology, Jackson tries to distance himself from the view that SOSM encompasses all systems thinking in a way that can be used to select context-appropriate systems theories. Jackson suggests that the purpose of the meta-methodology is to provide a set of methodologies so that any one of them can be critiqued from within any one of the others, rather than from the perspective of an overall methodology because that would conflict with his commitment to pluralism.

The final element of Jackson's critical systems thinking is what he calls Total Systems Intervention (TSI), which is described as a meta-methodology. This takes different views on the problem situation and combines different methodologies to address them in three phases: the creativity phase, where metaphors are used to stimulate thinking; choice of the appropriate systems-based methodology; and implementation, which is the use of a particular systems methodology to implement specific proposals. The tools of TSI, consisting of lists, metaphors and models, are available to assist this process and the outcome is co-ordinated change which brings about improvement:

> *The task during the choice phase is to choose an appropriate systems-based inter-vention methodology (or set of methodologies) to suit the particular characteris-tics of the organization's situation as revealed in the creativity phase. The tools provided by TSI to help with this stage are the system of system methodologies and, derived from that, knowledge of the particular strengths and weaknesses of different systems methodologies. (pp. 369–70)*

The essentials of critical systems thinking are commitment, pluralism and eman-cipation or improvement. It aims to help individuals realise their potential. The point of pluralism is to enable the best use of methodologies, methods, models, tools and techniques in any intervention. Critical systems thinking is thus very clearly an ideology. It is not a description or explanation of what people in organ-isations are actually doing but a set of prescriptions for how people should approach problem situations. The ideology is precisely the commitment to pluralism, emancipa-tion and improvement.

Comment

Jackson makes a significant move to encompass the social nature of decision making. However, despite his arguments to the contrary, he does seem to me to set up a meta-paradigm to include all systems thinking in what he calls a pluralist framework. As soon as one posits a set that includes all systems thinking and the relationships between them, one is inevitably taking a view that cannot simply be located within any one of them. I would then argue that if one really takes a pluralist viewpoint, then even Jackson's meta-paradigm is only one amongst many. For example, the process view taken in Part Three of this book falls quite outside Jackson's meta-paradigm of systems. To achieve the aim of being as comprehensive as possible, we would therefore need a meta-meta-paradigm that incorporates both systems and process thinking. I will be arguing that these two ways of thinking are mutually excluding so that it becomes difficult to envisage what this meta-meta-paradigm could be. Even if one found such a paradigm, however, there would no doubt be some way of thinking not included in it and an even higher-level paradigm would be required, taking us once again to the problem of infinite regress.

Furthermore, the causal duality characteristic of all of the systems thinking so far reviewed is apparent in Jackson's thinking. He writes about someone choosing an appropriate systems-based methodology. This immediately implies autonomous individuals subject to the causality of free choice. The person(s) choosing between different types of systems thinking are exercising some kind of choice based on their observation of context and systems methodology. Someone, the researcher, consultant or manager, has to form a judgement about the nature of the context of a problem situation and select the appropriate methodology. However, once the person has selected a methodology, that methodology is then applied to interacting humans, including the person(s) choosing the methodology. They are then subject to the formative causality of the system they have chosen. This is the dual causality and 'both . . . and' thinking that eliminates paradox. There is no sense in Jackson's discussion of the inherent paradox of observing that which includes oneself as participant.

There also seems to be an underlying systemic notion that if one does not at least attempt to encompass the whole, then it is not reliable thinking. Despite talking about being involved, this approach relies on someone standing outside of human interaction, defining context and selecting method.

My comments are as follows:

1 Jackson classifies systems thinking in a number of ways and states that two of them (functionalist and radical structuralist) do presuppose that the system has an external reality, is observed and is modelled, or at least causal regularities are identified. This hard, first-wave systems thinking does not deal with the problem of humans being inside and outside the system at the same time. However, second-order systems thinking does recognise the problem. I argue that second-order systems thinking does not deal with this problem in a manner that avoids infinite regress, which must be either ignored or mystified.

2 Jackson says that in the interpretive and humanist paradigms we see that free individual agents are creating the system. What are they creating? They are

creating a system as a set of interactions within a boundary. So they must be creating a boundary and they must be creating, that is, specifying and designing, the nature of their interaction and its purpose. If they create a system it must be so that they can be parts of it and they then have to act in accordance with the specified interactions they have chosen in advance. If the system is to be a system then they must be its parts in order to realise it as a system, even if only in their minds. They are then no long free in the spontaneous sense. Implicitly, Jackson senses the point about human freedom because he talks about coercion and the need for emancipatory systems thinking. However, he does not see the lack of freedom as necessarily part of systems thinking. It is just a possibility calling for more systems thinking. In fact, freedom becomes an ideology rather than an essential part of the explanation. The point I am making about the difficulty in systems thinking with human freedom is not ideological at all. It is a point about explanation. If you have a population of free individuals making their own individual choices in the ordinary course of their everyday lives, then the behavioural patterns they together produce will differ from those of a population of individuals acting as parts of a system. If they are parts of a system they will be acting according to the system's imputed intention. If you use an explanation modelled on this assumption and apply it to the population of individuals exercising ordinary freedom then you will not understand what is going on.

3 The point about novelty is not recognised. There is no explanation of this other than the creativity of individuals.

4 The claim is that interpretive and humanist paradigms do recognise that the system is not an external given but is the creation of human beings having intention and free will. The systems thinker therefore has to get involved, understand the intentions and look for constraints. Getting involved has a particular meaning here. It is understood as an 'intervention' in the activities of the people creating/constituting the system. Getting involved means that the systems thinker employs tools and techniques to enhance the debate, uses sets of metaphors, follows list of questions, analyses contexts and selects appropriate methodologies. The stance of the systems thinker who intervenes is that of the problem solver who takes a pluralist view of the problem situation. In all of this the systems thinker is still apart – the systems thinker is outside the interactions and contexts and is intentionally selecting pre-given methodologies. The systems thinker makes his/her intervention in terms of meta-paradigms and meta-methodologies.

Critical system thinking, therefore, has in common with all other forms of systems thinking the employment of central notions of wholes and boundaries. Difficulties with the concept of the whole are recognised and it is argued that they are inevitably incomplete. Difficulties with the notion of drawing boundaries and the infinite regress to which this leads are also recognised. However, these difficulties, and the inevitable causal dualism that goes with them, are not regarded as practically important. It is suggested that in practice they are overcome by pluralism.

Pluralism

Pluralism means taking many different perspectives on a problem situation and selecting those that are most helpful in a specific situation. The metaphor of lenses is often used. It is claimed that individuals have the capacity to change perspectives rather in the same way that one changes lenses in a pair of spectacles. The belief is that decision-making processes in groups, organisations and societies can be greatly improved if those involved avoid commitment to a particular perspective. Instead, they should engage in dialogues, hold their assumptions in abeyance and explore with each other different ways of understanding their situation. I would argue that this is a highly idealised notion and I do not think that it is possible for people to follow this advice The perspective we take on the world is intimately tied up with our very identities and we cannot easily change who we are as if our identities were simply interchangeable lenses.

In the next section, I examine Wenger's arguments that meaning and identity are interlinked. In Part Three, I will make much the same argument. If the way we together make sense of our world is so much a part of who we are, is in fact a vital aspect of our identities, then putting on one lens after another would mean frequently changing identities, and pluralism implies that this is as easy as changing our spectacles. This is simply an idealised way out of conflict. People do not simply alter perspectives as if they did not matter – they kill each other for them because they are aspects of collective identity. Despite the concern with the social, with political action, power and freedom, the systemic way of looking at these does not accommodate their ordinary conflictual nature and it retains the primacy of the individual. Its dualistic thinking eliminates paradox.

9.4   Communities of practice

So far, this chapter has been exploring the way in which more recent developments in systems thinking have taken into account ethical, ideological, social and political factors and processes of learning. Another development that focuses very much on social relationships and is receiving growing attention is the notion of communities of practice (Brown and Duguid, 1991; Lave and Wenger, 1991; Wenger, 1998). This section reviews the work of Wenger (1998) as an illustration of thinking about communities of practice.

Wenger regards engagement in social practice as the fundamental process through which people learn and so become who they are, thereby making a close link between social practice and identity formation. Not only do people form communities of social practice, they also are formed by the process of learning in which they engage in their communities of practice. From this perspective, then, one can think of an organisation as a community of practice, that is, as a collective identity that shapes and is shaped by individual identities. An organisation then becomes what it becomes, it forms strategies, in the learning process of a community of practice.

Wenger builds a theory of *community*, social *practice*, *meaning* and *identity*, in which learning is a process of social *participation*. Learning is not simply an individual process but the lived experience of participation in local situations in the world as the production and reproduction of specific ways of *engaging* in the world. Through *local interactions*, learning *reproduces and transforms* the social structure in which it takes place and the *identities* of those who participate. These are all matters that will be very much the focus of attention in Part Three of this book. However, the explanation it will put forward is significantly different to that of Wenger.

First consider Wenger's definition of the key concepts in his argument. For him, practice is essentially an experience of everyday life and meaning is located in the process of negotiating meaning. *Practice is essentially the process of negotiating meaning.* He closely associates practice with the formation of communities, defined as those engaged together on a joint enterprise. It is this joint enterprise that distinguishes communities of practice from cultures and social structures. Practice is the source of coherence in communities of practice and it has three dimensions:

- *Mutual engagement* in actions whose meaning is being negotiated. Mutual engagement has a history and it defines membership of a community, which is not just a social category, a matter of who knows whom, or of geographic proximity. Being included (in gossip, memos, friendship, etc.) is what matters. Mutual engagement does not entail homogeneity; indeed it is diversity that makes a practice possible. People gain unique identities in their engagement and mutual engagement gives rise to both homogeneity and diversity. There is no connotation of peaceful coexistence because mutual engagement generates tension and conflict as well as alignment.

  > *In real life, mutual relations among participants are complex mixtures of power and dependence, pleasure and pain, expertise and helplessness, success and failure . . . friendship and hatred. Communities of practice have it all. (Wenger, 1998, p. 77)*

- *Joint enterprise*, which is a collective process of negotiation creating relations of mutual accountability. This does not mean agreement, because disagreement is a productive part of the practice. The process of negotiation always takes place in a wider institutional context but is never fully determined by it. Power exerted by the context outside the community is always mediated by the community's production of its practice.
- *Shared repertoire* consisting of routines, words, ways of doing, stories, gestures, symbols and genres. This repertoire reflects history and is always ambiguous, which is a source of new meaning. The repertoire provides the resources used in negotiating meaning and ambiguity. Shared beliefs are *not* what shared practice is about.

Wenger describes (1998, pp. 96–7) these three dimensions as 'interdependent and interlocked into a tight system', combining 'an open process (the negotiation of meaning) and a tight system of interrelations'. He talks about small perturbations rapidly having 'repercussions throughout the system' so that learning 'involves a close interaction of order and chaos'. Practice as a shared history of learning creates discontinuities between those participating and those not, and in so doing creates boundaries and also connections with other communities across boundaries. Wenger associates learning with *boundary* crossing. Furthermore, a practice is local but there are interactions between local and global *levels*. What I am stressing here is the way in which Wenger uses the terminology of systems thinking and its central concepts such as boundaries and hierarchical levels.

Wenger focuses on the person, understood from a social perspective, and extends the focus to issues of participation and exclusion, addressing identity as an integrated aspect of practice, community and meaning. A person's identity includes the ability/inability to shape the meanings that define communities and forms of belonging. Wenger focuses on the person without taking the individual self as point of departure. He says that building an identity consists of negotiating the meaning of the experience of membership of communities of practice and that practice entails the negotiation of ways of being a person in a community. Identity is the pivot between the social and the individual so that each has to be talked about in terms of the other as mutual constructions. He links identity to multi-membership of communities as the living experience of *boundaries*, which creates a *dual* relationship between identities and communities of practice. They reflect and shape each other.

Power has a dual structure reflecting identification and negotiability.

> On the one hand, it is the power to belong, to be a certain person, to claim a place with the legitimacy of membership; on the other it is the vulnerability of belonging to, identifying with, and being part of some communities that contribute to defining who we are and thus have a hold on us. Rooted in our identities, power derives from belonging as well as exercising control over what we belong to. It includes both conflictual and coalescing aspects. (p. 207)

The importance Wenger attaches to the negotiation of meaning and the relationship between individual and social he postulates are themes that will be taken up in Part Three. However, these issues will be dealt with in a different way.

Running throughout Wenger's exposition there is the central role accorded to the negotiation of meaning. This is the centrepiece of his theory so how does he understand this process?

The negotiation of meaning

Wenger understands the negotiation of meaning to be a process and distances his theory from functional, cybernetic or system-theoretical accounts. When he does this (p. 286, n. 5), he means something quite specific. He wants to exclude things (like computers) from the status of participant in the negotiation of meaning. He does not want to think in terms of a total system in which both things and persons are actors. He wants to understand how meaning is negotiated and only people can negotiate and recognise experience of meaning in each other. However, as I have already pointed to above, he does refer to the dimensions of learning as interlocked into a tight system, to interrelations between people as a tight system, and to the importance of boundaries. So it seems to me that while he mostly talks in terms of the process of negotiation, he does couple it with a notion of a system of interrelationship. Wenger seems here to be moving away from hard to soft systems thinking.

How does he think about the negotiation of meaning as a process? He argues that the negotiation of meaning is the interplay of two constituent processes that form a duality. He calls these processes participation and reification. They are *both* distinct *and* complementary in that they come about through each other. The negotiation of meaning is the seamless interweaving of these two distinct and complementary processes and the experience of meaning is this duality. To explain what he means by a duality he makes a comparison with a dichotomy. A dichotomy is a sharply defined division into two, a binary classification, which requires us to make an 'either . . . or' choice. A duality is a single conceptual unit formed by two inseparable and mutually constitutive elements whose inherent tension and complementarity give the concept richness and diversity. He understands the negotiation of meaning in terms of a duality of participation and reification. What does he mean by these terms?

Participation

Participation is an active process of human bodies, of human persons, engaging together in a practice. This is mutual engagement in action as a shared historical and social resource. Participation is both action and connection. The actions are the personal and social acts of doing, teaching, talking, conversing, thinking, reflecting, feeling and belonging. Participation is a process characterised by mutual recognition, which is a source of identity. Identity is constructed through relations of participation. Participation is more than mere engagement in a practice, in that participation becomes part of our identity as we become part of each other. In participation we recognise ourselves in each other. As members of a community of practice, people embody a long diverse process of participation, of mutuality, both collective and personal. He links this with intuition.

Reification

Reification is also a process of engagement with the world but this time it has to do with things. Reification is the production of the artefacts of a practice and they embody a long diverse process of reification. It is a process in which people project meanings on to the world and then perceive those meanings as existing in the world and having a life of their own. In reification we project ourselves on to the world, do not recognise ourselves in our projections and attribute to our meanings an independent existence. Reification *gives form to our experience*, so creating points of focus around which negotiation is organised. An understanding is given form and the form becomes the focus. He provides the following examples of reifications: all symbols (including all words and so language), writing something down, creating a procedure, producing a tool, abstractions, stories, terms, concepts. The process of reification includes making, designing, representing, naming, encoding, describing, perceiving, interpreting, using, re-using, decoding, recasting. Recipes, theories, speeches, smoke signals, pyramids, logos, concrete trucks, information processing systems, simple words, complex arguments, glances, silences are all examples of the reification process. They all congeal experience, although they do not capture it, and they contribute to the experience of meaning. Reification is personal in the sense that it is projection and collective in the sense that it co-ordinates actions.

The process is an evocative shortcut to meaning and is always incomplete. It is not an articulation of something that already exists.

Notice here how Wenger seems to be postulating experience as something to which form is given by language. This is a very different notion of experience to that which will be taken up in Part Three.

The duality

Taken together, participation and reification are inseparable elements of the duality of the negotiation of meaning. This is not a paradox because although they interweave at the same time in tension with each other, they are distinct processes in which there is no inherent contradiction. They are dual modes of existence through time because they exist in different realms (p. 87). They continually converge and diverge, unfolding in different media. The duality operates as follows. Participation organises itself around reifications such as words. Conversation is said to be a powerful form of communication because it is the interweaving of participation, the action of talking to and mutually recognising each other, and of reification, the words or argument we are using. The words (reification) take advantage of shared participation to create shortcuts to communicational meaning, while participation produces and uses reification.

Participation and reification make up for each other's shortcomings. Reification makes up for loose, confusing, ephemeral participation, and participation makes up for the rigidities of reification. Notice again the notion of the experience of participation as something ephemeral to which some kind of shape is given.

As distinct modes of existence, participation and reification act as distinct forms of remembering and forgetting. Reification produces forms that persist and change according to their own laws. The process allows practice to leave enduring footprints that focus the future around them and compels us to negotiate the meaning of its past products. Reification takes on an open-ended life of its own through interpretation. Participation is a source of remembering and forgetting through our memories and the shaping of our identities. Remembering and forgetting in practice stem from the interplay of reification and participation and we are connected to our histories by this dual process.

The simultaneous investment of practice in participation and reification is a source of both continuity and discontinuity. For example, some participants move to new positions, change their lives, but others stay where they are. In reification new artefacts are produced, old ones become extinct and yet others are unchanged. He links the process of change to the arrival of newcomers in the community. He also says that participation and reification are dual modes of existence in time, dual modes of remembering and forgetting, dual sources of continuity and discontinuity.

Wenger also refers to two distinct forms of *power*. Power in participation includes influence, personal authority, nepotism, rampant discrimination, charisma, trust, friendship and ambition. Power in reification is different and refers to legislation, policies, institutionally defined authority, expositions, argumentations, statistics, contracts, plans and designs.

Participation and reification act as sources of social discontinuity (boundaries) and as connections (continuity across boundaries). Sometimes boundaries are reified with explicit markers of membership (titles, dress, degrees and initiation rites). Products of reification can cross boundaries and enter different practices. Or people can introduce new elements into practice because they participate in multiple communities. Practice is the source of its own boundary because participation forms close relationships.

An identity is a layering of events of participation and reification. Engagement in practice gives us experience of participation and what our communities pay attention to reifies us. Bringing the two together through the negotiation of meaning we construct who we are. Identity is the constant work of negotiating itself. Our experience of life becomes one of identity through the interplay of participation and reification. We define ourselves through the practices we engage in as well as the ones we do not, so that non-participation also becomes important.

Discussion

As I understand it, Wenger is saying that communities of practice are fundamentally social processes of negotiating meaning, which is the same as learning. Participation and reification are distinct processes, or modes of existence, operating in different realms, in different media with their own laws. However, they are also complementary and the process of negotiating meaning is the continuous interplay of the processes of participation and reification, which together constitute an inseparable, interwoven unity. The realm of participation is the actions and interactions of people. It is their doing, talking, thinking, feeling, reflecting and belonging. The realm of reification is another mode of existence, namely the process of projecting meaning on to objects, that is, artefacts, tools or abstractions treated as if they were things. In addition to material artefacts and tools, reifications are also all symbols, including language, and also any bodily expression of feeling, or communication such as glances and silences.

It is the interplay of the processes of participation and reification that constitutes the negotiation of meaning. I understand this to mean that the meanings forming in the interaction of participation, say talking, are projected on to objects, say words, and these objects then focus attention so that participation, and hence the negotiation of meaning, is organised around them. The source of coherence in the process of negotiation of meaning lies in mutual engagement (participation) defining membership of the community, joint enterprise and shared repertoire of reifications. Wenger describes these sources as a tight system of interrelationships, which are combined with an open process of negotiation of meaning. Wenger, therefore, thinks in the 'both . . . and' terms of a duality in which the parts are different and come together to constitute the unity and he clearly distances his explanation from any notion of paradox. He uses the term 'ambiguity', not paradox, and the thinking about ambiguity is also clearly in the 'both . . . and' mode. Aspects of the duality and the multiple aspects of ambiguity are always there, and one can think of them alternatively, first in terms of one and then in terms of the other, in a figure-ground way.

What Wenger is doing here, I think, is moving from a micro-description of communities of practice to an abstract, macro-level explanation of the process. He provides a detailed description of the ordinary, daily experience of a woman engaged in a community of practice of claims processors. In constructing a theory to illuminate and explain their practice, he moves away from the daily lived experience and talks in terms of abstract (in the sense of removed from direct experience) macro processes called 'negotiation of meaning', 'participation' and 'reification'. In doing this he splits the experience of action and interaction into two distinct but complementary aspects constituting the unity of a duality. In other words he adopts a 'both . . . and' mode of thinking in that his view of experience as the negotiation of meaning consists of *both* participation *and* reification. Although he sometimes says that in their interweaving they take place at the same time, there is nothing paradoxical about this because they are separate and distinct modes of existence.

Notice here how theory and practice are separated. The practice is described in one way, namely the experience of events of daily interaction between claims processors and their clients. However, the theory, which 'accounts' for the practice, is cast in terms of processes abstracted from direct experience.

The reifications take on a life of their own, subject to laws that apply to that realm. In other words, they constitute a system, and people are operating as Kant suggested, in ascribing an 'as if' regulative idea to this system and then testing (negotiating) for veracity. The negotiation of meaning then becomes an interaction between two systems, one being people participating in mutual engagement and the other being a system of symbols and tools. In the interplay, participants are negotiating the meaning of the system of reification, which is then forming their participation. The two systems are forming each other. Although Wenger argues in places that he is not thinking in systems terms, and although he mainly uses the word process, it seems to me that the 'both . . . and' and 'as if' features of Kantian systems thinking are very much evident in his framework.

Implications

Wenger's main practical conclusion from his analysis has to do with what can and cannot be designed. By design he means a systematic, planned and reflexive colonisation of time and space.

- Communities of practice exist before design and cannot be designed, only recognised, supported, nurtured and encouraged.
- Practice is not amenable to design either, since neither patterns nor procedures that can be articulated produce practice. Instead, practice unfolds. However, one can design systems of accountability and policies for communication levels, although one cannot design the practices that will emerge as a response to such systems.
- Roles can be designed but not the identities that will be constructed though them. One can design visions but not the allegiances required to align energies behind them.
- Learning cannot be designed, only designed for, that is, facilitated or frustrated. Although learning cannot be designed, the social infrastructure that fosters it

can. Those who can translate insights of the informal yet structured, experiential yet social, character of learning into designs will be the architects of the future.

Wenger says that participation and reification are dimensions of practice that create two avenues for influencing the future. They are two complementary aspects of design that create two kinds of affordances for negotiating meaning. In designing for participation one must make sure that the right people are at the right place at the right time in the right kind of relation to make something happen. In designing for reification one must provide some artefacts (tools, plans, procedure and schedules) so that the future will have to be organised around them. He says that design for practice is always distributed between participation and reification and the realisation of practice depends on how they fit each other. The process of design involves decisions about what to reify and when, with respect to what forms of participation, that is, who to involve, when and where, and with respect to what forms of reification. Through these choices, design becomes a resource for the negotiation of meaning. The approach to practice here seems close to that of soft and critical systems thinkers. There is the same causal duality of designers as autonomous individuals, and the system being designed, which is subject to formative causality. Again, there is no sense of the paradox of a person being free to choose as designer but not free to choose as part of the learning system.

Wenger talks about identifying and 'getting right' the mix of participation and reification, so immediately implying an outside position. He says that we produce the reification we need to proceed with practice. The dual forms of power (participation and reification) offer two kinds of lever available to shape the future, to maintain the status quo or redirect the practice. Wenger says:

> *You can seek, cultivate, or avoid specific relationships with specific people . . . You can produce or promote specific artefacts to focus future negotiation of meaning specific ways. (p. 91)*

Again this sounds to me like someone stepping outside of the duality and choosing how to move it. He also says:

> *Because of the complementarity of participation and reification, the two forms of politics can be played off against each other. As a result of this complementarity, control over practice usually requires a grip on both forms of politics. (p. 92)*

> *Because the negotiation of meaning is the convergence of participation and reification, controlling both participation and reification affords control over the kinds of meaning that can be created in certain contexts and the kind of persons that participants can become . . . The combination of the two forms of politics is powerful indeed when it affords a hold on the development of a practice . . . No form of control over the future can be complete and secured. In order to sustain social coherence of participation and reification within which it can be exercised, control must constantly be reproduced, reasserted, renegotiated in practice. (p. 93)*

Wenger says that practice and identity have their own logic and that design is only one structuring element. The structures of practice and identity are also emergent, always constructing themselves, both highly perturbable and highly resilient. It is this that gives practice and identity their ability to negotiate meaning. Improvisation and innovation are essential in an unpredictable world. It follows that the relation of design to practice is always indirect in that practice is an emergent response to design. There is an inherent uncertainty between design and practice. He says:

> The challenge of design is not a matter of getting rid of the emergent, but rather including it and making it an opportunity. It is a balance. (p. 233)

> design requires the power to influence the negotiation of meaning. In order to have an effect it must shape (or form) communities and economies of meaning. (p. 235)

A design must offer facilities for modes of belonging. Wenger says that organisations are social designs directed at a practice and the latter are key to the competence of the former. He distinguishes the designed organisation from the lived practice.

Wenger says that learning cannot be designed but that it is a response to design. For him, designs then lead to a learning response and he implies some degree of control exercised by the designer over at least the occurrence of learning. Wenger's move to talking about designing participation and reification implicitly suggests that someone can step out of the processes and design the whole, while others in the community of practice are subjected to the designed aspects of participation and reification. This is the systems idea that people are part of an already existing system, although Wenger makes it clear that this is not what he is trying to do. For the appearance of novelty, Wenger relies on the separate systems of participation and reification taking on a life of their own and amplifying differences. This, it seems to me, creates a problem for personal freedom because persons are subject to these macro processes of participation and reification which have a life of their own.

This section has devoted as much attention to Wenger as it has because it signals a move from systems thinking to the kind of process thinking that will be the concern of Part Three of this book. He is also shifting from the individual-centred psychology of cognitivism to a relationship psychology in which personal identities emerge. However, he presents his argument in terms of dualities, including a duality of design and emergence. This preserves the dual causality of designers subject to rationalist causality and their 'designs for learning' subject to formative cause. This implies that what emerges is the unfolding of what the designers have enfolded. Once again, the problems of freedom and explaining novelty are not dealt with.

● ● ● ● 9.5   Summary

This chapter has reviewed the development of soft and critical systems thinking towards the end of the twentieth century. I have argued that while these developments have introduced very important social, ethical, ideological and political aspects of the decision-making processes encountered in organisational life, they do not depart from certain key aspects of systems thinking. Like all systems thinking they are based on the spatial metaphor of an inside and an outside. The inside is a whole separated from others by a boundary. This immediately introduces a dualist way of thinking in which one causality applies to the inside, another to the outside. The inside moves according to formative causality and the outside, ultimately in the form of autonomous individuals who draw boundaries, is still subject to rationalist causality. The problem of infinite regress that this leads to is not solved in even the latest developments of critical systems thinking. The way of thinking, therefore, is that of the 'both . . . and' mode that is inevitable when reasoning is conducted in dualisms. This eliminates paradox, for example the paradox of the observing participant and any paradox to do with freedom of choice. As with other systems thinking the source of novelty and the processes of transformation cannot be explained in systems terms.

The thinking explored in this chapter continues within the traditions of humanistic, cognitivist and constructivist psychology. Interaction between people is thought to create systems, even if they are only mental constructs. Critical thinking places much emphasis on pluralism in a normative, idealised way without exploring how such pluralism is possible when a person's very identity depends upon the way meaning is made.

Second-order, soft and critical systems thinkers take a clear ideological position in relation to improvement, freedom, liberation and participation and develop the social and participative aspects of decision making and problem solving in organisations. They are concerned with prescriptions to improve decision making rather than explanations of what people are actually doing. In developing systems thinking, the theories reviewed in this chapter regard hard systems theories as tools but they do not develop any new insights into the nature of systems as such. The complexity sciences to be reviewed in Part Two do contribute such developments.

The chapter then went on to explore the notion of communities of practice. This development is similar to soft systems thinking but does make the very important point about the intertwined nature of individual identities and communities of practice. However, the thinking remains in the systemic tradition of dualisms.

Further reading

Flood (1999), Midgley (2000) and Jackson (2000) all provide thorough accounts of the more recent developments in systems thinking described in this chapter. Wenger's (1998) book on communities of practice is an important source for understanding the notion of communities of practice.

PART TWO ● ● ● ● ●

The challenge of complexity

Part One of this book has described how the 1940s and 1950s saw the development of a number of closely related ideas. At much the same time engineers, mathematicians, biologists and psychologists were proposing the application of systems theories taking the form of open systems, cybernetics and systems dynamics. These systems theories were closely related to the development of computers and cognitivist psychology. Over the decades that followed, all of these theories and applications were used, in one way or another, to construct ways of making sense of organisational life. The central themes running through all of these developments are those of the autonomous individual who is primary and prior to the group, and the concern with the control of systems. In the first three theories of organisation surveyed so far, namely the strategic choice, learning organisation and psychoanalytic perspectives, there is a clear focus on the individual and how powerful individuals make rational choices about the purpose and direction of their organisations. It seems to me that the key differences between these three theories relate to how they understand the blockages to the process of rational choice, organisation-wide intention and control. These ways of talking about, understanding and acting in organisations are now so taken for granted that many people talk as if they are objective facts about organisations.

This first wave of twentieth-century systems thinking raised a number of problems that second-order, soft and critical systems thinking sought to address. The first of these problems had to do with the fact that the observer of a human system is also simultaneously a participant in that system. This led to a shift in the focus of attention from the dynamical properties of systems as such to the social practices of those using systemic tools in their thinking. Ideology, power, conflict, participation, learning and narratives in social processes all feature strongly in these explanations of decision making and change in organisations. These later developments in systems thinking moved from the realist position in which the world was thought to actually consist of systems to the Kantian idealist position in which they are thought of as mental constructs attributing 'as if' purposiveness to systems.

The 1970s and 1980s bear some striking similarities to the 1940s and 1950s in terms of the development of systemic theories. During the two later decades, physicists, meteorologists, chemists, biologists, economists, psychologists and computer scientists worked across their disciplines to develop new theories of systems. Their work goes under titles such as chaos theory, dissipative structures, synergetics, complex adaptive systems, nonlinear dynamics. What they have in common is the centrality they give to nonlinear relationships. Independently of this work in the natural sciences, similar ideas have also been appearing in sociology and psychology.

Unlike the development of second-order and criticial systems thinking in the social sciences, this new wave of interest in complex systems in the natural sciences has been very much concerned with the abstract dynamical properties of systems as such. This has brought new insights into our understanding of systems functioning. These new insights have picked up on Kant's emphasis on systems as self-organising and emergent wholes, which are features that are not very prominent in any of the systems thinking reviewed in Part One, apart from autopoiesis. In particular, the exploration of complex systems has directed attention to inherent uncertainty and paradox. However the development of the sciences of complexity continues to be systems thinking and the central concepts still relate to wholes and boundaries. In the main the theory of causality continues to be the dual one of rationalist causality applied to the observer and designer of the system and of formative causality applied to the system itself.

Part Two of this book will consider what the developments in the complexity sciences are and how they are being taken increasingly seriously in the field of management and organisational theory. This increasing interest is demonstrated in the growing number of academic papers and research programmes, the interest being shown by major corporations and the growing number of management books on these topics.

This part of the book first reviews the theories of chaos, dissipative structures, synergetics and complex adaptive systems. It then explores how these theories are being used by writers on management and organisation. I will be suggesting that most management writers regard chaos and complexity theories as extensions of systems thinking and retain the cognitivist understanding of human nature, the notion of the objective observer and the primacy of the individual. I will argue that this loses the potentially radical nature of the insights coming from complexity theory. The themes of individual autonomy, organisation-wide intention and control continue to be central, just as they were in the theories reviewed in Part One.

Chapter 10 ● ● ● ●

Chaos theory, dissipative structures and synergetics

10.1   Introduction

In the review of systems dynamics, Chapter 5 pointed to how it differed from both cybernetics and open systems theory in the emphasis that it placed on nonlinearity and non-equilibrium states. The system was mathematically modelled using nonlinear relationships. In other words, systems dynamics took account of relationships where the effects of a cause could be more or less than proportional and where there could be more than one effect for a single cause. When systems dynamics came to be used in learning organisation theory, the nonlinearity was incorporated by adding positive feedback loops to the negative feedback that formed the basis of cybernetic systems. Systems dynamics was thus used as an extension of cybernetics. This chapter is concerned with much the same kind of nonlinear relationship that systems dynamics was originally concerned with. These relationships, just as those explored in systems dynamics, are deterministic. This means that the relationships themselves do not change or evolve. To put it another way, these are systems that do not learn. It follows that they cannot be applied in any direct way to human relationships since humans do learn and evolve, but the systems of chaos theory may have some value as metaphors. Chapter 11 will examine systems that do evolve, namely complex adaptive systems. This chapter, however, outlines the development of three theories of nonlinear deterministic systems. These are chaos theory, the theory of dissipative structures and synergetics. The chapter will explore the potential implications of these theories.

10.2   Chaos theory

Section 5.2 used the logistic equation to illustrate the nature of systems dynamics. The equation was used to model the dynamics of population growth and decline, explaining how the dynamic is internal to the system and might be explained in terms of a switch from amplifying to damping feedback. To illustrate the theory of chaos I want to return to that equation and look more closely at its properties. To do this, I am going to use the logistic equation as a model of a ridiculously simple organisational interaction. I am not claiming in any way that this is a model of any organisational reality. I am simply using it to explain the properties of a particular dynamical system.

Suppose that the profit level P of a particular company in a time period t depends exactly upon its advertising outlay in that period. Suppose further that there is a simple nonlinear relationship between profit and advertising. The relationship would be such that increased advertising has a diminishing impact on consumers until eventually some increase in advertising brings in a profit which is smaller than the outlay, so that the total profit falls. Therefore, sometimes profit grows and sometimes it declines, just as the insect population did in Chapter 5 so that the logistic equation used in that chapter can therefore also be used to model profit.

$$P_t = cP_{t-1}(1 - P_{t-1})$$

This iterative nonlinear relationship will generate a sequence of profits over time for any value of c. The question is, what patterns will profit follow as the value of the parameter c (bigger impact of advertising on profit and/or bigger proportion of profit devoted to advertising) is raised?

At low levels of c, profit will settle into stable equilibrium paths of straight lines over time (values for c between 0 and 3), or of regular, repetitive cycles (values for c between 3 and 3.5). At high values for c (above 4), profits will show an unstable but uniform pattern of explosive growth to infinity. So, there are states of stable equilibrium at first and later on states of explosive growth that would lead to the disintegration of any real-world system. What happens at the borders between stable equilibrium and the highly unstable state (values for c between 3.5 and 4)?

To answer this question it is necessary to perform thousands of calculations on a computer, gradually increasing the value of c. For example, at $c = 3.2$, profits fluctuate along a regular two-period cycle with one peak and one trough. At a value for c of 3.5, a four-period cycle appears – two peaks and two troughs. If the parameter is 3.56 then the period doubles again to an eight-period cycle. By 3.567 the cycles are to period 16. Thereafter there are rapid period doublings until the parameter c takes the value of 3.58 (Stewart, 1989).

So, for low values of c, the system displays one form of behaviour. Chaos theorists call this a point attractor. An attractor is the state of behaviour into which a system settles. The point attractor is a state of stable equilibrium. As the parameter c is increased the system's attractor changes to two forms of behaviour known as a periodic or cyclical attractor. Further increases in c result in further changes in attractor to more and more complicated cyclical attractors. These are all perfectly predictable states of equilibrium, of the kind open systems and cybernetics focus on.

The pattern described above is shown in Figure 10.1. Here the final values reached by profit are plotted (on the vertical axis) against the value of the parameter c (on the horizontal axis). So for each value of c between 0 and 3 there is a single stable point, a higher point for each value of the parameter shown by the rising curve from 0 to 3. At 3 there are two final values for profit: the peak and the trough of the cycle. The line splits into two, or bifurcates. And the peaks and troughs diverge as the parameter moves from 3 to 3.5. At 3.5 there is a further bifurcation to show two peaks and two troughs. They in turn bifurcate and soon at 3.58 there

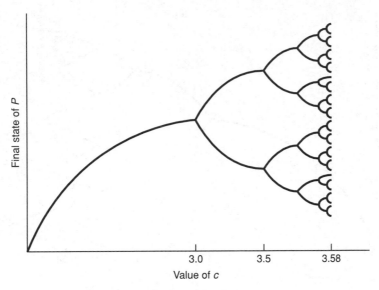

Figure 10.1 Mapping the logistic equation

Source: Adapted from R. Stacey (1991), *The Chaos Frontier: Creative Strategic Control for Business*, Oxford: Butterworth–Heinemann.

are infinitely many bifurcations. This diagram has been called a figtree diagram, showing how, at successive values of the parameter, the trunk of final values splits into boughs, the boughs into branches, the branches into twigs, the twigs into twiglets, and so on. The behaviour of the system is far more complicated than one could have imagined.

What happens as the parameter c continues to be tuned up? At the parameter value of 3.58 the behaviour of the system becomes highly irregular (instability), within fixed boundaries (stability). There are no regular cycles; the values from each iteration shoot all over the place (within boundaries) and never return to any value they previously had. No matter how many thousands of iterations are tried, this remains true. There are cycles that one can recognise as cycles, but they are always irregular. This is mathematical chaos, also known as a strange attractor. This is not a state of equilibrium but one of non-equilibrium. You could say that it is far from equilibrium. The key point about a strange attractor is that it has a shape, or qualitative pattern, but the path it traces over the long term is unpredictable. This is because tiny changes in the environment in which the system is operating can be escalated into completely different paths over time. You would have to be able to detect every tiny change and measure it with infinite precision in order to make long-term predictions. For this example this property, known as sensitive dependence on initial conditions, means that you will not be able to forecast what will happen to profit over the long term if the parameter value is 3.58 – and that has nothing to do with environmental changes or random shocks. Nothing changes outside the equation. The same constant rule is followed and the parameter value sticks at 3.58, but the consequence is an unpredictable path in profit over the long term, although there is predictability over the short term.

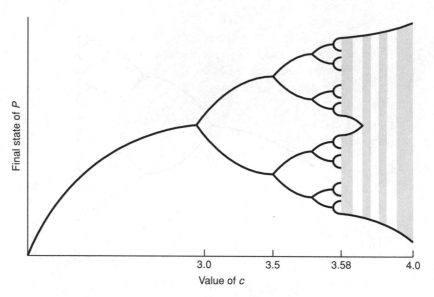

Figure 10.2   Further map of the logistic equation

Source: R. Stacey (1991), *The Chaos Frontier: Creative Strategic Control for Business*, Oxford: Butterworth–Heinemann.

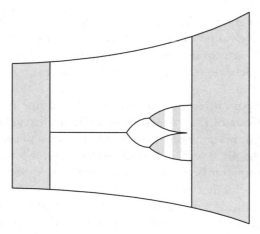

Figure 10.3   Yet another map of the logistic equation

Source: R. Stacey (1991), *The Chaos Frontier: Creative Strategic Control for Business*, Oxford: Butterworth–Heinemann.

Figure 10.2 shows a representation of many thousands of iterations for parameter values between around 3.3 and 4. The black areas are mathematical chaos and the white stripes within chaos are windows of order.

You can now examine the first white stripe at the right of Figure 10.2 by iterating for very small intervals of the parameter value which yields that white stripe. In effect, you 'blow up' the picture within the window of order, and you find that this magnified portion resembles the whole diagram. This is shown in Figure 10.3. If you repeat the blow-up procedure for the first white stripe in Figure 10.3 you will once again find a picture that resembles the whole diagram. The structure is infinitely deep; there are pictures within pictures forever and they are always similar.

The conclusion, then, is that a very simple nonlinear relationship, a perfectly deterministic one, produces a highly complex pattern of behaviour over time. Between stability and instability there is a complex border that combines both stability and instability. Note that although the word chaos is being used, it does not mean the utter confusion, the complete randomness, it usually means in ordinary conversation. On the contrary, mathematical chaos reveals patterns in phenomena previously thought to be random. It is just that the patterns are paradoxically regular and irregular, stable and unstable.

This dynamic of mathematical chaos is a paradox. It is stable and unstable, predictable and unpredictable, at the same time. You could call it stable instability or unpredictable predictability. It is not simply a combination of stability and instability, a unity in which the meaning of stability and instability remain the same as before. Instead, it represents a transformation of stability and instability. In this new dynamic of mathematical chaos, stability and instability continue but they are inseparably intertwined so that, in a sense, their meanings have changed. This is the first powerful insight from chaos theory: in certain circumstances, iterative, recursive, nonlinear systems operate in a paradoxical dynamic characterised by uncertainty.

Chaos in nature's systems

Chaos exists outside abstract mathematical equations, for example in the earth's weather system. The weather comprises patterns in interdependent forces such as pressure, temperature, humidity and wind speed that are related to each other by nonlinear relationships.

To model its behaviour, the forces have to be measured at a particular point in time, at regular vertical intervals through the atmosphere from each of a grid of points on the earth's surface. Rules are then necessary to explain how each of the sets of interrelated measurements, at each measurement point in the atmosphere, move over time. This requires massive numbers of computations. When these computations are carried out they reveal that the weather follows what is called a *strange* attractor, another name for a chaotic pattern. The shape of that attractor is shown in Figure 10.4.

What this shape means is that the weather follows recognisably similar patterns, but those patterns are never ever exactly the same as those at any previous point in time. The system is highly sensitive to some small changes and blows them up into major alterations in weather patterns. Chaotic dynamics means that humans will never be able to forecast the weather at a detailed level for more than a few days ahead because they will never be able to measure with infinite precision. The theoretical maximum for accurate forecasts is two weeks, one meteorologists are nowhere near reaching yet.

Although the specific path of behaviour in chaos is unpredictable, that behaviour does have a pattern, a qualitative shape. Figure 10.4 gives a simplified picture of that shape, the strange attractor, which the weather follows.

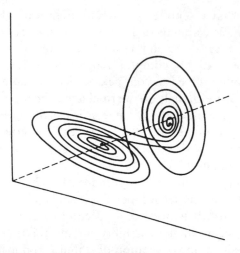

Figure 10.4   The strange attractor for the weather system
Source: R. Stacey (1991), *The Chaos Frontier: Creative Strategic Control for Business*, Oxford: Butterworth–Heinemann.

That figure shows how the weather, described in terms of air pressure, humidity, temperature and so on, varies over time, moving around one of the lobes of the shape and then suddenly switching to the other. The weather system moves end-lessly around this shape, never once returning to any point it previously occupied; the lines never intersect. (They appear to do so in Figure 10.4 only because this is a two-dimensional representation of a three-dimensional figure.)

So the specific path of the weather is unpredictable in the long term, but it always follows the same global shape. There are boundaries outside which the weather system hardly ever moves and, if it does so, it is soon attracted back to the shape prescribed by the attractor. Some weather conditions do not occur – snow storms in the Sahara desert or heat waves in the Arctic. There is an overall shape to weather behaviour because it is constrained by the structure of the nonlinear relationships generating it.

Because of this, the system displays typical patterns, or recognisable categories of behaviour. Even before people knew anything about the shape of the weather's strange attractor, they always recognised patterns of storms and sunshine, hurri-canes and calm and seasonal patterns. These recognisable patterns are repeated in an approximate way over and over again. They are never exactly the same, but there is always some similarity. They are similar to what went before and similar to what is occurring elsewhere in the system.

The category winter follows the category autumn and within a particular winter there are typical patterns of temperature, rainfall and wind speed. As one enters a particular winter, one does not know whether the temperature will be very low or very high for that time of the year, the rainfall heavy or light, the wind speed moderate or at gale force.

This means that it is not possible to identify specific causes that yield specific out-comes, but the boundaries within which the system moves and the qualitative nature of the patterns it displays are known. The very irregularity of the weather will itself be regular because it is constrained in some way – it cannot do just anything. The resulting self-similar patterns of winter weather can be used to prepare appropriate behaviour. One can buy an umbrella or move the sheep off the high ground. People can cope with the uncertainty and the lack of causal connection because they are aware of self-similar patterns and use them in a qualitative way to guide specific choices.

Throughout the 1970s and 1980s the principles of chaos were explored in one field after another and found to explain, for example, turbulence in gases and liquids, the spread of some diseases and the impact of some inoculation programmes against some diseases. The body's system of arteries and veins follows patterns similar to the branching pattern generated by the logistic equation. The growth of insect populations has chaotic characteristics. The leaves of trees are fractal and self-similar. The reason for no two snowflakes ever being the same can be explained using chaotic dynamics. The orbit of the moon Hyperion around Saturn follows a path which can be explained using the principles of chaos as can the Great Red Spot of Jupiter. Water dripping from a tap has been shown to follow a chaotic time pattern, as does smoke spiralling from a cigarette. One of the most intriguing discoveries is that healthy hearts and healthy brains display mathematical chaos. The heart moves into a regular rhythm just before a heart attack and brain patterns during epileptic fits are also perfectly regular. It seems that chaos is the signature of health.

The properties of low-dimensional deterministic chaos have been found to apply to nonlinear systems in meteorology, physics, chemistry and biology (Gleick, 1988). Economists and other social scientists have been exploring whether these discoveries are relevant to their disciplines (Anderson, Arrow and Pines, 1988; Baumol and Benhabib, 1989; Kelsey, 1988). There are some indications that chaos explanations may give insight into the operation of foreign exchange markets, stock markets and oil markets (Peters, 1991).

At this stage, I want to return to the point that I made in Chapter 5 on how the logistic equation is interpreted in systems dynamics. The description ran in terms of feedback loops. First, the system follows an amplifying loop when the population is low and then it flips into negative feedback when the population is high. There it is the level of the population that is causing the nature of feedback to change. This method of analysis in systems dynamics was taken into the way systems thinking is understood in the theory of the learning organisation. The system is understood as alternating between positive and negative feedback. The model is essentially cybernetic with the addition of the possibility of positive feedback. The analysis in chaos theory is different. It is the parameter, c, which reflects the rate of information or energy flow in the system, that causes the dynamics to change at any level of the population. For low values of c the dynamics is stable and for high values it is unstable. At a critical range, the dynamics is mathematically chaotic. It follows the pattern of a strange attractor. The strange attractor is paradoxically stable and unstable, regular and irregular, predictable and unpredictable, at the same time. This is a very different notion to that of a sequential flip from one dynamic to another and back again.

The point I am making is that if you interpret the operation of a dynamical system in feedback terms you are likely to introduce this sequential pattern. The insight that behaviour between stability and instability is a completely different dynamic, one that is simultaneously amplifying and damping or constraining, tends to get lost. This is not a notion of some sequence, but one of a continuously present tension between amplification and constraint.

It seems to me that it is not appropriate to use the concept of feedback when interpreting the meaning of nonlinear relationships such as the logistic equation. The system is not referring to some outside point and then amplifying or damping differences between its behaviour and that reference point. Instead, it seems more meaningful to interpret the system as referring back to itself. It is a self-referential system, not a feedback one. In other words, its state now depends only on its state last time, not on any comparison with an external reference point. I think that this distinction is important because if you interpret nonlinear systems in feedback terms, you are in danger of losing the insight about paradoxical behaviour. There is then very little difference between chaos theory and systems dynamics. Utilising chaos theory as a metaphor in theories of organisation will then rapidly lead to the same conclusions as systems dynamics and learning organisation theory.

There is another important point to notice. Systems dynamics pointed to the possibility of unexpected and unanticipated outcomes. Chaos theory provides an explanation of why this might be so and takes a further step by pointing to the impossibility of long-term prediction. It therefore makes a much stronger statement about dynamical systems.

Furthermore, it is important to note that chaos models of systems do not have the internal capacity to move spontaneously from one attractor to another. It requires some external force to manipulate the control parameter, c, for the system to move from the point attractor to the strange attractor. Finally it is important to note a related point about causality. Causality continues to be formative, just as it is in systems dynamics. The chaos model is unfolding the pattern already enfolded in its mathematical specification.

The next section continues the exploration of deterministic dynamical systems by briefly describing the theories of dissipative structures and synergetics.

●●●● 10.3   The theories of dissipative structures and synergetics

Dissipative structures

Prigogine (Nicolis and Prigogine, 1989; Prigogine and Stengers, 1984) has shown how nonlinear systems develop unpredictable forms of behaviour when they operate far from equilibrium. He points to a fundamental relationship between the dynamics of chaos on the one hand, and the development of forms on the other.

Chaos performs the important task of amplifying small changes, or fluctuations, in the environment, causing the instability necessary to shatter an existing behaviour pattern and make way for a different one. Systems may pass through states of instability and reach critical points where they may spontaneously self-organise to produce a different structure or behaviour that cannot be predicted from a knowledge of the previous state. This more complex structure is called a dissipative structure because it takes energy to sustain the system in that new mode.

For example, as energy is pumped into a particular gas the molecules are put into a more and more excited state. They all move randomly in different directions – a state of instability. This instability performs the function of amplifying or spreading the energy or information around the molecules in the gas. The instability also shatters any relationship the molecules bore to each other before the energy was pumped in. In this state the gas emits a dull glow. As further energy is pumped into this system, it reaches a critical point. At this point the molecules suddenly and spontaneously organise themselves so that all point in the same direction. The result is a laser beam casting its light for miles. The sudden 'choice' of molecules all to point in the same direction is not predictable from the laws of physics. There is no central law prescribing this behaviour; it emerges out of instability through a self-organising process.

Consider another example in a little more detail.

A liquid is at thermodynamic equilibrium when it is closed to its environment and the temperature is uniform throughout it. The liquid is then in a state of rest at a global level, that is, there are no bulk movements in it, although the molecules move everywhere and face in different directions. In equilibrium, then, the positions and movements of the molecules are random and hence independent of each other. There are no correlations, patterns or connections. At equilibrium, nothing happens and the behaviour of the system is symmetrical, uniform and regular. This means that every point within the liquid is essentially the same as every other and at every point in time the liquid is in exactly the same state as it is at every other. Time and space do not matter.

When the liquid is pushed far from equilibrium by tuning up the control parameter heat, then the system amplifies small fluctuations throughout it. So, if one starts with a layer of liquid close to thermodynamic equilibrium and then begins to apply heat to the base, that sets up a fluctuation or change in the environmental condition in which the liquid exists. That temperature change is then amplified or spread through the liquid. The effect of this amplification is to break the symmetry and to cause differentiation within the liquid.

So, at first the molecules at the base stop moving randomly and begin to move upward, those most affected by the increase in temperature rising to the top of the liquid. That movement eventually sets up convection so that those molecules least affected are displaced and pushed down to the base of the liquid. There they are heated and move up, in turn pushing others down. The molecules are now moving in a circle. This means that the symmetry of the liquid is broken by the bulk movement that has been set up. Each point in the liquid is no longer the same as all others: at some points movement is up and at other points it is down. There is diversity at the micro level.

After a time, a critical temperature point is reached and a new structure emerges in the liquid. Molecules move in a regular direction setting up hexagonal cells, some turning clockwise and others turning anti-clockwise: they self-organise. What this represents is long-range coherence where molecular movements are correlated with each other as though they were communicating. The direction of each cell's movement is, however, unpredictable and cannot be determined by the experimenter. The direction taken by any one cell depends upon small chance differences in the conditions that existed as the cell was formed.

As further heat is applied to the liquid, the symmetry of the cellular pattern is broken and other patterns emerge. Eventually the liquid reaches a turbulent state of evaporation. Movement from a perfectly orderly, symmetrical situation to one of some more complex order occurs through a destabilising process. The system is pushed away from stable equilibrium in the form of a point attractor, through bifurcations such as the limit cycle, and so on towards deterministic chaos. The process is one of destruction making way for the creation of another pattern.

What I have been describing is a laboratory experiment used to explore the phenomenon of convection. When it comes to the phenomenon in nature, rather than in the laboratory, there is an important difference. In the case of convection in nature there is no experimenter standing outside the system objectively observing it and turning up the heat parameter as there is in the laboratory experiment. Instead, the patterns of convection in the earth's atmosphere and oceans are caused by variations in the earth's temperature, which are in turn partially caused by the convection patterns. Outside of the laboratory, the system itself is changing the parameters and it is this that the experiment is trying to model.

So, self-organisation is a process that occurs spontaneously at certain critical values of a system's control parameters and it involves the system organising itself to produce a different pattern without any blueprint. Emergence here means that the pattern produced by self-organisation cannot be explained by the nature of the entities that the system consists of or the interaction. What is important is that there should be diversity, otherwise the system cannot spontaneously jump to a different attractor. The different pattern that emerges is a dissipative structure in that it easily dissolves if the system moves away from critical points in its control parameters. An equilibrium structure requires no effort to retain its structure and great effort to change it, while a dissipative structure requires great effort to retain its structure and relatively little to change it.

Prigogine (Nicolis and Prigogine, 1989; Prigogine and Stengers, 1984) has established that nonlinear chemical systems are changeable only when they are pushed far from equilibrium where they can become dissipative systems. Dissipative systems import energy and information from the environment that then dissipates through the system, in a sense causing it to fall apart. However, it also has structure taking the form of irregular patterns and it is capable of renewal through self-organisation as it continues to import energy and information. A dissipative system is essentially a contradiction or paradox: symmetry and uniformity of pattern are being lost but there is still a structure; dissipative activity occurs as part of the process of creating a different structure. A dissipative structure is not just a result, but a process that uses disorder to change, an interactive process that temporarily manifests in globally stable structures.

Thus, when nonlinearity and constraints are introduced into a system the result is to hold the system far from equilibrium in a state of some instability. In other words, the system is prevented from becoming adapted to its environment and this enables it to amplify small changes. That amplification makes it possible for the whole system to change. Stability dampens and localises change to keep the system where it is, but operation far from equilibrium destabilises a system and so opens it up to change.

It is important to note here that the kind of system described in the section on chaos theory cannot spontaneously move of its own accord from one attractor to another. Something outside the system has to alter the parameter for this to happen. However, with the kind of system described in this section such a spontaneous move is possible because the system is sensitive to non-average interaction with its environment (fluctuations) and the internal process of symmetry breaking creates microdiversity within it (Allen, 1998a and 1998b).

Note, however, that these are deterministic systems that do not evolve. Formative causality still applies but now the system can make spontaneous moves from one enfolded attractor to another. The suggestion is that a spontaneously changeful system is one that is constrained from settling down into equilibrium. It is one characterised by non-average relationships. You can see how this would have considerable implications for management practice if it said anything at all about organisations. Most management theory talks about success as a move to equilibrium and seeks to remove differences by getting everyone to share the same culture.

When Prigogine (1997) considers the wider implications of his work, he poses an important question: 'Is the future given, or is it under perpetual construction?' One could express the question thus: 'Is causality to be understood as formative or is it to be understood as transformative?' Prigogine sees the future for every level of the universe as under perpetual construction and he suggests that the process of perpetual construction, at all levels, can be understood in nonlinear, non-equilibrium terms, where instabilities, or fluctuations, break symmetries, particularly the symmetry of time. He says that nature is about the creation of unpredictable novelty, where the possible is richer than the real. When he moves from focused models and laboratory experiments to think about the wider questions of evolution, he sees life as an unstable system with an unknowable future in which the irreversibility of time plays a constitutive role. He sees evolution as encountering bifurcation points and taking paths at these points that depend on the micro details of interaction at those points. Prigogine sees evolution at all levels in terms of instabilities with humans and their creativity as a part of it.

Synergetics

Synergetics is the name applied to a field of research that seeks to understand how patterns form in non-equilibrium systems (Haken, 1977; Kelso, 1995). Synergetics is concerned with how the interaction between large numbers of parts of a nonlinear system co-operate to create different forms. Here similar concepts to those in dissipative structure theory are employed. Synergetics points to the importance of instability in generating different forms through a process of spontaneous self-organisation. Much of the research in this area is concerned with the brain. It suggests that the brain is a self-organising system subject to nonlinear dynamical laws. Since the concepts employed in synergetics are close to those used in the theory of dissipative structures I will not go into further detail. I did think it important, however, to at least refer to this body of work.

I want to turn now to the implications of the theories of chaos, dissipative structure and synergetics.

10.4   Implications

Since the times of Newton, Bacon and Descartes, scientists have tended to understand the natural world in terms of machine-like regularity in which given inputs are translated through absolutely fixed laws into given outputs. For example, if you apply a given force to a ball of a given weight, the laws of motion will determine exactly how far the ball will move on a horizontal plane in a vacuum. Cause and effect are related in a straightforward linear way. On this view, once one has discovered the fixed laws and gathered data on the inputs to those laws, one will be able to predict the behaviour of nature's systems. Once one knows how the system would have behaved without human intervention, one can intervene by altering the inputs to the laws and so get nature to do something different, something humans want it to do. According to this Newtonian view of the world, humans will ultimately be able to dominate nature.

This whole way of reasoning and understanding was imported into economics, where it is particularly conspicuous, and also into the other social sciences and some schools of psychology. This importation is the source of the stable equilibrium paradigm that still today exercises a powerful effect on thinking about managing and organising. That thinking is based on the belief that managers can in principle control the long-term future of a human system. Such a belief is realistic if cause-and-effect links are of the Newtonian type described above, for then the future of a system can be predicted over the long term and its future can be controlled by someone.

If one takes the perspective presented in the last section, nature is still understood to be driven by laws. The laws, however, are not ones of straightforward unidirectional causality; rather, they take the form of nonlinear relationships in which the system iteratively refers back to itself so that causality is circular.

More specifically, these theories say that, when a deterministic nonlinear system moves away from stable equilibrium towards the state of explosive instability, it passes through a stage of *bounded instability* in which it displays highly complex behaviour. One might think of this stage as a paradox in which two contradictory forces, stability and instability, are operating simultaneously, pulling the system in opposing directions. While the system is in this dynamic neither of these contradictory forces can ever be removed. Instead, there is a new paradoxical dynamic. When the system is in this dynamic it never behaves in a regular way that leads to equilibrium. Instead, it generates patterns of behaviour that are not only irregular but also unpredictable over the long term. Nonetheless, such behaviour has an overall, qualitative pattern.

These properties may be fundamental to all iterative nonlinear systems no matter where they may be found. They may be consequences of the nonlinear structure of the system itself, not due to any environment in which the system may operate.

Bounded instability far from equilibrium

So a key discovery about the operation of deterministic iterative nonlinear systems is that stable equilibrium and explosive instability are not the only *attractors*. Nonlinear systems have a third possibility: a state of bounded instability far from equilibrium in which behaviour has a pattern, but it is irregular. That pattern emerges through self-organisation. These are properties of the system itself, not the consequences of some external agent first applying positive feedback and then applying negative feedback. Either the system is driven by negative feedback and then it tends to stable equilibrium, or the system is driven by positive feedback and then it tends to explosive instability. If that instability is to be removed, then some agent or condition outside the system would have to 'step in and put a stop to it'. However, when systems are held far from equilibrium, they automatically apply internal constraints to keep instability within boundaries. This is so because of the nonlinear structure of the system.

When it operates in the paradoxical dynamic of stability and instability, the behaviour of the system unfolds in so complex a manner, so dependent upon the detail of what happens, that the links between cause and effect are lost. One can no longer count on a certain given input leading to a certain given output. The laws themselves operate to escalate small chance disturbances along the way, breaking the link between an input and a subsequent output. The long-term future of a system operating in the dynamic of stability and instability at the same time is not simply difficult to see: it is, for all practical purposes, unknowable. It is so because of the structure of the system itself, not simply because of changes going on outside it and impacting upon it. Nothing can remove that unknowability. If this were to apply to an organisation, then any decision-making process that involved forecasting, envisioning future states, or even making any assumptions about future states, would be ineffective. Those applying such processes in conditions of bounded instability would be engaging in fantasy activities.

Although deterministic iterative nonlinear systems may generate unpredictable specific behaviour over the long term, that behaviour nevertheless has an overall qualitative pattern to it. Perhaps the easiest way to think of this is as follows. Dynamic systems generate sequences of specific behaviours or events that fall into categories recognisable by 'family resemblance' types of features which the behaviour or events share with each other. But within those very general, rather vague and irregular categories, each piece of behaviour or event is different. There is endless individual variety within broad categories. If this applied to organisations, one would raise questions about decision-making techniques that involved step-by-step reasoning from assumptions about the future. One would have to rely instead on using qualitative patterns to *reason by analogy and intuition*. Those who succeeded would be those who saw patterns where others searched for specific links between causes and events.

Cause and effect

The discovery of the dynamic of bounded instability has implications for the nature of cause and effect. These important conclusions about cause and effect might apply to organisations. In a state of deterministic chaos a system operates to amplify tiny changes in starting conditions into major alterations of consequent behaviour. That sensitivity is so great that differences in the value of a variable or parameter to the thousandth or even the millionth decimal point can eventually alter the complete behaviour of the system. Tiny changes that could not possibly be detected, measured or recorded could lead the system to completely different, qualitatively different, states of behaviour. This means, for all practical purposes, that the links between cause and effect are lost in the detail of what happens. For all practical purposes the links have disappeared, making it impossible to identify the specific consequences of a specific action and to identify the specific cause of a specific event. Instead, it is necessary to think in terms of general qualitative patterns related to the system as a whole.

Systems dynamics recognises that the links between cause and effect become distant in complex systems and are hard to detect. Chaos theory suggests that it might be more extreme than that – the links can disappear altogether if the system operates in the dynamic of bounded instability.

Chaos, cybernetics and statistical relationships

You will recall that those who developed cybernetics (*see* Chapter 3) were concerned with what feedback meant for cause-and-effect links. They sidestepped the problem by saying that a feedback system is so complex that one cannot establish what the causal links are. But the way cybernetic models operate is based on the assumption that the links generate clear connections between inputs to the system and outputs from it. It is only because of this assumption that cybernetic control can be based on statistical relationships. Chaos theory suggests that this connection is broken when a system operates in deterministic chaos. This would make cybernetic control impossible. When the cause-and-effect links are in effect lost in the complexity of specific experience strong statistical associations in data from the past may be detected, but those associations will not continue into the future.

Going back in time

Consider what this loss of the ability to identify cause-and-effect links means. Suppose a system has moved from a particular state A many periods ago and now occupies another state B. Could one take control of this system and take it back to state A? One could, if it were possible to identify the links between the causes and effects of its behaviour and one had a record of those causes over the past periods. The system could then be made to retrace its steps and go back into its own history. If perfectly accurate records of past causes and precisely specified causal links were not available, the system could still be taken back to a position approximating A, provided that it did not escalate tiny differences. So, one could only take a system back to some previous state if it was operating in equilibrium. Only then are there the detectable connections between cause and effect and only then do tiny differences not escalate in an unpredictable way.

If, however, the system operates in bounded instability it will be impossible to make it retrace its steps. For, on its journey through time from state A to state B, it will have lost some information. It will have been impossible to keep infinitely accurate records of everything that happened to it, to measure with infinite accuracy to the millionth decimal place. This inability to retain every single scrap of information as the system moves from A to B is of great importance when the system operates in deterministic chaos. For, as the system moves backwards, it inevitably makes tiny mistakes in reproducing what happened to it. Before long those tiny mistakes take over and the system misses the state A that one is trying to take it back to. Time is irreversible and one can never give an entirely accurate explanation of why the system is where it now is (Prigogine and Stengers, 1984).

Going forward in time

The same points apply if one wants to control the movement of a system to a fixed point in the future. There is no fundamental problem of principle in doing this if the system is an equilibrium one. But, to control movement to a future point when the system is boundedly unstable, one would have to specify with infinite accuracy each event, each action, required to reach that future state. If one makes some tiny error in specification the system could well amplify this and end up somewhere completely different. One cannot then decide on some future state for the system, say C, and identify the events required to take it there. It is not possible to measure or record in the infinitely accurate detail required to allow this to happen. The tiniest error could escalate and swamp the behaviour of the system. Nor could one fix on some future point and then get there by trial-and-error action, because errors would not cancel out.

One could imagine this desirable state C and stipulate that that this is where one wishes to go, but there is an infinitely small chance that one will actually reach it. Stipulating the future state is then an illusion, a waste of time, when the system is operating in bounded instability. Making some assumptions about what that future state might be is also rather pointless because one will have to keep changing those assumptions. If an assumption is made about the specific future of a chaotic system, then the only useful thing to be said about that assumption is that it will not happen. It then becomes difficult to see how the assumption helps one to make a decision. The real drivers of behaviour become what has just happened, not some hypothetical and unrealisable assumption about what might happen. There is no option but to create where the system is going through action and discovering where it is going as it is going there. This is a process of learning in real time, provoked by paradox and conducted through reasoning by analogy.

It follows that no one can be 'in control' of a system that is far from equilibrium in the way that control is normally thought about, because no one can forecast the specific future of a system operating in bounded instability. No one can envision it either, unless one believes in clairvoyance or prophecy. No one can establish how the system would move before a policy change and then how it would move after the policy change. There would be no option but to take a chance, make the change and see what happens. Note that the long-term future of the system is inherently unpredictable. It is unknowable. It is not just that it is difficult to forecast accurately. It is impossible to do so. Such systems are an unravellable record of their own histories. You can see that if organisations were to display similar properties to the dynamical systems being discussed here, it would have major implications for how people think about and act in organisations.

Other perspectives

There is by no means widespread agreement on the kind of radical potential I have outlined above. Some scientists working in the field of nonlinear dynamics do take a radical perspective. For example, Prigogine speaks of a new dialogue with nature in which the purpose of science would not be that of dominating and controlling nature. Others, and they may well be the majority, do not see the kind of radical potential that Prigogine does. As an example, consider how Holland (1998) interprets chaos theory.

For Holland emergent patterns are predictable and regular. He points to how chaos theory is used to explain why it is that the long-term future of nonlinear systems is unpredictable. He accepts this but then takes the example of the weather system and says:

> *Because meteorologists do not know the values of all the relevant variables, they do not work at a level of detail, or over time spans, in which chaos would be relevant . . . Moreover, rather than trying to develop predictions based on remote initial conditions, as with the butterfly effect, meteorologists start anew each day, using the most recent data. These observations continually bring the state of the model into agreement with what has actually occurred. Under this regime chaos theory has little relevance. (p. 44)*

However, the procedure Holland describes still does not enable long-term prediction, only short-term prediction. What Holland does, then, is to dismiss the importance of long-term unpredictability and holds that it is possible to get by through focusing on the short term. In organisational terms it may be impossible to follow this advice. Sometimes organisations must make investments that take a very long time to produce results and those results depend on the fine details of what happens over long periods. Holland's approach is of little assistance in these circumstances because some method of making long-term decisions is still required. How is one supposed to do this if the long-term future is radically unpredictable?

●●●● 10.5 Comparisons with other systems theories

Open systems theory models a system at both the macro and micro levels while cybernetics focuses on the macro level. Both assume that systems naturally tend to states of stable equilibrium. Systems dynamics models systems at the macro level and assumes nonlinear relationships between variables in a system that does not move rapidly to equilibrium. The models are specified in mathematical terms in which the values of the variables (micro events) affecting the system are set externally by the environment. These variables, or micro events, are assumed to occur at their average rate (Allen, 1998a and 1998b). In other words, 'noise', or 'fluctuations', in the variables are assumed away, leading to the assumption that the most probable trajectory is the only one. This allows the modeller to use a deterministic, mechanical description of the system. It is also assumed that individual components in a given system are identical, or have a normal distribution around an average, or vary in a fixed, exogenously imposed manner. Models built on these assumptions display different dynamics; they occupy different attractors, at different parameter values, as set by the modeller. The assumptions made in systems dynamics models are such that the system itself cannot move of its own accord from one attractor basin to another but must await manipulation by the modeller, the objective observer who stands outside the system. Because the model of the system cannot move attractors of its own accord, it lacks the vitality of most of the systems we see around us.

How do the systems models discussed in this chapter compare?

Chaos theory

Chaos theory is an extension of systems dynamics. It demonstrates that the kind of equations used by systems dynamics modellers have:

- different possible stationary states;
- different possible cyclical states;
- chaotic motions of various kinds.

For different parameter values there are different basins of attraction. The modeller can alter the parameters and move the system from one basin to another. However, the system model can only follow trajectories within the basin of the initial conditions and cannot of its own accord jump from one basin to another. The model does not display self-organisation. There is no place for intrinsic novelty.

Various strange attractors can be shown to occur, given certain initial conditions/parameter values. The insight is that, in certain conditions, dynamical systems are characterised by sensitive dependence on initial conditions and radical long-term unpredictability at some level of description. At other levels of description and over the short term, predictability is still possible. Some modellers play down the property of radical unpredictability and focus on the short term and that level of description where some predictability is still possible. This is because the equations used in chaos theory are the same as those used in systems dynamics. They model at the macro level and they assume average relationships with the environment and average micro events and entities.

Dissipative structure

Prigogine's theory of dissipative structures takes a radical step from systems dynamics and chaos theory. Like systems dynamics, Prigogine's models are cast in nonlinear equations that specify changes in the macro states of a system and like systems dynamics the system is assumed to be a non-equilibrium one. In addition, however, the assumption that micro events occur at their average rate is dropped. In other words, the 'noise', or 'fluctuations', in the form of variations around any average are incorporated into the model (Allen, 1998a and 1998b). Prigogine's work demonstrates the importance of these 'fluctuations', showing how fluctuations impart to a nonlinear system that is held far from equilibrium the capacity to move spontaneously from one attractor basin to another. He calls this 'order through fluctuations' and shows how it occurs through a process of spontaneous self-organisation. This order takes the form of a dissipative structure.

It is important to note how the nature of self-organisation and emergence is conceived in these theoretical developments. Self-organisation and emergence are thought of as the collective response of whole populations. The process is described in terms of correlations and communication at a distance.

Insights

The move from systems dynamics and chaos theory to a theory of dissipative structures offers a number of insights:

1 Nonlinear systems operating in conditions far from equilibrium are sensitive to initial conditions and fluctuations and their long-term future development is radically unpredictable.
2 The capacity of a system to self-organise depends upon fluctuations in its environment and the diversity of its micro entities. Non-average behaviour is a requirement for the production of novelty.
3 The notion of an individual trajectory is replaced by that of collective, adaptive responses. Attention is thus focused on populations rather than individual entities or single paths of development.
4 Emergence and spontaneous self-organisation are central features of these models.

●●●● 10.6 Summary

This chapter has reviewed a number of developments in theories of systemic behaviour, namely chaos, dissipative structures and synergetics. These developments suggest a number of radical possibilities, which not everyone working in the field accepts. It is important for those trying to understand organisational life to consider the implications of these new systems theory developments. This is because current ways of understanding management and organisation were derived from the systems theories developed just after the Second World War, namely open systems theory, cybernetics and systems dynamics. If these are being superseded, in some sense by chaos and dissipative structure theory, then this could have important implications for theories of organisation. What if the future of a creative organisation is radically unpredictable over the long term? What if those long-term outcomes emerge from processes of self-organisation? What if difference, disorder and chance are essential to the creative evolution of an organisation? These are questions

I will return to in Chapter 16. At this point, however, the next chapter will outline the nature of complexity theory.

Further reading

On chaos there is the classic account of how chaos was discovered and what it means by Gleick (1988), and also Briggs and Peat (1989) and Kellert (1993). A more mathematical but accessible treatment is Stewart (1989). On self-organisation it is useful to read Prigogine and Stengers (1984), Davies (1987) and Nicolis and Prigogine (1989).

Chapter 11 ● ● ● ●

Complex adaptive systems

11.1 Introduction

Chapter 10 described how chaos theory identifies a dynamic between stability and instability, namely bounded instability. This paradoxical dynamic is both stable and unstable at the same time and it displays variety as opposed to the repetitive, uniform behaviour of the dynamics of stability. When a system operates in the dynamics of bounded instability, its short-term behaviour is predictable at a fairly detailed and quantitative level. Its long-term behaviour is predictable in a qualitative sense because it displays recognisable patterns called strange attractors and it may be predictable in a quantitative sense, but only at a coarse level of detail. However, prediction at a fine level of detail over the long term is impossible for all practical purposes. Long-term unpredictability and variety seem to go together.

This matter of variety and long-term unpredictability is of central importance in relation to the possibility of controlling a system. Suppose that the production of variety is a requirement for the successful development of a system. In other words, it must operate in the dynamic of bounded instability. Suppose also that the long-term success of any change made to the system depends only on the qualitative pattern and coarse level of quantitative detail produced by that change. Then, it will be possible for someone standing outside that system to determine in advance which changes should be made so as to secure outcomes selected well in advance of making the change. It will be possible to control the system over long time periods and actualise a comprehensive long-term intention in relation to that system as a whole.

However, if the long-term success of any change to the system depends upon the fine detail of the outcome, then the situation is completely different. Someone standing outside the system, or inside it for that matter, will not be able to predict outcomes to the required level of detail. It will be impossible to determine what system-wide outcomes will be in advance of action and so ensure success well in advance of making a change. The only alternative will be to make the change and deal with what happens. As chaos theorists put it, there is no shorter way than to run the program; that is, there is no shorter way of discovering the nature of an experience than that of living it. The question then becomes: how is one to understand the nature of management and the process of organisational change when the long-term future is unpredictable at the required level of detail?

One way of thinking about this question is provided by the developments in systems theory described in the last chapter. Chaos theory is a theory of systems that focuses on the same level of description as systems dynamics; that is, both focus on the level of the system as a whole. They both make assumptions about the entities comprising a system and their interactions, particularly with the environment. The assumption is that both the entities and their interactions are average, or normally distributed around an average. Dissipative structure theory develops the notions of self-organisation and emergence. It models the system of interest in terms of non-linear mathematical equations governing state changes at the macro level of the system, just as systems dynamics and chaos theory do. However, unlike the latter, the former models incorporate fluctuations, or variety, in exogenous variables, or micro events. In other words, fluctuations in the sense of non-average behaviour in the system's environment are incorporated in the former and not in the latter. The result is the phenomenon of self-organising order through fluctuations.

This is a very important point. It is only in the presence of non-average behaviour, that is diversity and difference, that a system has the internal capacity to move spontaneously from one attractor to another. Note also that self-organisation in dissipative structure theory is a collective response of the whole system. It takes the form of correlations and resonances between the entities comprising the system that emerge as new patterns or order.

Another approach to understanding complex behaviour is that taken by scientists working at the Santa Fé Institute in New Mexico, who formulate systemic behaviour in agent-based terms. Here there are no equations at the macro level. Instead, the system is modelled as a population of agents interacting with each other according to their own local 'if–then' rules. Note how this theory of systems differs from all of those so far surveyed in that it focuses attention at a lower level of description, namely the level of the individual agents that form the system. The models demonstrate how local, self organising behaviour yields emergent order for the whole system and also, in certain conditions, evolution in the form of emergent novelty. These models focus on a system's internal capacity to evolve spontaneously. Here self organisation refers to local interactions between agents in the absence of a system-wide blueprint, rather than the collective response of the whole system as in dissipative structure theory.

This chapter will be concerned with complex adaptive systems theory. I think it is important to look carefully at what the theory of complex adaptive systems is stating and how it is interpreted. I think this is important in order to avoid drawing loose and unjustified conclusions about organisations on the basis of complexity theory.

11.2   Complex adaptive systems

A complex adaptive system consists of a large number of agents, each of which behaves according to some set of rules. These rules require the agents to adjust their behaviour to that of other agents. In other words, agents interact with, and adapt to, each other. For example, a flock of birds might be thought of as a complex adaptive system. It consists of many agents, perhaps thousands, who might be following simple rules to do with adapting to the behaviour of neighbours so as to fly in formation without crashing into each other. A human being might be seen as a network of 100,000 genes interacting with each other. An ecology could be thought of as a network of vast numbers of species relating to each other. A brain could be considered as a system of ten billion neurones interacting with each other. In much the same way, an organisation might be thought of in terms of a network of people relating to each other. Complexity science seeks to identify common features of the dynamics of such systems or networks in general.

Key questions are these: how do such complex nonlinear systems with their vast numbers of interacting agents function to produce orderly patterns of behaviour? How do such living systems evolve to produce new orderly patterns of behaviour?

The traditional scientific approach to answering these questions would be to look for general laws directly determining the order and governing the evolution observed. The expectation would be to find an overall blueprint at the level of the whole system according to which it would behave. The approach taken by complexity scientists is fundamentally different. They do not look for an overall blueprint for the whole system at all but, instead, they model agent interaction, with each agent behaving according to their own principles of local interaction. In such a structure, no individual agent, or group of agents, determines the patterns of behaviour that the system displays or how those patterns evolve and neither does anything outside of the network. This is the principle of self-organisation: agents interact locally according to their own principles, or 'intentions', in the absence of an overall blueprint for the system they form.

A central concept in agent-based models of complex systems is that of self-organisation, which involves the emergence and maintenance of order, or complexity, out of a state that is less ordered, or complex. Self-organisation and emergence lead to fundamental structural development (novelty), not just superficial change. This is 'spontaneous' or 'autonomous', arising from the intrinsic iterative nonlinear nature of the system, sometimes in interaction with the environment. Some external designer does not impose it, rather, widespread orderly behaviour emerges from simple, reflex-like rules. Self-organisation is a bottom-up process in which the detailed input of the system itself determines what happens.

Since it is not possible to experiment with living systems in real-life situations, complexity scientists use computers to simulate the behaviour of complex adaptive systems. Some scientists argue that computer simulations are a legitimate new form of experiment but others hold that they show nothing about nature, only about computer programs.

How complex adaptive systems are studied

In the computer simulations, each agent is a computer program. This computer program is a set of operating rules and instructions concerning how that program should interact with other computer programs. It is possible to add a set of rules for evaluating those operations according to some performance criteria. It is also possible to add a set of rules for changing the rules of operation and evaluation in the light of their performance. Another set of rules can be added according to which the whole computer program is copied to produce another one. That set of replicating rules could take the form of a rule about locating another computer program to mate with. Another rule could instruct the first to copy the top half of its program and the second to copy the bottom half of its program and then add the two copies together. The result would be a new, or offspring, program. This is known as the genetic algorithm, developed by John Holland of the Santa Fé Institute.

You can see how such a procedure could model important features of evolution in that a population of computer programs interact with each other, breed and so evolve. The result is a complex adaptive system in the computer consisting of a collection of agents, each of which is a computer program. Each of the agents in the simulation, that is each computer program, is made up of a bit string, a series of ones and zeros representing an electric current that is either on or off.

Take a simple example, namely a flock of birds. Whenever I ask a group of managers how they think it is that thousands of birds manage to fly in formation, the usual reply is that they are following the leader. The following simulation indicates that this may not be the case. Reynolds (1987) simulated the flocking behaviour of birds with a computer program consisting of a network of moving agents called Boids. Each Boid follows the same three simple rules:

1 Maintain a minimum distance from other objects in the environment including other Boids.
2 Match velocities with other Boids in the neighbourhood.
3 Move towards the perceived centre of mass of the Boids in the neighbourhood.

These three rules are sufficient to produce flocking behaviour. So, Boids interacting with each other according to their own local rules of interaction produce an emergent, coherent pattern for the whole system of Boids. There is no plan, or blueprint, at the level of the flock. There is no overall intention in relation to the flock on the part of any Boid. Each does its own thing and orderly behaviour for the whole emerges. Flocking is an attractor for a system in which entities follow the three rules given above.

Another example of the operation of an adaptive system is provided by the trail-laying behaviour of ants. Ants set off from their nest in search of food and those who find it lay down trails of a chemical called pheromone. Other ants learn to follow the trail and find the food. This behaviour has also been simulated using what are called cellular automata. In the Vants simulation (Langton, 1996) each agent moved across a grid according to rules such as 'if you move into a square coloured blue then turn right and change the colour of that square to yellow'. As they did this, they left coloured trails that other Vants could follow just as ants do. The simulation starts from a random position in which the Vants simply move without pattern. There is no 'boss' or central programmer. However, once the table of rules has been established, bottom-up self-organisation takes over and coherent patterns of behaviour emerge out of the chaos of randomness: the Vants learn to follow a trail. This bottom-up process and its emergent outcomes are fundamental properties of complex adaptive systems. Trail-following behaviour is an attractor for a system whose entities follow the rules set out in the table of rules.

Note, in these examples, how all agents follow the same rules. Each agent is the same as every other agent and there is no variation in the way they interact with each other. Emergence here is therefore not the consequence of non-average behaviour, as was the case with dissipative structures in the last chapter. Instead, emergence is the consequence of local interaction between agents. Unlike dissipative structures, and because of the postulated uniformity of behaviour, these simulations cannot spontaneously move, of their own accord, from one basin of attraction to another. Instead, they stay always with one attractor and show no evolution. However, more complicated simulations of complex adaptive systems do take account of differences in agents or classes of agents and different ways of interacting. These simulations do then show the capacity to move spontaneously from one attractor to another and to evolve new ones. This is demonstrated by the simulation called Tierra (Ray, 1992).

The Tierra simulation

Organic life utilises energy to organise matter and it evolves, developing more and more diverse forms, as organisms compete and co-operate with each other for light and food in geographic space. An analogy to this would be digital life in which central processing unit (CPU) time organises strings of digits (programs) in the space of computer memory. Computer programs are used as the analogue of living organisms. Would digital life then evolve as bit strings and compete for CPU time? This is the question explored by Ray in his simulation.

What the programmer sets
In this simulation the programmer:

- sets aside a block of RAM in a computer, designating it as the space within which the digital organism can operate and evolve. The space is divided into blocks available for occupation by digital organisms.
- designs the first digital organism, hereafter referred to as a creature. This creature is a self-replicating assembler-language program. All programs are converted into machine code since it is this that directly manipulates bits, bytes, CPU registers and something called the instruction pointer. Ray likened assembler language to amino acids in biology. The first, or mother creature, is 80 instructions long; that is, it is a string of digits of a particular length with its beginning and end marked by a template. The code enables this creature to write, read and execute. In order to replicate it has to examine itself to identify where in memory it begins and ends. It calculates its size and allocates a block of adjacent memory of the same size for its daughter. It then copies, or writes, its code into this space and executes a divide instruction so that the daughter is now independent. After this, the mother cannot write in the daughter's space but can proceed to replicate again. The daughter too can now replicate. However, the independence is not complete because although no creature can write in another's space, it can read and execute code in spaces that are near enough to it. Interaction between creatures is thus possible.

- determines that the evolution of this system is to be driven by random mutations taking the form of bit flipping, some of this occurring in a background way and some occurring during replication. These mutations affect the process whereby the creatures examine themselves and calculate their size, thus potentially causing the production of offspring of different sizes.
- introduces a constraint taking the form of scarce computer time which works as follows. Agents are required to post their locations in the computer memory on a public notice board. Each agent is then called upon, in turn according to a circular queue, to receive a slice of computer time for carrying out its operational and replication tasks.
- introduces a further constraint on agent life span. Agents are lined up in a linear queue according to their age and a 'reaper' lops off some of these, generally the oldest. However, by successfully executing some parts of their programs agents can slow down their move up the linear queue while flawed agents rise quickly to the top.

The only task agents have is that of replicating in a regime of scarce CPU time and what happens is that new modes of doing this evolve. In other words, different categories of replication method appear. These changes can be observed in numerical terms by watching changing patterns of dots on a computer screen. An analogy is then drawn between this digital interaction and the biological evolution of species and the simulation is described in these biological terms. For example, categories of agents are said to develop their own survival strategies. It is important to remember that this is an analogy drawing attention to changes in categories of agent in the digital medium and changes in categories of species in the biological medium.

What happens in the simulation

The simulation was set off by introducing a single agent consisting of 80 instructions. Within a short time, the computer memory space was 80 per cent occupied by these agents but then the reaper took over and prevented further population growth. After a while agents consisting of 45 instructions appeared, but they were too short to replicate. They overcame this problem by borrowing some of the code of longer agents in order to replicate. This strategy enabled them to replicate faster within their allocated computer time. In other words, a kind of parasite emerged. The use of the term 'parasite' is obviously an analogy. What actually happens in the computer simulation is as follows. Through random mutation, code representing a template at either end of an agent appears in the middle of the bit string. When the instruction to identify the beginning and end of the string is carried out, the middle is mistaken for the end and a shorter version is copied into an adjacent space. This copy does not have all the required code. However, because it can read and execute in adjacent spaces it can match its template with code in an adjacent space.

Returning to the analogy, although the parasites did not destroy their hosts, they were dependent on them for replication. If they became too numerous in relation to hosts then they destroyed their own ability to replicate and so declined. In the simulation, the parasites suffered periodic catastrophes. One of these catastrophes occurred because the hosts stopped posting their positions on the public notice board and in effect hid so that the parasites could no longer find them. Some hosts had, thus, developed an immunisation to parasites by using camouflage as a survival strategy. But, in hiding, the hosts had not retained any note of their position in the computer memory. So, they had to examine themselves to see if their position corresponded to the position being offered computer time, before they could respond to that offer. This increased the time they needed for replication. However, although not perfect, the strategy worked in a good enough way so that the parasites were nearly wiped out.

Then, however, the parasites developed their own memories and did not need to consult the public posting board. Once again, it was the parasites' turn to succeed. Later, hyperparasites appeared to feed off the parasites. These were 80 instructions long, just like the hosts, but they had developed instructions to examine themselves for parasites and feed off the parasites by diverting computer time from them. These hyperparasites worked symbiotically by sharing reproduction code: they could no longer reproduce on their own but required co-operation. Although this was not yet cross-over replication, analogous to sexual reproduction, something close to it had emerged spontaneously as a strategy for survival without anyone programming it.

This co-operation was then exploited by opportunistic mutants in the form of tiny intruders who placed themselves between replicating hyperparasites and intercepted and used hyperparasite code for their own replication. The cheaters could then thrive and replicate although they were only 27 instructions long. Later, the hyperparasites found a way to defeat the cheaters, but not for long.

How the simulation is interpreted

I would like to emphasise, once more, what is happening in this simulation. I think that this is important because it is all too easy to slip into rather cavalier interpretations of what simulations like this mean for biological evolution and the evolution of human organisations. In terms of the computer simulation, this is what I understand to be happening. After the simulation has run for some time there are a number of bit strings, each arranged into operating instructions requiring them to replicate in a particular way, often in interaction with other bit strings. These bit strings fall into categories and all within a category replicate in the same way while bit strings in another category replicate in a different way. In complexity language, each of these categories is an attractor and there are a number of different attractors in the system. To put it another way, there is microdiversity in the total population of bit strings. During one round of replication, that is during a given short time period, the bit strings carry out their instructions, one after the other, and as they do so bits in some of the strings are randomly flipped. Over a series of runs the bit flipping and the interaction between the bit strings result in rearrangements in the bit strings themselves. In other words, new arrangements of bit strings appear, that is new categories of replicating instructions. At the same time older categories disappear because of the procedure of competitive removal of some of them.

In summary, the population of bit strings is a population of algorithms, or logical procedures. What running the simulation demonstrates is the logical properties of iteration (replication) and local interaction of algorithms (self-organisation in the absence of a blueprint for the whole) in the presence of random mutation and competitive selection. The simulation shows that it is logically possible for self-organisation, mutation and selection operating iteratively to display evolution – that is, emergent novelty that is radically unpredictable. This evolution is characterised by both destruction of some categories and emergence of new ones.

Anything more that is said about the simulation is an interpretation by way of analogy. So, Ray uses the simulation as an analogy for biology and calls the bit strings creatures. One category of bit strings is called hosts and another is called parasites. If the interpretation is done carefully, it may provide insight. For example, it may indicate that new biological forms can emerge from a process of self-organisation. If done carelessly it could produce unwarranted claims. For the purposes of this book, therefore, it is important to take great care in using insights about self-organisation and emergence in relation to organisations. The question becomes one of how to interpret, in organisational terms, the logic of iterative, nonlinear interaction between replicating algorithms and their self-organising and emergent properties. Even more fundamental is the question of whether it even makes sense to try to do this.

So, this simulation displays digital evolution. The digital forms are self-organising and new forms of interaction emerge. What emerges is unpredictable. Many other simulations display the same processes of self-organisation, emergence and unpredictability.

How is one to interpret the significance of these findings? What implications do they have for thinking about organisations? Increasingly researchers at universities are turning to complexity theory for a new frame of reference. Practising managers are also increasingly being exposed to these ideas. It is important, therefore, to look rather carefully at just how various people are interpreting the meaning of self-organisation and emergence. As soon as one does this, it becomes clear that there are significant differences between complexity scientists themselves. The next section will consider the nature of these differences. In the next chapter I will explore how those differences appear in the way researchers and writers are using the concepts in relation to organisations.

11.3   Different interpretations of complexity

It seems to me that there are at least four important matters on which those working in the field of complexity take different positions. These four matters are:

1 The significance of self-organisation.
2 The nature of emergence.
3 The importance of unpredictability.
4 The implications for the scientific method.

To illustrate how views on these matters differ (Griffin, Shaw and Stacey, 1998; Stacey, Griffin and Shaw, 2001), I will now review the positions of five leading figures in the field of complexity, namely, Langton (1996), Gell-Mann (1994), Holland (1998), Kauffman (1995) and Goodwin (1994).

Langton

Langton (1996) puts his work into the category of artificial life (AL), carefully distinguishing it from artificial intelligence (AI). He locates AL historically in the development of mechanical control systems that have complicated internal dynamics, such as clocks. He describes how clockwork mechanisms were used to make automata that imparted life-like movements to mechanical figures, such as those that strike a bell to mark the hours. Process control developed from this, leading to programmable controllers. Then, in the twentieth century there was the formalisation of logical sequences of steps that is the essence of a mechanical process. It was realised that the essence of a mechanical process was an abstract control structure or program, that is, a sequence of simple actions selected from a finite repertoire. The essence of the control structure could be captured in an abstract set of rules, a formal specification, without regard to the material out of which the machine was constructed. This logical form is an algorithm, that is, a step-by-step procedure for manipulating information. It is then a short step to viewing these abstract, formal specifications, or algorithms, as potential machines, or universal computers. Programmable controllers (cybernetics), calculating engines and universal computers (formal theory of machines) come together in the form of the general-purpose computer. Note how the origins of complexity theory, in Langton's view, can be traced through cybernetics.

Limits of computers

Langton then points to the limits of computers. First, there is the limit to computability in principle. There are some behaviours for which no formal specification can be given for a machine that will calculate that behaviour. In principle, an algorithm cannot be specified for such behaviour. Then there is the limit to computability in practice. Here, although algorithmic in principle, there are many behaviours for which an algorithm cannot yet be identified in practice. This makes it necessary to draw a distinction between the logical structure of a machine and the logical structure of that machine's behaviour. It may be possible to specify the structure of the machine but not the structure of its behaviour and the only way to understand its behaviour will then be to run the machine and observe its behaviour. In essence, this is what those studying AL do: they specify the structure of a system whose behaviour cannot be generated by an algorithm because of its nonlinear complexity and then they observe the behaviour that emerges.

So, Langton specifies the simple rules of interaction that each agent in his system will follow and then observes the behaviour that emerges, as in the Vants simulation described above. He stresses the radical unpredictability of the pattern that emerges. The inability to provide a global rule, or algorithm, for changes in the system's global state makes it necessary to concentrate on the interactions occurring at the local level. It is the logical structure of the interactions, rather than the properties of the agents themselves, which is important.

Langton sees organisms as extremely complicated and finely tuned biochemical machines and AL as the science devoted to abstracting the logical form of an organism. The fact that the organisms on earth are carbon-based constructions is not seen as essential and so the same logical form can be exhibited by silicon-based computer organisms (programs). In AL, life is thought of as an information structure, encoded for example in the DNA. This genetic information is manipulated to generate carbon-based life while computers are thought of as incubating information structures in silicon. Langton distinguishes AL from the AI project:

> *AI has based its underlying methodology for generating intelligent behaviour on the computational paradigm. That is, AI uses the technology of computation as a model of intelligence. AL, on the other hand, is attempting to develop a new computational paradigm based on natural processes that support living organisms. That is, AL uses insights from biology to explore the dynamics of interacting information structures. AL has not adopted the computational paradigm as its underlying methodology of behaviour generation, nor does it attempt to 'explain' life as a kind of computer program. (p. 50)*

> *The advantage of working with information structures is that information has no intrinsic size. The computer is the tool for the manipulation of information, whether that information is a consequence of our actions or a consequence of the actions of the information structures themselves. Computers themselves will not be alive, rather they will support informational universes within which dynamic populations of informational 'molecules' engage in informational 'biochemistry'. (Langton, 1996, p. 50)*

It is important to notice, I think, how AL retains the processes of information manipulation, of computation, but locates them at the level of the agents rather than the global level as AI does. This establishes a strong link with cybernetics and cognitivism. In both of the latter, the manipulation and processing of information is a central concept. The system as a whole is no longer a cybernetic one but it is composed of cybernetic entities which function in a cognitivist manner in that they process information. Algorithms drive the behaviour of the agents, although no algorithm can be identified for behaviour at the global level. This retention of an essential cognitivist view of the world has important implications for the ease with which the insights generated by AL can be assimilated into management discourses based on systems thinking.

Methodology

Langton holds that the field of Artificial Life is both mechanistic and reductionist, but in a new sense (Langton, 1996). What Langton appears to mean by this is that the old mechanism is one in which the components could be added to arrive at the whole in a linear manner. Parts have functions that fit together uniquely to determine the whole. The new mechanism he is talking about is one in which the parts interact according to recursive rules to produce a whole that is radically unpredictable. However, the system remains mechanistic in the sense that the recursive rules are computed and it is this running of the program that yields the resultant whole. The mechanism is the rules and the reduction is to the rules, so that there is nothing left unexplained. The system has subparts and the rules of the system specify how to modify the most elementary subparts. The rules are recursive to the context in which the subparts are embedded. There is an important feedback mechanism between levels of description. Intervention at local levels gives rise to global-level dynamics and this affects the lower levels by setting the local context within which each entity's rules are involved. The behaviour of the whole system does not depend upon the internal details of the entities, only on the details of the way they behave in each other's presence.

So, Langton's position on methodology is one that stays close to scientific ortho-doxy. The methodology remains deterministic, reductionistic and mechanistic. However, he stresses the radically unpredictable nature of emergent order. For him, self-organisation is an algorithmic interaction of a cybernetic kind and emergence is a fundamentally important phenomenon.

Gell-Mann

Gell-Mann (1994) gives a number of examples of complex adaptive systems: bio-logical evolution; the behaviour of organisms; learning and thinking; the evolution of human societies; the functioning of markets; the use of computers to make pre-dictions on the basis of past observations and to prepare strategies.

> *The common feature of all these processes is that in each one a complex adaptive system acquires information about its environment and its own interaction with that environment, identifying regularities in that information, condensing those regularities into a kind of 'schema' or model, and acting in the real world on the basis of that schema. In each case, there are various competing schemata, and the results of the action in the real world feed back to influence the competition among those schemata. (p. 17)*

> *complex adaptive systems . . . are collectives of co-adapting adaptive agents, which construct schemata to describe and predict one another's behaviour. (p. 318)*

The cognitivist frame of reference, and its cybernetic underpinnings, could hardly be put more clearly than this. Furthermore, the emphasis on evolution as competit-ively selected adaptation also clearly stands out. Gell-Mann then goes on to define effective complexity of a system in algorithmic, informational terms as the length of the schema used to describe its regularities, relative to the complex adaptive system that is observing it. He locates effective complexity as intermediate between order and disorder, stating that it is only here that a complex adaptive system can func-tion. Order is defined as too much regularity and disorder as too little.

> *Conditions between order and disorder characterize not only the environment within which life can arise, but also life itself, with its high effective complexity and great depth. (p. 116)*

Gell-Mann does not talk a great deal about self-organisation and emergence, at least not in the book that most now use when importing his ideas into organisation theory. Typical of his references to self-organisation and emergence is the following quotation:

In an astonishing variety of contexts, apparently complex structures or behaviors emerge from systems characterized by very simple rules. These systems are said to be self-organized and their properties are said to be emergent. The grandest example is the universe itself, the full complexity of which emerges from simple rules plus the operation of chance. (p. 100)

It is important here to note the use of the word 'apparently' to limit the notion of the complex and the emphasis that he places on self-organisation as a process of following *simple rules*. It is important to note this, I think, because the emphasis on apparent complexity and simple rules makes it very easy indeed to assimilate what Gell-Mann says into systemic perspectives on the nature of organisations. What Gell-Mann is doing is downplaying the importance of self-organising process and emergence and focusing on competitive selection as the driver of evolution in complex adaptive systems. This is made clear by the importance he attaches to 'frozen accidents':

The tree-like structure of branching histories involves a game of chance at every branching. Any individual coarse-grained history consists of a particular outcome of each of those games. As each history continues through time, it registers increasing numbers of such chance outcomes. But some of those accidents become frozen as rules for the future, at least for some portion of the universe. Thus the number of possible regularities keeps increasing with time, and so does the possible complexity. (p. 229)

So, like Langton, Gell-Mann stays with orthodox scientific methodology. He emphasises the importance of chance in the evolution of complex adaptive systems. Although this implies long-term unpredictability, Gell-Mann seems to me to downplay the implications of this and focuses instead on regularities and predictability. His emphasis on 'frozen accidents' and competitive selection is close to the orthodox ideas of neo-Darwinism, as is his lack of emphasis on self-organisation and emergence, which he clearly does not see as radical concepts in any way. Despite talking about the importance of interaction, he retains the primacy of the autonomous individual in the sense of agents and systems that individually represent a world and then act autonomously on those representations. For me, the potentially radical implications of complexity theory are readily assimilated by Gell-Mann into scientific orthodoxy. Complexity theory, in his version, is an interesting extension of orthodoxy. This, and the explicitly cognitivist frame of reference he works within, makes it almost inevitable that the importation of his work for theorising about organisation will not pose any radical challenge. Also, the kind of emphasis he places on simple rules has proved to be very popular amongst many of those who have applied the theory of complex adaptive systems to organisations. The validity of doing this will be explored in Chapter 12.

Holland

Modelling lies at the heart of Holland's way of understanding life:

Among living forms on earth, the construction of objects and scripts that serve as models is a uniquely human activity . . . It is less apparent that models are a pervasive part of everyday activity. Driving to or from work is model directed; we have a kind of internal map of the principal landmarks and turning points along the way. We are typically unaware of this map until we have to search for an alternative route . . . In that search we carry out virtual experiments, rather than actually testing the alternative routes. Herein lies a major value of models: we can anticipate consequences without becoming involved in time-consuming, possibly dangerous, overt actions. (Holland, 1998, p. 10)

Holland is particularly concerned with nonlinear agent-based models and he sets out the procedure for designing such models. The first step is to shear away irrelevant detail because the model must be simpler than that which it models. He then talks about specifying the mechanisms through which entities, or agents, relate to each other and how these mechanisms form the building blocks of the model. The configuration of the building blocks determines the state of the model at any particular moment and transition functions determine how it changes state.

the art of model building turns on selecting a level of detail that admits simple laws. (p. 46)

It is our ability to discern and use building blocks that makes the perpetual novelty of our world understandable, and even predictable. (p. 25)

The program is fully reducible to the rules (instructions) that define it, so nothing remains hidden; yet the behaviours generated are not easily anticipated from an inspection of those rules. (p. 5)

If the model is well conceived, it makes possible prediction and planning and it reveals new possibilities. (p. 11)

Holland's cognitivist frame of reference is quite explicit, as is his deterministic and reductionistic approach to science. He clearly takes the position of the independent observer of a system and talks about models needing to follow the designer's intent. Also, the model need bear no resemblance to what is being modelled. Repeatedly he talks about focusing on the time spans and the levels of detail that allow the uncovering of regularities and unchanging laws. He stresses how *simple rules* of interaction yield emergent pattern, how rules generate perpetual novelty. However, he rapidly follows such statements with others in which he says a phenomenon is emergent only when it is recognisable and recurring, although it may not be easy to recognise or explain. So, he points to chance, unpredictability and novelty and then rapidly backs away from these notions to advocate concentrating on time spans and levels of detail where predictability is possible and 'novelty' is regular.

The emphasis he places on the autonomous individual also comes out very clearly when he describes the individual agents in his models. He says that these agents must have strategies, that is, prescriptions telling them what to do as the game unfolds, approximating a complete strategy that tells them what to do in all possible situations.

It is next to impossible to predict the course of the game. Emergence and perpetual novelty are ever present in games where the opponents are adapting to each other. (p. 10)

This view of opponents' adapting to each others' strategies, encourages a more careful look at emergence in rule-governed systems. A computer, once supplied with the rules of the game, and the rules that determined the players' strategies and changes in strategies (setting aside chance moves), can, move by move, determine the course of the game. So the overall system is fully defined. Despite this, an outside observer will be hard put to determine what happens next, even after extended observation . . . what, if anything, shows the regularity and predictability we expect of emergent patterns? (pp. 10–11)

Above all, we've seen that models give us a way of compensating for the perpetual novelty of the world. (p. 243)

What I see here is someone pointing to radical unpredictability, emergent novelty through a radical notion of self-organisation and then immediately assimilating it into orthodox science and so neutering its implications. Again, I would argue that the principal route through which this is achieved is the retention of a cognitivist perspective on human knowing. As with Gell-Mann, I would argue that in the hands of Holland, complexity theory represents an interesting development of orthodoxy in the natural sciences. I am not trying to say that this is unimportant. I am simply pointing to the reasoning process being employed. Holland's views, even more so than Gell-Mann's, are immediately and easily assimilated into systems-based management thinking.

Kauffman

Kauffman's work has much in common with that of Gell-Mann and Holland but in some important respects it is radically different: his work holds much of the radical implications of complexity while that of the others slips into orthodoxy. The similarity is in his method. He simulates abstract living systems consisting of large numbers of autonomous adaptive agents in terms of information-processing systems. What he does is quite close to Langton's work on cellular automata. Once again, the agents and their *rules of interaction are simple* and, from this simplicity of interaction, complex novelty emerges. As with the others, his agents are cybernetic entities, cognitivist in nature. His methodology and the underlying cognitivist assumptions make it just as easy to import his modelling approach into systems-based theorising about organisations. However, the conclusions he draws from his work are radical.

Biology has come to seem the science of the accidental, the ad hoc, and we just one of the fruits of this ad hocery . . . We humans, a trumped-up, tricked-out, horn-blowing, self-important presence on the globe need never have occurred . . . Since Darwin, we turn to a single, singular force, Natural selection . . . Without it we reason, there would be nothing but incoherent disorder. (Kauffman, 1995, pp. 7–8)

I shall argue . . . that this idea is wrong . . . the emerging sciences of complexity begin to suggest that the order is not all accidental, that vast veins of spontaneous order lie at hand. (p. 8)

The first theme is self-organization. Whether we confront . . . the origin of life . . . or the patterns of co-evolution . . . we have found the signature of law. All these phenomena give signs of nonmysterious but emergent order . . . Selection is the second theme . . . powerful, but limited . . . the inevitability of historical accident is the third theme. (pp. 185–6)

So, Kauffman is taking a radical stand. This is one which places emergent novelty at the centre of life and as a consequence he accepts that one has to give up the dream of predicting the details. Instead, one has to pursue the hope of explaining, understanding and, perhaps, predicting the emergent generic properties of a system.

If I am right, the very nature of co-evolution is to attain this edge of chaos, a web of compromises where each species prospers as well as possible but where none can be sure if its best next step will set off a trickle or a landslide. In this precarious world, avalanches, small and large, sweep the system relentlessly . . . At this poised state between order and disorder, the layers cannot foretell the unfolding consequences of their actions. While there is law in the distribution of avalanche sizes that arise in the poised state, there is unpredictability in each individual case . . . In such a poised world, we must give up the pretense of long-term prediction. (p. 29)

The radical position Kauffman takes up here is directly contrary to management orthodoxy and it is this perspective I will be interested in exploring in relation to organisations in Part Three.

Goodwin

Goodwin (1994) also holds the radical implications of complexity theory, particularly emphasising relationship and participation. He points to two aspects of the development of form: an individual developmental cycle (Aristotelian evolution) and the evolution of species, or new forms. Neo-Darwinists see the individual development cycle as being determined by genes and markers on genes. In other words, the typical phases and features of individual development have causes that are to be found in the genes. Evolution of the genome then occurs through random mutation and competitive selection. The result is infinite variety, novelty, that is partly history determined and partly due to chance, all cobbled together without any internal, inherent order. Like Kauffman, Goodwin rejects this view and presents the following argument.

Goodwin takes the organism, rather than the gene, as the fundamental unit in biology. He thinks in terms of a network of interacting genes located within an environment, or context, which he calls the morphological field. This context is a constraint on the possible patterns of expression by the genetic network. The field limits the set of possible sequential trajectories. The field, as a constraint, is then a source of order. The field is a spatio-temporal order, a dynamic process with distinctive properties that result in the emergence of progressively more complex spatial patterns as development proceeds. The action of the genes takes place within, and contributes to, a context of spatio-temporal order, the morphogenetic field. Networks of genes lie at the interface between individual development and the evolution of form. For individual development to be stable, it must be insensitive to developmental and mutational noise. However, for evolution to occur, gene interactions must be plastic and capable of generating a large variety of dynamic sequences, which can be selected and stabilised. Paradox is at the heart of his explanation.

According to neo-Darwinism, one would expect a huge variety of leaf arrangements. In fact, there are only three: whorls, as in mint or a rose; distichous – that is, alternating from side to side of a stalk – as in maize and grass; spiral, as in ivy and most plants. He suggests that the mechanical behaviour of the meristem (stalk) constrains the leaf trajectories to three. Furthermore, 80 per cent of the 250,000 higher plant species have spiral pattern leaves. He thinks that this probably reflects the relative probability of morphogenetic trajectories. All three forms, however, might be good enough light collectors and so one does not confer greater survival benefit than another. Here natural selection does not generate form but is simply one factor in stabilising it.

By ensuring that parameter values fall within certain domains, genes contribute to the stability and repeatability of a life cycle, the biological memory, or heredity. But, organisms are entities organised dynamically by developmental and morphogenetic fields. Such fields are powerful particulars: that is, things with a particular kind of agency or causal power. Fields are wholes actively organising themselves. They are agents but they are also acted upon. Organisms influence, and are influenced by, their environment. He sees a species life cycle as an attractor and claims that genetic networks can undergo extensive reorganisation as the whole organisation responds to the environment.

What Goodwin is doing here is, to my mind, quite radical. Unlike all the others I have reviewed above, he relocates agency away from interacting individual components and places it at the level of the whole. This whole is the morphogenetic field, the interface between a network and its context. This is radical because the Western mind overwhelmingly locates agency in individuals. This shift in the location of agency can be seen quite clearly if one consider levels of description. It is common to regard physics as one level of description, from which emerges chemistry. The latter is constrained by the former but cannot be reduced to it. Similarly, the genetic could be thought of as a level of description that emerges from chemistry, being constrained by, but not reducible to, chemistry. One could then see biological organisms as a level of description that emerges from the genetic but is not simply reducible to it. What Goodwin is proposing, it seems to me, is the biological as one level of description. This is the morphogenetic field constituted by the interaction of genome and context, one forming and being formed by the other, at the same time, in the field.

I see a parallel between what Goodwin is proposing and what I will later present (Chapter 15) as a relationship psychology approach to the social and the psychological, with one difference, namely that while Goodwin talks in terms of wholes and fields, the approach I will be taking does not. It is usual, in the social sciences, to regard the biological as one level of description. The individual mind is then seen as a higher level that is constrained by, but not reducible to, the biological. The group and the social are seen as a yet higher level of description that is constrained by, but not reducible to, the individual mind. The debate then arises as to whether the individuals form the group or whether the group/social forms the individuals. The former is the position of cognitivism and psychoanalysis and the latter the position of the social constructionist. What I will be suggesting in Chapter 15 of this book, under the label of a relationship psychology approach, is that the individual and the group are one level of description. I will be suggesting that the individual is the singular and the group the plural of one phenomenon, namely relationships and communication between people. As Goodwin locates agency in the genes and the morphogenetic field, so I will locate agency in the individual and the group at the same time. I will argue that individual minds form and are formed by groups, just as groups form and are formed by individual minds, at the same time.

A summary

I have gone to some length to separate out what I see as different perspectives on the nature of complex adaptive systems. On the one hand, there is what seems to me to be an orthodox perspective, typified by the views of Holland and Gell-Mann and to some extent by those of Langton. From this perspective, a complex system is understood in somewhat mechanistic, reductionist terms and is modelled by an objective observer in the interests of predicting its behaviour. Self-organisation/emergence is not seen to be a new ordering principle in the evolution of the system. Evolution occurs through random mutation and competitive selection. The radical unpredictability of emergent new forms is not emphasised. The system is modelled as a network of cybernetic and cognitivist agents: they represent regularities in the form of schemas, the equivalent of mental models; they store those representations in the form of rules and then act on the basis of those rules. Complexity is reduced to simplicity and much emphasis is placed on complex patterns emerging from simple rules. On the other hand, there is what seems to me to be a radical perspective on the nature of complex systems. This is typified by the views of Kauffman and, even more so, those of Goodwin. From this perspective, self-organisation, rather than random mutation, plays the central role in the emergence of new forms. Those new forms emerge and they are radically unpredictable. Agency lies not at the level of the individual agent but at the level of the agent and the morphogenetic field.

This other radical distinction becomes a very important issue when organisational theorists use insights from agent-based modelling. The more orthodox viewpoint on complex adaptive systems can be brought to bear on organisational issues within a cognitivist view of human psychology and a systemic perspective on interaction. The result, I hope to show in the next chapter, is a theory of organisation that uses the terminology of complex systems but stays firmly within dominant systems-based thinking about organisations. Potentially radical insights from complexity theory are easily assimilated into the orthodox discourse. This is done by selectively concentrating on time periods and levels of detail that are predictable and talking about self-organisation and emergence as if they could be controlled by managers. When this is done, what is lost is the invitation to explore what managers do when time spans and levels of detail are radically unpredictable.

In the next chapter, I will be exploring how some writers have been doing just this, in my view. In Part Three, I will be exploring the consequences for organisational theory of the radical perspective on complexity within a framework of human psychology that is different to both cognitivism and psychoanalysis. I will be reviewing a process rather than a systemic way of making sense of life in organisations, a way that draws on analogies from the more radical expositions of complex adaptive systems.

Before doing that, however, I would like to return to the Tierra simulation described earlier and look at the insights it brings if one takes a radical perspective. In that interpretation I will use Ray's interpretation in terms of biology.

11.4   Insights into the dynamics of complex adaptive systems from a radical perspective

Returning now to the Tierra simulation described in Section 11.2, I would like to draw your attention to some of the major insights that this simulation provides on the nature of complex adaptive systems when one takes a radical perspective.

First, this system produces order of a changeable and diverse kind that comes about in a spontaneous, emergent way. It has not been programmed and there is no blueprint, grand design or plan. Furthermore, this spontaneous self-organising activity, with its emergent order, is vital for the continuing evolution of the system and its ability to produce novelty. However, what form that order takes – that is, the global pattern of behaviour, the system-wide strategies – cannot be predicted from the rules driving individual agent behaviour. In that sense the system is disorderly. This system continuously operates in a state of bounded instability: periods of relative stability are followed by upheavals as particular strategies for the survival of both hosts, and parasites emerge from spontaneous self-organising processes that appear to be so close to market competition. The experimenter is not introducing them and neither is an agent taking over and formulating the strategy.

The strategies are emerging unpredictably in a co-evolutionary arms race occurring in a dynamical, somewhat disorderly environment, driven partly by chance. First the strategy is small size, but then parasites change the rules and the most successful strategy becomes feeding off others. Then the hosts change the rules and the better strategy is camouflage. But the parasites change the rules of the game again and the best strategy becomes the development of a local memory. Competition and conflict emerge and the evolution of the system is driven by agents trying to exploit each other, but the game can go on only if neither side succeeds completely, or for long, in that exploitation.

This is self-organisation, or the collapse of chaos, in that the environment was at first random but as soon as an agent is introduced the collapse begins. From this perspective, the evolution of life in the universe does not occur primarily through random mutations selected for survival by the forces of competition, but primarily through an internal, spontaneously self-organising, co-operative process that presents orderly forms for selection by the forces of competition. Selection is not made by freely operating competition that chooses between random little pieces, but by a competitive process constrained to choose between new forms emerging from a co-operative process. Life in the universe, and life in organisations, arises from a dialectic between competition and co-operation, not from an unconstrained competition! The implications are both profound and, of course, contentious.

Secondly, this system has discovered, quite spontaneously, the importance of competition. But not competition all on its own, rather competition in tension with co-operation. Through an internal process of spontaneous self-organisation this system produces parasites and something approaching a predator–prey dynamic. This is behaviour that is, paradoxically, both co-operative and competitive.

Thirdly, this system has discovered symbiotic reproduction.

Note the common thread running through these three insights about complex adaptive system dynamics. Each is a paradox. Each is the simultaneous presence of stability and instability, order and disorder, tidiness and mess. Take the first. There is emergent order but it is unpredictable. Take the second. There is the tidy harmony of co-operation but it operates in tension with the dissonance of destructive and messy competition. The system has not yet discovered cross-over replication, that is sexual reproduction. However, when this is added to the system it produces even more novelty. Why is this? Well, in cloning an agent gets to copy itself only if it is relatively successful, so that less successful code is incrementally weeded out and the system moves progressively in the direction of improvement. In cross-over replication, however, a male agent copies half his code and splices it to a copy of half of a female's code, thus mixing up the code. This makes it possible for some inefficient and ineffective code to be passed on to the next generation, as well as effective code. Evolution is, then, not an incrementally progressive affair, but a rather stumbling sort of journey in which a system moves both forwards and backwards. And this, as I will now explain, is the most effective way to proceed.

Fitness landscapes

You can see why this is so if you think in terms of fitness landscapes, a concept Kauffman (1993, 1995) has used to give insights into the evolutionary process. Picture the evolution of a particular species, say leopards, as a journey across a landscape characterised by hills and mountains of various heights and shapes, and valleys of various depths and shapes. Suppose that movement up a hill or mountain is equivalent to increasing fitness and moving down into a valley is equivalent to decreasing fitness. Deep valleys would represent almost certain extinction and the high peaks of mountains would represent great fitness for the leopards. The purpose of life is then to avoid valleys and climb peaks.

The shape of the landscape

What determines the shape of this landscape, that is, the number, size, shape and position of the peaks and valleys? The answer is the survival strategies that other species interacting with leopards are following. So, leopards could potentially interact with a large number of species in order to get a meal. They could hunt elephant, for example. However, the elephant has a survival strategy based on size and if leopards take the elephant-hunting route they will have a tough time surviving.

Such a strategy, therefore, is a move down into a rather deep and dead-end sort of valley. Another possibility is to hunt rather small deer. In order to achieve this the leopard might evolve the strategy of speed, competing by running faster than the deer. To the extent that this works it is represented by a move up a fitness hill. Or, the leopards may specialise in short-distance speed plus a strategy of camouflage. Hence their famous spots. This strategy seems to have taken them up a mountain to a reasonably high fitness peak.

The evolutionary task of the leopard, then, is to journey across the fitness landscape in such a manner as to reach the highest fitness peak possible, because then it stands the greatest chance of surviving. To get caught in a valley is to become extinct and to be trapped in the foothills is to forgo the opportunity of finding one of the mountains.

Moving across the landscape

So, how should the leopard species travel across the landscape to avoid these pitfalls, given that leopards cannot see where the high peaks are? They can only know that they have reached a peak when they get there. Suppose the leopards adopt what strategy theorists call a logically incremental strategy. That is, they adopt a procedure in which they 'stick to the knitting' and take a large number of small incremental steps, only ever taking a step that improves fitness and avoiding any steps that diminish fitness. This rational, orderly procedure produces relatively stable, efficient, progressive movement uphill, consistently in the direction of success. Management consultants and academics in the strategy field would applaud leopards following this procedure for their eminent common sense. However, a rule that in essence says 'go up hills only and never downwards' is sure to keep the leopards out of the valleys, but it is also almost certain to get them trapped in the foothills, unless they start off with a really lucky break at the base of the highest, smoothest mountain, with no crevices or other deformities. This is highly unlikely, for a reason I will come to.

The point to note here is that the rational, efficient way to move over the short term is guaranteed, over the longer term, to be the most ineffective possible. What is the alternative? The alternative is to abandon this nice, neat strategy of logically incremental moves and travel in a somewhat erratic manner that involves sometimes slipping and tumbling downhill into valleys out of which a desperate climb is necessary before it is too late. This counterintuitive and somewhat inebriate method of travelling across their fitness landscape makes it likely that the leopards will stumble across the foothills of an even higher mountain than the one they were climbing before. So, cross-over replication, sex to us, makes it more likely that we will find higher mountains to climb than, say, bacteria which replicate by cloning, precisely because of the disorder of mixing the genetic code rather than incrementally improving it.

The whole picture becomes a great deal more interesting when you remember that the fixed landscape I have been describing for the leopard is in fact a fiction, because the survival strategies of the other species determine its shape and they are not standing still. They too are looking for peaks to climb and every time they change their strategy then what was a peak for the leopard is deformed and could become a valley. So, if the leopard increases its short-distance speed and improves its camouflage then it moves up towards a fitness peak on its landscape. But, if the deer respond by heightening their sense of smell, then that peak certainly subsides and may even turn into a valley.

The evolutionary journey for all species, therefore, is across a constantly heaving landscape and it is heaving about because of competition. Competition ensures that life itself never gets trapped. Species come and go but life itself carries on, perhaps becoming ever more complex. It is this mess of competitive selection that is one of the sources of order, the other being the co-operative, internal process of spontaneous self-organisation.

The insight is this. Systems characterised by dynamics that combine order and disorder, that operate at the edge of disintegration, are capable of learning faster than those that are purely orderly, those that operate well away from the edge of chaos in the stable zone. At the edge of chaos, at the edge of disintegration, systems are capable of endless variety, novelty, surprise – in short, creativity. Systems that get trapped on local fitness peaks look stable and comfortable, but they are simply waiting for destruction by other species following messier paths.

Kauffman is arguing, then, that the manner in which competitive selection operates on chance variations depends upon the internal dynamic of the evolving network, that is, upon the pattern of connections, that is, the self-organising interaction, between the entities of which it is composed. The fitness landscape is not a given space containing all possible evolutionary strategies for a system, which it searches for fit strategies in a manner driven by chance. Rather, the fitness landscape itself is being constructed by the interaction between agents. The notion of fitness landscape, its ruggedness, becomes a metaphor for the internal dynamic of a system, not an externally given terrain over which it travels in search of a fit position. These internal properties of the network are the connections between its entities and these connections create conflicting constraints. The internal dynamic is thus one of enabling co-operation and of conflicting constraints at the same time, a paradoxical dynamic of co-operation and competition at the same time. In human terms, connections between agents may be taken as analogous to relationships between people and relationships immediately constrain those in relationship. Power is constraint and conflicting constraints, therefore, translate, in human terms, to power relations.

While no agent is 'in control' of the evolution of the system, it is nevertheless evolving in a controlled manner and the source of this control lies in the pattern of conflicting constraints. This is a very important point because it is the conflicting constraints that sustain sufficient stability in a network at the edge of chaos. At the edge of chaos, a network configures itself into closely connected clusters, separated from each other to some extent, making it difficult for perturbations to cascade through it. This happens because of canalisation, which means that many agents follow the same rules so that there are many chances of the same responses and patterns of response being reproduced. Canalisation is the same as redundancy or loose coupling. It is not efficient but it preserves stability in a dynamic of change. At the edge of chaos, there are tendrils of contact between clusters of agents so that some but not all perturbations cascade through the network.

Another way of putting this is in terms of the power law. It is a property of the edge of chaos that many small perturbations will cascade through the network but only a few large ones will. In other words, there will be large numbers of small extinction events but only small numbers of large ones. It is this property that imparts control, or stability, to the process of change at the edge of chaos.

Redundancy or loose coupling

Another insight follows from the study of complex systems. Life survives at the edge of disintegration because of massive inbuilt redundancy. It is redundancy flowing from self-organising co-operation that is the source of constancy and order. Some kind of inefficiency is required to enable faster discovery and redundancy is required to be able to survive that disorder. The human brain, for example, is characterised by redundancy in that one part of it is capable of carrying out functions normally carried out by some other parts. Humans can, therefore, survive the destruction of fairly large parts of their brains. Slack resources, multitasking, overdeterminacy and loose coupling (*see* Section 5.3) are what make systems resilient enough to cope with the pressures of creativity at the edge of system disintegration. This certainly raises a question mark over the drive to remove redundancy in organisations across the world.

The inherent patterning capacity of interaction

Those who have developed the study of complex adaptive systems have been most interested in the analogy between the digital code of computer program agents and the chemical code in the genes of living creatures. One of their principal questions has been this: if in its earliest days the earth consisted of a random soup of chemicals, how could life have come about? You can simulate this problem if you take a system consisting of computer programs with random bit strings and ask if they can evolve order out of such random chaos. The answer to this question is that such systems can indeed evolve order out of chaos and this chaos is essential to the process.

Contrary to some of our most deep-seated beliefs, disorder is the material from which life and creativity are built and it seems that they are built, not according to some overall prior design, but through a process of spontaneous self-organisation that produces emergent outcomes. If there is a design, it is the basic design principles of the system itself, namely a network of agents driven by iterative nonlinear interaction to produce emergent outcomes that do have pattern. There is inherent order in complex adaptive systems which evolves as the experience of the system, but no one can know what that evolutionary experience will be until it occurs. In certain conditions, agents interacting in a system can produce, not anarchy, but creative new outcomes that none of them ever intended. It seems that even if no one can know the outcome and even if no one can be 'in control', we are not doomed to anarchy. On the contrary, these seem to be the very conditions required for creativity, for the evolutionary journey with no fixed, predetermined destination.

Causality

In Kant's philosophy, the scientist understands organism in nature as wholes consisting of parts. It is in the self-organising interaction of the parts that those parts and the whole emerge. The scientist understands the development of such a system by hypothesising that it is developing according to some 'as if' purpose, usually that of the whole realising a mature form of itself. Although Kant cautioned against applying this notion to human action, later systems thinkers did so and came to understand societies and organisations as systems, or Kantian wholes, unfolding some purpose ascribed to the whole. In doing so, they were applying the same causality as in Kantian thinking, namely formative cause. The cause of the development of the system was the process of unfolding its purpose. An example is when an organisation is understood to be moving in accordance with its Chief Executive's vision.

What the first wave of twentieth-century systems thinkers did not do, however, was to develop Kant's idea of systems as *self-organising* wholes. Instead, they emphasised self-regulation and self-influence. Autopoiesis theory did take up the notion of self-organising wholes, which conserved their identities. This emphasis on the conservation of identity amounts to a retention of formative causality. Although not stressing the conservation of identity, chaos and dissipative structure theories also have to do with systems moving according to formative causality. They are systems that unfold attractors already enfolded in the equations specifying them. The theory of formative causality continues to apply to homogeneous complex adaptive systems, where the agents are all the same.

However, heterogeneous complex adaptive systems, where the agents differ from one another, do what none of the other systems can. They display the capacity for spontaneous evolution to new forms, the unknown. Causality, therefore, is transformative. In other words, such systems take on a life of their own. This creates a problem for the notion of the whole because here the 'whole' is never finished but always evolving. One then has to talk about incomplete or absent wholes, notions that make rather dubious sense. It amounts to saying that there is something that is a whole but is not yet a whole and never will be. Heterogeneous complex adaptive systems then begin to point to a problem with one of the central concepts of systems thinking, namely wholes.

11.5   Comparisons with other systems theories

The chapters in Part One reviewed the theories of interaction upon which various theories of organisation and management are based. All of them are systemic theories of interaction. They are about entities interacting within a system, or systems interacting with each other. This also applies to the theories of chaos, dissipative structures and complex adaptive systems reviewed in the last chapter and this one.

The first of these systems theories, cybernetics, was reviewed in Chapter 3. It models a system at the macro level; that is, without paying attention to the nature of the entities comprising the system. They are implicitly assumed to be homogeneous, or average. The central concept is that of feedback in which the system's output is compared with some fixed reference point outside of it and the difference between that fixed reference point and its output is fed back as input into the next iteration of the system. In cybernetics, the only type of feedback considered is that of negative, or damping, feedback. This means that the system is self-regulating and its dynamic is that of a movement towards stable equilibrium. Such a system has no internal capacity to change spontaneously by moving to a different attractor or evolving a new one. It can move only within one attractor, that of equilibrium. Change has to come from outside the system. The methodology employed in studying such a system is that of the objective observer who is able to control the system by designing a move from one attractor to another.

The point was also made that the cognitivist view of human nature is essentially a cybernetic one. Together, cybernetics and cognitivism form the basis of strategic choice theory.

The second systems theory reviewed was that of systems dynamics. Here the system of interest is also modelled at the macro level, but this time using mathematical models consisting of iterative nonlinear equations that can be interpreted in both negative and positive, or amplifying, feedback terms. Again, the entities comprising the system are assumed to be homogeneous as are the interactions between them. These models produce the dynamics of non-equilibrium movement. These systems are rather unlikely to move to equilibrium because they are nonlinear, or as some interpret this, because they also take account of amplifying feedback. This system also has no internal capacity to move from one attractor to another and so change has to come from outside it. The methodology is once again that of the objective observer. This systems theory, together with cognitivist and humanistic psychology, is the basis of the theory of the learning organisation.

The third systems theory surveyed was open systems theory. This theory takes account of the entities of which a system is composed, its subsystems. However, nonlinearity is not a central feature and the system is assumed to move towards stable equilibrium in the absence of obstacles. The focus of this theory is on regulation at the boundary of the system to sustain it in equilibrium adaptation to its environment. Iterative replication does not feature in this systems theory. This forms the systemic foundations of psychoanalytic perspectives on organisations.

Together, these three systems theories constitute the first wave of twentieth-century systems thinking, which can be described as hard systems or first order systems thinking. They do not make any essential use of notions of self-organisation or emergence to be found in Kant's original systems philosophy but in their application in organisational theory they do reflect Kant's dual causality. The system unfolds the purpose already enfolded in it and the cause of its movement is formative unfolding. Organisations are understood as wholes in which some aspects of its members are thought of as parts. The causality applying to the observers and designers of such systems is that of rationalist causality. Contrary to Kant, however, both of these causalities are applied to human action.

This causal duality can be expressed as the problem of the observer also being a participant in the system, which led to second-order systems thinking, including its later development as soft and critical systems thinking. All of these developments, however, have retained the causal duality and so are unable to deal with the paradox of the participant observer.

One development of system thinking, namely autopoiesis, has emphasised the self-organising nature of a system but it too retains formative causality. When applied to organisations the rationalist causality of the observing manager is brought into the explanation.

Second-order systems thinking and the theory of autopoiesis, together with constructivist assumptions about human psychology, have been used as the basis of theories of knowledge creation and management in organisations. These theories stress the social, interactive, conversational nature of the knowledge-creation process.

Then, in this Part of the book, the last chapter reviewed more recent developments in thinking about the fundamental properties of systems in the form of chaos theory and dissipative structure theory. Chaos theory employs the same mathematical approach as systems dynamics, models at the macro level and makes the same assumptions about entities. It goes further than systems dynamics in identifying the different attractors that such a system can move to – most importantly, the possibility of strange attractors at critical parameter values. This theory clarifies the possibilities and impossibilities of prediction. However, as with systems dynamics, such a system has no internal capacity to move spontaneously from one of its attractors to another. The impetus for change has to come from outside the system.

Dissipative structure theory also models systems at the macro level by means of nonlinear mathematical equations. Here, however, fluctuations and symmetry breaking mean that there are non-average relationships between micro entities. In other words, small, chance variations in relationships between a system and its environment, the fluctuations, can amplify through the system when it is held far from equilibrium. The effect is to break the symmetry or uniformity of behaviour within the system. The consequence is a move to a different attractor and the possibility of evolving a new one. So, once microdiversity is introduced into the model it acquires the internal capacity to change spontaneously and unpredictably although only from one attractor to another that is already enfolded in the relationship. Change need no longer be imposed or triggered from the outside but can emerge from spontaneous self-organisation at certain critical points. Note how different this is from the nature of a cybernetic system. Although the methodology is still that of the objective observer and although causality is still formative, the system can change spontaneously although it cannot evolve.

Finally, there are the complex adaptive systems reviewed in this chapter. They differ from all of the others in locating the focus of analysis primarily on the micro level. They are concerned with the behaviour of the entities comprising the system. Some complex adaptive system models assume that the agents are homogeneous and that their interactions are all the same. Such systems, like the systems of chaos theory and all of the systems before that, have no internal capacity to move from one attractor to another. Self-organisation in these systems produces an emergent attractor that the system follows until some change is introduced from outside. Other models of complex adaptive systems, however, do include agent diversity and these systems show the internal capacity not only to move from one attractor to another but also to evolve emergent, radically unpredictable new attractors through the process of self-organisation. The new emerges in these models when the system displays the dynamics of the edge of chaos, or bounded instability, where the differences between entities, microdiversity, are amplified. Here the system produces not only the new but avalanches of destruction as well, with many small and few large extinction events. The methodology remains that of the objective observer. Some scientists do not see anything radical in this and some do.

In the review of all of these systems theories there has been a move from models that are linear, equilibrium seeking and lacking in any microdiversity to those that are nonlinear, far from equilibrium and full of microdiversity. The most striking change in the properties they display is the capacity for spontaneously developing new forms. Many would say that this is one of the hallmarks of living systems.

The important point to notice is that those complex adaptive systems characterised by microdiversity, such as the Tierra simulation discussed in this chapter, display the capacity to evolve in completely unpredictable ways. The causality is clearly no longer formative but transformative. Another way of saying this is that the system takes on a life of its own. This creates problems for the notion of the whole. It means that the whole is never complete and one therefore has to talk about absent wholes. The notion of a system with a life of its own brings other problems. If the system model has a life of its own how can we be confident that it actually models what it is supposed to? Surely the model and what it is trying to model would diverge. Also what would it mean for individual members of an organisation to think of themselves as parts of an organisational system that had a life of its own?

It is important to make the distinction between homogeneous and heterogeneous complex adaptive systems in order to avoid misleading categorisations. For example, in Chapter 9, I referred to the way in which Jackson (2000) categorises complex adaptive systems. He classifies systems according to whether they are simple or complex and according to whether they are unitary or plural. By unitary he means that the participants in the system are in a unitary relationship with each other in the sense of sharing values and interest. By plural he means that the participants have many different views. He locates complex adaptive systems in the category of complex unitary systems. This is true of homogeneous complex adaptive systems because all the agents are the same. However, it is not true of heterogeneous complex adaptive systems, which should, in his scheme, be located in the category of complex-plural systems. The work of Kauffman would also have to be classified as complex plural because of the emphasis Kauffman places on the conflicting constraints that agents in a complex adaptive system impose on each other. It should also be noted that the approach to be reviewed in Part Three does not fall into any of Jackson's categories simply because it is not systems thinking in any form – it is process thinking.

11.6 Summary

This chapter has reviewed complex adaptive systems theory, which models interaction between many agents comprising a system. It sets out the logical structure of algorithmic, that is digital-code-based, interaction and derives the properties of such interaction through the method of computer simulation. The digital code interaction is then used as an analogy for some other kind of interaction. For example, digital code is used as an analogy for the genetic code of biological organisms. The properties of digital code interaction are then inferred to apply to biological code. In other words, an act of interpretation is required in order to utilise the insights derived from the logic of digital code interaction in relation to some other kind of interaction.

I have distinguished between what seem to me to be orthodox and radical interpretations of the implications of digital code interaction. From an orthodox perspective, the insights yielded by complex adaptive systems simulations do not represent a radical departure from previous scientific theories. Predictability is stressed and self-organisation is not seen as a new ordering principle. Other scientists, however, take a more radical perspective, stressing unpredictability and the radical importance of self-organisation.

From a radical perspective, the key insights yielded by agent-based modelling of systems are as follows:

- *The dynamic at the edge of chaos.* This is understood to be a dynamic of paradox, that is, simultaneous stability and instability, which is a requirement for the emergence of novelty.
- *Emergence of the new and extinction.* Although the dynamic at the edge of chaos is required for novelty to emerge it does not provide a guarantee of survival. In addition to the emergence of the new there are many small and a few large extinction events.
- *Diversity as a prerequisite for the emergence of the new.* A system displays the internal capacity to change spontaneously only when agents comprising it are different from one another – microdiveristy.
- *Radical unpredictability over certain time spans and levels of detail, which renders problematic the possibility of top-down control.* What agent-based modellers have consistently identified is that, in certain critical conditions, complex adaptive systems, consisting of large numbers of interacting agents, display a paradoxical dynamic of simultaneous stability and instability. Some call it effective complexity, lying between order and disorder; others call it the dynamics of the 'edge of chaos'. When a system operates in this dynamic it displays radical unpredictability over certain time spans at certain levels of detail. The insight is that uncertainty is inevitable in an evolving system.
- *The self-organising capacity of a complex adaptive system and its ability to produce emergent novelty when it operates in the dynamic at the edge of disorder.* Self-organisation here means interaction between agents on the basis of local organising principles. Emergence means the appearance of novel forms arising from this local interaction, in the absence of any overall programme or design, in a context that may be characterised by chance events. An insight here is that the creative and the new arise in relationships in the absence of any overall design. Those relationships create the context within which they themselves take place. Complex adaptive systems co-evolve, participating in the collective production of their own future in the absence of any external imposition. The system is recursive and causality is mutual. Another insight is that creativity is a collective phenomenon.

- *The capacity that iterative nonlinear interaction has to pattern itself.* Local interaction between entities produces emergent coherence and this is what self-organisation means.
- *Most agent-based modellers locate agency at the level of interacting individual entities in a complex adaptive system, that is at the level of the autonomous agent.* A more radical perspective locates it at the level of the interaction of system and context. System and context form and are formed by each other at the same time.
- *The most interesting simulations of complex adaptive systems are those that are heterogeneous and because of this take on a life of their own.* This means that they are charaterised by transformative rather than formative causality.

It is these insights that I wish to explore in relation to organisations because I believe that they have the potential for making more useful sense of life in organisations. I do not believe that the modelling and simulating approach of agent-based modellers holds much potential for understanding the nature of organising and managing. I think that it is the insights about the nature of systems that hold the potential, rather than the methodology. In other words, I will be arguing that the simulations of heterogeneous complex adaptive systems provide a source domain for analogies with human organisations but it is not sensible to simply apply them to organisations.

Why might these insights be important? Their importance lies, I think, in the possibility of a radically different theory of organisation. This can be seen by comparing the above insights with the organisational theories reviewed in previous chapters.

Strategic choice theory holds that an organisation changes because its top managers choose new strategic directions. Learning organisation and knowledge management theories hold that organisations develop in new ways because top managers identify leverage points in the system from which they can control it or they develop systems through which they can capture the knowledge of individuals. These theories also hold that new directions flow from changes in the mental models of people in an organisation and that these changes can be managed. From the psychoanalytic perspective, an organisation changes when its managers can regulate the boundary between their psychic lives and their roles so that task performance is not impaired.

The insights coming from heterogeneous complex adaptive systems suggest a completely different possibility. Managers may be making strategic choices, operating at leverage points and managing boundaries. However, from a radical complexity perspective they are agents in the system, not external observers of it. They cannot therefore know the long-term outcome of the choices they are making. Instead new directions for an organisation emerge from both their choices and the patterns of responses these evoke from others in a self-organising way. In other words, the widespread patterns that are an organisation emerge in many, many local interactions in the absence of any blueprint or plan and no one is intending or in control of what emerges. Part Three will be exploring such possibilities but before doing so, the next chapter explores the approach being taken by most of those who write about complexity and organisations.

Further reading

Useful reviews of complexity theory are provided by Waldorp (1992), Casti (1994), Cohen and Stewart (1994), Goodwin (1994), Kauffman (1993, 1995) and Levy (1992). Boden (1996) provides a useful review of the philosophy and methodology of complex adaptive systems.

Chapter 12 ●●●●

Systemic applications of chaos and complexity theory to organisations

12.1 Introduction

It seems to me that during the 1970s and 1980s there have been developments of a fundamental conceptual nature in the thinking about systems. In the last two chapters, I have summarised and reviewed what I think are the main features of this development, namely chaos theory, the theory of dissipative structures and synergetics, and the theory of complex adaptive systems. These systems theories, like the first wave of twentieth-century systems theories, have been developed by natural scientists. I have argued that they are potentially radical in that they point to the self-referential, self-organising capacities of such systems. What this means is that agents in a complex system interact locally with each other on the basis of their historically evolved identities. They do so without knowing in advance how the whole system is going to evolve, or even understanding its current state as a whole. However, despite lack of knowledge about the whole and its future, local self-referring, self organising interaction itself generates emergent new forms in the absence of any blueprint or programme for the system as a whole. These insights are a radical departure from earlier systems theories in that new forms are now seen to emerge from interaction, but only in the presence of diversity. The emphasis is placed on the local, differentiated, evolving relationships between entities rather than on essentially some view of the whole. This potentially displaces the cognising individual from the central position occupied in the earlier systems theories. Furthermore, the creative novelty that emerges is unpredictable. This raises question marks over the nature of control, another central feature of the earlier system theories.

However, in the last two chapters I have also tried to show how the theory of complex systems in the natural sciences does not depart completely from cybernetics. This is because, in some formulations, the agents making up a complex adaptive system are defined in cybernetic and cognitivist terms. Furthermore, they continue, of course, to be systems theories. Despite the radical potential of some complexity theories, stressed by a few, most of the natural scientists working in this area seem to me to remain, more or less, with a basically orthodox perspective and, of course, all of them continue to think within the system paradigm. Organisational theorists using chaos and complexity theory also continue to think in terms of systems and, I suggest, most of them focus on those expositions in which the notion of feedback is used as an explanatory device and those simulations in which agents are cybernetic entities. They continue with an individual-based psychology drawn from cognitivism, constructivism or humanistic perspectives.

The objective observer

There is another important sense in which those developing complex systems theory seem to me to be continuing in the cybernetics, open systems and systems dynamics traditions. This is the matter of methodology. Just as the earlier systems theorists did, most complexity theorists in the natural sciences adopt the stance of the objective observer who stands outside the 'real' system and models it.

What I mean by this is the following. Flocks of birds and colonies of ants existed long before Reynolds and Langton constructed models to mimic and explain their behaviour. Reynolds (1987) and Langton (1996) were concerned with a pre-existing reality. They stood outside the flock of birds and the colony of ants and observed the patterns in their behaviour. They had to do this, of course, because they are not birds or ants. They then experimented with different computer simulations of the behavioural rules that individual birds and ants might be following as they interacted with each other. They were able to identify a small number of simple rules, which if followed by the birds and the ants would lead to the emergence of flocking and trail setting. In doing this, they were able to show that it is, in principle, possible for processes of self-organisation to produce emergent global order. Ray (1992) did a similar thing when he considered how species might evolve. He observed what is known about a pre-existing reality, the species that have evolved over the past, and constructed a computer simulation to demonstrate how processes of self-organisation could, in principle, lead to the unpredictable emergence of new species.

In the main, organisational theorists adopt the same methodology. They stand outside what is assumed to be the pre-given reality of an organisation and observe its behaviour. Some use computer modelling and simulation techniques and can quite rapidly incorporate chaos and complexity into their work. Others research organisations, describing how successful organisations function and in effect constructing qualitative models of them. They then derive prescriptions for the successful conduct of all organisations. The great majority build models and make prescriptions on the implicit assumption that organisations are cybernetic systems, or systems of the systems dynamics type, made up of individuals who behave according to the principles of cognitivism. So, most organisational theorists share a methodology with what I have called orthodox complexity scientists and they share the same view about the nature of the agents constituting the system. What they have not shared, until some recent writings, is the same view of systems, namely the processes of self-organisation and the possibility of unpredictably emergent new forms. However, the fact that organisational theorists and complexity scientists share the same fundamental methodology, and the same views about individual agents, makes it comparatively easy for the former to incorporate a complex system perspective into their models. In doing this, as I explain in the next sections of this chapter, they lose the radical implications of complexity theory.

For me, the problem in adopting the position of the external, objective observer of a pre-existing organisational reality is this: according to complexity theory, new forms emerge unpredictably in a complex system through the process of self-organisation. To reiterate, this means that the agents in the system interact with each other at their own local level on the basis of their historically evolved identities. In other words, they are always participants and the system evolves only because they participate in this local way. It is the very essence of self-organisation that none of those individual agents is able to step outside the system and obtain an overview of how the whole is evolving, let alone how it will evolve. It is the very essence of self-organisation that none of the agents, as individuals, nor any small group of them on their own, can directly design, or even directly shape, the evolution of the system as a whole. The impact of any agent, no matter how powerful, on the systems is indirectly through their local interaction only. In their interaction with each other, they are co-creating the whole system's evolution but none of them, individually or in small groups, is organising the interaction, the self-organisation, across the system. No agent is setting the simple rules for others to follow and then 'allowing' them to self-organise. If they were, the system could no longer be described as a self-organising one.

The methodological position of the external observer is a possibility if I want to study birds and ants, because I am neither. However, if I want to study the behaviour of a group of people, it seems to me that I have to take account of the fact that I am one of them. As soon as one loses sight of this and talks about a complex system of human beings from an external position, it is easy to slip into the tendency of prescribing this external position as the management role. The question then becomes how the manager needs to be able to identify whether the organisation is operating in the dynamic of bounded instability so that it has creative potential. Or whether it is operating in stable equilibrium and needs to be nudged, by the manager, into bounded instability. Or the prescription becomes to find the set of simple rules and prescribe them for the members of the organisation. This is supposed to ensure that they self-organise to produce the emergent pattern that the manager wants. That immediately implies a pre-given reality and the possibility of prediction rather than the emergence of new forms. In other words, the tendency is to focus on an individual who is able to exert some kind of control or impart some kind of coherence to a self-organising system.

As soon as this is done, it seems to me, it results in the loss of the radical implications of complexity theory for understanding life in organisations. If a human group or organisation is thought of as a complex adaptive system then the questions become: What is it like to be an agent in such a system? What is it like to be such a system? What does diversity mean in human relationships and how do people respond to it? How does an agent in such a system cope with radical unpredictability? What is it like to participate in self-organising processes? To what extent can agents in such a system articulate emergent patterns? How does doing this help? It seems to me that as soon as one starts to seriously consider questions such as these, one begins to question the whole notion of applying systems thinking to organisations or any other form of human action.

The point I am making is this. I think the insights coming from complexity theory offer an opportunity for theorists and practitioners to explore a different way of thinking about life in organisations. However, this opportunity is rapidly lost if the insights are imported into organisation theorising from the methodological position of the external observer, implicitly based on the assumption of the powerful, autonomous individual so central to cognitivism. Even more than this, I will argue in Part Three that thinking of organisations as systems of any kind, including the systems of complexity theory, is inappropriate. Most organisational theorists using complexity theory continue to think of organisations as systems and when they do, they mainly re-present existing organisational theories in new terminology derived from complexity theory.

I will illustrate what I mean by looking at some recent books and papers that use notions from complexity theory.

12.2   Modelling complex systems in organisations

One approach to applying the theories of chaos and complexity to organisations is to use the mathematical and modelling techniques of the natural scientists. I point to some examples of that approach in this section and draw attention to how there is no shift from the systems thinking and psychological assumptions to be found in the theories reviewed in Part One.

Forecasting of financial markets

A number of writers and researchers (Hsieh, 1989; Peters, 1991; Schenkman and Le Baron, 1989) have explored the hypothesis that the financial markets exhibit low-dimensional deterministic chaos and are attempting to build forecasting models using nonlinear equations. This involves accepting that long-term developments cannot be predicted but offers the hope that well-specified models might enable superior short-term forecasting.

Production and inventory scheduling

Here researchers (Morley, 1993, 1995) employ some of the simulation techniques of complexity theory, such as the genetic algorithm, to develop methods of production and inventory scheduling. The approach is to regard production processes as complex systems that are capable of learning. In the genetic algorithm computer programs breed new computer programs, so evolving in a manner akin to learning. So, instead of preparing a comprehensive design or plan for production lines or inventory levels the computer programs are left to find beneficial schedules themselves. This holds the promise of a more flexible approach more suited to customised production methods. These developments are in their infancy.

The psychology of perception and learning

Here, researchers (Abraham, 1995; Guastello, 1995) apply nonlinear mathematics to the measurement of perception and learning. This is, of course, firmly grounded in cognitivist psychology.

Modelling industries

Another approach is to model the dynamics of whole industries. This section looks at three examples of this. The first uses Prigogine's work, the second employs chaos theory and the third makes considerable use of fitness landscapes.

Allen

Prigogine's theory of dissipative structures, briefly described in Chapter 10, represents a potentially radical shift in the domain of the natural sciences. I argue, however, that when these radical theories are imported into the domains of social, economic and organisational theory they are subtly reproduced as theories of strategic choice and the learning organisation, cast in a new vocabulary. I suggest that this happens because those making the transfer continue to employ systems terms and adopt an essentially cognitivist view of human psychology, emphasising the primacy of the individual who knows through making representations of reality and behaves on the basis of these representations. As I keep reiterating, this is an essentially cybernetic view of human knowing and behaving, one that is entirely compatible with systemic management and organisational theory. The result is that the potentially radical implications of Prigogine's theory are not realised in relation to the management of organisations.

To illustrate what I mean, take Allen's (1998a) analysis of the fishing industry. He contrasts the conclusions produced by equilibrium (cybernetic system), systems dynamics and what he calls self-organising and evolutionary models of that industry. The equilibrium model produces a policy recommendation to constrain fishing effort at, or just below, the maximum that yields a sustainable fish population. However, the dynamics of the fish population and fish markets rapidly render any selected sustainable level of fishing highly inaccurate. A systems dynamics model allows for variations in fish populations and in economic conditions. However, the model uses average data for all of these factors.

Allen then introduces 'noise' into the equations to represent random fluctuations in fish populations and the model produces boom-and-bust oscillations in fishing fleet catches. He concludes that management should concern itself with overcoming this cyclical behaviour rather than discussing fishing quotas. He introduces a variable to represent the rate of response of the fleet to fish availability, another for the level of technology and yet another for price responsiveness. Now there is still a boom-and-bust attractor, but in addition, another attractor emerges, one of a small high-priced niche where fish becomes a luxury food. He offers this as the kind of strategic insight modelling can yield.

He then goes on to incorporate different levels of information acquired by each fishing fleet and different attitudes to risk. He assumes that fishing fleets are boundedly rational decision-makers and so imports cognitivism as his theory of human psychology. The model demonstrates that optimal use of information increases profit in the short term but not necessarily in the long term. Cautious optimisers get locked into the existing situation while more adventurous risk-takers open themselves to the possibility of finding new strategies. The model identifies a tendency to follow short-term profit-maximising strategies at the expense of the long term.

Finally, Allen specifies what he calls an evolutionary complex model:

Not only do we have uneven and changing patterns of fish stocks in the system, but we are also not going to consider that the 'taxonomy' of boat types and fleet behaviours is fixed. We can now develop a model that will explore the relative effectiveness of different strategies, and will search for success, not just in geographic space, but also in strategy space, and will discover robust fishing strategies for us. (1998a, p. 33)

From this analysis, he reaches the conclusion that sustainability does not lie in efficiency, or in allowing free markets, but in creativity. Creativity is rooted in diversity, cultural richness and the will and ability to experiment and take risks. Another conclusion is that uncertainty is inevitable:

Innovation and change occur because of diversity, non-average individuals with their bizarre initiatives, and whenever this leads to an exploration into an area where positive feedback outweighs negative, then growth will occur. (1998a, p. 36)

Allen very clearly demonstrates the importance of diversity in generating new forms as he moves from one way of modelling the fishing industry to another. He clearly identifies the radical nature of models that incorporate high levels of diversity. However, what he suggests as application in terms of management falls quite easily into the systemic management discourses reviewed in Part One. For example, his whole methodology implies a cognitivist view of human beings who use rational constructs to explore scenarios in the interest of gaining insight. This easily allows one to sidestep the possibility that management itself is an evolving process. The implication is that managers can step outside their system and model it as the basis of making decisions to manipulate it. The insights he produces are radical but the prescriptions are not.

Levy

Levy (1994) simulates an industrial supply chain using nonlinear equations of the type that can produce mathematical chaos and concludes that the model can be used to guide decisions concerning production location, sourcing and optimum inventory levels. He says that complex systems must be understood as a *whole*. For him, goals are to be achieved through indirect means. So, here chaos theory is being used to model an operational system at the macro level in order to aid decision making. Levy clearly equates the manager's role with that of the model builder or programmer who stands outside the system and controls it.

I think that the radical potential of theories of chaos and dissipative structures for organisational theory tends to be obscured by simulations of this kind because the agents in the system are treated in an impersonal way. This is a problem if you are interested, as I am, in the nature of organising and managing in terms of human relationships. Attempts to model people, as agents driven by rules, immediately introduces cognitivism and loses the rich texture of emotional and embodied relating.

Levy focuses his analysis at an even higher macro level, that of the industry. He argues that industries can be modelled as dynamic systems that exhibit both unpredictability and underlying order. He notes the point that human systems are not deterministic:

> *Human agency can alter the parameters and the structures of social systems, and it is perhaps unrealistically ambitious to think that the effects of such intervention can be endogenized in chaotic models. Nevertheless, chaotic models can be used to suggest ways that people might intervene to achieve certain goals. (p. 169)*

He concludes that, although short-term forecasting is possible, long-term planning is impossible and says that this has 'profound implications for organisations trying to set strategy based on their anticipation of the future' (p. 170). He concludes that strategic plans should take account of a number of scenarios and that firms should not focus too narrowly on core competences. For him, strategy becomes a set of simple guidelines that influence decisions and behaviour. This is the notion of 'simple rules' so popular amongst those applying complexity theories to organisations. Furthermore, firms need to change these guidelines as industries and competitors change. Levy also says that the system as a whole must be understood if one is to understand indirect and counterintuitive means to an end.

Notice again how this argument proceeds. It recognises the impossibility of long-term prediction. However, instead of asking how managers are actually now proceeding in the absence of forecasts or foresight, Levy says they should foresee a number of scenarios and set simple guidelines. Again the notion seems to be that complex systems can be managed if one can identify the right set of simple rules. He also recommends, just as the systems-dynamics-based theory of the learning organisation does, that organisations must be understood as a whole and that this can be done by computer simulation. Clearly, Levy takes the position of the external observer and is implicitly recommending that this is the position managers should also take. The idea that an organisation can be modelled and then influenced and controlled is implicitly cognitivist and cybernetic. What is lost here is the question of what it is like for a manager to be a member of a complex system, interacting at a local level, when it is not possible to see the organisation as a whole.

Marion

Marion (1999) describes the development of the microcomputer industry and uses it to illustrate his perspective on organisational complexity. He describes how mainframe computers became commercially available in 1952 and how in the mid-1960s microprocessors were developed and incorporated in hand-held calculators. Small packets of technology were, therefore, emerging in a moderately coupled network of industries over the 1950s and 1960s. Then in 1975, MICS produced the first microcomputer, the Altair, which was cheaper and more accessible to a wider market than mainframes. Micros had a different architecture to mainframes and calculators and during the initial stage of market development, competition in the micro sector had more to do with architectures than anything else. There were, and still are, only two architectures. One is based on the Intel chip and the other on the Motorola processor. A number of operating systems were built around these chips: CP/M; the Apple system; IBM DOS; and systems for the Commodore, Tandy, Texas Instruments (TI), NCR, NEC, Olivetti, Wang and Xerox microcomputers.

The early market niche for micros was thus crowded with architectures and operating systems when, in 1981, IBM entered the micro market. The entry of IBM immediately put the fastest growing operating system, CP/M, out of business. By the mid-1980s, IBM's architecture was dominant and others adopted it in order to survive. At the same time, Apple introduced the Mac, which was not as cumbersome and difficult to learn as DOS. Later, Microsoft brought some simplicity to DOS but it is still not able to match the elegance and simplicity of the Mac. During this period, microprocessor technology was also developing: the earliest processors were 4 bit and were soon replaced by 8- and then 16-bit processors. By the mid-1990s, 32-bit technology was dominant.

Marion describes a development, then, in which there were a few people dreaming of microcomputers in 1974, a great many people wanting one by 1976 and explosive growth in the ensuing two decades. It looked as if microcomputers had suddenly appeared out of nowhere. However, the pieces were coming together long before microcomputers were ever envisioned: microcircuits, microprocessors, ROM and RAM memory chips were being used in calculators, while computer language logic was being documented in mainframes. The microcomputer was built from these pieces.

Marion uses the Kauffman framework described in Chapter 11 to make sense of these developments. Just as Kauffman argues that emerging connections between molecules became the chemical basis of life, so Marion argues that bits and pieces of already existing technology come together as emergent microcomputers. He continues with Kauffman's framework to argue that the early micro niche was occupied by a large number of architectural species. These early producers were small organisations driven by a few engineering personalities. They were relatively simple organisations, lacking much internal complexity and having few internal connections. They also displayed relatively few connections with other players in the niche, since producers specialised in sub-niches, for example, Apple in the education market and Commodore at the low end of the home market. Competitive interaction was thus limited. Kauffman's models show that such patterns of connection produce highly unstable, chaotic dynamics and this was evident in the rapid and unpredictable development of the microcomputer market in the early days. The industry was characterised by frequent and strong shocks, or large avalanches of extinction.

Then in the 1980s, the number of players in the architecture field diminished until IBM DOS and Mac dominated that field. In addition, the entry of an internally complex organisation, IBM, and the rapid growth and development of Apple, meant that internal complexity rose, that is, there was a greater number of connections between agents within the competing organisations. At the same time, the number of connections between organisations in the niche increased because both of the main players competed with each other in all of the market niches. In Kauffman's models, this pattern of connections produces the dynamic at the edge of chaos, which combines both stability and instability. Marion argues that this intertwining of stability and instability was also characteristic of the microcomputer industry at the end of the 1980s and on into the 1990s, when changes became much smaller and more incremental, with large extinction events a rarity. IBM DOS came to dominate the architecture niche, despite the technical superiority of the Apple

Mac. This is technological 'lock-in', which occurs as more and more users come to rely on a particular technology so that the costs of change become too high and users stay with the technology they have, even if it is inferior. However, there was still change as the number of micro producers increased, IBM lost its market dominance and Microsoft increased its power. The changes, of course, continue to this day.

Marion is showing how an industrial network evolves through its own internal dynamic to the edge of chaos. He emphasises the radical unpredictability of such evolution and the continuing unpredictability when a network operates at the edge of chaos. He draws on three characteristics to reach this conclusion. The first is sensitive dependence on initial conditions (*see* Chapter 10), which he argues can be seen in the sensitivity of human interaction to small events. Unpredictability here is due to human inability to monitor and observe infinite detail. Secondly, he refers to Prigogine's work on potential energy and Poincaré resonances to argue that intrinsic unpredictability is also a feature of complex systems. Thirdly, he brings in the power law (*see* Chapter 11) to argue that despite its great stability and robustness, a network at the edge of chaos will be subject to many small, and a few large extinction events and that these are impossible to predict.

He argues that all of these factors are sources of radical unpredictability in the evolution of human networks that makes it impossible for an individual to be in control of such a network. In other words, no single organisation in the industrial network chooses the future direction of the industry, and this means that it cannot choose its own evolution either. This suggests that managers who claim to be planning the future of their organisation will not actually be doing so. Furthermore, no single organisation can choose the dynamics of the industry as a whole and therefore no organisation can choose its own dynamic either. In the early stages of the development of the micro industry, the dynamics was chaotic because of the large number of simply structured competitors, loosely connected to each other. None of them chose this. It flowed from the nature of the interaction between them. The entry of IBM was a deliberate choice but the reduction in the number of competitors and the increase in the range of competitive interaction between the survivors was not simply IBM's choice. It depended upon what the others did too. The evolution from chaos to the dynamic at the edge of chaos was co-created through the interaction of the organisations, not chosen by one in isolation. Outcomes and dynamics continued to change in unpredictable ways, outside the power of individual organisations to choose, as the number of micro producers increased and Microsoft gained greater power over the market. Nowadays, the power of Microsoft is being challenged by lawsuits and freely available operating systems on the Internet.

Marion is making an important point here because many who take up complexity theory in relation to organisations may accept that organisations cannot choose future outcomes but then claim that they can deliberately choose the dynamic in which they operate.

However, Marion also repeatedly stresses that unpredictability does not lead to the conclusion that there is no control. Attractors at the edge of chaos are bounded and demonstrate a family-like similarity. Therefore, it is not possible for just anything to happen. He also argues that the power law is itself a form of control because, at the edge of chaos, the numbers of extinction events both large and small are smaller than they are in the dynamics of stability, on the one hand, and chaos, on the other. Because of the relatively small number of large extinction events, change spreads through a network in a controlled manner. In the other dynamics, change spreads through the network in a highly destructive, continuous manner. Furthermore, the edge of chaos is characterised by coupling between agents and systems that is neither too tight nor too loose and this, equivalent to walls separating attractors, contains the spread of change through a system when it is at the edge of chaos.

Marion, therefore, focuses at the macro level of a whole industry and talks about a population of impersonal organisations (IBM and Apple for example) interacting with each other in a self-organising manner, driven by an urge to survive. He is talking about this population and the organisations of which it consists as if they were no different from a population of organisms. However, what are these organisations? They are not organisms, or anything like organisms but, rather, patterns of joint human action. Marion reifies organisations and treats them as if they were things, or organisms, apart from, or outside of humans, interacting according to principles that apply to them at a macro level, split off from the humans that constitute them. The principles governing these systems are taken to be the same as those governing non-human systems.

To this Marion adds the deliberate purposefulness (teleology) of human beings, by which he means what has been called the rationalist causality in Part One. The result is that humans, acting according to rationalist causality, find themselves having to act within a system that is somehow independent of them, operating according to the causal principles of self-organisation. The latter considerably restricts the scope humans have for realising their intentions. Patterns in human action, then, emerge as the 'both . . . and' paradigm of both human choice and a system with a life of its own.

Marion's assumptions about human psychology are clearly individual centred and cognitivist. He argues that social behaviour arises from the selfish need of the individual. Selfishness is local and personal, an individual trait that does not depend upon any external force. Humans are said to co-operate because that is the best way of achieving individual goals. In addition, he says that humans assign meaning to symbols and mental constructs that catalyse human action to create complex social structures. This clearly places the individual as fundamental and thought before action. Before there can be the social there have to be individual humans with their selfish interests and before they act, they think and make selfish choices.

The split that Marion makes between an individual and a social level becomes clearer when one considers his argument about social forces. He takes from Dawkins (1976) the concept of the meme, the social equivalent of the gene. From a neo-Darwinian perspective, the genes of an organism are a blueprint that determines the biological structure of that organism. Marion argues that memes, that is ideas, concepts, beliefs, scientific theories, ideologies, fads and fashions, provide the blueprint for social and organisational structure. These memes produce the content of culture, that is, the shared understanding of how things should be. Just as there are mechanisms that translate genes into biological structure, so there are mechanisms that translate memes into social, cultural and organisational structure. These mechanisms are processes of mimicry, interaction, correlation, teaching and learning through which societies and organisations imprint people with the memes of the parent culture, for example, the beliefs of an organisation's founder.

For Marion, memes are the agents, or species, in a complex adaptive system that interact co-operatively and competitively to evolve in potentially novel ways through cross-fertilisation between species of memes. Cross-fertilisation is made possible because people, imprinted by memes, belong to more than one group. While genes are efficient causes of biological structure, that biological structure never causes the genes. With memes, he argues, it is different because although memes cause social structure, individuals in that structure can deliberately affect the memes. This makes it possible for cultural evolution to proceed much faster than biological evolution: major novel changes in memes can appear fully blown and be transferred to the young within a single generation. Competitive selection means that less fit memes perish while fitter ones survive, modifying cultural and organisational structures so that they fit the environment.

Memes, then, are portrayed as somehow existing above the level of the individual as a kind of group mind or transpersonal process. They are described as the agents of a complex adaptive system with a life of its own, reproducing and potentially changing. They form a cultural blueprint, quite apart from the individuals upon whom they act. Memes are said to be translated into social structures as they imprint individuals who reproduce them through processes of mimicry and learning. Memes produce and choose behaviour. However, in turn, individuals can deliberately choose to influence memes but the memes will choose which of these efforts is to succeed. Marion's main argument splits individuals and groups into two distinct but interactive levels. There are both individual and group processes and they affect each other but in a sequential rather than a simultaneous manner. Each individual is like an attractor and when individuals come together to form a group, they resonate with each other, producing through their communication the social attractor. The split comes at this point because social attractors are now said to reproduce themselves and in the process they may change. Marion says that under the surface of the social, individual resonances harmonise in the sense that they develop a shared view. One operates within one kind of causal framework and the other operates according to another. Marion stays within the dualistic, 'both . . . and' thinking that is easily assimilated into the systemic theories of organisations reviewed in Part One.

However, another part of his argument does pick up on a radical insight coming from complexity theory. He argues that the very nature of the irrational and the random is essential to the emergence of novel structures. He ties creativity and the emergence of novelty firmly to the unpredictable aspect of the dynamic at the edge of chaos. He argues that without irrationality there would be stagnation. He sees irrationality as the social equivalent of the Poincaré resonances that Prigogine regards as essential to the emergence of new structures in nature. The diverse and surprising order in the world arises because life takes unexpected directions. Marion thinks about human learning as a process of tinkering, often without much thinking. People tinker, and as they do so they sense patterns. These patterns organise their perception and understanding, and as they tinker further those perceptions and understandings restructure, which in turn affects what people observe. He claims that learning occurs because humans are irrational. Perfectly rational decision-makers have nothing to discover and hence nothing to learn. Heroic leaders do less than we think they do, but they do act as symbols of a cause and they do rally unified behaviour.

However, having taken a radical position on causality, predictability, equilibrium, limits on human ability to change social processes through deliberate action alone, and so in many ways decentring the individual, Marion ends up with a view of human psychology and social relating that is not particularly radical, apart from the way he stresses the irrational and the need for deviant behaviour. He stays within the systemic paradigm to the extent that he sees human behaviour resulting from a mimetic blueprint that humans have limited capacity to change of their own choice, with any choice having, in a sense, to be ratified by the memetic blueprint. He implicitly ends up with rather mysterious notions of a social mind or transpersonal processes. What has happened to the non-mysterious, fundamentally self-organising nature of human action that Marion refers to, action that produces emergent patterns of behaviour in the absence of a blueprint? What has happened to the importance of relationship? What he ends up with is a split between human action explained according to one causal framework and human choice explained according to another, just as other systems thinkers do.

12.3   Seeing organisations as complex systems

In this section, I will look briefly at a number of publications that import theories of chaos and complex adaptive systems into theorising about organisations in a qualitative way.

Thietart and Forgues

Thietart and Forgues (1995) review chaos theory and conclude that mathematical chaos can be found 'when there is the simultaneous influence of counteracting forces' (p. 23). The authors then review relevant literature on organisations to show that organisations are characterised by counteracting forces. Some of these forces push an organisation to stability, namely the forces of planning, structuring and controlling. Other forces, however, push an organisation towards instability and disorder. These forces include innovation, initiative and experimentation. They argue that when these forces are coupled they produce the chaotic organisation. On this basis, Thietart and Forgues present a number of propositions based on the theory of chaos, such as:

- Organisations are potentially chaotic.
- Organisations move from one dynamic state to another, namely stable equilibrium, periodic equilibrium or chaos.
- Forecasting is impossible, especially at a global scale over the long term. Change, therefore, has an unpredictable long-term effect.

- When in the chaotic state organisations are attracted to an identifiable configuration.
- Similar actions taken by the same organisation will never lead to the same state.

They conclude as follows:

> *The combination of the forces of stability and change can push the organization towards the chaotic domains where deterministically induced random behavior is the rule. Furthermore, because of the dissipative nature of open systems such as organizations, chaos has an underlying order: the strange attractor or the organizational configuration. As a consequence chaos contains the seeds of new stabilities. It is an organizing force. Thus, organizations face two contradictions: first, let chaos develop because it is the only way to find new forms of order. Second, look for order but not too much, because it may be a source of chaos. (p. 28)*

There are a number of points to note about this kind of analysis. First is the level at which the analysis is conducted, namely the macro level of the organisation as a whole. Secondly, it combines notions from chaos theory and the theory of dissipative structures. Thirdly, it adopts the position of the objective observer. Fourthly, there is a hint of an underlying cognitivist perspective in that organisations, presumably those who manage them, are assumed to be able to choose how much chaos or order to have. Again, there is the notion that the role of managers is to move their organisation between different dynamic possibilities. I would like to sound a note of caution in pursuing this kind of analysis. Chaos theory is a theory of deterministic systems but human systems are not deterministic. The behaviour of people is not driven by unchanging rules. The 'rules', if that is what they are, change as people learn.

Morgan

Morgan (1997) uses chaos and complexity theory as the basis of one of his metaphors for organisations, namely the organisation as flux and transformation. Having outlined the key elements of chaos and complexity theory he draws a number of conclusions with regard to organisations. First, he says:

> *But the message of chaos and complexity theory is that while some kind of ordering is always likely to be a feature of complex systems, structure and hierarchy can have no fixed form, hence cannot function as predetermined modes of control. (p. 266)*

He repeats this *always* on a number of occasions. However, this is not necessarily so. A complex system can self-organise into disintegration just as it can into a rigid, repetitive pattern. Furthermore, even when it operates at the edge of chaos there is the potential for the emergence of a new form, the shape which no one can know of in advance, and it may well not be one that leads to survival. The power law is a property of the edge of chaos and it means that there is no guarantee of survival.

Like most of the other writers surveyed in this chapter, he then points to the order that can emerge from interaction governed by a few simple rules. He equates this with his notion of 'minimum specs': that is, avoiding a grand design and specifying a small number of critical variables to attend to. He says the minimum specs define an attractor and create the context within which the system will move to it.

There are problems with this idea of 'simple rules'. If the requirement is some new form then the rules, or the context, that will produce that form do not exist yet. If the emergence depends critically on small changes then there is no way to specify what they are in advance. You could not ensure that you have detected all of them or measured them accurately enough. Morgan passes over this and recommends that managers should manage the context and allow self-organisation to do the rest. Here again there is the notion of manager, not as participant in a difficult-to-understand complex system but as one who stands outside it, identifies the minimum specs and then creates the context for it to produce self-organisation. Note the talk about a manager 'allowing it to happen'. This seems to assume that self-organisation is some new form of behaviour rather than a different way of understanding how people have always behaved. The question is whether such self-organising behaviour produces patterns that block or enable change.

Morgan also recommends identifying the small changes, or leverage points, that will transform the system. I have already explained above why I think that this does not fit with the notion of a complex system. He also recommends identifying the existing attractor that is locking an organisation into a stable position and identifying whether it should be changed. If it is to be changed, then managers are supposed to work out how the transition is to be achieved and how small changes can be used to do so. In advance, they are supposed to identify what the new ground rules are supposed to be. They must consider how they are going to manage through the 'edge of chaos'.

For me, the essentials of cybernetics and cognitivism are all firmly in place in this argument. The focus is on the autonomous individual who stands outside the system and in effect controls it, even if in a much looser way than is usually supposed. The reasoning remains, I think, firmly within the systemic tradition and the invitation to explore a radical perspective is passed by.

Nonaka

Nonaka (Nonaka, 1988, 1991; Nonaka and Takeuchi, 1995) also uses chaos theory in his perspective of creation of knowledge in organisations (*see* Chapter 8). Nonaka and Takeuchi use the words 'self-organising' but in a very different way to my understanding. They see self-organisation, not as the local interaction of agents that produces emergent patterns, but rather as autonomous or free individuals. They describe a self-organising team as a structure in which individuals can be free to diffuse their ideas in a team (p. 76). They link this with Morgan's (1997) 'minimum critical specification'. In complexity theory, self-organisation is a process in which agents interact locally on the basis of their historically evolved identities. This does not necessarily imply freedom to diffuse ideas.

A key insight from complexity theory is that of the paradoxical dynamics of stability and instability at the 'edge of chaos'. Again Nonaka and Takeuchi use similar words but for them they have little to do with characteristics of relationships that generate the dynamic. Rather, they equate chaos with crisis and assign top management the role of injecting it into the organisation in order to break down routines, habits and cognitive frameworks. I cannot see any justification for equating mathematical chaos with human crisis, a matter I briefly take up below.

Sanders

Sanders (1998) starts her book like this:

> *In the last decade, scientists attempting to understand chaos, complexity, and change, and organizations trying to survive them, reached the same conclusions: Chaos, complexity, and change are everywhere! Mastering them requires new ways of seeing and thinking . . . at the heart of the new science is the discovery that beneath what appears to be disorder there is order – a type of self-organizing pattern that emerges through the rich web of tangles, connections, and interrelationships in the system observed. And the most exciting discoveries relate to the dynamics, or 'hows' of this process. By applying the insights from the new science to our lives and businesses, I believe that I have found a way to show you how to anticipate, respond to, and influence change as it is emerging and before a crisis arises . . . And at last we have a way to develop the much-needed skill of strategic thinking. (pp. 6–7)*

Note how she talks about observing the system, so implicitly taking the position of manager as objective observer rather than participant. She defines dynamics as hows, that is as prescriptions. Dynamics, however, refers to patterns of movement and to the stability and instability characteristics of this movement. It is difficult to see what is prescriptive in this. She also claims to have found the answer. The basis of the claim seems very unclear to me.

The book depicts and describes the Lorenz strange attractor of a simplified model of the weather that I described in Section 10.2. It is then claimed that this picture allows 'scientists to *see*, for the first time' (p. 59) the order hidden in disorder. She concludes from this image that it is possible to identify any system's initial conditions because it is deterministic, but that it is difficult to predict its future state because it is nonlinear. If you return to Chapter 10, you will see that this statement is wrong. It is in practice impossible to forecast the long-term state of the kind of system she is talking about precisely because it is not possible to identify the initial conditions to the infinite exactness required. Infinite precision is required because the nonlinear structure of the system may amplify even the tiniest failure to identify and precisely measure the initial conditions. Without this, long-term prediction would be possible because the system is deterministic. Determinism is a theory of causality and it implies nothing whatsoever about the ability to measure initial conditions.

She then says that despite an inability to make predictions of long-term states it is possible to provide qualitative descriptions of whole system behaviour over time. This is true, but only for the attractor the system is currently drawn to. It would not be possible to describe any new attractor that some system was capable of spontaneously jumping to, until the jump occurred. This is Prigogine's point about bifurcation, which I described in Section 10.3. Furthermore, human systems are not deterministic because even if there are 'rules' governing them, these rules change over time. If one is to think of the human in terms of systems then one at least needs to think of them as learning and evolving and producing new forms. In other words, they have to be thought of as moving to entirely new attractors, the 'shape' of which cannot be 'seen' before the move is made, according to complex adaptive system simulations capable of generating new forms. So, you can only 'see' the shape of the attractor you already know about. To the extent that strategy is about producing creative, innovative new forms of business, it would not be possible, in terms of complexity theory, to 'see' that form before it emerges.

Sanders tries to get around this by saying:

> 'Perking' information is the term I use to identify the new initial conditions to which your system may be sensitive – changes or developments that are already taking shape just below the surface, and which can only be seen with peripheral vision or well developed foresight skills . . . The key to foresight is learning to recognize your system's initial conditions as they are emerging, so that you can see change coming, respond early, or influence it to your advantage. It's important to recognize your system's initial conditions BEFORE they erupt as an unexpected strange attractor. (p. 74)

> if you want to influence the future, you need to identify your system's perking information or changing initial conditions – and apply your resources here. These are your new leverage points. (p. 77)

This attempt runs into the same problem as before. It is not possible to identify all of the initial conditions and measure all of them with infinite accuracy. There are too many and they may be very small indeed. It follows that objective detection and measurement cannot be relied upon. Instead, she proposes peripheral vision and foresight. What is the former? How can you have foresight if you cannot predict? All the radical potential is lost and all that is left is straightforward strategic choice theory. Managers can carry on identifying leverage points and there is no threat to the possibility of control. The use of chaos theory is quite unnecessary and simply amounts to a change of vocabulary.

As far as I understand it, what I have summarised above is the conceptual core of the whole book and underlies all the prescriptions it makes. Sanders clearly takes the stance of external objective observer who sees an organisation as a chaotic system. Implicitly, she is prescribing this as the stance that a manager should take too. Managers are supposed to look at the system as a whole and then identify the pre-existing order, the strange attractor, hidden in apparent disorder. Then they are supposed to detect new initial conditions and take hold of them, master them she says, before they do something that is unexpected or not wanted. Not only is the manager to be the objective external observer but also the heroic individual who can master chaos and find hidden order. Unpredictability is mentioned and then, in effect, ignored. The words are from complexity science but the concepts are from cybernetics and cognitivism. In the process, any new insight is lost and orthodox prescriptions are simply presented in different language.

Consider now how Shona L. Brown and Kathleen M. Eisenhardt (1998) apply complexity theory to management in their book, called *Competing on the Edge: Strategy as Structured Chaos.*

Brown and Eisenhardt

Brown and Eisenhardt start their book as follows:

> *Given the pervasiveness of change, the key strategic challenge is managing that change . . . Given this challenge, what strategy is successful in rapidly and unpredictably changing industries? The answer is a strategy that we term competing on the edge. (p. 3)*

> *At its heart competing on the edge meets the challenge of strategic change by constantly reshaping competitive advantage even as the marketplace unpredictably and rapidly shifts. The goal is reinvention through a relentless flow of competitive advantages. In terms of strategy, competing on the edge ties 'where do you want to go?' intimately to 'How are you going to get there?' The result is an unpredictable, uncontrollable, and even inefficient strategy that nonetheless . . . works. (p. 4)*

Again, the authors claim to have found the answer using complexity theory. The questions posed, however, are the conventional ones of strategic choice theory: where do 'you', the masterful individual, want to go and how will you get there?

Having stated that their strategic solution involves a strategy that is unpredictable and uncontrollable they then immediately state what managing change means. It means reacting to the unexpected as a defensive tactic. It also means anticipation:

> *By anticipation we mean gaining insight into what is likely to occur and then positioning for that future . . . Anticipation means looking ahead to the needs of the global market and then lining up ahead of time the right resources . . . Or it could mean foreseeing the emergence of a new customer segment. (p. 1)*

This is still seen as defensive, however, so they claim that the highest level of managing change is leading change by dominating markets, setting the rhythm and pace for the others. So, on the same page they talk about a strategy that is unpredictable and uncontrollable and then prescribe foresight and the domination of markets. They imply that this is a choice that it is possible for managers to make all on their own. Having said that the future is unpredictable, they immediately call for anticipation and foreseeing the emergence. Surely, this is a logical contradiction. This is straight back to the theory of strategic choice. It implicitly assumes the presence of the heroic individual manager who can do all of these things in a cognitivist fashion. How do they use complexity theory?

The central concept they employ from complexity theory is that of the 'edge of chaos', which they define as being only partially structured. Notice how the notion of paradox is immediately lost. This is not a state of contradictory forces that can never be resolved. It is simply a balance: not too much structure and not too little.

Too much structure produces stability and too little produces chaos. Being at the edge also means letting a semi-coherent strategy emerge from the organisation, that is, one that is not too fixed, nor one that is too fluid. Of the edge of chaos they say:

The power of a few simple structures to generate enormously complex adaptive behaviour – whether flock behaviour among birds, resilient government (as in democracy), or simply successful performance by corporations – is at the heart of the edge of chaos. The edge of chaos captures the complicated, uncontrolled, unpredictable, yet adaptive (in technical terms self-organized) behaviour that occurs where there is some structure but not very much. The critical management issue at the edge of chaos is to figure out what to structure, and as essential, what not to structure. (p. 12)

It is worth spending a little time unpicking what is being said here. The notion of the dynamic at the edge of chaos is a rather sophisticated one. It is a dynamic to which a system evolves, or self-organises. This is the notion of self-organising criticality. The edge of chaos is a dynamic that occurs when certain parameters fall within a critical range. For example, at critical rates of flow of information, critical degrees of connectivity between agents, and critical degrees of agent diversity, the edge of chaos dynamic occurs. These authors take the notion of the edge of chaos across into organisations and immediately collapse these parameters into one of organisational structure and it then becomes a choice for managers to make. The choice is to install just enough structure to move their organisation to the edge of chaos where it can experience relentless change. Self-organisation is equated with adaptiveness and the notion of local interaction amongst agents producing emergent outcomes is lost. The analogy of the birds is used and then quite effortlessly coupled with successful organisations.

However, flocking is one attractor for bird behaviour, one that already exists. The few simple rules that produce it will not produce spontaneous jumps to new attractors. Surely, success for corporations over the long term requires just such a move to new attractors. Furthermore, a key feature of the edge of chaos is the power law. This means that small numbers of large extinction events occur periodically while large numbers of small extinctions occur. There is no guarantee of survival at the edge of chaos, only the possibility of new forms emerging that might survive. Nowhere do the authors mention this power law. Instead, they make a simplistic equation between being at the edge of chaos and success.

Among the prescriptions they derive from complexity theory there is, first, the injunction to improvise:

successful managers rely on a few key rules to innovate adaptively while consistently executing products and services on time, on target and on budget. These managers neither fall into rigid routines nor do they become chaotically undisciplined. Rather, they solve the dilemma of how to achieve adaptive innovation and consistent execution. Here improvisation is the first building block of competing on the edge. (p. 22)

In the managerial situation, improvisation is about extensive, real-time communication in the context of a limited structure with a few sharply defined responsibilities, strict priorities, and targeted deadlines. Improvisation is what enables managers to continuously and creatively adjust to change and to consistently move products and services out of the door. (p. 33)

Human behaviour is reduced to a few key rules. It is assumed that they can ensure success. And it is assumed that managers solve dilemmas rather than face paradoxes. The authors provide a questionnaire that managers can use to identify whether they are at the edge of chaos or trapped in one of the other dynamics (pp. 30–31). They give examples from their research of a company in each of these states and, of course, the only successful one is reported to be at the edge of chaos. They then give prescriptions for moving to the edge, if they are not already there. Managers should foster frequent change in the context of a few strict rules. They should keep activity loosely structured but at the same time rely on targets and deadlines. They should create channels for real-time, fact-based communication within and across groups.

So, the strategic choice now relates less to outcomes and more to a few simple rules, frequent changes to keep people on edge and fact-based communication channels. Why is it necessary to appeal to complexity theory for these prescriptions?

I think I have said enough to show that, once again, researchers have made some very loose interpretations of what complexity theory means and quite easily subsumed it into orthodox organisational theory. The prescriptions and the descriptions rely implicitly on cybernetics and cognitivism, even though the language is drawn from complexity theory. The result is a watered-down strategic choice theory.

Wheatley

Griffin (2001) provides a critique of Wheatley's (1999) reliance on chaos and complexity theory. He points out how she sees chaos and complexity theories providing an insight into the simplicity of all living systems in nature. If leaders come to understand their organisations as living systems then they will be able to use the insights from chaos and complexity theories to find a much simpler way of organising human affairs. For her, it is by recognising and working with the living system, by participating in a higher-level whole, that leaders can achieve a more human and a more creative organisation. She also attaches much the same importance to the notion of vision as learning organisation theorists do but she understands vision as a field of real but unseen forces influencing human behaviour. Having conceived of an organisation as a living whole in which people participate, Wheatley argues that those people exhibit a self-organising capacity just as in nature's living systems. Wheatley suggests that organisations are quite literally alive and must be understood, using the complexity sciences, just as other living systems in nature are thought of.

For Wheatley, the essence of living systems is the *simple rules* according to which they function. If leaders of organisations are to lead in a simpler way then they must identify the simple rules and they can do this by turning to the complexity sciences, which she sees as the rediscovery of ancient wisdom. In her thinking about leadership, Wheatley clearly displays the 'both . . . and' thinking of causal duality. There is a living system having it own purpose and an autonomous individual, the leader, also having purpose and what she is arguing for is for leaders to align their individual purpose to that of the greater living whole. For her, it is an overriding system that assures the emergence of order and she often refers to this in mythological terms, for example, as the order of Gaia emerging from Chaos. Wheatley affirm the mysterious nature of this level of system and being a part of such a system is what participation is about. She speaks of finding the self in participation in higher wholes. Not to participate, she says, leaves one isolated as an individual. Those who participate in the whole are 'healthy'. Ethical action is equated with conforming and submission to harmonious wholes (*see* Griffin 2001 for extended critique). Note how her view of organisational life is essentially the same as learning organisation theory and emphasises the rather mystical aspects of that theory (*see* Chapters 6 and 8).

Lewin and Regine

Griffin (2001) discusses the work of Lewin and Regine (2000), who also state that organisations are living systems, which they understand as complex adaptive systems, drawing on the work of Stuart Kauffman. They are concerned with the individual's soul being allowed to be present in the workplace and with the emergence of the collective soul of the organisation, thereby displaying the same kind of dualistic, 'both . . . and' thinking as Wheatley. Individuals *both* are agents in complex adaptive systems, where the simple rules governing their interactions have to do with ensuring *caring* relationships, *and* have souls, that is, they are autonomous individuals responsible for their actions in a way that is independent of the self-organisation of the complex adaptive system. There is a distinction between individuals as agents in the system making choices that are caring and participative, so contributing to the health of the system (organisation), and individual agents making other choices which are selfish and make the system (organisation) an unhealthy place to work in.

For Lewin and Regine, the implication of the complexity sciences is that leaders must come to a new understanding of themselves, putting aside their egos to serve others. The new form of leadership requires nothing less than a personal conversion, which is a painful process of learning to let go of the illusion of control. However, they also talk about the leader as the one who changes the culture. The leader on the one hand, is capable of changing the culture and, on the one hand, must give up the illusion of control.

Just as Wheatley did, so Lewin and Regine emphasise the 'few simple rules' idea, arguing that rich, creative, complex behaviour emerges from a few simple guidelines. They, along with so many others, cite the Boids simulation (*see* Chapter 11), which reproduces flocking patterns on the basis of only three simple rules of interaction among individual agents. They argue that when leaders formulate a few simple rules and leave the rest to self-organisation they will unleash human creativity. However, as Chapter 11 made clear, simulations based on a few given rules produce no creativity whatsoever. What the simple rules thinking represents is simply a different form of control (Stacey, Griffin and Shaw, 2000).

Lewin and Regine express the source of commitment and ethical action in terms of idealised wholes. Individuals must give up themselves in order for this whole to emerge, which then becomes the basis for the action already taken. This means that the participants are not focused on the everyday potential emerging from conflict and difference, but rather on an idealised and harmonious whole. Again, what Lewin and Regine present is little different to the more mystical aspects of learning organisation theory.

Pascale

Pascale (Pascale *et al.*, 2000) also claims that organisations are living organisms, and that as such they are complex adaptive systems. It is not just a metaphor for organisations. Nevertheless, he uses the terminology in both metaphorical and literal senses. For example, he views the mathematical term 'attractor' as a key concept in understanding complex adaptive systems but also uses it in the metaphorical sense of a 'vision' drawing the organisation forward. In a manner which is very similar to that of Lewin and Regine, Pascale describes the leader as being in a 'both . . . and' position. Operational leadership is to be applied in conditions of relative equilibrium. Adaptive leadership, on the other hand, makes happen what would not otherwise have happened. The individual leader must choose the appropriate form of leadership. It is taken for granted that the leader can observe the system from outside and choose among possible alternatives to apply to the system.

However, Pascale differs significantly from Wheatley and Lewin and Regine in his focus on conflict as the most important quality of relationship in looking at the organisation as a complex adaptive system. The leader, again from a position external to the system, judges when adaptive leadership is necessary and then considers how much the system needs to be disturbed. Pascale says that this is achieved by communicating the urgency of the adaptive challenge, establishing a broad understanding of the circumstances creating the problem, clarifying why traditional solutions will not work and keeping up the stress until guerrilla leaders come forward with solutions. Leaders intentionally generate anxiety and tension when an adaptive style is called for. They push their organisation to the edge of chaos. Social interaction is driven by conflict but the leaders introduce the source of the conflict into the team.

Griffin (2001) argues that Pascale and his co-authors present a view of leadership that is unethical in Kant's sense. To induce crisis into human teams in order to take advantage of 'productive' self-organisation for the survival of the whole is using humans as a means to an end and so contravenes Kant's ethical imperative.

The problem with 'living systems' and 'simple rules' as a theory of organisation

Griffin (2001) makes a number of criticisms of those who present a theory of organisations as living systems. First, those proposing this view frequently make emotive appeals for a return to ancient wisdom, supposedly now made scientific by the complexity sciences. However, it is far from clear that the ancients were any wiser than we, or that the complexity sciences are rediscovering this ancient wisdom, including Far Eastern spirituality. These are simply assertions. Secondly, the suggestion that an organisation is a living system sets up a whole outside of the experience of interaction between people, a whole to which they are required to submit if their behaviour is to be judged ethical. This distances us from our actual experience and makes it feel natural to blame something outside of our actual interaction for what happens to us. It encourages the belief that we are victims of a system, on the one hand, and allows us to escape feeling responsible for our own actions, on the other. Or it alienates people. They come to feel that they are insignificant parts of some greater whole and that there is nothing much they can do about it. The third difficulty is that organisations are not things at all, let alone living things. They are processes of communication and joint action. Communication and joint action as such are not alive. It is the bodies communicating and interacting that are alive.

Those prescribing 'simple rules', as the new way to manage complex organisations, hope to accomplish two rather attractive states. On the one hand, they hope that simple rules will replace complicated procedures, plans and other forms of bureaucracy, so freeing people to act creatively. On the other hand, they implicitly hope that this replacement of a bureaucracy by autonomous people freely following a few simple rules will not erode the control of the leaders. What these writers tend not to notice is the ideological basis of their prescription. This is an ideology of harmony in which people voluntarily submit themselves, often somewhat mystically, to a greater living whole in which they display caring behaviour and get in touch with their true selves, their souls. Griffin (2001) points to how this distracts our attention from the essentially conflictual nature of human interaction and so covers over inevitable power relations. Griffin draws on Mead's (1923) distinction between cult and functional values. Cult values are idealisations in which real-life obstacles to what we want to achieve are ignored. Cult values provide a feeling of enlarged personality. Functionalised values are interpretations of cult values in ordinary, real-life situations. On the rare occasions in which humans do directly follow the simple rules (cult values) without functionalising them, they form a cult. However, organisations are rarely cults. Mostly, they are collectives of people who are interpreting or functionalising the cult values in their interactions with each other.

Those prescribing 'simple rules' in this way usually draw on the Boids simulation (*see* Chapter 11) to justify their view that simple rules can generate complex behaviour. This demonstrates a complete misunderstanding of the Boids simulation. In that simulation, all the Boids are the same – they are homogeneous. They each precisely follow the same three simple rules and only those three rules. They do not interpret or functionalise them. They are the equivalent of cult values directly applied to conduct and they can only produce one pattern of complex behaviour, namely flocking. The Boids are in no sense free, just as the members of a cult are not free. If they were free, then each Boid would be interpreting or functionalising the three rules in their own unique way and they would then not flock. They would produce some other pattern and we cannot know what that pattern is until we see it.

If the leaders of an organisation do prescribe a few simple rules (cult values) for the members to follow, then it is highly likely that the members will interpret or functionalise the values in many different ways. The overall pattern of behaviour they would produce would be unpredictable. The simple rules prescription can, therefore, not be a means for retaining control and as the leader tried to influence the interpretations, more and more rules would be added. If, on the other hand, people did slavishly follow the simple rules then they would constitute a cult, which is incapable of creativity.

I am here emphasising the need for a careful study of what the complexity simulations are actually doing before jumping to simplistic prescriptive conclusions.

12.4 How the four questions are dealt with

The above sections have briefly reviewed some of the growing literature taking a complex systems view of organisations. Some employ the simulation methods of complexity scientists to model organisational processes at the macro level of the organisation as a whole. Others use the theory of complex systems as a metaphor that gives insight into the management of organisations. The analysis here is usually at the macro level, but sometimes at a more micro level. In the latter case, the emphasis tends to be on prescription rather than analysis.

I would like now to do what I did in relation to the theories of organisation reviewed in Part One of this book and examine how the theories surveyed in this chapter deal with the four questions posed at the end of Chapter 1.

The nature of interaction

As with strategic choice, organisational learning, knowledge management and psychoanalytic perspectives, interaction in organisations is seen in systemic terms, this time in terms of chaotic or complex systems. Analysis of these systems may be at a macro level in which diversity in agents and their interactions is not postulated. In that case, the system may follow equilibrium attractors or some strange attractor, but it does not have the internal capacity to move from one attractor to another. In this regard, there is relatively little difference from systems dynamics. What is different is the identification of strange attractors and the use of the concept of self-organisation to explain how movement around the strange attractor emerges. Alternatively, the system may be modelled with a focus on the micro level to include agent interaction and microdiversity. In this case, the system does display the internal capacity to move spontaneously from one attractor to another or to evolve new ones. Self-organisation is now understood as the process that produces emergent novelty. This is a major difference from all of the other systems models reviewed in this book because here the system takes on a life of its own.

It seems to me that the literature reviewed in this chapter mainly uses the first of the above complexity models, namely the one that does not place microdiversity at the centre. This is evidenced by the focus on identifying a few simple rules and on someone operating on the conditions, or model parameters, to move the system to the edge of chaos. Apart from Allen and Marion, it is rare for those utilising complexity theory to talk about the importance of diversity, which in human terms amounts to deviance and eccentricity and this is central to that kind of self-organisation that might produce emergent novelty. As a result, the causality of the system is always formative and even those who do focus attention on diversity do not develop the implications of a move to transformative causality.

Complex systems at the edge of chaos display the dynamics of order and disorder, stability and instability, regularity and irregularity, all at the same time. When this is interpreted in organisational terms, by the authors reviewed in this chapter, it is often translated as 'crisis'. I suppose that from an orthodox perspective it might be crisis. However, the dynamics of the edge of chaos is not at all the dynamics of crisis, but rather, of paradox and ambiguity. For me, this connotes a mature ability to hold a difficult position, not a state of crisis. Equating the edge of chaos with crisis leads on to the prescription to inject crisis into an organisation. Surely, this is a misinterpretation of what mathematical chaos or complexity might mean in human terms.

The nature of human beings

The above applications of complexity theory to organisations all make implicit assumptions about human psychology. These are drawn from cognitivist and humanistic psychology. This is evident in the emphasis placed on the individual. It is the individual who learns and chooses, even though that individual may be part of a team. Further evidence is given by the use of the notion of mental models and the idea that people can pass tacit knowledge from one individual to another, quite separately from explicit knowledge. This means that the notion of a complex system is being interpreted in organisational terms from the same psychological perspective as those theories based on cybernetics and systems dynamics. Given the tendency also to interpret complex systems from the orthodox perspective, it would be surprising to find enormous differences between the theories surveyed above and those of strategic choice, organisational learning and knowledge management.

Methodology and paradox

The methodological position of the theorists reviewed above is no different from that of those proposing strategic choice, learning organisation and knowledge management theories. They all take the position of the objective observer, understood in terms of rationalist causality, who stands outside the system and models it in the interest of controlling it. The prescriptions derived from these theories all implicitly place the manager in the same position. It is the manager who must produce and impose the few simple rules that will produce the desired attractor. It is the manager who must alter the parameters, or create the conditions, that create the edge of chaos dynamics. This is then simplistically equated with success.

Although paradox seems to me to be at the heart of what the dynamics at the edge of chaos means, it does not feature at the centre of the theories described in this chapter. The paradox of observing participant is eliminated in the 'both . . . and' thinking of dual causality (Griffin, 2001).

Focusing attention

The approaches using chaos and complexity theory reviewed in this chapter focus attention on much the same factors as the systemic theories reviewed in Part One of this book. There is the same emphasis on the agency of the autonomous individual. There is the same concern with control. There is the same downplaying of the importance of unpredictability and diversity. There is the same belief in the possibility of an organisation moving according to some organisation-wide intention.

It seems to me that what is happening is this. Complexity theories, particularly those modelling systems with a life of their own, have potentially radical implications for thinking about organisations. The most radical potential implication, it seems to me, is to question systems thinking itself. Continuing to think of human interaction as 'system' makes it impossible to move away from all the other systemic theories and the problems with them that Kant identified so long ago. Added to this, the theories of complex systems are combined with a cognitivist theory of human behaviour. Cognitivism has close links with cybernetics and systems dynamics and as soon as the cognitivist perspective is brought to bear cybernetics and systems dynamics assumptions come with it. The result, I think, is theoretical developments that start off with radical promise but then rapidly slip back into the same systemic theories as those reviewed in Part One. It seems to be very hard to hold on to the radical perspectives of complexity theory while retaining the perspective of systems, the assumptions of cognitivism and the methodology of the independent, external observer.

What are these radical implications?

First, iterative nonlinear interaction patterns itself. This immediately brings process to the fore.

Secondly, groups of people are creative only when their behaviour displays the paradoxical dynamics of stability and instability at the same time. In psychological terms, this dynamic has to do with the ability to live with the ambiguity and paradox of life, as well as the anxiety they generate.

Thirdly, the creative process is also destructive. It involves not only co-operation, but also competition that takes place in the medium of ideas, communication and power relations. The creative process in human relationships, therefore, inevitably involves difference, conflict, fantasy and emotion; it stirs up anger, envy, depression and many other feelings. To remove the mess by inspiring people to follow some vision, to indoctrinate them to share the same culture and follow the same simple rules, is to remove the very raw material of creative activity.

Fourthly, neither creative processes nor their outcomes can be planned or intended because long-term outcomes are unknowable in the paradoxical dynamics of stability and instability at the same time. Links between people's next actions and their long-term outcomes disappear so that no one can be 'in control'. This becomes far less anxiety provoking once it is accepted that the consequence is not necessarily randomness and anarchy. This is because spontaneous self-organisation produces emergent strategies; that is, the interaction itself creates patterns that no agent individually intends or can foresee. Emergence means that it is not possible to foresee the global outcome of interaction between individuals, nor is it possible to reduce the global pattern to the behaviour of the agents.

For me, the key message coming from the sciences of complexity is this. It is possible, with much effort, for someone, or some small group of powerful people, to predict the outcomes of group, organisational and societal behaviour and, therefore, to remain 'in control' of them. However, this is possible only while there is enforced stability. The result could be stability for a long time, but it will be the death of creativity and innovation. So, organisations cannot survive by following some blueprint. Instead, the potential for, but not the guarantee of, survival is created by the capacity to produce emergent new outcomes. This is controlled by the process of spontaneous self-organisation itself.

12.5 Summary

This chapter has reviewed the way in which a number of writers are interpreting chaos and complexity in organisational terms. It has suggested that the common approach is to retain a systems view of interaction and a cognitivist approach to human psychology and to interpret chaos and complexity from that perspective. This amounts to retaining the assumption of the autonomous, even heroic, individual and the prescription of the manager as the objective observer of the organisation as a system. I have argued that the result is the re-presentation of strategic choice, learning organisation and knowledge management theory in a different vocabulary. The emphasis on control and organisation-wide intention remains intact. For me, this means that the opportunity to explore what it means to operate as a participant in a setting in which the future is unknowable is lost. No further understanding of the process of how strategy might emerge from local interaction is obtained. The interpretation of chaos and complexity thus remains within management and organisational theory orthodoxy. The essentially dual causality, formative and rationalist, remains.

Part Three of this book reviews a very different way of interpreting the insights of the complexity sciences for organisations. This moves from systems thinking to thinking in terms of process and from individual-centred to relationship psychology.

Further reading

The publications reviewed in this chapter are examples of the most recent work in this field. For further reading I suggest Axelrod and Cohen (1999), Goldstein (1994), Goerner (1994), Hurst (1995), Kiel (1994), Nilsen (1995), Wheatley (1992) and Zimmerman (1992). If the applications to economics are of interest the following are suggested: Anderson, Arrow and Pines (1988), Arthur (1988), Baumol and Benhabib (1989) and Kelsey (1988). In addition to those reviewed in this chapter, other recent publications you might want to refer to are: Wood (2000); Ralls and Webb (1999); Axelrod and Cohen (1999); Lissack and Roos (1999); Rycroft and Kash (1999); Baets (1999); Petzinger (1999); Stickland (1998) and Kelly and Allison (1999). An in-depth critique of the use of complexity theories can be found in Griffin (2001).

PART THREE ● ● ● ● ●

Complex responsive processes perspectives on strategy and organising

This Part explores how one might think about organisations and their strategies as temporal processes rather than as systems. Part One reviewed the main theories of strategic management and organisational dynamics, pointing to how they are all based on the theoretical foundations of systems thinking and individual-centred theories of human psychology. Part Two described the development of theories of chaos and complexity, pointing to the potentially radical nature of the insights they provide, which most of those applying complexity to organisations do not take up. I argued that because they continue to think of organisations as systems and because they continue to base their thinking on individual-centred psychology, mainly cognitivism, writers on organisational complexity end up using new words to re-present the systems theories described in Part One. This Part of the book will move away from thinking in terms of systems altogether and away from individual-centred theories of psychology. Instead, organisations will be thought of as complex responsive processes of relating. The key word here is process, signalling that human interaction is to be understood not as a system but as processes of relating and communicating, signalling a theory of human psychology based firmly on relationships between people rather than on the individual.

Chapter 13 will explore what I mean by process. This notion of process is based on an essentially temporal metaphor and the significance of the shift can be seen by comparing this with the essentially spatial metaphor upon which systems thinking is based. Central to systems thinking is the spatial notion of an 'inside' and an 'outside'. A system is a 'whole', an 'inside', separated from an environment, an 'outside', by a 'boundary'. This immediately establishes hierarchical levels. At one level there is a system and at another level there is the environment, usually thought of as a suprasystem, or more encompassing whole. Interaction between subsystems produces the system and interaction between systems produces the global suprasystem or whole. For example, the human individual may be thought of as a cognitive system consisting of interacting mental models and the group is then a suprasystem of interacting individuals. The individual and the group are at different hierarchical levels of being and need to be understood in different ways. In other words, systems thinking inevitably involves causal dualism in which individuals are understood to act according to rationalist causality when in the position of the observer and according to formative causality when in the position of participant in the system.

In moving to the temporal notion of process, one altogether abandons thinking in terms of an 'inside' or an 'outside', a 'whole' and a 'boundary'. One also abandons thinking about different hierarchical levels of existence or explanation, at least as far as human action is concerned. If one is concerned with the temporal processes of human interaction, one is concerned with the actions of human bodies such as walking, talking and thinking. Take walking, for example. The notion of anything inside or outside of walking makes no sense, nor does it make much sense to describe walking as a whole separated by a boundary from something else. One could say the same about the bodily action of thinking. Most importantly, process thinking moves away from dualisms and the elimination of paradox. It is based on a unitary, paradoxical causality of emergent continuity and transformation at the same time.

Chapters 14 to 17 will explore just what it might mean to focus attention on the temporal processes of interaction between human bodies as the basis of an explanation of human organising. Chapter 18 will explore how thinking in process terms focuses attention in relation to strategy and organisational dynamics. Moving from systems thinking to process thinking about strategy and organisational dynamics has a number of important consequences. Strategy ceases to be understood as the realisation of someone's intended or desired future state for the whole organisation. It ceases to be understood as the intentional design and leveraging of whole organisational learning and knowledge-creating systems. Instead, strategy is understood as evolving patterns of organisational and individual identities. Strategy is then about what an organisation is, the collective or 'we' identity and who its members are, the individual or 'I' identities. Evolving organisational and individual identities are understood to emerge in the local communicative interacting and power relating of the people who constitute an organisation.

The focus of attention is then not on some abstract systemic whole but on what people are actually doing in their relationships with each other in the living present. It is in these relationships that strategy continually emerges. It is in interaction, particularly ordinary, everyday conversation, that members of organisations perpetually construct their future as continuity and potential transformation at the same time.

Chapter 13 ● ● ● ●
Process thinking

13.1 Introduction

Chapter 2 explored the origins of modern systems thinking in the philosophy of Kant, with its dualistic way of thinking. On the one hand, there is reality, the noumenal, which is unknowable, and on the other hand, there is the appearance of reality, the phenomenal, which is knowable. On the one hand, there are subjects, that is, autonomous individual humans, who can freely choose goals and actions through their reasoning capacity and are therefore subject to rationalist causality. On the other hand, there are objects, the natural phenomena, which human subjects can know because they have innate mental categories by means of which they can classify and causally connect phenomena. Humans come to know phenomena by means of the scientific method, which means that they formulate hypotheses about phenomena and then test them. These hypotheses can take the form of mechanistic 'if–then' rules, that is, efficient cause, or they can take the form of regulative ideas, which means that the objective observer ascribes an 'as if' purpose to phenomena, understood as systems. The system is understood as unfolding the purpose ascribed to, or enfolded in, the idea of the system. Nature is then understood to move according to the formative process of the system, that is formative cause. The result is another dualism in which human action is understood to be subject to rationalist causality and nature is understood to be subject to either efficient or formative causality.

The essence of Kantian thinking, therefore, is the dualism. This way of thinking has a 'both . . . and' structure in which one side of the dualism applies at one time or place and the other side of the dualism applies at another time or place. First one side is the figure and the other the background and then this is reversed. The effect of this dualistic, figure–ground way of thinking is to eliminate paradox. Locating the opposites of the dualism in a sequence avoids the need to hold the two together *at the same time*, which is the essence of paradoxical thinking (Griffin, 2001).

Kant was not claiming that the world really consists of systems, only that humans have the innate mental idea of system through which they can understood the world 'as if' it were a system. The first wave of twentieth-century systems thinkers took a realist position and claimed that reality was a system but the more recent development of soft and critical systems thinking moves back to the Kantian position and holds that systems are mental constructs. In Chapter 9, for example, I examined Jackson's claims that human thought is fundamentally systemic.

Kant cautioned against thinking about human action as a system because this was incompatible with individual autonomy. However, all of the system thinkers of the twentieth-century have ignored this caution and applied systems thinking not only to nature but to human action and interaction as well. In Part One, I argued that this application of systems thinking to human action created problems for our understanding of organisations and their strategic evolution. In addition to the problem with human free choice, there is the inability of systems thinking to account for novelty in systemic terms, simply because its fundamental causality is formative, that is, unfolding what is already there. Novelty is then an unexplained capacity of autonomous individuals. Furthermore, in Chapter 12 I argued that when the insights of the natural complexity sciences are applied to organisations in systemic terms, including the systemic psychology of cognitivism and constructivism, the result is mainly the re-presentation of strategic choice and learning organisation theories in new jargon with no essential difference in implications.

This chapter explores an alternative to systems thinking about organisations. The philosopher, Hegel, argued against Kant's dualisms and their elimination of paradox. Instead, for him, thought is essentially paradoxical. Unlike Kant, who located human knowing in the innate capacities of the individual mind, Hegel presented a view of human knowing that was essentially social and, as later chapters will explain, this immediately signals a move away from individual-based views of human psychology. The next section briefly reviews Hegel's thinking and how the sociologist Elias thought in essentially the same terms. The section after that suggests that the insights of the natural complexity sciences can be interpreted in human terms using the kind of process thinking that derives from Hegel and Elias. This provides a substantially different way of understanding complex human processes to that afforded by systems thinking. The purpose of this chapter is to clarify the sense in which systems and process thinking provide two completely different and quite incompatible ways of understanding human organisations. Later chapters will explore the consequences of thinking in process terms about strategy and organisational dynamics.

●●●● 13.2 Process thinking

In the late eighteenth and early nineteenth centuries, the philosophers known as romantic idealists (Fichte, Schelling and Hegel) responded to the problems created by Kant's dualisms of subject and object and ideal and real, by identifying the object of knowledge with the process of knowing to be found in the self. They were particularly concerned with self-consciousness where the subject is an object to itself. It is the self that is real and all experience is carried back to this immediate experience of the self so that the reflexive position becomes central. Kant held that the mind encountered contradictions when it attempted to go beyond the phenomenal world to the noumenal and these contradictions were warnings of a mind going beyond its limits. For the romantic idealists, however, contradictions were inherent in the movement of thought. The romantic idealists moved away from a Kantian innate logic, with already given forms of thought outside of experience (transcendental), to a dialectical logic in which human consciousness and self-consciousness as experience is central to knowing. Furthermore, individual selves and social relations were understood to be intimately interconnected and experience was understood as historical, social processes of consciousness and self-consciousness. This represented a powerful break with the notion of the autonomous individual.

Hegel

In Hegel's philosophy, the development of thought takes place through conflict and the world of our experience is the world we are creating in our thought. Hegel held that one cannot begin, as Kant had done, with an isolated individual subject experiencing the world and then ask how a world of objective experience gets built up out of the inner world of purely subjective experience. Rather, one must begin with an already shared world of subjects making judgements in the light of possible judgements by others. Hegel also emphasised the idea of mutual recognition to argue that there was an intersubjective unity of mutually recognising agents. He argued against any separate realm outside of experience. In this, he moved decisively away from the Kantian notion of a system lying outside of experience and causing it. He accorded central importance to recognition, linking it to desire, particularly the desire for the desire of the other. Here he is emphasising the co-operative aspects of society, although power and competition are also central to his view.

For Hegel, the notions of person and subject are historically specific and are given content only by the social institutions in which each individual achieves social identity through interdependence and mutual recognition. Mind or consciousness is manifested in social institutions, that is, ways of life, which give identities, self-concepts, to individuals. Each person is self-consciously, purposively directing herself or himself but each is also dependent on the other. The self maintains and leads a life and so discriminates experience, objectively tied to the real properties of the world but also necessarily relational. How we come to understand our own desires, interpret their intensity and priority, how we categorise objects to satisfy our desires, is not fixed or determined by our natures or the real world but depends on the concepts we employ and these are socially evolved. Self-determination by a free subject can only occur through another person who is also a self-determining subject and is doing the same. Another self-conscious subject offers resistance to the realisation of my desires by testing or challenging me and my self-world conception. It is inevitable that two self-determining, self-conscious subjects will conflict and struggle. In their struggle each negates the other as a subject. They become an object to each other. Paradoxically, however, each also confirms the subjectivity of the other in genuine mutual recognition. This is the dialectical process of the social in which we come to know.

Hegel argued that individual autonomy could only be achieved in a social context. He held that individuals are fundamentally social practitioners and what they do, think or say takes form in the context of social practices, while these practices provide the required resources, objects of desire, skills and procedures. In contrast to Kantian thinking, where there is a duality of the individual and the social, Hegel presents a perspective in which they cannot be separated. Indeed, individual consciousness and self-consciousness arises in social relations, which they are simultaneously constructing. This is clearly a paradoxical or dialectical perspective in which individual minds are simultaneously forming and being formed by social relations at the same time.

Hegel's dialectical method of thought is reflected throughout his discussion of the social evolution of consciousness, self-consciousness and knowledge. Dialectic refers to the social processes of power difference and mutual recognition in which self-consciousness arises. The dialectic is the experience of self-consciousness consisting of self-examination, that is, the subject–object identity, in which one is an object to oneself. This is not a dualism in which the subject simply observes itself as an object but a paradox of participant observation in which the subject and object are moments in one action.

Hegel's dialectic, in purely technical terms, is a way of thinking, a particular kind of logic to do with the paradoxical movement of thought. It is a logic in which there is the apprehension of the unity of opposites in their dissolution and transition, that is, *aufhebung*. Aufhebung means transformation in which opposites are retained but their meanings change. The concept of mathematical chaos provides a technical example of this logic. In thinking about the weather, one notices its stability, for example, in terms of the seasons predictably following each other. However, one also notices the instability as storms unpredictably alternate with sunshine. One could think about the weather in Kantian dualistic terms as both stability and instability, locating stability in one place or time and instability in another place or time. In other words, one could think of the weather moving from the dynamic of stability to the dynamic of instability and back again. The thesis of stability and the antithesis of instability are then combined in the synthesis of the weather system. This is a Kantian dialectic in which the two opposites or antimonies are preserved with their meanings unchanged in a synthesis that does not yield anything substantially new and in a way that paradox is resolved or eliminated. However, when one thinks of the weather as a distinctive dynamic, described as mathematically chaotic, which is stability and instability at the same time, then the opposition of stability and instability is preserved but at the same time it is destroyed because these opposites can no longer be separated and so do not mean the same as they did. Instead the opposition is transformed, is raised, to a new unity, a new dynamic, in which stability is always found in instability and vice versa. New meaning emerges in the tension of opposites and the paradox remains. Indeed the paradox is the source of the new meaning. The 'edge of chaos' is also a concept of a dynamic characterised by stability and instability at the same time. In all of these cases there is no notion of moving from stability to instability and back again – the opposition of stability and instability is always present at the same time.

However, Hegel's dialectic is not just a technical logic but the movement of thought as a social process expressing a human self-consciousness encountering, desiring and recognising the self-consciousness of others where the unity is that of meaning and the social. In terms of Hegel's dialectic, one thinks of the individual and the social in much the same way.

Now consider how these ideas are reflected in the sociology of Elias.

Elias

Following the tradition of Hegel, Elias did not think about the relationship between the individual and society in terms of any spatial distinction between inside and outside, nor did he adopt any kind of systemic formulation that abstracts from direct experience. Instead, he understood both individual and social purely in process terms. He did not think of the individual and society first existing and then subsequently affecting each other (Elias, 1991, p. 456). He argued against metaphors of individuals and groups interpenetrating each other because this obscures an understanding of the relationship between the individual and the social. He suggests that we can see the connection between individual structures and social structures more precisely if we refuse to abstract from the process of their development. For him, 'structures of personality and of society evolve in an indissoluble interrelationship' (1991, p. 456). Elias developed an activity theory of human psychology and sociology and argued against the spatial notions of inside and outside.

> If instead of the usual substance-concepts like 'feeling' and 'reason' we use activity-concepts, it is easier to understand that while the image of 'outside' and 'inside', of the shell of a receptacle containing something inside it, is applicable to the physical aspects of a human being mentioned above, it cannot apply to the structure of the personality, to the living human being as a whole. On this level there is nothing that resembles a container – nothing that could justify the metaphors like that of the 'inside' of the human being. (Elias, 1991, p. 480)

He also dismissed attempts to retain the concepts of inside and outside by postulating an interaction between them. Instead of seeing some irreducible wall between one human and another, he sees an

> irreducible intertwining of individual beings, in which everything that gives their animal substance the quality of a human being, primarily their psychical self-control, their individual character, takes on its specific shape in and through relationships to others. (Elias, 1991, pp. 31–2)

In rejecting the notion of the individual mind as an 'internal world', he also argues against thinking of the social as an organic unity or supra individual by taking models

> primarily from the natural sciences, particularly biology. But here, as so often, the scientific modes of thought easily and imperceptibly merge with religious and metaphysical ones to form a perfect unity. A society is conceived, for example, as a supra-individual organic entity which advances ineluctably towards death through the stages of youth, maturity and age . . . Sometimes the members of this latter camp . . . ascribe to whole social formations or to a mass of people a soul of their own beyond the individual souls, an anima collectiva or a 'group mind'. (Elias, 1991, pp. 5–6)

Elias had much the same view of concepts of society as some kind of whole:

> By a 'whole' we generally mean something more or less harmonious. But the social life of human beings is full of contradictions, tensions and explosions.

> *Decline alternates with rise, war with peace, crises with booms. The communal life of human beings certainly is not harmonious. But if not harmonious, at least the word 'whole' evokes in us the idea of something complete in itself, a formation with clear contours, a perceptible form and a discernible, more or less visible structure. But societies have no such perceptible form. They do not possess structures that can be seen, heard or touched directly in space. Considered as whole, they are always more or less incomplete: from wherever they are viewed they remain open in the sphere of time, towards the past and the future . . . it is in reality a continuous flow, a faster or slower change of living forms; in it the eye can find a fixed point only with difficulty. (Elias, 1991, p. 12)*

What Elias is doing here is moving completely away from any notion of human interaction as a system and any notion of some whole existing outside of that interaction and causing it. Instead, he is focusing entirely on the processes of interaction between human bodies. Elias argued that the concept of the whole applied to human action simply created a mystery in order to solve a mystery.

In order to understand the nature of human interaction, Elias made a detailed study of changes in the way Western people experienced themselves over hundreds of years and pointed to how social order emerges in interactions between people.

The emergence of social order

Elias argued that what we now call Western civilisation is not the result of any kind of calculated long-term planning. Individual people did not form an intention to change civilisation and then gradually realise this intention through rational, purposive measures. It is not conceivable that the evolution of society could have been planned because that would suppose that modern rational, calculating individuals with a degree of self-mastery already existed centuries ago, whereas Elias's research shows that such individuals did not exist then but were, rather, themselves the products of social evolution. Societal changes produced rational, planning kinds of individuals, not the other way around. In medieval times, people experienced their self-consciousness in a completely different way, in a completely different kind of society, compared to the way we experience our self-consciousness in modern society.

> *Though it is unplanned and not immediately controllable, the overall process of development of a society is not in the least incomprehensible. There are no 'mysterious' social forces behind it. It is a question of the consequences flowing from the intermeshing of the actions of numerous people . . . As the moves of interdependent players intertwine, no single player nor any group of players acting alone can determine the course of the game no matter how powerful they may be . . . It involves a partly self-regulating change in a partly self-organizing and self-reproducing figuration of interdependent people, whole processes tending in a certain direction. (Elias, 1991, pp. 146–7)*

Elias argued that change in society occurred in an unplanned manner but nevertheless displayed a specific type of order. His research demonstrated how the constraints imposed by others were converted into self-restraints and how many human bodily activities were progressively pushed behind the scenes of communal social life and invested with feelings of shame. Although this transformation could not have been planned and intended, it was not simply a sequence of unstructured changes (Elias, 2000, p. 365). Elias looked for an explanation of how it was possible that orderly formations, which no human being had intended, arose in the human world:

> *It is simple enough: plans and actions, the emotional and rational impulses of individual people, constantly interweave in a friendly or hostile way.* This basic tissue resulting from many single plans and actions of men can give rise to changes and patterns that no individual person has planned or created. From this interdependence of people arise an order sui generis, an order more compelling and stronger than the will and reason of the individual people composing it. *It is the order of interweaving human impulses and strivings, the social order, which determines the course of historical change; it underlies the civilizing process. (Elias, 2000, p. 366)*

Although it is highly unlikely that Elias was ever aware of the complexity sciences, what he is describing here is what complexity scientists call self-organisation and emergence. Elias is arguing that individuals and groups are interacting with each other, in their local situations, in intentional, planned ways. However, the widespread, global consequences of the intermeshing of these intentions and plans cannot be foreseen by any of them – long-term global consequences emerge. Elias explains that long-term consequences cannot be foreseen because the intermeshing of the actions, plans and purposes of many individuals constantly gives rise to something that has not been planned, intended or created by any of those individuals. Elias pointed to the important fact that individuals pursuing their plans are always in relationship with each other in a group or power figuration. While individuals can plan their own actions, they cannot plan the actions of others and so cannot plan the interplay of plans and actions. The fact that each person depends on others means that none can simply realise their plans. However, this does not mean that anarchy, or disorder, results. Elias talks about a trend or direction in the evolution of the consequences of the interweaving of individual plans and intentions. In other words, he is talking about self-organisation and emergence and this immediately suggests to me the potential for greater insight into the process that may be found in the complexity sciences, which are concerned with the same kind of process.

Elias talked about an essentially paradoxical process in which individuals form groups while being formed by them at the same time. This is a fundamentally different way of thinking to the dualism of individual and social to be found in systems thinking. In Elias's process theory, change occurs in a paradoxical transformative process – change is self-organising, emergent processes of perpetually constructing the future as continuity and transformation. Elias argued that we cannot identify self-organising social order with the order of nature, or with some kind of supra-individual. Instead the order arises in specific dynamics of social interweaving in particular places at particular times.

> *Our thinking today is still extensively governed by ideas of causality which are inadequate to the process under discussion: we are strongly inclined to explain*

any change in a particular formation by a cause outside that formation. (Elias, 1991, pp. 45–6)

To summarise, Elias argued that social evolution could not be understood in terms of social forces, cultural systems, supra-individuals, suprasystems, spirit, *élan vital*, or any other kind of whole outside of experience. Instead he argued for a way of understanding that stayed with the direct experience of interaction between people. He suggested a kind of circular, paradoxical causality in which individuals form the social while being formed by it at the same time and he acknowledged the link between this view and the philosophy of Hegel. Elias held that there is nothing mysterious about the simultaneous evolution of social order and individual personality structures. He posits processes of interweaving intentional actions of people that produce transformation, which is not unstructured or chaotic change even though none of the interacting people planned or intended the change. He talked about self-regulating change in self-organising and self-producing figurations of interdependent people. He described this as the autonomous dynamics of a web of relationships in particular places at particular times.

If it makes sense to think of societies and their 'strategies' in this way, then there is no reason why we could not think about organisations in this way too. This is what Chapters 14–17 will be doing.

Elias developed his process sociology during the 1930s and 1940s well before the emergence of the complexity sciences. He continued to develop his theories until his death in 1990 but it is unlikely that he knew anything about the developments in the natural sciences just referred to. However, these developments provide considerable support for what Elias was arguing. What these sciences are pointing to is the ubiquitous presence in nature of the unpredictable emergence of order in disorder through processes of spontaneous self-organisation. The sociology of Elias, and others in the Hegelian tradition, therefore, provides an alternative to systems thinking for interpreting the insights of complexity theories into human terms. Elias's process sociology also provides a distinctive way of thinking about the relationship between the individual and the group.

concepts such as 'individual' and 'society' do not relate to two objects separately but to two different yet inseparable aspects of the same human beings . . . both aspects (and human beings in general) are normally involved in structural transformation. Both have the character of processes, and there is not the slightest necessity, in forming theories about human beings, to abstract from this process character . . . The relation between individual and social structures can only be clarified if both are investigated as changing, developing entities. (Elias, 1991, pp. 455–6)

For Elias then, the individual and the group are two aspects of the same process of human relating. He talked about society being a society of individuals and about the individual as being thoroughly social. He saw the relationship between the group and the individual in paradoxical terms in which each simultaneously forms and is formed by the other. There is only one kind of causality here – that of a transformative process. This is very different to the foundations of systemic theorising about organisations reviewed in Part One, which was based on the dual causality of the formative system and the rationalist observer.

●●●● 13.3   Chaos, complexity and analogy

In presenting some elements of Elias's process sociology, I pointed to the similarity between his notion of social process and the processes of self-organisation and emergence in chaos and complexity theories (*see* Chapters 10 and 11). This section explores how the abstract relationships studied in the complexity sciences might provide analogies for human interaction understood from the perspective of Elias's process sociology. First, consider whether it is reasonable to regard chaos and complexity theories as source domains for analogy with human interaction.

Chaos theory

Chaos theory reveals the properties of iterative, deterministic, nonlinear mathematical relationships (i.e. algorithms) in which the output of one iteration becomes the input of the next. These are not cybernetic relationships and they cannot be called feedback ones. In cybernetic feedback, the output of one iteration is compared with some target, or some environmental state, outside the iterative process, and the difference between the output and the target or environmental state becomes the input for the next iteration. The relationship between this input and the subsequent output is such as to dampen the difference between that output and the target or environmental state – the negative feedback of cybernetic and open systems. Systems dynamics is also usually understood in the organisational literature in feedback terms but here the system can either amplify or dampen difference, or alternate sequentially between the two.

In the relationships modelled by chaos theory, it is the whole output of one iteration that becomes the input for the next iteration. There is no comparison with an outside reference point. The relationships modelled by chaos theory, therefore, are more accurately described as self-referential than as feedback. In other words, the current state is determined by referring, through a deterministic nonlinear algorithm, to its own previous state. When a control parameter is held at a critical point by some external force, then this self-referential relating takes the form of a strange attractor. While the control parameter is held at that critical point, the pattern of relationships takes one, and only one, form, namely that of the particular strange attractor generated by the particular algorithmic relationship specified. This is the simultaneous operation of amplification and constraint, that is, a paradox. It is not a sequential alternation between constraint and amplification.

Chaos theory, therefore, presents abstract mathematical models of iterative nonlinear interactions between entities that form a system. The system is modelled as a set of mathematical equations whose properties are identified through analysis and iteration. The mathematical models are not reality but simply logical structures created by mathematicians. The physicist, meteorologist, chemist, biologist, or any other scientist in any other field, then has to interpret how these abstract logical structures might apply to the field they are interested in. They do this by calling upon what is already known, through scientific experiments, about the phenomena in their field of study. They also perform new experiments suggested by chaos theory in order to provide empirical support for the claim that the abstract mathematical models they have developed do apply to the phenomena in their field of interest.

In Chapter 12, I referred briefly to the work of economists and some organisational theorists who adopt exactly the same approach. They use data on macro events, such as foreign exchange rates, to explore whether the mathematical equations of chaos theory fit the data. As soon as they do this, they make implicit assumptions about the nature of human interaction. They assume that human beings are such that patterns in their interaction can be described at the macro level in terms of deterministic equations. Alternatively, other organisational theorists use the properties revealed by the mathematical models of chaos as metaphors to describe organisations. For example, Chapter 12 reviewed the work of a number of researchers who describe an organisation as chaotic. As soon as they do this, they too are making implicit assumptions about the nature of human interaction.

It is very important not to jump straight from a mathematical model to an application in a particular field without examining how the model is being interpreted in that particular field. In other words, the implicit assumptions being made about human action need to be made explicit. If one applies chaos theory directly to any form of human action, including organisations, then one is assuming that human interaction is deterministic. This immediately means that one is assuming away any form of human freedom, that is, any possibility of individuals making any kind of choice. Since this is so directly contrary to our experience, it follows that chaos theory cannot be directly applied to human action. Furthermore, chaos theory cannot offer analogies for human action. In reasoning by analogy, we take relationships, without any attributes, from one domain and argue that these relationships apply in some other domain. The relationships in chaos theory are abstract relationships between mathematical symbols of a deterministic kind and the attributes are patterns in those symbols, for example patterns called strange attractors, fractal or chaos. I have already argued that we cannot take abstract deterministic relationships as analogous to real human relationships because that would mean that humans do not exercise choice. However, we might still want to reason using metaphor. When we reason by metaphor we take the attributes of phenomena in one domain to another domain without taking the nature of the relationships. So, one could use chaos theory to provide metaphors for human interactions. For example, one might want to say that human interactions are patterned like the paradoxical patterns of mathematical chaos, strange attractors or fractals. Chaos theory, then, can only ever provide what might be experienced as provocative metaphors, which might give us some kind of poetic insight into patterns of human action.

Complex adaptive system theory

The theory of complex adaptive systems differs from chaos theory in that it reveals the properties of iterating the interaction between separate algorithms comprising a system, rather than those of iterating algorithms modelling the system as a whole. The former focuses at the micro level while the latter focuses at the macro level. I want to distinguish between two substantially different kinds of complex adaptive system simulation. The first is where the algorithms, or agents comprising the system, are all the same as each other, as for example in the Boids simulation discussed in Chapter 11 (Reynolds, 1987), and the second is where they differ from each other, as for example in the Tierra simulation discussed in Chapter 11 (Ray, 1992).

Complex adaptive systems with homogeneous agents

In some simulations of complex adaptive systems, the agents are algorithms, or computer programs, that are all the same as each other. Take Reynolds' simulation of Boids, described in Chapter 11. The system consists of a number of computer programs, each comprising the same three instructions that organise the interaction of each computer program with other programs. Each instruction is a bit string, a sequence of ones and zeros. This model, then, is a number of bit strings, symbols, that are arranged in a particular sequence specifying an agent's interaction with others. In other words, the model is simply a large number of symbol patterns. Each symbol pattern interacts with other symbol patterns. Furthermore, the algorithms or computer programs are cybernetic entities. This is so because the output of one, say its velocity in the case of the Boids, is compared with that of a neighbour, and the difference is fed back so as either to increase or to decrease its velocity. The agents in complex adaptive systems of this kind are deterministic, cybernetic algorithms.

The simulation then reveals that this interaction between each separate symbol pattern with some others yields an overall pattern in the relationship between all of them. They clump together. When each bit string is represented as a dot on the computer screen, the clumping pattern can be seen and the programmer can observe how it persists in various forms over time. Reynolds then makes an interpretation. He calls each bit string, or symbol pattern, a 'Boid' and he calls the pattern they produce 'flocking'. He makes a further interpretation when he suggests that the Boids are logically equivalent to real birds and that the model points to how real birds produce flocking behaviour. He then points to how a few simple rules can yield emergent patterns of a very complex kind, without the need for any overall blueprint to determine them. Each symbol pattern interacting with a few others at their own local level of interaction is sufficient to produce an overall pattern of relationships between them. What the iteration of their interaction reveals is the emergence of a coherent collective pattern, that is an attractor for the whole system. Such a system has no capacity to move spontaneously from one attractor to another.

Let me emphasise the point. The Boids simulation simply reveals the logical consequences of the interaction between separate symbol patterns, where each pattern is the same as all the others. The simulation demonstrates the overall pattern that unfolds, the attractor, as symbol patterns of a very specific kind interact. The attractor is enfolded, as it were, in the interacting symbol patterns and revealed by iterating their interaction. One interpretation of this phenomenon is that as soon as the symbol patterns, or rules, are specified, they imply a given reality. However, that reality cannot be logically deduced or predicted from the rules and there is no blueprint for it. It emerges. Once the program has been run, the programmer can predict that these particular symbol patterns will lead to the emergence of a particular type of overall pattern that might then be called flocking. However, the programmer cannot predict the specific qualitative form that the flocking will take as the symbol patterns interact since this depends upon the specific context in which they interact. This system of separate, interacting symbol patterns is described as a self-organising system.

But what is organising itself in the Boids simulation? Each separate Boid is a little blueprint, doing only what the program enables it to, and it is constrained by that program from doing anything else. Therefore, it cannot be they, as separate individual symbol patterns, that are organising themselves. Instead, it is the overall pattern of interaction that is organising itself because there is no blueprint for that. The pattern of interaction called flocking turns back on itself, so re-creating itself through the interaction of the separate symbol patterns and providing the context within which the separate symbol patterns interact.

There is a very important point to note about simulations, such as the Boids one, where each interacting symbol pattern is the same as all the others. This is interaction where there is no diversity amongst the symbol patterns, no non-average interaction between them, no noise, no fluctuations in Prigogine's terms. Because of this lack of diversity, the simulation cannot display spontaneous moves from one attractor to another, nor can it spontaneously generate a new attractor (Allen, 1998a, 1998b). The symbol patterns, or rules, always yield the same attractor and change can occur only when the programmer changes the individual symbol patterns.

I have made this point a number of times before in previous chapters. I repeat it here because I believe that it is very important when it comes to interpreting complexity theory in the setting of human organisations. This touches on another very important point that is worth continually emphasising, namely that any use anyone makes of a simulation is an interpretation that they are making.

Organisational interpretations

Consider how some organisational theorists interpret simulations like Boids. They use the simulation to justify the following conclusion. If a manager wants his or her organisation to produce an overall pattern, or strategy, of a highly complex kind then it is not necessary to formulate and implement an overall strategy. It is not necessary to provide a blueprint that sets out what the strategy is and how it is to be implemented. Instead, the manager should establish a few simple ground rules and this is held to unleash the power of self-organisation. In this interpretation, the manager is, without any explicit justification, equated with the programmer. Reynolds, the programmer, took the position of the objective observer, standing outside the pre-given reality of birds flocking, and induced rules that might produce flocking. He then simulated them in the computer and showed that they do produce the equivalent of flocking. This is what the manager is now supposed to do. Implicit in the prescription to formulate a few simple rules that all in the organisation are to follow is the notion that the manager must first choose which attractor he or she wants the organisation to be drawn to. The manager then has to induce the few simple rules that will produce it.

However, note the consequence of this. Suppose that the manager succeeds in identifying the right set of rules and people do follow them. Then the required attractor will indeed emerge. However, that is all that will emerge. The organisation will follow this attractor until the manager changes the rules, because a system in which the separate entities are all following the same rules does not possess the capacity for spontaneously moving to another attractor, nor does it possess the capacity to generate new attractors spontaneously. The prescription ensures that the organisation will not be creative. The only change from strategic choice theory is that the manager is now relieved from having to formulate detailed overall plans. This is not a radically different insight since it was long ago concluded that detailed long-term plans were not very helpful in turbulent times and that what managers needed to do was set the direction in the form of a few guidelines.

Now consider whether complex adaptive systems, such as the Boids one where all the agents are the same, can provide a source domain for analogies with human behaviour. The abstract relationships in such systems are relationships between cybernetic entities defined as deterministic, simple rules. It follows that such complex adaptive systems cannot provide analogies with human interaction for exactly the same reasons as chaos theory cannot. Such simulations can only ever provide metaphors that may or may not provoke thinking about human interaction.

Interpreting agent-based models with heterogeneous agents

Now consider another simulation in which the interacting algorithms (agents) do not all follow the same rules and can change from one iteration to another through random mutation and/or cross-over replication. This means that the algorithms in the population fall into different categories, so that difference is located between categories and sameness within a category. An example of this kind of system is provided by the Tierra simulation in Chapter 11.

In the Tierra simulation, Ray designs one bit string, one symbol pattern. This is not a few simple rules but 80 instructions specifying in detail how the bit string is to copy itself. He then introduces a mechanism to generate diversity. This is random mutation in the bit string and a selection criterion, namely speed of replication. He does this by limiting the computer time available for replicating and limiting the total time period over which an individual bit string has the opportunity to replicate. In other words, he designs rules to generate random mutation in, and impose constraints on, the replicating system that come from outside that system. He is imposing conditions that both enable and constrain, and in doing so, he introduces chance, or instability, into the system. This instability within constraints makes it possible for the system to generate novel attractors, as follows.

An overall pattern of interaction rapidly emerges in the form of an increase in the number of bit strings encoding the 80 instructions. The attractor is that of exponentially increasing numbers, which eventually impose a constraint on further replication. The overall pattern is continually moving from sparse occupation of the computer memory to overcrowding. The bit strings are also gradually changing through random bit flipping. In other words, they are gradually differing from each other and increasing diversity is appearing.

A new attractor

Soon, this random mutation and the selection pressure of limited computer time in the presence of large numbers provide the context for the emergence of a new attractor. This is the appearance of smaller bit strings. Now there are distinctively different kinds of bit strings, namely long ones and short ones. The constraints on computer time favour smaller ones and the overall pattern is now decline in long bit strings and increase in numbers of short ones. The system has spontaneously produced a new attractor.

New forms of individual bit string and new overall patterns have emerged at the same time. There can be no pattern of increase and decline without simultaneous change in the length of some individual bit strings. There can be no sustained change in bit string lengths without the overall pattern of increase and decline. Individual bit string patterns, and the overall pattern of the system, are forming and being formed by each other, at the same time.

Another new attractor

Later, another kind of bit string emerges, that is another symbol pattern, taking the form of instructions to read the replication code of neighbouring bit strings. Another new attractor has emerged.

At the overall level this is a pattern of fluctuating numbers of the new kind of bit string and the old kind. The new bit strings are very short and require the presence of the others in order to perform their replication task. If the short ones increase in numbers too much, then they cannot find enough partners to replicate with and so they decline. This is the new attractor that has emerged at the level of the population of bit strings as a whole. However, at the same time new kinds of bit string have emerged. The new attractor is evident both at the level of the whole population and at the level of the individual bit strings themselves at the same time.

The important point is that the programmer has not programmed the new attractors in advance. They emerge because the system is organising itself within the constraints that the programmer has set, but the programmer is not able to predict what they will be before they emerge. Once they have emerged, the programmer can of course repeat the program and the same attractors will emerge again. However, now they are not new. The new comes about through self-organisation, not design. At the start of that simulation, one algorithm copies itself to generate another algorithm of the same kind. The output of the algorithm's operation is another algorithm, not an input into its next iteration. Instead of taking a previous output as the input for the next operation, the algorithm is simply repeated, with some random mutation. Here there is no feedback; rather the algorithm refers to itself in order to operate. Exactly the same point applies to its copy. The only possibility of any change, or evolution, lies in the random mutations. In the case of cross-over replication, two algorithms produce an output that is combined to form another one. This new one is not utilised as input into the next iteration of the original two. Therefore, there is no feedback, only reference by each to itself. Now variety can arise in the system because of the mixing of code to produce another algorithm. The nature of the system, namely the scarce CPU time and the limited number of iterations allowed for each algorithm, provides a constraint on the possibility of each algorithm performing its iteration. The key point here is that the agents are different from each other and the nonlinearity of the iterating system can amplify tiny differences into major qualitative changes in global pattern. This micro-diversity is what enables the system to evolve in the sense of producing emergent, unpredictable, novel forms (Allen, 1998a, 1998b).

Note that the agents are not cybernetic entities and the interactions between them are not deterministic but evolving and that capacity for evolution arises because of the presence of micro-diversity in the interaction between entities.

Instead of using macro-level mathematical models, agent-based modellers construct computer models consisting of large numbers of interacting agents and then explore their behaviour through simulation.

The action of complex adaptive systems is explored using computer simulations in which each agent is a computer program, that is a set of interaction rules expressed as computer instructions. Since each instruction is a bit string, a sequence of symbols taking the form of 0s and 1s, it follows that an agent is a sequence of symbols, arranged in a particular pattern specifying a number of algorithms. These algorithms determine how the agent will interact with other agents, which are also arrangements of symbols. In other words, the model is simply a large number of symbol patterns arranged so that they interact with each other. *It is this local interaction between symbol patterns that organises the pattern of interaction itself* since there is no set of instructions organising the global pattern of interaction across the system. The programmer specifies the initial rules, that is, symbol patterns, and then the computer program is run, or iterated, and the patterns of interaction across the system, the attractors, are observed. Simulations of this kind repeatedly produce patterns of behaviour that are coherent and sometimes novel. In other words, the models are a demonstration of the possibility of interaction patterning itself. They provide a 'proof' of existence in the medium of digital symbols arranged into algorithmic rules.

The pattern of interaction organises itself

So, what is organising itself here? It seems to me that it is the pattern of interaction that is organising itself and doing so simultaneously at the level of the individual agents and at the level of the population as a whole. Indeed, it now seems rather problematic to separate them out as levels, since they are emerging simultaneously. They are forming while being formed at the same time. The argument for claiming this is as follows. No individual bit string can change in a coherent fashion on its own. This is because continual random mutation in an isolated bit string would eventually lead to a completely random one. In interaction with other bit strings, however, advantageous mutations are selected and the others are weeded out. What is organising itself, through interaction between symbol patterns, is then the changes in the symbol patterns themselves. Patterns of interacting are turning back on themselves, imperfectly replicating themselves, to yield changes in those patterns of interaction and this is possible only because there is a mechanism for generating diversity. New attractors can only emerge when the process of replication is imperfect.

When Ray (1992) introduces another form of generating diversity, the bit strings evolve in ways that are more complex. This other form of diversity generation is that of cross-over replication, the genetic algorithm referred to in Chapter 11. Here bit strings are mixed up in replication, so that replication is even more imperfect.

So, this simulation is very different to the Boids one. The latter displayed only one attractor and could not spontaneously move to another. The programmer had to change the symbol patterns for this to happen. In the Tierra simulation, the system does spontaneously move to other attractors and indeed spontaneously produces emergent new ones. The programmer had, however, to introduce a mechanism for generating diversity in the replication process. The model spontaneously produced a new attractor, one that had not been programmed in. In other words, new forms of individual bit string and new overall global patterns emerged at the same time, for there can be no global pattern of increase and decline without simultaneous change in the length of individual bit strings and there can be no sustained change in individual bit string lengths without the overall pattern of increase and decline. Individual bit string patterns, and the overall pattern of the system, are forming and being formed by each other, at the same time. To repeat, the new attractor is evident both at the level of the whole population and at the level of the individual bit strings themselves at the same time.

Furthermore, the new attractors are not designed but emerge as self-organisation, where it is not individual agents that are organising themselves but, rather, the pattern of interaction and it is doing so simultaneously at the level of the individual agents and at the level of the population as a whole. It is problematic to separate them out as levels, since they are emerging simultaneously. No individual bit string can change in a coherent fashion on its own since random mutation in an isolated bit string would eventually lead to a completely random one. In interaction with other bit strings, however, advantageous mutations are selected and the others are weeded out. What is organising itself, through interaction between symbol patterns, is changes in the symbol patterns themselves. Patterns of interacting are turning back on themselves, imperfectly replicating themselves, to yield changes in those patterns of interaction.

Ray, the objective observer external to this system, then interprets the changes in symbol patterns in his simulation in terms of biology. Using the model as an analogy, he points to the evolution of life and claims that life has evolved in a similar, self-organising and emergent manner. Other simulations have been used to suggest that this kind of emerging new attractor occurs only at the edge of chaos where there is a critical combination of both stability and instability.

Important points to note

Complex adaptive system models of interaction between heterogeneous algorithms present abstract nonlinear interactions between patterns of digital symbols. The abstract relationships of such models are *interactions* between patterns in digital symbols and the attributes are the *digital* nature of the symbols and the patterns of change in them. One could appeal to models of this kind as a source of metaphor for human organisations in much the same way as complex adaptive system models of the homogeneous kind or those of chaos theory. However, with models of the heterogeneous kind just discussed there is the possibility of reasoning by analogy. This is because the agents in these models are not deterministic or cybernetic but evolving, or learning. One can, therefore, explore the transfer of abstract relation-ships from the model domain to the human domain and this will require some kind of interpretation that adds human attributes. While agents in the models interact in the medium of digital symbols, humans interact in the medium of other kinds of symbols, particularly those of language.

The computer simulations demonstrate the possibility of digital symbols arranged as algorithmic rules self-organising in the dynamics at the edge of chaos to produce emergent attractors of a novel kind, provided that they those symbol patterns are richly connected and diverse enough. Natural scientists at the Santa Fé Institute and elsewhere then use this demonstration of possibility in the medium of digital symbols as a source of analogy to provide explanations of phenomena in particular areas of interest such as biology. My argument is that the abstract, non-linear, iterative relationships of heterogeneous complexity models are analogous to the interactive process of social evolution proposed by Elias.

In the subsequent chapters of Part Three, I will argue that the interaction between patterns of digital symbols described above provides an abstract analogy for human interaction, if that interaction is understood from the perspective of Elias's process sociology and also from the perspective of Mead's (1934) thought on mind, self and society.

Just what are the analogies I propose using? First, *there is no analogy between the programmer of the complex adaptive system model and anything in human interaction.* There is no possibility of standing outside human interaction to design a program for it since we are all participants in that interaction. When Ray and others use a model of complex adaptive systems to simulate life they are quite clearly trying to simulate the evolution of a process where there is no outside programmer or designer. They are trying to model self-organising and emergent phenomena in nature, that is, phenomena that evolve without design. Since, they are using a model for this purpose, they naturally have to design the model. But they do not propose any analogy in nature for the modeller of the system – on the contrary they argue that there is no designer outside nature. If one is trying to understand human organ-isations as self-organising and emergent phenomena then one cannot find an ana-logy for the programmer.

Furthermore, following the arguments of Elias, I suggest that *there is no analogy between systems and humans.* Throughout Part One, I pointed to the ways in which it is inappropriate to think of human interaction in systems terms, since that per-spective reifies what is an ongoing process and ascribes a causality to human action that does not take account of individual capacities to choose actions and does not explain the possibility of novel forms. Furthermore, the simulations of heterogen-eous complexity models begin to pose problems for systems thinking, even though they are models of systems. For example, as I have explained above, these simula-tions can be understood in a way that does not involve hierarchical levels, which is a central concept in systems thinking. Then there are problems created for that other central concept in systems thinking, namely the 'whole'. Heterogeneous com-plexity models take on a life of their own, that is, they evolve in unpredictable and novel ways. It follows that the 'whole' is not there until it has emerged and since it is always evolving it is never complete. One then has to talk about incomplete or absent wholes and this begins to undermine the usefulness of the very concept of the whole itself. The explanation of the unpredictability and the novelty has nothing to do with the 'whole'. It lies in the *intrinsic properties of the process of interaction between diverse entities*. The notion of a model that takes on a life of its own also creates problems for the use of the models. If one is modelling a phenomenon with a life of its own then the phenomenon and the model will soon diverge from each other. The usefulness of the model is then restricted to the insight it gives into the general nature of the dynamics.

With regard to human action, the *analogy begins with the interaction* of entities in the complexity models. This interaction is analogous to the kind of interweaving of individual human intentions and plans described by Elias, discussed Section 13.2. Furthermore, the *digital symbols of the complexity models are taken as analogies* for the symbols humans use to interact with each other. In other words, it is the aspects of process in the complex adaptive system models that I suggest provide analogies for human interaction, not the systemic aspects of those models. From a process point of view *there are no levels of operation*, only degrees of detail in which the phenomenon of interest is examined. Elias's description of societies forming individual minds while being formed by them at the same time is analogous to populations of algorithms forming individual algorithms while being formed by them.

Finally, the transformative causality displayed by interaction between heterogeneous entities in the complexity model is analogous to the transformative causality that Elias posits in relation to interaction between people. This represents a move away from the dual causality of the theories described in Part One to the paradoxical transformative causality of 'forming and being formed by at the same time' that will be the basis of the theory developed in the subsequent chapters of this Part.

What I hope to do in the subsequent chapters of Part Three is to explore the implications of taking a process view of human action rather than a systemic one. I want to explore what happens when organisational analogies are sought for in simulations in which there is agent diversity and hence the spontaneous capacity to change. Instead of thinking about the manager as the analogue of the programmer I would like to consider the consequences if the manager is a participant in process of relating, and human interaction is thought of, not as a system or a network, but as processes. Since humans do not always adapt to, or fit in, with each other, it might then be useful to think of human relating, not as adaptive, but as responsive. I will suggest that the human analogues for complex adaptive systems in the simulations are complex responsive processes of relating in an organisation. I will explain what I mean by this in Chapter 16.

Table 13.1 summarises the different ways in which complexity theory is used as a source domain for systems and process thinking.

Organisational interpretation

I want to return now to how most organisational theorists are using complexity theories (*see* Chapter 12). The question is how these theories of algorithmic interaction are interpreted in organisational terms to say something about organisational life.

The analogue of the algorithmic agent in a complex adaptive system is often unquestioningly taken to be an individual human being. The translation of agent as

Table 13.1   Human analogues of simulations of complex systems

Computer simulations	Systemic analogue	Process analogue
The programmer	CEO	None
The whole is a complex adaptive system	The whole is a complex adaptive system	None
Consisting of interacting digital symbols	Consisting of interacting individuals with minds	Complex responsive processes of relating between people in medium of symbols
Arranged as algorithmic rules called agents	Arranged as schemas and mental models as basis of individual as agent	Arranged as narrative and propositional themes that organise experience
Reproduced through replication with random mutation and cross-over replication	Reproduced through individual choice to change mental models	Reproduced through interaction with conflict, negation, misunderstanding and deviance as source of transformation
What organises itself is arrangements in the digital code and the pattern of the whole attractor at the same time	What organises itself is individual humans	What organises itself is themes in conversations that are individual mind and group at the same time
What emerges is rearrangement in code/attractor	What emerges is detail of action	Novelty emerges as re-patterning of conversational themes
Novelty emerges at the edge of chaos, i.e. paradox of stability and instability	Edge of chaos defined as crisis and stress	Paradoxical processes of human interaction simultaneously predictable and unpredictable, continuity and transformation
Radical unpredictability	Unpredictability played down	Radical unpredictability
Boundaries set by programmer	Boundaries set by CEO, i.e. simple rules	Constraints of power relations and dynamics of inclusion and exclusion emerge

cybernetic entity in a computer simulation to human being as a cognitive entity is all too easy to make. A rapid jump is then made to prescribing a few simple rules that all agents should follow. No account is taken of the implication. The unquestioned assumption of the primacy of the individual results in implicitly equating the manager, especially the most powerful executive, with the programmer who designs the organisation as a system. It is then deduced that, like the programmer of the simulation, the manager must introduce some mechanism for generating sufficient instability and variety and a mechanism for selection into the system. The prescriptions for introducing instability are to set stretching targets, put people under pressure and create crises. The equivalent to cross-over replication is to promote mental cross-fertilisation through cross-functional contacts and multidisciplinary team working. The selection mechanism is increased competition between individuals and groups. Having put these mechanisms in place managers are then supposed to leave the teams to operate in what is called a self-organising way. The factor that receives little serious attention is that the new behaviours that will emerge are unpredictable according to the very complexity theory these writers are using to justify their prescriptions.

The problem, as I see it, lies with the equation of manager and programmer and with the equation of the organisation with a system. In other words, the problem is with the notion of the objective observer and with the whole idea of applying systems thinking to human action. What the agent-based modellers are trying to show is how a complex system operating within enabling constraints has the capacity to organise itself, from within itself, into emergent new attractors. They are trying to point to the plausibility of novelty emerging in the absence of a design or a designer. Of course, they cannot avoid some initial designing activity themselves because they are dealing with computers and not the reality they are trying to model. However, if an organisational theorist is trying to keep to the spirit of what they are trying to do, namely understand the internal capacity of a system to produce novelty spontaneously, then it is necessary to avoid equating the chief executive, or any other manager, with the programmer. Instead, all managers, no matter how powerful, need to be understood as participant. Furthermore, as individuals with at least some degree of choice, they cannot be understood as parts of a system, nor can their organisations be understood as systems.

13.4   The difference between systems thinking and process thinking

The kind of process thinking outlined in this chapter is completely different from systems thinking, starting with the meaning of process. Systems thinkers use the word process to mean the interaction of parts of a system to produce that system, whether that system be real or a mental construct. In human terms this amounts to the assumptions that in their interaction, people either actually produce a system or they understand their interaction as a system. In process thinking, the interaction between people is understood to produce further interaction between them. In process thinking people are not thought of as parts producing a system but as people in relationships producing relationships, which produce them at the same time. In the kind of process thinking I am talking about there is no notion of system at all.

There is also no notion of hierarchical levels in human action. Instead of thinking that individuals produce society as another level, which shapes their identities, individual identities and the social are thought of as the same processes. In process thinking, people interacting are intrinsically social and what they produce is further interaction with widespread patterns, not some higher-level system or whole. In systems thinking, emergence relates to levels in that interaction at one level produces an emergent system at another level. In process thinking, relationships are emerging in relationships and the question of levels does not even arise.

It follows that there is no notion of a 'whole' in process thinking and no notion of boundaries around human interaction. The key concepts of systems thinking, namely wholes and boundaries, are thus completely absent in process thinking. While systems thinking is holistic, process thinking is not. It focuses attention not on abstract wholes but on the actual micro, local interaction between people in the living present.

Process and systems ways of thinking differ because they are based on completely different theories of causality. Systems thinking assumes a dual causality: the rationalist causality of the autonomous individual applies to the human observer or designer of the system and human thinking about the system, while formative causality applies to the operation of the system. The system unfolds what is enfolded in it so that the future is in a sense already there. The systems that humans produce in their interaction emerge as a higher level than the individuals and those higher levels have their own causative powers. The system produced in interaction acts back on that interaction as formative cause. For example human interaction is said to produce social structures or cultural systems that then cause the actions of individuals. Novelty cannot be explained in systemic terms, only in individual-centred terms. In process thinking the theory of causality is unitary and transformative in that patterns of interaction emerge as continuity and potential transformation in the iteration of interaction itself. The future is thus under perpetual construction in the interaction between people and it is the process of interaction between differences that amplifies these differences into novelty. The explanation of novelty lies in the properties of the processes of interaction. The individual and the social are at the same level. There is nothing above, below, behind or in front of interaction exercising any causal power on it. Instead of thinking in terms of dualism, process thinking is conducted in terms of paradox and dialectic.

It can be seen immediately that systems thinking and process thinking make completely different assumptions about human psychology. Systems thinking is based on the individualistic psychologies of cognitivism, constructivism, humanistic psychology or psychoanalysis, while process thinking takes a relationship, social perspective on individual psychology, a point that will be explained in Chapter 14.

Systems thinking is based upon a spatial metaphor of inside and outside. It is built upon a linear notion of time in which the past is factually given, the future is yet to be unfolded and the present is simply a point dividing the two. Process thinking avoids any spatial notion of inside and outside and takes a circular, paradoxical view of time. This means that the past is not actually given but is being reiterated, retold in the present in the light of the expectations people are forming in the present for the future. Expectations for the future are affecting how the stories of the past are being retold and those stories are affecting expectations for the future, all in the present. In a sense the future is changing the past just as the retelling of the past is changing the future, all in the present. The present is thus living in the sense that it has a time structure incorporating both the past and the future.

Participation also means something completely different. In systems thinking people are thought to participate in a system, a whole. In process thinking, participation means direct interaction between people in local situations in the living present.

In current critical systems thinking, much stress is laid on the need for pluralism. This is the notion that people should approach problem situations from a number of different perspectives. The metaphor of a lens is often used. People are thought to be able to change the lens, the perspective through which they view what is going on. The individual mind is thus thought of as being capable of some kind of self-engineering. Individuals can change the way they see the world. It will become clearer in Chapter 14 why this is not seen as a possibility in process thinking. Briefly, this is because the meaning of any action depends not simply on the individual making it but on the response it calls forth from others. Meaning is not located in an individual mind but in the recognition and counter-recognition of people in interaction with each other. Since meaning is thus continually arising in relationships it becomes impossible to think of any individual unilaterally deciding to see things first in this way and then in that way. Furthermore, in process thinking, meaning and identity, who one is, are intimately intertwined. To say that one can simply see the world first in one way and then in another is tantamount to saying that one can easily change who one is, first to this and then to that.

The shift from systems thinking to process thinking also entails a different way of thinking about theory and practice.

Theory and practice

First consider how theory and practice are thought about from the perspective of, say, soft systems thinking. People facing a problem situation are advised to come together and construct a rich picture of their problem situation, that is, the world in which they understand themselves to be operating. Then they are encouraged to abstract some aspects of their rich description in order to formulate systems models of their problem situation (*see* Chapter 9). In other words, they select a number of features of their descriptions of their situation and understand these features as interconnected parts producing some purposive whole with boundaries around it. For example, the whole could be a framework of ideas, a set of values, a grouping of participants or a system of interests. When they do this, systems-aware people are not saying that the real world is a system. They are saying that they are forming systemic mental constructions of their world and using these models to facilitate their discussion. They are then doing exactly what Kant recommends as a way of thinking about nature. They are taking the position of autonomous individuals who have the capacity for making choices about goals, what they will attend to and what they will not. Also they are formulating hypotheses in the form of 'as if', regulative ideas about the purposive movement of their postulated system. This conceptual system must be subject to formative cause because it can only unfold what has been designed into, or hypothesised about it. So, soft systems thinkers are not claiming that the world is a system but they are thinking about it as if it were a system following a purpose that they have ascribed to it. Each person involved in the problem situation will draw out a different systemic perspective and all must be taken into account. This inevitably means positing a system that is understood as a context within which the observing autonomous individuals act. The problem comes when this procedure is applied to the observing autonomous humans themselves because if we are to think of ourselves in terms of systems, then each of us must in some way be a part of the system we are mentally constructing. So we will then have to think of ourselves in terms of two causalities between which we alternate, namely, the causality of freedom when we are hypothesising and formative causality, in which there is no freedom, relating to what we have formulated hypotheses about. The problem is that it is ourselves that we are hypothesising about and so we are ascribing two completely different forms of causality to ourselves.

This way of thinking amounts to saying that in our interaction with each other we are creating conceptual wholes as a context within which to make sense of our direct experience of interaction. We make sense by thinking that these constructed wholes are acting back on us and causing our interaction. As soon as one talks about people constructing a system one implies two different causalities, one for the constructor and another for the constructed. Soft and critical systems thinkers do not claim that people actually do form wholes in their interactions with each other. But they are proposing to explain what they are doing as if they were forming wholes so the theory or explanation is, potentially at least, different from the experience of direct interaction.

We have come to make distinctions between acting, doing or practising, on the one hand, and accounting, explaining and theorising, on the other. But what do we mean by acting, doing and practising? These words refer to performances of bodies. In times past it may well have made sense to differentiate between bodily performances involving the manipulation of physical things in problem situations and bodily performances involving the manipulation of sound as in talking, with the former designated as action or practice and the latter as accounting or theorising. However, in the age we now live in, most of us spend most of our time in communicative interaction with others. The distinction between different kinds of bodily performance hardly matters now because talking is doing, explaining our actions is acting, and accounting for our practice is practice. When we come to talk to each other about what we have just done or might do, so accounting for our practice, we are not doing anything significantly different from what we have just done or might do as practice.

The important point is that there are different ways in which can now talk together about what we have just done or might do next. We can talk together employing systems tools with the result that we focus our attention on the systems tools themselves. In doing this we implicitly distinguish between, on the one hand, what we are now doing in our explaining, theorising or accounting as using systems tools, and on the other hand, what we were doing or might do in our acting, doing or practising as the experience of direct interaction. As a result, our current mode of talking is not the same as it was or will be in what we refer to as our practice because we are now constructing rich pictures and extracting systemic models, which is not how we normally go about interacting with each other. We normally talk to each other, shaping and being shaped by the themes emerging in our talking. We do not normally talk to each other, in ordinary, everyday conversations, in terms of rich pictures and systemic models. The systemic mode of explaining focuses our attention on wholes, interaction between parts producing wholes and boundaries around wholes. But this it not how we proceed in an ordinary, everyday way in which decisions on what to do next are emerging between us in conversational processes.

On the other hand, we can now talk together about what we have just been doing or might do in the future in a process way and this focuses our attention on the conversational processes themselves without constructing pictures or extracting models. Instead, we carry on communicating now in much the same way as we were communicating in what we have just been doing and will continue to communicate in what we might 'do' next. In other words, we carry on in conversational ways to make sense of what we were doing in ordinary conversational ways and will carry on doing in conversational ways. The processes of our current explaining and our past or future doing are much the same, although we might be using different terminologies. We focus on the experience of the thematic patterning of our recent and prospective interactions and the way it is emerging in a narrative way and in so doing the narrative continues to evolve. It then makes no sense to ask what we will be doing differently in our practice as a result of our explanation or theory because we are now already 'doing' differently. When we are exploring together what we have been doing, or what we are now doing, in everyday life we are gesturing and responding, that is, interacting communicatively just as we were when we were doing what we were doing. We are now simply doing more of the same in process terms although we may, of course, be using different words. It is distracting for us now to hypothesise that what we were doing had the quality of some whole when this was not what we were doing in the ordinary way of things.

From the perspective of complex responsive processes, to be developed in Chapters 14 to 17, theory and practice are, therefore, thought of in a way that is different to systems thinking. Instead of separating theory and practice, the process perspective is a theory of the *unity of theory and practice*. Consider how this is so. Instead of starting with a problem situation as the focus of attention, as systems thinkers do, it is people communicating and relating to each other in conversations and other forms of interaction that is the focus of attention. What they are doing is evoking and provoking responses from each other. In doing so they are creating their reality, including their very identities. These identities emerge as continuity and potential transformation. What is emerging is always thematic patterning and all that emerges is thematic patterning. Interaction patterns itself and does not construct anything other than thematic patterns in itself. So we are not talking about people coming to a special type of discussion about an identified problem situation and constructing rich pictures or anything else, for even then the conversational processes are still going on. Instead we are focusing attention on the way in which people are constructing the everyday patterning of their interactions with each other in the course of which problem situations arise and in their resolution trigger yet other problem situations in endless iteration. People are forming patterns of interaction while being formed by them. This is what one means by practice from a complex responsive process perspective. It is simply what we are doing together and we do not do something and then try to explain it as if the explaining were a different kind of activity to doing. We are explaining as we are doing. In fact explaining is doing.

When, in an ordinary way, we explain or make sense of our practice in retrospect, we do not construct some conceptual whole outside of the experience of interaction. Instead the process of explaining is simply a continued iteration of what we were doing in the so-called practice. The subsequent interaction is the same process as the interaction being explained. The explanation is also a conversational process of evoking and provoking responses in which thematic patterning is emerging. There is no construction of conceptual wholes, only the continuing emergence of themes of meaning. So in our explaining of our recently experienced interaction we could say to each other, 'let us now hypothesise what was going on between us as a whole with boundaries and then explore how this whole affected us'. Or we could point to aspects of the themes that are now emerging in stories about our previous interaction, and as we do so other themes will continue to emerge. What we are now doing as we together explore what we were doing in the past or what we might be doing in the future is the same process of communication or power relating as we were or might be doing. What system thinkers are suggesting is that what we are now doing, that is making hypotheses, is different from what we were or might be doing. In positing some whole we are pointing to something outside of the process going on now. As soon as you think in systems terms you are thinking of autonomous individuals making hypotheses, that is, you bring in cognitivist psychology. The theory of complex responsive processes talks about forming and being formed. It implies a different psychology or sociology.

When we now explain, theorise or talk about what we have done or will do, we are interacting with each other and themes are now emerging just as they did (or will do) when we were doing or will be doing what we are now talking about. The causality is the same now as it was then and will be later. This is transformative causality in which themes are emerging characterised by continuity and potential transformation and it applies to all our forms of doing, including theorising. There is no dual causality because the identity of the observing participant is emerging in the observing participation. There is the same spontaneity now as there was then and will be in the future. In this approach there is no notion of anyone observing the 'whole' and making hypotheses about it. When I enunciate a hypothesis about our interaction, I am simply making a gesture as everyone else is doing and this calls forth some response just as everyone else's does. I am then observing and participating at the same time. In systems thinking, however, we posit the 'there' as a system we identify or design and so formative causality must apply to it. However, this causality cannot apply to our acts of identification and design because otherwise we cannot explain how we can choose. The spontaneity is located in the observer and not in the system. In this 'both . . . and' structure, observation (identifying and designing the system) is separate from participation (the system) and separate causalities apply to them.

The move from systems thinking to process thinking, then, is not a move from one way of accounting for practice to another way of accounting for practice. It is, rather, a transformation in theory-practice, which means focusing differently on what we are doing and the act of focusing differently is itself change. In focusing differently we are already doing differently. The concern is not with what we should be doing in the future but with what we are doing now as we iterate our pasts in expectation of our futures. In thinking like this we are paying attention to our local interactions rather than trying to be comprehensive and we are focusing upon the wider process of communicative interaction between us rather than just on specific problem situations.

● ● ● ● 13.5 Summary

This chapter has presented arguments for interpreting the relevance of complexity theories for organisations from a process perspective.

Process thinking involves moving away from any form of systems thinking when it comes to human action. The key properties of complex adaptive systems to be used as analogies for complex responsive processes of human relating in the rest of this Part of the book are:

- The intrinsic patterning properties of interaction as self-organisation or emergence.
- The paradoxical dynamic of simultaneously predictable and unpredictable interaction.
- The importance of connectivity and diversity in the dynamic at the edge of chaos and how this is essential to the emergence of novelty.
- The emergence of continuity and transformation at the same time.

If these aspects of abstract relationships in computer simulations are taken as analogies for human relating, the consequences are:

- Focusing attention on the detailed local interaction between diverse people in the living present as patterning of experience, emergent identity and transformation.
- This means communicative interaction in the form of conversation and how it patterns experience in narrative-like forms. This emphasises the importance of the informal and the narrative rather than the prescriptive and instrumental.
- The importance of conflicting constraints emerging as power and the dynamics of inclusion and exclusion and the links to how people deal with anxiety.
- The simultaneous emergence of continuity and novelty, creation and destruction, in the iteration of nonlinear interaction and its amplification of small changes.

I will be arguing that a perspective along these lines forms a coherent way of thinking that directs attention to the narrative forms of human experience. The focus is on lived experience in local situations in the present, paying particular attention to the diversity of relationships within which individual and organisational identities emerge.

Further reading

The arguments presented in this chapter are explored in Stacey, Griffin and Shaw (2001). Further information on the differences between Kantian and Hegelian thinking can be found in Ameriks (2002).

Chapter 14 ● ● ● ●

Strategy as the emergence of organisational identity

14.1 Introduction

The last chapter referred to Elias's explanation of how individual personality structures and society emerge simultaneously and evolve over long periods of time. The organisations of both personality and social structures emerge together in the intertwining of individual plans and intentions but those structures themselves are not planned – they emerge without overall intention. The last chapter also argued that abstract heterogeneous models of complex interaction could be regarded as a source domain for analogies with the human interaction that Elias talked about. These abstract models provide us with insight into the general nature of the dynamics of interaction. The abstract complexity models simulate interaction between entities and demonstrate how change in both the entities themselves and the widespread patterns of their interaction emerge in self-organising processes of interaction. Self-organisation here means local interaction proceeding without any overall blueprint governing that interaction.

Elias's process sociology is also, at the same time, a theory of individual psychology, simply because individual and social identities are emerging at the same time. This, however, is a psychology that differs markedly from those that were reviewed in Part One. The latter were based on the individual and accorded primacy to the individual whereas the Eliasian theory does not. The purpose of this chapter is to explore the kind of relationship psychology that forms the basis of Elias's thinking. The concern is with how one might think about the individual and the group and about how the organisations of both emerge at the same time in the interaction between individuals. What I will be doing here is describing the theory of complex responsive processes.

If one adopts this approach, then one comes to think about an organisation's strategy in a very different way to the theories described in Part One. Strategy comes to be understood as the evolving patterns of an organisation's identity. Strategy is about what an organisation does, what it is, and this is exactly what identity means. Strategy is about the evolution of what an organisation does and how it becomes what it becomes. In other words, it is about the evolution of organisational identity. It is about the recognition of the community that the organisation serves and how this recognition evolves. Strategy as the identity of an organisation is continuously constructed and enacted in the interaction of organisational practitioners. The question then becomes just how human futures are perpetually constructed. From the perspective of complex responsive processes, the future is perpetually constructed in the ordinary, everyday relating between human bodies in local situations in the living present. The next section explores the theory of human psychology that underlies this view.

●●●● 14.2 The individual and the group

Chapter 3 described how the cognitivist approach to understanding human behaviour placed the individual as prior to, and primary over, the group, so that groups are seen as collectives formed by individuals. Those collectives might then affect how individuals behave. There is no notion of individual minds being somehow constructed in group relationships. Chapter 7 described some psychoanalytic perspectives. These also give primacy to the individual in that inherited drives provide the energy and the motivation for behaviour. However, psychoanalysis does see individual minds as emerging from the clash between inherited drives, or inherent fantasies, and the external reality of the group. Once again, groups consist of individuals but from this perspective their minds are structured by the clash between their inheritance and the conformity required by the group. Furthermore, the individual's behaviour, indeed his or her thinking capacity, is affected by the group context. Groups play a far more important role from this perspective than they do from a cognitivist one.

There are other perspectives that ascribe much more importance to the role of the group in creating individual minds. These are social constructionism (Gergen, 1982, 1985, 1991; Harre, 1983, 1986; Shotter, 1993), intersubjectivity theory in psychoanalysis (Atwood and Stolorow, 1984; Stolorow, Atwood and Brandschaft, 1994) and group-analytic perspectives (Dalal, 1998). All three of these approaches see relationship as primary in some sense but they often take a systemic perspective in that they use the spatial metaphor of mind inside a person and the social as a system outside the person. In relating to each other people create, and are created by, their social reality. Here the mind is not structured by a clash between an inherited, internal force and an external reality. Instead, mind is seen as emerging in relationship, taking the form of a phenomenon between them. Mental phenomena, including the sharing of meaning with others, all arise in social, or group, relationships, although they may be experienced as phenomena pertaining to the individual. It is this kind of perspective that I want to describe in this section.

From this perspective, genetics and biology create the potential for the fundamental human attribute, namely the need, and the capacity, to form social relationships. However, it is the experience of relating that actualises this potential in terms of unique individual minds, thoughts and behaviours and the capacity to resonate to a common meaning and hold similar beliefs. In the tradition of Hegel, the sociologist G. H. Mead (1934) argued that an individual mind is the silent conversation and private role-play of an individual body with itself, equivalent to social processes.

Silent, private conversations

Behaviourist psychology focused on the behaviour of the isolated individual, explicitly excluding any mental phenomena and implicitly excluding the importance of social relations between individuals. From this perspective behaviour is the response of the individual to a stimulus, and whether the stimulus is provided by a thing or another human matters little. The meaning here lies in the stimulus, for if it rewards, the human responds in one way, and if it punishes, the human responds in another way.

Mead argues that humans cannot be understood in isolation and that the phenomenon of mind cannot simply be ignored. He explains the phenomenon of mind in the context of the evolution of the human animal and its emergence in behaviour, but social rather than isolated individual behaviour. The fundamental unit of analysis then becomes the social act: that is, not simply a stimulus or a response but both together. This is important because, for all social organisms, other organisms provide most of the stimuli to which each organism responds and each response is itself the stimulus to yet other responses. Mead held that the meaning of a stimulus lies not only in the stimulus itself but also in the response to it, where stimulus and response are both aspects of one social act. Most stimuli are gestures made by one animal and most responses are returned gestures made by another animal. The stimulus calls forth the response and the meaning lies in this response. For example, one dog may approach another and bite it and this may call out a violent response in the other. This social act then means aggression, attack and anger. Alternatively, the first dog might bite the second in a manner that calls forth the response of a counter-nip. The meaning of this social act is then play. The stimulus on its own is not sufficient to establish what the meaning is. The gesture, then, is the first phase of an act. It carries with it the attitude of the one making the gesture, that is the emotion that underlies it. The gesture means this attitude and it calls forth the response of the other.

In this way Mead shows how all social animals communicate with each other through a conversation of gestures, movement, touch, sound, visual display and odour. At this point, however, while there is meaning, there is no mind or consciousness. Mead argues that mind evolved in humans when they came to use vocal gestures more and more. This is because the vocal gesture, more than any other, can be experienced by the one making it in the same way as it is experienced by the recipient. We cannot see the facial expressions we are making to another but we can hear the sounds we make just as they do. This opens up the possibility that the vocal gesture can call forth the same response in the one making it as in the other. This then becomes what Mead calls a significant symbol because it means the same thing to the maker of the gesture and the recipient.

It is now possible for the maker of the gesture to be aware, in advance, of the likely response of the recipient. The maker of the gesture is, thus, conscious and can think; that is, hypothesise likely responses to a gesture. The maker of the gesture now has a mind. Mind means being conscious of the possible consequences of actions and exploring them, in advance of action, by means of a silently conducted conversation of gestures in the form of significant symbols. The maker of the gesture has a mind in the sense that he or she can have some notion of the consequence of his or her actions, can think, can reflect.

All of this is possible only because of the evolution of significant vocal symbols, that is language. Mead is at pains to stress that he is providing an explanation of how a gesture can come to call forth the same response (meaning or idea) in the one making it as in the one receiving it. He is saying that meaning is shared through social relationships conducted in significant symbols. The shared meaning arises, and continually re-arises, in the conversation of gestures, in the action and inter-action. Meaning is not something that is going on in a mind or that even requires a mind. Mind is silent conversation, the action of a body directed to itself, which is private meaning, or consciousness. The silent conversation is the same process as the conversation of gestures between bodies and in this sense mind is always a social phenomenon. Mead's theory of mind is also firmly linked to the body because mind as a silent conversation of gestures requires a body. Although the use of language has been stressed, this is not the only form of communication between human bodies. The non-verbal gestures between people are also extremely important.

Reflexivity and self-consciousness

The explanation of mind as conscious thinking in the form of a private silent conver-sation is one based on reflexivity. This is so in the sense that the conversation is about the response one's own stimulus is calling out in one's self as well as in the other. This kind of reflexivity gives humans consciousness but not yet self-consciousness. To become self-conscious one must, as a subject, become an object to oneself, a further reflexivity.

Mead explains the process that makes this possible. To be an object to them-selves, an individual man or woman must experience themselves from the stand-point of others; they must talk to themselves as others talk to them. This happens as they learn to take up the roles of others in a form of role-plays with themselves, eventually becoming able to take the position of the whole group. They move from taking the attitude of specific individuals towards themselves to taking the attitude of the whole group towards themselves. Mead calls this taking the attitude of the 'generalised other'. When he or she does this, the individual here takes the attitude of the whole community towards himself or herself, as well as the attitude of others towards herself or himself and the attitude of others towards each other. It is through this generalised other that the community exerts control over the individ-ual. This is a social process and is possible only in language. It follows that the self is a social construction and only animals that possess language can possess a self. This does not mean that an individual cannot have the solitary experience of a self. One can never start life as a hermit, but once having evolved a self one can go off and be a hermit.

Note here how in this theory, the social is not a constraint and the mind or self does not emerge out of a clash between something that is already there in the individual and that constraint. Mind is emerging in social relationships and it is itself in pro-cesses of relating. It needs to be stressed that this is a very different notion of mind to that in cognitivism, humanistic psychology and psychoanalysis. The individual mind is not primary and prior to the group. Instead, the individual mind and the web of relationships that are a group are emerging simultaneously. Individuals are forming and being formed by the group at the same time. There never was a time when there was just an individual, nor was there ever a time when there was just a group. Both have to be there at the same time. The individual is social to the core (Foulkes, 1948). The individual is the singular, while the group is the plural of the same phenomenon, relationship (Elias, 1978, 1989).

Language, ideology and power

Elias (1978, 1989) also held that human beings were born with an inherited, instinctual nature, but as a constraining potential rather than a determining force. Humans are enabled to see and hear what they do because of this inherited potential and that inheritance also constrains them from seeing or hearing in any other way. Like Maturana and Varela (1987), and like Mead (1934), Elias emphasised the selecting or enacting nature of biology and evolution.

Part of the inheritance is a species-specific set of reactions and symbols, such as smiling and grimacing. Another part is the capacity for learning that breaks the rigid link between instinct and behaviour. The key element in this capacity to learn is the ability to develop a community-specific symbol system in addition to the species-specific one. The community-specific symbol system is, of course, language. Elias was of the view that symbols do not represent the world but are rather a medium of social orientation in the world and to the self. He also claimed that experience was multidimensional and could not be reduced to symbols. Symbols allowed humans to take a view of their world that was somewhat detached and could have some distance from their fears, but only somewhat. Experience was always invested with emotion to some extent. Elias defined the human mind in terms of the capacity to utilise symbols to explore potential reactions to an action before undertaking that action. He also stressed the use of language and symbols of all kinds in the elaboration of private fantasies.

He saw people interacting with each other through the use of both species- and community-specific symbols to form what he called figurations. By figuration, he meant the pattern of interdependence, a kind of order. These figurations were formed by the competitive and co-operative relationships between people and reflected power disparities between individuals and groupings of them. Relationships constrain and constraint is what power is about. Note how power is located in the relationship. It is not simply one individual imposing his or her will on another. Power relations are co-created. Elias pointed to how particular uses of symbols, particular ways of talking, could be used to signal and enhance power:

> *By figuration we mean the changing pattern created by the players as a whole – not only by their intellects but also by their whole selves, the totality of their dealings in their relationships with each other. It can be seen that this figuration forms a flexible lattice-work of tensions. The interdependence of the players, which is a prerequisite of their forming a figuration, may be an interdependence of allies or of opponents. (1978, p. 130)*

In this way, people are emotionally bound together through the medium of symbols. (p. 137)

So, figuration is the pattern of bonding, that is the web of interdependence, between people upon which human existence utterly depends. Individuals cannot develop, and having developed they can only rarely exist, outside a web of relationships. The immediate consequence of such interdependence is that the behaviour of every individual is constrained by the demands of others. Constraints are what power is about and as soon as one sees this, it becomes clear that figurations are structured by power. What Elias is presenting here is a clearly self-referential, reflexive process in which individual minds are formed by power relationships while they are, at the same time, forming those power relationships. He writes about these processes in a way that shows how he thought about them as self-organising processes that produced emergent patterns in themselves. He was very alive to the paradoxical nature of the processes he was describing. For example, he defines individuals as interdependent people in the singular and he defines society as interdependent people in the plural, so emphasising the point that he sees individual and society as two aspects of the same phenomenon.

Elias then explains how the interdependence between people in a figuration is expressed in symbolic form. He insists that language, reason and knowledge, speaking, thinking and knowing are different words for exactly the same phenomenon: they all have to do with handling symbols. For him, language is not a tool used to express a thought because a thought is already in language. Thinking is born of concrete activity that takes place between people. It is because people are interdependent that they must communicate if they are to survive and the means of communication is language. Language, therefore, expresses the power relations of the social figuration. Language orients one in the world – that is, it is knowledge – and its themes organise experience. Elias equates mind with silent conversation, just as Mead did before him, and mind, therefore, emerges in social relationships. In fact mind is the same process as social relating and is, therefore, just as much structured by power relationships as social figurations are.

Ideology and the preservation of power relations

One of the principal ways in which power differentials are preserved is the use of differences to stir up hatred (Elias and Scotson, 1994). It is not that a racial or religious difference generates hatred of itself, but rather that such differences are used to stir up hatred in the interests of sustaining power positions. Elias and Scotson studied the events following the influx of a working-class group into a new housing estate adjacent to an older estate, also occupied by working-class people. Although there was no material difference between the two groups, hostility soon appeared in which the older inhabitants denigrated the newer ones.

Elias and Scotson explained this in terms of the cohesion that had emerged over time in the already established group of inhabitants. They had come to think of themselves as a 'we', a group with common attachments, likes, dislikes and attributes that had emerged simply because of the passage of time. They had developed a 'we' identity, which is an important aspect of everyone's 'I' identities. The new arrivals lacked this cohesive identity because they had no history of being together and this made them more vulnerable. The more cohesive group therefore found it easy to 'name' the newcomers and ascribe to them hateful attributes such as being dirty or liable to commit crimes.

So, although there was no obvious difference between the two groups, one group used the fact that the other was newly arrived to generate hatred and so maintain a power difference. This was, in a sense, 'accepted' by the newcomers who took up the role of the disadvantaged. Dalal (1998) points to this as an unconscious social process. The hatred between the groups emerged from an essentially self-organising process that no one was really aware of or actually intended.

Another, and closely related, way in which power differentials are preserved is through the use of what Elias and Scotson called the 'weapon' of ideology, also an unconscious process that emerges in a self-organising way. A key aspect of ideology is the binary oppositions that characterise it and the most basic of these is the distinction between 'them' and 'us'. Dalal (1998) links this tendency to set up binary opposites to the structure of language itself. Humans categorise or partition experience in order to deal with it and this act of naming is intrinsically binarising: the deep structure of language is a binary logic in that things are categorised as 'A' or 'not-A'. There seems to be an inevitable tendency, as humans frame their experience, to binarise and polarise it. Dalal argues that the very act of naming or categorising inevitably binarises and polarises an experience and at the same time the process of thinking makes the experience both heterogeneous and homogeneous. So, when some in a group are named 'British', the others all become 'not-British', and symmetrical thinking is immediately applied to both 'British' and 'not-British' in that homogeneity is imposed on each group. Within each group the differences between members are obliterated and the fact that this is being done is unconscious.

Dalal then makes a very important point about identity and difference. At the centre of identity there is an unconscious symmetry that cannot be tested without destroying that identity. He links this with discourse. Within each discourse there are certain categories taken to be natural, the equivalent of identities, and these are homogenised and so hidden from questioning. What is being made unconscious is the power differential. People cluster around their similarity to hide the difference of power. I will return to these points about power, ideology and the social unconscious in Chapter 16 when I talk about 'shadow' relationships.

Ideology is thus a form of conversation that preserves the current order by making it seem natural and in this way, just like all other conversation, it organises the experience and behaviour of the group. As a form of conversation, as an aspect of the power relations in the group, ideology is taken up as that silent conversation which is mind in individuals. It is important to note how these authors are talking about ideology as a mutually constructed conversation that is continually repeated, not a 'thing' that is shared or stored. The ideology exists only in the speaking of it.

Elias and Scotson point to how ideology emerges in self-organising processes of gossip. Streams of gossip stigmatise and blame the outsider group while similar streams of gossip praise the insider group. The gossip builds layer upon layer of value-laden binary pairs such as clean–dirty, good–bad, honest–dishonest, energetic–lazy and so on. The result of the gossip is to attribute 'charisma' to the powerful and 'stigma' to the weak. In this way the power differences are reinforced. In established, cohesive groups, streams of gossip flow along well-established channels that are lacking for newly arrived groups. The stigmatisation, however, only sticks where there is already a sufficiently large power difference. Again these are social relations that are taken up as the silent conversation of mind, conferring feelings of superiority on the powerful and feelings of inferiority on the weak.

Elias, therefore, introduces a fundamental aspect of social relationships, namely the constraints they impose on members of a group and, thus, the power differentials they create. He points to a basic social impulse, namely to maintain power differentials, and how this is exercised by using any difference between groups to arouse the hatred needed to preserve power. He links this to the role of ideology, which categorises groups into binary opposites, making power-preserving behaviour feel natural. He identifies how that form of conversation known as gossip plays a central role in constantly reinforcing the ideology and so preserving power differences. What Elias has done, therefore, is put power, ideology and emotion at the centre of social relationships and therefore at the centre of conversation. All of these factors will, thus, characterise the silent conversations individuals have with themselves. Minds too will be taken up with power relationships, ideological and emotional interchanges of a body with itself, some of which will be the voices of group opinion.

Elias's analysis extends Mead's notion of mind as silent conversation. Elias places great emphasis on fantasy, the propensity of individuals to elaborate silent conversation in highly imaginative ways. Individuals do not simply take 'real' social relationships into their private, silent conversations with themselves. Whatever is so taken in is subjected to a process of elaboration that can rapidly diverge from external conversations and actions. Of course, those private elaborations may well find expression in public gestures, so evoking responses in others in the same way as any other gesture.

Unconscious processes

Elias talks about the automatic, self-compulsive nature of self-control instilled in individuals brought up in the kind of society that has evolved in the West, in which so much is banished behind the scenes. The impact of charisma on one group and stigmatisation on another and how this is tied up with the evolution of 'we' and 'I' identities are all processes that are largely unconscious. This is both social and individual at the same time as are the unconscious ways in which ideology sustains power relations in shifting dynamics of inclusion and exclusion. The same applies to that constellation of processes to do with shame, anxiety, inclusion or exclusion and aggression, all of which are destructive of social and individual mental life. Throughout, these unconscious processes are simultaneously individual and social, as is conscious communicative interaction and power relating.

The main point I am trying to make is that mind is silent conversation. If this is so, mind must be organised in much the same way as ordinary everyday conversations between people are organised. Mental processes must, therefore, be equivalent to conversational processes. There is only one difference. Public conversation between people requires vocalisation that is directed towards other people with the purpose of evoking responses from them. The private conversation that is mind is silent gestures of the body to itself, one 'voice' evoking responses from others. Public conversation discloses to others, while private conversation conceals from others, at least initially. However, in terms of nature and structure, public and private conversation, it seems to me, must be equivalent. Understanding the nature of ordinary, everyday conversation then becomes crucial to an understanding of human behaviour, of group processes and of organisations.

How conversation constructs social realities

Bakhtin wrote in the 1920s and, after a long period of official banishment during the Stalinist regime, again in the 1950s and 1960s. His thinking bears some striking similarities to that of Mead and Elias, although as far as I know he was not aware of their work, nor they of his. As for Mead and Elias, so for Bakhtin, all social phenomena are constructed in the ongoing dialogical relationships between people. He stressed the multiplicity of discourses, symbolising practices and speech genres that are to be found in any culture. He talked about language as simultaneously structuring and being structured by people so that individuals were not simply the effects of social relations but nor were social relations simply the sum of individuals.

Bakhtin stressed the unpredictable and unfinished nature of dialogue and its capacity to produce the novel:

> *An utterance is never just a reflection or an expression of something already existing and outside it that is given and final. It always creates something that never existed before, something absolutely new and unrepeatable, and moreover, it always has some relation to value.* (Bakhtin, 1986, pp. 119–20)

He also stressed the paradoxical, tension-filled nature of dialogue. The tension was between centripetal forces seeking expression in unity, merging, agreement and monologue, on the one hand, and centrifugal forces seeking expression in multiplicity, separating, disagreement and dialogue, on the other. These forces that characterise dialogue account for the emergence of official ideologies: centrifugal forces push towards unity and order giving voice to particular beliefs while the centripetal forces of multiplicity and diversity come to be denied expression. This is the point about power again. Power relations determine which words can be used officially and which can only be used unofficially.

Official and unofficial ideologies

Bakhtin paints a picture of official ideological unity on the surface that covers over a multiplicity of unofficial ideologies. He places considerable emphasis on what he calls 'carnival' as the process that subverts the official ideology and is thus a force for change. By carnival he means humour and parody, the grotesque and the sensuous, all of which are means of turning the official ideology on its head. Bakhtin saw this as a non-violent process of change. Carnival stands for the processes that create the conditions of fluidity and ambiguity that are required if change is to occur. It may be argued that carnival is not a good metaphor because carnivals are officially sanctioned and that what they actually do is allow people to discharge emotion so working to sustain the official ideology. It seems to me that the grotesque, the humorous and the sensuous could work either to sustain or to undermine the official ideology depending on the context. I will be returning to this matter later. Here I want to point to how Bakhtin focuses attention on the processes he calls 'carnival'. He claims that Carnivals give a voice to those at the margins and that this is associated with the potential for change in some way.

Shotter and Billig (1998) build on Bakhtin's distinction between official and unofficial ideologies to talk about a 'dialogic unconscious':

> *We see it as operating, not within the heads of individuals, but in our use of certain words at certain times in certain ways, while repressing or ignoring the use of others. In such a view there would be a dialectical relationship between consciousness and unconsciousness, for, as the very words we use in our dialogues with others draw attention to certain issues, it is drawn away from others. As dialogic consciousness, or attention, is focused on particular aspects of language, so others slip by, as it were unnoticed. (p. 20)*

They are arguing that ideology is reproduced in the unconscious aspects of language and they point to how the very ability to continue in dialogue with others requires repression of impulses to rudeness. The intricate codes and rituals of polite relating and conversing must be observed if one is to stay in the dialogue, and this underlies the unconsciously repressive aspect of language.

The final point I want to mention in relation to Bakhtin is how he stressed that although dialogue constructs meaning, that meaning does not lie in the words themselves. Dictionaries may set out the common features of words but the meaning always resides in a communication made by a specific person in a specific context. The meaning is not, however, in the intention or control of the speaker. This is because a word has already been spoken by someone else and what it means will also depend on the one to whom the word is addressed. Meaning is determined by whose word it is and for whom it is intended. In order to fill a word with meaning the speaker uses particular intonations and places words in different relationships to each other. For the other to whom the word is addressed to understand it that other must recognise these context-dependent novelties. Understanding meaning depends upon understanding the novelty of the communication rather than the abstract identity of the word. I think this is a very important point, and one to which I will return later. What it is saying is that the sophisticated negotiation of meaning in ordinary everyday life depends heavily on the human capacity to detect difference and novelty in the communications of others, rather than the capacity to extract regularities from an environment that cognitive psychology emphasises so much.

The discussion in this chapter may seem to have strayed some way from the phenomenon of organisations. However, what I have been describing is a way of understanding how the organisations, or patterning, of the social ('we' identities) and individual minds ('I' identities) both emerge together at the same time in the interaction between human bodies. An organisation is a social structure and its identity emerges in the interactive processes I have been describing in this chapter. In order to understand the emergent strategies, the evolving identities of organisations, therefore, we need to understand the human dynamics of communicative interaction, power relating, inclusion or exclusion, and anxiety. It is in these dynamics, in local situations in the living present, that organisational strategies emerge. Chapter 16 will be taking these processes up in relation to organisations.

14.3   Complex responsive processes compared to other psychological theories

In Chapter 3, I briefly outlined the view of human knowing and acting presented by cognitivist psychology. The immediate focus of attention from this perspective is a single individual, particularly a single individual brain. Cognitivism postulates that the human brain is an information-processing mechanism in much the same way as a computer. While a computer processes symbols taking the form of on/off electric currents, the brain processes electrochemical discharges between the neurones of which the brain consists. In computer language terms, the on/off electric current is represented as digital symbols, ones and zeros. In mental terms, the brain's electrochemical discharges are represented in symbols mainly taking the form of sounds and pictures.

The symbols are representations of an external reality that already exists before the representation is made. That representation is made through the senses of seeing, hearing, smelling and touching. The representations are stored in the brain/mind, as they are in computers, in short- and long-term memory banks. Through repeated experience of similar sensations the individual brain/mind builds up a more and more accurate picture of external reality taking the form of a template, a map, a model, schemas, scripts or rules relating to behaviour. These rules, maps, models, schemas or scripts then form the basis upon which the individual acts. These models are assumptions about the world, including other people. They are predictions of the reaction of others to any action a person takes

When one individual interacts with another, he or she does so in a manner determined by his or her mental model. An individual acts on the basis of the assumptions and predictions of which the model consists. A group of people is a collection of individuals who are interacting with each other on the basis of their mental models. Those mental models will include assumptions and predictions of how groups of people behave. It is through mental models that an individual interprets the response of other individuals in a group and it is in this way that the group affects the individual. Group and individual are two different levels of analysis. First there are individuals and then there are groups composed of individuals.

Individuals, according to this theory, are essentially cybernetic entities who can take the position of objective observer of an external reality, although that observation might be distorted by their mental models. I have argued that this view of human psychology is fundamental to the theories of strategic choice, the learning organisation and knowledge management. I have also argued that it underlies the way most people seem to be interpreting chaos and complexity theory in an organisational setting.

In Chapter 3 I mentioned humanistic psychology, and then in Chapter 6 I pointed to how it plays an important role in the theory of the learning organisation. Humanistic psychology also immediately focuses attention on the individual, but in a way rather different to cognitivism. The central tenet here is the belief that the human individual is fundamentally motivated by self-realisation, or self-actualisation. Human knowing and acting, and therefore human learning, are driven by the need to find the self. Others, in the form of community, are very important to emotional well-being but it is not postulated that the group or the community actually forms the individual. In fact, the self-actualising individual has to find his or her true self despite group pressures to conform.

In Chapter 7 I briefly summarised some psychoanalytic understandings of human beings. Again, the primary focus is on the individual. An individual is born with instincts and these provide the energy and the motivation for living. The instincts are represented as drives in the psyche and they seek satisfaction through discharge. Individuals, however, also need others to survive and so cannot discharge any drive in any way they please. Individuals are constrained by the prohibitions of society and this clash between drives and social prohibition structures the mind. Later developments in psychoanalysis stressed the importance of inherited mental fantasies and how these were shaped in relating to others. So the later developments of psychoanalytic theory increasingly emphasised the importance of relationships in forming the psyche of an individual. Mostly, however, the primacy of the drives as the source of energy and motivation has been retained, with the exception of relational and intersubjectivity theory.

In psychoanalytic theory the group consists of individuals but exerts a far more powerful effect on how individuals behave than is the case in cognitivism and humanistic psychology. Individuals anonymously contribute emotions to groups and are then affected by them in the form of basic assumption behaviour.

The way of thinking that I have described in this chapter, drawing primarily on the work of the sociologists Mead, Elias and Bakhtin, points to what I will call a complex responsive processes view of human psychology. There are strong similarities between this and relational/intersubjectivity theory in psychoanalysis (Stolorow, Atwood and Brandshaft, 1994). This holds that one person is not an object that affects another, but that they are subjects interacting with each other. In their interaction, they form the experience of each other. The work of the psychoanalyst and developmental psychologist Stern (1985, 1995) also emphasises the importance of relationship in the formation of the infant mind. Group-analytic theory, to which I will turn in the next chapter, also emphasises the formative importance of the group and the social. In one way or another, I suggest, all of these developments point to some aspects of complex responsive processes. The major difference is that these later developments in psychoanalytic thinking are very much built on systems thinking, while the work of Elias, Mead and Bakhtin represents process thinking and it is on this basis that the theory of complex responsive processes is built.

The essence of the complex responsive processes view of psychology is the notion that an individual mind is a silent conversation of voices and feelings, more or less hidden from others. This private, silent conversation arises in relationships between people, while being experienced in their bodies. Relationships between people are expressed in the same medium as mind, namely conversation and feeling states. The two – relationships between people and relationships between voices in a silent conversation – are equivalent to each other. They form and are formed by each other at the same time. Unlike any of the other psychological theories, this one does not see individuals at one level of description and groups at another. They are the same phenomenon seen from different angles: one is the singular of relationship and the other the plural of relationship. This does not mean that all individuals are the same because each develops unique, private fantasies around public conversation. Furthermore, I suggest that the development of mind is sensitive to small misunderstandings, or differences in understandings, which can easily escalate into very different silent conversations, that is very different minds.

As I have said, cognitivist, humanistic and psychoanalytic psychology all postulate the individual as primary. For cognitivists, relationships between people do not play any fundamental part in how humans know anything. Each individual knows in the way he or she does because of the architecture of the brain. Humanistic psychology attaches importance to relationships between people in so far as a sense of community is part of the actualisation of an individual self. Psychoanalysis puts relationships in a much more central position but often retains the assumption that psychic energy and the motivation are located in an individual's inherited drives or inherited fantasies and it almost always sees individuals creating group or social systems.

Relationship psychology, as I have explained above, makes a radical departure from all of these by decentring the individual, without moving to the opposite extreme of giving the group, or the social, primacy either. It does so by postulating that individual minds are formed by and form relationships at the same time. The energy and the motivation for individual and joint action arise simultaneously in relationship. Relationship immediately constrains and so establishes power relations. Relationship is communication and it is this communication that forms and is formed by power relations.

From the perspective of an individual-centred psychology, the analogue of a complex adaptive system in human terms is easily assumed to be a group of individuals. The analogue for an agent in that system is easily assumed to be an individual human. The analogue for self-organisation is then individuals organising themselves in a group, or, more likely, a team. The analogue of the complex adaptive system programmer is easily taken as the manager. Through this route, people immediately think that complexity theory applied to organisations implies the manager standing outside the complex system; altering the conditions so that the dynamics of the edge of chaos is obtained; setting the rules to secure the desired attractor; and then leaving the members of a team to organise themselves. These prescriptions are no different from those of strategic choice or the learning organisation. They are simply presented in a new vocabulary.

What happens, however, if one looks for analogues from the perspective of complex responsive processes of relating? The analogue for the digital code in a simulation is the symbols people use to communicate with each other. Since the agents of a complex adaptive system simulation are nothing other than arrangements of digital code, it seems reasonable to say that the analogue in the case of humans is arrangements of symbols, that is themes, stories and propositions. In other words, the analogue of agents is the themes organising conversation, communication and power relations. What is organising itself, therefore, is not individuals but the pattern of their relationships in communicational and power terms in the public vocal arena and, at the same time, in the silent, private arena that is mind. The analogue of a complex adaptive system in human terms is then the self-organising processes of communicating in power relations.

The next chapter will explore this analogy more fully.

14.4 Managers as participants in self-organising processes

I find that there is a typical response whenever I suggest to a group of managers that they might think of themselves, and also their chief executive officer (CEO), as participants in self-organising processes. They claim that if they cannot be the designer and if they cannot know the outcomes of what they are doing then they have no role. They claim that they would simply give up if they thought that this was true. Alternatively, they point to examples of CEOs who do form overall intentions for their organisation, who set out compelling visions and missions and do thereby transform their organisation. They conclude that the notion of self-organisation does not apply to them. Why do they think this?

It seems to me that they are immediately understanding self-organisation in terms of the individual: the unquestioned assumption of the primacy of the individual again. Self-organisation is taken to mean that it is the individual members of the organisation who organise themselves. This then leads to the view that self-organisation means all or some of the following:

- Something that happens no matter what anyone does. This means that there is no point in doing anything. One should simply sit back and just wait for fate or destiny.
- Full-blown democracy in which all agents are equal and nothing is done without complete consensus.
- Anarchy in which everyone does whatever they please.
- The empowerment of the lower echelons in the organisation and then leaving them to get on with it.
- The disempowerment and incapacitation of the higher echelons who no longer have a role.

It is important to stress that the notion of self-organisation as it is employed in complexity theory does not mean any of these things. People think it does because they hear these words from the perspective of the autonomous individual and think that it means that individuals are organising themselves without any constraint. However, if you look carefully at the simulations intended to demonstrate the nature of self-organisation you will notice two points.

First, there are conditions that both enable and constrain the interactions between agents at the same time. Take the Tierra simulation (Ray, 1992) discussed in Chapter 11. Agents are enabled to replicate because computer time is allocated to them, but this is also a constraint because they only have limited time. In organisations, all managers are both enabled and constrained by the availability of resources. In the simulation, agents are constrained by the mode of replication and by the competitive selection applied to them. In the simulations, the programmer imposes all of these constraints but in the reality the programmer is trying to model, they all emerge in evolving interaction. So self-organisation is certainly not a constraint-free form of behaviour.

Secondly, that which is organising itself is not the separate individuals on their own. It is the overall pattern of relationships that is organising itself at the same time as the nature of the agents is changing. The agents are forming and being formed by the overall pattern of relationships (Griffin, 2001). They are, I think, the same phenomenon viewed from different perspectives. The system and its agents are emerging together, simultaneously constraining and being constrained by each other. Once this perspective is taken there is no justification for making any of the interpretations of self-organisation in the bullet points above. Instead:

- Far from there being no point in doing anything, everything one does, including nothing, has potential consequences. Far from the outcome being a matter of fate or destiny, it is the co-creation of all interacting agents.
- There is no reason at all why agents should be interacting in a democratic way. They might, but they might not. Furthermore, they are not all equal in a simulation such as Tierra. Some are pursuing more powerful strategies than others, in terms of survival. There is certainly no requirement for consensus but, rather, the tension between competition and co-operation.
- There is no anarchy because no agent can do whatever it pleases. There are a number of constraints, not least those provided by the actions taken by other agents.
- There is no connection whatever between empowerment of the lower echelons in an organisation and self-organisation, a matter I will explore next.
- There is also no connection whatever between disempowering the higher echelons and self-organisation, also to be explained in the next section.

The roles of the most powerful

Self-organisation means that the agents in a system interact with each other according to their own local principles of interaction. This means that they respond to others according to their own capacity to respond. They are enabled to respond in certain ways and constrained from responding in others by that capacity, which has emerged from their histories of interacting with others. There is no reason whatever why some agents should not have wider-ranging capacities than others do. Indeed the evolution of relationship virtually ensures this. Some have capacities that enable them to respond more effectively and more successfully than others do. This can be translated into organisational terms by saying that some members have more knowledge, more understanding and more power than others do.

Furthermore, there is nothing in the notion of self-organisation that says that each agent should interact with the same number of agents, nor that they have to be nearby in spatial terms. The simulations tend to limit the number of connections and specify them in relation to spatially nearby agents, but this is simply a matter of convenience. So, there is no reason why some agents in a self-organising system should not be much more powerful than some others, nor any reason why some agents should not interact with many more agents than some others.

In organisational terms, the top executives have more power than others, that is a greater capacity to instruct, persuade or even force others to do what they want. Furthermore, those top executives interact with a great many more people than the less powerful. A CEO may communicate with, and issue instructions to, hundreds of thousands of others in his or her organisation through email, for example. If they all responded according to some blueprint the CEO, or others, had designed, then there would clearly be no self-organisation. However, if they responded according to their own local capacities, and their responses had some effect on the CEO, leading to further responses from the CEO, then this would be self-organisation.

Greater understanding also confers power. Unlike agents in computer simulations, human beings are able to stand back and understand something of the larger processes in which they are participating. Note that this is not the same thing as stepping outside those processes and understanding them from the perspective of the objective observer. A human being trying to understand human processes cannot stop being human. Human emotion and the impact of the one trying to understand on those that the individual is trying to understand make it impossible to step outside. What I am talking about is reflecting, as a participant, on the nature of what is happening. Humans are able to reflect on, and articulate something about, the widespread patterns that are emerging.

So, a CEO might form certain views about the nature of his or her organisation, the nature of leadership, the direction the CEO would like it to go in, a vision or a mission for it and so on. These are all actions the CEO is taking that are likely to call forth some kind of response from many others in the organisation. A small group of powerful people at the top of an organisation might take a decision to enter a new market or to negotiate with a small group of powerful people in another organisation to merge with it. All of these actions would evoke and provoke a multitude of responses from others, both within and outside the affected organisations. If the pattern of these responses were simply the expression of some overall blueprint then the system could not be called self-organising. However, if others were responding according to their own local capacities to respond, it could be self-organising.

The point I am making is this. Small groups of very powerful people at the top of an organisation allocate resources and in so doing both enable and constrain other members of the organisation. They design sets of procedures and hierarchical reporting structures. They legitimise some actions and not others. They communicate with very large numbers of others. They make statements about visions and missions. They make decisions and take actions that greatly affect a great many others. What they cannot do, however, is programme the responses those others will make. The powerful may identify what kind of responses they would like by making statements about values and required cultures and behaviours. They may try to motivate others to adopt all of this. However, people will still only be able to respond according to their own local capacities to respond and the most powerful will find that they have to respond to the responses that they have evoked and provoked. This is what I think self-organisation means in human terms. It is a process of interaction that is ever present in all human situations and would only cease if people really did respond like automatons to statements about the values and behaviours they were supposed to display.

There is another aspect to the self-organising nature of what I have just been describing. I have been talking about powerful people who state and implement intentions that affect many others in an organisation. How did they come to have such intentions? They would doubtless have emerged in numbers of conversations and political interactions that, I will be arguing later, are themselves self-organising processes.

In this section I have been stressing how one group of people takes actions that evoke and provoke responses from many others, the latter in turn evoking and provoking yet further responses from the first group. Since all are acting according to their own local capacities, it is impossible to predict how this pattern of responses will unfold past a certain point in the future. All together will be forming and being formed by this overall pattern of responses. In describing behaviour in this way I have, in effect, avoided taking the perspective in which the individual is primary. Instead I have been suggesting that neither the individual nor the group is primary since they form and are formed by each other at the same time.

●●●● 14.5   Summary

The mind, that private conversation a body has with itself, is made possible by social relationships. The mind and the social are two facets of the same phenomenon. One cannot exist without the other. Mind is conversational in nature. It continuously arises between bodies while being experienced in an individual body. The silent, private world of mind is, however, essentially social in nature, the symbols having been taken up through actual experience of social relationships in conversation.

Mind, as a mental process, always arises between people but, at the same time, is always experienced in an individual body. Mind is thus paradoxical in that it is at the same time between individuals but experienced in their individual bodies. Mind is also paradoxical in another sense: it is formed by the social/the group at the same time as it is forming the social/the group.

The mind does not process symbols to produce representations of a pre-given reality and nor does the ordinary everyday conversation that gives rise to mind. Gestures people make to each other, the vocal ones of language as well as the cues of body movements, are symbols and in that sense they represent something other than themselves. However, they are not symbols or representations in the cognitivist sense of an accurate picture of an already existing reality that is stored as a template, map or program. Rather, the symbols of language and body cues are gestures, that is a phase in an act that points to the later unfolding of that act, in effect warning and signalling to another how the act will unfold. Such symbols convey meaning to both the presenter and the recipient of the symbol and in so doing call forth responses that are the meaning of the gesture. Symbols of this kind, gestures and responses that together create meaning, do not have to be stored anywhere for the meaning is in the act. Nor is there any 'thing' that needs to be shared in order for people to have common beliefs and undertake joint action. This is because there is no 'thing' to share. There are only continuously emerging patterns of social relationship, which emerge in conversation that is being taken up in the private sphere of conversation called mind. It seems unlikely that any two individuals will privately take up exactly the same themes. Even if they did the capacity for fantasy would soon lead to variety. This does not cause a difficulty for joint action because joint action does not mean that all do exactly the same thing – it means that all more or less fit in with each other. The way they do this is through the continual negotiation of ordinary everyday conversation.

The important point about this silent conversation is that it is reflexive. The maker of the gesture is turning its meaning back on him- or herself. The silent conversation is frequently even more reflexive than this when it becomes one about how the maker of the gesture takes the perspective of others to him- or herself. This is self-consciousness. To understand what a phenomenon is it is also necessary to understand what it is not. An understanding of what consciousness means requires an understanding of how the unconscious arises. This chapter has presented arguments suggesting that unconscious processes are those concealing the power relations and creating the ideology to make those power differentials feel natural and unquestionable. If one understands organisations to be continually iterated patterns of collective and individual identity, then these are the processes in which organisational strategies as the continuity and transformation of identities will emerge.

Further reading

Useful further reading is provided by Burkitt (1991), Bell and Gardiner (1998), Dalal (1998), Shotter (1993), Steier (1991), Stolorow, Atwood and Brandschaft (1994) and Turner (1994).

Chapter 15 ●●●●

The narrative structure of self-organising experience

15.1 Introduction

Chapter 14 outlined the basis of a complex responsive process view of psychology. The basic proposition of this theory of human knowing and acting is that people relate to each other in the medium of symbols. These symbols are gestures that call forth responses, which are themselves symbols that call forth further responses in a conversation of gestures. Mind and group are aspects of the same processes of evolving identities. An organisation is the process of communicative interaction and power relating between people and organisational strategies are the evolving patterns of collective and individual indentities. This chapter explores the narrative structure of interactive experience and the importance of processes of ordinary conversation for the emergence of identities. The argument will be that ordinary conversation is the medium in which organisational identity, strategy, emerges.

The symbols that are the medium of human communicative interaction can be regarded as the human analogue of the digital symbols, or code, that are the medium of computer simulations of complex adaptive systems. The simulations reveal a number of possibilities. First, random collections of interacting digital symbols can self-organise into orderly patterns. Secondly, interaction between a number of homogeneous digital symbol patterns (e.g. Boids) can produce particular emergent collective patterns, or attractors (e.g. flocking). These attractors are patterns of interaction so that interaction is producing emergent patterns in itself, through self-organisation. Thirdly, interaction between a number of heterogeneous digital symbol patterns can produce novel emergent patterns of interaction. In other words, new attractors can emerge and they are simultaneously new patterns of collective interaction and rearrangements of the individual symbol patterns. Interaction is producing new patterns in itself, through self-organisation. I suggest that there is a human analogue for this process of digital symbols organising patterns in themselves. The analogue is to be found in another fundamental notion in relationship psychology. This is the proposition that human experience is organised by themes, stories and conversations. This chapter will explore what is meant by this proposition.

● ● ● ●   15.2   The organisation of experience

It might be useful to start the exploration of how human experience is organised right at the beginning of life.

Symbols

Stern (1985, 1995) has drawn together a body of experimental evidence to offer an explanation of how an infant's self emerges in the mutual relationships between the infant and his or her family members. As soon as an infant is born, the conversation of gestures begins. Parents hold the infant. They make sounds and they look at the infant. These gestures evoke responses from the child who cries, stops crying, makes noises and returns the parental gaze. In this manner infant and parents, as well as other people, communicate with the infant who communicates with them in ever more elaborate ways. This communication is the infant's experience just as it is the experience of those relating to the infant.

It is important to note how these are bodily experiences, or feeling states. Feeling states can be thought of as rhythms in the body (Damasio, 1994): rhythms of breathing, heart beating, digestion, brain functioning and so on. There is never a time when a living body is without feeling states. Furthermore, as bodies interact with each other, the feeling state of one body affects those of other bodies. One might say that bodies resonate with each other. For example, a crying infant immediately evokes feeling states in the bodies of caregivers. The same thing happens, of course, between adult bodies. Emotions are heightened feeling states of a specific kind, such as anger or pleasure. At the start of life, then, communication is in the medium of gestures and responses taking the form of looking, vocalising, listening, touching and smelling, all expressive of feeling states in bodies. These gestures and their evoked responses are symbols that constitute the meaning of interactions. A cry when responded to with food that brings satisfaction means hunger. I will call symbols of this kind *protosymbols*; that is, the first, original or elementary symbols.

Stern presents a picture of an infant in a family whose members are continuously responding to each other. He suggests that each member relates to other members in accordance with principles that organise their experience of being with each other. He calls these organising principles schemas-of-being-with. Stern uses the cognitivist language of schemas and suggests that they are representations of relational experiences. I think it is important to avoid using this cognitivist language in a psychology of relationship. It is possible to do so by interpreting what Stern is saying using the terminology of intersubjectivity theorists (Stolorow, Atwood and Brandschaft, 1994). They talk about principles that organise the experience of a person interacting with another.

Stern's schemas-of-being-with then become principles that organise the interactive experience of being-with a particular person in a specific, repetitive way. For example, an infant would repeatedly experience being hungry and waiting to be fed. As the infant's experience of relating to others continues, that infant develops more and more organising principles and some of them become tied together by a common theme or feature. For example, they may cluster around the themes of feeding, playing or separation. Another possibility is that they become organised around particular emotions, for example being-sad-with or happy-with. Alternatively, they may be organised around particular people.

Qualities of relational experience

The important point to notice is this: Stern is suggesting that, in the infant's experience of relating to others, themes emerge around the *qualities* of that relational experience. These are reinforced by repeated experience and become expectations and so come to structure the infant's responses to the gestures of others. In other words, themes of being-with others that have emerged in a particular history of relating to others then organise the subsequent experience of relating. These themes are the infant's emerging self, always arising in relationship while being experienced in the infant's body. Themes that organise the experience-of-being-with trigger others, which trigger yet others. At some point, particularly when the infant begins to talk, its gestures come to call forth the same response in itself as in the others to whom they are directed. At that point one might say that the infant is conscious and the symbols being used are what Mead (1934) called *significant symbols*. However, the child does not abandon the use of protosymbols and use significant symbols instead. Both are present together. In fact it is not possible to communicate in significant symbols alone because it is a body that is communicating and bodies always have feelings. Communication has moved from the medium of protosymbols alone to an inseparable intertwined medium of protosymbols and significant symbols.

Later, as the child develops and comes to take the attitude of others towards itself, one may say that it is self-conscious. Meares (1992) has related the fullest sense of a self to that point, around four years old, when a child discovers that he or she can have a secret. In other words, the child comes to know that he or she has thoughts that others do not know about until he or she discloses them. The development of mind, consciousness and self in Stern's studies is quite consistent with Mead's theorising.

From this perspective, then, self is the patterning of interacting themes as a body relates to itself, rather than some mental apparatus, such as a mental model. This patterning of interacting themes is the same process as the social, which is the patterning of themes in the interaction between bodies. It is not only infants and their caregivers that interact in the manner I have just described. This is how people relate to each other throughout their lives.

It is important to notice the difference between interactive themes that organise experience, on the one hand, and the notion of mental models (*see* Chapter 6), on the other. The former arises in relationship *between* people, while the latter are located *in* individuals. In the former, self and mind are not located in a person; rather, they both continuously arise out of the relationship between them. Mind/self and relationship are forming and being formed by each other at the same time (Griffin, 2001). I think that this is a radical perspective because the individual is no longer prior to the group, nor is the individual primary. From the relationship perspective, the individual and group continuously and simultaneously co-create each other. Furthermore, the notion of human experience being organised by interactive themes captures more of the rich texture of human relationship, I think, than the idea of individual mental models consisting of simple or even complicated rules.

Stern's descriptions show how organising themes evolve in the interactive experience of the infant being with the mother, the father and other family members, and their being with the infant. His descriptions demonstrate how an infant self emerges in this evolution. The mother's experience is also organised by themes-of-being-with, for example her infant, her mother, her husband, herself. These interact with her infant's themes that organise the experience-of-being-with the mother. The personality emerges from the continuous interaction between all of these themes. Furthermore, mind, self, personality and identity are not formed in this way and then fixed for life. They continuously evolve throughout life, always arising in the relationships with others. As the pattern of relationship changes so the selves, the minds, the personalities and the identities change too. At the same time minds, selves, personalities and identities exhibit long-term stability. Here the notions of mind and self are paradoxical, displaying the interwoven stability and instability that is typical of complex processes.

As I have already mentioned, it is not only Stern who talks about themes organising experience. Those writing from an intersubjective psychoanalytic perspective adopt a similar formulation. Stolorow, Atwood and Brandschaft (1994) talk about recurring patterns of interaction that result in the establishment of invariant principles that unconsciously organise an infant's subsequent experiences. They see these principles as the process of personality development and this process as continuous throughout life. The organising principles provide distinctive configurations of self and other that shape and organise a person's subjective world. They think of these configurations as systems of ordering or organising principles, through which a person's experiences assume their characteristic forms and meanings.

A social constructionist perspective

Some social constructionists take a similar view in some respects. For example, Shotter (1993) talks about experience being organised in what he calls the rhetorical-responsive conversations of ordinary, everyday life. What he means by this is that people continually account for themselves to each other. They continually respond to what others are doing and try to persuade others to take the position they want. This conversational activity organises experience. Shotter explores how groups of people come to a more articulate grasp of their practices from within their ongoing conduct of them. Shotter and Katz (1997) talk about a relational-responsive form of understanding between people in their ordinary everyday conversation. In their ordinary forms of language they:

> deconstruct the routine links and relations between things once constructed and then taken for granted. In this way, new possibilities are revealed. People do this in the directive use of words: by saying 'Look at that', 'Look at this', people can lead others and themselves to notice important features of their circumstances. In ordinary conversation, people arrest or interrupt each other in order to deconstruct and destabilise so that they can make new distinctions and so create new knowledge. They also use analogies, metaphors, and other ways of making comparisons

to develop new ways of talking. It is in talk like this that people are moved. (Shotter and Katz, 1997, p. 5)

This is a very important point: new knowledge can emerge in ordinary, everyday talk.

The point I am making is that throughout life people's experience is organised by interactive conversational themes in the medium of protosymbols and significant symbols. These themes endlessly trigger other themes that trigger yet others in turn. Later in this chapter, I will return to how these themes take a narrative form, but here I want to refer to another form of symbol in which communication takes place.

Returning to the development of a child, the child is taught to read and write at some point and then goes to school. I think that the symbols that constitute reading and writing lead to what I will call *reified symbols*. These are symbols taken to be the reality they point to. People use written symbols to construct models and frameworks of many kinds and the tendency is to equate the model with the reality being modelled. The reified symbol becomes a thing in itself rather than just a means of communication. While protosymbols and significant symbols are patterned as narrative themes, reified symbols tend to be patterned as propositional themes. Tsoukas (1997) draws a distinction between propositional and narrative knowledge that is relevant here. Propositions make causal and prescriptive statements about experience, such as if you shout then people will get angry. Since reified symbols are also made by bodies, they too will be interwoven with protosymbols. The point is that experience may be organised by both narrative and propositional themes.

Themes organising the experience of being together

Each member of a group has his or her own personal organising themes that have been taken up in the silent conversation, or mind, of that individual. They reflect his or her own personal history of relations with, and between, others. As soon as members of a group meet each other, they all actively, albeit largely unconsciously, select and so organise their own subjective experience of being in that place with those people at that time. They do this according to personal organising themes that reflect their own individual histories. However, what those particular themes are at that particular moment will depend just as much on the cues being presented by others as upon the personal history of a particular individual. Each is simultaneously evoking and provoking responses from others so that the particular personal organising themes emerging will depend as much on the others as on the individual concerned. Put like this, it becomes clear that no one individual can be organising his or her experience in isolation because all are simultaneously evoking and provoking responses in each other. Together they immediately constitute intersubjective, recursive processes. These are continuous back-and-forth circular processes in which themes emerge that organise the experience of being together out of which further themes continuously emerge.

Relationships between people in a group can then be defined as continuously replicating patterns of *intersubjective themes that organise the experience of being together*. These themes emerge, in variant and invariant forms, out of the interaction between group members as they organise that very interaction. I want to stress, however, that I am not suggesting that these themes are disembodied interactions. Although the themes emerge between people, and therefore cannot be located 'inside' any individual, the experience is nevertheless always a bodily experience. I am suggesting, then, that both personal and group themes always arise between people but are always at the same time experienced in individual bodies as changes, marked or subtle, in the feeling tones of those bodies. Consider an example of what I mean.

An example

During a social meeting between three people, one person, Mary, may complain that the other two are taking no account of how she feels about a troublesome relationship with her boyfriend. Her friend, Helen, may take this as a direct criticism of her and aggressively suggest that there is nothing stopping her from talking about this relationship. Helen's partner, Fred, may support her and complain about Mary always wanting to be the centre of attention. Mary may then slump back into her seat, adopting a silent, sulky pose. She may then announce that their remarks have simply confirmed what she already knew, namely that they do not like her. Therefore, remarks by one person evoke feelings and remarks from another, which in turn trigger other remarks and feelings in others in a self-organising way. The personal and group themes are so intertwined that they cannot be separated. There may be an invariant and, therefore, largely predictable strand in the themes that emerged here. On many occasions before, Mary may have complained to Helen and Fred that people do not take account of her feelings and they may usually have responded angrily. However, on each occasion, the particular form this sequence takes, and when it occurs, may well be very different and so quite unpredictable.

This simple example makes it clear that the interweaving of organising themes of being together does not mean that all share the same theme. Each member is responding differently around a theme that has to do with dissatisfaction with each other, of being liked or not liked. This clarifies why there is no need to postulate the sharing of any kind of mental content. Nothing is being shared as people resonate individually around a common theme to do with being together. They are responding to each other in a meaningful way, not sharing something.

I am suggesting, then, that a large number of themes organise the experience of being together in the group. The entities in this interaction are these themes that organise experience and they are simultaneously arising between people and being experienced in their individual bodies. The entities are not simply individuals. Thus, in the case given above, Helen's feeling that she is being criticised is evoked by Mary's comment. Mary's remark in turn evokes a reaction from Helen and a statement from Fred, and as he makes his remark, Mary slumps in her chair. Even where there is no apparent change in posture, I am suggesting that there will always be subtle changes in body rhythms as changes in feeling states accompany the emergent themes organising experience. From the perspective I am suggesting, the themes interact in a self-organising manner so that patterns of relating continuously emerge. These patterns are changes in the themes organising local interaction as group members seek to negotiate with, and respond to, each other in some way. The pattern of organising themes is continually re-creating itself in a self-referential, reflexive way as people continuously experience these changes in their bodies.

These themes create power relations. In fact, they are power relations. Remember that power is not simply an individual imposing his or her will on others. Relating is a process of constraining and constraints are power. It is not an individual imposing power but the process of relating that inevitably creates power relations. The pattern of relating is thus also a pattern of power relations. It is another way of describing the same phenomenon.

Another important point to be made here about organising themes is that they arise in a particular place at a particular time. The bodies interacting with each other in a group are located in a wider context of a community and a society that has a history. This means that the group/individual themes are resonating with wider themes that organise the experience of being in a community and a society at a particular point in its history. The themes arising in a particular group, at a particular time, will thus be influenced by the figuration of power relations in the wider grouping. They will also reflect the pattern of control over economic resources and, therefore, the material, technological and physical nature of the place at a particular historical moment. The focus on the importance of a particular group at a particular time can easily lead to neglecting the constraining nature of the social and material and technological world in which the group themes are arising.

So, organising themes are continuously arising in the interaction between people, while simultaneously being experienced in their bodies, located in a particular community, in a particular place, at a particular point in the history of community and group. Note that this is very different to saying that members of a group share the values of the community and the society in which they are located. It is saying that at a particular time there will be salient themes organising the experience of being together in a community. They will evoke themes organising the experience of being together in a particular group. The theme evoked in the group might be quite different to the theme in the community. For example, a theme organising the experience of being together in a community might have to do with condemning gypsies. Groups of residents and groups of gypsies in the community will not be sharing a common theme. However, both groups will be responding to the theme in a different way.

The analogy with complex adaptive systems

I want to return now to how complexity theory might provide an analogue of human behaviour. Computer simulations are the equivalent of laboratory experiments for those studying complex adaptive systems. The simulations are conducted in the medium of digital symbols.

In human terms, the analogue of digital symbols is the protosymbols, significant and reified symbols that are the medium of human relating. The symbolic medium of human relating and communicating is therefore very much more complicated than the digital symbols of the computer simulations. However, the logic of interaction revealed by the interaction in the medium of digital symbols may nevertheless provide further analogies for human interaction and thus further insight.

The digital symbols in the computer simulations are arranged into patterns taking the form of algorithms, that is 'if–then' calculating procedures. These algorithms, or agents, interact with each other and in the presence of diversity they self-organise to produce emergent changes in themselves. Overall, patterns of interaction and the individual symbol patterns evolve simultaneously in the absence of an overall blueprint. The analogue in human terms could be described in the following way. Protosymbols interwoven with significant symbols are patterned primarily in the form of narrative themes that organise people's experience of being together with others and with themselves. Protosymbols interwoven with reified symbols are arranged into propositional themes that organise people's experience of being with others and with themselves. These themes interact with each other in the presence of diversity in a self-organising way to produce emergent changes in themselves. Themes organising the experience of being together in a group and themes organising the silent conversation of mind evolve simultaneously in the absence of an overall blueprint. In other words, public, vocalised conversations between people and the private, silent conversations of mind evolve simultaneously. The analogue of agents in human interaction is themes that organise experience.

Note again how very much more complicated it all is in the case of humans. Some of the themes organising human experience may take an algorithmic form, namely, what I have called propositional themes. However, human experience is mainly organised by narrative themes in conversation and this is not algorithmic at all. Nevertheless, insights drawn from the logic of interaction between algorithms may illuminate interaction between narrative themes.

The computer simulations reveal patterns of interaction that are called attractors. The analogue of an attractor in human interaction would be a recognisable pattern in sequences of organising themes triggering organising themes. So, in the example given above, the attractor would be Mary complaining that people do not take account of her feelings, triggering an angry response from those to whom she is complaining, triggering in turn further complaints that they do not take account of her feelings.

In the computer simulations, diversity and thus the capacity to evolve spontaneously are provided by random mutation and cross-over replication. The analogue in human interaction would be the imperfect communication between people, misunderstanding, and the partial taking up in silent conversation by one person of ways of conversing acquired from others in the course of public conversations. I will return to this matter later in this chapter.

Another analogy is that between the interaction of digital agents in a simulation and interaction between human bodies. In the simulations, interaction between agents is complex and adaptive. However, although human interaction is certainly complex, to describe it as adaptive is to miss the full complexity. People do not simply fit in with, or adapt to, each other. Often they negotiate a lack of fit with each other. I suggest then that the key feature of human interaction is that it is responsive, and in this responsiveness it may be adaptive or it may not.

Finally, in computer simulations it is the pattern of digital symbols that is organising itself. The analogue of this in the case of human interaction is the manner in which themes organising experience are organising themselves. In fact, human experience *is* these themes. So to say that the themes organise experience is to say that they organise themselves. The primary medium for this self-organisation is conversation. Conversation organises itself through bodies.

To ground what I am talking about I now recount an experience I shared with two of my colleagues when we were employed to run a workshop at a major company, which I will call Excel. After that, I will return to the important matter of conversation.

The workshop at Excel

We were working with human resource executives of Excel's European subsidiary and with members of another institution to develop ways of introducing managers to the insights of complexity theory. Through some contact we were unaware of, a senior executive in the management development function at the head office in the United States, Stan, got to hear about this work and asked us to run a workshop there. Initially, the workshop was to consist of a group of line managers. However, when Stan's boss, Steve, heard about this he insisted that novel material of this kind had to be seen first by himself and his colleagues before they risked it with people outside the department. There was some discussion between them and us around this point but we eventually agreed to go ahead on Steve's terms.

We drove from the airport to one of Excel's locations, which consisted of a number of low stone and glass buildings in parkland with a rather severe, grim appearance. We entered the building through two sets of automatic doors and went to a reception desk where a very sharp young woman told us we would have to pay for our stay. We managed to get her to understand that we had come as speakers whose costs were being paid for by Excel. She did not appear very interested in this because the subcontractor who ran the building on behalf of Excel employed her. Then she gave us instructions to the effect that we had to park the car in a particular car park, unpack our luggage and then wait for transport to take us to our rooms. She told us, rather severely, that we were not allowed to drive cars to the building where the rooms were. The three of us felt that we had been treated like children and all of us felt rather depressed.

After unpacking, we met Stan in the room we were to use. It was a long narrow room with a long narrow table of such weight that it could not be moved. One of my colleagues and I felt so depressed by this time that we pleaded jet lag and went to our rooms, leaving our other colleague, by now rather alarmed, to make preparations. Later, the other colleague and I returned and Stan found us a room that we could rearrange and took us out to dinner. Stan seemed rather disconcerted by our room rearrangement.

So, a number of cues were presented to us, in the form of the building itself, the infantilising reception, the rigidity of the room and the surprise of Stan at our wanting to rearrange it. These cues directly conveyed tones of the themes that organise experience at Excel. Our experience of being together on that evening at those Excel offices was being organised, most importantly, by protosymbolic themes to do with the rhythm of the place and the rhythms, or feeling states, being evoked in us. One might say that, as a group, we were resonating in some way with the experience of the Excel community. We experienced a rather rigid and depressing quality of life there.

On the next day, the morning workshop went quite well. It was interesting how Steve, a striking, powerful-looking man, came in and immediately moved his chair. At first, he looked almost angry and withdrawn but eventually asked quite a number of questions and became very involved with the material. After lunch, we tried to link what we had been talking about in the morning to a particular project we knew about at Excel. We asked the person who was most concerned with this project to talk about it. Steve objected to this, saying it was not how he wanted to spend the afternoon. This silenced the person we had invited to speak.

Steve then aggressively asked us how complexity theory was to be applied. I felt irritable about the way he twisted his chair and body away from the group in a rejecting manner and then made aggressive demands. It may have been this irritation that prompted me to stand up and give a short lecture. Steve and some of the others liked this and it sparked some discussion. The pattern we then fell into, for nearly an hour and a half, was quite striking. The three of us tended to give long speeches, one after the other, with interjections from Steve. We tended to look at him and the others hardly ever said anything. We kept talking about the importance of conversation, but none of us really engaged in one. I noticed what we were doing and that we were very much colluding with each other in this, but I felt it impossible to say anything like this.

My colleagues later said that they too felt disabled. We do not usually work in this way and we do not usually feel powerless to point to, or stop colluding with, this kind of group process. We were not really relating to each other or using our relationship in our work. We were simply making speeches, one after the other. We were talking about complexity as an intellectual construct and not working at all with the psychological implications and the behaviour in the room.

One might understand this as follows. This session was characterised by a push to use intellect to cover up feelings. We were caught in a power dynamic in which the more powerful have to provide for others who take up a dependent position. There was something disabling about the atmosphere in this company when it came to anything but an intellectual approach. There was something about the relative unimportance of relationships compared with doing a task. These are all recognised aspects of Excel's culture, confirmed for us the next morning by Stan and Steve. Steve arrived for this meeting rather later and we learned that he had been at Excel, noted for its long-serving employees, for only a year. As we talked about these matters, he eventually disclosed how tired and depressed he was at constantly having to justify what his department did. He felt pressed by those above him and unsupported by his staff. He talked about how tiring it all was and how lonely he felt. This felt to us like a real shift. Apparently, he had not spoken like this before.

So, how was it that the three of us came to be so totally sucked into the themes organising this company's experience, to the point where we seemed to have little power to avoid its organising our experience? Culture is often thought to be transmitted by imitation, as something people share. However, our experience on this occasion points to some direct way that one rapidly becomes part of a culture. The whole context of building, room settings, the manner in which one is treated, the ways in which members of the group and their managers respond to us and to each other, are all protosymbolic. They were rhythms that evoked bodily rhythms, feeling states, in us.

In this account, I have been stressing the relevance of protosymbols but of course we engaged in ordinary conversation and in the use of reified symbols organised into theoretical propositions in a lecture. There were a great many narrative themes organising our experience of being together with each other and with the members of Excel, for example, the difficulties Steve was having in adjusting to the culture of Excel.

I return now to the important matter of conversation, which I have suggested is complex responsive processes.

15.3   Conversations in organisations

Ethnomethodologists (Garfinkel, 1967; Goffman, 1981) study the finely ordered detail of local action, including an analysis of the detailed flow of ordinary conversation (Jefferson, 1978; Sacks, 1992; Shegloff, 1991).

Self-organising turn taking

Conversation analysts have used recordings of ordinary conversations to build up a picture of how such conversations are patterned and how they produce orderly interactions between people. What they point to, as the fundamental organising principle of conversation, is the process of turn taking. Starting with Mead's notion of the conversation of gestures between animals, and between human infants and their caregivers, this principle is everywhere in evidence. Turn taking is at the heart of all social activity in that it establishes a temporal and spatial location for social interaction. From it flows the back-and-forth rhythm of social relationships. Turn taking:

> creates the rhythms of daily life, from the formal, public rituals and ceremonies of ancient religions and national states to the most intimate of human intercourse. (Boden, 1994, p. 66)

Sack's research pointed to the way in which turns to speak are valued, distributed across speakers, competed for, abandoned and held on to. Turn taking is, thus, one of the important ways in which power differentials are established and sustained in conversations, very much a reflection of the process to which Elias points. The process also has all the hallmarks of self-reference as participants respond to each other in a back-and-forth way. The response of one calls forth a further response from another, in turn calling forth a response from the first. It is also a reflexive process since none of the participants can get outside the conversation, observe it and control it, at least without destroying its very nature as ordinary, everyday conversation. Furthermore, the process is very clearly a self-organising one that produces emergent patterns of meaning for participants. I am suggesting, then, that conversations are complex responsive processes. Speakers take turns that are organised by certain principles that have themselves emerged out of the history of interaction in the community of speakers to which they belong.

The principles I am referring to have to do with: how one person speaks at a time; how it may, or may not, be permissible to interrupt or talk over others; how the number and order of speakers varies; how turn sizes vary; how turn transition is accomplished; what kind of gaps and overlaps occur in turn taking; how the turns themselves are allocated. These organising principles evolve, and so come to differ from one historical period to another and from one locality to another.

Sacks and others have also pointed to the manner in which turns tend to be organised into what they call 'adjacent pairs'. So conversational exchanges may be organised into greeting–greeting, question–answer, invitation–acceptance (rejection), summons–answer, request–response and so on. Speakers create turns with recipients in mind and listeners are motivated to hear their turn, all in a self-organising manner. Speakers tend to pursue a response until they are acknowledged and those being addressed are under pressure to respond to the meaning. This requirement to respond does not mean that grammatical sentences are always used. In fact, ordinary conversation is characterised by grunts, other noises like 'mm', pauses and fragments of sentences. The listener is thus co-creating the meaning by a constructive process of filling in. The result is the highly associative nature of ordinary, everyday conversation.

Boden talks about different kinds of conversation:

> From the basic elements of conversational turn taking, what Sacks and his collaborators proposed was that other speech exchange systems such as meetings, classrooms, interviews, debates, and even the most ritual of ceremonies would span a kind of continuum. The central differences between casual, freely occurring conversation and the kinds of exchanges listed depend primarily upon such issues as: allocation and duration of turns, selection and order of potential speakers, and designation and order of topic, as well as a specific method for ensuring that each speaker is heard and that discussion does not break down into mini conversations. In meetings and on conference calls, the structuring methods of turn-taking are indeed modified . . . but the core of organizational communication remains this simple, reciprocal and self organizing system. (Boden, 1994, pp. 72–3)

The self-organising nature of ordinary, everyday conversation can be very easily seen by asking a group of people to play a word game. One member of the group is asked to start with any word he or she chooses and the others are asked to respond. What always happens is this. One word triggers a response, usually by association, from another person and that response triggers yet another and so on. Within a very short time, a theme emerges. For example, the theme may have to do with the weather, with body parts, with places, with moods, or whatever. Some people may try to break the associative links and if they succeed another theme begins to emerge. Even when people try very hard not to associate but to keep breaking the links, it turns out to be rather difficult to keep it going. This is exactly what happens in conversation: a theme emerges and the talk swirls around this theme, until some remark triggers the emergence of some other theme.

Free-flowing conversation

Consider how the conversational life of a group can be thought about in a dynamic way. As people participate in a conversation, the details of the context of place and time those people are embedded in may change. Others may join in the conversation while some leave it, for example. The themes emerging in and organising the conversation, therefore, keep changing. This is what happens in lively, energising conversation. However, a group of people may get stuck in repetitive, emotionally dulling exchanges. Foulkes (1948) made a strong association between this kind of stuckness and mental ill health. He defined health as free-flowing communication through a group or community. He saw mental illness as, at its roots, a disturbance, a blockage, in the free flow of communication and he pointed to how this blockage could become located in one or more of the members of a group or community. This was one of his key concepts, ill health as a blockage in communication that may become located in one or more of the members of a group. This process of location and blockage is clearly self-organising. Such a group is caught in repeating a similar conversation.

Since the mind is a silent conversation reflecting the experience of social processes, the silent conversation must have the same features of the social interaction discussed in the above paragraphs. I think that my own efforts at introspection, and the reports of others about the results of their introspection, provide ample support for this claim. People often talk about different parts of themselves and they frequently refer to voices in their minds talking to each other. Introspection reveals a stream of thoughts, which, as Elias (1989) emphasised, are exactly the same as conversations, one thought triggering others in a manner that one cannot design or control. There is a kind of turn taking shown by the great difficulty, at least for me, of sustaining a consistent train of thought. In fact, the distinction rapidly blurs between the vocal conversation of each person engaged in an interaction and their silent conversations that are going on at the same time. What I am talking about is the same phenomena, viewed from different vantage points. If one takes the viewpoint of the individual, one identifies silent conversation, and if one takes the group viewpoint, one identifies vocalised conversation. However, they are so intimately interlinked with each other that they cannot be separated.

The point about mental disturbance can be seen from the group point of view, as was done above. Alternatively, one can view it from the point of view of the individual. Not surprisingly, there is no real difference because the phenomenon is the same. It is only the perspective that is different. So, mental disturbance displays itself in an individual as a blockage in the free flow of silent conversation. This is an extremely distressing and painful state to be in. It is a state of a silent conversation that has lost its free-flowing nature and come to alternate repetitively between a few positions. The number of voices in the private role-play has been severely curtailed. So, for example, one obsessively ruminates about some slight or even about some deep hurt. Peace and happiness are states of fluid, free-floating, silent conversation. The link with the social is ever present because the silent conversation resonates with vocalised conversations throughout life. Note the analogy here between the dynamics of stability in complex adaptive systems and the repetitive nature or blockage in conversation. Note also the analogy between the dynamics at the edge of chaos for a complex adaptive system and the pattern of free-flowing conversation amongst people.

Conversation and power

I have been arguing then that conversations are complex responsive processes of themes triggering themes through self-organising association and turn taking that both reflect and create power differentials in relationships. These conversational processes are organising the experience of the group of people conversing and from them, there is continually emerging the very minds of the individual participants at the same time as group phenomena of culture and ideology are emerging. Individual and group phenomena emerge together in the same processes, co-creating each other. In fact, one can say that they are the same phenomena simply looked at from different standpoints. This is a very radical view of the nature of the relationship between the individual and the group. It is saying that change in the behaviour of a group and change in the behaviour of individual members is exactly the same phenomenon. Furthermore, it is saying that change can only occur when the pattern of conversation changes. Individual behaviour can only change when individuals' silent conversation changes because it is this that organises their experience. However, that silent conversation can only change through processes reflecting conversational change in a group. It is only as individuals experience change in social relationships that they can change psychologically and, of course, their relating to others can only change as they change psychologically. It is in this sense that change in groups and in individuals is the same thing. They can only occur together since both are forming and being formed by each other at the same time. This view of culture change or change management has far-reaching implications that will be explored in Chapter 16. Briefly, it means that it is only when people in an organisation talk differently to each other that their organisation will change. Facilitation of change is facilitation of different forms of conversation.

I want to return now to the notion of conversation as a self-organising process from which themes emerge. Ordinary, everyday conversation is themes organising themes into stories and narratives.

Stories and narratives

A story is an account of a sequence of specific actions, feeling states and events, while a narrative is a story line linked by reflections, comments upon, and categorisations of, elements of the story line. So, a narrative contains within it a story but it is a more complex form of communication than a story because it involves some kind of evaluation. It seems to me that the associative, turn-taking processes of ordinary, everyday conversation produce emergent, co-created narrative. One person tells an anecdote that evokes some evaluative comment from another and an associated anecdote from a third as together they spin narrative themes. These narrative themes structure their historic experience and their current experience of being together, so creating personal and group realities (Gergen, 1982; Shotter, 1993).

Bruner has identified some of the key features of narrative processes of constructing experience. Narratives create a sense of temporality in experience, linking present experience to past ones and pointing towards the future evolution of the experience. They focus upon departures from what is expected, from what is taken for granted as ordinary and acceptable, and thereby they reinforce cultural norms. Stories that simply recount expected routines are not particularly interesting, but those that describe the unexpected are, and such stories usually have a 'moral' that reinforces the culture or ideology of the group. Stories also impart something about the subjectivity of the narrator or about the subjectivity of the characters in the story. In other words they disclose some aspects of individuals' silent conversations and provide the means for people to experience each other's subjectivity.

People also use stories to describe and deal with ambiguity. Bruner (1990) points to the essential ambiguity of stories themselves in that it is quite difficult to tell just what is fact and what is fiction in a story, thereby opening up the possibility of the fantasy potential to which Elias attached so much importance. An essential aspect of narrative, therefore, is the scope it offers for the exercise of imagination and the spinning of fantasy. Bruner also emphasises the constructive role of the listener in storytelling, because people do not just listen to stories. They select and fill in meanings and indeed storytelling techniques employ devices to encourage this active participation in the co-construction of meaning in narratives. Bruner talks about stories as 'trafficking in human possibilities rather than settled certainties' (1986, p. 28).

Sarbin (1986) points out the link between narrative and feelings – emotional states are located in narratives and passions are 'storied'. McCleod (1996) emphasises the problem-solving function of stories in that they are used to put chaotic experiences into causal sequences and explain dilemmas and deviations:

> *In co-constructed narratives, the listener or audience may feed their own alternative accounts into the story that emerges, or may seek clarification by asking questions. So, the act of telling a story makes available a communication structure that not only conveys a sense of a world of uncertainty and ambiguity, but also provides a means of reducing dissonance and re-establishing a sense of control and order, by assembling an account that becomes more complete or ordered through the process of being told. (p. 37)*

I wish to emphasise the self-organising character of narratives and the emergence of meaningful themes in their telling. Conversations, stories and narratives are complex responsive processes of symbols interacting with each other to produce emergent themes of meaning that organise the experience of those engaged in the conversational activity.

Furthermore, if mental phenomena are simply social processes taken up in the silent conversations of individuals then mind can also be usefully thought of as having the same characteristics as social interaction. In other words, an individual's mind can be thought of as complex responsive processes of symbols, that is language and feelings, self-organising into narrative themes that organise the experience of the individual concerned. The psychoanalyst Schafer (1992) points to how people construct story lines to account for important events in their lives and how one of the most important of these story lines is the self-narrative. As with social constructionists, he sees the self as an autobiographical story a person tells about him- or herself, a story that is endlessly retold and can change in the retelling.

Intention

One response to the theory I have outlined in the previous chapter, and in this one, is that it leaves no room for intention, choice and free will. This, however, is not so.

Intention is a communication between people, and like any other communication it is expressed in the medium of symbols. It is a particular kind of theme and it organises experience just as any other theme does. An intention may be expressed explicitly or implicitly in a propositional theme. For example, if you do this for me, then I will do that for you; or we are going to buy a car. When managers communicate statements about strategic direction, mission, vision and values, they articulate propositional themes. An intention may also be expressed explicitly or implicitly in a narrative theme. All of these intentional themes are gestures that provoke or evoke responses in others. Those articulating the intention then find that these responses, in turn, evoke or provoke responses from them and they will not be able to know in advance just how these responses, and response to responses, will evolve.

The question arises as to where intention comes from. The theories of strategic choice, the learning organisation and psychoanalytic perspectives on organisations take intention for granted. They assume that the formation of an intention is not problematic. People simply decide. However, when one comes to regard intention as a theme that organises the experience of being together it becomes clear that intentions emerge in relationship just as any other organising theme does. Intention, then, emerges in the conversational life of a group of people. A single individual does not simply 'have' an intention. Rather the intention an individual expresses has emerged in the conversational interaction with others. Intention and choice are not lonely acts but themes organised by and organising relationships at the same time.

Where does this leave human free will? The response that any individual can make to a gesture is both enabled and constrained by the history of that person's relationships with others, as reflected in his or her current silent conversations with him- or herself. I am not free to choose to do what I am not able to do. However, I am free to respond to a gesture in a number of different ways that do fall within the repertoire available to me. Thinking about human relationships as self-organising complex responsive processes does not therefore mean that individuals have no free will. It simply means that people have the freedom to respond within the constraints of who they are and the relationships they are in.

The patterning of complex responsive processes

This section explores the insights that complexity theory brings to human relationships. Complexity theory demonstrates that the dynamics of a complex network of interacting agents is determined by the nature of the relationships across the network. In general, as information/energy flows increase, as connectivity between agents and diversity in the nature of agents increase, the dynamics of the network shifts from repetitive, predictable stability towards the dynamics of randomness and disintegration. At some critical range in information/energy flow, connectivity and diversity, the dynamics of bounded instability appears, that is the simultaneous presence of stability and instability, order and disorder. It is in this dynamic, at the edge of disintegration, that novel forms of relationship may emerge. I think that these factors have immediate and quite obvious relevance to groups of people. It is widely known that groups of people fall into repetitive patterns of behaviour when they have little access to information or to the stimulation of high enough interaction with others who are sufficiently different to be stimulating. In other words, the themes organising experience are impoverished through too little content, connection and diversity. It is also well known that people can be incapacitated by information overload and by too many contacts with people who are too different from each other to form any kind of agreement. In these conditions human relating disintegrates. In other words, themes organising experience are so diverse, interconnected and full of content that communication is random. It is in the dynamic in between that free-flowing conversation arises.

In human terms, of course, other factors affect the dynamics. There are two such factors which seem to me to be of particular importance (Stacey, 1996). The first of these is power difference. Those who exaggerate power difference by behaving in an autocratic manner, or even in too directing a way, are likely to evoke either compliance in group members, the dynamics of stability or rebellion, the dynamics of instability and disintegration. On the other hand, ignoring or abdicating from the position of power altogether is likely to provoke the dynamics of 'sibling' rivalry as members seek to fill the power vacuum. Part of the skill of managers and leaders, therefore, lies in exercising power difference in a manner that steers between directing and abdicating. There will also be power differences between people because some are more persuasive, more frightening, more dominant than others and the manner in which these differences are exercised could have similar effects to those outlined above.

The second major factor influencing the dynamics of the human system has to do with the holding of anxiety. Where anxiety is avoided, the group dynamic is one of stability and regularity. This is evident when a group moves into a conversational mode similar to that of a dinner party – here there can be no change or evolution in the pattern of themes organising the experience of being together. On the other hand a group can become so suffused by anxiety that it defends against by engaging in patterns of dependency, fight–flight or pairing (Bion, 1961). This produces an unstable dynamic disintegrative of work as the group shifts in a volatile manner, operating almost entirely on the basis of fantasy. The patterning of themes of being together fluctuates in a virtually meaningless way. However, when the pattern of relationships can contain the anxiety in a 'good enough manner' then there is the possibility of change. What changes then is the pattern of themes that organise the experience of being together and by being taken into the inner conversation of the individuals involved, this changes them too.

●●●● 15.4 Comparison with the notion of communities of practice

Chapter 9 reviewed that perspective which regards organisations as communities of practice. The way in which this perspective focuses attention on organisational matters is very close to that of the complex responsive process perspective. However, the explanation of what is going on in a community is somewhat different and an exploration of the differences may help to clarify the meaning of complex responsive processes of relating.

Chapter 9 argued that Wenger thinks in the 'both . . . and' terms of a duality, while the theory of complex responsive processes is about thinking in terms of paradoxical 'at the same time' processes. Right at the beginning, therefore, his conceptual approach differs from that described in this chapter, which is a paradoxical way of thinking.

Wenger argues that in their participation as members of a community of practice, people are producing reifications (e.g. symbols), which focus attention and enable sharing in their participation. In their negotiation of meaning, people are interrelating with each other through talking, say, and in that talking they are projecting meanings on to objects, say words, which they are then using in their talking. Taken together as a unity, this dual process of participation (talking) and reification (projecting meaning on to words) constitutes the negotiation of meaning, which is essentially what a practice is. There is a sense of participation and reification taking place at the same time but as dual processes, not as the movement of paradox or dialectic. We do not get the reification producing the participation at the same time as the participation is producing the reification. The process of negotiating meaning (learning) is a participative activity that both produces and uses reification. Wenger seems to use participation as the action of negotiating and the term reification for the object/content/focal point of the negotiation. He seems to be assuming that participative interaction taken on its own cannot explain the negotiation of meaning.

In the perspective described in this chapter, interaction is participation and this process on its own produces emergent meaning. This is an explanation that relies heavily on self-organisation/emergence as the main feature of the process. There is no separation of symbols from the interaction. Drawing on Mead and Elias, the act of talking, say, is the gesture of a body and this gesture is itself a symbol, which finds its meaning in the response and that too is the action of a body, a symbol. It is in the interaction of symbols understood as living acts that the meaning emerges. The meaning is not negotiated around the symbol, but rather, the meaning is the symbol. People are not negotiating meaning in their interaction but rather their interaction is negotiation and it is meaning. In their interaction people are not pointing to any process or product other than their interaction because their interaction is the meaning. I distinguished between protosymbols, significant symbols and reified symbols. I argued that all interaction has aspects of all of these symbols at the same time. In their use of reified symbols, the gestures of people refer to the reified symbols (abstract-systemic frameworks), as do the responses. The gesture is then not calling forth the response in the direct way of significant symbols and protosymbols. There is a reference to some tool outside the direct interaction. However, this is only ever an aspect of a wider process of communicative interaction in which gesture and response are directly linked. Wenger takes this one aspect of symbols, their reified aspect, and makes of it a separate process that people have to employ in addition to their interaction. In the perspective of complex responsive processes there is no duality, only the paradox of those responding having the response called forth by the gesture at the same time as it is being selected on the basis of history so that the response is never simply an intentional choice or simply due to the gesture. Emergence does not feature in an essential way in Wenger's argument.

In Wenger's understanding of the process of negotiating meaning, people participate, that is, they interact to do or say something and in doing this they produce an 'as if' object, which they then use in their action. From a complex responsive process perspective this is not what people are primarily doing in their everyday interaction. Instead, participation means communicative interaction or power relating in the medium of symbols, sometimes using tools such as artefacts that reify symbols. There is only one process with its paradoxical nature. Since interactions are negotiation there is no need for objects around which to negotiate. If it is an intrinsic property of interaction to pattern itself, then there is no need to postulate an object around which a pattern forms. For Wenger, symbols are *given* meaning by a process of projection whereas for the perspective described in this chapter, symbols *are* meaning. The gesture-response is not a duality but one action. In complex responsive process theory, meaning does not organise itself around objects but rather meaning is the patterning of interaction, that is, the emergent narrative themes organising the experience of being together. Some of these themes become habitual, are institutionalised, and it is this that imparts repetition and stability to a process that is at the same time unstable and transformative.

While Wenger moves from a micro-description of communities of practice to an abstract, macro-level explanation of the process, the complex responsive process perspective stays with the micro interaction and understands widespread pattern to emerge from it. The complex responsive process perspective is concerned with much the same phenomenon as that described by Wenger but provides a very different kind of explanation. First, the explanation does not abstract from the direct experience of interaction. Instead of moving to macro levels and positing overall processes or systems, it stays with the interaction, exploring its micro details. Instead of macro processes (systems) of participation and reification, the theory of complex responsive processes is one micro process (one social act) of gesture-response in which meaning emerges. This micro process is at one and the same time communicative interaction and power relating. There is no duality here but rather the paradox of gesture forming while at the same time being formed by the response. The paradox is one of the response being called forth by the act of the gesturer and the history-based selection of the responder. Then I would argue that the ordinary, everyday experience is not that of negotiating meaning. As soon as one says that we are *negotiating* meaning that implies, to me, a conscious deliberateness. Sometimes, for example in a scientific debate, this is what we might be doing, but in an ordinary, everyday way what we are directly doing is acting and interacting. To the extent that we are negotiating then what we are negotiating is our mutual conduct, the actions and the interactions themselves. The meaning of what we are doing emerges in the interaction and is not normally the direct subject of negotiation. What we are doing in our interactions is 'going on' together and the meaning this has emerges in our 'going on together'.

Conceptual differences of the kind discussed in this chapter matter because of their implications for practice, which will be taken up in Chapter 17.

● ● ● ● 15.5 Summary

This chapter explored how complexity theory might provide a framework for thinking about the process of mind and self-formation. A complex adaptive system consists of a great many agents interacting with each other according to their own local rules and in doing so they are adapting to each other. When this is interpreted in a human context it is easy to postulate a human system in which the agents are individual people adapting to each other according to their own mental models. I suggested another interpretation. First, humans are not simply adapting to each other according to given mental models. I find it more useful to think of humans as continuously responding to each other. Humans continuously make gestures that evoke and provoke responses from each other. The word responsive, therefore, seems more apt than the word 'adaptive' when it comes to humans. I also want to move away from the notion of human interaction constituting a 'system'. I therefore proposed using the concept of process instead. Human relating is complex responsive processes.

Complex responsive processes are interacting themes that organise human experience and they largely take a narrative form. Each individual mind is many narrative themes that are interacting with each other and with those of other people to produce emergent patterns of family, and any other group, relationships that constitute the further evolution of their narrative themes. These relational, responsive narrative themes are continuously replicated, or re-created, and as this happens there is the possibility of novel emergent relational patterns. In other words, as people relate to each other, the complex responsive relational themes evolve. Those themes consist of protosymbols, significant symbols and reified symbols. These symbols are all intricately interwoven with, and endlessly triggering, each other to form narrative themes, and also propositional rules, that organise the experience of being together in a particular place at a particular time. Distinguishing between these categories of symbols in this way is important, I think, in emphasising the way in which themes, both personal and group, organise experience. The conversational experience is not organised in language or significant symbols, alone. It is also organised through the medium of body, that is protosymbols, and in the context of a material, technological world expressed in reified symbols.

These complex responsive processes take the form of coherent thought and communication. By demonstrating the possibility of self-organising processes and the emergent coherence they produce, complexity theory offers a way out of having to postulate some designer, programme, system or group mind to explain how the coherence comes about.

What I am suggesting here is a very different interpretation of complexity theory in relation to humans to those reviewed in Chapter 12. I described there how there seems to be a general tendency to interpret human affairs from a complexity perspective in the following way. It is unquestioningly postulated that the agents in a human complex adaptive system are the individual members of a group or organisation. Each of the individual agents then possesses a mental model according to which they adaptively interact with others. I think that this general tendency is based on the unquestioned assumption of the autonomous individual, prior and primary to the group. I suggested that this leads to the incorporation of complexity theory into systemic management and organisational theory. When one moves to the relational view I have been describing it becomes impossible to equate agency with individuals. Instead, agency lies simultaneously with individuals and the group since they form and are formed by each other. It is because I want to signal this shift that I want to use the term complex responsive processes. In complex responsive processes, the entities are themes that organise experiences of relating. The individual person and the group are simply different aspects of the one phenomenon, namely relating.

Further reading

The book by Boden (1994) is highly recommended.

Chapter 16 ● ● ● ●

Understanding organisations as complex responsive processes

16.1 Introduction

In taking a process view of organisations and their strategies, this Part of the book is suggesting that we think of an organisation as the continually iterated processes of relating and communicating between people. It is in their complex, responsive relating to each other that people become who they are, both collectively and individually. Organisation is, therefore, a reflection of human identities, where identity means what an organisation is and who its members are. Identity has to do with being recognised by others for being and doing something and with people recogising themselves in that recognition. For example, GE is recognised as perhaps the world's largest corporation, which provides a wide range of products and sevices. It presents itself to, and is recognised by, many of us as a competitive company that operates with integrity and values its people. In other words, GE is a recognisable collective identity and as such is a key aspect of the identities of the people who work there. They take pride in telling people that they work for GE and experience a real sense of loss if their part of GE is sold to another corporation.

Once one understands that any organisation is essentially collective and individual identities, then the 'organisational' strategy refers to the manner in which its identity evolves. Strategy is concerned with how an organisation has become what it is and how it will become what it becomes, that is, how its identity evolves.

The central argument of the complex responsive process perspective is that strategy is the evolving pattern of collective and individual identities emerging in the ordinary, everyday local interactions between people. This ordinary, everyday interaction is a continual iteration of communication/power relating patterned as themes that organise the experience of being together. As they continually interact, people form and are simultaneously formed by narrative and propositional themes that emerge as continuity and potential transformation at the same time. The rest of this introductory section summarises the key points about the complex responsive processes perspective and the subsequent sections explore the nature of the thematic patterning of experience in organisations. The strategy of an organisation is the evolution of this thematic patterning.

In Chapters 13 to 15, I have been suggesting that the human analogue for a complex adaptive system is complex responsive processes. The perspective of complex responsive processes provides a process rather than a systemic explanation of inter-action. I also explained how complex responsive processes constitute a theory of human psychology, which takes as fundamental the processes through which people relate to each other. While the systemic theories reviewed in Part One combine a theory of interaction with a theory of human psychology, the complex responsive processes perspective is a theory of human psychology that is also a theory of inter-action. Interaction and human nature are the same phenomenon. While systemic theories distinguish between individual and group as different levels of analysis, the complex responsive process perspective is one in which the individual is the singular of relating while the group is the plural of relating. This perspective can be expressed in the following propositions:

1 Humans relate to each other in the medium of symbols, which are always gestures and responses interwoven with feeling states or emotions.

2 These symbols form themes that organise people's experience of being together and being alone. The themes interact with each other in a self-organising way. Themes trigger themes that trigger themes so that they are continuously repro-duced and transformed in relationships through conversations between people.

3 An individual mind is a silent, private conversation resonating with vocal, public conversations. Mind and group/society are the same phenomenon. They form and are formed by each other, at the same time, in an essentially self-referential process. That process is also reflexive in that people evoke, provoke and res-onate with each other in ways that are both enabled and constrained by their own histories of relating.

4 The organising themes are dynamical. They may display stable patterns in which the same themes are continually reproduced in a stable way. They may also display patterns analogous to the edge of chaos in which there is simultaneously both stability and change in their reproduction so that there is the potential for some kind of transformation. Conversation then takes a spontaneous free-flowing form.

5 The organising themes of one moment emerge from interaction between themes of the previous moment and what so emerges may take propositional or narrat-ive forms. Both are emergent but the former takes a more stable and often more persistent form while the latter form is more fluid and fleeting. Both forms of theme are expressed in conversation. Intention is an organising theme that emerges from conversation and organises experience. The intention of one is a gesture and its meaning lies in the response it evokes from others.

6 Relationships organised in conversation by propositional and narrative themes both enable and constrain what may be said, done and even thought. In other words, conversations configure, and are configured by, power relations between people.

7 Ideology is organising themes that either justify current power relations or justify the undermining of these current power relations. Dominant ideology makes current power relations feel natural, while ideologies at the margin make opposition feel natural. Official ideology is themes organising what may be openly and safely talked about. Official ideology legitimises some kinds of

conversation and banishes others. Unofficial ideologies are themes organising the relationships and conversations banished from the legitimate arena. They may either collusively support current power relations or potentially undermine them.

8 Ideological themes organising experience, whether official or unofficial, binarise and polarise experience into sameness and difference, them and us, inclusion and exclusion.

9 People are usually unaware of how ideology polarises experience and makes differences seem natural in the interest of sustaining or opposing current power relations – unconscious processes.

10 Another aspect of unconscious processes is the fantasies that groups and individuals develop around power relations and take up in their silent conversations that are their minds.

11 Official ideologies are sometimes maintained and sometimes undermined through processes of gossip and ridicule.

12 Change in individuals and groups means change in the themes organising the experience of being together and hence change in power relations.

13 The responsive nature of the processes of relating means that the evolution of relationships displays the paradox of predictability and unpredictability. Since any gesture could call forth a variety of responses, and those responses could provoke a variety of further responses, the possibility of predicting how they will unfold rapidly diminishes. Human responses are sensitive to small variations in gesture.

This chapter will explore how an organisation, as part of a population of organisations, might be understood as complex responsive processes.

●●●● 16.2   Organising themes, power relations and ideology

The theoretical perspective I am suggesting draws on complexity theory to posit that organisations are complex responsive processes analogous to complex adaptive systems but also significantly different from them. I do this because the logical properties of interaction revealed by simulations in digital symbols provide, I believe, a powerful analogy for interaction in the protosymbols, significant and reified symbols that are human communication.

Digital symbols are arranged in algorithmic forms that organise interaction between themselves, that is they self-organise. This is analogous to the arrangement of protosymbols, significant and reified symbols into propositional and narrative themes that organise themselves as people's experience of relating to each other. Instead of taking a cognitivist, constructivist, humanistic or psychoanalytic view of human psychology that leads straight to defining organisations as complex adaptive systems in which the entities or 'agents' are individual humans, I am taking a relationship psychology perspective. Consequently, an organisation is not immediately thought of as an adaptive thing-like system or network but, rather, as responsive processes. The self-organising entities are then not individual human beings but the symbols, arranged as propositional and narrative organising themes, through which they relate to each other. What emerges is the reproduction and potential transformation of the propositional and narrative themes themselves, that is the pattern of relationships between people. This is analogous to the computer simulations of heterogeneous complex adaptive systems in which the self-organising entities are arrangements of digital symbols in the form of algorithms that interact with each other. What emerges here is the reproduction and potential transformation of the algorithms, that is the pattern of relationships between them.

Algorithmic and human interaction

Given this analogy, I suggest that the insights about nonlinear interaction in heterogeneous complex adaptive systems point to a radically different way of thinking about creative change in organisations. The insights I am referring to have to do with the self-organising, emergent nature of the interaction, the paradoxical dynamic at the edge of chaos and the potential for creativity, and the radical unpredictability arising in that dynamic. I am suggesting, then, that the similarity between algorithmic interaction and human relating resides in the iterative nonlinear nature of both, implying a similar logic to, and similar properties of, interaction in both cases. I believe that a careful exploration of these similarities is a fruitful theoretical strategy, but one requiring detailed attention to the enormous differences.

The enormous difference between algorithmic and human interaction relates to the significant difference between digital symbols and the symbols humans use in communication. The symbols in human communication are not digital, they are primarily not algorithmic in form, and they are not processed or disembodied. The symbols of human communication are patterned as narrative and propositional themes that organise the responsive experience of those individuals in their being and doing together and their experience is these themes. It is the themes that interact and these themes are always experienced in individual human bodies. In other words, an organisation is thought of, not just as a group of individuals, but as responsive processes of relating, that is communicative interaction between them.

Organisational action, then, is never simply the act of an autonomous individual but always occurs in the relationships that people have with each other. Drawing on the analogy of heterogeneous complex adaptive systems, I want to suggest that the complex responsive processes of human relating are self-organising. By this I mean that the interacting responsive processes, operating at any one time, organise themselves, with reference to themselves, into emergent processes of relating at the next point in time. Responsive processes of relating continuously reproduce and transform themselves. This in no way denies the possibility of an individual choosing or intending anything. It simply posits that such choice and intention is itself a theme that organises experience and emerges in the same way as any other theme. Intentions emerge in conversations as gestures that call forth responses from others in an ongoing conversation. This may sound as if I am saying that processes of relating between people organise themselves in some abstract way not involving individual bodies. However, I am not saying this at all for reasons that follow.

People relate to each other through gestures made by one body to another that evoke responses in other bodies that are gestures to the first. There can be no relationships without this circular connection between gesture and response. As soon as the connection is broken the relationship ceases. All gestures and all responses are the actions of bodies. They can take place either directly between bodies in the presence of each other, or through the medium of some technology or artefact. Whether the self-referential, reflexive gesture-response cycle takes place directly or through technology or artefact, it does so in the medium of symbols.

I have distinguished between protosymbols, significant and reified symbols. To recapitulate, protosymbols are body rhythms experienced as feeling states. They are bodily responses to gestures made by the body itself, by other bodies and the material environment of the body.

Significant symbols are bodily gestures potentially calling forth the same response in oneself as in others. The most important form of significant symbol is vocal language. Since significant symbols are bodily gestures, they are always interwoven with protosymbols and they are organised into narrative themes that organise the experience of being together. Narrative themes are always interwoven with emotion in that people care, often passionately, about the narratives that organise their experience. Narrative themes have the potential of organising experience of a fluid kind with multiple meanings.

Reified symbols are those that tend to be used as if they have an independent reality. They tend to be arranged into propositions that organise the experience of being together. Usually, reified symbols are stated in written form or vocal recordings. Through this means there may be a long delay between the gesture and the response. However, the words or recordings have no meaning until someone reads or hears them, responding with an interpretation. Since bodies express and, after some delay, bodies interpret propositional themes, they too must be the interweaving of reified symbols and protosymbols. People may be no less passionate about certain propositional themes organising their experience than they are about narrative ones. Propositional themes may be arranged in the form of procedures, maps of role relationships, flows of tasks, models of organisational activity and organisational environments, all of which are often called systems. Experience organised in this way tends to be rather stable.

Organising themes

Narrative and propositional themes, both conscious and unconscious, organise themselves into conversations, both the public and vocal and the private and silent of mind, and can take a number of forms, for example:

- fantasies
- myths
- rituals
- ideology
- culture
- gossip

- rumour
- discourses and speech genres
- dialogues
- discussions
- debates
- presentations.

In all of these forms of relating, narrative and propositional themes are organising that experience of relating in a number of ways, for example by:

- selecting what is to be attended to;
- shaping how what is attended to is to be described;
- selecting who might describe it;
- accounting by one to another for their actions;
- articulating purpose in the form of themes expressing intentions;
- justifying actions in the form of themes that express ideology.

Organising themes of an ideological nature are fundamental to human relating because it is these themes that make current power relations feel natural, so justifying them. Relationships always impose constraints on what may be done, what feelings may be acknowledged and even on what may be thought. Such constraint is power. The narrative and propositional themes express and are expressed by, they shape and are shaped by, power relations between people in organisations. Power, from this perspective, is not located in one individual who somehow manipulates or dominates others, but in the relationship between people. Relationships between people constrain all of them. The patterns of constraints arising in relationship is what is meant by the figuration of power relations.

From this perspective, then, an organisation is complex responsive processes of relating, that is various forms of communicating, in the form of conversation. Conversation is complex responsive processes of organising themes or, to put the same phenomenon in different words, relational constraints. I am suggesting that it is useful to think of an organisation as a pattern of conversation and organising and managing as responsive processes of relating in conversation. How people talk, what patterns that talk displays, is of primary importance to what the organisation is and what happens to it. The processes of conversation are also of great importance to how individual members of an organisation experience themselves. This is because the silent, private conversation with oneself is one's mind and self, and this conversation inevitably resonates with the vocalised, public conversations taking place in an organisation. In other words, individual and collective identities emerge simultaneously in human interaction.

If one takes this perspective, that an organisation is a pattern of talk (relational constraints), then an organisation changes only in so far as its conversational life (power relations) evolves. Organisational change is the same thing as change in the patterns of talk and therefore the patterns of power relations. Creativity, novelty and innovation are all the emergence of new patterns of talk and patterns of power relations. In other words, the strategic direction an organisation follows emerges as a pattern in the way people talk and so configure power relations. Note that public, vocal conversations (group relationships) and private, silent conversations (individual minds) are both aspects of the same phenomenon. Change in one means some kind of change in the other. Organisations and their individual members change together. It is not a matter of changing the people first and then changing the organisation. Change is possible when conversational life is free flowing and flexible and impossible when conversational life remains stuck in repetitive themes. The key questions then become: How do themes organise the experience of organisational life? What facilitates and what blocks the emergence of new patterns of talk?

I now want to explore how themes organise experience of life in organisations, starting with how they organise what can, and what cannot, be talked about.

16.3   Legitimate and shadow themes

If there is one thing that everyone knows about life in organisations, or any other grouping of people for that matter, it is this: it is not possible to talk freely and openly to just anyone, in any situation, about anything one likes, in any way one chooses, and still survive as a member. Relationships impose powerful constraints on what it is permissible to say, to whom and how. There is another thing that everyone knows about life in organisations and it is this: it is sometimes quite acceptable to act but quite unacceptable to discuss freely and openly the reasons for doing so. Alternative reasons that cover up the 'real' reason are disclosed instead. This is the basis of the distinction I make between legitimate and shadow themes that organise relationships in organisations.

Legitimate themes organise what people feel able to talk about openly and freely. They organise conversations in which people give acceptable accounts of themselves and their actions, as well as imputations about the actions of others. They are the kind of conversation you readily engage in with others, even if you do not know them well. Shadow themes organise conversations in which people feel able to give less acceptable accounts of themselves and their actions, as well as of others and their actions. They are the kind of conversations you would only engage in informally, in very small groups, with others you know and trust. Shadow themes organise what people do not feel able to discuss freely and openly.

The distinction between legitimate and shadow themes is intimately related to ideology, which can be either official or unofficial. It is ideology that legitimises a conversation. In particular, it is the ideology sustaining current power relations that makes conversation feel natural, acceptable and safe – that is, legitimate. One would normally expect that ideology to be official; that is, the values that are publicly pronounced as those people are to live by. This official ideology may well exert a powerful influence on what may or may not be freely spoken about. However, it need not necessarily determine what may or may not be done. Despite the official ideology, people may act in ways consistent with unofficial ideologies, even though they cannot talk about how their actions are justified by unofficial ideologies. Instead, they will have to find some other, plausible reason consistent with the official ideology. When people engage in shadow conversations, they also do so on the basis of some ideology that makes it feel natural and justifiable to talk as they do, but this time secretively. Here too, the underlying ideology could be official or it could be unofficial.

Let me give an example to clarify the distinction. Although the organisation I am about to describe is a fiction, it is nevertheless constructed from experiences in a number of real organisations.

Example: equal opportunities

This company's board of directors consists of eight men. The group of 30 senior executives who report to them also consists entirely of men. There are some 150 senior managers reporting to them, and of these, 12 are women, mostly in the human resources, public relations and marketing functions. For the past ten years, the directors have emphasised the company's formal equal opportunities policy for recruitment and promotion and its policy on the harassment of women and minorities. Virtually everyone in the organisation is aware of this official ideology of equality, for example between men and women, and it exercises a powerful constraint on what may be talked about freely and openly. It is widely felt to be unacceptable to talk freely and openly about whether women, for example, are in general suitable for the most senior positions. It is also unacceptable to ask openly why there are no women in the upper echelons despite the equal opportunities policy. Even the 12 senior women managers in the company do not feel that it would be wise to talk to directors about this matter. The fear seems to be that such comments would be interpreted as accusations of hypocrisy. The organising theme has to do with it being unwise to point to openly, let alone question, the policies of equal opportunities and harassment in any way.

This is what I mean by themes organising the legitimate experience of being together. Some of these themes are formal, propositional and quite conscious in nature, such as the policy statements on equal opportunities and harassment. Others are narrative, informal and possibly unconscious in nature. The unconscious aspect may lie in the reasons why the women managers do not challenge top executives. For example, it might be a fantasy that the latter would interpret any comment as an accusation of hypocrisy. It is legitimate in this organisation to talk openly and freely only in terms of the equality that is part of the official ideology but it is also quite legitimate to appoint only men to the upper echelons. In other words, it feels right and natural to appoint men only, but it does not feel right to talk openly about this. Note here how the ideology underlying current power relations is a mixture of official and unofficial ideology.

However, people do talk about inequality in private, but only to those who they trust and expect to agree with them, or in the form of a joke. For example, some of the directors and senior managers can be heard to tell disparaging jokes about women, occasionally in the presence of one of the 12 female managers. Female managers also sometimes make disparaging remarks about men, often in their presence. Because the exchange takes place in the form of jokes, any serious intention underlying them can be denied if need be. Privately a few men express their unwillingness to report to a woman. Although women are sometimes interviewed for director and senior executive posts, a good reason has so far always been found for not appointing them. In each separate case, the reasons produced are indeed plausible but the pattern over a long period of time is curious. The senior women managers also talk in private, often amongst themselves but also with male colleagues who are known to be sympathetic. They talk about glass ceilings and hypocrisy.

These are all examples of what I mean by shadow themes that organise the experience of being together. They organise conversations that can only be conducted in private with people whom one knows and trusts, or in the form of jokes. These conversations express the organisation's unofficial ideologies. Unofficially, some have an ideology that does encompass discrimination and yet others believe that top executives are hypocrites. Note how the themes organising shadow conversations are mainly narrative in nature. Also, note the unconscious aspect. Those making decisions to appoint women are usually not cynically ignoring the equal opportunities policy and most of them would strenuously, and probably quite genuinely, deny that they are discriminating. After all, they provide very careful and convincing reasons why they have not appointed a woman in each separate case. The female managers may not be aware of how they are colluding in maintaining the situation by their public silence. Note how the ideologies underlying shadow conversations are usually unofficial but could be official. The official ideology of equality underlies some of the shadow conversations.

Clearly, unofficial ideologies are undermining official ideology. It is also easy to see that one powerful unofficial ideology, in part unconscious, is sustaining current power relations in which men get the top jobs. It can also be argued that the unofficial ideology of the women and some of the men who support them contributes to sustaining current power relations. It looks as if official ideology is about changing current power relations and unofficial ideologies are resisting this. However, a different argument can be made. In today's social climate, it would be unacceptable not to have public policies about equal opportunities and harassment. It is also probably helpful to have them from a legal point of view. The policies may well be providing an official ideology that meets the requirements of public opinion and in the process covers up the unofficial ones that really make action feel right. This interpretation is strengthened when one of the human resources directors recounts how he raised the topic of equal opportunities over the two years before it was incorporated in personnel policies. He did so privately with a few of his colleagues to get the necessary support to take it to the board. His most persuasive argument was the weight of public opinion.

I am using this example to argue that it is neither the official nor the unofficial ideologies on their own that are sustaining current power relations. Rather, it is the complex interplay between them, between legitimate and shadow organising themes, that sustains current power relations. I am also using it to point to how what is the officially stated ideology today in fact emerged from shadow conversations some time ago.

I want to take this example one step further. A few of the female managers become increasingly frustrated and begin to talk privately about how they can influence the situation. Some of them talk, as people do, at dinner parties about their experience of discrimination in the workplace. A guest at one of these dinner parties is an influential journalist, well known for her championing of women's rights. She interviews the chairman and writes a sarcastic piece in a major newspaper about the all-male management cast at this particular company. Most people in the company talk about the article and they now feel able to talk more openly and freely about why there are so few women in top management. What was a shadow conversation has now emerged into the legitimate arena. A few months later two women are appointed to the senior executive ranks and a prominent businesswoman is appointed to the board as non-executive director. Clearly, the meaning of the equal opportunities policy has changed and with it the pattern of power relations.

Again, what I am illustrating here is the complex interplay between shadow and legitimate themes organising experience in an organisation and how new themes, new meanings, can emerge in this interplay. This interplay has generated greater diversity and variety in the management of the company.

Another example

Consider another example of the interplay between legitimate and shadow themes. Fonseca (*see* Management narrative 1 in this book) reports a development in a water utility in Lisbon. The manager and his colleagues in the Operations and Maintenance Department talked about the waste involved in having to consult many different maps showing the location of utilities in the streets before they could carry out any repairs on the water supply system. They decided that it would be a good idea to digitalise all the existing maps so that repair crews would only have to consult one up-to-date map. However, the manager of the department knew that investment priorities lay elsewhere and that any request for funds for the digitalisation project would be turned down. Without approval, the manager nevertheless started the project, freeing up some time for the four engineers who were enthusiastic and finding small amounts of funding from other budgets.

The project could not be talked about openly and freely to anyone because it was not in the legitimate arena. This did not mean that no one else knew about it. Senior managers did know about it and tolerated it. However, it still could not be talked about openly. Conversations about it were organised by shadow themes. The reason is obvious. The official ideology on control was one in which the use of resources had to be approved by senior executives. It is immediately evident how such a control ideology sustains current power relations and how going around the approval procedures subverts them. After some time, the project reached a stage at which there was enough evidence of its potential usefulness to seek and obtain official approval. As it further developed, it led to significant shifts in power relations between different departments in the organisation. The complex interplay of shadow and legitimate themes led to the emergence of a new technology.

A key point to notice here is how shadow themes can organise collusive maintenance of existing power relations or subvert them. The complex dynamics of interactions between legitimate and shadow themes, between official and unofficial ideologies, establishes the power relations of who is 'in' and who is 'out', who is at the 'centre' and who is at the 'margin'. I will return to this below when the importance of diversity and deviance is discussed.

The distinction between legitimate and shadow themes is not one that is made in the organisational theories reviewed in Part One. The distinctions made there were between formal and informal, conscious and unconscious aspects of organising. Consider first how they are defined and then how one might understand the relationship between them and how they differ from the legitimate-shadow distinction.

Formal and informal

All of the theories reviewed in this book draw much the same distinction between the formal and the informal aspects of an organisation. The formal is identified in terms of an organisation's purpose, its mode of fulfilling its purpose, that is its task, and the individuals who are assigned roles in carrying out the task. The formal organisation is defined in terms of the role it promises to fulfil in its larger community and it is defined in terms of those formally authorised to be its members. The organisation's identity here is defined in terms of formal propositions as to membership, roles and relationships between roles, tasks and purposes.

The informal organisation consists of all relationships not formally defined by their roles or clearly related to their tasks. All personal and social relationships fall within this category. These personal relationships extend into other organisations, making it difficult to define the membership. As everyone knows, no organisation can function without these informal relationships and an organisation, therefore, has to be understood in terms of both formal and informal relationships.

In the terms I am using in this chapter, some of the themes that organise the experience of being together, and therefore some aspects of power relations, may be described as formal. These are primarily propositional themes, frequently expressed in written form setting out reporting structures, procedures and policies of various kinds. The propositions model the hierarchy and the bureaucracy and set out the official ideology. However, the formal organising themes also encompass some of a more narrative kind. For example, there are unwritten understandings of how people should conduct themselves at formal meetings and the kind of deference they should display in conversations with those more senior to them in the hierarchy. The themes that organise informal experience take a narrative form.

Note that this distinction between formal and informal is very different to the distinction between legitimate and shadow. The former distinction relates to the degree of formality and the latter to the degree of legitimacy.

Conscious and unconscious

Learning organisation theory distinguishes between assumptions people are aware of and those that they are not aware of. The concept of mental models used in this theory postulates that most of the content of the models is below the level of awareness. A distinction is also drawn between tacit (unconscious) and explicit (conscious) knowledge. Psychoanalytic perspectives distinguish between what members of an organisation do consciously and what they do unconsciously and it attaches particular importance to the notion of unconscious group processes. This theory pays particular attention to the impact of unconscious fantasy on organising how people experience being together and to the unconscious deployment of defences against anxiety. In terms of this chapter's focus, there is the notion of unconscious processes in which people are unaware of how they use ideology to justify power relations and patterns of inclusion and exclusion.

People are usually conscious of the formal propositional statements that organise their experience of being together. Reflective members of a group are also usually aware of a number of the narrative and protonarrative themes that are organising their experience of being together. However, most of the themes organising experience are likely to be unconscious. It is unusual for people to struggle publicly to identify what these themes are. Certain categories of themes are particularly likely to be unconscious and will be linked with other themes that protect them from exposure to consciousness. In Chapter 14 one such category was identified around the unconscious preservation of power relations through talking and acting on differences that are used to stir up hatred.

This is the dynamic of those who are 'in' and those who are 'out'. While people will be aware of who is 'in' and who is 'out', what they tend to be unaware of is the purpose this categorisation is serving. People in groups also unconsciously categorise experience into binary opposites that become entrenched as ideologies, which make their behaviour seem right and natural. Here the ideology will be conscious but its dubious basis will be unconsciously excluded from consideration. Then the very categorising and logical procedures of language work to highlight certain differences and obliterate others in what is ultimately an arbitrary way. The difference is conscious but what it obliterates becomes unconscious.

To summarise, people in a group will normally be conscious of the propositional statements organising their experience of being together. They will also normally be conscious of some of the narrative themes organising their experience of being together. In particular they will be conscious of themes that include certain people in informal groupings but exclude others and they may be conscious of the ideological reasons for doing this. What they are far less likely to be aware of is that the reason for their classification of who is in and who is out is to preserve power differences. They will be unaware of how they exclude any examination of the ideological basis on which they are discriminating between those who are in and those who are out. Of potentially great importance is the manner in which logic itself unconsciously obliterates differences within categories of people and focuses attention on arbitrary differences between categories of people.

How organising themes interact

This section examines how organising themes of the formal–informal, conscious–unconscious and legitimate–shadow type relate to, and interact with, each other. The connections between them are depicted in Figure 16.1. The key point I hope to make in using this diagram is that although one may focus attention on a part of it, the processes it points to are always simultaneously operating in any organisation. Each category in the diagram is a description of themes that organise the process of relating and together they constitute the complex responsive processes of relating

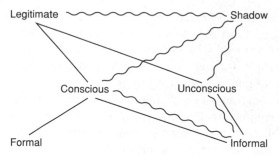

Figure 16.1 Legitimate and shadow

that are the organisation. All of the categories have to do with the reproduction and potential transformation of power relations.

The straight lines in the diagram identify all the interconnections between organising themes that can be described as legitimate, while the wavy lines describe those that can be described in terms of shadow themes. I have already described how the complex interplay between legitimate and shadow organising themes, official and unofficial ideology, either supports or undermines current power relations. This interaction is depicted by the wavy line running between legitimate and shadow in the diagram. The following subsections examine other important interactions.

Legitimate interactions

From the definition given above, it is obvious that all formal themes organising experience are also conscious and legitimate. This is depicted in the diagram as the straight-line connections between these categories. These are the organising themes that strategic choice theory focuses attention on. The organising themes here are primarily propositional in nature and are arranged in models and maps of one kind or another. Plans and budgets, management information and control systems, reward systems and all the other systems and techniques discussed in the chapters on strategic choice theory, all take this form.

However, the formal–conscious–legitimate themes never interact in isolation from the others. To illustrate this, I suggest that you turn to Management narrative 2 in this book. This is an account of a perfectly normal formal meeting to review a budget submission that is to be made to senior executives. It is about propositional themes falling into the conscious and legitimate categories described above. The problem is how to deal with a substantial budget overrun. The first striking point is how personal ambitions and interpersonal rivalries are all part of the process. This immediately brings in organising themes of an informal and even a shadow nature. The story reveals the emotional undercurrent and the anxiety, first of not knowing just how realistic the figures are, and, secondly, of not knowing how senior management will receive them. This points to the probability of unconscious organising themes as a response to anxiety. The story also points to the way in which interaction between various organising themes supports or threatens current power relations. The point is that even as routine and rational an activity as reviewing a budget cannot be understood purely in terms of formal, conscious, legitimate interaction.

What emerges from the budget meeting emerges from the interaction of all the categories of themes.

This example also helps to clarify the nature of intention and control. All arrive at the meeting with an intention, namely to reduce the budget estimate. This is their response to the gesture made by senior management. Each participant also arrives with an individual intention, namely to reduce his or her part of the budget as little as possible and with the hope of even increasing it. Whether this intention materialises, or not, depends upon the responses it evokes from the others. These intentions and the responses they evoke are all themes organising their experience together. It is relatively predictable that they will reduce the budget estimate. However, what they are all well aware of is that they might find themselves in a similar position next year. After all, when they prepared the original estimate some time ago they did not intend that it should quadruple. What happens over the next year will emerge, just as what happens to the detail of the estimate emerges in this meeting. The self-organising interaction of the themes organising their experience and the emergent outcome does not imply in any way that people are interacting without intention.

A similar point applies to the issue of control. A prime requirement of the managers' role is that of controlling their activities and the expenditure they generate. It is the purpose of this meeting to carry out that requirement. However, the managers are well aware that they have not succeeded in controlling the expenditure since the last estimate and they clearly realise that this might happen again. Nevertheless, they do not take this as a cause of despair and so abandon the whole attempt. They, and the situation they are in, cannot be described as out of control. This is what Streatfield (2001) refers to as the paradox of control. In situations of great uncertainty managers are in control and not in control at the same time. The matter of control will be taken up in Chapter 17.

Returning to Figure 16.1, you will see that I have connected informal, conscious and legitimate with straight lines. This is because some organisations are run on informal lines and carry out informally what others would do formally. I have also connected informal, unconscious and legitimate with straight lines indicating that some legitimate organising themes can be informal and unconscious. What I have in mind here is the point made above, namely that people may be interacting informally with each other according to quite legitimate ideology but be unconscious of how in doing so they are sustaining current power relations.

I now want to turn to the wavy-line connection between informal, conscious and shadow organising themes in Figure 16.1.

Covert politics

In learning organisation theory, reviewed in Chapter 6, Argyris (1990) identifies behaviour in organisations that blocks learning. He calls it organisational defence routines. For example, people make certain issues undiscussable, and they also make undiscussable the fact that they are undiscussable. They do this, according to Argyris, because they fear embarrassing, and being embarrassed by, others. He ascribes this behaviour to a defective mental model of the learning process located in the minds of individuals. This model is one in which a person enters a discussion with assertions about others that are not disclosed, knowing that others are doing the same. Each also assumes that they are engaging in the discussion to win and not to lose. His prescription is then that individuals should become aware of their defective mental model of the learning process and change it. The new model requires them to enter into open dialogue and disclose the assertions they are making about each other. He recognises that this will be very difficult and reports that, despite training, people hardly ever do this.

From the perspective I am pointing to this finding is hardly surprising. People hardly ever move to the learning process Argyris recommends because it is a completely unrealistic requirement. It amounts to requiring people to disclose the shadow themes organising their experience, so making the shadow public and legitimate. However, they cannot do this without taking the chance of openly undermining the current power relations and incurring the retaliation of those they threaten. Some ideologies are unconsciously justifying current power relations and others are unconsciously justifying covert attempts to undermine them. People are passionate about these ideological underpinnings. Requiring people to move to the kind of position Argyris has in mind is the same as requiring them to abandon passion and expose not only their ideological position but the largely unconscious purpose they serve. This is only remotely plausible if you put the individual at the centre of your theory of psychology.

Once you place relationship at the centre, it is evident that the basic nature of human relating, the power relations it immediately implies and the ideologies that underpin these relationships would all have to change completely before the Argyris prescription could work. I cannot imagine that human beings will stop engaging in the kind of covert politics that Argyris has so perceptively identified. These complex responsive processes are always likely to characterise life in organisations. However, while they cannot be removed they can be understood, as can their impact on how an organisation evolves.

Covert politics is clearly informal, shadow themes organising experience and the themes are mostly conscious, although the underlying reasons for them may not be. However, it is not organising experience in isolation from or as an alternative to other combinations of theme. For example, over many months colleagues and I engaged in just the kind of covert politics Argyris talks about. One faction in the company I worked for formed around the chief executive and favoured a strategy of investing in the existing business while another faction formed around another powerful figure and favoured diversification by acquisition. I found myself in the latter faction. The chief executive did not publicly dismiss the diversification strategy, although we all knew that he did not favour it. Instead, he called for it to be carefully examined and commissioned a paper on acquisition criteria. After discussion of this, a lengthy report was prepared on possible acquisition targets. At the end of the discussion on this report the chief executive called for a rewording of the acquisition criteria. By the time this had been discussed most of the acquisition targets had been bought by other companies. A further report was prepared. This went on for many months, during which time one small investment after another was made in the existing business.

Everyone engaged in this process knew what was going on and knew that others, including the chief executive, knew what was going on too. No one, however, spoke about this at executive meetings, only privately. Conversations about what was going on were organised by shadow themes while legitimate themes organised silence. Note how the themes were informal, quite conscious and of the shadow. However, the reasons for keeping the conversation in this form were probably less conscious and much of the interaction between the two factions took place at formal meetings organised by legitimate themes. It was all going on at the same time.

From the perspective I am suggesting, covert politics is a social process. In ordinary conversations, legitimate and shadow themes interact in complex ways as people bolster, undermine and shift power positions. Action to remove people from their positions, from the chief executive to the office clerk, all begin as ordinary conversations organised by shadow themes. The important point here is that this form of conversation can shift power relations and patterns of talking but it can just as easily block any such shifts. Obviously this affects how an organisation evolves.

Unconscious themes

Consider now how relationships might be organised by themes that are informal and unconscious and have shadow characteristics.

An example of what I mean occurred during a meeting of a group in which I was a consultant. The chief executive for this company expressed considerable frustration with a group of his most senior executives, claiming that he had empowered them to get on with meeting their targets. Instead of doing this, he said that they still kept referring everything to him and he felt that this was a cause of their company's falling profits. He was unwilling to reflect on why this was happening. Instead, he instructed the managers to attend a meeting at which they were to define their roles in such a way that they took more responsibility. I was to be a consultant at this meeting. He started the meeting by berating them for their lack of initiative and then left them to go through the exercise of defining their roles. They refused to do this and spent the entire day in an emotional attack on the chief executive's leadership style. They complained about the unreasonableness of being required to meet conflicting targets. One reported overhearing the chief executive promising to fire the next executive who failed to meet any target whatsoever. This provoked outrage on the part of the managers. How could they be held responsible for changes over which they had no control? During this time, any comment I made was simply ignored and they decided that when the chief executive returned on the next day they would confront him.

However, the next morning one of the executives advised caution and gradually their resolve to confront him ebbed away. Instead they prepared a number of colourful overhead projector foils and made a presentation to the chief executive about some rather safe business issues. He responded with a lecture. During the course of this lecture it became clear that there was little truth in the rumour that he would remove anyone who failed to achieve all targets no matter what happened. It was only on the following day, in a somewhat depressed state, that they were able to reflect on what they were doing. We talked about some of the themes organising their experience of being together at that time. For example, one clear theme that they seemed to be unconscious of was one that might be summarised as follows: 'Every casual remark the chief executive makes is an instruction or at least about to become one.' An example was the statement all took to be true that they had to achieve all targets or they would be fired. Other themes were those around flight from their task, the fight dynamic around the chief executive and the dependency on presentations of safe issues. These are the basic assumption behaviours of the psychoanalytic perspective (*see* Chapter 7), understood here as unconscious themes organising the experience of being together. On the chief executive's next visit they were able to discuss their relationship with him.

The themes organising the experience for much of this meeting were informal, unconscious and of the shadow. However, the meeting took place legitimately and when the chief executive appeared it took formal, conscious and legitimate form. However, even when this happened the feelings and silent communications between the senior executives clearly reflected the informal, unconscious and shadow themes organising their experience. Again, interaction between all the kinds of theme differentiated in Figure 16.1 are taking place simultaneously. What emerges does so through the complex interplay of legitimate and shadow, conscious and unconscious and formal and informal themes. How all this is at the same time forming and being formed by power relations is also evident in the example. Again, these processes affect how an organisation evolves.

One of the most important aspects of shadow organising themes is the socially unconscious form they take. What is unconscious here is how members of a group collectively employ, in their talk and their actions, differences between themselves (senior executives in the above example) and other groups (the chief executive and those who report immediately to him) to stir up anger (even hatred) against the others in order to preserve unconsciously sensed power differences. They do this by collectively categorising their experience into binary opposites (meet all the targets or get fired) that become entrenched as ideologies, which make their behaviour seem right and natural. Furthermore, they collectively obliterate some differences and highlight others, so polarising experience.

16.4   The importance of diversity

Let me reiterate what I mean by shadow themes that organise experience. Legitimate themes are legitimate because they conform to official ideologies. The opposite of legitimate is, of course, that which is illegitimate or illegal. This is not what I mean by the organisational shadow. Shadow themes form conversations, that is power relations, that arise between the legitimate and the illegitimate or illegal. The shadow is neither legitimate nor illegitimate. In a sense, one might say that it is both legitimate and illegitimate at the same time. Shadow themes/power relations are shadow because of the manner in which they are expressed in conversation. Such conversations always take place informally between small numbers of people and their distinguishing feature is that they do not conform to the official ideology. Some unofficial ideologies may collusively support current power relations while others seek to undermine them and both can be taking place at the same time. This does not mean that such conversations only take place between the less powerful. The most powerful participate in them too.

In using the term shadow, I am trying to capture some of the points reviewed in Chapter 15. The first is that made by Elias (1989) when he talked about people challenging the official ideology from the margin. Conversations in the shadow are conversations at the margin. I am also trying to capture the point Bakhtin (1986) made about 'carnival'. Frequently, conversations in the shadow take humorous forms. Conversations in the shadow are a form of play, transitional phenomena in the sense of Winnicott (1965). It is in the complex interplay of legitimate and shadow themes that ordinary, everyday conversations create organisational reality (Shotter, 1993).

To summarise, organisations exist to enable joint action and people can only act jointly through their relationships with each other. People relate to each other through complex responsive processes that can be understood in terms of inter-acting propositional and narrative themes. It is these themes that organise the experience of relating between people. The themes take many forms. They may be ideological themes. They may take the form of intentions, expressions of emotion, descriptions and so on. Simultaneous interaction between many themes taking dif-ferent forms constitutes the conversational life of an organisation. The process of relating through conversation constrains that relating and so establishes power rela-tions. Conversation and power relations are simply different words for the same phenomenon, namely that of relating between people. An organisation is pro-cesses of relating, that is its pattern of power relations, its conversational life. Conversational life cannot develop according to an overall blueprint since no one has the power to determine what others will talk about all the time. Conversation is thus a self-organising phenomenon and this self-organisation continuously pro-duces emergent patterns in itself. In other words, themes organising the experience of relating in conversation continuously reproduce themselves and in so doing may transform themselves. Creativity, innovation and learning are all transformations of organising themes as they reproduce themselves. It is important, therefore, to understand how such transformation occurs. The key to transformation is diversity.

The reproduction and transformation of conversational themes

In the language of complexity theory, system transformation means that the system moves from one attractor to another. More fundamentally, transformation is move-ment not just from one attractor to another that already exists, but to a new one that is evolving. Chapter 11 described the conditions that must be satisfied if a sys-tem is to display the internal capacity to move spontaneously from one attractor to another and to evolve new ones. These conditions have to do with the heterogeneity of the entities comprising the system and the heterogeneity of their interactions. Transformation is possible only when the entities, their interactions with each other and their interaction with entities in the system's environment are sufficiently het-erogeneous, that is sufficiently diverse. The fundamental requirement for transform-ation is non-average, deviant, maverick or eccentric behaviour on the part of the entities comprising a system (Allen, 1998a, 1998b). In simulations of complex sys-tems, such diversity is generated in the course of reproduction through random mutation, that is chance changes, in the digital code and through cross-over replication, that is the mixing of two sets of digital code. Of course, if the rate of mutation is too high, the system becomes totally disorganised. Transformation therefore requires a rate of mutation within a critical range where it is neither too high nor too low. A similar point applies to cross-over replication. If the mixing of the code during replication is totally random the system will soon become completely disorganised. However, cross-over replication, as with sexual reproduction, is not a totally random mixing of digital, or genetic, code. Blocks of code from one 'mate' are joined to blocks of code of the other, so preserving some structure, but not too much.

What then is the analogue of random mutation and cross-over replication in the conversational life of an organisation? In other words, what generates the variety upon which continuing diversity depends? I have already argued that there is no analogy for the system in human interaction but that the interaction between digital entities can be taken as analogous to human communicative interaction in the mode of protosymbols, significant and reified symbols. Just as variety is generated by random fluctuations in the reproduction of pattern, so variety in human communicative interaction is generated by the lack of perfection in communication.

Misunderstanding

As everyone knows, human communication is far from perfect. When people converse about any matter that is at all complicated, they only partially understand each other, at first anyway. The back and forth movement of conversation is a process of trying to clarify meaning. In other words, there is usually some degree of misunderstanding in human communication. This is the analogue of random mutation. Meaning, that is themes organising conversational life, has the potential for being transformed when there is a critical level of misunderstanding (Fonseca, 2001). If misunderstanding is too extreme, then communication fails, and if it is very mild, then nothing novel is being communicated. The analogue for cross-over replication is the interaction of different patterns of conversation. This occurs, for example, when people from one discipline, say biology, talk to people from another, say management (Fonseca, 2001). These two groups of people use different vocabularies and concepts but in talking to each other, trying to understand each other's ways of talking, new meaning may be generated. This is cross-fertilisation and emergent transformation in the reproduction of conversation.

This suggests that it is through the diversity generated by misunderstanding and cross-fertilisation of different ways of talking that transformation in organising themes and thus patterns of conversing occur. Individuals and small groups become identified with this diversity, attracting the labels of conforming and deviant, normal and eccentric, responsible and maverick, orthodox and radical, us and them and so on. This is clearly the identification and description of power relations in terms of what conversational themes and which people are 'in' and 'out'. All of these distinctions are ways of describing the distinction between legitimate and shadow. That distinction between legitimate and shadow is important because the tension between the two is the potential source of the diversity that is critical to the capacity to change spontaneously in novel ways.

The organisational shadow, then, is those organising themes/power relations that are in some sense deviant and this deviance encompasses the despicable and the destructive, on the one hand, and the heroic and the creative, on the other. Shadow communications take the form of ordinary, everyday conversations, gossip, rumour, inspirational accounts, stories that express humour and the grotesque, tales that take the form of elaborate social fantasies or touching personal contacts. Shadow communications shape and are shaped by power relations, some of which collusively support and others of which covertly undermine the legitimate. I am suggesting that it is important to distinguish between legitimate and shadow organising themes because the potential for the emergence of new organisational direction arises when legitimate and shadow themes are in tension. In other words, creative potential arises from the subversion of legitimate organising themes by shadow themes. What emerges then is new forms of conversation, that is shifts in power relations. In other words, just as with any complex system (Allen, 1998a), an organisation's internal capacity to move spontaneously to a new form depends upon the degree of diversity in its conversational themes.

The dynamics of conversation

Chapter 11 described the different dynamics characteristic of complex adaptive systems, namely the dynamics of stable equilibrium, bounded instability at the edge of chaos or disintegration. It also pointed to the conclusion that such systems produce novel emergent forms when they operate in, or near to, the dynamics of the edge of chaos. That dynamic occurs at critical rates of information flow, critical degrees of connection between agents and critical levels of diversity in agents and their interactions. I think that convincing analogues for the dynamics of complex adaptive systems and the factors that alter this dynamics are to be found in the complex responsive processes of human relating, that is in patterns of conversation.

You can see this when you reflect upon how changes in patterns of conversation sometimes arise spontaneously and at other times get caught in patterns of repetition where change is blocked. Repetitive patterns of conversation that block change are the analogue of equilibrium attractors in complex adaptive system. Free-flowing, flexible conversation that spontaneously shifts to new patterns (Shaw, 2002) is the analogue of the complex attractors at the edge of chaos. Highly emotional miscommunication would be the conversational analogue of the dynamics of disintegration. Organisational health has to do with the capacity to change, to produce new forms, and this depends crucially on free-flowing, flexible conversation, that is conversation displaying the dynamics of bounded instability. Organisational illness, on the other hand, is an inability to change that occurs when conversational life follows stable attractors in which themes are simply repeated with only superficial change.

Consider now the analogues for those factors that determine whether the dynamics is that of stable equilibrium, bounded instability or disintegration. The first two are the rate at which information flows through the system and the number of connections between agents. The human analogues of information flow and connectivity in complex adaptive systems are the number and quality of the connections between themes that organise the experience of relating. In other words, the richness of the themes organising the experience of relating have an impact on the dynamics of conversation. When relationships between people are organised by a small number of loosely connected themes, conversational patterns become repetitive, the dynamics of stable equilibrium. For example, neighbours may see each other regularly as they come in and out of their homes but the themes organising their relating may be few in number and they may not trigger many associations with other themes. They may organise the conversation around how the others are, what they feel about the weather and sometimes a report about some local matter, such as planning permission for some building alteration. These conversations are repetitive and predictable. They lack any spontaneous and free-flowing qualities.

Relationships between colleagues in work situations, on the other hand, may be organised by a large number of themes triggering many associations with other themes. The complex interaction of these themes is likely to produce conversations of a free-flowing nature. When conversation is organised by very many themes triggering very many associations with others, communication is likely to become highly disorganised. The conversational equivalent of bounded instability at the edge of chaos is thus likely to occur in some critical range of richness in organising themes. If the themes are too impoverished then the dynamics is stable and if they are too rich then the dynamics is disintegrative.

Diversity

The third determinant of the dynamics in a complex adaptive system is the diversity in agents and their interaction. The analogue in human relating is the diversity in organising themes. As discussed above, that diversity arises in misunderstanding and in the cross-fertilisation of concepts through interaction between different patterns of conversation. Again, the dynamics of free-flowing conversation is associated with critical levels of misunderstanding and cross-fertilisation. If there is little misunderstanding between people forming a group with well-established concepts and ways of talking to each other, their conversations are likely to be repetitive. If there is too much misunderstanding between people drawn from very many disparate groups then there is the disintegration of communication, a 'tower of Babel'. The conditions for creative, free-flowing conversations lie in some critical range between these extremes. This is where the tension between legitimate and shadow themes becomes important in that this tension expresses the relationship between orthodoxy and deviance. It is this deviance that imparts the internal capacity to evolve spontaneously new patterns of conversation, that is new conversational attractors.

There are some additional factors affecting the dynamics of human relating that are not evident in simulations. Human relationships are relationships between bodies and the medium of relating is symbols that are always felt in bodies. It is essential then, in understanding the dynamics of relating, that is of conversing, to understand the impact of bodily interactions. I suggest that the most important additional aspects to incorporate in thinking about complex responsive processes of relating are the nature and impact of anxiety and the emotional responses to power relations.

Anxiety

Anxiety is a generalised form of fear. While fear has a known cause, anxiety is a very unpleasant feeling of general unease, the cause of which cannot be located.

Chapter 7 on psychoanalytic perspectives reviewed the important contribution that psychoanalytic perspectives make to an understanding of the organisational effects of anxiety. First, there are the defences people use to avoid feeling anxious. These may take the form of structures and procedures having the ostensible purpose of enabling some rational task, but actually operating as defences. For example, people may prepare forecasts of future states that are impossible to predict and develop strategic plans on the basis of these forecasts. Such plans may then have little impact on what is actually done but by creating a sense of certainty defend people against the anxiety of feeling uncertain. The result is stable, repetitive conversational dynamics around strategies that are simply a continuation of what is already being done. An alternative form of defence is what Bion (1961) called basic assumption behaviour. Here people in groups are overwhelmed by volatile fight, flight, dependency and other dynamics that disable their thinking capacity. Conversations are organised by fantasy themes that produce highly unrealistic conversational stability or conversational disintegration. The former are present when the basic assumption is dependency and the latter when it takes the form of fight–flight.

Chapter 7 also introduced the important psychoanalytic concept of 'good enough holding'. Here conditions are such that people are able to hold the simultaneous excitement and anxiety of conversations that test the boundary of what they know. The 'good enough holding' of anxiety is an essential condition for the free-flowing conversational dynamics that is the analogue of the edge of chaos. I suggest that 'good enough holding' is a quality of the themes organising the experience of relating. When these take the form of trusting interaction, they are themselves then forms of 'good enough holding'. In other words, when the quality of relating is characterised by trust, conversation can take free-flowing forms. This interpretation of 'good enough holding' differs from the psychoanalytic interpretation in that it does not locate the 'good enough' in a leader or a consultant (Stapley, 1996) but in the quality of conversational interaction itself.

Closely related to the 'good enough holding' of anxiety there is the matter of the quality of power relations. Themes organising relating between people may be highly constraining so that power relations have the qualities of force, authoritarianism, dictatorship and so forth. The responses that these qualities evoke are either submission or rebellion. The former produce highly repetitive, stable conversational patterns, while the latter produces disintegration in communication. Sometimes, the themes organising the relating between people impose very little constraint. This is equivalent to saying that relational ties are very weak and, therefore, patterns of conversation are likely to be disrupted. The conversational dynamics is disintegrative. Again, it is a critical range that is associated with free-flowing conversation, this time a critical range in the constraining qualities of relating. This is a quality of the themes that organise relating.

Free-flowing conversation

The crucial distinction I am making here is that between free-flowing conversation and patterns of conversation that take on a repetitive, stuck form. This is crucial, because it is only in the former that potential creativity, that is emergent new patterns of conversation, lie. A healthy, functioning organisation is one that continually responds; that is, provokes and evokes responses from other organisations and reacts to the provocations and evocations of other organisations so as to survive and prosper. For this to happen, communication must flow freely and not get caught in repetitive themes. This means that the themes organising experience must interact so as to flow continually along new pathways and this will happen only if new shadow themes emerge to become legitimate. An ailing organisation is one in which communication is blocked.

This is essentially the same as Foulkes's (1948) view of mental ill health. He defined health as the free flow of communication between people in a group. For him illness was a state in which communication was blocked and he argued that this blockage gets located in an individual or group of individuals. That individual or group is then said to be ill but it is really the whole pattern of relationships that is ill, the illness merely being located in particular people or groups. The 'cure' is to attend to the blockage and free it.

In organisational terms, I suggest that the quality of free-flowing conversation is closely associated with the interplay between legitimate and shadow themes organising conversational life. Conversations arise in the organisational shadow as a response to the inhibition that legitimate power relations, and the official and unofficial ideologies that support them, impose on talking. They take place, often in fleeting snatches, in small groups of people, usually as they are going about other, legitimate business. They occur in corridors, on aircraft, in cars, in someone's office, in the bar, over dinner, around the photocopier and so on. Their key feature, however, is that they are expressions, and explorations, of deviations, eccentricities and other matters that do not fit with what is legitimate. In such conversations, people question the wisdom of decisions made, they complain, they suggest other possibilities, they talk about highly personal differences and difficulties, they spread gossip and rumour, they express cynicism, they fill gaps in their knowledge with fantasies, they tell jokes, they express their feelings of anger and frustration, enthusiasm and excitement, hatred and affection, pride and disappointment, trust and mistrust. Conversations in the shadow provide a means to vent emotion and to test the boundaries of what is acceptable. They deal with the unexpected and the ambiguous. They are a form of play.

The kinds of conversation I am describing are usually thought of as an unproductive waste of time at best, and normally even worse than this, a destructive deviation from consensus and the capacity for joint action. What purpose do they serve from the perspective I am suggesting? Ordinary conversations are complex responsive processes evoking and provoking responses in a continuing back-and-forth rhythm. Each response is made on the basis of local organising principles in the absence of any overall blueprint. Complexity theory suggests that it is just this kind of interaction that has the potential, in certain conditions, for producing emergent new forms.

I suggest, then, that an organisation's potential for creativity lies in these shadow conversations and their tension with the legitimate. Complexity theory also suggests that the dynamics of creativity is also that of destruction. So, conversations in the shadow are potentially both creative and destructive. The key condition for the kind of free-flowing ordinary conversations to have the potential for creativity, and destruction, is that of trust. When people who trust each other engage in shadow conversation they feel able to test boundaries, particularly those of current power relations, talk about what is possible and what is not, and how the impossible might be rendered possible.

The kinds of conversation arising in the shadow are therefore crucial to an organisation's capacity to produce novel strategic directions. When shadow conversations collusively support the legitimate then the organisation cannot change. The potential for change lies in the extent to which shadow conversation undermines current power relations and legitimate forms of talk.

The capacity for emergent new ways of talking is fundamental to organisational creativity. If this is so, then it is a matter of considerable strategic importance to pay attention to the dynamics of ordinary conversation, particularly those in the shadow. The purpose of this attention is not to control the conversation or somehow produce efficient forms of it, but to understand it and particularly to understand what blocks it. So what are its chief characteristics?

Conversation in the shadow is always informal and it is organised by complex and subtle principles. It is a self-organising, rhythmical process of vocal gestures and response. This turn taking is organised by implicit principles relating to who may speak next, who may interrupt whom and so on. Although a response to the inhibition opposed to the official ideology, it too is organised by power relations expressed in ideology, this time deviant, or even subversive, ideologies covering up deviant power relations. The content of these conversations is organised by narrative themes, rather than propositional ones.

The conversational life of an organisation may be characterised by the repetition of the same kinds of shadow conversation over and over again in ways that never emerge as shifts in legitimate conversations; for example, repetitive complaints about poor management and lack of direction; or repetitive complaints about poor-quality staff who do not do as they are told. This is the dynamics of stability. Or, people may engage in highly destructive attacks on others, undermining their credibility and tearing their reputations apart – the dynamics of instability. New forms of conversation and other action may emerge at the edge of chaos in free-flowing conversations that begin to appear in legitimate form. The conditions for this to happen are trust and the holding of anxiety, power relations that are both co-operative and competitive, and conversational practices that do not block exploration.

What conversational practices block the kind of flexible, exploratory conversations characteristic of the dynamics of the edge of chaos? What practices trap groups of people in highly repetitive conversations? Some of the answers to these questions are provided by paying attention to the rhetorical ploys that people employ in their conversations.

All ordinary conversations employ some kind of rhetorical ploy. In such conversations, people are giving accounts of themselves to others, explaining to each other why they feel as they do and why they want to do what they want to do. Rhetoric is the conversational art of giving such accounts persuasively. They are conversational organising principles.

Rhetoric

Springett (1998) categorises rhetorical ploys as follows. Amongst the many he identifies, there are moves that:

- influence the path of conversation. Under this heading, he includes statements that invoke a sense of purpose, as when someone says, 'these are *the* objectives'. Then there are silencing moves such as not responding to a point made but rapidly raising another. There are also moves that bound the path, such as 'this is really Stone Age stuff'. Some moves contract the line of conversation, such as 'let's concentrate on the key points'. Other moves expand the line of conversation, such as 'there must be other ways to think about this'. Yet other moves give emphasis, such as 'this is the way we must go'.
- provide frames of reference. This takes place when someone uses other companies as examples of the successful application of their ideas.
- make claims to be the truth, such as 'the latest research shows', or 'customers feel'.
- destabilise, such as 'Does that really add anything?'
- influence beliefs about what is real and possible. Examples are making the intangible seem tangible, such as talking about a merger as a 'marriage', referring to a company as if it were a person and using statements like 'let me walk you through this'. Another example is a move that implies pre-existence, such as talking about unlocking a company's potential.
- construct urgency, such as 'there is a short time window'.

The point is this: without even being aware of it, people in ordinary conversation may be using conversational devices to dismiss the opinions of others and close down the development of a conversation in an exploratory direction. If this way of talking to each other is widespread in an organisation, it will inevitably keep reproducing the same patterns of talk. The use of some rhetorical device is therefore one of the most important blockages to free-flowing, flexible conversation and thus the emergence of new knowledge. Other usages of rhetorical devices could have the effect of freeing these blockages.

I want to draw attention to one further analogy between complex adaptive systems and human complex responsive processes. The dynamics of the edge of chaos in relation to complex adaptive systems is characterised by a power law (see Chapter 11). This means that there are a large number of small extinction events and a small number of large extinction events during some time period. In other words, a system at the edge of chaos has the potential for emergent new forms but there is no guarantee of survival for these new forms. Some will survive and others will not, because of competitive selection. The same point applies to complex responsive processes. The dynamics of bounded instability displayed in free-flowing conversation in organisations creates the potential for the emergence of new forms of conversation, power relations and thus activities. However, the pattern of conversation and activity that emerges will be subjected to selection in competition with other patterns emerging in other organisations. Some will succeed and others will not. There is no general recipe for success. While stability guarantees ultimate extinction, bounded instability creates the potential, but not a guarantee, of survival. Notice how frequently I have used the word 'quality' in talking about the conditions in which an organisation displays the internal capacity to change spontaneously.

Figure 16.2 summarises the key points that this chapter has made about the dynamics of complex responsive processes.

> **Figure 16.2**
>
> ## Complex responsive processes: main points on organisational dynamics
>
> - Organisations are complex responsive processes of relating between people. Since relating immediately constrains, it immediately establishes power relations between people. Complex responsive processes take the form of propositional and narrative themes that organise the experience of relating and thus power relations. The themes organise the conversational life of an organisation.
> - These themes take many forms. Of great importance are the official ideological themes that determine what it is legitimate to talk about in an organisation. Of even greater importance are the unofficial ideological themes that make current power relations feel natural and the unofficial themes that organise the subversion of current power relations. In other words, unofficial ideologies may be supporting or subverting official ideologies. This dynamic is an aspect of the organisational shadow.
> - Themes organise patterns of conversation and power relations. These patterns are the analogues of attractors in complex adaptive systems.
> - Conversational patterns may take stable forms of repetition in which people are stuck. They may also take more free-flowing forms, analogous to the dynamics of the edge of chaos.
> - Change occurs in novel ways through the presence of sufficient diversity in organising themes. This is expressed in free-flowing conversation in which shadow themes test the legitimate.
> - The evolution of free-flowing conversation and the emergence of creative new directions are radically unpredictable.
> - Free-flowing conversation becomes possible when the pattern of relating has the quality of good enough holding of anxiety.
> - It is qualities of relationship that determine whether an organisation has the internal capacity for creativity.
> - There is no guarantee of success.

16.5   The social structure of organisations

So far, this chapter has explored the kinds of thematic patterns that emerge in the interaction between the people who are an organisation. These patterns display the dynamics of both continuity and potential transformation at the same time. They may take on a fluid form in which change emerges or highly repetitive patterns may continually emerge in which people become stuck and so cannot change. However, rather repetitive patterns are also what impart enough stability to social relations to enable people to go on together. This kind of stability is what is meant by the term social structure.

Social structure is usually defined as the repetitive and enduring patterns of recurring relations between people in their ongoing dealings with each other. Examples of social structures are economic phenomena such as patterns of relationships between the owners of capital and the providers of labour. Markets are patterns of relationship between suppliers and demanders of goods and services and as such constitute social structures. Other examples of social structures are state and government functions; legal relationships; technological development; the family; religious practices; language; demography. Institutions and social structures not only are characterised by repetition and endurance but also may be described in widely accepted language. Organisations may be thought of as institutions with a significant element of formal description of roles, relationships between members and the tasks they perform. Closely linked to the ideas of social structure, institutions and organisations are the notions of habits, customs, traditions, routines, mores, norms, values, cultures, paradigms, beliefs, missions and visions. These are all ideas about the repetitive, enduring, shared practices of people in their ongoing dealings with each other in institutional life.

Culture and social structure can, therefore, be defined in terms of repetitive and enduring values, beliefs, traditions, habits, routines and procedures that many people have in common. From a complex responsive process perspective, these are all social acts of a particular kind. They are couplings of gesture and response of a predictable, highly repetitive kind. They do not exist in any meaningful way as a thing in a store or artefact anywhere. They are aspects of the continually iterated interactions between people. In other words, they are habitual themes organising the experience of being together. However, even habits are rarely exactly the same. They may often vary as the contexts and participants in interactions change. In other words, there will usually be some spontaneous variation in the repetitive reproduction of patterns called habits. Social habits and routines, values and beliefs are emerging aspects of the thematic patterning of interaction between people. Habits here are understood not as shared mental contents but as history-based, repetitive actions, both private and public, reproduced in the living present with relatively little variation.

The institutional themes organising the experience of being together tend to take the formal, conscious, legitimate form and they have the effect of limiting the connections between people, so preserving stability. Hierarchical reporting structures in an organisation are an example of this. In hierarchical structures, people mainly interact with their immediate superior, who in turn interacts with a person higher up in the hierarchy. This clearly cuts down on the number of connections. The accomplishment of hierarchy, habits, customs and traditions is to replace many potentially conflicting constraints with a few in the interests of ongoing joint action. When current power relations are sustained by this means, stability emerges. Social structures, cultures, bureaucratic procedures and hierarchical arrangements emerge, often as intentions and designs, in the self-organising process of communicative interaction. This is a way of thinking about, say, hierarchy that is more encompassing than the usual way of simply identifying it as a designed structure. What is more encompassing is the inclusion of hierarchy and decisions about hierarchy in the wider process of communicative interaction.

The social process may be one that patterns communicative interaction as clusters of strong connections linked to other clusters by much weaker connections. Such clusters of strong connections would constitute institutions and organisations, in turn patterned as clusters of strong connections with weaker links to others, for example, as departments and project teams within an organisation. This could be understood as an intrinsically stabilising process in that it reduces numbers of connections and hence the numbers of conflicting constraints. In this process, closely linked clusters establish power differences both within and between clusters, so constraining both those within the cluster and those in other clusters. The strong connections take the form of habits. In this way powerful institutions and organisations emerge that constrain the choices open to people.

However, institutionalisation as formal, conscious, legitimate themes organising the experience of being together is only one aspect of the process. At the same time experience is also being patterned by, for example, informal, unconscious, shadow themes. These too form clusters as people organise themselves into shadow pressure groups in organisations, sometimes displaying the kind of fluid communication between people that tends to be stifled by institutionalised themes. These pressure groups and their shadow themes will frequently be antagonistic to institutionalised themes and it is in the tension and the conflict between them that change in institutionalised themes emerges.

The tools of communicative interaction

Communicative interaction between people in organisations involves the use of highly sophisticated tools. Obvious examples are telephones, the Internet, email, documents of all kinds and the wider media of television and newspapers. Less obvious, perhaps, are those tools that are usually mistaken for communication itself, indeed for the organisation itself. I am referring here to management systems of information and control, including budgets, plans of all kinds, monitoring, evaluation and appraisal systems, databases and so on. Even less obviously, perhaps, tools of communicative interaction include statements of visions, missions, values, policies and so on.

When people interact with each other in the living present of their local situations in an organisation they talk to each other in ways that have reference to all of the kinds of systems and procedural tools referred to in the previous paragraph. Meaning does not lie in the tools but in the gestures and responses made with the tools.

For example, a decision on whether to make an investment or not emerges in the communicative interaction between a number of senior managers. Their communication around this issue is patterned in an emergent way by a great many themes forming while being formed in their conversations with each other. Many of those conversations take place between small groups of two or three managers and the kinds of themes patterning their interaction will have all the aspects, legitimate and shadow, conscious and unconscious, formal and informal, discussed earlier. Their conversations with each other may refer to documents setting out discounted cash flow analyses, risk factor appraisals, mission statements and other communicative tools. In other words, they will be using documents that set out specific abstract-systematic frameworks as tools in their communicative interaction. They will refer to the documents as rhetorical tools to persuade others of their opinion. The documents are tools in the process of negotiating with each other and accounting to each other for the positions they take. The constraints provided by an organisation's budget and financial policies are used in similar ways, as are the procedures laid down for obtaining investment approval. All of these tools are essentially aspects of the process of institutionalisation and the constraints it imposes on action.

However, it is *important not to mistake the tools for communicative interaction itself* because this leads to obscuring the nature of the themes patterning the decision-making process, creating the illusion that the decision is largely a calculation. This then acts as a defence against taking into account the underlying ideological processes and the ways they are sustaining or shifting power relations, as well as any anxiety provoked by the potential for transformation of organisational, sub-group and individual identities. Most significant investment decisions shift power relations to some extent and also potentially transform identities of one kind or another. The debate around such decisions has as much to do with such shifts in power relations and identities as with monetary aspects.

The local nature of communicative interaction

Communicative interaction always takes place in specific local situations in the living present. The local nature of these situations is often not hard to see, but particularly when it comes to managers and leaders at the top of an organisational hierarchy, the local nature of interaction might require some explanation. After all, it is supposed to be the role of the chief executive, for example, to act in relation to the whole of an organisation. However, I suggest that closer examination, of what a chief executive actually does, points to another interpretation. A competent chief executive will indeed be thinking and talking about the organisation as a whole but to whom does he or she talk in this way? A chief executive, like anyone else in an organisation, talks most frequently about matters of greatest concern to a relatively small group of trusted others. The chief executive's important communicative interactions take place, therefore, in the local situation of other senior executives. Their communicative interaction is patterned by the processes of themes shaping themes, formal and informal, conscious and unconscious, legitimate and shadow, just as anyone else's is.

There are, of course, differences as well as similarities between the processes of communicative interaction involving a powerful chief executive and those involving the much less powerful. When a chief executive makes a public gesture it potentially calls forth responses in much larger numbers of others than is the case with the less powerful. However, just what those responses will be cannot be arranged by the chief executive, as anyone in that position knows only too well.

For example, suppose the chief executive of a major multinational corporation announces his new vision of the 'corporation as global leader in network solutions'. Perhaps one hundred thousand people around the globe hear the gesture and a great many feel called upon to respond in some way. However, the meaning of the vision, like the meaning of all gestures, does not lie in the gesture. What it means will be created in the responses. Will most just pay lip-service to it and carry on doing what they were doing before? If they do not, just what will they do? The gesture may call forth the response of many meetings around the globe as people discuss what it means and what they are supposed to do about it. The meaning of the chief executive's gesture, and its impact on the organisation, will emerge in many local situations, including his or her own, in the living present of conversations around the globe.

From a complex responsive processes perspective, no one can determine the dynamic of interaction within an organisation because that dynamic depends upon what others both within that organisations and in other organisations are doing. In other words, an individual, or a group of individuals, powerful or otherwise, can make gestures of great importance but the responses called forth will emerge in local situations in the living present where an organisation's future is perpetually being constructed.

Powerful managers, such as chief executives, do have major, widespread effects. However, what a chief executive does emerges in his or her local communicative interaction and the nature of the impact on the organisation emerges in many other local situations, all in the living present. The focus of attention, in trying to make sense of what happens, shifts from the chief executive's statement or new tool to the processes in which the statement or tool arises and to the widespread local situations in which they have their effects. Instead of taking it for granted that powerful chief executives actually individually change organisations directly through their intended actions, the complex responsive processes perspective focuses attention on the communicative processes in which the mere presence of, the images of and the fantasies about leaders all affect local processes of communicative interaction in the living present.

16.6   Summary

One of the important insights contributed by the theories of dissipative structures and complex adaptive systems, reviewed in Chapters 10 and 11, relates to the importance of diversity. A system only has the internal capacity to move spontaneously from one attractor to another, and to evolve new attractors, when it operates in the presence of diversity. In other words, a system can produce novel, creative behaviour only when it has the internal capacity to generate and respond to variety. Variety arises through processes such as cross-over replication, random mutation, internal and external fluctuations or 'noise', or heterogeneity in the entities comprising a system. In terms of human organisations this means that organisations can only evolve new strategic directions, change in creative ways, produce innovations if they have the internal capacity, that is enough diversity, to generate and respond to variety.

This internal capacity to sustain diversity and generate variety has to do with the nature of the complex responsive processes that are an organisation. Organisational change is change in the themes organising the experience of being together in an organisation. Novel change takes place when these themes self-organise to produce emergent changes in themselves. In other words, organisations change in novel ways when new patterns of conversation and the power relations embedded in them emerge. The required diversity and variety, and the emergent change conditional on their presence, can be understood by making a conceptual distinction between two inextricably intertwined forms of organising theme. The distinction is that between themes that are felt to be legitimate and those that I describe as shadow themes. Creative change arises in the tension between shadow and legitimate themes that organise the experience of relating.

Further reading

Additional material on the points covered in this chapter can be found in Stacey (2001).

Chapter 17 ● ● ● ●

Control, leadership and ethics

17.1 Introduction

Chapters 14 to 16 have outlined the basis of a complex responsive process theory of organisations. This is a process theory and from its perspective, organisations are patterns of interaction between people, that is between human bodies. The theory stresses two ever-present, inextricably intertwined aspects of human interaction. First, interaction is always communication and communication always takes place in the medium of symbols. Symbols are always social acts, that is, the gesture of one body responded to by another and as such symbols are meaning. Particularly important are the vocal symbols of language, and ordinary, everyday conversation is a particularly important form of communicative interaction in the medium of language. Secondly, interaction between human bodies is always power relating because in relating to each other people are always simultaneously constraining and enabling each other's actions. The term 'complex responsive processes of relating', therefore, always encompasses power relating and communicative interaction. Complex responsive processes are synonymous with meaning and it is in such responsive processes of relating that human beings accomplish joint action of any kind. The key feature of all human groups, organisations, institutions and societies is this joint action. Joint action is only possible because complex responsive processes of relating are patterned in coherent, that is meaningful, ways.

The theory postulates that these coherent, meaningful patterns of interaction take the form of narrative and propositional themes that organise and are simultaneously organised by people interacting with each other. In other words, interaction is self-organising in that meaningful patterns emerge in local interactions between people in the living present, in the absence of any prior design, blueprint or plan. People do design and they do use blueprints and plans but these are all tools they use in their communicative interaction with each other. They are not designs, blueprints or plans for the interaction itself and the tools emerge in the interaction between people. Although interaction is always local, the emergent patterns of meaning may be very widespread due to the fact that people do not interact in one local situation only. A particular understanding of experience follows. Experience is the direct interaction between human bodies and the joint action accomplished in that interaction. Experience is participation in direct interaction, not participation in some hypothetical whole.

The thematic patterning of communicative interaction has many continuously intertwining, inseparable aspects. These aspects are formal and informal, conscious and unconscious, legitimate and shadow themes organising and being organised by the experience of interaction. Furthermore, interaction is always evolving as the past is iterated in the living present in which the future is perpetually constructed. Other important aspects of interaction, therefore, are continuity and the spontaneity of the transformation of organising themes at the same time. In other words, in the continual iteration of the living present, thematic patterns are reproduced as habits, norms, routines, customs and so on. Social structures, cultures organisations, institutions and societies, therefore, are not things but perpetually reproduced thematic patterns of relating between people taking habitual forms. Change, or evolution, in these rather repetitive patterns is only possible because in their iteration they are never exactly reproduced. This is because of the diversity of the people interacting, the imperfection of reproduction (memory) of past habitual interaction, and the inherent spontaneity or human capacity to choose responses, at least to some extent. Since human interaction is nonlinear, its iteration has the capacity to amplify small differences caused by imperfect reproduction into major qualitative changes in patterns of relating. It is in this manner that human interaction evolves in novel ways and it is in this sense that human interaction may be said to have the intrinsic capacity to pattern itself in simultaneously repetitive and novel ways.

The theory of complex responsive processes, therefore, reflects a theory of transformative causality. This means that the causality of human interaction is not a dual one as in systems thinking. In systems thinking there is, on the one hand, formative unfolding of that which is already enfolded (the known) in the system of which people are parts through, say, design or some pre-given motivation such as a vision. On the other hand, there is rationalist individual choice. Instead, in process thinking, human interaction is perpetually constructing the future as the known-unknown, that is, as continuity and potential transformation at the same time. This is a fundamentally paradoxical theory of causality.

Furthermore, what is being perpetually constructed as continuity and potential transformation is human identity, that is human meaning. Human identity has two inseparably interwoven aspects, namely, individual and collective, that which Elias called 'I' and 'we' identities. From a complex responsive process perspective, *an organisation is evolving identity*. In talking about organisations, the normal practice is to focus almost exclusively on collective or 'we' identities. The complex responsive process perspective, however, encourages us not to lose sight of the fact that interacting 'I' identities are simultaneously forming and being formed by 'we' identities. This intertwining of 'I' and 'we' identities is immediately apparent when you ask someone to introduce themselves, to say who they are. It does not take long for them to tell you what organisation or institution they belong to, that is, the collective from which they derive essential aspects of their identity. This view of identity makes sense of the trauma individuals experience when they are ejected from an organisation or when their organisation is dissolved or merged with another. What is threatened is far greater than economic well-being; it is the very identities of people that are threatened.

This immediately leads us to the definition of strategy implicit in the theory of complex responsive processes. Strategy is the evolving pattern of organisational identity. It is the evolving pattern of what an organisation is. An organisation is what it is because of the history of relating and it will become what it becomes in the local communicative interaction and power relating between people in the living present. If we want to understand strategy, then we need to understand the evolving complex responsive processes of relating between people who constitute an organisation.

The purpose of this chapter is to explore how one might think, from the complex responsive processes perspective, about very practical matters that preoccupy organisational practitioners, researchers and thinkers alike, namely control and leadership. If organisations are continually iterated, self-organising processes of relating and if strategy is continually emerging, evolving collective and individual identities, the question becomes what happens to control and what the role of leaders is. When one takes the perspective of complex responsive processes on these matters, one cannot escape the link to ethics or the importance of ordinary conversation. Consider first the question of control.

17.2   Control

In the systemic theories of organisation reviewed in Part One, the role of the manager is always thought to be that of formulating the purpose (visions, aims, goals, objectives, performance targets) of the organisation and controlling its movement into the future so as to achieve its purpose. It is recognised that this is difficult and cannot be perfectly achieved but it is thought that managers nevertheless need to be in control as much as possible, designing and using systems for this purpose. To be 'in control' means to more or less control the movement into the future of the whole organisational system through some kind of monitoring of its progress. Control means ensuring that movement into the future realises or unfolds a future state already enfolded in the present or past as the intention or desire of top managers, or of the democratic intention or desire of organisational members. Control requires organisational members to conform and sustain consensus. The implicit view is that without such control there would be anarchy. Control is ensured through conscious, formal, legitimate decisions based on the possibility of reasonably useful predictions of the future. Some opposites of being 'in control' are taking piecemeal decisions, reacting, not knowing and conflicting. In systemic theories of organisation, effective managers remove the characteristics of 'not in control' so as to avoid 'drifting' or anarchy. Figure 17.1 summarises the characteristics of being 'in control' and 'not in control' and how systemic approaches to management conceptualise them.

For a long time now, management research has frequently pointed to the messiness of actual decision-making processes in organisations. For example, Lindblom (1959) talked about organisational decision making as 'muddling through', while March and Olsen (1972) referred to it as 'garbage can' decision making and Mintzberg and Waters (1985) pointed to *both* deliberate *and* emergent strategies in the sense that strategy is sometimes the former and sometimes the latter. It is rare for management theorists, or practitioners for that matter, to think of organisational control in paradoxical terms.

'In control'	'Not in control'
Focusing on the whole	Piecemeal
Intended/selected/designed/planned	Evoked/provoked/emerging
Aim/goal/objective/target/vision	Exploring/searching
Detecting/correcting deviation	Amplifying deviation
Forming	Being formed
Known	Unknown
Predictable/certain	Unpredictable/uncertain
Stable	Unstable
Order/regular pattern	Disorder/irregular pattern
Conformity/consensus/sharing	Diversity/conflict
Clarity	Confusion
Formal/legitimate	Informal/shadow
Conscious	Unconscious
Habitual movement/culture	Spontaneous movement

Systemic perspective

Focuses attention on:	***So as to remove:***
Movement of whole system	All aspects of 'not in control'
Unfolding a future that is enfolded	
Continuity	
Meaning in the past/future	
Individual objective observer	
Hierarchical power	

Figure 17.1 Control from a systemic perspective

Source: Adapted from P. Streatfield (2001), *The Paradox of Control in Organizations*. London: Routledge.

Streatfield (2001) does think about control in paradoxical terms and in exploring his own experience of control as a manager at various hierarchical levels in organisations and has this to say:

> *My experience is that of one communicatively interacting with others at all times in the known and the unknown at the same time. I would certainly not label what my colleagues and I were doing as 'muddling' or as an inferior kind of 'garbage can' decision making. I have been arguing for a way of thinking about the dynamics of human relating and joint action, that is, the dynamics of organizations, which is essentially paradoxical. This is the paradoxical dynamic of being 'in control' and 'not in control' at the same time. The apparently messy processes of communicative interaction I have been describing are not some second best but, rather, the only way we know of living with paradox. The very dynamics of organizational life call for the kind of complex responsive processes of relating that I have been describing. It is in these processes that the dynamic is created. The processes only appear to be messy and less than competent from the perspective of mainstream thinking about management. From the complex responsive process way of thinking, management skills and competencies lie in how effectively managers participate in*

those processes. They provide a way of thinking about what competent managers actually do to live effectively in the paradox of organizing. And what they actually do is continue to interact communicatively, especially in the medium of conversation, in spite of not knowing and not being simply 'in control'. (p. 128)

Streatfield argues that instead of collapsing to either the 'in control' or the 'not in control' pole, we can make more sense of the activities of the manager if we understand that organisational life requires living with paradox. Managers are 'in control' and 'not in control' at the same time and they display the courage to continue participating in the making of meaning in paradox. The essential function of managers cannot be to control the paradoxical movement of continuity and transformation, of the known-unknown, because it is impossible for any participant to be in control of it. But this does not simply mean that managers are not in control. Instead, managers are simultaneously 'in control' and 'not in control' in the sense that they intend their next gestures, which are simultaneously evoked by previous responses. There is coherence, which emerges as continuity and potential transformation of identity in the perpetual construction of the future. The distinguishing feature of management is not control but courage to carry on creatively despite not knowing and not being in control, with all the anxiety that this brings. The paradox of control is summarised in Figure 17.2.

The central notion of systemic thinking, that of the manager being 'in control', is therefore much more problematic than is usually assumed because managers are both 'in control' and 'not in control' at the same time. The key question then becomes how managers operate effectively and maintain reasonably orderly states of affairs if they are not simply 'in control'. From the perspective of complex responsive processes, it is transiently stable, self-organising patterns of meaning that maintain a sense of order and therefore a sense of control as managers go about their daily activities. Intentional goal-oriented acts emerge in the conversations of managers at a local level and those conversations function as patterning, meaning-making processes. These communicative interactions constitute the way in which managers, individually and collectively, maintain their sense of self and their defences against anxiety. An organisation is self-organising processes in which intention and meaning emerge and anxiety is lived with. These interconnected processes across an organisation generate collective emergent outcomes that cannot be traced back to specific actions. Processes of decision making, change and performance achievement emerge in the self-organising patterns of meaning in which each individual struggles, in participation with others, to maintain a sense of self in an uncertain world. This is the process of an organisation's evolution.

This emergent pattern of evolution arises in self-organising interaction and creates a felt sense of meaning, order or control in the midst of uncertainty and anxious feelings of 'not being in control'. The paradox of being 'in control' and 'not in control' at the same time pervades all hierarchical levels in an organisation: the individual; individuals in conversation; the department; the business unit; the corporate level; and the industry. Streatfield discusses this as follows:

Are managers in control of organizations in which they work? My experience now suggests to me that this is the wrong question. The key management ability

'In control'	'Not in control'
Reflecting on widespread patterns	Piecemeal
Intended/selected/designed/planned	Evoked/provoked/emerging
Aim/goal/objective/target/vision	Exploring/searching
Detecting/correcting deviation	Amplifying deviation
Forming	Being formed
Known	Unknown
Predictable/certain	Unpredictable/uncertain
Stable	Unstable
Order/regular pattern	Disorder/irregular pattern
Conformity/consensus/sharing	Diversity/conflict
Clarity	Confusion
Formal/legitimate	Informal/shadow
Conscious	Unconscious
Habitual movement/culture	Spontaneous movement

Complex reponsive process perspective

Movement in local situation, self emergence/emergence perpetually constructing the future.
Movement of paradox as gesture-response
Simultaneous continuity and potential transformation.
Identity and difference
Meaning in the living present
Participation in subjective interaction in groups
Power as emergence of enabling constraints, including hierarchical constraints, ideology and dynamics of inclusion/exclusion
Anxiety and courage

Figure 17.2 The paradox of control from the complex responsive processes perspective
Source: Adapted from P. Streatfield (2001), *The Paradox of Control in Organizations*. London: Routledge.

is not that of being 'in control' but the ability to participate creatively in the formation of transient meaning, which enables all of an organization's members to continue living with the anxiety generated by change. It is this meaning that creates a felt sense of order, coherence, pattern or control. The ability to participate creatively in the construction of meaning develops as managers struggle to cope with the paradox of control, using legitimate control mechanisms as tools in a wider dynamic of self-organizing communicative interaction. I believe that management practitioners continually hone and develop the capacity to live with paradox as they go about their practice, even if they are not all that aware of doing it. (2001, p. 136)

Streatfield is making it clear that when one understands that organisations are self-organising, emergent processes of communicative interaction and power relating, one does not conclude that things just happen. Instead, he points to how what happens is due to the detail of what managers as interacting individuals are doing, particularly in their ordinary, everyday conversations with each other. Streatfield has written

Management narratives 2 and 3 to be found at the end of this Part. In these narratives, he tells the story of an ordinary budget meeting and a major performance-management project. He describes the sense in which he and his colleagues were in control and not in control at the same time. In these narratives, another point becomes clear about the perspective of complex responsive processes. Emphasising the self-organising, emergent nature of social interaction in no way lessens the accountability and responsibility of the interacting individuals. On the contrary, one can no longer blame a system for what is happening, because what happens is due to the detail of how each of us is interacting with others. Each of us has to take ethical responsibility for what we do. The next section explores this matter of ethics and its connection to leadership.

17.3   Ethics and leadership

Griffin (2001) argues that from a systemic perspective, leaders are understood as autonomous individuals who formulate visions and values to be directly applied to an organisational or cultural system. In other words the whole system is reified in thought and ascribed intentions or qualities such as 'harmonious', 'caring' or 'soul'. They are then understood as idealised wholes, which provide leadership to those individuals participating in them. The result is a dual notion of leadership being provided *both* by individual leaders who define the values and purpose of the whole system *and* by a system, which incorporates those values and purposes as the leading principles its members are to follow. Individuals following the principles of the whole are regarded as 'good' or 'compassionate', while those who do not are characterised as 'bad' or 'selfish'. In other words, leadership and ethics become matters of explicating the rules or qualities of the harmonious whole and of individuals conforming to it. Griffin is drawing attention here to how notions of leadership are inextricably interwoven with questions of ethics.

Griffin argues against this view of leadership and ethics because he says that it eliminates paradox and mystifies leadership, abstracting ethics from direct experience and locating it in some kind of external, idealised whole. As a result, people experience themselves as the victims of the systems they think they have created.

Griffin traces systemic thinking on ethics and leadership back to Kant's categorical imperative. By this, Kant meant that the principles behind an ethical action would reflect a universal law. Autonomous individuals could objectively observe their own conduct, just as they could objectively observe nature, and judge their actions, which could be understood 'as if' they were actions that could be performed by everyone. As people proceed in this way, different formulations of the categorical imperative emerge, for example, 'treat others as you want them to treat you' and 'do not treat other people as means to an end since all people are ends in themselves'. These imperatives have the character of universals but they do not dictate what to do in any specific situation. In specific situations people have to choose what to do by formulating hypothetical imperatives and then, in their acting, testing them against the categorical imperatives, also using such a procedure to justify what they have done. In this way, just as we can progressively build up a body of knowledge about the timeless universal natural laws governing nature, so we can progressively build up a body of knowledge on timeless, ethical imperatives for human conduct. Ethics here is firmly based on the reasoning capacity of the autonomous individual who can discover the universal principles of good conduct through what amounts to the scientific method.

Kant, then, presented a notion of ethics as a body of universal imperatives that already exist, just as natural laws do, to be discovered by autonomous individuals, just as natural laws are, and expressed in a body of timeless ethical imperatives, just as natural laws are timeless and universal. From this perspective, the principles of actions do not depend upon social or natural contingencies, nor do they reflect the bias of the particulars of individuals' plans for their lives, the particular desires, aims or aspirations that motivate them. It is this notion of ethics that forms the basis of traditional business ethics today – a notion of universal codes of conduct discovered or formulated by autonomous rational individuals as the basis upon which they are to judge their own and each other's conduct. In this way of thinking, the leader is an autonomous individual, as is everyone else, charged with developing ethical behaviour.

Contrary to Kant (see Chapter 2), however, systems thinkers today apply the notion of systemic wholes to human interaction. This leads to an ethics that is quite contrary to Kant in that now autonomous individuals are required to participate in, submit themselves to, some larger whole or greater good. No longer are the autonomous individuals trying to discover in their actions what the ethical imperatives reflecting the not-to-be-defined whole are. Instead they are required to submit themselves to the visions and values revealed to them by their leaders. In doing so, they lose their autonomy. In the Kantian sense of autonomy, the endorsement of the vision statements of top management by others is in effect the surrender of their autonomy. In organisational theory of this kind, it is only senior managers who are leaders in the Kantian sense of being fully autonomous individuals and they allow others to share in this autonomy. Participation becomes participating in the leadership of the leaders, where that leadership is the values ascribed to the organisational system.

Griffin suggests that the theory of complex responsive process of relating provides an alternative way of thinking about leadership and ethics. Here participation is the direct interaction of persons with each other, not participation in some whole. This is an approach that stays with our experience of interaction and regards the ethics of action as a process of perpetual negotiation that does indeed depend upon personal desires, aims and aspirations as well as natural contingencies. This process of communicative interaction is one in which we together create what happens to us and it is one in which small differences can be amplified to transform global situations. What each of us does matters even though we cannot know what the outcome of our actions will be. Griffin regards this as an empowering perspective that also makes it impossible for one to escape the responsibility for one's own actions by ascribing the causes of what happens to some whole system outside of our direct experience of interacting with each other. He argues that instead of leading us to feel hopeless, victimised or rebellious, this perception encourages us to pay attention to what we are doing and to believe that this is effective in some way, even though we cannot know how.

Griffin draws on Mead (1934) to develop this argument. For Mead, those who emerge as leaders are those who display a greater spontaneity and have the ability to deal with the ongoing purpose or task for which others are interacting. The leader is an individual who is able to enter into the attitudes of others, so enhancing connection and interaction between group members. Notice how this notion of a leader does not simply locate leadership in the individual by ascribing leadership purely to the personal attributes of the leader. This is because the leader is actually constructed in the recognition of others. It does not matter what leadership attributes one has if no one recognises them. And, of course, one cannot be a leader if one does not recognise the recognition of others and so recognise them. Leaders, therefore, emerge in complex responsive processes of mutual recognition.

Mead refers to the way in which groups tend to recognise the leader role in those who have acquired a greater spontaneity, a greater ability to deal with the unknown as it emerges from the known context. Mead argued that the ethical interpretation of action is to be found in the action itself, in the ongoing *recognition* of the meanings of actions that could not have been known in advance. In other words, ethical meaning does not reside in external universals to be applied to interaction but continually emerges in the interaction itself. Ethics are being negotiated in the interaction. Moral advance, for Mead, then consists not in adapting individuals to the fixed realities of a moral universe, but in constantly re-constructing and re-creating the world as individuals evolve.

Cult and functional values

Mead argued that individualising a collective, and treating it 'as if' *it* had overriding motives or values, amounted to a process in which the collective constitutes a 'cult'. The actions of members of such 'cults' are driven by the cult's values. A cult provides a feeling of enlarged personality in which individuals participate and from which they derive their value as persons. 'Cult values' are an idealisation of the collective, experienced as an enlarged personality that often justifies the terrible actions people take. Cults are maintained when leaders present to people's imagination a future free from obstacles that could prevent an organisation from being what they all think it should be. The use of visions and value statements in modern corporations is a striking example of this technique. The idealisation functions to divert people's attention from the ethics of their daily actions. This diversionary function of cult values follows not only from negative ideals but also from positive ones, such as family values and democracy.

Idealised, or cult, values emerge in the historical evolution of any institution, to which they are ascribed, and they become functional values in the everyday interactions between members of the institution. For example, the cult value of a hospital might be to 'provide each patient with the best possible care'. However, such a cult value has to be repeatedly functionalised in many unique specific situations throughout the day. As soon as cult values become functional values in real daily interaction, conflict arises and it is this conflict that must be negotiated by people in their practical interaction with each other. Functional ethics is this negotiation.

In stressing functional values, Mead was alerting us to the dangers of focusing on the cult values themselves, on the values of the personalised institution or system, and directly applying them as overriding universal norms, conformity to which constitutes the requirement of continuing membership of the institution. This is the usual understanding of a 'cult', namely an idealised group that is thought of as having values to which individuals must conform; if they do not they are judged to be selfish or sinful, and their failure raises questions about their continued membership of the group. Instead of focusing attention on the daily, necessarily conflictual functionalising of cult value, this idealisation of the organisation involves the direct application of the cult values as universal norms abstracted from daily life and people are said to be selfish when they do not conform to them.

The distinction between cult and functional is also relevant to understanding leadership. One aspect of a leader is his or her idealisation as cult leader. This idealisation is functionalised in the role of the leader in the everyday conflicts of interaction. The functionalised role of leader emerges in the interaction and those participating are continuously creating and re-creating the meaning of leadership themes in the local interaction in which they are involved. However, there always remains a strong tendency for a group to idealise the leader, who thereby becomes a cult leader, that is, leader of a group of people directly enacting idealised values, cult values, to which they are subtly pressured to conform to. This blocks the functionalising of the ideals, which is what an organisation needs in order to come alive in the present.

Chapter 12 referred to the way in which many people are using complexity theories to justify the formulation of simple rules and their application to an organisational system as an alternative to detailed plans. The hope seems to be that through specifying simple rules, we can still get the whole to do what we want it to. From the complex responsive perspective, these simple rules are cult values and what really matters is how they are functionalised in daily life. It is this functionalising that brings in the conflict and uncertainty, which will defeat our hope of controlling the whole unless it is indeed a cult. Management narrative 6 tells the story of a project to introduce diversity into an organisation. One could understand this as an attempt to formulate and apply a cult value, that is, the idealisation that people could respect each other's differences without any conflict. The narrative describes how difficult the managers in this organisation found it to functionalise this cult value. Management narrative 7 tells of an attempt to apply global competences to the global system of an organisation. One again one could understand this as an attempt to directly apply lists of idealised management competences to all the managers in this organisation and once again the story demonstrates the difficulties of functionalising such cult values.

17.4   Change, decision making and the importance of conversation

From the perspective of complex responsive processes, organisations are continually iterated processes of human communicative interaction figured as power relations. The conversations people continually engage in as they work are the most important feature of organisational life. Fonseca (2001) argues that innovation and change can be understood as the conversational processes of transforming both collective and individual identities and that misunderstanding is an essential aspect of transformative processes. He explores three innovation stories in some detail and concludes that in each of these cases it is impossible to locate the meaning that came to be the innovation at any particular point in time or space, or in one individual, even when one person was a very prominent figure in the story. The innovations studied were not the result of some purposeful search or sequential process formulated in advance. Instead, he argues, the innovations emerged in streams of conversations, characterised by high levels of redundancy, diversity and misunderstanding, over long periods of time.

Fonseca argues that no one is able to control the conversational process or the emergent meanings in the evolution of innovations. It follows that no one can manage innovation. He also noticed that those who engaged in the conversations from which innovations emerged were not located within a single organisation. It was this that enabled critical levels of diversity to be reached, a prerequisite for the potential for new meaning to emerge. Fonseca has written Management narrative 1, which provides an illustration of the kind of innovation experience on which he bases his views.

Shaw (2002) draws attention to the importance of ordinary conversations in organisations as the processes in which change emerges. In such ordinary conversations what is being talked about is necessarily unclear in many respects because some lack of clarity is the very reason for having the conversation. We come to know what we are talking about from within the development of the conversation itself, even when a topic has been agreed in advance. Shaw argues that ordinary conversations do not take the form of one person saying something, others listening in order to understand what is said, and then formulating a response. Instead, people speak into one another's responses, so responsively shaping what they say in the very process of conversing. When people understand what they are doing in conversation as clarifying information, reaching shared understandings, developing orderly agreements and plans and capturing outputs, they lose awareness of the ongoing mutually constructive nature of what they are doing together. Shaw argues that the widespread demand that management meetings should be carefully planned and prepared actually kills the spontaneity of ordinary conversation in which new meaning can emerge. She points out how consultants and managers try to agree, in advance of starting a conversation, on the ground rules for good communication, such as listening carefully, respecting the views of others, suspending judgements and surfacing assumptions. The result is a set of idealised rules that change the nature of the conversation and limit its ordinary spontaneity.

As a consultant, Shaw seeks to foster free-flowing conversation through her participation in ordinary conversations in organisations. She does not decide in advance what role she is going to take at a meeting. Instead, she joins the meeting and leaves unspecified what the rules of interaction should be. After the meeting she does not try to abstract what was learned, nor does she make summaries and action plans to provide feedback to anyone anywhere. She argues that as people continue to meet and talk with others in other settings they will remember what was relevant in previous conversations. She does all this to avoid the rigidity that people impose on meetings in organisations and to restore something of the ordinary spontaneity of conversation.

What Shaw is drawing attention to is those aspects of processes of change that are excluded in orderly accounts of organisation change initiatives. She is drawing attention to the importance of ordinary conversation in processes of change and such ordinary conversation is characterised by random as well as intended encounters. As people go about conversing in an ordinary manner, they purposefully make connections with others but often without a set of clearly defined objectives. They participate in situations where they have only an incomplete grasp of what is happening. In doing this ordinary process of relating, they are forming and transforming, they are perpetually constructing their future in the living present.

I now want to compare the approach that Shaw is describing with that described by systems thinkers.

Comparisons with systemic approaches

When I read accounts of the work that second-order and critical systems thinkers (for example, Ison and Russell, 2000; Jackson, 2000; Midgley, 2000; reviewed in Chapters 8 and 9) give of their work in organisations, I am struck by a number of differences between what they do and what one does when informed by the perspective of complex responsive process.

The problem situation
First, the immediate concern of these systems practitioners is with some problem issue or situation about which some group of people feel that they need to make decisions and take actions in order to bring about some improvement. The practitioner aims to *intervene* in this situation in order to identify how this issue or situation *should* be formulated, how the decision *should* be taken and how it *should* be implemented. The purpose is to specify some kind of procedure that the group *should* follow in order to improve the situation, recognising that it will probably be impossible to optimise the decision outcome. Improvement is understood as securing some desired or intended outcomes. The unquestioned assumption is that problem formulation/analysis, decision making and implementation are separate activities. They may overlap, they may circle around many iterations, but conceptually they are separate. The assumption is that thought is apart from action.

The practitioner operating from the complex responsive process perspective does so on the basis that thinking and talking are action. What is of interest is the conversational process in which a group of people are coming to feel that there is some kind of issue or situation of concern even though as yet they do not know what it is. The perspective is then not what people should be doing but what they actually are doing as the practitioner joins them. Here the practitioner joins a group of people as a participant in their conversations seeking to understand something of the organising themes that are emerging in these conversations.

Preparing for the intervention
Secondly, the systems practitioner prepares for an intervention by gathering data and interviewing those involved or affected by the situation in order to formulate some kind of view of what is going on. The systems practitioner has various techniques

for doing this, such as preparing a 'rich picture' of the situation or summaries of evaluations of the situation made by various participants (*see* Chapter 9). This information is prepared as some kind of presentation or feedback to those who will participate in the intervention and it is the basis on which the practitioner advises on who the appropriate group of participants should be.

From a complex responsive process perspective, the practitioner does not join a group with the intention of structuring or shaping the situation or the conversations in which an issue is emerging. The practitioner has no intention of creating the right conditions for better conversations or identifying the right people to be involved in them. There is no intention to design anything, improve it, or make it right or more creative. Instead, the intention is the same as that of other participants, namely to understand what they are all doing together, what they are talking about and why. So, for example, Shaw explains how she asks people how they came to be involved in the current conversation because their stories begin to indicate what they are actually doing in the living present. In participating in this storytelling she draws attention in certain ways rather than others by emphasising certain moments rather than others and using certain forms of expression rather than others. In so doing she is drawing attention to how these stories create meaning, changing in emphasis as people go on thinking and speaking about them. People resonate with each other's stories and so sustain their relationships. This process does not simply reaffirm existing ideas but enlivens the senses of participants, stirring them from the habits of familiar ways of drawing attention to awaken a fresh appreciation of their experience.

For Shaw, there is no intention to prepare for the work to be done at some later point because in their already conversing, the work is under way in what she calls gatherings. Instead of selecting a key group influencer, formal or informal, to initiate change, she pays attention to the way in which influence is spontaneously arising in webs of relationships in particular contexts, reflected in people gathering together in some way. Gatherings are provoked by the urgent need to make sense of some dimly perceived issues, making it inevitable that their conversation will be characterised by a vague sense of why they are there. Instead of a clear formulation of an inquiry and special invitations to a representative sample of stakeholders, Shaw seeks ways to connect people so that gatherings will arise spontaneously because of some interest in common. Such gatherings are not representative, fair or consultative but, rather, they are active. The point is to work with the potential for change, finding ways of convening forums which tap people's interests, enthusiasms or frustrations and which demand an intensive interaction to create meaningful forms of activity that 'move things on'. These discussions have an 'everyday quality' – they are messy, branching, meandering, associative and engaging. They are similar to the mode people value and recognise in many informal kinds of conversation. They include formulating and making reference to proposals, analysis and frameworks. They involve speculation, anecdotes and personal revelation. They are shot through with the feeling tone and bodily sensation which all are resonating and responding to in different ways. It is a very active, searching, exploratory form of communication in which the way the future is under perpetual construction is more than usually evident.

Intervening in the system

Thirdly, the systems practitioner designs some kind of intervention event such as a meeting, workshop or learning event in which participants explore the nature of the issue/situation and possible responses to it. The systems practitioner has a collection of methodologies, methods, tools and techniques to draw upon in designing the intervention events. For example, there are various heuristics, procedures and models developed by systems thinkers for application to ambiguous problem situations characterised by power differences and ideological features. The methods and techniques aim to surface multiple evaluations of the situation in what is a pluralistic approach. All of these methodologies, techniques and so on, are systemic. This means that they focus attention on some *whole* or system and the interconnections that produce the system. The implicit assumption is that it is only by affecting the whole that improvement can be assured. This is because complex interconnections could overcome attempts at partial improvement. The systems practitioner is seeking to assist people draw boundaries around the problem situation, identifying the whole system of which it is an aspect. They recognise the difficulties of doing this in complex situations and so advocate the drawing of multiple boundaries and the exploration of ethical and power implications of doing so. Each mode or system identified is recognised as only a partial view of the whole, one that depends upon the particular paradigm of those drawing the boundary.

Systems practitioners think of themselves as facilitators who structure, shape and guide workshops and other intervention events using the methodologies of systems thinkers. They keep it rational, to the point and following the agenda. For example, they present lists of questions to workshop participants asking them to evaluate their current situation and how they plan to do things differently. They support workshop participants in looking at where they want to go. Such information may then be used to design subsequent learning events. They give exercises to participants in learning events, such as imagining that they have just climbed out of a time capsule five years into the future.

In relation to the group faced with the problem situation, the stance of the systems practitioner is one of involvement in that the work is done with the people involved. The systems practitioner joins the group but always does so in a particular manner, namely, as the bringer of systematic sets of conceptual paradigms, a system of methodologies, a plurality of methods, techniques, heuristics, lists of questions. The systems thinker analyses the situation in order to select appropriate paradigms and methodologies for the situation in accordance with some kind of metaparadigm or metamethodology. In other words, the systems thinker sets some kind of agenda.

In the stages leading up to these events, and in the events themselves, then, systems practitioners see themselves as participating with those whom they are advising in the formulation and exploration of the problem situation. However, in an important sense they are all taking the stance of the objective observer of the situation simply because they analyse the situation, design the intervention events and select the appropriate models. The participants also then take this objective position in applying the models to their situation.

From the complex responsive processes perspective, Shaw argues that meetings which are carefully orchestrated and over-specified in advance increase the likelihood of people reconstructing the familiar. Outcomes, procedures for working together, agendas, roles to be taken up by those present, form of contribution and prepared slide presentations, all conspire to reduce the experience of uncertainty as the experience of acting into the known is engineered. She argues that under-specification increases the experience of diversity and multiplicity, disturbing routine responses and increasing the potential for novelty. For Shaw, facilitating means participating as fully and responsively as possible, voicing one's opinions, associations and ideas along with everyone else. In doing this she is sensing the move towards and away from agreement, of shifts in power difference, the development and collapse of tensions, the variations in engagement, the different qualities of silence, the rhetorical ploys, the repetition of familiar turns of phrase or image, the glimpsing and losing of possibility, the ebb and flow of feeling tone, the dance of mutual constraint. She tries to participate in the conversation in a way that helps to hold open the interplay of sense making rather longer than would occur in her absence, to hold open the experience of not knowing. In doing this she is resisting the enormous pressure for closure.

Notice the difference between the systems and complex responsive processes accounts of practice. The systems practitioner arrives at the situation with a set of methodologies, techniques and so on, to shape the discussion. There is a design and something of an agenda. From the complex responsive processes perspective the practitioner's methodology is the ordinary everyday conversational process that is already under way. The practitioner does not set any agenda at all but seeks to understand the shifting thematic patterning of the self-organising process as the basis on which to contribute to it, just as all the other participants are doing. There is little emphasis on facilitating in the sense of structuring, summarising, writing bullet points on flip charts, calling for feedback. Instead, by responding to what others are saying, by linking themes, the practitioner is helping to articulate emerging themes and in so doing influencing the further patterning of the conversation. It is these shifts in communicative patterning that constitute organisational change.

This means that unlike the systems practitioner, the practitioner from a complex responsive processes perspective is not concerned with any whole or system at all but with the detail of the local interactions between people in the living present.

Implementation

The fourth step in systemic practice is that of working in the intervention to make decisions and take actions to improve the situation. For the complex responsive processes practitioner, the action and the work has been going on all the time and in this work decisions and actions are continually emerging or being blocked.

Systems practitioner are well aware of the highly complex, ill-structured, messy nature of the situations that groups in organisations face. Their response is pluralism, which means employing combinations of given paradigms, methodologies and methods. Instead of proposing a single, or even a few consistent hypotheses, they encourage those they work with to explore many hypotheses, selecting particular models according to what the culture allows. From the complex responsive processes perspective, one is sceptical of this notion of pluralism, that is, identifying and selecting different paradigms for evaluation. Instead the practice is concerned with what is emerging and since what is emerging is individual and collective identities, one is sceptical about the possibility of simply switching paradigms as systemic practice suggests. In the kind of practice I am describing the focus of attention is on emerging themes and there is no notion of anyone drawing boundaries around a system.

Shaw has written Management narratives 4 and 5 to be found at the end of this Part. They both illustrate the points made in this section about the approach to organisational change that a practitioner takes from the complex responsive processes perspective.

• • • • 17.5 Learning and knowledge creation in organisations

The theory of complex responsive processes focuses attention on the importance of local communicative interaction in the living present, particularly its thematic patterning, its gesture-response structure and its reflection in ideologies and power relations. This represents a way of understanding the emergence of knowledge in which people use both the tools of communication and the tools and technologies with which they transform their material environment. This view of knowing as process counters the widespread tendency to focus attention on knowledge as artefact or systems tool used in the active process of communicative interaction. Instead of focusing attention on the tool, the perspective I am suggesting focuses attention on how the tools are used.

The tools are used in wider processes of communicative interaction in which particular ways of talking are 'in' and others are 'out'. A concern with the knowledge-creation process would, therefore, involve an exploration of this dynamic as it manifests in local situations in the living present. What kind of exclusion is operating? What impact does this have in terms of obstructing or encouraging the emergence of new knowledge? Such questions soon lead to reflection on the manner in which ideologically based power relations are being sustained and challenged. What impact does this have on communicative interaction and the emergence of knowledge? A concern with the knowledge-creating process also involves an exploration of the identity-threatening and anxiety-provoking aspects of the process, so focusing attention on these and other aspects of the conversational life of an organisation and its transformative potential.

This refocusing of attention raises important questions with regard to mainstream thinking about knowledge creation in organisations. What can it mean to talk about managing knowledge creation in organisations when knowing is action in local situations in the living present? What can it mean to create a learning organisation? What can it mean to talk about measuring and managing the intellectual capital of an organisation?

As part of the knowledge management theory reviewed in Chapter 8, a number of writers call for steps to measure intellectual capital on the grounds that what is measured can be managed. The aim of measuring intellectual capital is that of managing its contribution to shareholder value. From the perspective of complex responsive processes, meaning, and therefore knowledge, arises in the local, detailed, ordinary communicative interaction of people in organisations in the living present. Knowledge creation is an evolutionary process of reproduction and potential transformation at the same time. In other words knowledge is neither stored nor shared because it is not an 'it' at all but a process. Knowledge cannot be grasped, owned by anyone or traded in any market and its creation is a process of communicating and power relating that is both stimulating and anxiety provoking at the same time. If one takes a view of knowledge creation along these lines, then it is not only impossible to manage knowledge, even asking the question makes no sense. The whole notion that an organisation can own 'intellectual capital', that is, can own the attitudes, competence and intellectual agility of individuals is a dubious one.

A central feature of the systemic theory of knowledge creation in organisations (*see* Chapter 8) is the split it makes between tacit and explicit knowledge. Tacit knowledge is assumed to arise in individual minds and this is thought to create a problem for organisations. The assumption is that humans are reluctant to share their individual tacit knowledge with others. To the extent that they do, it is in informal exchanges, and systemic views tend to express a profound mistrust of these informal exchanges. This leads to the major emphasis on the conversion of individual tacit knowledge into explicit form and the storing of that explicit knowledge in systems. The complex responsive processes perspective, however, holds that tacit and explicit knowing are facets of the same communicative process and, therefore, that it makes no sense to talk about them separately or to believe that one is converted into the other. Furthermore, knowledge is not simply located in individual minds, nor is it stored in any straightforward sense. Instead knowledge is continuously replicated and potentially transformed in the communicative interaction between people. Knowledge is not understood to be 'property' at all but active relational processes between human persons and a reflection of human identity, which cannot be captured, stored or owned.

If one starts from the basic assumption that the origins of knowledge are located in tacit form in the heads of individuals, it is a natural step to advocate that organisations pay particular attention to hiring and retaining a professional elite. From the perspective of complex responsive processes it is not particularly clear that simply hiring and retaining individual professionals has very much to do with knowledge creation. If knowledge arises in communicative interaction, then what matters is the process of relating that individual professionals engage in, not simply how clever or competent they are as individuals.

Systemic views of knowledge creation and management also present prescriptions concerned with spreading knowledge around an organisation. If knowledge is created in individual heads, and if human nature is such that individuals selfishly seek to keep it to themselves, then it becomes a prime management task to design structures, systems and behaviours to overcome these selfish tendencies and spread knowledge around the organisation. However, if knowledge is not a thing but a process of making meaning, where meaning is continuously reproduced and potentially transformed in the action of communicative relating between human bodies, then one cannot speak of sharing it, or of spreading it around an organisation. Any concern with 'improving' knowledge-creating capacity becomes a concern with the qualities and the dynamics of human relating in the living present. Attention is then focused on the power relations being sustained and shifted in communicative inter-action and on the ideologies unconsciously making patterns of power relations feel natural.

Closely linked to prescriptions for hiring and retaining of professionals are those for training and developing people. Again, these prescriptions reflect the underlying assumption that knowledge is stored in individual heads. The aim of training and development follows, namely, to increase the competence, skill and knowledge of the individual, including the capacity to work as a member of a team. The emphasis is placed on managing not just the activities of training and development but the quality of the learning process itself. Again, management is understood in systemic terms and the prescriptions relate to the design and operation of a system to ensure the quality of the learning process. However, this usually ignores the impact of learning processes on human identity.

Aram (2001) argues that learning is individually experienced processes of incre-mental transformation of identity, which happen in groups and to groups. The pro-cess of learning is also characterised by the dynamics of inclusion and exclusion simply because some participants are changing in the learning process and others are not and even when they are changing, people change at different rates in differ-ent ways. This establishes subgrouping and patterns of inclusion and exclusion. These processes, therefore, inevitably involve anxiety and potential shame because the learning process challenges identity. Learning, therefore, is as a paradoxical pro-cess of personal change, of transformation of identity, and also of continuity. From this perspective, one focuses not on designing learning systems but on understand-ing the highly complex psychodynamics of human learning processes.

17.6 Summary

This chapter has explored how one might understand some central concerns of strategic management.

The first of these concerns is the matter of control. The first section of the chapter therefore examined how control is understood as a paradox when one takes a com-plex responsive processes perspective. Instead of there being a focus on control as the realisation of intention and the removal of uncertainty as in systems thinking, con-trol is understood as the manager's continual grappling with the paradox of being in control and not in control at the same time.

The second concern is with the intertwined issues of leadership and ethics. Instead of the dual notion of leadership and the rule-based notion of ethics found in systemic theories of strategic management, a complex responsive processes perspect-ive leads to a different view. Leadership is understood to emerge in the process of mutual recognition in the interaction between people, and ethics is understood as the continual negotiation of what is appropriate action. An important distinction was drawn between cult and functionalised values. The former is the direct applica-tion of idealised values to a situation, while the latter is the negotiation of what cult values actually mean in a specific situation. Traditional views on business ethics tend to focus on cult values alone while the complex responsive processes perspective focuses attention on how cult values are functionalised in the ordinary interaction between people in local situations in the living present.

Finally, this chapter looked at the importance of conversation in the emergence of innovation and change. It compared the structured approach to change of the systemic practitioner with the concern of the complex responsive processes practitioner's with the emergence of meaning in ordinary conversations.

Further reading

The subject matter of this chapter is developed in Streatfield (2001) on control in organisation, Griffin (2001) on leadership and ethics, Fonseca (2001) on innovation and conversational processes and Shaw (2002) on change practice and the conversational life of organisations.

Chapter 18 ● ● ● ●

The implications of understanding organisations as complex responsive processes

18.1 Introduction

In Chapter 1, I suggested that this book would be dealing with the following questions. How do populations of organisations, and the individual members of those populations, change and evolve over time? How do these populations and their members come to be what they are and how will they come to be whatever they come to be? How can one make sense of the observation that new organisations are continually forming while many small and a few large ones disappear or merge into others? In other words, how does one explain the dynamics of populations of organisations and their members? What do strategy, strategic direction and strategic thinking mean? How does a strategy come into being and how is it manifested? I also suggested that the way one answers these questions depends upon the frame of reference from which one approaches them and in the rest of the book I reviewed a number of different frames of reference.

In this chapter, I want to explore how a theory of organisation as complex responsive processes deals with questions like these and in so doing compare this theory with the others reviewed in this book.

18.2 How the theory of complex responsive processes answers four key questions

Four important questions were posed in Chapter 1 and used to explore important features of a number of theories of organisation. These questions relate to:

1 How the theory in question understands the nature of interaction.
2 What views the theory takes on human nature.
3 The methodological position that the theory adopts.
4 The manner in which it deals with paradox.

This section will examine how the complex responsive processes theory of organisation deals with these questions and how this differs from other theories.

The nature of human interaction

Strategic choice theory is built on a systemic notion of interaction in which organisations adapt to their environments in a self-regulating, negative-feedback (cybernetic) manner so as to achieve their goals. The dynamics, or pattern of movement over time, is that of movement to states of stable equilibrium. Prediction is not seen as problematic. The analysis is primarily at the macro level of the organisation in which cause and effect are related to each other in a linear manner. Microdiversity receives little attention and interaction is assumed to be uniform and harmonious.

Learning organisation theory also adopts a systemic perspective on human interaction, but one that takes account of positive as well as negative feedback. From the systems dynamics perspective the dynamics is that of non-equilibrium in which unexpected outcomes appear. However, this theory holds that when managers understand the positive and negative feedback structure of the whole system they will be able to identify leverage points through which they can control it. This theory does not explore the implications of radical unpredictability. Here too, the analysis is at the macro level of the organisation but this time connections between cause and effect take nonlinear forms in which the connections might be distant over time and space. Again, little attention is paid to microdiversity and successful interaction is still assumed to be harmonious, although this theory does recognise obstacles to the achievement of such harmony.

The third theory reviewed also takes a systemic perspective on interaction, this time open systems theory, which focuses on regulation at permeable boundaries between system and environment and between subsystems of the system. The dynamics of human open systems is somewhat turbulent and the importation of primitive human behaviour disrupts organisational learning. This possibility requires careful management of boundaries and radical unpredictability does not feature as an important characteristic. This theory sees the purpose of management as intervention aimed at enabling equilibrium adaptation to the organisation's environment. The analysis here is at a far more micro level than is the case with strategic choice and the learning organisation, taking account of the behaviour of members of an organisation, particularly the unconscious causes of that behaviour. Microdiversity is recognised and success is a state of adaptation to reality.

These three approaches to organisations are, therefore, based on a systemic theory of interaction. This means that interaction between people is assumed to create a whole, a system, of which they are parts and so subjected in some way to the purpose of the whole. Later developments in systems thinking in the form of autopoiesis, second-order, soft and critical systems thinking all continue on the basis of a theory of systemic interaction. Various strands of systems thinking may differ according to whether they view systems as reality itself or mental constructs of reality but they continue to take a systemic perspective on interaction. This also applies to more recent developments in organisational theory to do with knowledge management.

A number of writers have been moving to a systemic perspective on human action drawn from chaos and complexity theory. Attention is drawn to the dynamics of the edge of chaos and the self-organising, emergent properties of the system.

Attention is also drawn to the possibility of unpredictability, but this is often not seen as essential and requiring further exploration. The analysis tends to be at the macro level of the organisation as a whole, although some do focus upon microdiversity to some extent. Most writers apply complexity theory to organisations within the systemic theory of interaction.

The complex responsive processes perspective described in Chapters 14 to 16 is built upon a completely different theory of interaction. It regards interaction between people as iterated processes of communication and power relating. There is no notion here of a whole or a system, and what people are producing in their interaction is further patterns of interaction. The theory of complex responsive processes, therefore, represents a move from a spatial metaphor of inside and outside to a temporal metaphor of continual reproduction and potential transformation. I have taken complex responsive processes of relating as the human analogue of the interaction modelled by complex adaptive systems. These complex responsive processes are fundamentally conversational in nature, forming and being formed by power relations. The analysis focuses at a micro level and concentrates on the dynamics of bounded instability in which self-organisation might produce emergent novel forms in relating and conversation. This perspective emphasises the importance of diversity and deviance as essential to the internal capacity to change spontaneously. In this evolving, potentially creative process, unpredictability is central, inviting further exploration of how people act into the unknown.

The comparison that I have made above between organisational theories suggests a move from one theory of interaction to another so that uncertainty and unpredictability, and their relationship with diversity and creativity, are increasingly taken into account.

Human psychology

Strategic choice theory takes a cognitivist view of human nature. Here mind is understood to be a property of the individual brain. The brain/mind processes symbolic information, forming representations and models of a pre-given reality. Humans then act on the basis of their mental models. The individual is primary in that knowing and behaving do not depend fundamentally on relationships between individuals. Knowing and behaving, including relating to others, are characteristics of individual minds/brains. Individuals form groups and being part of a group may then affect individual behaviour. This theory places great emphasis on the importance of the intentions formed and expressed by individuals. Emotion is seen as a dangerous disruption of rational choice capacity and power is understood as an attribute of an individual, mainly in terms of official authority. Creativity is an attribute of an individual.

Learning organisation theory employs the same theory of human nature. However, it also combines this with notions from humanistic psychology in which the central motivation for behaviour is the urge individuals have to actualise themselves, finding their true selves as it were. Again, individuals form groups and these groups may affect their behaviour. Leadership is a competence possessed by individuals and intention is a characteristic of individuals. Emotions of a positive kind are emphasised. Power as an attribute of charismatic individuals comes to the fore. Creativity is in the end seen as an attribute of an individual, although a role is also ascribed to cohesive teamwork.

Psychoanalytic perspectives on organisations combine open systems theory with a view of human nature derived from psychoanalysis. The fundamental motivation for human behaviour here is the mental ideas of inherited animal instincts called the drives. Aggressive and libidinal drives blindly seek satisfaction but encounter social prohibition. Individual mental processes are structured by this encounter with the social. Individuals form groups but much greater account is taken of the impact group processes have on individual behaviour, particularly those that are unconscious. The theory focuses on how regression to primitive behaviour can destroy rational thinking and learning. An important insight into the nature of the relationship between individual and group is that about leadership. Individuals may be sucked into leadership positions by unconscious dynamics of the group. Leadership is no longer simply a competence of the individual. Emotion and power play a much more important role in understanding the development of an organisation than they do in the theories of strategic choice and the learning organisation. The impact of emotions of a negative kind and of individual and group fantasy life is taken into account, as are the negative aspects of power. Creativity is an individual attribute arising in the ability to hold anxiety and engage in play.

Many of those developing the knowledge management perspective on organisations, as well as those understanding organisations as communities of practice, adopt a constructivist view of psychology, sometimes combined with the theory of autopoietic systems. Here, individuals are thought of as selecting or enacting the world into which they act. In this way, interacting individuals co-create their worlds. However, the individual still remains primary, although much more importance is attached to social interaction.

The writers reviewed in Chapter 12 import a theory of interaction drawn from chaos and complexity theory into their theory of organisations. They combine this with the same cognitivist, constructivist and humanistic views of human nature as those found in strategic choice, learning organisation theory, knowledge management and communities of practice perspectives. The individual, therefore, remains central, and as a result these writers do not go further, in my view, than the other systemic theories reviewed in Part One. More attention may be paid to the creative aspects of instability but the same views on control are retained and creativity continues to be regarded as an attribute of an individual.

The complex responsive processes theory of organisations makes a radical departure when it comes to forming a view on human nature. The fundamental proposition is that individuals and groups form and are formed by each other simultaneously. Individual minds are not seen purely as a process of brain computation, nor are they seen as motivated by primitive drives formed in mind by the clash with the social. Instead, mind is the singular of relating while the group is the plural of relating. The fundamental motivator of human behaviour is the urge to relate. From this perspective, there can be no human individual outside of relationship. Mind is a silent, private conversation structured by, and always resonating and changing with, vocal, public conversations in groups. This theory radically decentres, while not losing sight of, the individual. It moves away from the notion of the autonomous individual containing a mind as an internal world to the notion of social selves. Power relations and the ideologies supporting them, emotions and fantasies are all central to this theoretical perspective. Since this view of human nature is basically one of human interaction, the theory of interaction and that of human nature are the same. Intention is no longer an attribute of an individual. Instead, it emerges in conversational relationship to be articulated by an individual. Leadership is no longer simply an individual competence but a form of relationship. Creativity arises in patterns of relationship in which there is sufficient deviance and subversion.

When the individual is treated as primary, the immediate tendency is to equate agents in complex systems with individual human beings. The notion of self-organisation is applied to them and the result is a concept that does not differ from orthodox notions of delegation and empowerment. From the complex responsive processes perspective, the analogue of agents is themes that organise experience. What is organising itself is then these themes and a radical notion of self-organisation and emergent unpredictability is retained. A move is made from the causal dualism (formative and rationalist) of systems thinking to the paradoxical transformative causality of complex responsive processes.

Methodological position

The methodological position adopted by strategic choice and learning organisation theorists is that of the objective observer who stands outside the organisational system and observes it as a pre-given reality. The purpose is to manipulate and control the system. This is part of cognitivist thinking. When the writers reviewed in Chapter 12 take chaos and complexity theory into theorising about organisations, they adopt the same methodological position. The manager is implicitly ascribed the same role and prescriptions are made as to how the manager may control, direct or at least disturb or perturb the system.

Those adopting psychoanalytic perspectives move some way from this position in that they adopt methodologies analogous to the clinical. They advocate action research in which the researcher participates with members of an organisation and uses his or her feelings as information. However, some notion of objective observation is retained. The researcher, and the manager, takes a position at the boundary of the system in order to avoid being sucked into unconscious group processes (Stapley, 1996).

Those who take second-order, soft and critical systems perspectives, as well as some of those who talk of communities of practice and knowledge management, adopt a reflexive and participative methodological position. They display great awareness of the co-constructed nature of knowledge and many actively look for multiple perspectives on any situation.

Many move from the position of the objective observer to methodologies of participative enquiry (Reason, 1988) where researchers understand themselves to be participants in processes of enquiry. This is a reflexive methodology (Steier, 1991) in which organisations are understood to be social constructions (Gergen, 1982).

However, while seeking to deal with the fact that humans are both observers and participants in their own action, the writers in the traditions just referred to continue to do so from a systemic perspective. They still understand human interaction as producing a system. This inevitably leads to a methodological dualism in which people move from the participant position to the observer position and back again. Critical systems thinking develops this kind of dualism into a whole system of methodologies.

The complex responsive processes perspective seeks to sustain a methodological position in which people are both participants and observers at the same time.

This has implications for how the role of the manager is understood. Neither researcher nor manager can step outside the conversational processes that are the organisation simply because their work requires them to talk to others. What they say affects what they hear and what they hear affects what they say. From this perspective, then, a manager cannot stand outside organisational processes and control them, direct them or even perturb them in an intentional direction. All such intentions are gestures made to others in an organisation and what happens unfolds from the ongoing responses. One might call this a methodology of emergent enquiry.

This perspective on the nature of management leads to a completely different understanding of the dynamics of bounded instability. The writers reviewed in Chapter 12 tend to equate the dynamics of the edge of chaos with crises. They tend to see the manager as one who stands outside the system and pushes, or nudges, it into instability, disturbance and crisis. One prescription is to place people under more stress so that they will be motivated to change and so unleash the power of self-organisation. The notion of the edge of chaos derived from a complex responsive processes perspective is completely different. The analogue of this dynamic is free-flowing conversation. People can only engage in this when the pattern of their relationships provides good enough holding of the anxiety of facing the unknown. Crisis and stress are not relational qualities that contain anxiety, rather they increase it. The edge of chaos, from the perspective I am suggesting, is safe enough, exciting enough patterns of relationships, not terrifyingly stressful ones.

Paradox

Paradox is not central to the theories of strategic choice, learning organisations, knowledge management and communities of practice or the importation of chaos and complexity theory into organisational thinking through cognitivist and constructivist perspectives on psychology. Contradiction, tension and dilemmas are recognised but they are seen as resolvable. It is indeed the purpose of management, according to these theories, to resolve them. The reason is that all of these theories are fundamentally systemic and it is of the essence of systems thinking to eliminate paradox in dualistic thinking.

Paradox plays a much more important role in psychoanalytic theories and is seen as fundamental to human life. The theory of complex responsive processes places even more emphasis on paradox in that the individual and the group are paradoxically formed by and forming each other at the same time. Particularly important is the emphasis placed on the paradox of predictability and unpredictability at the same time. Paradox, of course, cannot be resolved or harmonised, only endlessly transformed.

In this section I have compared the answers to four key questions given by various *systemic* theories of organisation with those provided by complex responsive *processes* theory. I suggest that the move from systems to processes leads to a radically different understanding of organisational evolution. It is radical in that it abandons the assumption of the autonomous individual and the position of the objective observer. It replaces these assumptions with those of the simultaneous social construction of group and individual and the position of participative enquiry. Another move is away from thinking of oneself as manager in terms of the objective designer, towards thinking of oneself as an active participant in complex processes. In the next section of this chapter, I want to explore how this theoretical shift focuses the attention of practitioners and researchers on factors that are, in some respects, very different to the other theories. This in turn has implications for how management and leadership competences are defined and what strategic management means.

18.3   Refocusing attention: strategy and change

In the title of this chapter, I have intentionally used the word 'implications' rather than 'applications' or 'prescriptions'. Strategic choice, learning organisation and knowledge management theories take the methodological position of the objective observer where the manager stands outside the organisation understood as a system and thinks in terms of controlling it. These theories, therefore, immediately have an application to do with the intentional control of the system by the observing manager. It is then a natural step to formulate general prescriptions for the application of control. The prescriptions take the form of tools and techniques of analysis and control. Furthermore, some test of the validity of the tools and techniques is required. This is provided by pointing to how organisations that use particular tools and techniques, or have particular attributes, are successful while those that do not use, or possess, them fail.

It seems to me that psychoanalytic perspectives on organisations hold the position of the objective observer much less firmly. The concern with application then becomes less central and the focus shifts more to understanding what is happening in an organisation. Rather than straightforward prescriptions, those working from a psychoanalytic perspective provide hypotheses for joint discussion with members of an organisation in specific, rather than general, cases.

A theory of organisations as complex responsive processes of relating makes a methodological move away from the notion of the manager as objective observer. Managers are understood to be participants in complex responsive processes, engaged in emergent enquiry into what they are doing and what steps they should take next. They may also be enquiring into the nature of their own complex responsive processes of relating. This is what it means to be reflexive. This theory provides an explanation of what managers are doing, rather than of what they should be doing. Application has little meaning in this endeavour. If you are trying to explain what managers are doing now, you can hardly use this as a prescription. They are already doing it. The whole purpose of the theoretical shift I have been suggesting is to focus attention on processes that managers are held to be engaging in, but which the other theories either do not focus upon or tend to do so in a prescriptive way. The purpose is not to apply or prescribe but to refocus attention. When people focus their attention differently, they are highly likely to take different kinds of actions. However, a theory that focuses attention on self-organising processes and emergent outcomes can hardly yield general prescriptions on how that self-organisation should proceed and what should emerge from it. The theory would be proposing to do the opposite of what it is explaining. Instead, the theory of complex responsive processes invites recognition of the uniqueness and non-repeatability of experience.

If you focus your attention according to strategic choice, learning organisation and knowledge management theories, the lack of application and prescription implied by complex responsive processes theory is highly unsatisfactory. The tendency is to dismiss it as useless for this reason. However, if you take the perspective of complex responsive processes theory, rather than trying to make it fit into some other theory, you might come to value what it does, namely refocuses attention. I have found that even if managers accept this, they immediately ask for examples of where people have refocused attention in the way suggested and whether they were then successful. Again, this is approaching the theory of complex responsive processes from the frame of reference of the other theories. One of the main properties of the dynamics of bounded instability is the escalation of small changes into qualitatively different patterns. Patterns of bounded instability may be similar to each other but they are never repeated in the same way. They are unique and not repeatable at important levels of detail. Organisations characterised by the dynamics of bounded instability will therefore all be unique in some important way. The experience of one cannot be repeated, at important levels of detail, by another. Giving examples of success in one organisation to managers in another is likely to be spurious. Perhaps this is why the track record of identifying attributes of successful organisation is so poor. Instead of looking for understanding in other people's experience one might look for it in one's own experience.

Consistent with the nature of the theory I am talking about, therefore, I will not be providing applications or prescriptions. What I will be trying to point to is how the theory shifts the focus of attention. First, consider how attention is focused on the quality of participation.

Focusing attention on the quality of participation

Whenever I talk to managers about the complex responsive processes perspective, they immediately ask what it says that 'you' need to do to bring about the success of an organisation. When I ask who this 'you' is, they usually say that they mean the top executives of an organisation. The main issue here is how one is thinking about what top executives of an organisation are doing. From the dominant systemic perspective they are implicitly thought of first as standing outside the organisation understood as a system and operating on it in some way, and then as participating in the system as parts of it. From the complex responsive processes perspective, top executives are thought of as participating with other members in evolutionary processes of communicating and power relating. The meaning of participation is completely different in the two perspectives. In the systemic perspective, participation means participating in an abstract 'whole' or system and in the complexity perspective it means participating in direct interaction with other people. In the fomer case participation creates a whole outside of the direct experience of interaction and in the latter case participation means creating further interaction.

Strategic choice theory holds that the top executives can form organisation-wide intentions for an organisation's future evolution. It also holds that if they then appropriately motivate other members of their organisation, those members will move according to the intention that top executives have ascribed to the system. In the language of complex responsive processes theory, this amounts to saying that top executives can make an intentional gesture for the whole organisation and they can more or less determine the responses to that gesture throughout the organisation. Responses of a deviant kind are to be forestalled by appropriate motivation and unexpected responses from other organisations are to be handled by making further, organisation-wide, intentional gestures. Innovation and creativity are also understood to be intentions formed by top executives. There is no fundamental place for the unexpected.

Learning organisation and knowledge management theory theory does take account of unexpected response to the organisation-wide, intentional gestures of top executives. However, it holds that they can intentionally operate at leverage points so as to get the responses they want, more or less. Creativity here is the intentional change of mental models by individuals. From psychoanalytic perspectives, top executives can choose task and role definitions and design structures that will hold disruptive unconscious processes at bay. Those employing complexity theory in what I have called an orthodox way point to unpredictability of responses and to their self-organising and emergent nature. However, they hold that top executives can choose simple rules or intentionally create crises that will move their organisation to a dynamic in which it can be successful.

In critical systems thinking, researchers, consultants and managers evaluate a problem situation, invite the 'right' participants to engage with it, encourage them to interact, trigger their enthusiasm and present them with the selected systems models that they think are appropriate to the problem situation. In the communities of practice perspective, someone formulates a design for learning.

In all these cases, the top executives are making choices about how they are to operate on the system as a whole and it is being assumed that they can determine the responses their gestures call forth. In effect this assumes that there is a special category of person in an organisation who alone has free will and choice, or agency, with all the others reduced to automata. Even members of that special category then have to become a part in the system they have designed, implying that they are only free while they are designing the system.

From the complex responsive processes participative perspective, no manager can stand outside an organisation and choose how it is to operate. Instead, all managers are active participants with each other in the interactive processes that are the organisation. Top executives can and do form organisation-wide intentions about their organisation. They can and do identify leverage points. They can and do design structures to contain unconscious processes and sometimes they do set simple rules and intentionally cause crises. They can and do prepare designs for learning and they do try to identify the 'right' people. They can and do select and recommend systems models that they think are relevant to particular problem situations. However, all of these intentions and designs emerge in the conversations top executives have with each other and with other people. Furthermore, top executives can never design the responses to these gestures. Small changes may escalate and people will engage in self-organising conversations and power relations, often organised by shadow themes, from which unexpected responses may well emerge. Attention is then focused on the thematic patterning of interaction, such as the pattern of power relations, the patterns of inclusion and exclusion, the ideological themes sustaining them and the feelings of anxiety and shame aroused by shifts in patterns of identity.

I am suggesting, then, that in moving from the position of manager as objective observer/system part to that of manager as participant in emergent enquiry, attention is focused on the unexpected and complex patterning of the responses of organisational members to managers' intentions. Intention and design are understood as emergent and problematic processes. The emphasis shifts from the manager focusing on how to make a choice to focusing on the quality of participation in self-organising conversations from which such choices and the responses to them emerge. It becomes a personal matter of reflecting together on the quality of participation.

Focusing attention on the quality of conversational life

In organisations relationships between people are organised in conversations that form and are formed by the power relations between them. Conversational relating is organised by themes of an ideological nature that justify the pattern of power relations. Intentions emerge as other themes organising the experience of relating, as do the responses these intentions call forth. New themes emerge as people struggle to understand each other and as their conversations are cross-fertilised through conversations with people in other communities and disciplines. Organisations change when the themes that organise conversation and power relations change. Learning is change in these themes. Knowledge is language and meaning emerges as themes interact to form conversations.

Attention is thus focused on the conversational life of an organisation as the changing, evolving, self-organising processes of communicative interaction and power relating patterned as intention and design and using communicative tools such as systems models. The quality of that conversational life is thus paramount. Increasingly, systemic theories are focusing on conversations, story and narrative. However, the tendency is to seek to design special forms of conversation known as dialogue and special forums such as communities of practice. From the complex responsive processes perspective the emphasis is on ordinary, everyday conversation. The key role of managers is their participation in those conversations and power relations, and their facilitation of different ways of conversing. A key implication of this way of understanding life in organisations has to do with being sensitive to the themes that are organising conversational relating. Another is awareness of the rhetorical ploys that are being used to block the emergence of new conversational themes. From this perspective, effective managers are those who notice the repetitive themes that block free-flowing conversation and participate in such a way as to assist in shifting those themes. They may do this, for example, by repeatedly asking why people are saying what they are saying. Effective managers will seek opportunities to talk to people in other communities and bring themes from those conversations into the conversational life of their own organisation. They will be particularly concerned with trying to understand the covert politics and unconscious group processes they are caught up in and how those might be trapping conversation in repetitive themes. They will also pay attention to the power relations and the ideological basis of those power relations as expressed in conversations.

Focusing attention on the quality of anxiety and how it is lived with

A theory of organisation as complex responsive processes focuses attention on the importance of free-flowing conversation in which people are able to search for new meaning. Anxiety is an inevitable companion of shifts in themes that organise the experience of relating because such shifts create uncertainty, particularly uncertainty around individual and collective identities. Themes organising the experience of relating are not only expressed in the vocal, public conversations between people. They also resonate with and change the silent, private conversations that are individual minds. Change in organisations is also, at the same time, deeply personal change for individual members. New ways of talking publicly are reflected in new ways of individuals making sense of themselves. Such shifts unsettle the very way in which people experience themselves. They threaten personal and collective identities. It is because of these deeply personal reasons that shifting patterns of conversation give rise to anxiety, but without this there can be no emergence of creative new themes.

When one thinks in this way, the manner in which people live with anxiety is crucial to organisational change and innovation. When managers focus attention on this matter they begin to pay attention to what it is about particular work, at a particular time, in a particular place, that gives rise to anxiety. They pay attention to the nature of this anxiety. They ask what makes it possible to live with the anxiety so that it is also experienced as the excitement required to enable people to continue struggling with the search for new meaning. This a matter for managers to reflect upon. What are we doing that enables us, or disables us, from living with the anxiety that change generates? Central to this possibility is sufficient trust between those engaging in difficult conversations. Attention is then focused on what in a particular organisation, at a particular time, is promoting or destroying trust. This is also very much the focus of attention in psychoanalytic perspectives.

What will be seriously questioned from the perspective of complex responsive processes are prescriptions that have to do with setting stretching targets and placing people under stress in the belief that this will move them to try harder. What this may do is simply make them feel more anxious and so less likely to develop the kind of conversational life that makes creativity possible.

Focusing attention on the quality of diversity

One of the most distinctive aspects of a theory of complex responsive processes is the way in which it focuses attention on diversity. The other theories reviewed in this book tend to focus attention on consensus. Strategic choice theory focuses attention on the importance of members of an organisation sharing the same commitment to its policies and its chosen strategic direction. Learning organisation theory focuses attention on the importance of people in an organisation being committed to the same vision and working together harmoniously in cohesive teams. Psychoanalytic perspectives focus attention on the importance of people understanding the nature of boundaries and having shared understandings of their roles and tasks. Those who import complexity theory into their theorising about organisations in systemic ways stress the importance of people sharing a few simple rules. The theory I am suggesting takes a more paradoxical perspective.

The paradox is this: if members of an organisation have nothing in common at all, then obviously any kind of joint action will be impossible. However, if they conform too much then the emergence of new forms of behaviour is blocked. Organisations only display the internal capacity to change spontaneously when they are characterised by diversity. This focuses attention on the importance of deviance and eccentricity. It focuses attention on the importance of unofficial ideologies that undermine current power relations. Such unofficial ideologies are expressed in conversations organised by shadow themes. A condition for creativity is therefore some degree of subversive activity with the inevitable tension this brings between shadow and legitimate themes organising the experience of relating.

It is difficult to get one's mind around what this means. It does not make much sense to me to move from noting the importance of deviance to thinking that managers, in their legitimate roles, should promote deviance. It would then not be deviance. It makes little sense to advocate harnessing shadow conversational themes in order intentionally to generate creativity. The shadow so harnessed is no longer the shadow. It makes little sense to say that managers should take steps to unleash self-organisation. This implies that it is not going on already, when the whole point of the theory of complexity is that it is explaining how things already are.

For me, the implication of recognising the importance of deviance has to do with people making sense of their own engagement with others in the shadow conversations that express deviance. It means paying attention to how what they are doing may be collusively sustaining the legitimate themes organising experience, so making change impossible. It means developing a greater sensitivity to the unconscious way in which together people create categories of what is 'in' and what is 'out' and the effect that this has on people and organisations. These dynamics of power relating, inclusion-exclusion and shame are central to the complex responsive processes perspective but do not feature in critical systems thinking or in theories of communities of practice.

Focusing attention on unpredictability and paradox

Perhaps the most radical implication of complex responsive processes theory is the limits to certainty and predictability that it points to. This is a major departure from other theories of organisation, which either virtually ignore or at least downplay the radical unpredictability of the long-term evolution of organisations. What does paying attention to such unpredictability imply?

First, for me, it means thinking about how to cope with not knowing and the potential for feelings of incompetence and shame that this arouses. Managers in organisations often find themselves in situations in which they must act without knowing what the outcome of their actions will be over long time periods. They must act because failure to act will also have unpredictable long-term outcomes. Furthermore, managers can and do act, often very creatively, when they do not know what the long-term outcomes of their actions will be.

These situations are made much more difficult, I think, when management is understood from perspectives that lead people to believe that long-term predictability is possible if one is well informed and competent enough. When the inevitable surprise comes then this view leads to a search for whom to blame. The perspective that predictability is possible leads to the view that the surprise must be due to ignorance, incompetence or some form of bad behaviour in that people did not do what they were supposed to do. In my experience, this judgement is frequently completely unjustified in that very intelligent managers do the best they can and still the surprises come. When you take the complex responsive processes perspective then surprise is part of the internal dynamic of the processes themselves. Surprise is inevitable no matter how well informed, competent and well behaved everyone is. Surprise is inseparable from creativity. I believe that thinking in this way is itself a way of living with the anxiety of not knowing. It is quite natural not to know and this does not have to incapacitate one. It is possible to carry on working together even in the condition of not knowing. Self-organising conversational processes operating in the state of not knowing produce emergent meaning, often of a new and creative kind.

This way of thinking encourages one to pay more attention to what one actually does as one holds the position of not knowing long enough for the new to emerge. One implication of this position has to do with the criteria used to judge a quality action. The systemic theories reviewed in Part One implicitly assume that the criterion for selecting a quality action is its outcome. Quality actions are those that produce desired outcomes. However, in an unpredictable world, the outcomes of an action cannot be known in advance. It is necessary to act and then deal with the consequences. This does not make action impossible or futile. It simply means that people select actions on the basis of other criteria for quality. For example, in a highly uncertain world a quality action is one that keeps options open for as long as possible. A quality action is one which creates a position from which further actions are possible. That is why the option of doing nothing is such a poor response to uncertainty. If the response to uncertainty is to stay at home then the options opened up by journeying forth will never be available. Another criterion for a quality action is that it should enable errors to be detected faster than other options. Finally, the most important criteria for quality actions are moral and ethical in nature. An action may be taken without the actor's knowing its outcome simply because the action is judged to be good in itself. One is not absolved of responsibility simply because one does not know the outcome. Even if I do not know how my action will turn out, I am still responsible and will have to deal with the outcome as best I can.

Just as the unpredictability arising in complex interactions imposes limits on what it is possible to know about outcomes of actions, so the complexity of the interactions itself imposes limits on how much of it can be understood. Managers often cannot know the long-term outcomes of their actions and they usually cannot understand the full nature of the complex responsive processes of organising. However, this does not disable action either because the process of self-organisation is one in which local interaction produces an emergent global pattern. It is not necessary to understand the whole in order to act; it is simply necessary to act on the basis of one's own local understanding. This is a very different notion to that in, say, learning organisation theory, which prescribes system thinking, that is understanding the whole system, as essential to learning. Unlike systemic theories of any kind, one is not seeking the whole or trying to be comprehensive.

The focus on long-term unpredictability has implications for the meaning of control. As it is normally understood in other theories of organisation, control is a cybernetic process. It is an activity that ensures the achievement of chosen outcomes. In highly complex processes with emergent and unpredictable long-term outcomes, this form of control is impossible. This does not mean that there is no control, however. It simply means that control has to be understood in a different way. Control then takes the form of constraint. As I have often pointed out in previous chapters, all acts of relating impose constraint on all of those relating. Control takes the form of relating itself, that is mutual constraint. Self-organisation is a process of mutual constraining and hence a form of control.

Notions of complexity, long-term unpredictability and control as constraint have implications for many activities that are currently taken for granted by managers. If these notions are taken seriously, they lead to a number of questions. For example: Why do people prepare long-term forecasts if it is impossible to make useful long-term forecasts? Why do they adopt investment-appraisal methods that require detailed quantitative forecasts over long time periods? Complexity theory suggests that it is impossible to make such forecasts so why do people carry on doing it? If organisations are not simply cybernetic systems why is so much effort expended on cybernetic systems of quality control? One important implication of a complex responsive processes theory of organising may have to do with putting a stop to many initiatives and abandoning control systems and procedures that are not fulfilling the purposes they are supposed to fulfil. The savings in time, resources and human stress might be considerable.

The theory of complex responsive processes particularly focuses attention on the paradoxical nature of organisational life.

- Organising is at the same time self-organising emergence and intention. Intention emerges in self-organising processes of conversation while at the same time organising that conversation.
- Conversational patterns in an organisation enable what is being done and at the same time constrain what is done.
- The performance of complicated tasks requires that they be divided up but at the same time they have to be integrated.

- The same processes of self-organising emergence creatively produce new forms while at the same time destroying others. New conversational themes and power relations emerge while older ones are destroyed.
- Themes organising the experience of relating in conversation are both stable and unstable at the same time.
- The emergence of new themes organising the experience of relating is both predictable and unpredictable at the same time.
- Managers operate in a state of knowing and not knowing at the same time.
- Complex responsive processes organise both conformity and deviance at the same time.

Managing is then a process of continually rearranging the paradoxes of organisational life.

Implications for management competences

I have been arguing that the main implication of the complex responsive processes perspective is the way in which it refocuses attention, not on what members of an organisation should be doing, but on what they are already, and always have been, doing. If there is a prescription, it is that of paying more attention to the quality of your own experience of relating and managing in relationship with others. This is a reflexive activity requiring each one of us to pay more attention to our own part in what is happening around us. This requires a reflective development of self-knowledge. It means taking one's own experience seriously. The reward, in my experience, is to find oneself interacting more effectively, not only for one's own good, but also for the good of those with whom one is in relationship.

However, the skills and competences required for this are difficult to develop and just as difficult to sustain. They are competences that do not usually feature in the skill sets prescribed for managers. Examples of the necessary skills are the capacity for self-reflection and owning one's part in what is happening, skill in facilitating free-flowing conversation, ability to articulate what is emerging in conversations and sensitivity to group dynamics. These skills become essential to notions of leadership and the role of top executives because their greater power renders their impact on others all the greater. Furthermore, these skills are not easily taught, perhaps they cannot be taught, in an abstract way. They are essentially acquired in the experience of exercising them.

Systemic theories of organising and managing encourage a belief in the possibility of identifying necessary skills in a clear way and defining steps to go through in order to acquire them. The essential skills I am pointing to are much fuzzier and the steps to achieving them even more nebulous. The response might be to stay with systemic management perspectives. After all, they have applications and prescriptions that are much easier to grasp. However, I believe that this easier option is not viable in the increasingly complex world of organisations. Effective participation in complex responsive processes seems to me to require an increasing commitment to grappling with the issues I have been pointing to in this chapter.

Finally, what are the implications for strategic management?

Strategic management

In Chapter 1, I suggested that the phenomenon that strategic management is concerned with is that of the population of interacting organisations and the population of interacting groups and individuals within any organisation. The key question relates to the nature of the processes through which these populations evolve over long time periods.

I have argued that it is too simple to suggest that they evolve in directions chosen separately by groups of senior executives within each of them. The interaction between them simply makes this impossible. Nor can change in any one organisation be chosen by groups of senior executives. The complex interactions between groupings of people within an organisation make this impossible too. I am not arguing that senior executives do not, cannot or should not make such choices. They do, they can and they should. What I am arguing is that these choices are gestures in an ongoing conversation of gestures out of which the evolution of organisations emerges.

What I have been pointing to is a theory of emergent strategy. Strategies emerge, intentions emerge, in the ongoing conversational life of an organisation and in the ongoing conversations between people in different organisations. Strategic management is the process of actively participating in the conversations around important emerging issues. Strategic direction is not set in advance but understood in hindsight as it is emerging or after it has emerged. This is because if small changes can escalate to have enormous consequences, then the distinction between what is strategic and what is, say, tactical becomes very problematic. The distinction can only be identified after the event. Complex responsive processes theory therefore leads to a different conceptualisation of strategy and strategic management.

18.4   Summary

Systemic theories of organisation see strategy as the usually rational choice or intention of some or all of the members of an organisation and the intentional overcoming of obstacles to the implementation of such choices. The psychoanalytic approach pays particular attention to how irrational processes might interfere with this choice or intention. Intention is understood as the choice, or design, made by autonomous individuals, usually taking the position of the independent observer. The criteria for the choice focus on desired, predetermined outcomes.

The complex responsive processes perspective makes a substantial move in a number of ways. First, it directs attention to how intention emerges in the self-organising process of ordinary conversation between people. This replaces the notion that intention is the expression of an autonomous individual who reflects and makes choices in the light of expected outcomes, as it were, after consulting with others. So, the first move is to focus on how intention emerges rather than on what it is. The second move is to postulate that any novel intention initially emerges only in the tension between legitimate and shadow themes organising the experience of being together, that is, in ordinary conversations at the margins of the organisation.

Management narratives

●●●● Management narrative 1: Innovation in
a water utility

by Jose Fonseca

Over the period from 1994 to 1998, I spent some time talking to people at Lisbon's water utility. They came from a number of levels in the hierarchy and different departments. I was interested in how a particular innovation at that company had come about and how it was unfolding. I will start by recounting some of what I learned in my conversations with people about this organisation's background and the beginnings of the innovation I was interested in up to my arrival in 1994.

EPAL's background

EPAL is the state-owned supplier of water to Lisbon and surrounding areas. The possibility of privatisation had been a matter of public discussion for some time but it was widely accepted that the monopoly in the water sector would eventually be broken up. Many feared that this would enable foreign entry into the industry and in order to be prepared for this threat, EPAL was investing in a substantial modernisation of the distribution network.

EPAL was organised into departments having the following functions:

- Production, that is capturing the water and transporting it to Lisbon.
- Treatment, that is making the water drinkable.
- Distribution, that is delivering the water to consumers.
- Consumer relations, that is registering consumers, measuring consumption, invoicing, collecting receivables and generally solving problems with households.
- Planning and construction of extensions to the distribution network.
- Maintenance and improvement of the distribution network.

The government appoints the members of the EPAL board for three- to four-year periods and the majority of the members do not normally serve for more than one term. Since 1989, the company had undergone three significant changes in organisational structure recommended by consultants. However, these involved only limited compulsory redundancies and few changes in physical locations, tasks and workflow. Sometimes departments were reorganised but tasks and processes remained the same. On other occasions, departments were given new names, but people carried on doing what they were doing before. The typical decision-making process at EPAL takes the form of conversations between heads of department, in which they accommodate each other's expectations and interests in order to reach a compromise. A decision is then presented to the board which legitimises it. Power lies with the heads of department who have usually been in the company for long enough to understand its culture.

That culture might be described as a culture of artisans, that is one of learning by doing and being taught by artisans. This 'craftsmanship' culture was expressed in a number of ways. For example, there was considerable peer pressure to do things 'right' as opposed to doing things cheaply. Self-improvement was valued more than 'doing things by the book'. People mentioned pride in belonging to this company and sharing its technical culture and professional attitude. On several occasions, I took part in conversations between workers about corporate heroes from the past. They had become heroes because of their professional expertise and their ability to improvise good technical solutions to difficult problems. Older employees transmitted to younger colleagues a sense of belonging and of pride in being members of a company reputed for its technical expertise and improvisational flexibility. People were interested in new ways of doing things and in new materials.

However, technical processes had been changing markedly over the past ten years. These changes, mainly to do with automation, were initiated and developed from within the company, with the co-operation of consultants and suppliers. Because of such technological innovation, the company was moving from its culture of 'craftsmanship' to one of disciplined scientific knowledge. This meant moving from a company that possessed an elite of artisan workers to an engineering company. This move was, in turn, altering perceptions of the value and status of various departments within the company. It was also altering patterns of conversation.

Within the above context, I was interested in an innovation that had to do with repairs to the water distribution system.

Repairs to the water distribution system

A number of people explained to me what the procedure was that led to repairs being made in the distribution system. Customers would telephone to report leaks in the street or interruptions to the supply of water to their premises. The sequence of communications their calls triggered is depicted in Figure MN1.1.

The Customer Service Department received the call and passed the information to the Operations Department (OD). An inspector travelled to the location and assessed the problem. In order to make an assessment the inspector needed an updated map of the area and a survey of the underground pipe network in that area. This enabled identification of which valves should be closed in order to stop the flooding. The inspector notified OD, where priorities were set and an order for repair issued and sent to the Maintenance Department. Typically within the day, a crew left the nearest company site to repair the leaking pipes. This crew also needed charts containing updated records of the type and dimension of pipes in place. On completion of the repair, a report was prepared on the work done, recording components replaced, types of material used and the nature of the damage to the failed components. The reports were used to update the charts of the network.

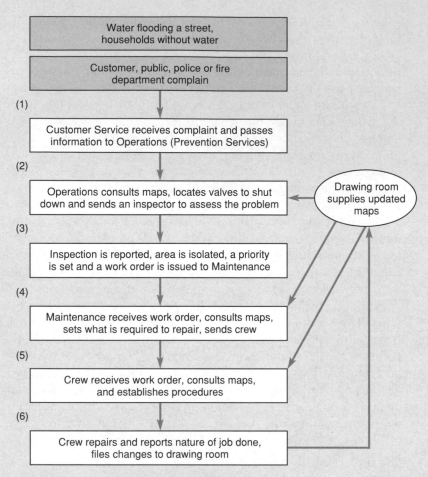

Figure MN 1.1   The flow of information in EPAL

On average, there were more than 300 repairs of this kind each day and the drawing room could not cope with the flow of information. The charts therefore tended to be updated on a piecemeal basis so that several versions of the same charts existed at any one time. People responded to the consequent unreliability of the charts by keeping their own private databases with different ways of recording and retrieving data. Unbeknown to senior managers, these private databases had proliferated throughout the company. People reached for whatever was to hand (PCs, paper cards, sheets of paper, recording books, writing directly on their charts) to store information they expected to need in the near future.

This way of dealing with the information people required to do their work gave rise to a number of problems:

● Customer Service did not know when a complaint related to a problem had already been reported and so passed redundant information to Operations. Customer Service staff had no way of knowing what was being done further down the line and so could not answer customer enquiries about how their complaints were being handled.

- Under the pressure of work in peak periods, they may well not have recorded the most recent components installed on site.
- Even when charts had actually been updated, confidence was so low that people did not believe that they had been updated and so checked up on what the charts showed. Each service organised its own set of charts (38 covering the city area), believing that its own charts were more likely to reflect what was actually under the ground.
- Crews often had to contact the office to obtain more up-to-date information on the site they were working on.

The result was the daily production of huge quantities of data, much of which were duplicated and stored in ways that were incompatible with each other. Many people talked about how useful it would be if these data were recorded and disseminated in real time. Those operating the pipeline system would then be able to function much more efficiently. So over the years there had been conversations about digesting the surveys of the pipe network and storing these surveys on computer where they could be accessed at work sites. In this way, the most up-to-date information could be accessed and any change made to the network could be immediately recorded electronically on to the digitised charts.

Developing a digitised cartographic system

In 1989, the head of the Distribution Department decided to pursue the idea of developing a digitised survey of the network. The departmental budget could not accommodate the significant cost of the technology and labour that would be required for this endeavour. Furthermore, the head knew that this issue was not, at that time, a major concern of the board. Their investment priority was the development of the distribution network. So, the head set in motion a less ambitious project within the department, using internal resources without formal approval. Two new engineers were hired and although their roles had nothing formally to do with the digitisation project, they were chosen because they had skills relevant to it. Soon, they were spending most of their time on the digitised survey. Later, in spite of financial constraints, a consultant was appointed to assist on the project. During this phase the development of the project depended on the motivation and effort of four people. Although their actions had not been legitimised, they were tolerated in a culture that emphasised technical progress and technical expertise.

This first phase of the project consisted mainly of the digitisation of the existing maps of Lisbon. Existing charts were drawn to different scales and this made it difficult for people to move from one chart to the next. Clearly, this would not do for an instrument that was supposed to be used as a tool for rapid identification of which pipeline branches to shut down. All charts would, therefore, not only have to be digitised but also reduced to a common scale if the system was to work. The routine work of loading the information was subcontracted to a consultant who placed people in-house to work under the supervision of a team leader from EPAL. It was intended that in this phase the work should be conducted in two shifts using two digitisation tables. However, the co-operation of other departments required for this was never obtained and therefore a smaller group of people carried on loading and monitoring the quality of the work being done. Because of resource constraints, the work had to be done on a small PC, but it could not accommodate the processing speed and quantity of information required for a digitised survey.

The task was becoming impossible. Each day, charts were being changed as much as they were being digitised, so that catching up with the changes became a vicious cycle. This went on until 1994.

Despite its apparent failure, however, this first attempt had been very important in drawing attention to the survey and in establishing a general agreement on the need for such a system. During this period, 'know-how' was developed on the way such processes could be carried out and what requirements and difficulties this entailed. Agreement was also reached on the symbols to be used so that the maps could be understood by all who would refer to them. Most importantly, these initial efforts were developing the skills within EPAL that are required to digitise geographical information systems, a technology that had so far only been developed by the military. EPAL was, therefore, a pioneer in Portugal in this field. During 1990–1 Lisbon's local government heard about this work and expressed interest in acquiring the digitised maps in order to control more effectively other companies that were burying structures beneath the city soil. However, this had the consequence of slowing down the development of the digitisation project, because the project director was required to attend many city council commissions addressing the survey issue, none of which produced anything concrete. However, the reputation EPAL was developing in this area was to become one of the foundations of a number of strategic moves that the company is now making in international markets. It is now being used as a basis for a bid that EPAL is making for work in Brazil.

By 1994, when I first began to talk to people about this innovation, the product concept of digitised charts was in the process of being revised. It was beginning to be redefined as a wider information system and it was decided that a database function should be included. I was very interested in how this redefinition was taking place.

Revision of the concept

As far as I could tell the main reason for the redefinition was that the project moved from the Distribution Department to the Information Technology Department. The move took place because the head of the Distribution Department was promoted and the head of the IT Department became interested in speeding the process up because it fitted in with what the head was already doing. The IT Department already possessed some knowledge of digitised surveys since it had been developing such a system for the large pipeline coming from the dams in the north (internally known as the production system).

The digitisation work done in OD was taken over by staff in IT who had available a UNIX platform, more powerful programming tools and consultant expertise in geographic systems and graph technology. Naturally, given who was now developing it, the project was redefined as an IT project and coupled with the other project that was then under way for the production system. The project was no longer simply to develop a digitised survey of the distribution network to assist engineers in carrying out repairs. It was now a project to develop a more dynamic information system. Therefore, relational database programming was introduced. In 1995, there was another shift in the platform used to develop the project as it changed to a Windows NT environment.

What I particularly noticed here was the shift in the nature of the conversations about digitised surveys. The dominant conversation of mechanical engineers was yielding to other conversations that were acquiring greater legitimacy. The vocabulary and the concepts in these new conversations were coming from information sciences, biology, management sciences and organisational psychology.

The years that followed this move saw a growing consensus on the importance of the project. It became more and more public, receiving official recognition, and its improving priority in the investment programme resulted in an increased budget. By the end of 1995 all cartographic data (names of streets, topographic heights) were introduced into the databases, but up-to-date information about technical data, such as pipe dimensions and type of material, valves and faucets, was still absent. The early maps that had been digitised were not being updated. Another six months were spent trying to bring the system in line with current changes in the materials installed in the ground. By mid-1996, other departments were brought in to contribute to the improvement of the system. It was at this stage that several unofficial databases came to light.

The pilot survey was ready for testing in October 1996 and a dialogue began with user departments. Several technical issues emerged during this dialogue and were addressed. Furthermore, participating in the dialogue made the system less threatening to people. In the last quarter of 1996 the first of a number of programmes took place to train people in how to use the new system. Three workstations were placed in each department that had to use the system, namely Customer Service, OD and Maintenance. People were invited to 'play' and comment on the use of the system. They were asked to absorb their 'private' databases into the new system. People in technical sections appeared to be willing to co-operate since it meant official recognition and appreciation of activities they had engaged in for years.

I was interested in how people had developed their own databases in order to overcome the inadequacies of the formal information systems. They had done so over the years in conversations that were quite unknown to those higher up in the hierarchy. The existence of these private databases came as a surprise during the programmes to train people to use the new system. The informal databases now began to affect the design of the new system. For example, new entry fields in the databases of the new system were added. It became clear that contextual information about the precise site conditions in which repairs would have to be conducted in different locations could not be depicted on the charts. They could not depict, for instance, that cars were parked in a particular street in such a way as to obstruct the work. This was usually dealt with by workers going into nearby cafés to ask who the car belonged to and request its removal. This took less time than the prescribed, formal procedure of summoning the police. For me, the interesting point was how the digitised survey had been able to absorb the narrative knowledge that had emerged from within the departments. In other words, the innovation 'absorbed' previous 'unrecorded' innovations that were the emergent result of people's conversations about the way they could simplify their lives or about how they could solve practical problems they faced in their day-to-day activities.

People on the training courses welcomed the new system. Indeed they were so enthusiastic that they began to complain about the quality and speed of the computers they had been given to learn from. They began to complain about a lack of commitment to the new system on the part of upper management. There did seem to be a lack of decisive direction on the part of upper levels in management. Budgets for the required number of computers and plotters were still not confirmed by February 1997. However, an extensive training programme was approved and the person who had been working in the project since 1994 trained more than 30 future operators.

One interesting consequence of the training programmes was the expectations they gave rise to. Operators were expecting the digitised system to be immediately usable in a perfect state. They complained that the survey would never be perfect enough because it would never be up to date with current realities on sites. It appears that when it came to the operational phase, they forgot the lessons from the development phase, where there were many surprises as the process unfolded. People seemed to forget the fact that the charts had never been up to date and required them to improvise. Now they demanded that the survey be absolutely fault proof if they were to use it. They seemed to have lost sight of the fact that if they did not operate with the system in its current state and so feed it with updates, it would never be updated, just as the charts never were.

The digitised survey system is a horizontal process running through nearly all departments. It is perceived as enabling those who create and manage it to acquire a new 'power tool'. There is a feeling that those who manage the system will acquire an internal visibility that might threaten the former status of people. The main issue seems to relate to the fact that within a water utility, those who graduated in mechanical engineering used to expect to climb the corporate ladder, whereas other people had more limited career expectations. However, in recent years the main pattern of talk has shifted from the vocabulary and concepts of mechanical engineers to those of computer scientists. This disturbs the pattern of power and status.

During the training sessions, there were many discussions on how the survey should operate, what kind of information it should store and how it would be retrieved. These discussions led the sector leaders to suggest the use of the survey for transmission of information about work and repair orders. By January 1997, the system was reconfigured and a new function was introduced. The communications between departments regarding work orders would be done through the survey. The survey would no longer simply be an information platform but would become a control system as well. This notion led to the installation of flow of work procedures.

In the new system, a repair order is processed in the following states:

1 Opening state (after communication from some external entity warning that there is a disruption in distribution).
2 Inspection state (when Operations receives the communication and sends someone to assess the problem).

3 Execution state (when a work order is issued and passed on to Maintenance).
4 Closing state (when work is done and a report is filed in the system and is waiting for validation).

It is not possible to alter the information as it passes from one state to another.
The computer automatically registers the time of recording and expedition of this
information. Costs of repair, materials used and recovered, labour costs, are all
stored in this system for each work order. The president of the company can, if
desired, see which repairs are being done, and so can anyone else in the company,
provided that they can access the system. This is very easy since workstations will
be situated in all departments.

The digital survey has clearly changed from simply being an enabling tool. It is
not just a tool to increase efficiency. It is also an instrument of control and of performance evaluation. Since the system identifies the time when a communication
takes place, it can be used to analyse time differentials between issuing the order
and completion of the repair. In addition, it identifies who sent, received and issued
communications. This is no longer a geographic information system; it is now a
process control system.

One of the most interesting aspects of this story for me, as I took part in conversations about it between 1994 and 1998, was the way in which it changed its
nature. As the conversations about it evolved, as changes in the context were occurring (technologies, organisational structures, technological updating of processes),
the project was being reconfigured and redefined. It started as a faster process of
updating information. It moved to a horizontal information-sharing platform. It
became an efficient problem-solving system. It moved to an operational information
support system. Finally, it was defined as part of an integrated information management system that is really an online device for management control. The curious
thing is that the system itself was even then not yet in full operation.

This project started as a tentative, limited and located process. It then moved to a
traditional top-down re-engineering process comprising a clear purpose, a detailed
budget and a detailed phase schedule. However, a much more messy and emergent
development process was really changing the outcomes and the meanings of this
innovation. The more formal approach to the process did not envisage, for instance,
that the innovation would accommodate previous innovative actions developed by
those who had simply responded to the demands they faced every day.

© Jose Fonseca

●●●● Management narrative 2: The budget meeting

by Phil Streatfield

The background to the meeting I am going to describe in this narrative was as
follows. In 1996, Axil plc initiated what was called the Chain 2000 programme.
The purpose of this programme was to improve supply chain processes across the
worldwide operations. The main objective was to integrate and standardise supply
chain processes and systems into the same time frame required for millennium

compliance. A number of benefits were expected. First, the risks associated with millennium compliance for supply chain systems would be reduced. Secondly, financial and volume forecasting would be linked, so improving the quality of operational and financial planning. Thirdly, operational efficiency would be improved by the introduction of formal trading relationships between businesses within the company. Fourthly, an infrastructure would be created to underpin the achievement of strategic objectives for optimising plant-to-market business. In October 1997 the corporate plan established a time scale for substantial delivery of the solutions before the end of 1998.

What I want to describe now is a meeting to review the Chain 2000 programme budget that took place in early 1998. The Chain 2000 team had put forward a budget for around £50 million. Now it needed to be challenged and debated to assess its robustness. A meeting of the ten managers who formed the Chain 2000 team was called for this purpose, each of whom had their own motives in assessing the budget.

The time for the meeting came and people crowded into a small room. Each had a copy of the budget document and together they began a struggle to make sense of what they called 'this damn thing'. They all knew that they had to put forward a sensible budget proposal that would be acceptable to the chief executive.

Colin Masterson, who was chairing the meeting, opened by saying, 'How did I get into this damn thing in the first place. I've got to go to my boss with this. He ain't going to be happy. Last year I told him it would be £12 million. Now it's more like £50 million.' I could feel the tension rising. Colin continued: 'I want to go through this line by line – we've got to get it down to something more sensible. Equally, though, you guys have got to be confident that we can deliver – so let's not put ourselves in an impossible position.'

The following people were sitting around the table listening to these opening remarks. There was the director of Information Resources (IR) whose agenda was that of standardising global systems. The director of Supply Operations (SO) also wanted this done so he could implement his global supply strategy. The Chain 2000 Programme director wanted everything tightly planned and managed according to his project methodology. The IR director was behind schedule in delivering his part of the project and had spent £2.5 million above plan. He wanted to get the budget number accepted at the highest possible level to cope with climbing resource requirements and turnover costs. The director of Chain 2000 Solution Delivery had been swinging back and forth between wanting to be in and out of the project. He had done as much as possible to evade any tangible responsibility for delivery. Two months later, he would go back to his job in IR and proceed to undermine the project from afar. The Corporate Finance director was really only there to ensure that his functional boss got what he wanted before he retired. He also wanted to curb the IR team who he thought were out of control. The Supply Chain director idealistically thought that he could really get this project to come to life. Finally, there was a consultant who had much to gain on the fee front, but also much to lose on the reputation front if he was associated with a project that did not work. This was a group, then, consisting of people with varying degrees of commitment to the success of the project and with their own anxieties about their reputations, credibility and career prospects.

The group started to review the IR development costs. The meeting really got going with the question of an extra £6 million for a new approach to communications software. The original software approach, brought in from a previous project, had failed in testing and was then shown to be non-millennium compliant so it was a write-off anyway. There were knowing glances exchanged as the Finance representative turned up the heat on the IR team. Old differences emerged as people took positions. It seemed that there was no other way forward than to spend the £6 million. If the project were to be achieved then the communications software had to be budgeted at the higher figure. There were sighs of relief in the IR corner. There was also more ammunition for the future for the Finance team who promised to come back to look at any potential overspends.

The Programme director then reminded everyone that the scope of the project had not changed and that the old budget of £12 million was seed-corn money anyway. He said that this was the first time anybody had even tried to assess the true costs of the project. That seemed to help Colin who was still very agitated at being the bearer of bad news to his boss. Others volunteered to help defend the position should he need assistance. The big unknown was what the business should be spending on this project anyway. 'Have you got any comparisons?' was the question put to the consultant. 'Not on this scale', he replied. So there was not much solace there, then.

'OK. Let's try to get rid of the ALPHA systems installations. We've already spent £400,000 on this development and got nothing yet. Can we take them out of scope and make some savings?' The group discussed this question. 'I suppose it's only 5 per cent of the sales not included in the demand pattern,' contributed one person. 'Yes, but if you don't get their inputs it can disrupt supplies to other parts of the business,' added another. Someone else replied, 'This is bloody difficult to assess without having some input from them.'

Then the Finance team's agenda surfaced: 'We believe the company should go for standardising on DELTA and get rid of ALPHA.' This was quite a change because they had advocated ALPHA for small market installations only months previously. 'Not possible at this time,' said the IR team almost as one. 'Too close to the millennium to take the client–server version of DELTA.' There was a pause as £250 million of sales supply support capability hung in the balance. 'We could just leave them as they are. How much is their cost again?' asked Colin. 'About £1.2 million,' came the reply. 'Look. As this would be a good step forward for these markets perhaps we should argue to leave them in?' 'Yes – key from my viewpoint,' said the SO director, who really needed this if he was to improve supplies to these markets. 'OK, it's worth a fight to keep it.' So the meeting progressed.

The glances, the sighs, the raised eyebrows, were all part of the processes of communication as alliances formed and broke over various topics and issues. Old scores came to the surface and new opportunities appeared from the background. There were those 'I never knew that' moments, leading rapidly into the 'I told you so' bits, and then some agreement around an issue, or some failures to agree. Sometimes there was logical argument and then some raw emotion and frustration: 'I'll never get that one past him.' Various experiences were introduced to support the arguments. Sometimes there was a complete lack of structure when everyone tried to talk at once. There was laughter at the sudden joke and the humour of the situation. There was giving and taking, total intransigence on some issues, table thumping to make a point strongly. There was also the unknown of whether it could really be afforded, followed by 'well, we've started so we'll finish.'

As I reflected on what was going on at this meeting, I was struck by just how complex it was. All desired to maintain credibility and power. The interactions were very real and filled with emotion. There was fear and desire to make a difference. There was resentment when one felt that one was being taken advantage of. It was tiring trying to take in all the inputs and manage all the engagements. There were smiles and then frustration at the lack of progress. People showed how irritating the numbers were and how they feared having to justify them, particularly when someone else had put them forward. There was pleasure in getting a point over and annoyance at not being heard. There were connections with some and disconnection with others, feeling of some kind of movement, then feeling stuck again. The conflict of interests between consultant and managers and between different managers was clear.

Eventually, the group somehow arrived at a figure of £42.8 million that seemed to be acceptable to those present in that it did not make it impossible to continue with the project. The arguments practised during the review were to be written up to support the situation arrived at. The anxiety abated as the satisfaction of knowing that they had got somewhere, almost in spite of themselves, settled on the group. Everyone had managed to get something of what they wanted and yet nobody had got everything. The outcome represented the transient sense the group had collectively made of this project at this point in the context of the business in which they were operating.

© Philip Streatfield

Management narrative 3: Performance measurement

by Phil Streatfield

During January 1996 two important members of the Board of Axil plc left. Roger Creighton, Technical Director, left at the end of January to take up a post in another company and Albert Peters, Director of Technology, left 'to consider the next moves in his career'. The current Chief Executive, Geoff Ingles, announced the departures two weeks before they happened. In doing so he seemed to be confirming strong rumours that things were moving on. On to what though?

At the time I was a member of a team working on a project called 'Project Control Panel'. This was an attempt to put together a set of performance measures, to be reported to the Board to indicate where the organisation was and where it was going. This provided me with a unique opportunity to talk to site leaders about how they saw things and to discuss their views with some of the leadership team. The following captures some of those conversations.

As part of my role in the project I visited sites and talked to their leaders. The first questions about the measures were usually, 'What do they want these for? Are they going to sit in the centre of the organisation and try to manage me? Of course we know that Geoff stands for control. He is trying to take away our freedom to act. Roger was good at giving us freedom to do things. He indicated what we needed to do and we got on with it. This new regime hasn't told us what it wants. If only it would tell us we'd get on and do it. Do these measures tell us where we are going? What is it we are trying to achieve? How can these people micro-manage what we do in the plants from the centre of the organisation?'

This led to some kind of second-guessing about what Geoff really wanted so that people could adjust what they were doing or their positions on issues so as to fit in. When I asked them about why they were looking at things this way they told me that the environment in the organisation over the last year had changed radically. 'Whilst Geoff seems to want to encourage debate over future strategy, he clearly doesn't want to listen to anything that doesn't fit with where he wants to go.' 'If I stand up and open my mouth on these things then I am going to be branded as somebody who doesn't support the new regime. If I keep my head down and just get on with things then I can survive – later on we can adjust the operations to get back to where we were.'

At the same time, however, there was a general acceptance that things had to change so that the company stayed competitive. 'We have achieved a lot under Roger – Geoff brings a fresh challenge. However, he seems to want to tell us what to do rather than to let us get involved in figuring it out.' There was also fear of engaging in any challenge to the way things were at that time. Many of the site leaders I spoke to were under intense pressure to deliver very stretched performance goals. Most were trying to deliver two years' worth of improvement in one year. Their expectations were that if they did not deliver they would be punished in some way. This was triggering all kinds of actions to deliver targets. Sometimes the actions reinforced each other and sometimes they worked against each other. The idea of reporting against more measures in this environment was very threatening to them. 'What will they do with this information?' 'Surely the measures are supposed to show us whether we are achieving or not – but achieving what?'

After responses of the kind from managers of operating units I had a number of conversations with members of the Board. I will give some examples of the remarks made by A and B and a report of conversation between Person C and me.

Person A

'Our capital spends are out of control.'

'We must get the capital in this business under control. People aren't managing their balance sheets properly.'

'We don't know where our finances really are at the moment. The measures will get this thing under control. There has been too much focus on the Customer Service front in the organisation. The inventory levels are too high and people can't tell me why it is there. We are clearly paying too much for the service levels we are achieving.'

'Sure the sites are trying to deliver from their perspective – but they are too focused on the local situation. We should manage the business by supply chains not by sites. It is key that we start to look at EVA [Economic Value Added] returns on our assets and that we adjust our measures to do this.'

'Geoff wants to pressure the business to deliver more – he doesn't know when he has squeezed too much though. We need the measures to tell us when we have pushed too hard.'

'There is a team working on the strategic part of the plan. This would give us more of an idea of where we are going – but we can't wait for them to deliver. Their timings have now slipped to October – we need to know where we are now – we can feed in the other stuff later on.'

Person B

'I think I have some kind of rapport with Geoff. I helped him out once before when he was running another section of the business. Others let him down over that but I rescued him so I hope he will value me as a result. I also worked on a project that he sponsored and got on with him OK so I hope that will help.'

'This is not the time to directly challenge though. We have to try to educate him so that he understands more about this business. He is under intense pressure from shareholders, though, to secure some significant performance improvements.'

'We shouldn't forget what it was like when the company was last reorganised. We had to work hard to establish the organisation. Geoff has got a hard time getting the commercial managers to support him – in fact they are challenging him. Although he is putting a lot of pressure on us, this, in a way, is not surprising because of the pressure he is under.'

'There is not a consistent view of where we are going at the leadership team table at the moment. We don't have the strategic plan worked out yet. To a certain extent that is because the company hasn't got its overall position really well set. Geoff wants us to be a single enterprise but we really don't know what that means for us at the moment.'

'As long as we continue to deliver then we will have some chance to influence things. On the influencing front it is important not to push too hard. Geoff is conscious that he has been relying on his old team and is beginning to open up to others in the team. So doing anything that pushes them together again will not be helpful. We know, though, at present, that they are possibly the only routes to really get things through.'

Person C

C: *'Hi. How are you keeping?'*

Me: *'Pretty good – I'm glad we have managed to get some time together because there seems to be a lot going on . . .'*

C: 'I am very frustrated. I can't find the right questions to ask to unlock this thing at the moment. Maybe if we spent some time going through what we see at the moment it might help me to formulate something. I'm seeing Geoff on Monday and I want something to put in front of him to keep my conversation going with him.'

Me: 'OK' (jumping up and standing at the dry marker board). 'Where do you want to start? What about where we think things are going at the moment?'

C: 'OK. We are currently organised as factories reporting by area through to Geoff and we are engaged in the FR [Factory Rationalisation] project. I believe that we should be looking at the chains of supply as an opportunity for the future.'

Me: 'What about organisation by product supply chain?'

C: 'This may be something we get to – it could be constrained by the overlap use of different pieces of capacity. At this point in time, though, I think that the chains are the transition piece. We might look at specific products later on. There is the strategic plan team looking at the future. This is a bit like deep thought, though. They are currently trying to analyse future demands and scenarios in order to come up with the approach we should take. This will be delivered as the answer 42 I expect – and then we will be left asking what the question was.'

Me: 'How about Geoff then?'

C: 'I met somebody the other day who had been at a managers meeting that Geoff had been speaking at. He apparently came over very well. People felt motivated by his comments. To me this suggests that he is beginning to connect with people and to get things moving.'

Me: 'This is interesting. I met someone else who had been at the same meeting. They said that Geoff had been complimentary about some aspects of their business – but then laid into them saying that they should be doing much better. He said that they should be focusing on some other things than they were. They had not been contributing as much to the business as they might and they all had to try harder. This person reported that it was like they weren't being recognised for all their good efforts. This individual also reported that they were demotivated and threatened by the whole experience. They indicated that the group had not received the messages well.'

C: (pausing) 'Maybe one way of making sense of this is that the person I spoke to could see a future for themselves in the organisation that Geoff would like to have. The person you heard from, Ian, maybe cannot see a future in the organisation for themselves.'

Me: 'Interesting way of looking at it. To me it tells us that the message reaching these people is mixed. Equally, people are reinforcing their perceptions of Geoff. One framework we have used in the past to look at this type of thing is the situational leadership model. In this case the organisation could be considered as task immature in operating differently – it might be appropriate for there to be some *form of centralisation in the short term to direct things in terms of moving forward. In which case any shift back from delegation will be exaggerated – especially in this environment where many people seem to be feeling threatened. It also indicates there is no selling of a potential future going on in the organisation – or of any coaching of what people need to do/be in order to contribute. This is making for a very uncomfortable situation.'*

C: *'What about Geoff himself? What sort of a person is he? Some time on this might help me with my approach.'*

Me: *'OK. For me I haven't seen him in action to form a firm opinion. The times I have seen him he has been very challenging in his questioning of what has been presented to him. There is a picture of him in the organisation – somebody who doesn't let people get close to him – who doesn't trust people – who doesn't provide much space for others to put their piece before he disagrees.'*

C: *'Yes. It is almost as if he is hiding behind a mask. I believe he is somewhat insecure in the sense that he wants to win and doesn't know how to. He is under pressure at the top table. He is seen as coming to this role from what was seen as a second class business and is now trying to establish a position of strength. He needs to do something radical to have an impact though. It's much more difficult when you are in supply chain leadership, you are generally playing with small numbers with less impact on the business. So, big EGO to satisfy – yet little to really shout about. A person who does not easily trust others. He also likes to play with models as long as you can show him their practical application.'*

C: *'I think his bark is worse than his bite. The other day he told me that people think that he holds grudges. He doesn't. Once the fight has gone he forgets about it. So it's the perception that is left which is working against him. He also has a similar Myers Briggs to me – INTP – so I have a similar approach to things which is helping.'*

(Time runs out at this point. The board is covered with many drawings/representations used during the conversation, which took about two hours.)

Person A (again)

Another meeting on another day:

Me: *'I believe we could do more with this measurement set. We seem to be designing it for short-term control. We need to bring it alive in terms of the organisation seen as product chains too, so we can play with the outcomes and see what this information tells us. We can then start looking at how we want to use it. This will get us thinking about where we go with this concept.'*

A: *'Ian – I like the sound of going ahead with this approach. Where would we get the information, though, on the chains – won't it take us some time to do this?'*

Me: *'Two years ago there was a project started to create a manufacturing supply database – the owner of it lives three offices down from you in this building!'*

A: 'Wow! I never knew that. Give me their name – I'd like to have a look at this stuff.'

Me: 'One thing you will find is that as sites have progressed over time they are beginning to organise in cells for production. One way of looking at our chains is to consider them as linked cells, rather than linked sites. I also believe we should look at specific products and play with those to see what we can get, rather than major chains.'

A: 'I am interested in doing this too – I feel that the major chains may still be too big.'

Me: 'I sense from your comments you want to get on with this. I had arranged to see PW [a consultant] to get this moving in March. I guess we could start earlier.'

I want to say something now about the sense I was making of these conversations. The idea of engaging in a performance measurement project seemed very straightforward on the surface. The classic closed-loop, negative-feedback, control mechanism was what was in mind when the project was started. At the first meeting of the project team it was made very clear to us that all that we were to define were the most appropriate measures for the new organisation and propose a mechanism to put them in place. A balanced approach was required that would bring both the financial and operational measures together. The project would also pave the way for an EVA management approach to be brought into the picture by 2000.

The purpose of the early conversations with people was to explore which measures should be used to indicate how we were doing in the company. So, we developed a list of what we thought was relevant and took it to a sample of site leaders and board members to validate our proposals.

We developed definitions of the financial and the operational requirements and set off to the meetings that I have reported on. I was surprised to find myself repeatedly drawn into conversation about the motives and behaviour of the new leader of the organisation. More and more people wanted to spend time on this, rather than the performance measures themselves. It was almost as if I was engaged in a rolling conversation with people trying to make sense of the world in the context of this man being at the head of the table. The task of developing and implementing the performance measures became almost incidental. The real project in this seemed to be a network of people trying to make sense of what was happening.

It was as if everyone involved was accustomed to the regime under Roger. Rumour had it that he was being removed for being too soft and undemanding on the cost front. He had let too much go to the site leaders who were seemingly being encouraged to run their sites as if they were their own businesses. Anxieties were running high. What was driving the anxiety, though? It was almost as if people were searching to see how to adjust their behaviour in order to survive something that they perceived to be some kind of threat. This shift in the person in the lead role in the organisation had generated a sense of the unknown into which seemed to be projected some sense of impending doom, gloom and disaster.

The new leader was almost built up as some kind of fantasy figure in the conversations in which I found myself. With virtually no first-hand data at all, people were forming judgements and coming to conclusions which in turn seemed to be affecting their behaviour quite considerably. This shift challenges the planned change school of thought: things were shifting without any kind of plan at all, just in the exploration of making new sense.

Questions around the motives for the measurement brought forth this picture of a man sitting in an office, somewhere in the world, knowing all and being able to dictate the next actions for those working in the organisation. Ironically, the very act of beginning the conversation about making the measurement in the first place sent many of the people into a mood of 'how can I stop this man taking control of me?' They seemed to fear that the performance measures would expose some activity that they had under way. In many ways this was strange because, of course, they were already reporting according to a raft of performance measures.

An important part of the conversation seemed to be the search to understand the intent of another so that there could be a matching of agendas such that basic beliefs or values were not compromised. Suspicion seemed to surround Geoff. People feared he would use his hierarchical power negatively. Where intent was not stated then one was formulated and used to make sense of what was happening. Some made sense of Geoff's behaviour in the context of him being put under pressure by others and so he was doing the same: 'Geoff has got a hard time getting the commercial managers to support him – in fact they are challenging him'.

Some people felt very distant and disconnected. Those who had tried to connect and exchange their views with Geoff were feeling bruised and ignored in many cases. Some were hanging on to some threads of a relationship: 'I helped him out once so hopefully he'll remember this'. Others were feeling strong because they were really close to Geoff. Person A was already used to working with Geoff and felt some kind of a bond. This person had some insight into what Geoff was really looking for, namely a feeling of some degree of influence over what was happening. That person's comments are much more confident than those of others who are still trying to establish some kind of rapport with the man.

Roger had begun in his period of leadership by holding what he called focus groups and also one-to-one discussion sessions where he talked to, and listened to, people who wanted to offer him views on where the organisation should go. He seemed to have tuned into the flow in the organisation and, having made some sense of it for himself, acted in such a way as to tackle what seemed to be the major issues of the day. I think he had also tapped into the collective sense-making processes in the organisation. The various senses that people made in conversation with him helped them to develop both the relationship and the sense made. So by addressing the task he also addressed the relationships. By making himself available and accessible he was able to develop a degree of trust with those who interacted with him. This degree of trust seems to be crucial in the connectedness that develops and the subsequent meaning made in the interactions.

This sense of connectedness seemed to help ensure that energy was being focused into moving forward on the basis of relatively high degrees of trust and openness. Perhaps the available free energy in the organisation was being channelled more into maintaining the transient, jointly constructed meanings which in turn meant that the energy was channelled into greater aligned action rather than into continued remaking of meanings. It was possible to make more effective closure as individuals and to move on to the next issue because Roger had provided the opportunity.

Geoff, on the other hand, had studiously maintained a distance between himself and the others in the organisation, so much so that he had instigated confidentiality arrangements with those working with him on significant projects in the organisation. Put in place for legitimate reasons the very introduction of these had immediately suggested a lesser level of trust than previously. On top of this his natural tendency not to visit production sites and to work only with a very small clique of people seemed to feed the image of someone who was very centrally controlling and centrally focused.

In this regime people were reduced to studying the man from a distance, unable really to make sense of his intentions or needs of them. Feeling excluded they were then spending time and energy handling the implications of the negative images they had developed. Amazingly, when I reflect on this now, it was a year into the tenure of Geoff in his role and yet much energy was still being expended coping with him. The 'reality' gap was filled with fantasy.

The conversations I have been engaged with contain significant content that is, in a sense, redundant to the supposed task at hand of 'creating economic value added', for example. This content, and the feelings that go along with it, are somehow important to achieving the tasks that those of us conversing are involved in. The conversations that took place and views that were shared with me occurred quietly in people's offices behind closed doors. I surmise that the sense-making process involves some kind of risk or exposure that requires trust to be present to contain the anxiety with which it is associated.

© Philip Streatfield

Management narrative 4: Consulting and culture change

by Patricia Shaw

In late 1995 an American-owned multinational announced a decision to create a 'spin-off' company. This sent shock waves through the system as some 8,000 people were faced with a compulsory change in employment. The sheer size and diversity of the corporation's operations throughout the world and its benevolent 'family' values had made lifelong job security seem guaranteed. Now employees moved to the new organisation were banned from reapplying to the parent company for two years. There was also a wave of redundancies, mostly voluntary, but not entirely. Unlike the situation of a takeover when there is the need to assimilate or merge different organisational cultures, the issues here were those of encouraging the evolution of a new entity with different characteristics. Some months later, I returned home to find three messages on my answerphone.

The first was from Greta, a woman who was putting together a team of external consultants to help develop and lead a programme to create the new culture of this 'spin-off' company. She wanted me to join this venture, together with some other consultants with whom I had worked before. The second message was from Alex, the head of HR in the new company. He wanted to speak to me about developing the new company. The third message was from Donald, recently appointed as Director of Operations for the new company. I had worked with him on various assignments over the past ten years. He expressed his misgivings about the consultants' proposals for culture-change programmes. It was not immediately clear if all three phone calls were connected.

When I called Greta, she explained that there had already been a series of 'Planning for Success' workshops. Groups of employees had been asked to brainstorm the changes in culture that were needed as the new company left the corporate fold. They were also asked for the ten best ideas in each Region for building a successful future. She had been involved in these sessions because of her organisation development role, and thought that they had gone very well. The material generated was being typed up, summarised and collated across all the Regions by the central transition team.

I wondered aloud what they would do with this 'output' abstracted from the contexts in which it had been generated. 'Of course,' Greta continued, 'we know there is a problem about creating this new culture as we carry over all the people and habits of the existing corporation with us. That is why I have suggested that we run a series of workshops to be attended by all managers before the official launch of the new company. I came up with the idea of focusing on the question "What happens when the customer calls on July 1st?" This is something Donald has also been asking as he goes round talking with employees. I believe we should aim to deliver a new corporate identity via the phone all over Europe on that day.'

I was bemused as I listened. Was she suggesting some kind of telephone training for everyone? I could hardly believe that she was contemplating this for all managers. And why ask me? She must know this was not the kind of work I was interested in. When I voiced my hesitations, she brushed them aside. No, no, I had not understood. This was to be a major initiative to create the new company, 'to shift people's minds, motivation and attitude. The way they answer the phone will be the visible result of the first but magic step into a new culture. The project will be implemented top down. I have the support of Donald and Alex, and I have already spoken with Daniella and Gertrude [the other two external consultants], and they have agreed enthusiastically.'

I felt that I was being invited into a situation that was already well formed. I wanted time to think. I said that I was not sure that this was a project I could usefully contribute to. I imagined puzzlement, a slight withdrawal in the short pause that followed. Obviously my willingness to be involved had been taken for granted. 'Look Greta,' I said, 'I have to be honest and tell you that this doesn't really make sense to me yet. I would like to better understand the thinking behind this initiative.' Greta replied that there was no problem, and she would fax through some papers that afternoon.

I could feel some tension as I put down the phone. This was a company containing people with whom I had significant working relationships. I was already part of the network of connections in which events were unfolding, and the web of expectations, trust and influence in which I was embedded was itself shaping and colouring my reactions as my mind raced. I had noticed the eagerness in Greta's voice. No doubt, this project was a significant one for her. She had pulled in an existing set of collegial relations amongst the external consultants she was wanting to employ, no doubt thinking that this would speed the design and implementation of her ideas. I had forgotten to ask whether Donald had already suggested to her that he would like to see me involved.

I decided to wait until I received the faxed information. This included a letter addressed 'Dear consultants' and copies of some messages that had passed between Greta and others by electronic mail. Here are some extracts from the letter:

> *Employees want the new company to become famous among customers as quickly as possible. Employees will bring across to customers that we are a company that takes care of them, we are responding quickly, with a high degree of quality, we are close to them, we offer as quickly as possible solutions to their problems, we offer total service around them. They are the centre of all we do. Employees want that we appear to customers in a similar way all over the world. A kind of uniformity.*
>
> *We have set up a task force 'Corporate Identity via the phone'. On 2nd of May I will give a presentation to the global HR/OD team on this project. In June all workshops will take place in Italy, France, Benelux, Scandinavia, UK, Spain, Germany and Central Region.*
>
> *On July 1st we will see the results: All employees (that means top down) will transfer the Corporate Identity via the phone. They will sound, appear and behave like they are by then: highly motivated to guarantee from their function the new company's success and to bring across all the things they mentioned in the Planning for Success workshops. There is no option to take or leave it. There is only an option about how to say and the sequence of what to say. There is a must about what to say at least. No exception.*
>
> *Your project will be:*
>
> - *to design a pragmatic workshop*
> - *to write a short and easy to handle manual for everyone who answers the phone*
> - *to prepare a presentation for May 2nd for me with your draft design and charts etc.*
> - *to offer dates in June when you will be available*
> - *to give me an offer about your cost. (You will not be paid for the draft design first. We will handle this when you officially get the contract after the final global buy in.)*

I was astonished by this document. If this was a sample of what was afoot in the new company, then there must be some very nervous people around. Greta seemed to be thinking of culture change as a major internal PR exercise, getting everyone to march in step into a brave new future. Yet, when I had spoken with her I sensed that she was advocating activity that she genuinely believed would generate lasting change. Her phrase 'a magic step into a new culture' was telling.

I wondered if I was the only one with severe doubts about the value of this activity. To find out, I called Gertrude, one of the consultants I had worked with before. It was clear that she was very keen on the project. She saw it as a useful way to start working with the company that would lead to less constrained opportunities. She was sure that we could come up with some creative ways of working within the brief. If I had reservations, it would be even more valuable to have me in the team to ensure these views were incorporated.

After this I sat for a while, slightly agitated. I was tempted to claim that I was not available for the period of this project. However, my curiosity was aroused. I realised that I was already enmeshed in the interplay of mutual influence, always only partly articulated, from which an initiative was emerging into the formalised life of the organisation. I felt that the emergent form was not yet stable but open to further evolution if I was willing to engage with what was happening. Would it be possible to bring attention to and work with what was already evolving in the new company, rather than focusing on a 'magic' step into a new identity? I knew I was already working, although I had no formal contract. I was probing, searching to discover what kind of project I might play a part in shaping.

Typically at this stage, a consultant would be concerned about finding and meeting the sponsoring client to hear the presenting situation and to agree the purpose, goals, terms and conditions of the proposed consulting assignment. Instead, I was more interested in adding my voice to the web of conversations sustaining the initiative that was crystallising, so that the meanings arising in it might continue to move. I knew that the conversations I had already had with Greta and with Gertrude had touched off some reactions whose consequences I could not know. By declaring myself uneasy with what was proposed, I had avoided reinforcing existing patterns of thinking, but I did not know how significant this would be.

It was in this spirit of probing the stability or otherwise of the emerging activity that I called Donald. I was also calling upon what seems to me an essential skill, if skill is the right word. This is the willingness to pick up a telephone at just the point when some sense of purpose is rising in me, but before its exact nature has become clear. I dialled Donald's number and got through immediately. I told him of Greta's invitation to join the team she was forming, and of my surprise that the company was about to embark on this kind of programme. He sighed and said: 'I've had my doubts, but Greta is very keen to do all this stuff and I don't like to dampen her enthusiasm.'

I then said, 'But you and Alex have given your formal support to her suggested initiatives, so that there is a gathering momentum. I have seen no sign that anyone is questioning the proposal.' He replied, 'No, well her boss in Germany is right behind her and is trying to position her for a European job within the Service operation. Anyway, I wanted you to speak to Alex about the development of the new company's culture. I wasn't thinking of Greta's project.' I made it clear to him that others were seeing Greta's project as an attempt to create a particular kind of culture. I pointed out that it would have all sorts of effects on the way people behaved. He agreed and asked me to call Alex.

I called Alex. It transpired that it was he who had suggested that I should be involved in the project, but he too was uncertain about the wisdom of it. As he spoke, I wondered if the real issue was the challenge of not knowing what to do in the face of pressure to create a new culture for success. Since the businesses were not making adequate profits to satisfy Wall Street financial analysts within the Mainline corporation, the new company needed to become different, fast. Actually no one knew how to do this, and I hypothesised that what was currently being learned in the new company was how people and ideas and activities would come to populate this unknown territory. Cascades of programmes were the well-worn route that the corporation had regularly chosen to enter such terrain, so I wasn't surprised that this was the kind of suggestion that was calming people's nerves. Fundamentally, the difficulty seemed to be the idea that the desired 'newness' had to be predetermined, agreed and implemented, quickly. I asked Alex if he believed that this is how genuine 'newness' developed in practice. 'No', he said bluntly, 'I don't, but what else can we do?' Since Alex was going to be in the UK in a few days' time we arranged to meet and talk.

At the end of the week, I drove over to the UK office of Mainline, where Alex had suggested we meet. He was not there. A secretary told me that his plane had been cancelled and he had decided not to travel that day. Thrown off the path I was on by this chance event, I asked if I could use an empty office to make some calls. I sat and looked at the telephone wondering who I might call, what thread I might pick up. I remembered that Donald had mentioned Gordon's name in his telephone call to me, so I asked for the internal directory and dialled his number. I explained what I was doing at the Mainline office and asked if he could make time to talk. 'Stay where you are,' he said, 'I'll be over in five minutes.'

Here was another person who said that he was very doubtful about Greta's initiative. In fact he was more than doubtful. He thought it was a disastrous idea because it belonged to an old way of thinking and ought to be stopped. Had he tried to argue against it? Well, no. He was hoping it would just die. He was also grappling with his own ideas, as head of the 'transition team', about how to launch a new organisation. He wanted some unexpected things to happen on the first day of the new company's life to mark a clear divide between the past and the future. He thought of hiring magicians, conjurors and jugglers to wander round the offices. Alternatively, he might arrange for some unexpected and funny messages to flash on every computer screen during the morning. Perhaps every location should be encouraged to celebrate with a party.

I noticed the desire for a 'trick', a waving of a magic wand to change the corporate Cinderella into a bright and successful princess overnight. As it happened, he was expecting to meet with Donald and Alex on Monday. I said I would join the three of them. Over the weekend, I wrote one page summarising the ideas I had introduced in all my conversations so far.

On Monday I met with Gordon, Alex and Donald for an hour. I did not use the notes I had made, but listened and joined the kind of conversation they were having. The spin-off created the opportunity to shed considerable operating costs in terms of numbers of employees and cumbersome structures so that cash generation would automatically improve in the short term, but then what? The company would need to explore the emerging digital arena to compete; this would mean acquisitions and some radical shifts in the way the business was managed and the relations with the market. The release from the big corporate fold generated some resentment, anxiety and grief aroused by feelings of being kicked out of the nest.

However, it was also an exciting period of free-fall, or take-off, in which people were discovering new freedoms of thought and action. The idea exercising Donald was that somehow the 'plane must not land' – how to encourage people to accept the new turbulence and openness as a way of working and not a temporary aberration. Only that way he felt would new structures develop quickly enough.

At this point I talked about edge of chaos conditions in which a complex network paradoxically experiences both stability and instability, that is the capacity to sustain some existing patterns, but also generate real novelty. However, such self-organisation was of necessity uncontrollable in the usual sense and unpredictable in the longer term. The Corporate Identity initiative belonged to the domain where ideology was used to secure formal agreement as uncertainty increased. However, it would not be working with the self-organising processes far from certainty and agreement where people really did not and could not know precisely what they were doing, as they acted into an unfolding situation. As I spoke about these ideas Donald lit up. Clearly his imagination was caught. 'Exactly, exactly. This is what is happening. This is what we need. I keep trying to say to people – this uncertainty is IT!' Alex spoke of his sense of the potential he felt was stirring, as so much that was taken for granted was open to question. 'So can you help us with this?' Donald asked. 'Write something down, brief please.' I said I would draw up a one-page offer about how I would work with the new company.

'What about the "Corporate Identity via the phone" initiative?' There was an uncomfortable pause. 'Alex, you need to speak with Greta,' Donald said. 'I think she does an excellent job in management training in Germany, but I don't think she should be let loose on organisation development.' I winced inwardly. I knew that in pursuing my own convictions about how organisations change, and in trying to secure conditions in which I could work in ways that made sense to me, I had played a role in changing Greta's immediate fortunes. I had not intended this as a political act, but my participation had damped one loop of activity and amplified the seeds of another. Apparently, Greta's potential role in the company had already been discussed on several occasions. Only Heinrich, her boss, was pushing for an expanded role beyond the German Region.

Uncomfortably, I said, 'None of you seemed to have expressed any doubts to Greta, about her proposal; you encouraged her to continue, yet you all claim to have had doubts.' Alex apologised, saying that Greta had been very unwell and that it was important not to demotivate her. Gordon said nothing. Donald sighed. I felt acutely alive at that moment to the webs of conflicting feelings in which so-called rational decisions are made: self-protection, honesty, concern, anxiety, hope, determination. 'I just want to emphasise', I said, 'that what everyone does and says matters in unexpected ways. It is important to stay alert to that, to notice what keeps unfolding. That is how the culture of this new company is already being created moment by moment.' I stopped. I felt that I was moving unhelpfully out of conversation, into a slightly preaching style. We ended the meeting.

I knew that Alex was going to speak to Greta about putting a halt to the other initiative, so after a few days I called her to talk through what had happened. She was bemused and disappointed. I said that I had acted from my own convictions about what would constitute effective work, and I was aware that one consequence of that had been to surface vague and unarticulated doubts about the usefulness of her proposal. 'But they all seemed to support the idea,' she said. 'Yes, I know,' I said. 'I believe that people did not know what to do and were therefore genuinely willing to go along with a suggestion to take some kind of action. They were not entirely comfortable but the discomfort was not clear enough to be articulated, so the best thing was to keep going, in order to learn more. Your initiative has set off a train of activity, which has included stimulating me to say some things that have resonated with three people who have the power to support or not an official initiative. I have not planned to stop your initiative; I have been acting in my own interest to try to create conditions in which I feel confident to work. This was not a carefully planned campaign to undermine you, although it may feel that way. In fact you are as much a part of the unpredictable chain of events as I am.' 'So', she asked carefully, 'are you willing to work with me?' 'Yes, of course,' I said, 'I'll send you copies of the documents I've circulated and let's try to meet and talk about what you want to do and what I want to do.'

I called Donald to get his reaction to my contract proposal. 'Fine,' he said. 'Go ahead. I don't quite see what you are going to do, but we're all happy for you to start.' 'We will start by phoning people and talking, trying to enter the networks and conversational life of the organisation.' He chuckled. 'I recognise that's what you're already doing.'

© Patricia Shaw

●●●● Management narrative 5: Culture change at a factory

by Patricia Shaw

As part of my consulting assignment with Imtech, I had a lunch meeting in the UK with the Technical Services Team. I happened to mention that I had been visiting the factory at Pisa in Italy. There was the usual pessimism about the factory but one or two said that there were a few signs of change. Some of the managers at the Pisa factory seemed more open and collaborative. I asked who they were and wrote their names on a paper serviette. Over coffee I joined another group and asked them who they were working well with at the Pisa factory. Over the next few weeks I asked people about their experiences of successful collaboration with people at the plant and slowly added to my list.

One name was mentioned three times. It was that of Alessandro, a young manager in the technical support area. It seemed to me that he was a node in a dense web of relationships inside and beyond the plant. One morning in early September I called him. I asked if he knew who I was. He did not. I explained briefly about the work Doug and I were doing. I told him that his name kept cropping up as I worked around Europe as someone who was 'getting it' at the plant, whatever that meant. I said that Doug and I were planning another visit to the plant and hoped to talk with him and a network of others who were perceived as 'getting it'. I read out the list of names I had. He was interested. Yes, he could understand why I might have many of these names. The majority had experience outside of the plant, had worked in the United States and other parts of the company in Europe, and had a broad range of relationships. However, he felt that some important names were missing from my list. I asked whether he thought he might convene an informal gathering of at least some of these people so that they could talk together about how the factory was evolving. He agreed and asked if I would write a brief note to help him. I wrote a few paragraphs and faxed the following to Italy:

> *We know that a different culture cannot be announced or imposed by an act of will. Culture develops itself day by day in the practical interaction of doing business in the new circumstances. Sometimes people believe that the Pisa factory is less affected than other parts of the company by the spin-off and so feel less impetus for change. At the same time, others already see significant shifts in the way people are thinking and working at the factory. They talk of people beginning to 'get it'. What might this mean? In what kind of relationships is this emerging? It is very hard to pin down the complex understanding that is compressed in this phrase. Our invitation is to ask a group of you to help us explore and elaborate what this is all about.*

The autumn found us with ten Italians in a room at the Pisa factory. This was in one of the few new buildings on the site. It was light and colourful, with a very different atmosphere to that of the wood-panelled solemnity of the directors building or the dark mazes of the other office buildings. Those gathered round the table included Alessandro, Franco, the youngest manager on the site committee, and one of the people I had met on another project at the factory. Mostly, they knew one another despite working in many different parts of the plant. Alessandro mentioned the names of several others who had been interested in joining this discussion, but had been unable to attend at such short notice. There seemed to be no expectation that we would try to define any goals or outcomes for our meeting. I realised that Alessandro had conveyed that this was a chance for a very open-ended exploration.

We found ourselves flowing between English and Italian so that any part of the conversation was always hard to grasp in detail by at least some of those present. We attempted no structured questioning. Doug and I talked about our experiences at the plant and they talked about theirs. The conversation flowed irregularly, from one association to another. We lingered for some time on the subject of telephones. It was very significant to these people that access to direct dial international lines was available only to the upper echelons of management. There was frustration that people at their level could not just pick up a telephone and call others anywhere else in Europe or the United States without going through the switchboard. The brainstorming sessions had thrown this up very early on and it was felt that the managerial response had been slow. Franco insisted that this had been taken seriously and an updated system was being installed.

Linked with this sense of narrow channels of communication was a long discussion about the poor perception of the plant in the rest of the company. What was the pattern of these perceptions? How did they seem to arise? Why did they seem so long-lived and difficult to shift? We told stories of our experience of how difficult it was for outsiders to penetrate beyond the official managerial welcome of the plant.

They told stories of their experience of how few people ever tried to make more direct connections or to spend more time there. So much was actually happening and changing in their daily experience, but they felt this was not apparent to enough people. They believed that a mutual feeling of collaboration was rare and this had led to the identification of them as 'getting it'. They thought there were networks of people who saw the move to Imtech as a release into a freer climate of more experimental action.

The meeting had started at ten in the morning and it was now 11.40. I knew the Italians tended to lunch early. Someone suggested a coffee. We trooped down to the basement. The coffee machines at the factory all seemed to be located in the basements. We continued talking. I felt some tension rising in me. What if nothing apparently came of this discussion? It felt rich. There was real concern and interest in the subjects that flowed. Was that enough? I knew also that no stronger shape could be forced if it was not emerging of its own accord. We returned to the room a little after 12.00. We all sat down again. The theme organising the conversation was still that of the factory as fatally unable to change. No one seemed particularly keen to leave. Does everyone have the same sense as I do, I wondered to myself, that we are seeking a pattern to talk and act into? The idea organising the conversation was still the perception of factory as fatally unable to change.

Suddenly I glimpsed something. I said, 'What is unique about the group in this room today is that it is part of a network that crosses factory areas and is linked to other parts of the company. Can we intensify that? What if you take the initiative to invite unusual groups of people to the plant? They could take part in some open-ended meetings around issues that are scarcely yet formed.' As I spoke I got up and started drawing circles on a flip chart, some small and some large, and links between them. 'Who would you want to ask? What would you want to talk about?'

Alessandro picked this up immediately and I was convinced that he too was looking for what might be amplified in our discussion, without worrying exactly where it was going. He began to talk about who he would like to have a conversation with about the way the strategy for the factory was forming. I interrupted and handed him the pen. 'Sketch out for us the groupings you have in mind. Who do you want to bring together? What are the relationships you feel are there? What is the potential you see?' After a little while I asked whether others were beginning to think about conversations that they would like to convene. I suggested that we took some time for people to develop their thoughts alone or in a small group. I was aware that I had shifted from flowing with the movement of the conversation to offering the chance for more structure to emerge. Very quickly, the group organised itself into two pairs and a foursome, while Alessandro and one other each worked alone.

The clock ticked round to well past one o'clock. I pointed out the time. Was this OK? Did anyone need to go? Everyone wanted to stay, lunch was unimportant. Doug and I looked at one another in mute delight. The excitement in the room was tangible. Something had taken off! The groupings began to share their ideas with one another. By now, much of the conversation was in Italian and Doug and I had only a rough idea of what each proposal was about. However, we knew that this did not matter. The important question was whether this energy would build up into further action or dribble away once we had left. 'Would anything stop you just doing this?' we asked. 'Why not take yourselves seriously and start talking with people to see if you can bring these conversations about? We will join and support you in whatever way we can.'

Over the next few months, the ideas that had emerged in the first meeting with Alessandro and his contacts flowered into activity. The foursome had focused their attention on the very sparse connections between those generating marketing and distribution strategies and people in manufacturing. The most committed member of the original group of four, Walter, told me that there had been many conversations since our meeting about how to create a richer web of communication. However, they were finding it difficult to get people to come to the factory. It was expensive and time consuming to make the journey and difficult to justify. They would have to find and use an opportunity when some of the people were coming anyway. For example, several of the people they would like to talk with would be attending the regular business meeting of the European Operating Committee. This group would be meeting next month in Rotterdam. I suggested that he persuade the business head to switch the venue and add some extra time to the meeting. I felt his nervousness. He would have to check with his boss first. Why not try it the other way round? Check out the business head's reaction to the proposal and then talk to his boss about what might then be developing as a real possibility? Would I have a word with the business head first? I explained that I thought this would have much less impact than if he called and talked about what he and his colleagues hoped to do. 'Remember,' I said, 'we were talking about the pattern of perception people have about not being really welcomed at the Pisa factory. You would be cutting right across that ingrained expectation by the act of calling him yourself. He will be surprised, it is true. But then you will have the chance to move into unknown territory with him.' That is how change may begin.

A week later I received a call from Tom, the head of the business. 'Listen,' he said, 'I've agreed to move the whole meeting from Rotterdam to the Pisa factory. Walter was so insistent and I was so astonished that an initiative like this was actually coming from the plant that I said yes, there and then. I gather you are somehow implicated in this, that they are working with you.' I told him that our role had been simply to amplify existing possibilities. The people at the plant knew exactly what they wanted to do. 'They have asked me to add on a whole day before the formal meeting. It seems a lot, wouldn't half a day be enough?' 'Look,' I said, 'you said yourself that this is an unusual step. If you are willing to explore what may come of it, don't squeeze it down. You have the authority to open this space, it's the best use of your power I can think of.'

A few weeks later I helped a group of seven people in manufacturing at the factory to think about how they wanted to use the day. My participation took the form of tracing the evolution of the ideas that had first motivated this gathering and bringing attention to any moves to collapse it into familiar patterns of activity. They had talked to about 25 people, all involved in different aspects of managing production at the factory. They wanted the marketing people to have the experience of bypassing the usual meetings in the directors building. They wanted them to spend the whole day in different small groups in offices all over the plant, talking about the business and sharing views and perceptions of what was happening. They would all meet in a large room they had found and explain very briefly what they wanted to do. They wanted to create the possibility of new networks forming and new understandings, questions and ideas emerging. There would be no brainstorming and no limits to the agenda. They divided the day into five potential 'conversation spaces', one of which would be over lunch.

At first they thought they would pre-set the membership of all the groupings through the day, but I pointed out that they could not know what would begin to emerge and their plan could constrict the spontaneous formation of groups. It might be better to give everyone a simple guideline. For example, 'Please keep moving into a new configuration with other people you are interested in speaking with, so that by the end of the day you have talked with most people, but not necessarily everyone.' Would this not be a mess? Only if they ignored the fact that the first conversations would occur in the context of existing conversations and relationships and would rapidly generate motivations and interests that would influence where people wanted to go next. By way of illustration I asked them to construct the first set of groupings. I suggested that this should not be a random mix as they had first thought. Instead they could use their existing knowledge, hopes, intuitions and curiosity about the relations between the population that was coming together. They spent about an hour doing this and came up with groupings of about five people that were full of meanings and potential for them. Some groupings were serious and some, I guessed, were rather wickedly provocative.

As far as output was concerned, we agreed that we would simply ask participants to log promising connections between people and ideas that had begun to emerge at the end of the day. I reminded them that there would be many connections that would only come alive later as further interactions were generated after the day. Self-organisation takes time to generate new forms that become strong enough to be recognised as such.

The day took place in early December and I participated along with everyone else. The group that convened at the start of the day was larger than I expected. The grapevine had carried news of this unusual occasion and a number of people had asked to participate. The strict rhythm of small groups and short milling sessions worked well to contain the open-endedness of the discussions. The same procedure had been used to create the groups of five or six who had lunch together and the level of sound in the dining room was unusually high even for an Italian gathering.

At one point I fell in step with Tom as we walked to one of the meeting offices. 'Who are all these people?' he said to me. 'I've been coming to business meetings here for 15 years and I have never met two-thirds of these people or set foot in these different parts of the plant. It is a bit humbling. I had no idea how constricted my round of interaction here was.' I met Cesare, one of the managers, over coffee after lunch. He was glowing with the satisfaction of meeting one of the people responsible for a particular contract for distribution in France. These people had made many complaints about product quality. Cesare had persuaded this person to invite members of Cesare's team to France to discuss what was going wrong and how people were working to improve quality at the factory. 'At last', said Cesare, 'I feel I have broken through to direct contact with all the parties concerned with the problem.'

During the afternoon, further energy was generated when one group discovered that there was a small group working on new product development at the factory. This was news to the marketing group who were also working on new directions for the business. I persuaded Walter to telephone Luigi, the head of this new group, and persuade him to come over immediately. Within five minutes, Luigi bustled in, wreathed in smiles, to be greeted by a rain of questions. He raised his hands deprecatingly, and said he could only spare ten minutes, but gave a good outline of his remit and the people he was working with. He quickly agreed to join the next day's meeting to collaborate further with the new business strategy group. Another small group emerged from the day offering to pursue some ideas for integrating aspects of the marketing and manufacturing organisations.

The groupings that organised that day, and those that emerged from it, could not locate themselves, or be located by anyone else, according to any existing organisational structure or rationale. It was not surprising, therefore, that people were asking, 'Who decided to convene this particular group of people?' This implied that someone must have orchestrated this event in a controlling way. However, it seems more realistic to see the meeting as a fluctuation in the existing political and social field of organisational interaction. We all slowly relaxed as we explored and created our own meaning in the ambiguity of the event. We encouraged a mode of dialogue in which people told of their own experience of recent decisions in the company. How had events unfolded? How did each person perceive and contribute to the unfolding of events? We did not try to trace decisions backwards, but instead picked up the threads of intertwined stories of situations unfolding out of the past into the present and still moving. I felt that I was part of a group who were developing their ability to speak about participating in developing patterns of activity. People were no longer distinguishing talking and acting; the organisation of action was taking shape moment by moment, rather than being planned and then implemented. This kind of exploration surfaced many differences but because they were of a narrative rather than a propositional kind, they did not produce oppositions or attempts to seek consensus.

© Patricia Shaw

●●●● Management narrative 6: The diversity project
by David Scanlon

In late 1999, as an internal consultant to a project on the implementation of a Balanced Scorecard, I interviewed the senior R&D management team. I knew that 'Build, develop and diversify our talent' had become one of five stated key strategic drivers in the R&D strategy. So, I was surprised to discover in the interviews that hardly anyone in the senior management team seemed to know what 'Diversify' meant. This led to a proposal to define diversity and draw up an action plan to implement the diversify strategy. I began to see this Diversity Initiative as an opportunity to work in a different way in the organisation. I thought I could work with intact work and management teams on group dynamics and awareness raising in relation to the diversity issue in order to change the behaviour of managers. Also, I was not a member of the Human Resources Department and I saw the Diversity Initiative as a means of working with HR professionals to develop my OD skills. I had no idea how to get involved in this particular initiative, but I knew that the senior management team had been asked to nominate people to attend a workshop on diversity.

Through my work on the Balanced Scorecard project I had come to know Mary, the HR manager who started work on the Diversity Initiative in March of 2000. Mary's work led to an R&D workshop in August 2000 to discuss diversity, define what it meant, and develop an action plan. I used my connections with the Head of R&D Facilities, and my head of department, to wangle an invitation to the event.

At the R&D workshop, a process consultant ran the whole process. Her style was soft, gentle and non-confrontational, and throughout the sessions there was soft music in the background. She presented information about how other companies had successfully delivered diversity projects. We were asked to describe how it would feel to work in a diverse organisation. All the words which were written down on the post-it notes and stuck on flip charts were positive: excitement, happiness, smiles, understanding, creativity, warmth, and so on. As I heard this, I reflected on how it had felt for me over the last few months studying on an MA programme as part of a diverse group whose thinking was being strenuously challenged by the programme faculty. I had found that the experience of movement to a different way of thinking had promoted a great deal of anxiety, as well as feelings of being rejected, and had led to angry responses.

As I thought about this, it seemed to me that as members of the workshop we were somehow colluding in a process of defining idealised situations in which there would be no conflict or anxiety. This did not sound like the kind of experience I have had in dealing with differences between people. So I said, 'I think that an organisation which was like this would give rise to a great deal of anxiety and conflict would be common place.' I caught people's attention and was asked to explain why this was the case. It felt at that moment as though I was not playing the game. I felt anxious. I explained my rationale, 'In a diverse group there would be times where I would be confronted by issues that challenge my own values which would lead to anxiety I would need to be able to manage myself in the face of the anxiety to go on working with the group.' This seemed to change the nature of the conversation.

Later in the workshop I found myself in a group discussing actions for training to promote diversity. At this time I had formed the concept of needing to bring reflective understanding to real-life experience rather than useful but limited-impact training courses. Bringing this into the group discussion seemed to make sense but I found myself in conflict with a training manager from HR. Nevertheless, I reported on our discussion to a later plenary meeting. Towards the end of the workshop, volunteers were called for to lead various streams of work. I sensed that people were happy to commit to a couple of days to talk about the issues but were less willing to devote more time. In many ways this was the start of a pattern that has continued throughout the Diversity Initiative. Rather anxiously, I volunteered to lead Diversity Training and was relieved when I saw a number of people nodding in agreement.

Why this interest in diversity

Clearly the issues around human diversity are not new but where have the diversity programmes many companies are developing come from? Certainly they have been around in the USA for many years (Mercer, 1996) but appear to be newer in Europe. Often-cited reasons for the present need are: increased globalisation in organisations through mergers and acquisitions and the required cultural integration; equal opportunities legislation which looks to prevent discrimination; increasing emphasis on corporate social responsibility brought on by triple bottom-line accounting, environmental, financial and social.

There have been legal implications with regard to equal treatment for many years; politicians have made strides to make society more inclusive. In Europe the major driving force is the 1957 Treaty of Rome. Article 48.2 refers to discrimination: 'Such freedom of movement shall entail the abolition of any discrimination based on nationality between workers of the Member States as regards employment, remuneration and other conditions of work and employment.' On gender and pay Article 119 refers to: 'Each Member State shall during the first stage ensure and subsequently maintain the application of the principle that men and women should receive equal pay for equal work. For the purpose of this Article, "pay" means the ordinary basic or minimum wage or salary and any other consideration, whether in cash or in kind, which the worker receives, directly or indirectly, in respect of his employment from his employer.' On diversity Article 128.1 refers to: 'The Community shall contribute to the flowering of the cultures of the Member States, while respecting their national and regional diversity and at the same time bringing the common cultural heritage to the fore.' This is the basis of all subsequent European laws and is signed up to by all Members of the European Community. It has been further supported in European Law by the Convention for the Protection of Human Rights and Fundamental Freedoms 1998. Article 14 Prohibition of Discrimination states: 'The enjoyment of rights and freedoms set forth in this Convention shall be set forth without discrimination on any ground such as sex, race, colour, language, religion, political or other opinion, national or social origin, association with a national minority, property, birth or social status.'

While these laws have been in place for some time discrimination and issues around equal opportunity and pay are still issues today. This link between HR and the legal environment, the protection from potential expensive litigation, provides me with a picture of HR as protecting the organisation: policing practices to ensure that organisations are compliant.

Diversity is a popular concept in the world of HR. Diversity management is quoted as being a new paradigm for human resource management (Thomas and Ely, 1996). In their article they differentiate between different strategic perspectives: the discrimination and fairness paradigm; the access and legitimacy paradigm; and the learning and effectiveness paradigm. The latter is stated as the paradigm which gives rise to successful diversity initiatives, as defined by actual improvements in business performance. They talk of eight preconditions for making the shift: leadership must truly value the variety of opinion and insight embodied in the different perspectives of a diverse workforce; leadership must recognise the difficulties that different perspectives present, it is a long process; the culture must create an expectation of high standards and performance from everyone; the culture must stipulate personal development through the design of jobs and the provision of training; the culture must encourage openness to sustain debate and constructive conflict; the culture must make people feel valued; a well-articulated vision is essential to ensure that work discussions stay focused on the accomplishment of goals; it must be an egalitarian and non-bureaucratic organisation. Diversity initiatives are also popular in the USA. According to a study by the society for Human Resource Management in Alexandria, Virginia, 3 out of 4 Fortune 500 companies have formal diversity programs in place, over half of which (58%) have staff members dedicated to these issues.

In terms of likely benefits, a recent article, based on interviews with human resource managers of Fortune 100 companies, cited the five top reasons for engaging in diversity management as: better utilisation of talent; increased marketplace understanding; enhanced breadth of understanding in leadership positions; enhanced creativity; increased quality of team problem solving (Gilbert and Ivancevich, 2000). In another study, the most frequently carried out initiatives are stated as: formal induction programmes for new recruits; criteria for selection and advancement that are open to all; having a policy on equal opportunities. Most cited benefits include: retention of employees; enhanced organisational flexibility; improved public image; and better morale. Driving forces behind initiatives were: good personnel practice; legislation; business sense; organisational commitment to equal opportunities (Kandola and Fullerton, 1994). A comprehensive guide for all HR managers is available, which apparently gives all the information needed to be successful (Kandola and Kandola 1998).

The corporate bash

Against this wider background, the Diversity Initiative proceeded. A global workshop of 30 people gathered in October 2000 to define the 'Corporate Diversity Strategy'. When I thought about the event and read the attendance list it was like reading a 'Who's Who' of my company. I had never worked before in such exalted company and felt both privileged and nervous. The global workshop was facilitated by a well-known consultancy firm in the area of diversity whose task it was to develop in 'real time' a strategy we could walk away with. I reflected how many times recently I had been involved in these situations, how often they broadened their purpose to include many other organisational issues, and how often I felt either railroaded or that the answer was already there. I felt that I knew, in some way, what was to come.

As I walked in the door I saw the familiar face of Mary, we smiled and I made my way to an empty chair at the end of the room. I came in part-way through the presentation of the lead consultant who called herself a futurologist: 'I know what is coming'. She was in the process of describing the process. It was very familiar to me: unfreeze, mobilise, realise, reinforce and sustain. She was focusing on diversity leadership, communication, involvement, change skills, competences and measurement. We were going to hear best practice in each area and build the strategy over the next day and a half. The consultant spoke at a very fast pace and appeared to me to have a very large ego, everything was centred on what 'I' have done. I was wondering how the northern Europeans in the room were responding to this very American presentation. I knew from previous experience that they often switch off in these situations and do not respond well to overt focus on individual success. For my part I tried to stay focused and attentive, but I soon slipped into checking out the room and working with my own internal reflections.

The meeting broke up for an exercise in understanding our own diversity. The message from the consultants was that 'we need to learn from the vast experience around us and focus on the future'. We were also offered a model to aid our discussion. In this model there were four concentric circles meant to represent different levels of diversity: organisational (functional, work content field, division, seniority, work location, union affiliation, management status); secondary (geographic, income, personal habits, recreational habits, religion, education, work experience, appearance, parental status, marital status); primary (age, gender, sexual orientation, physical ability, ethnicity, race); and core personality. We were all asked to write what we saw in ourselves. A woman who was warm and felt authentic led the session. She talked in a very calming voice and I saw her as a therapist since she used a number of Gestalt terms and talked of systems extensively. I was amazed at how compliant everyone was. People got involved. We were also introduced to John, who was very matter of fact and constantly reiterated, 'So what I am hearing you say is . . .'. I found myself feeling irritated at this refrain.

As the day went on, a number of things started to happen which created conflict. A number of people from the USA started to dominate the discussion. They were clearly very passionate about the issue of race and repeated themselves over and over again. One of them kept interrupting people as they were speaking. I started to wonder why she was doing this. What was she out to prove? I started to notice that whenever she spoke people looked away in complete disinterest in much the same way I was doing myself. It was starting to feel tense in that room. Even in a syndicate meeting to talk about strategic objectives this person attempted to dominate. She spoke as though no one else knew what they were talking about. The conversation went on in a very disjointed way, partly because other work was being done in parallel and we could not define objectives without this other work.

The next syndicate looked at methodologies for data collection. We were informed that there were only four methods of collecting the data: questionnaires, focus groups, interviews or personal narratives. Members of the syndicate argued that we already had all the data we need but the consultants ignored this and advocated focus groups. They seemed to be pushing for the extra business of supporting these focus groups. I agreed to present the syndicate discussion back to the plenary. It seemed a simple message: we have lots of data and although we might want to collect more, the key point was to promote dialogue on the issues both within the business and external to the business. As I finished my presentation, the facilitator stated that I had missed something and went on to say, 'We agreed, focus groups should be supported by external consultants'. The other groups presented a force field analysis and everyone still seemed to be very compliant.

The next day, we slipped back into the same routine: best practice presentation and then syndicate discussion. The message was that the right answer was on the overheads and that this is what we should be discussing. A number of attempts at taking the conversation somewhere else were made but all were rejected in favour of the process. The final straw came when the consultants were making a presentation on affirmative action. The VP for legal stated, 'I'm sorry this isn't right. I know that in Europe we have a lot to learn from the US but it is not the US. Here we have different issues. We need a vision that captures everyone.' I suggested that 'the group seems to be split between those who are focusing on relationships and those focused on affirmative action'.

At lunch, the conversations were more animated than before. The northern Europeans began speaking together in their native tongue. The pressure for compliance combined with the oppressive facilitation process contributed to everything boiling over. The things people couldn't say in the room were said outside. 'This is not good' 'Some of the meeting behaviour is appalling.' Whereas inside the meeting the discussion was focused on future plans and issues of organisational change, outside the meeting the conversations I was involved in were focused on the very thing we were here to discuss: diversity; meaning the pain and discomfort that different views were arousing; how particular characters were not being 'aware' of their impact; cultural stereotyping. These conversations felt more like gossip aimed at pointing the finger and alienating people. These feelings were, of course, also being experienced in the formal meeting but they were not talked about. How can this be explained in the context of the discussion about planning a better organisation? This was the enlightened group, who knew the issues well and yet we were still demonstrating intolerance of difference. Maybe we could have been seen as an embodiment of the organisation? Certainly we were in the mess. But the consultants were in control, or so they thought.

After lunch an executive who would have to present the output of the global workshop to the board gave a summary of his view of the events before lunch and asked people to decide what was needed now. People engaged with this and seemingly agreed a way forward, namely, to define what exactly we mean and generate a compelling story for the senior executive team. The tension seemed to have gone and the meeting was handed back to the consultants. 'We have a process to do this,' were the first words I heard. It seemed as if we went back to the process as though the discussion hadn't occurred. We discussed the next topic and I noticed how a number of us were looking at one another in amazement. The loud woman and another person, a facilitator by training, continued as before. There was more best practice and another syndicate. This was enough for me. I said, 'I'm losing the plot. This isn't what we agreed.' Others seemed to agree but the facilitator said, 'I know it is tiring but let's stay with it.' More best practice and another syndicate. I made another attempt, 'Is it just me or does anyone else feel that this practice isn't right. Many of the companies cited are struggling and yet we are saying this work adds to the bottom line.' The discussion changed and those who had switched off came in strongly and added their own points.

Output of the two workshops

The output of the two workshops so far described was a definition of diversity which was as follows:

Diversity means recognising, understanding, valuing and gaining benefit from differences for us as individuals, for our business and our customers, and for the communities in which we work. It refers to 'all the ways we are different'. It is not just a gender and race issue. It applies equally to other visible differences such as culture, language, age, disability, stature, etc. It also includes less visible differences that our employees experience within the company. These include education, grade level, regional, national, work/life, cross-functional, staff to business, HQ to sites, etc.

This was translated into an R&D vision for diversity, which was:

At R&D Diversity is Great business! In R&D, we recognise and value the richness of our differences and utilise them to gain advantage for the benefit of the business. The diverse mix of characteristics we bring to the team reflects the R&D shared Values.

The output of the two workshops was presented to the senior executive team and the R&D management team. For R&D there was now not only a definition of diversity but also a diversity action plan, an organisational structure, an organisational scope, a senior sponsor, and a list of the perceived long-term benefits of the work. The benefits included: increased efficiency, effectiveness, creativity, innovation and problem solving; valuing and enhancing the contribution of all employees, promoting the release of latent talent; stimulating receptiveness to change and willingness to share best practice; increased ability to attract, retain and develop people from all groups; improved team effectiveness; enhanced external image, maintaining the organisation's reputation as a good employer. Five priority areas for action were set out: diversity at all levels, with the objective of identifying and removing barriers to performance; development and progression enabling all employees to contribute to their full potential; ensuring that legal and practical requirements are being met in each country; providing diversity training, to increase understanding of the issues and benefits of diversity in daily work; communication and marketing plan to inform all R&D employees and relevant external parties of R&D's commitment to diversity and the actions being taken. So, at the end of 2000, R&D had achieved the goal. They had a definition and an agreed action plan.

The diversity training project

Over the next few months, as leader of the 'Diversity Training' initiative and a member of the core action team, I attempted to engage the team appointed to work on the project. I sent out e-mails to engage the discussion and forwarded relevant material I came across. I attempted to organise a meeting but was unable to get everyone together. I left voicemail messages which were not responded to. This was not my full-time role but I seemed to be spending more time working on it than anything else. I knew that the other people involved were very busy and that their schedules were difficult to co-ordinate but even so, the level of interest seemed low. However, I had agreed to deliver on five actions: ensure that global managers have appropriate cultural and legal understanding of the countries in which they manage by end 2001; design a short 'Diversity Dialogue' process for teams which includes the team identifying their own positive and negative behaviours relating to Diversity by Q3 2001; design and offer a 'Valuing Difference' workshop for teams (up to a day); make Diversity learning materials available on the Intranet for individual learning; ensure inclusion of Diversity into R&D Management, Leadership, Induction and other training programmes. In my desperation, and growing sense of inadequacy, I relinquished my desire to facilitate a team effort and started to work on my own.

One of the activities we had agreed to was to identify ongoing training activities in the organisation that might support the Diversity Initiative. I consulted widely and a number of issues came to a head: there was no structure for global delivery of programmes in R&D; there were many programmes which supported 'awareness' raising and cultural understanding at local levels but no system for sharing the information across sites; different parts of the organisation approached training from different perspectives; diversity was covered well by the Leadership programmes. I started to wonder what it was that I needed to do. The most obvious thing was to link all the activities across the various sites using the Intranet but this I saw as an HR system issue that was outside the scope of our project. I started to realise that we might need consultant help and formed a relationship with a consultant from a leading HR consultancy whom I had met in the course of my other work. Eventually I did manage to get the team together and presented them with the material I had gathered. Although one of the four-member team was unable to attend, at late notice, we made good progress and hammered out what we needed to do and agreed who was doing what. I thought that we had started.

Throughout this time, Mary was pushing me to spend the money she had in the budget but I had no clear idea what was wanted and how to deliver it. In addition she had not yet presented the material from the global workshop to the senior management team in R&D and the Diversity Steering Group was still to be formed. In many ways the authority to act was not clear to anyone.

I was beginning to get anxious about my performance. It was only when the core action team met in December that I realised I was not alone, all the other members of the team, who were responsible for other aspects of Diversity, were equally unsuccessful at getting anything moving. It was particularly difficult to get any interest from HR where this initiative was not one of their objectives and so they were reluctant to contribute. Throughout, I had experienced the most resistance from HR. The overall sponsor of the Diversity Initiative had never hidden his views that this was not a HR project and that projects that come from HR always fail.

In the New Year, a new VP was appointed for HR in R&D. I had met him a number of times on the Balanced Scorecard project. At the same time I had a new boss, and when I talked to him about my involvement in the Diversity Initiative, it was agreed that I should work with the new VP of HR. What I felt was needed was a discussion about what Diversity meant for the teams in the way they interacted together, drawing attention to what was really going on rather what 'ought' to be the situation. Asking what are we actually doing when we talk about Diversity seemed to me like a legitimate question. However, when I made this suggestion at meetings, I was told what I needed to do. 'The teams need to walk away with a plan and measures about how they will bring about change. I think what you are trying to do is too abstract for people. Come to our meeting and talk us through your plans so that we can roll out the dialogues.' I felt powerless; all attempts to talk in another way met either agreement, yet supported by words that emphasised something different, or rejection, in terms of not fitting a particular model. Other conversations with people outside HR did not have this characteristic and seemed to generate more spontaneous and interesting conversations.

In February the Senior Implementation Team was in place and had their first meeting. It was a meeting that Mary prepared for with the purpose of reviewing the work to date. The plans were once again scrutinised, analysed and reviewed, and roles and responsibilities for the different groups were agreed. I was left with the same feeling I had at my R&D workshop. There was no real drive to make this happen, but a lot of fine words about Diversity planning though. I also sensed real protectionism from HR and defensiveness about its role.

In March 2001 the pressures of work and family became too much for Mary and she decided to leave the company. It had taken a year to get this far and now there was no leader. We agreed, however, that I would be the acting leader until a replacement could be found.

© David Scanlon

●●●● Management narrative 7: Global competencies
by Jane Blacketer

With the growth of globalisation, companies are increasingly debating which business decisions should be taken from a global perspective and which should be decided locally. The pull towards local decision making is evident in the tendency to favour local marketing strategies. However, while differences between customers and consumer populations are recognised by marketing professionals, it seems that HR professionals are less aware of differences between employees when they call for global competencies. The pull towards globalisation drives HR functions to feel the need for standardisation in employee competencies across the whole organisation, irrespective of local cultural differences. The thinking seems to be that HR professionals need a rational basis on which to act and to be able to be in control of the HR aspects of a business. To do this they need to define HR systems, processes and procedures to be applied across the whole business.

For example, HR functions argue for a standardised process for moving people from one country to another, so it is clear to those involved what they need to do to achieve these moves in a consistent way. Global Competency sets are the latest example of these standardised procedures. These define the skills that particular categories of job holders are required to possess. They are supposed to provide the ability to recruit better employees, to assess them more objectively and to develop them more effectively. One of the positive consequences of introducing global competencies into the business is supposed to be the triggering of new thinking. For example, a manager who recruits against competencies needs to think about such questions as: What does the job involve? What is needed to perform these activities and achieve these results? This in turn should lead to considering what kinds of skills and capabilities a candidate would need to be successful in the job. People can then be selected against these skills set out in the Competency Profile.

In defining competencies, therefore, managers are looking for a simple tool that will help them drive up the performance of all their employees in excess of expectations. They believe that superior results can be achieved by individuals conforming to given approaches and behaviours as set out in Global Competency Profiles. Competencies are understood to be generalised, codified behaviours, a 'homogenised view' of what managers do, which is mostly quite different to what managers actually do. Whilst generalisations may sometimes help, they also obliterate difference and may stifle individual flair because there is a pressure to do things according to the defined behavioural indicators. Competency definitions can also prevent genuine enquiry into how a manager *actually* gets things done. The question then is how to bridge the gap between the codified behaviours and living experience.

The project

Early in 2001, I was appointed as a member of my organisation's Global Competency Project under the leadership of the Vice President of Learning and Development. We were charged with developing competencies for the Corporate Resource Group (CRG), which is the most senior management group in the company.

In preparation for the first week of the project, the project leader sent a set of articles, compiled for her by the Leadership Council, to members of the project team. These all put forward the positive value of developing Global Competencies. No significant obstacles, concerns or difficulties were raised in these articles. Equally, there was no questioning of the validity of Competencies, particularly in a global context. There were no examples of companies which had 'got it wrong' and the lessons that could be learned from the difficulties they may have had. There was no evaluation of the positive and negative impact of competencies.

To me it all felt too neat, positive and uniform and did not fit with my experience. Within just a few weeks of hearing of my involvement in the project and chatting to people whom I thought might have valuable experience, I had heard of two large organisations which had started to develop Global Competencies and had shelved the initiative or deemed their efforts a failure. Yet, there was nothing of this in the articles! Was this a sanitised picture we were being given? It appeared so, but I doubt it was a conscious act. I found myself reflecting on the question: 'What does this mean for the "space" for challenge within the project group?' I started to wonder if it would be possible to talk about what was really going on, when there seemed to be an unquestionable general agreement on the value of global competencies within the project group.

I thought that it was not only the sanitised preparation for the first project team meeting that would constrain genuine discussion. There was also the 'elitism' of belonging to the project team. It was seen as a privilege to be involved in the project group and this would make it difficult to challenge the fundamental nature of the project and question whether we should do it at all, or even question the validity of the proposed approach in order to explore how to do it well. It all felt risky and made me ask myself, 'Is my thinking valid?' It felt as if questioning *certain* aspects of the project group's work would amount to questioning many other assumptions, beliefs and well-established patterns of behaviour. It felt that certain questions could not be asked because they might unravel a whole set of associated meanings and understandings.

So what would I say?

I had compiled some notes before the project started and saw the purpose of these notes as one of helping me to marshal my thoughts so that I could articulate my views more effectively in the group. Initially, I was hesitant about expressing these points, in case the project leader and the group members did not see them as valid. At the outset of the project I was unclear how much experience and expertise the other group members had. However, I realised that whether my views were initially seen as valid by others or not, it was important that they were raised, since no one else was going to do this.

At the first meeting of the project group in May, I wondered what everyone else's views were on competencies. It was a dilemma for me. Others seemed to be total believers in competencies and this project, while I had reservations. I had moved from 'unquestioning believer' to 'sceptic' and I wondered how others would view my questions. Would I be seen as a saboteur out to undermine progress?

The meeting began with the project leader introducing herself and revealing her great conviction of the value of competencies. She said, 'My previous organisation lived by them. They were the glue that held things together. They gave us a common language.' Then she added, almost under her breath, 'Perhaps they can be a little restrictive.' I saw this as an opening for discussion but wondered if it would stay open. When she referred to the competencies as the 'glue' that held things together, I started to silently question what was behind her comment. I assumed she was suggesting that the competencies built a common language, which helped build a sense of cohesion and belonging. I was uncomfortable with the word 'glue' because it implied compliance and constraints. It suggested having to comply with the given ideology of the organisation. It had a controlling tone to it, as if I was being told: 'You either comply with this set of norms and have a chance of being included, or not.' It also implied being stuck and fixed. These are two states that are contrary to what I believe is required in successful organisations today.

In introducing myself to the others, I mentioned that I had questions about competencies and their use. 'I no longer see them as the 'be all and end all' but a tool that can be helpful in certain circumstances but which also has limitations and drawbacks.' It felt as if I was seeking permission to challenge. Another member came in, 'I too am a bit sceptical about competencies.' In that moment I thought I had an ally and was comforted by this, believing that I would not be the lone challenging voice. I raised a number of points at different times during the week. For example, I made particular mention of the need to be sensitive to the differing needs and language patterns of people in different countries. I was not alone in recognising the cross-cultural sensitivities since another member was from Hungary. He based his comments on specifics, namely things that would not work for people in his country. I tended to be challenging from a more generic perspective, asking questions without necessarily having the answers such as, 'How would that come across to a Korean or a French person?' Since neither of these countries was represented in the group, we could only speculate about the answers. Interestingly, the Russian representative seemed less vocal on the issue of cross-cultural differences. Perhaps her youth and relatively junior position was a significant factor in this.

The timetable

On the first day of our first meeting, the project leader announced that the Global Competencies for the CRG had to be delivered by 24 September for the Global Conference in Vienna. This would be a convenient date for communicating the results to a large group of senior managers and stakeholders. We all fell silent. This seemed a tight deadline, given our other commitments and the apparent size of the task in hand. Gradually, we started to question whether this was the final deadline or whether it could be a staging-post where we talked about progress. After further discussion, we reached the conclusions that the final deadline should be for the Competencies and Performance Management Scheme to be in place in good time for use in January 2002.

We had negotiated a later deadline amongst ourselves but later on, towards the end of our second meeting in July, this was changed again. The Executive Vice President of HR had declared that we would either be ready with our competences by 1 September or he would be using a McKinsey set. Earlier that day, we had prepared a project plan gearing ourselves up for the later deadline. We reflected on the ultimatum over night and decided that with help we could achieve the new deadline.

Returning to the first meeting, some of us wanted to conduct a SWOT on Competencies on the second day. I saw this as an opportunity to flush out the weaknesses of competencies. At the start of the day, however, it looked as if the SWOT was not going to be included. I lobbied to retain it. The project leader replied, 'We will not conduct a SWOT on competencies *per se* – this is not the place for that.' She looked directly at me as she said this. I took this look to be a power play to silence my challenge. It worked – I agreed!

However, we did list the strengths and weaknesses we had observed from our experience of *using* competencies (rather than strengths and weaknesses of competencies *per se*). When the lists were completed, the weaknesses were viewed from a limited perspective: they were rationalised away by attributing them to others getting the competency development wrong, or failing to implement them properly. The weaknesses were seen as matters that we could rectify through superior processes. So this information was treated as part of a feedback loop (lessons learned) to help us do it better next time. This meant that there was no fundamental questioning of whether there were some inherent weaknesses in the competencies approach.

Later in the week, I chose not to ask who would be interviewing the EVPs (Executive Vice Presidents) to identify what the competencies are at their level. I was concerned that if I raised it, I would be volunteered to do these interviews. Why my concern? First, there were my reservations about competencies. I feared that they would 'show through' and I could risk sounding unauthentic. Furthermore, there was the fact that I had no previous experience of conducting interviews for identifying behaviours for a competency model (let alone doing it at this level of seniority). I also had minimal knowledge on what operating at this level of seniority involved and I assumed that such knowledge was important in conducting interviews to tease out valuable data for Competency modelling, including what contributes to excellent performance and what does not.

So, during our first meeting, the question of interviewing the EVPs was not mentioned, although I for one thought about it several times. Instead of conducting interviews, we were invited to arbitrarily define a list of competencies for senior executives. This was referred to as a straw-man, and it became the goal of our work that week. This goal took over in the interests of speed, and somehow we were invited to ignore our unease about its arbitrary nature. The two most senior and experienced members of the group seemed relaxed about the validity of developing a straw-man in isolation. They viewed it as 'something to be knocked down and if necessary changed beyond recognition by members of the CRG'. 'It is easier to start from something than from nothing.' I noticed that this was precisely part of my concern – starting from what seemed like an arbitrary list of behaviours is likely to shortcut the thinking process. The things that are likely to get overlooked are the activities and behaviours that are not popular, not done frequently or those people are not good at. I found myself doubting the validity of my reservations.

Most uncomfortable moment

On Thursday evening, as I sat in my hotel room, tired from the first week, thinking of packing for home, I noticed that I felt a sense of discomfort. It felt as if, over the week, I had been caught up in the process of the group and I was not now entirely committed to what we had produced. It felt as if I could not challenge what had been decided because I had been part of the group and was jointly responsible for what we had done. I wondered how this happened and I chastised myself for not re-reading the notes I prepared beforehand, and for not being 'stronger'. However, the way the goal was articulated with a predetermined end-point – a straw-man to be defined by Thursday (and therefore, by definition, in isolation from the business) – forced certain assumptions. I also realised that things can and should change in the process of discussion, but how come the changes had led us to where we ended up – a place I found hard to justify?

As we left the workshop, we were all tasked with taking the straw-man, the arbitrary list of senior management competencies we had put together on Thursday, and word-smithing it. The brief was to stick with the eight areas of competency that we had already defined and polish up on the wording. We needed to put forward preferred titles, draft short descriptions of two to three lines for each title and edit the lists of behaviours to produce a shorter set of bulleted behavioural indicators. So, in the week we went from enquiry mode which I considered to be valuable, to 'word-smithing' where enquiry seems to get closed down.

I decide to ask my boss to help me with my 'word-smithing'. I explained what had happened at the workshop and how we had all committed to the word-smithing task. Then to my disbelief, she said, 'I won't help you draft these words – I disagree with the process. I was not there so the words mean nothing to me. You will have to do it yourself as you were there and therefore it will mean something to you.' I was in shock. First, I had relied on gaining her support and felt completely exposed without it. Secondly, I had never been in a similar situation before where a boss whom I respected had 'withheld their support' on a significant corporate project.

Then she suggested that I just did not do it. I said that I had made a commitment to the group, so for me that was not an option. However, I felt I was unlikely to be able to do justice to the task and therefore would be letting the group down. This could reflect poorly on me and the UK business in the eyes of the project team. I was concerned that this could impact my future in unforeseen ways. I mentioned this to my boss who reassured me but I was not convinced. In retrospect, this extremely uncomfortable moment was a turning point for both me and my involvement in the project. It resulted in a challenge to the process and the involvement of experts. It also amplified my dissatisfaction with our development process and contributed to my seriously questioning my membership of the project group. This in turn gave me a sense of freedom and increased power, when I later raised the matter publicly.

That evening I was so unsettled, I thought that I would speak to the project representative from Hungary. He was surprised to hear from me, and sounded equally surprised to hear me questioning the approach we agreed. He still felt our agreed approach was entirely rational. That evening I tried to work out why he and I felt so differently. I wondered if it was because my boss and I have previously been involved in developing competency models in thorough and well-researched ways.

The following morning I met with the HR Director as suggested by my boss. I explained what had happened and asked for his views on the situation, given that he was likely to be in the target group for the competency set and that I am his representative on the group. His approach was so practical that I found it very re-assuring. He reminded me of the organisation's culture of relying on speed and pragmatism rather than relying solely on robust methodologies at the expense of speed. He highlighted the fact that we do not 'own' this group of people and there-fore cannot control what happens and will have to accept compromise. He also said the competency set was unlikely to be cascaded further down into the UK business because it was aimed at a strategic level, and that we could adjust it as and when further cascading was appropriate. This conversation freed me up to move forward.

I met with another contact and together we developed a refined set of com-petencies based on both her research and my first draft. We discussed the draw-backs in the straw-man set, such as overlap between a number of the competencies, 'behavioural indicators' not written in behavioural terms and so on.

When I circulated my revised set, I started to seed the idea with the group of interviewing all the EVPs and possibly involving an expert in this. At this time there seemed no possibility of this happening. The project leader seemed strongly averse to the use of consultants and she was not alone in this view. In subsequent commun-ications, however, I gently repeated my point. Eventually she agreed to invite con-sultants to talk to us in July and shortly thereafter we involved them in the project.

Following that first meeting, each project group member produced individual submissions and the next stage was to consolidate these into one. This was done by the member of the group with availability rather than the most experienced.

Think of a number – any number!

I set up a meeting to brief our MD on what had been happening and took the HR Director with me. We mentioned that the Competency Group's methodology was different to what we would do in the UK. We therefore urged him to challenge the content of the competency set when he was invited to review them – he was a delegate on the Global Leaders Programme where the set was to receive its first airing.

I notice what a balancing act this is. The political line would be to talk the process up and one's own part in it. In doing so one potentially builds belief/confidence in the outcome and this may diminish the level of challenge and questioning. The challenging route would be to influence the MD into rejecting the framework and questioning the capabilities of the people who produced it as a way to sabotage the whole process. This didn't occur to me as an option until suggested by a colleague. The honest approach is to draw attention to the drawbacks of the process and outline ways to address them. However, the MD seemed comfortable with what we had discussed.

I spoke to our MD after he had attended the programme. To my surprise and annoyance, the project leader had unilaterally changed the eight competencies into six: she had deleted 'Personal Mastery' and 'Valuing Diversity'. They were only alluded to in the other competencies. For example, Global Perspective mentioned 'Diversity'. I had assumed that what we had agreed as a project group would be what was used. I subsequently discovered that this type of behaviour (unilaterally changing the group decision) was how things were conducted in parts of our organisation. This gave me a different understanding of her unilateral actions but I intended to challenge the 'rules of engagement' when we next met.

At the start of the second meeting of the Competency Project Group in July, the project leader briefed us on the various groups with whom she had shared the competencies. Even before I had a chance to ask her why she had changed them she said, 'I couldn't walk in with that'. I wondered why she had not presented that challenge to us as a group, when the consolidated set had been circulated, which was well before she first had to use them. I for one would have been glad to help her work on them. She also added, 'My EVP had in his mind three or four – I thought our number was over the top.' I was interested that an arbitrary number held so much sway. To me this demonstrates the effect of power differentials. She can change things we have agreed. She in turn has to satisfy her boss. Yet neither is an expert in competency development!

Ultimatum

After this, I began to realise that I could not go on with the way things were. I felt trapped. Even if I put my reservations about global competencies aside and stayed on to attempt to influence the project for the better, I could not support methodologies that seem 'arbitrary' rather than based on sound best practice. My dilemma was that if I stepped down from the project and asked to be replaced, then the challenge that I could bring would be lost.

I realised that I wanted to find ways to speak into the situations in which I found myself. In particular I would address my sense of feeling trapped. I wanted to speak in ways that created a chance of changing things – in ways I didn't know yet.

I resolved to speak to my boss to discuss whether to continue on the project or not. I felt a sense of relief just in deciding to speak about my discomfort and to question whether I wanted to continue in the group. A colleague said he would like to join if I chose to stand down. I met with my boss and talked about my issues around continuing in the group, about my fundamental problem with some aspects of the global competencies project, and the fact that I recognised that as long as I did not have a better recommendation, I would have to 'park' my difficulties. I noticed how if someone comes up with an alternative solution, it is unlikely to be seen by others as 'better' if it challenges their ideological perspective. Surprisingly my boss was pleased with my challenging attitude.

We discussed my options. As a result I chose to remain in the group and continue to influence from within. I was getting a sense that my various attempts to steer the group's methodology were beginning to be picked up and accepted by the project leader and the others. The very act of considering leaving the group, and discussing it openly, gave me the freedom to choose to stay.

© Jane Blacketer

References

A

Abraham, F. D. (1995), *Chaos Theory in Psychology*, Westport, CT: Praeger.

Ackoff, R. L. (1981), *Creating the Corporate Future*, New York: Wiley.

Ackoff, R. L. (1994), *The Democratic Organization*, New York: Oxford University Press.

Allen, P. M. (1998a), 'Evolving complexity in social science', in Altman, G. and Koch, W. A. (eds) (1998), *Systems: New Paradigms for the Human Sciences*, New York: Walter de Gruyter.

Allen, P. M. (1998b), 'Modelling complex economic evolution', in Schweitzer, F. and Silverberg, G. (eds) (1998), *Selbstorganisation*, Berlin: Dunker and Humblot.

Ameriks, K. (ed.) (2002), *The Cambridge Companion to German Idealism*, Cambridge: Cambridge University Press.

Anderson, P. W., Arrow, K. J. and Pines, D. (1988), *The Economy as an Evolving Complex System*, Menlo Park, CA: Addison-Wesley.

Ansoff, I. (1990), *Implanting Corporate Strategy*, Hemel Hempstead: Prentice Hall.

Aram, E. (2001), 'The Experience of Complexity: Learning as the potential transformation of identity', Unpublished PhD thesis, University of Hertfordshire, UK.

Argyris, C. (1957), *Personality and Organization*, New York: Harper & Row.

Argyris, C. (1990), *Overcoming Organizational Defenses: Facilitating Organizational Learning*, Boston: Allyn & Bacon.

Argyris, C. and Schon, D. (1978), *Organizational Learning: A Theory of Action Perspective*, Reading, MA: Addison-Wesley.

Arthur, W. B. (1988), 'Self-reinforcing mechanisms in economics', in Anderson, P. W., Arrow, K. J. and Pines, D. (eds) (1988), *The Economy as an Evolving Complex System*, Menlo Park, CA: Addison-Wesley.

Ashby, W. R. (1945), 'The effect of controls on stability', *Natura*, vol. 155, pp. 242–3.

Ashby, W. R. (1952), *Design for a Brain*, New York: John Wiley.

Ashby, W. R. (1956), *Introduction to Cybernetics*, New York: John Wiley.

Atwood, G. E. and Stolorow, R. (1984), *Structures of Subjectivity: Explorations in Psychoanalytic Psychology*, Hillsdale, NJ: Analytic Press.

Axelrod, R. and Cohen, M. D. (1999), *Harnessing Complexity: Organizational Implications of a Scientific Frontier*, New York: The Free Press.

B

Bacharach, S. B. and Lawler, E. J. (1980), *Power and Politics in Organizations*, San Francisco: Jossey-Bass.

Baddeley, A. (1990), *Human Memory: Theory and Practice*, Hove, Sussex: Lawrence Erlbaum Associates.

Baets, W. (1999), *A Collection of Essays on Complexity and Management*, London: World Scientific Publishing Co.

Bakhtin, M. M. (1986), *Speech Genres and other Late Essays*, Austin, TX: University of Texas Press.

Bales, R. F. (1970), *Personality and Interpersonal Behaviour*, New York: Holt.

Bateson, G. (1972), *Steps to an Ecology of Mind*, New York: Ballantine Books.

Baumol, W. J. and Benhabib, J. (1989), 'Chaos: significance, mechanism and economic applications', *Journal of Economic Perspectives*, Winter, vol. 3, no. 1, pp. 77–105.

Beck, P. W. (1982), 'Corporate planning for an uncertain future', *Long Range Planning*, vol. 15, no. 4.

Beer, Stafford (1959/67), *Cybernetics and Management*, London: English Universities Press.

Beer, Stafford (1966), *Decision and Control: The Meaning of Operational Research and Management Cybernetics*, London: John Wiley.

Beer, S. (1979), *The Heart of the Enterprise*, Chichester: Wiley.

Beer, S. (1981), *The Brain of the Firm*, Chichester: Wiley.

Beiser, F. C. (ed.) (1993), *The Cambridge Companion to Hegel*, Cambridge: Cambridge University Press.

Belbin, R. M. (1981), *Management Teams: Why They Succeed or Fail*, Oxford: Heinemann.

Bell, M. M. and Gardiner, M. (eds) (1998), *Bakhtin and the Human Sciences*, Thousand Oaks, CA: Sage.

Bennis, W. G. and Shepard, H. A. (1956), 'A theory of group development', *Human Relations*, vol. 9, pp. 415–57. (Republished in Gibbard, G. S., Hartman, J. and Mann, R. D. (eds) (1974), *The Analysis of Groups*, San Francisco: Jossey-Bass.)

Bion, W. (1961), *Experiences in Groups and Other Papers*, London: Tavistock.

Blauner, R. (1964), *Alienation and Freedom*, Chicago: University of Chicago Press.

Boden, D. (1994), *The Business of Talk: Organizations in Action*, Cambridge: Polity Press.

Boden, M. A. (ed.) (1996), *The Philosophy of Artificial Life*, Oxford: Oxford University Press.

Bohm, D. (1965), *The Special Theory of Relativity*, New York: W. A. Benjamin.

Bohm, D. (1983), *Wholeness and the Implicate Order*, New York: Harper and Row.

Bohm, D. and Peat, F. D. (1989), *Science, Order and Creativity*, London: Routledge.

Borgatta, E. F., Couch, A. S. and Bales, R. F. (1954), 'Some findings relevant to the great man theory of leadership', *American Sociology Review*, vol. 19, pp. 755–9.

Boulding, K. E. (1956), 'General systems theory: The skeleton of science', *Management Science*, vol. 2, pp. 97–108.

Briggs, J. and Peat, F. (1989), *The Turbulent Mirror*, New York: Harper & Row.

Brown, J. S. (1991), 'Research that reinvents the corporation', *Harvard Business Review*, Jan.–Feb.

Brown, J. S. and Duguid, P. (1991), 'Organizational learning and communities-of-practice: toward a unified view of working, learning and innovation', *Organization Science* vol. 2, no. 1, pp. 40–56.

Brown, S. L. and Eisenhardt, K. (1998), *Competing on the Edge: Strategy as Structured Chaos*, Boston: Harvard Business School Press.

Bruner, J. S. (1986), *Actual Minds, Possible Worlds*, Cambridge, MA: Harvard University Press.

Bruner, J. S. (1990), *Acts of Meaning*, Cambridge, MA: Harvard University Press.

Burkitt, I. (1991), *Social Selves: Theories of the Social Formation of Personality*, London: Sage.

Burns, T. and Stalker, G. M. (1961), *The Management of Innovation*, London: Tavistock.

Burrell, G. and Morgan, G. (1979), *Sociological Paradigms and Organizational Analysis*, London: Heinemann.

Burton-Jones, A. (1999), *Knowledge Capitalism: Business, Work and Learning in the New Economy*, Oxford: Oxford University Press.

Buzzell, R. D. (1984), 'Citibank: marketing to multinational customers', in Buzzell, R. D. and Quelch, J. A. (eds) (1988), *Multinational Marketing Management*, Reading, MA: Addison-Wesley.

C

Campbell, A. and Tawady, K. (1990), *Mission and Business Philosophy: Winning Employee Commitment*, Oxford: Heinemann.

Casti, J. (1994), *Complexification: Explaining a Paradoxical World through the Science of Surprise*, London: HarperCollins.

Chandler, A. D. (1962), *Strategy and Structure*, Boston: MIT Press.

Checkland, P. B. (1981), *Systems Thinking, Systems Practice*, Chichester: Wiley.

Checkland, P. B. (1983), 'OR and the systems movement: mapping and conflicts', *Journal of the Operational Research Society*, vol. 34, p. 661.

Checkland, P. B. and Holwell, S. (1998), *Information, Systems and Information Systems*, Chichester: Wiley.

Checkland, P. B. and Scholes, P. (1990), *Soft Systems Methodology in Action*, Chichester: Wiley.

Child, J. (1984), *Organisation*, London: Harper and Row.

Churchman, C. West (1968), *The Systems Approach*, New York: Delacorte Press.

Churchman, C. West (1970), *The Systems Approach and its Enemies*, New York: Basic Books.

Cohen, J. and Stewart, I. (1994), *The Collapse of Chaos: Discovering Simplicity in a Complex World*, New York: Viking.

Cohen, M. D., March, J. G. and Ohlsen, J. P. (1972), 'A garbage can model of organizational choice', *Administrative Science Quarterly*, vol. 17, pp. 1–25.

Cooke, S. and Slack, N. (1984), *Making Management Decisions*, Englewood Cliffs, NJ: Prentice-Hall.

D

Dalal, F. (1998), *Taking the Group Seriously: Towards a post-Foulkesian Group Analytic Theory*, London: Jessica Kingsley.

Damasio, A. R. (1994), *Descartes' Error: Emotion, Reason and the Human Brain*, London: Picador.

D'Aveni, R. (1995), *Hypercompetitive Rivalries*, New York: Free Press.

Davenport, T. H. and Prusak, L. (1998), *Working Knowledge: How Organizations Manage What they Know*, Cambridge, MA: Harvard University Press.

Davies, P. (1987), *The Cosmic Blueprint*, London: William Heinemann.

Dawkins, R. (1976), *The Selfish Gene*, New York: Oxford University Press.

De Board, R. (1978), *The Psychoanalysis of Organizations*, London: Tavistock.

Dunphy, D. C. (1968), 'Phases, roles and myths in self analytic groups', *Journal of Applied Behavioural Science*, vol. 4, pp. 195–226.

E

Elias, N. (1978), *What is Sociology?* London: Hutchinson.

Elias, N. (1989), *The Symbol Theory*, London: Sage.

Elias, N. (1991), *The Society of Individuals*, Oxford: Blackwell.

Elias, N. (2000), *The Civilizing Process*, Oxford: Blackwell. First published 1939.

Elias, N. and Scotson, J. (1994), *The Established and the Outsiders*, London: Sage.

Etzioni, A. (1961), *Complex Organizations*, New York: Holt, Reinhart & Winston.

F

Fayol, H. (1916), *Industrial and General Administration*, London: Pitman (reprinted 1948).

Festinger, L., Schachter, S. and Back, K. (1950), *Social Pressures in Informal Groups: A Study of a Housing Project*, New York: Harper & Row.

Fiedler, F. E. (1967), *A Theory of Leadership Effectiveness*, New York: McGraw-Hill.

Flood, R. L. (1990), 'Liberating systems theory: Towards critical systems thinking', *Human Relations*, vol. 43, pp. 49–75.

Flood, R. L. (1999), *Rethinking the Fifth Discipline: Learning within the Unknowable*, London: Routledge.

Fonseca, J. (2001), *Complexity and Innovation in Organizations*, London: Routledge.

Forrester, J. (1958), 'Industrial dynamics: a major break-through for decision-making', *Harvard Business Review*, vol. 36, no. 4, pp. 37–66.

Forrester, J. (1961), *Industrial Dynamics*, Cambridge, MA: MIT Press.

Forrester, J. (1969), *The Principles of Systems*, Cambridge, MA: Wright-Allen Press.

Foulkes, S. H. (1948), *Introduction to Group Analytic Psychotherapy*, London: William Heinemann Medical Books.

G

Galbraith, J. R. and Kazanian, R. K. (1986), *Strategy Implementation: Structure, Systems and Process*, St Paul, MN: West.

Gardner, H. (1985), *The Mind's New Science: A History of the Cognitive Revolution*, New York: Basic Books.

Garfinkel, H. (1967), *Studies in Ethnomethodology*, Englewood Cliffs, NJ: Prentice-Hall.

Garven, D. A. (1993), 'Building a learning organization', *Harvard Business Review*, July–Aug.

Gell-Mann, M. (1994), *The Quark and the Jaguar*, New York: Freeman.

Gergen, K. J. (1982), *Toward Transformation in Social Knowledge*, New York: Springer.

Gergen, K. J. (1985), 'The social constructionist movement in modern psychology', *American Psychologist*, vol. 40, pp. 266–75.

Gergen, K. J. (1991), *The Saturated Self: Dilemmas of Identity in Contemporary Life*, New York: Basic Books.

Gibbard, G. S., Hartman, J. J. and Mann, R. D. (eds) (1974), *Analysis of Groups*, San Francisco: Jossey-Bass.

Gick, M. L. and Holyoak, K. J. (1983), 'Schema introduction and analogical transfer', *Cognitive Psychology*, vol. 15, pp. 1–38.

Gilbert, J. A. and Ivancevich, J. M. (2000), 'Valuing diversity: A tale of two organisations', *Academy of Management Executive*, vol. 14, no. 2, pp. 93–105.

Gleick, J. (1988), *Chaos: The Making of a New Science*, London: William Heinemann.

Goerner, S. J. (1994), *Chaos and the Evolving Ecological Universe*, Langehorne, PA: Gordon Breach.

Goffman, E. (1981), *Forms of Talk*, Philadelphia: University of Pennsylvania Press.

Goldsmith, W. and Clutterbuck, D. (1984), *The Winning Streak*, London: Weidenfeld & Nicolson.

Goldstein, J. (1994), *The Unshackled Organization: Facing the Challenge of Unpredictability through Spontaneous Reorganization*, Portland, OR: Productivity Press.

Goodwin, B. (1994), *How the Leopard Changed its Spots*, London: Weidenfeld and Nicolson.

Goodwin, R. M. (1951), 'Econometrics in business-style analysis', in Hansen, A. H. (ed.) (1951), *Business Cycles and National Income*, New York: W. W. Norton.

Goold, M. and Campbell, A. (1987), *Strategies and Styles*, Oxford: Blackwell.

Goold, M. with Quinn, J. J. (1990), *Strategic Control: Milestones for Long Term Performance*, London: Hutchinson.

Gordon, R. (1993), *Bridges: Metaphors for Psychic Processes*, London: Karnac Books.

Gould, L., Stapley, L. and Stein, M. (eds) (2001), *The Systems Psychodynamics of Organizations: Integrating the Group Relations Approach, Psychoanalytic and Open Systems Perspectives*, New York: Karnac.

Gouldner, A. (1964), *Patterns of Industrial Bureaucracy*, New York: Free Press.

Greiner, L. E. and Schein, V. E. (1988), *Power and Organization Development: Mobilizing Power to Implement Change*, Reading, MA: Addison-Wesley.

Griffin, D. (2001), *The Emergence of Leadership: Linking Self-Organization and Ethics*, London: Routledge.

Griffin, D., Shaw, P. and Stacey, R. (1998), 'Speaking of complexity in management theory and practice', *Organization*, vol. 5, no. 3, pp. 315–34.

Griffin, J. D., Shaw, P. and Stacey, R. D. (1999), 'Knowing and Acting in Conditions of Uncertainty: A Complexity Perspective', *Systemic Practice and Action Research*, vol. 12, no. 3, pp. 295–310.

Guastello, S. J. (1995), *Chaos, Catastrophe, and Human Affairs*, Hillsdale, NJ: Lawrence Erlbaum Associates.

Gustafson, J. P. and Cooper, L. (1978), 'Toward the study of society in microcosm: critical problems of group relations conferences', *Human Relations*, vol. 31, pp. 843–62.

H

Haken, H. (1977), *Synergetics: An Introduction*, Berlin: Springer.

Hamel, G. and Prahalad, C. K. (1989), 'Strategic intent', *Harvard Business Review*, May–June, pp. 63–76.

Hamel, G. and Prahalad, C. K. (1990), 'The core competence of the corporation', *Harvard Business Review*, vol. 68, no. 3, pp. 79–81.

Hamel, G. and Prahalad, C. K. (1994), *Competing for the Future*, Boston: Harvard Business School Press.

Handy, C. B. (1981), *Understanding Organisations*, Harmondsworth: Penguin.

Harre, R. (1983), *Personal Being: A Theory of Individual Psychology*, Oxford: Basil Blackwell.

Harre, R. (1986), 'An outline of the social constructionist viewpoint', in Harre, R. (ed.) (1986), *The Social Construction of Emotions*, Oxford: Basil Blackwell.

Henderson, B. D. (1970), *The Product Portfolio*, Boston: Boston Consulting Group.

Hersey, P. and Blanchard, K. (1988), *Organizational Behavior*, Englewood Cliffs, NJ: Prentice-Hall.

Hertzberg, F. (1966), *Work and the Nature of Man*, Cleveland, OH: World.

Hertzberg, F., Mausuer, F. and Snyderman, N. (1959), *Work and the Nature of Man*, New York: John Wiley.

Hirschorn, L. (1990), *The Workplace Within: Psychodynamics of Organizational Life*, Cambridge, MA: MIT Press.

Hofer, C. W. and Schendel, D. (1978), *Strategy Evaluation: Analytical Concepts*, St Paul, MN: West.

Holland, J. (1998), *Emergence from Chaos to Order*, New York: Oxford University Press.

Hsieh, D. (1989), 'Testing for nonlinear dependence in daily foreign exchange returns', *Journal of Business*, vol. 62, no. 3.

Hurst, D. (1995), *Crisis and Renewal: Meeting the Challenge of Organizational Change*, Boston: Harvard Business School Press.

Hurst, D. K. (1986), 'Why strategic management is bankrupt', *Organizational Dynamics*, Autumn, pp. 4–77.

Hurst, E. G. (1982), 'Controlling strategic plans', in Lorange, D. (ed.) (1982), *Implementation of Strategic Planning*, Englewood Cliffs, NJ: Prentice-Hall.

Hussey, D. E. (1991), 'Implementing strategy through management education and training', in Hussey, D. E. (ed.) (1991), *International Review of Strategic Management*, vol. 2, no. 1, Chichester: John Wiley.

I

Isaacs, W. (1999), *Dialogue and the Art of Thinking Together*, New York: Doubleday.

Ison, R. and Russell, D. (2000), *Agricultural Extension and Rural Development: Breaking out of Traditions*, Cambridge: Cambridge University Press.

J

Jackson, M. C. (2000), *Systems Approaches to Management*, New York: Kluwer.

Jacques, E. (1955), 'Social systems as a defence against persecutory and defensive anxiety', in Klein, M., Heinmann, P. and Money-Kyrle, P. (eds) (1955), *New Directions in Psychoanalysis*, London: Tavistock. (Also published in Gibbard, G. S., Hartman, J. J. and Mann, R. D. (1974), *Analysis of Groups*, San Francisco: Jossey-Bass.)

Jefferson, G. (1978), 'Sequential aspects of storytelling in conversation', in Shenkein, J. (ed.) (1978), *Studies in the Organization of Conversational Interaction*, New York: Academic Press.

Johnson, G. and Scholes, K. (2001), *Exploring Corporate Strategy* (6th edition), Harlow: Pearson Education.

K

Kandola, R. and Fullerton, J. (1994), *Managing the Mosaic: Diversity in Action*, London: Institute for Personnel and Development.

Kandola, P. and Kandola, R. (1998), *Tools for Managing Diversity*, London: Institute for Personnel and Development.

Kauffman, S. A. (1993), *Origins of Order: Self Organization and Selection in Evolution*, Oxford: Oxford University Press.

Kauffman, S. A. (1995), *At Home in the Universe*, New York: Oxford University Press.

Kellert, S. H. (1993), *In the Wake of Chaos*, Chicago: University of Chicago Press.

Kelly, S. and Allison, A. (1999), *The Complexity Advantage: How the Science of Complexity can Help your Business Achieve Peak Performance*, New York: McGraw-Hill.

Kelsey, D. (1988), 'The economics of chaos or the chaos of economies', *Oxford Economic Papers*, vol. 40, pp. 1–31.

Kelso, J. A. Scott (1995), *Dynamic Patterns: The Self-Organization of Brain and Behaviour*, Cambridge, MA: MIT Press.

Kets de Vries, M. F. (1989), *Prisoners of Leadership*, New York: John Wiley.

Kiel, L. D. (1994), *Managing Chaos and Complexity in Government*, San Francisco: Jossey-Bass.

Kiersey, D. and Bates, M. (1978), *Please Understand Me: Character and Temperament Types*, Del Mar, CA: Prometheus Nemesis Books.

Klein, M. (1975), *The Writings of Melanie Klein*, London: Hogarth Press.

Kleiner, A. and Roth, G. (1997), 'How to make experience your best teacher', *Harvard Business Review*, Sept.–Oct.

L

Langton, C. G. (1996), 'Artificial life', in Boden, M. A. (ed.) (1996), *The Philosophy of Artificial Life*, Oxford: Oxford University Press.

Lave, J. and Wenger, E. (1991), *Situated Learning: Legitimate Peripheral Participation*, New York: Cambridge University Press.

Lawrence, P. R. and Lorsch, J. W. (1967), *Organization and Environment*, Cambridge, MA: Harvard University Press.

Leonard, D. and Strauss, S. (1997), 'Putting your company's whole brain to work', *Harvard Business Review*, July–Aug.

Levy, D. (1994), 'Chaos theory and strategy: theory, application, and managerial implications', *Strategic Management Journal*, vol. 15, pp. 167–78.

Levy, S. (1992), *Artificial Life*, New York: First Vintage Books.

Lewin, R. and Regine, B. (2000), *The Soul at Work*, London: Orion Business Books.

Likert, R. (1961), *New Patterns of Management*, New York: McGraw-Hill.

Lindblom, L. (1959), 'The science of muddling through', *Public Administration Review*, vol. 19, pp. 79–88.

Lindblom, L. and Norstedt, J. (1971), *The Volvo Report*, Stockholm: Swedish Employers Confederation.

Lissack, M. and Roos, J. (1999), *The Next Common Sense: Mastering Corporate Complexity through Coherence*, London: Nicholas Brealey Publishing.

Luhmann, N. (1984), *Social Systems*, Stanford, CA: Stanford University Press.

M

March, J. G. and Simon, H. A. (1958), *Organizations*, New York: John Wiley.

March, J. G. and Olsen, J. P. (1972), 'A garbage can model of organizational choice', *Adminsitrative Science Quarterly*, vol. 17, no. 1.

Marion, R. (1999), *The Edge of Organization: Chaos and Complexity Theories of Formal Social Systems*, Thousand Oaks, CA: Sage Publications.

Maslow, A. (1954), *Motivation and Personality*, New York: Harper & Row.

Matte-Blanco, I. (1975), *The Unconscious as Infinite Sets: An Essay in Bi-Logic*, London: Duckworth.

Maturana, H. R. and Varela, F. J. (1987), *The Tree of Knowledge: The Biological Roots of Human Understanding*, Boston and London: Shambala.

Mayo, E. (1945), *The Social Problems of an Industrial Civilization*, Cambridge, MA: Harvard University Press.

McCleod, J. (1996), 'Qualitative research methods in counselling psychology', in Woolfe, R. and Dyden, W. (eds) (1996), *Handbook of Counselling Psychology*, London: Sage.

McCulloch, W. S. and Pitts, W. (1943), 'A logical calculus of ideas imminent in nervous activity', *Bulletin of Mathematical Biophysics*, vol. 5.

Mead, G. H. (1923), 'Scientific method and the moral sciences', *International Journal of Ethics*, vol. 33, pp. 229–47.

Mead, G. H. (1934), *Mind, Self, and Society: From the Standpoint of a Social Behaviourist*, Chicago: Chicago University Press.

Meares, R. (1992), *The Metaphor of Play: On Self, the Secret and the Borderline Experience*, Melbourne: Hill of Content Publishing Co.

Menzies Lyth, I. (1975), 'A case study in the functioning of social systems as a defence against anxiety', in Coleman, A. and Bexton, W. H. (eds) (1975), *Group Relations Reader*, Sausalito, CA: GREX.

Mercer, W. M. (1996), *Mercer Work/Life and Diversity Initiatives Benchmarking Survey*.

Merton, R. K. (1957), 'Bureaucratic structure and personality', in *Social Theory and Social Structure*, New York: Free Press.

Midgley, G. (2000), *Systemic Intervention: Philosophy, Methodology, and Practice*, New York: Kluwer.

Miller, E. H. (1983), *Work and Creativity*, Occasional Papers, London: Tavistock.

Miller, E. H. (1993), *From Dependency to Autonomy: Studies in Organization and Change*, London: Free Association Books.

Miller, E. J. (1977), 'Organisational development and industrial democracy: a current case-study', in Cooper, C. (ed.) (1977), *Organisational Development in the UK and USA: A Joint Evaluation*, London: Macmillan.

Miller, E. J. (1989), *The Leicester Conference*, Occasional Papers, London: Tavistock Publications.

Miller, E. J. and Rice, A. K. (1967), *Systems of Organization: The Control of Task and Sentient Boundaries*, London: Tavistock.

Mills, T. M. (1964), *Group Transformation: An Analysis of a Learning Group*, Englewood Cliffs, NJ: Prentice-Hall.

Mingers, J. (1995), *Self-Producing Systems: Implications and Applications of Autopoiesis*, New York: Plenum Press.

Mintzberg, H. (1994), *The Rise and Fall of Strategic Planning*, Hemel Hempstead: Prentice Hall.

Mintzberg, H. and Waters, J. A. (1985), 'Of strategies deliberate and emergent', *Strategic Management Journal*, vol. 6, pp. 257–72.

Mintzberg, H., Théorêt, A. and Raisinghani, D. (1976), 'The structure of the unstructured decision making process', *Administrative Science Quarterly*, vol. 21, no. 2, pp. 246–75.

Mirsham, E. J. (1980), *Cost/Benefit Analysis*, London: Allen & Unwin.

Mirvis, P. and Berg, D. (1977), *Failures in Organizational Development and Change*, New York: John Wiley.

Morgan, G. (1997), *Images of Organization*, 2nd edn, Thousand Oaks, CA: Sage.

Morley, D. (1993), 'Chasing chaos in Santa Fe', *Manufacturing Systems*, February, p. 40.

Morley, D. (1995), 'Chaos 3.0', *Manufacturing Systems*, August, p. 14.

N

Nelson, R. R. and Winter, S. G. (1982), *An Evolutionary Theory of Economic Change*, Cambridge, MA: Harvard University Press.

Nicolis, G. and Prigogine, I. (1989), *Exploring Complexity: An Introduction*, New York: W. H. Freeman.

Nilsen, T. H. (1995), *Chaos Marketing*, Maidenhead: McGraw-Hill.

Nonaka, I. (1991), 'The knowledge-creating company', *Harvard Business Review*, November–December, pp. 96–104.

Nonaka, I. and Takeuchi, H. (1995), *The Knowledge-Creating Company: How Japanese Companies Create the Dynamics of Innovation*, Oxford: Oxford University Press.

O

Oberholzer, A. and Roberts, V. Z. (1995), *The Unconscious at Work: Individual and Organizational Stress in the Human Services*, London: Routledge.

P

Pascale, R. T. and Athos, A. (1981), *The Art of Japanese Management*, New York: Simon & Schuster.

Pascale, R. T., Millemann, M. and Gioja, L. (2000), *Surfing the Edge of Chaos: The Laws of Nature and the New Laws of Business*, New York: Crown Business.

Perrow, C. (1984), *Normal Accidents: Living with High Risk Technologies*, New York: Basic Books.

Peters, E. E. (1991), *Chaos and Order in the Capital Markets: A New View of Cycles, Prices and Market Volatility*, New York: John Wiley.

Peters, T. J. (1985), *Thriving on Chaos*, New York: Macmillan.

Peters, T. J. and Waterman, R. H. (1982), *In Search of Excellence*, New York: Harper & Row.

Petzinger, T. (1999), *The New Pioneers: The Men and Women who are Transforming the Workplace and Marketplace*, New York: Simon & Schuster.

Pfeffer, J. (1981), *Power in Organizations*, Cambridge, MA: Ballinger.

Phelan, S. (1999), 'A note on the correspondence between complexity and systems theory', *Systemic Practice and Action Research*, vol. 12, no. 3, pp. 237–46.

Philips, A. W. (1950), 'Mechanical models in economic dynamics', *Econometrica*, vol. 17, pp. 283–305.

Polanyi, M. (1958), *Personal Knowledge*, Chicago: Chicago University Press.

Polanyi, M. (1960), *The Tacit Dimension*, London: Routledge and Kegan Paul.

Polanyi, M. and Prosch, H. (1975), *Meaning*, Chicago: University of Chicago Press.

Porter, M. (1980), *Competitive Strategy: Techniques for Analyzing Industries and Competitors*, New York: Free Press.

Porter, M. (1985), *Competitive Advantage: Creating and Sustaining Superior Performance*, New York: Free Press.

Porter, M. (1987), 'From competitive advantage to corporate strategy', *Harvard Business Review*, May–June, pp. 43–59.

Porter, M. (1990), *The Competitive Advantage of Nations*, London: Macmillan.

Prigogine, I. (1997), *The End of Certainty: Time, Chaos and the New Laws of Nature*, New York: The Free Press.

Prigogine, I. and Stengers, I. (1984), *Order out of Chaos: Man's New Dialogue with Nature*, New York: Bantam Books.

Q

Quinn, J. B. (1978), 'Strategic change: logical incrementalism', *Sloan Management Review*, vol. 1, no. 20, Fall, pp. 7–21.

Quinn, J. B. (1980), *Strategic Change: Logical Incrementalism*, Homewood, IL: Richard D. Irwin.

Quinn, J. B., Anderson, P. and Finkelstein, S. (1996), 'Managing professional intellect:

making the most of the best', *Harvard Business Review*, March–April.

R

Ralls, J. G. and Webb, K. A. (1999), *The Nature of Chaos in Business: Using Complexity to Foster Successful Alliances and Acquisitions*, Houston TX: Gulf Publishing.

Ray, T. S. (1992), 'An approach to the synthesis of life', in Langton, G. C., Taylor, C., Doyne Farmer, J. and Rasmussen, S. (eds), *Artificial Life II*, Santa Fe Institute, Studies in the Sciences of Complexity, vol. 10, Reading, MA: Addison-Wesley.

Reason, P. (1988), *Human Inquiry in Action: Developments in New Paradigm Research*, London: Sage.

Reynolds, C. W. (1987), 'Flocks, Herds and Schools: A Distributed Behaviour Model', Proceedings of SIGGRAPH '87, *Computer Graphics*, vol. 21, no. 4, pp. 25–34.

Richardson, G. P. (1991), *Feedback Thought in Social Science and Systems Theory*, Philadelphia, PA: University of Pennsylvania Press.

Roos, J. G., Dragonetti, N. C. and Edvinsson, L. (1997), *Intellectual Capital: Navigating the New Business Landscape*, London: Macmillan Press.

Rowe, A. J., Mason, R. O., Dickel, K. E. and Snyder, N. H. (1989), *Strategic Management and Business Policy: A Methodological Approach*, Reading, MA: Addison-Wesley.

Rush, J. C., White, R. E. and Hurst, D. C. (1989), 'Top management teams and organizational renewal', *Strategic Management Journal*, vol. 10, pp. 87–105.

Rycroft, R. W. and Kash, D. E. (1999), *The Complexity Challenge: Technological Innovation for the 21st Century*, New York: Pinter.

S

Sacks, H. (1992), *Lectures on Conversation*, ed. Jefferson, G., Oxford: Blackwell.

Sanders, T. I. (1998), *Strategic Thinking and the New Science: Planning in the Midst of Chaos, Complexity, and Change*, New York: Free Press.

Sarbin, T. R. (1986), 'The narrative as a root metaphor for psychology', in Sarbin, T. R. (ed.) (1986), *Narrative Psychology: The Storied Nature of Human Conduct*, New York: Praeger.

Schafer, R. (1992), *Retelling a Life: Narration and Dialogue in Psychoanalysis*, New York: Basic Books.

Scharmer, C. O. (2000), 'Presencing: using the self as gate for the coming-into-presence of the future', Paper for conference on Knowledge and Innovation, 25–6 May 2000, Helsinki, Finland.

Schein, E. H. (1988), *Process Consultation Volume II: Lessons for Managers and Consultants*, Reading, MA: Addison-Wesley.

Schenkman, L. and Le Baron, B. (1989), 'Nonlinear dynamics and stock returns', *Journal of Business*, vol. 62, no. 3.

Senge, P. M. (1990), *The Fifth Discipline: The Art and Practice of the Learning Organization*, New York: Doubleday.

Shannon, C. and Weaver, W. (1949), *The Mathematical Theory of Communication*, Urbana, IL: the University of Illinois Press.

Shapiro, E. R. and Carr, Wesley A. (1991), *Lost in Familiar Places*, New Haven, CT: Yale University Press.

Shaw, P. (2002), *Changing the Conversation: Organizational Change from a Complexity Perspective*, London: Routledge.

Shegloff, E. A. (1991), *Reflections on Talk and Social Structure*, in Boden, D. and Zimmerman, D. H. (eds) (1991), *Talk and Social Structure*, Cambridge: Polity Press.

Shim, J. K. and McGlade, R. (1984), 'The use of corporate planning models: past, present and future', *Journal of Operational Research Science*, vol. 35, no. 10, pp. 885–93.

Shotter, J. (1983), ' "Duality of structures" and "intentionality" in an ecological psychology', *Journal for the Theory of Social Behavior*, vol. 13, pp. 19–43.

Shotter, J. (1993), *Conversational Realities: Constructing Life through Language*, Thousand Oaks, CA: Sage.

Shotter, J. and Billig, M. (1998), 'A Bakhtinian psychology: from out of the heads of individuals and into the dialogues between them', in Bell, M. M. and Gardiner, M. (eds) (1998), *Bakhtin and the Human Sciences*, Thousand Oaks, CA: Sage.

Shotter, J. and Katz, A. M. (1997), 'Articulating a practice from within the practice itself: establishing formative dialogues to the use of a "social poetics"', *Concepts and Transformations*, vol. 2, pp. 71–95.

Simon, H. A. (1952), 'On the application of servomechanism theory in the study of production control', *Econometrica*, vol. 20, p. 2.

Smith, P. B. (1969), *Improving Skills in Working with People: The T Group*, London: HMSO.

Springett, N. (1998), 'Producing strategy in the 1990s: the rhetorical dynamics of strategic conversation', Complexity and Management Centre Working Paper no. 21, University of Hertfordshire.

Stacey, R. (1991), *The Chaos Frontier: Creative Strategic Control for Business*, Oxford: Butterworth-Heinemann.

Stacey, R. (1996), *Complexity and Creativity in Organizations*, San Francisco: Berrett-Koehler.

Stacey, R. (2001), *Complex Responsive Processes in Organizations: Learning and Knowledge Creation*, London: Routledge.

Stacey, R. D., Griffin, J. D. and Shaw, P. (2000), *Complexity and Management: Fad or Radical Challenge to Systems Thinking?*, London: Routledge.

Stapley, L. F. (1996), *The Personality of the Organisation: A Psycho-dynamic Explanation of Culture and Change*, London: Free Association Books.

Steier, F. (1991), *Research and Reflexivity*, Thousand Oaks, CA: Sage.

Stern, D. N. (1985), *The Interpersonal World of the Infant*, New York: Basic Books.

Stern, D. N. (1995), *The Motherhood Constellation: A Unified View of Parent-Infant Psychotherapy*, New York: Basic Books.

Stewart, I. (1989), *Does God Play Dice? The Mathematics of Chaos*, Oxford: Blackwell.

Stickland, F. (1998), *The Dynamics of Change: Insights into Organizational Transition from the Natural World*, London: Routledge.

Stolorow, R., Atwood, G. and Brandschaft, B. (1994), *The Intersubjective Perspective*, Northvale, NJ: Jason Aaronson.

Streatfield, P. (2001), *The Paradox of Control in Organizations*, London: Routledge.

Sveiby, K. E. (1997), *The New Organizational Wealth: Managing and Measuring Knowledge-Based Assets*, San Francisco: Berrett and Koehler.

T

Taylor, F. (1911), *Scientific Management*, New York: Harper Brothers.

Teece, D. J., Pisano, G. and Shuen, A. (1992), 'Dynamic capabilities and strategic management', Harvard Business School Working Paper.

Thietart, R. A. and Forgues, B. (1995), 'Chaos theory and organisation', *Organisation Science*, vol. 6, no. 1, pp. 19–31.

Thomas, D. A. and Ely, R. J. (1996), 'Making differences matter: A new paradigm for managing diversity', *Harvard Business Review*, Sept.–Oct., pp. 81–7.

Trist, E. L. and Bamforth, K. W. (1951), 'Some social and psychological consequences of the long wall method of coal getting', *Human Relations*, vol 5, pp. 6–24.

Tsoukas, H. (1997), 'The firm as a distributed knowledge system: a constructionist approach', Complexity and Management Papers, no. 10, Complexity and Management Centre, University of Hertfordshire Business School.

Tuckman, B. W. (1965), 'Developmental sequences in small groups', *Psychological Bulletin*, vol. 63, pp. 384–99.

Turner, S. (1994), *The Social Theory of Practices*, Cambridge: Polity Press.

Turquet, P. (1974), 'Leadership: the individual and the group', in Gibbard, G. S., Hartman, J. J. and Mann, R. D. (eds)

(1974), *Analysis of Groups*, San Francisco: Jossey-Bass.

Turton, R. (1991), *Behaviour in a Business Context*, London: Chapman and Hall.

Tustin, A. (1953), *The Mechanism of Economic Systems*, Cambridge, MA: Harvard University Press.

U

Ulrich, W. (1983), *Critical Heuristics of Social Planning*, Bern: Haupt.

V

Varela, F. J., Thompson, E. and Rosch, E. (1995), *The Embodied Mind: Cognitive Science and Human Experience*, Cambridge, MA: MIT Press.

von Bertalanffy, L. (1968), *General Systems Theory: Foundations, Development, Applications*, New York: George Braziller.

von Foerster, H. (1984), 'On constructing reality', in von Foerster, H. (ed.), *Observing Systems*, Seaside, CA: Intersystems.

von Krogh, G., Roos, J. and Slocum, K. (1994), *Strategic Management Journal*, vol. 15 (Special Issue), pp. 53–71.

Vroom, V. H. and Yetton, P. W. (1973), *Leadership and Decision Making*, Pittsburgh, PA: University of Pittsburgh Press.

W

Waldorp, M. M. (1992), *Complexity: The Emerging Science at the Edge of Chaos*, Englewood Cliffs, NJ: Simon & Schuster.

Webster, G. and Goodwin, B. (1996), *Form and Transformation: Generative and Relational Principles in Biology*, Cambridge: Cambridge University Press.

Weick, K. (1969/1979), *The Social Psychology of Organizing*, New York: McGraw-Hill.

Weick, K. (1977), 'Organizational design: organizations as self-organizing systems', *Organizational Dynamics*, Autumn, pp. 31–67.

Weick, K. (1995), *Sensemaking in Organizations*, Thousand Oaks, CA: Sage.

Wenger, E. (1998), *Communities of Practice: Learning, Meaning and Identity*, New York: Cambridge University Press.

Wernerfelt, B. (1984), 'A resource-based view of the firm', *Strategic Management Journal*, vol. 5, no. 2, pp. 171–80.

Wheatley, M. J. (1992), *Leadership and the New Science: Learning about Organisation from an Orderly Universe*, San Francisco: Berrett-Koehler.

Wheatley, M. J. (1999), *Leadership and the New Science* (revised edition), San Francisco: Berrett and Koehler.

Wiener, N. (1948), *Cybernetics: Or Control and Communication in the Animal and the Machine*, Cambridge, MA: MIT Press.

Wilson, R. M. S. (1991), 'Corporate strategy and management control', in Hussey, D. E. (ed.) (1991), *International Review of Strategic Management*, vol. 2, no. 1, Chichester: John Wiley.

Winnicott, D. W. (1965), *The Maturational Processes and the Facilitating Environment*, London: Hogarth Press.

Winnicott, D. W. (1971), *Playing and Reality*, London: Tavistock. (Reprinted in 1993 by Routledge.)

Wood, R. (2000), *Managing Complexity: How Businesses can Prosper in the Connected Economy*, London: Profile Books.

Woodward, J. (1965), *Industrial Organisation: Theory and Practice*, Oxford: Oxford University Press.

Z

Zimmerman, B. J. (1992) 'The inherent drive towards chaos', in Lorange, P., Chakravarty, B., Van de Ven, A. and Roos, J. (eds), *Implementing Strategic Processes: Change, Learning and Cooperation*, London: Blackwell.

Index